Communicating *for* Results

A Canadian Student's Guide

Updated Second Edition

Communicating
for Results
A Canadian Student's Guide

Carolyn Meyer

OXFORD
UNIVERSITY PRESS

OXFORD
UNIVERSITY PRESS

Oxford University Press is a department of the University of Oxford.
It furthers the University's objective of excellence in research, scholarship,
and education by publishing worldwide. Oxford is a registered trade mark of
Oxford University Press in the UK and in certain other countries.

Published in Canada by
Oxford University Press
8 Sampson Mews, Suite 204,
Don Mills, Ontario M3C 0H5 Canada

www.oupcanada.com

First Edition published in 2007
Second Edition published in 2010

Library and Archives Canada Cataloguing in Publication

Meyer, Carolyn Margaret, 1962–
Communicating for results : a Canadian student's guide / Carolyn
Meyer. — Updated 2nd ed.

Includes index.
ISBN 978-0-19-900630-4

1. Business communication—Canada–Textbooks. 2. Business
writing—Canada—Textbooks. I. Title.

HF5718.M49 2013   651.7   C2012-907571-X

Cover image: Rami Halim/iStockphoto

This book is printed on permanent (acid-free) paper ⊖ which
contains a minimum of 10% post-consumer waste.

Printed and bound in the United States of America.

1 2 3 4 — 16 15 14 13

Brief Contents

Contents

Getting the Message Across 1

Getting Started: Planning and Writing Business Messages 36

Business Style: Word Choice, Conciseness, and Tone 57

Business Style: Sentences and Paragraphs 87

Memorandums, E-mail, and Routine Messages 116

Routine and Goodwill Messages 143

7

Delivering Unfavourable News 186

Persuasive Messages 217

Communicating for Employment 248

10

Informal Reports 287

11

Proposals and Formal Reports 358

Oral Communication 406

Appendix A
Business Usage—A Style and Mechanics Guide 441

Appendix B
Grammar Handbook 471

Appendix C
Social Media and Networking 491

Summary of Writing Samples

From the Publisher

In today's fast-paced, globally connected world, effective communication is essential to successful business practices. Now, more than ever, with the expansion of the knowledge-based economy, Canadian employers are increasingly interested in hiring individuals who are able to communicate clearly and effectively. Globalization poses new challenges to traditional modes of communication, as traditional spatial barriers virtually cease to exist. New technologies can provide solutions to long-distance communications barriers, but in order to be effective, these technologies must be understood.

In addition to understanding the changing business environment, businesspeople must possess strong language skills. It is not enough to know what needs to be said, but how to say it. An effective writing style begins with a consideration of the basics: grammar, tone, word choice, conciseness, and rhetorical techniques. But advanced business writers know that they must also consider strategic composition strategies and persuasive document planning; and they must have a thorough understanding of their audience's needs.

Building on the foundation set out in the much used and much respected first edition of *Communicating for Results*, this new edition continues to address these needs by providing students with a thorough understanding of how to effectively communicate in Canadian business environments. A unique, hands-on approach engages students in the processes of critical thinking, stylistic development, and content evaluation. Extensive models and organizational plans for letters, e-mails, reports, and presentations—in addition to extensive exercises based on real-life situations—help to simplify the writing process, banish writer's block, and ease fears about public speaking. Quick-access checklists, along with the handbooks to grammar and mechanics found in the appendices, summarize key points for both immediate review and future reference.

Throughout, this approach emphasizes practical knowledge that will give students a head start in the business world. With practice, students will develop confidence in their skills, and confidence is key to success. Ultimately, students will have everything they need to become competent communicators whose spoken-word skills hold audiences and whose documents get the message across, get noticed, and get results.

Highlights of the Second Edition

- **A fully revised introductory chapter** that introduces current trends in the workplace—from the globalization of business practices to the focus on team-based work environments to the ever increasing reliance on new technologies such as Web 2.0—and identifies how these trends impact how we communicate

- **New discussions** of informational and analytical writing styles, trends in communication research, privacy strategies for safeguarding personal and sensitive information, and cultural differences in communication

- **Updated guides** to using voice mail, Internet-based job searches, electronic resumés, PowerPoint presentations, and meeting-planning technologies

- An array of **new full-text writing samples** that includes goodwill messages, incidental reports, job-completion reports, and problem-investigation reports

- **Fully updated APA and MLA documentation guidelines** for business reports

- Extensive **boxed checklists** that summarize important points

- **Marginal glossary** definitions of key terms and concepts

- Updated end-of-chapter **communication exercises**

- Comprehensive **guides to style and mechanics** (Appendix A) and **grammar** (Appendix B)

- Added **coverage of social media and networking** (Appendix C)

- A vibrant new **full-colour design**

- An extensive suite of **online ancillaries**

- **Full-text writing samples**
  that respond to real-life situations present students with solid examples of what their own letters and memos should look like. Marginal tips draw students' attention to important features of the samples, and "ineffective" samples show students what to avoid in their own writing.

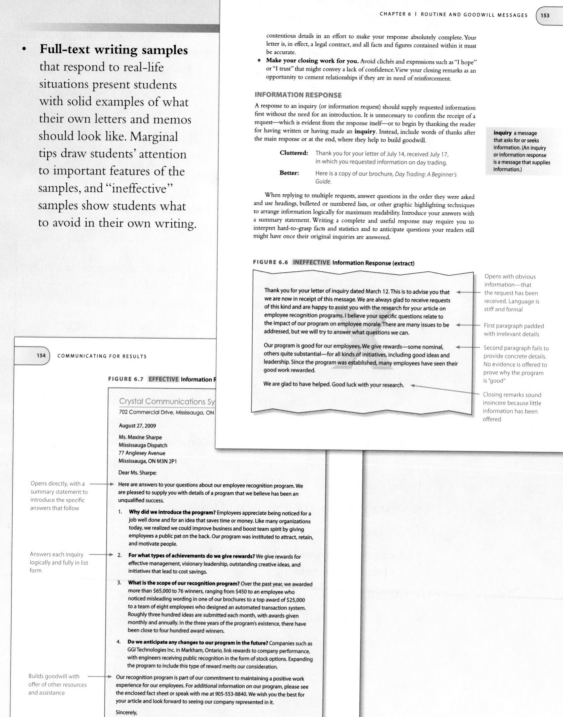

contentious details in an effort to make your response absolutely complete. Your letter is, in effect, a legal contract, and all facts and figures contained within it must be accurate.

- **Make your closing work for you.** Avoid clichés and expressions such as "I hope" or "I trust" that might convey a lack of confidence. View your closing remarks as an opportunity to cement relationships if they are in need of reinforcement.

INFORMATION RESPONSE

A response to an inquiry (or information request) should supply requested information first without the need for an introduction. It is unnecessary to confirm the receipt of a request—which is evident from the response itself—or to begin by thanking the reader for having written or having made an **inquiry**. Instead, include words of thanks after the main response or at the end, where they help to build goodwill.

inquiry a message that asks for or seeks information. (An inquiry or information response is a message that supplies information.)

| **Cluttered:** | Thank you for your letter of July 14, received July 17, in which you requested information on day trading. |
| **Better:** | Here is a copy of our brochure, *Day Trading: A Beginner's Guide*. |

When replying to multiple requests, answer questions in the order they were asked and use headings, bulleted or numbered lists, or other graphic highlighting techniques to arrange information logically for maximum readability. Introduce your answers with a summary statement. Writing a complete and useful response may require you to interpret hard-to-grasp facts and statistics and to anticipate questions your readers still might have once their original inquiries are answered.

FIGURE 6.6 INEFFECTIVE Information Response (extract)

Thank you for your letter of inquiry dated March 12. This is to advise you that we are now in receipt of this message. We are always glad to receive requests of this kind and are happy to assist you with the research for your article on employee recognition programs. I believe your specific questions relate to the impact of our program on employee morale. There are many issues to be addressed, but we will try to answer what questions we can.

Our program is good for our employees. We give rewards—some nominal, others quite substantial—for all kinds of initiatives, including good ideas and leadership. Since the program was established, many employees have seen their good work rewarded.

We are glad to have helped. Good luck with your research.

Opens with obvious information—that the request has been received. Language is stiff and formal

First paragraph padded with irrelevant details

Second paragraph fails to provide concrete details. No evidence is offered to prove why the program is "good"

Closing remarks sound insincere because little information has been offered

FIGURE 6.7 EFFECTIVE Information R

Crystal Communications Sy
702 Commercial Drive, Mississauga, ON

August 27, 2009

Ms. Maxine Sharpe
Mississauga Dispatch
77 Anglesey Avenue
Mississauga, ON M3N 2P1

Dear Ms. Sharpe:

Opens directly, with a summary statement to introduce the specific answers that follow

Here are answers to your questions about our employee recognition program. We are pleased to supply you with details of a program that we believe has been an unqualified success.

1. **Why did we introduce the program?** Employees appreciate being noticed for a job well done and for an idea that saves time or money. Like many organizations today, we realized we could improve business and boost team spirit by giving employees a public pat on the back. Our program was instituted to attract, retain, and motivate people.

Answers each inquiry logically and fully in list form

2. **For what types of achievements do we give rewards?** We give rewards for effective management, visionary leadership, outstanding creative ideas, and initiatives that lead to cost savings.

3. **What is the scope of our recognition program?** Over the past year, we awarded more than $65,000 to 76 winners, ranging from $450 to an employee who noticed misleading wording in one of our brochures to a top award of $25,000 to a team of eight employees who designed an automated transaction system. Roughly three hundred ideas are submitted each month, with awards given monthly and annually. In the three years of the program's existence, there have been close to four hundred award winners.

4. **Do we anticipate any changes to our program in the future?** Companies such as GGI Technologies Inc. in Markham, Ontario, link rewards to company performance, with engineers receiving public recognition in the form of stock options. Expanding the program to include this type of reward merits our consideration.

Builds goodwill with offer of other resources and assistance

Our recognition program is part of our commitment to maintaining a positive work experience for our employees. For additional information on our program, please see the enclosed fact sheet or speak with me at 905-553-8840. We wish you the best for your article and look forward to seeing our company represented in it.

Sincerely,

Audrey Bryant

Audrey Bryant
Vice President

WORKSHOPS AND DISCUSSION FORUMS

1. **Research Employment Prospects.** Using library resources, the Internet, or your local white pages, compile a list of five companies that might present promising prospects for employment. Record basic contact information and instructions on how to apply. Take note of information (about corporate culture, size of the company, etc.) that might be used in a prospecting letter or help you compile a list of questions to ask at an informational interview.

2. **Prepare a Professional Data Record.** Evaluate your qualifications by compiling personal data

relating to your education, work experience, skills, activities, awards, and references. Use action-oriented words to describe your skills and accomplishments.

3. **Revise Your Application Letter.** Working in groups of three or four, analyze the following application letters. How could their tone, professionalism, and overall expression be improved?
   a) What opinion do you form from reading the following extract from this applicant's letter? Collaborate on a revision that is less *I*-centred.

I respectfully submit my strong application for the position of regional sales manager. I have attached my resumé. I have a great deal of experience in the fashion retail industry. I believe this position is tailor-made to my considerable skills and talents. I am more than ready to meet the challenges of this position. I believe I have earned the opportunity to work for a prestigious and well-respected employer such as Bryant McKay.

I hold a degree in Business Administration from the University of Western Ontario, where I was an outstanding student. I completed all of my marketing courses with top honours. I am now a great salesperson. My communication skills are much better than those of my peers. I take pride in my ability to work well with others in a managerial capacity. Although I do not have any public-relations experience, I am a quick learner and should be able to master public-relations skills in no time. My only regret in my short career is that my previous employers did not value the tremendous contributions I made to their organizations.

It would be a shame if you were to miss out on the opportunity to hire me. I look forward to interviewing with you and to the possibility of earning $100,000 a year with your company.

- **Extensive end-of-chapter exercises**—which focus on workshop and discussion forums, writing improvement exercises, case study exercises, and online activities—provide realistic business situations to encourage students to develop their abilities to think critically, solve problems, and work collaboratively in a group setting.

ONLINE ACTIVITIES   http://www.

1. **Online Career Tests:** For various online career tests, check out Job Star Central. Its "What Do I Want?" section features five tests, including the "Keirsey Temperament Sorter" and a personality-style test based on *The Platinum Rule* by Tony Alessandra.
   http://jobstar.org/tools/career/career.php

2. **Government of Canada Online Training and Career Quizzes:** Log on to this site and complete up to six quizzes that will help you discover your work preferences, values, and learning style. You can

5. **Research Companies Online:** What can you find out about a company through its website? Log on the following sites for Canadian companies and prepare a brief fact sheet on each. What distinguishes the companies in terms of size, corporate culture, products, etc.?

Research in Motion	www.rim.net
Schneider Foods	www.schneiders.ca
Bombardier	www.bombardier.com
Sobeys	www.sobeys.com

6. **eResumé Tutorial:** Visit the following site, where you can view a sample resumé, which will open in a separate window, as you work through this tutorial. Gain practice in listing job titles and responsibilities, choosing an appropriate resumé format, and creating a keyword summary.
   http://eresumes.com/eresumes_practice.html

7. **Government of Canada Training and Careers Online Resumé Builder:** Click on "Resume Builder" and create a user account to be able to create resumés for your personal use or to apply online for federal government jobs.
   www.jobbank.gc.ca

WRITING IMPROVEMENT EXERCISES

1. **Action Verbs for Resumés:** Rewrite the following descriptions of significant work duties and accomplishments in appropriate resumé style. Eliminate personal pronouns, begin points with strong and specific action verbs, make points concise, apply parallel structure, and quantify accomplishments where possible.
   a) Administrative Assistant Position:

   I was responsible for the reorganization of procedures and implementation of cost-containment policies. I also monitored the production of all printed materials and ordered supplies and maintained on- and off-site inventories. I also did many mass mailings.

   b) Sales Manager/Production Assistant Position:

   I did a study of automobile accessory needs of fifty car dealerships in the Greater Toronto Area. I was responsible for marketing and sales for a manufacturer of automobile accessories. I also developed new accounts and maintained existing customers. I headed a sales team that generated orders for sales of $3 million annually. In this capacity, I monitored and trained a sales staff of seven to augment a high standard of

   service and increase profitability. I also travel to off-road functions to promote products.

2. **Descriptive, Action-Oriented Language for Resumés:** Improve the following job descriptions by using more precise, action-oriented language.
   a) Gave advice to sales staff on meeting monthly sales quotas.
   b) Did all bookkeeping functions, including internal audits, once a month.
   c) Talked with regular clients all the time to do technical support.
   d) Did a study of cost–benefit to bring about the updating of PCs to make network integration for two hundred users a lot better.
   e) Got together a team to train staff in new safety procedures.

3. **Objective Statements:** From a job site or the careers pages of a newspaper, select three advertisements for jobs that closely match your qualifications. For each one, write a one- to three-line objective statement targeted to the position.

4. **Writing a Letter of Application:** Using information from Mitra Das' resumé (Figure 9.2, "Chronological Resumé," on page 259), write a cover letter that answers the advertisement on page 285.

- **Easy-to-use review checklists, quick-reference guidelines, and tip sheets** give students practical advice and provide a concise summary of key points to keep in mind as they plan and revise their own work.

Quick Reference Guidelines for Memos

- Fill in appropriate information, including a strong subject line, after headers.
- Be as brief as your message allows you to be.
- Follow the style guidelines of your organization.
- Be direct and begin with your most important point when relaying routine news or information.
- Provide only as much background or evidence as your reader needs to act on your instructions or information.
- Itemize supporting details, related questions, and additional requests in bulleted or numbered lists in parallel form.
- End courteously with a request for specific action, reason for the request, and deadline.

E-mail

Few technologies have had such dramatic impact on the business world as e-mail has in recent years. Few are as loved and hated as this essential medium of communication has come to be. E-mail is now an unavoidable fact of business life; it is an indispensable, multi-use tool of management work and the most common means of transmitting workplace documents and files. Its advantage—and ironically its disadvantage—is that messages can be produced easily and quickly and transmitted instantaneously. E-mail's versatile capabilities and wide availability make it an ideal productivity tool—a cheap [and efficien]t way to access, exchange, and process information. Collaborative work [carries] out more easily than before, due in no small part to the interaction and [pa]rticipation that e-mail fosters. E-mail has revolutionized the workplace in [way]s, helping to improve customer service, boosting the quality and quantity [employe]es share with their colleagues, and giving managers an effective way of [people] who report and are accountable to them.

[Rece]ntly has e-mail become a source of corporate embarrassment—a smok-[ing gun that] can offer incriminating and permanent proof of companies' wrongdo-[ing. E]-mail can end up anywhere and compromise confidential and classified [data. M]any organizations have been forced to clamp down on e-mail use and [even] monitor it closely, even going as far as requiring employees to save their [e-mail for s]everal years as proof of ethical conduct.

[E-m]ail has certainly changed the way companies do business, many of the [practic]es that are meant to boost efficiency can result in poor, lazy behaviours [that wast]e and energy and leave recipients frustrated and vexed by unwanted [e-mail. Not] surprisingly, e-mail has its own special set of problems: clogged inboxes; [huge] distribution lists; serious privacy violations; uncooperative servers; unso-[licited,] inflammatory, or undeliverable messages; and difficult-to-follow "thread"

Report-Writing Checklist

The Whole Report

- [ ] Does the report fulfill your original intentions? Does it present a solution that is practical, financially feasible, and appropriate?
- [ ] Is the report professional in its presentation? Is the title complete and accurate? Does the transmittal letter tell readers what they need to know about the report? Does the table of contents offer an overview?
- [ ] Is the report shaped according to the needs of its primary and secondary audiences?

Introduction

- [ ] Has the problem or report situation been sufficiently analyzed? Does the purpose statement reflect this analysis?
- [ ] Does the introduction set the stage for the report? Does it supply information that brings readers up to speed and guide them through the report?

Findings

- [ ] Is the problem subdivided for investigation?
- [ ] Does each heading cover all the material under it? Are all subheads under a heading in parallel form?
- [ ] Is your analysis given in sufficient detail?
- [ ] Are facts and assertions supported by evidence?
- [ ] Have you used sources that are reliable and appropriate for the type of information you are expected to present?
- [ ] Do you cite your sources using appropriate documentation style?
- [ ] Is your language moderate and bias-free?
- [ ] Do visuals, if they are needed, support and clarify written material, without distortion? Are they straightforward and clearly labelled?

Conclusions and Recommendations

- [ ] Do facts and findings support conclusions and recommendations? Are recommendations linked to purpose?
- [ ] Have you achieved what you wanted to achieve in writing your report?

effort not to reciprocate any unpleasantness in your response. If you overhear nasty asides from the audience, single out and ask the person responsible to share his comments with the group. If asides turn to heckling, you have several options: finesse your way out of the situation with a humorous reply, give a serious answer, carry on as if you have not heard the remark, appeal for a fair hearing, or ask that the heckler be ejected.

9. **End by thanking the audience for their questions and feedback.** Show that you value the question period as part of the communicative process.

TEAM-BASED PRESENTATIONS

Working together in a group of two or more can enhance the scope and complexity of a presentation, but it can also make the presentation more difficult to plan and execute. When there is a lack of coordination, speakers might end up contradicting or repeating each other, or not covering key topics. The presentation can lose its focus and clarity. Such problems can be avoided with proper planning and team effort.

Quick Tips for Team-Based Presentations

- Come to an agreement about who will cover which topic areas (conducting research, providing visual materials and handouts) and decide how the group will be governed (by majority rule, by consensus, or by shared leadership).
- Establish ground rules for the group, and give priority to presentation development meetings.
- Develop a work plan and set deadlines, working backward from the date of the presentation.
- Know what opinions each person will express to better prepare you to deal with questions and avoid controversy; agree how questions are to be handled.
- Allow time for rehearsals; plan the use of visual aids and how each person can help others use them; coordinate all presentation parts and visuals for consistency; and identify handover cues when one person takes over from another.
- Appoint a team leader to introduce speakers and help the group maintain its focus.
- Use previews, transitions, and summaries to help the audience understand how parts of the presentation interrelate. Provide a bridge to the next presenter with an introduction such as "Vanessa will now discuss time management."
- Adhere strictly to the allowed time for each speaker, but be flexible enough to accommodate last-minute changes and defer to the expertise of other group members.

FIGURE 8.1 Maslow's Hierarchy of Needs

Self-actualization is the highest level of need, met when people use their talents and problem-solving skills to serve humanity and live up to their potential.

Esteem is first among what Maslow termed "growth needs." The need for status, appreciation, and recognition leads people to strive for status symbols, work promotions, positions of authority, or good reputations.

Love and a sense of belonging are at a slightly higher level of need. Most people seek acceptance, companionship, and group identity. They don't want to be alone—they need to be needed.

Safety and security represent the next level of need. People are often motivated by the fear of not having a comfortable standard of living, a good health insurance or pension plan, reliable investments, job security, home security, or a pleasant work environment. They want to hold onto the money and resources that give them a sense of security.

Physiological needs include basics such as food, shelter, clothing, medical care, and a safe working environment.

- **Consider design and layout.** Opinions are often formed before a message is read, based on its appearance alone. A proper layout—one that conveys non-verbal messages through proportioning, typography, and use of white space—puts a document in a positive light and makes it look both attractive and professional.
- **Be positive and accurate.** Plan on adopting a sincere, confident tone and using positive, you-centred language. Match your phrasing to your relationship with the reader and avoid giving the impression that you are handing out orders. Stick to the facts—don't distort information just to get your way.
- **Anticipate objections and plan how to deal with them.** Persuasion is necessary whenever you expect resistance or when you think readers would prefer to keep things as they are. It is important to consider why readers might object to what you have to say and to be prepared to offer clear and compelling counterarguments to refute the opposing view. Overcoming opposition is a delicate matter best done in a non-threatening and balanced way. Readers are naturally more receptive and more likely to change their minds when their views have been respected, taken into account, and not simply labelled wrong. Try [ ] persuasive request as a win-win proposition. A concession statemen[ ] acknowledge those objections in a non-judgmental way before you [ ] tal that proves that what you are asking for makes sense and needs t[ ] *although the new system may cause some disruptions at first, it will speed pro[ ] cally and give us access to all relevant company-wide databases.*

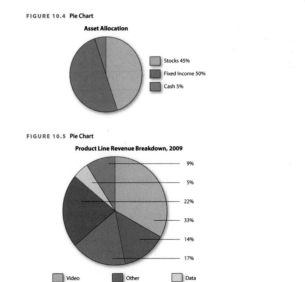

FIGURE 10.4 Pie Chart

Asset Allocation

Stocks 45%
Fixed Income 50%
Cash 5%

FIGURE 10.5 Pie Chart

Product Line Revenue Breakdown, 2009

9%
5%
22%
33%
14%
17%

Video   Other   Data
Wireless   Long distance   Local and access

Source: Telephone Services Annual Report 2009

either **horizontally** (when labels are long) or **vertically** (when labels are short). The higher or longer the bar, the greater the value it represents. Bars have different meanings depending on their colour or shading, which also helps to distinguish them from the background. Arranged in logical or chronological order, bars can be **segmented**, **divided**, or **stacked** to show how the components of each add up (e.g., how a municipal tax dollar is budgeted or allocated). In this way, a **divided bar chart** (Figure 10.9) is much like a pie chart (Figures 10.4 and 10.5), but it can also be used to present complex quantitative information (Figure 10.10). A particular kind of bar chart called

segmented bar chart (or divided bar chart) a visual consisting of a single bar divided according to the different portions that make up an item as a whole.

- **New full-colour design** adds clarity to the various elements, making them much more accessible to students.

Supplements

Communicating for Results, second edition, is supported by an outstanding array of ancillary materials for both instructor and student, all available on the companion website: **www.oupcanada.com/Meyer2e**.

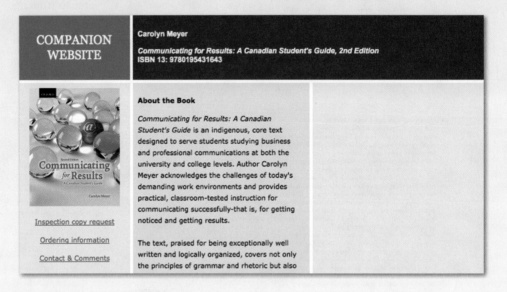

FOR THE INSTRUCTOR

- An **instructor's manual** includes chapter overviews, demonstrative examples, suggestions for discussion topics, recommended resources, and additional homework assignments.
- A **full answer key** provides solutions to both the in-text exercises and the new online case-study workbook for students.
- **PowerPoint slides** summarize key points from each chapter and incorporate figures from the textbook.
- A **test generator,** with both multiple-choice and short-answer questions, creates both chapter-specific and multiple-chapter tests.

FOR THE STUDENT

- A brand new **case-study workbook**—containing 15 new case studies along with questions for critical thinking—provides real-life examples taken from both general and discipline-specific situations.
- Interactive **self-grading practice quizzes** for each chapter, along with a practice mid-term and a practice final exam, allow students to test their level of comprehension.
- A **study guide** presents chapter summaries, learning objectives, and key concepts.
- Annotated **web links** and an **online directory of business resources** provides a starting point for Internet research.

Acknowledgements

The development of a new edition is a process that involves the expertise, insights, and dedication of many people. I am grateful to have worked alongside and in collaboration with an Oxford University Press team that values consideration and thoughtfulness in this process, and I wish to thank all those involved with the acquisition, editing, and production of this edition for their generous support, advice, and assistance. My special thanks go out to developmental editor Jodi Lewchuk and acquisitions editor Jacqueline Mason for their enthusiasm and unwavering commitment to expanding the book and to Janice Evans, Eric Sinkins, and Amanda Maurice for their editorial diligence and precision. I express my special gratitude to David Stover, president of Oxford University Press Canada, and Sophia Fortier, vice-president and director, Higher Education Division, for their responsiveness to questions and continuing support for this project.

To my students and consultancy clients I owe a debt of gratitude for what they have added to my own learning and understanding of the day-to-day challenges of professional and managerial communication. To my many colleagues in the School of Professional Communication at Ryerson University, I extend my gratitude for their formal and informal feedback and for their continuing support of the book.

I also thank the many reviewers from across Canada who originally recommended the project and who have since offered insightful recommendations that helped in the process of shaping and re-shaping *Communicating for Results* to meet the needs of faculty and students. In addition to those who provided anonymous feedback, I would like to recognize the following individuals:

Lyn Bennett, Dalhousie University
Paula Crooks, Conestoga College
Mary Daniels, Algonquin College
Steven Moore, Queen's University
Sonia Perna, SAIT Polytechnic
Brad Quiring, Mount Royal University
Daniel Rorai, St. Clair College of Applied Arts and Technology
Philip Savage, McMaster University
Beth Ann Wiersma, Lambton College

Finally, on a personal level, I want to thank my family—Margaret Meyer, the late George Homer Meyer, Dr. Bruce Meyer, Kerry Johnston, and Katie Meyer—whose unfailing support, kindness, and patience have made it possible for me to produce the first edition and to do it all again a second time.

Carolyn Meyer

To my mother, Margaret
—and in memory of my father, George Homer

1

Getting the Message Across

In this chapter you will learn to

1. Identify how effective business communication is linked to personal career success.

2. Identify key changes and trends in the workplace.

3. Describe the communication process.

4. Identify communication barriers and apply strategies for overcoming them.

5. Analyze the systems and mechanisms for communicating inside and outside organizations.

6. Analyze the flow of communication within organizations.

7. Explain the importance of non-verbal communication.

8. Identify the goals of ethical business communication and apply standards to avoid ethical lapses.

9. Contrast the communication differences between high-context and low-context cultures.

10. Ease the flow of communication between and across cultures.

11. Identify workplace privacy issues and apply strategies to safeguard personal information.

Business Communication as a Path to Success

Good communication matters—now more than ever in business. In today's diverse, wired, global business environments, everyone communicates for a living. It is impossible to work in an office setting without having to write a report, dash off a quick e-mail message, compose a formal letter, take part in a meeting, carry on a telephone conversation, network and collaborate with colleagues and associates, make a presentation, or use Web 2.0 technologies to carry out any of these functions. Spoken and written communication that is focused, reliable, and disciplined has the power to influence opinion and shape perceptions on which an organization's competitiveness, productivity, and success depend. Good communication plays a crucial role in building credibility and upholding standards of accountability in a global business environment where relationships thrive on trust. How you write, speak, and listen on the job reflects who you are professionally, how you treat others, and how you do business.

Done well, your communication can empower you and be the means to promotion and success. Language is, after all, a powerful tool worth the effort of learning to use well. Effective communication can cut through the complexities of business, clarifying fuzzy concepts and making masses of data both meaningful and manageable for those who must use it and make decisions based on it.

Successful communication on the job doesn't merely happen by chance. It is the result of learning how to structure your information strategically—of using text, design, and technologies to achieve an intended purpose for a clearly defined audience. Delivering information effectively can depend on a fine balance between you and your audience, between a commitment to your business goals and an awareness of the needs of your audience. Delivering information at Internet speed, as so many jobs now require, may demand a little more than simply familiarizing yourself with the basic rules of grammar, spelling, and punctuation. It is also a matter of keeping up with changes and developing an accessible, functional style that is flexible enough to be applied to the many forms of communication in your workplace.

Good communication makes good business sense. Even though the ability to communicate effectively is thought of as a "**soft skill**"—one of the social and self-management behaviours that help people take action and get results—as opposed to a "**hard skill**"—the know-how, tools, and techniques that equip people to work in a professional capacity—research has shown that communication is important to success. In a 2005 publication entitled *SUCCESS,* the Canadian Advanced Technology Alliance (CATA) revealed that, among 100 Canadian business leaders, communication was a top attribute linked to leadership skills. Communication capabilities are not just a pathway to career advancement, but a route to a healthy bottom line. According to an estimate from the U.S. National Commission on Writing, based on a survey of 120 human resource directors, American businesses spend $3.1 billion annually training their employees to write (www.writingcommission.org/prod_downloads/writingcom/writing-ticket-to-work.pdf). With the enormous cost of poor communication, the ability to communicate effectively is now a skill top-ranked by Canadian employers, as noted in the Conference Board of Canada report *Employability Skills 2000+* (www.conferenceboard.ca/Libraries/EDUC_PUBLIC/esp2000.sflb). According to this report, progress in the work world depends on the ability to do the following:

- read and understand information in many forms,

soft skill a social, interpersonal, or language skill that complements a person's technical skills.

hard skill a technical skill a person requires for a specific job.

- speak and write to command attention and promote understanding,
- actively listen and appreciate other points of view,
- share information via a range of technologies,
- use scientific and technological skills to clarify ideas,
- manage information by gathering and organizing it through use of technologies and information systems, and
- apply and integrate knowledge and skills from other disciplines.

Besides being a base for further development, these skills bring lasting benefits to those who can apply them, the organizations where they are practiced, and—more indirectly—the stakeholders who must interact with them. Benefits include

- enhanced problem-solving and decision-making;
- increased efficiency, workflow, and productivity; and
- improved professional image, business relationships, and group dynamics.

Communicating for a Changing Workplace

According to Industry Canada (www.ic.gc.ca/eic/site/ict-tic.nsf/eng/Home), our country is on the cusp of an advanced technology revolution and is actively committed to a culture of creativity and innovation. Profound changes are now taking place in the Canadian workplace—and beyond—with implications for learning, job requirements, sought-after business talent, hiring, and the quality of work life. This transformation encompasses a changeover to a knowledge-based Internet, the adoption of revolutionary information and communication technologies (ICTs), new team-based work environments with flattened hierarchies and a more diverse employee base, and highly competitive global markets. Communication is the cornerstone in the new and rapidly evolving workplace, bringing together core functions.

The knowledge economy. Where Canada's economy used to be based on the products people made from raw materials through manual labour, today's economy in the age of information is knowledge-based. The knowledge worker makes and sells some kind of idea-based product: software, consulting and financial services, music, design, or pharmaceuticals. The advantage knowledge products have over those produced through manual labour is that their value can dramatically increase as the global market expands; the challenge in a knowledge economy is to ensure there is continued funding for research and development (R&D), to continue to draw on an educated workforce—trained in critical thinking—and to fight the problem of "brain drain," the loss of experts to other countries.

Spurring the spread of information, utilities and search engines such as Google and open-access business information engines have become equalizers, helping to make the acquisition of knowledge more democratic so that everyone can, potentially, know almost anything they seek to know, at any given time. It is understood that workers should have both the skills to utilize such resources to find and evaluate information and the know-how to process and communicate it effectively. The age of information makes researchers of us all, no matter what our occupation or job profile. Shared workspaces—or areas hosted by a web server where colleagues can share information and documents—and company intranets—where employees can share insider information in a protected web environment—are prime examples of how the information age is radically reshaping business environments.

Flatter organizations. Organizations are by tradition layered and hierarchical. Managers from the top-down at many levels are entrusted with making the decisions and setting the strategies for action-taking to be carried out by front-line employees with whom they may or may not be in direct contact. As organizations strive for greater cost-savings, efficiency, competitiveness, and sustainability, management hierarchies may be flattened, with fewer divisions. This decentralization and democratization of the workplace, with fewer managers in the middle to pass along and interpret directions, makes for shorter communication chains, and because of this, every individual must be a skilled communicator if company products and services are going to make it into the market. As business guru Thomas J. Friedman, author of *The World Is Flat*, observes, ". . . when the world starts to move from a primarily vertical (command and control) value-creation model to an increasingly horizontal (connect and collaborate) creation model, it doesn't just affect how business gets done. It affects everything."[1] The old autocratic style of business management is being replaced with a more participatory one, where communication helps to build trust and understanding and motivate others.

Business on a global scale. The world's economy is becoming increasingly global—to the point where, since 2000, the world seems to have shrunk. This is due, in large part, to several key factors:

- Netscape, promoting connectivity and the free-flow of information;
- software (such as PayPal) and other communication platforms promoting wider co-operation;
- open-sourcing (or software in the public domain that users are permitted to change and improve);
- outsourcing and offshoring (designing at home and redistributing customer service functions and production facilities to far-flung countries); and
- "amplifiers" that are digital, virtual, mobile, and personal (cellphones, smartphones, chips, file sharing, VoIP, WiFi).

The globalized structure for business is providing new opportunities as well as challenges for Canadian workers and their organizations. Canadian products must compete in international markets, yet the brands we may think of as 100 per cent Canadian may in fact be produced, in whole or in part, in other countries. For example, Canadian aerospace and transportation giant Bombardier has facilities in 29 countries (www.bombardier.com/en/corporate/about-us/worldwide-presence). At the same time, investment from foreign-based companies and emerging super-economies such as China has jumped dramatically, from 3 per cent in 1996 to over 26 per cent in 2002 (www.ic.gc.ca/eic/site/061.nsf/eng/01435.html), and the trend toward outsourcing and offshoring customer service functions continues. The need to explore new and emerging markets, negotiate, buy and sell overseas, market products, and enter into joint ventures is anchored in effective communication with people from around the world, without which none of these functions could be carried out. The ability to communicate across cultural barriers, time zones, and language divides—and to exercise intercultural sensitivity by respecting differences in customs, lifestyles, religions, and business etiquette—is crucial to the success of operations in this new global economy.

More diverse employee base. Most employee constituencies in Canada today reflect differences in ethnicity, age, race, gender, physical abilities, and sexual orientation. This diverse, multi-generational workforce is not simply the outcome of Canada's success in attracting talented immigrants or in cultivating social responsibility through fair and equitable employment policies; it is a matter of good economic sense, as companies capitalize on the talents, expertise, creativity, and age-defined generational strengths across diverse groups. Without this deep talent pool, Canada could very well lose out on opportunities for growth. RBC Financial Group refers to this as "the diversity advantage" and cites this as a defining trend of business in the twenty-first century (www.rbc.com/newsroom/pdf/20051020diversity.pdf). Because of the demographic makeup of most workplaces, extra effort has to be made by way of corporate practices to sustain an inclusive work environment where all individuals are valued and their voices heard.

Team work environments. Teams are the way businesses do business in the twenty-first century. According to IBM strategist Joel Cowley, "we are not just communicating more than ever before, we are now able to collaborate—to build coalitions, projects, and products together—more than ever before."[2] Collaboration through cross-functional teams, in which individuals of different areas of expertise come together to share information for a common goal, makes the most of the creative potential of a workforce by increasing individual involvement in decision-making and project development. Working in teams, however, depends on good communication and the interpersonal skill to overcome conflicts that arise when people with differing viewpoints must make joint decisions. Special training is often required to help teams boost performance by managing conflict and practising open communication. Innovations in information technology and mobile communications have made it possible for employees to be part of virtual project teams, which can eliminate time and space barriers—by allowing team members to work from home or other off-site locations beyond a strict 9 to 5 workday—and still provide quality, low-cost solutions to organizational problems.

Advancing communication technologies. Technology and language use as shaped by technology now filter our perspective of the world. Our communications are mediated through many different technologies and electronic forums, most of which did not exist 30 years ago: fax machines, laptops, e-mail, hand-held wireless devices, instant messaging (IM), text messaging, voice mail, personal digital assistants (PDAs), space-defying video conferencing and web conferencing, presentation software such as PowerPoint, interactive software that allows users to change the sequence of information, weblogs, wikis, and virtual worlds. Not only do these technologies allow us to communicate farther and faster, they also enable us to communicate around the clock—to the point where we are always using one technology or another.[3] As Michael Sandel comments in *The World Is Flat*, ". . . developments in information technology are enabling companies to squeeze all the inefficiencies and friction out of their markets and business operations."[4]

Connectivity through Web 2.0 technologies. Web 1.0 was invented in the early 1990s and continues to enable users to find information through tools such as browsers, search engines, and portals, and to exchange information through applications such as e-mail. Web 2.0 applications such as blogs, wikis, peer-to-peer file sharing, social networking platforms, and virtual worlds represent a great leap forward because they allow users to create, distribute, and share content.

- **Social networking sites: Facebook, MySpace, and Twitter**. Facebook began as a tool—or what the Facebook site calls "a social utility"—for meeting new people and for business. Communication without the involvement of a partner, or partners, is like a tennis match with just one player. Communication can be understood in terms of being

- **situated** (it is embedded in a particular environment or socio-cultural context);
- **relational** (it involves the ability to interact effectively and ethically according to what is needed at a given moment); and
- **transactional** (it is a co-operative activity in which people adapt to one another).

Communication isn't simply something that is *done* to others; it is something that is conducted together—a process in which both sender and receiver are involved in a necessary if not entirely equal partnership.

In conceptual terms, communication can be thought of not as a thing but as a process of transferring data from a sender to a receiver as efficiently and accurately as possible. This takes place through the use of a code—a language or a set of signs and symbols (e.g., words or gestures)—that transmits a thought through a channel and carries an agreed-upon meaning within a particular context, with the aim of eliciting a response from the receiver. The receiver must be able to understand, with certainty, what is significant about the data and make meaning out of it in order for this active, ongoing, and ever-changing process to be truly effective. Through communication we assign meanings and take possession of the world around us, though the realities we create are shaped by our different cultural experiences and individual knowledge.

ELEMENTS OF THE COMMUNICATION PROCESS

One of the first conceptual models of communication was developed over sixty years ago by Claude Shannon, an engineer at Bell Telephone Laboratories, and Warren Weaver. Their findings came about through their attempt to establish how a message, when converted into electronic signals, could be transmitted from one point to another in the quickest, most efficient, most error-free way. What they came up with was a broad definition of communication as "all of the procedures by which one mind may affect another"[11] and a model for communication that represented it as a dynamic two-way process. For communication to occur, according to this mathematical theory, there

FIGURE 1.1 Transactional Communication Model

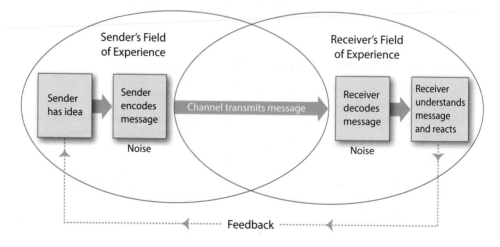

must be both a source and a destination—someone at one end to formulate and launch the **message** and someone at the other end to receive it and respond to it. The success of this process depends on the extent to which a message received corresponds to the message transmitted or to which the input and the output correlate. The goal is for the message to be understood as it was intended. The process, unfortunately, is not always as simple and straightforward as it sounds. Difficulties with transmission, reception, and interference have the potential to disrupt the process.

message any type of oral, written, or non-verbal communication that is transmitted by a sender to an audience.

Sender

The **sender**, also known as the transmitter or communicator, is the person or group with a particular idea or purpose in mind and an intention to express that purpose in the form of a message. The form the idea ultimately assumes—its content, tone, emphasis, and organization—is shaped by the sender's context, knowledge, attitudes, background, and other assumptions based on the sender's experience. The act of taking ideas and putting them into a code—signals comprising words or gestures—is known as **encoding**. The message can be encoded verbally or non-verbally—in writing, speech, or gestures—with the goal that it will eventually be understood. For this to happen, however, the sender must consider the receiver's context, knowledge, attitudes, and communication skills and then choose the right symbols—words, gestures—that convey the intended meaning; otherwise the communication transaction can fail.

sender the participant in the transaction who has an idea and communicates it by encoding it in a message.

encoding the act of converting ideas into code in order to convey a written, oral, or non-verbal message.

Channel

The **channel** is the medium by which the message is physically transmitted. Delivery can be by spoken word, letter, memo, report, telephone, computer (e-mail), voice, or gesture. Choosing the optimal channel depends on a variety of factors discussed later in this chapter. A medium can be synchronous (i.e., enabling the communication to take place directly, at the same time or in real time) or delayed or asynchronous (i.e., allowing for a transfer of information that is stored or archived and accessed later, so that sender and receiver do not need to be present at the same time). Face-to-face conversations, telephone conversations, synchronous text chat, and audio and video conferencing involve synchronous delivery and allow for the most spontaneous interaction and rapid feedback. E-mail, faxes, weblogs, and discussion boards allow for asynchronous delivery, which allows for more time to reflect on a message.

channel a communication pathway or medium over which a message travels.

Receiver

The **receiver** is the person or group at whom the message is directed. The receiver is responsible for **decoding** the message—extracting meaning from its symbols. The receiver's life experiences, knowledge, attitudes, and context can influence how he or she will interpret and respond to the message.

receiver the person for whom a message is intended, who decodes the message by extracting meaning from it.

decoding the act of extracting meaning from spoken, written, and non-verbal communication.

Feedback

Feedback is the discernable response of the receiver to a sender's message. It can be non-verbal, like the nod of a head during a face-to-face conversation; oral, like the "umms" or "ahhs" heard during a telephone conversation; or written, like the e-mail message reply that conveys the receiver's reaction. Feedback is a vital part of communication, allowing for clarification and ensuring that the message has been properly

feedback the receiver's response to a message that confirms if the original message was received and understood.

noise any form of physical or psychological interference that distorts the meaning of a message.

communication barriers problems that can affect the communication transaction, leading to confusion or misunderstanding.

channel overload the inability of a channel to carry all transmitted messages.

information overload a condition whereby a receiver cannot process all messages due to their increasing number.

emotional interference a psychological factor that creates problems with the communication transaction.

semantic interference interference caused by ambiguity, jargon, language, or dialect differences, and different ways of assigning meaning.[12]

bypassing misunderstanding that results from the receiver inferring a different meaning from a message based on the different meanings of the words that are used.

physical and technical interference interference external to the sender and receiver.[13]

understood. Making no provision for feedback, and choosing a medium whereby feedback is delayed when it is immediately required, can bring the communication process to a frustrating conclusion.

BARRIERS TO EFFECTIVE COMMUNICATION

Anyone who has experienced a dropped cellphone call or had an argument as a result of a misunderstanding can appreciate that the course of communication does not always flow smoothly. In today's fast-paced business environments, there is always the potential for miscommunication. The average workplace is not immune to human error or spared from the fact that trained professionals are sometimes imperfect people. The technology on which an organization relies may not be reliable 100 per cent of the time.

Noise refers to **communication barriers** and physical and psychological obstacles that can interfere with every aspect of the communication process, creating misunderstanding anywhere, at any time. Noise can be any factor that makes the outcome of the communication process less predictable, but it also might be called the Murphy's Law of the communication process. If something can go wrong with a message, it will go wrong unless you understand potential communication barriers and take precautions to prevent them.

- **Channel overload**. This problem occurs when the number of messages transmitted through a channel exceeds the capacity of the channel to handle them. You may, for example, try to leave a voice-mail message for a business contact only to find that his or her voice-mail box is full.
- **Information overload**. Another common problem, information overload occurs when a channel simply carries too much information for the receiver to absorb it easily or when too many messages are transmitted at a time for the receiver to properly handle them. Too much information is sometimes too much of a good thing because it can leave receivers annoyed and confused.
- **Emotional interference**. Strong feelings of joy, anger, hostility, and resentment can interfere with an individual's ability to communicate objectively, thus preventing the person from either encoding or decoding a message satisfactorily. Flamed e-mail messages, composed in the heat of anger and certain to inflame tempers, demonstrate the damage emotional interference can cause.
- **Semantic interference**. Words do not have assigned or fixed meanings, thus creating at times a wide margin for misinterpretation. In fact, one word may mean different things to different people, and its meaning can also change in various contexts. This type of misunderstanding is known as **bypassing**. Shifts in meaning, faulty diction, and misplaced emphasis can all lead to miscommunication.
- **Physical and technical interference**. Every so often, technical difficulties arise—phone lines jam, computers crash, and cellphone connections fade.
- **Mixed messages and channel barriers**. Some messages give off conflicting signals, resulting in misunderstanding when the receiver can't decide which signal to observe. A speaker might say that he agrees with an idea, but raise his eyebrows as he speaks, suggesting that he still harbours a few doubts or reservations. Likewise, choosing the wrong communication channel—for example, by e-mailing a contentious message or transmitting a message through too long a communication chain—can lead to a breakdown in communication.

Paralanguage (vocalics). **Paralanguage** refers to the acoustic or non-verbal vocal qualities of verbal communication—the way in which a message is spoken in terms of three classes of vocalic cues:

- **Vocal qualities**—the properties that make each voice unique, including intonation, pitch, volume, speed or tempo, rhythm, emphasis or inflection, intensity, resonance, nasality, and articulation.
- **Vocal characteristics**—sounds that may be recognized as speech but that primarily express emotion—such as laughing, crying, and yelling.
- **Vocal segregates**—pauses or fillers—the "umms," "ahhs," and "you knows"—that punctuate but get in the way of fluent speech.

These voice patterns, because they can reveal underlying emotions and are used to infer personality traits, sometimes come across more strongly than the actual words that are spoken, at times creating mixed messages when the words and vocal cues clash. Shifts in meaning can occur with the subtlest changes in volume and emphasis. A change in vocal inflection can turn a general observation, such as "Oh, really," into an expression of sarcasm. "We can't fill your order" is a factual statement when delivered at normal volume but may have the potential to terminate the customer relationship if it is shouted. "I'm very concerned about this problem" delivers a different message than when you say "*I'm* very concerned about this problem" (other people may not be), "I'm *very* concerned about this problem" (my concern is strong), or "I'm very concerned about *this* problem" (there are other problems). Becoming an effective speaker is a matter of learning to capitalize on paralanguage and the specific qualities of your own voice to complement and reinforce the words you use.

Body language (kinesics). Kinesics is a field of research that examines communication through body movements, based on the assumption that all humans—consciously or unconsciously—act and react to situations both verbally and non-verbally. The meaning of these signals and their positive and negative value can shift depending on the receiver's culture, personality, and experience.

1. **Gestures**. Various hand and arm movements and specific body positions express special meanings—often culturally determined ones—that may both complement and contradict other forms of communication. Psychologists Paul Ekman and Wallace Friesen suggest that gestures can be categorized into five types:

- Emblems—gestures that can be easily translated into unequivocal verbal statements, for example waving goodbye or holding a palm outward to signal "stop."
- Illustrators—non-verbal behaviours that accompany speech and depict what is said verbally, such as wagging a forefinger at another person in a verbal interaction that involves reprimand or disagreement.
- Affect displays—gestures that convey emotion, primarily through the face, such as a smile.
- Regulators—gestures that control interaction, such as leaning forward to signal entry into a conversation.
- Adaptors—body movements that aid in the release of bodily tension due to new or anxious situations, for example crossing your arms, running your hand through your hair, or tapping a pencil.[19]

paralanguage (vocalics) non-verbal vocal qualities of communication.

body language (kinesics) non-verbal communication conveyed by gestures, eye contact, posture, and facial expressions.

Most gestures convey unconscious messages on the sender's part, so excessive gesturing is a distraction that should be kept in check.

2. **Posture**. Open body positions (arms uncrossed and away from the body, legs uncrossed, leaning forward) suggest openness, ease, comfort, and agreement. Closed body positions (arms folded across the torso, legs close together or crossed, hands in pockets) may be signs of defensiveness, a lack of receptivity, or physical or psychological discomfort.

3. **Eye contact**. Eye contact is a powerful form of communication. What it conveys depends very much on its degree, duration, and context. It can mean different things in different cultures. Direct and purposeful eye contact is a sign of honesty, sincerity, respect, and recognition. It is difficult, after all, to fake eye contact or to look someone in the eye and lie. More than a passing glance between strangers, however, can make both parties uncomfortable. Prolonged eye contact in any situation can prove to be a source of intimidation. Averting the eyes can communicate stress or dishonesty; deliberately averting the eyes can indicate anger or a lack of interest, although in some cultures it is interpreted as a sign of deference. Knowing how to maintain good eye contact is important to the success of public speakers and presenters, who may use it as a means of holding an audience and assessing their receptivity, levels of interest, and attitudes.

4. **Facial expressions**. On the basis of eye contact, it is possible to read a face through its range of expressions. Most expressions are short-lived, but each is an indicator of personality traits, judgments, attitudes, and emotional states. There are, regardless of culture, six universally recognized facial expressions: happy, sad, afraid, surprised, angry, and disgusted. Facial expressions provide a useful, if not always reliable, source of feedback. It is easy to misjudge how people feel by the expressions on their faces, just as it is often common for people to mask their true feelings, especially in a professional environment. Individuals may have their own "display rules," such as "never show your anger in public," which inhibit emotional displays and limit their expression or cause them to replace a genuine expression with a more socially acceptable one.

5. **Image**. Clothing, possessions, and grooming communicate specific messages about an individual's integrity, professionalism, status, trustworthiness, interests, education, and work habits. Clothing especially sends out certain signals about an individual's willingness to conform to company standards as outlined in unofficial rules or dress code.

◖◗ Communicating in Organizations

INTERNAL AND EXTERNAL COMMUNICATION

internal communication
communication through
the channels of an
organization.

To stay in business and be successful, businesses today must communicate with two main audiences: the organization's internal audience—employees and owners—and its external audience—customers, government officials, suppliers, and the general public. **Internal communication** stays within an organization and involves the back-and-forth sharing of ideas and information among superiors, co-workers, and subordinates.

Although the speed, instantaneousness, interactivity, and relative informality of e-mail messaging make it the most popular and logical choice for use within a company, internal communications systems are also supported by other pathways such as memos, department reports, in-house newsletters or magazines, face-to-face conversations, group meetings, opinion surveys, speeches, and telephone conversations. Functioning together, they provide the means for organizations to detect and solve problems, coordinate activities, foster decision-making and policy-setting, introduce and explain procedures, and persuade employees and managers to accept change.

Through **external communication**, organizations establish themselves in the marketplace; foster good public and media relations; and work to keep their operations functional, efficient, and productive. Some of the functions of external communication are to influence consumer decisions through advertising and promotion, process orders and collect payment, answer customer service inquiries and handle complaints, respond to government agencies, and carry out purchase transactions. Though customer communication can take a variety of forms, most external communication with businesses consists of letters sent on a company letterhead. Whether an externally directed message is written or spoken, it carries its company's reputation and corporate values with it. Today's businesses recognize the importance of using communication with outside stakeholders as an opportunity to build prestige and a favourable public image by fostering goodwill and establishing solid business relationships. While the general functions of business communication are to (a) inform, (b) persuade, and (c) promote goodwill, it is the third function that assumes increasing importance in external communication.

> **external communication** communication with audiences who are part of an external environment.

ESSENTIAL SKILLS FOR WORKPLACE COMMUNICATION

To perform basic business functions well requires not only the ability to speak and write effectively but also proficiency in the complementary skills of reading and listening.

Reading. On the job, you may spend almost as much time reading as you do writing. Well-developed reading and comprehension skills enable you to absorb and analyze masses of sometimes complex and technical written information, and to do so quickly, even when faced with distractions. Effective responses start with knowing and understanding what you are responding to.

Active listening. There is a big difference between hearing—an auditory function—and listening—the act of decoding and interpreting a sound message. The most important thing a listener can do is pay close and respectful attention to everything that is said, not just a portion of the message, and to synthesize that information in her own words so it is both memorable and manageable. Part of this process involves developing an awareness of **cognitive dissonance**—the tendency to reject a message based on personal value systems. It may be necessary to tune out the emotional filters—strong opinions about the subject or speaker—that prevent you from thinking objectively and understanding a message. Effective listening means knowing the difference between types of listening. Polite, passive listening is a kind of mechanical listening that doesn't involve real response, just a pattern of pre-formulated statement and counter-statement. It is usually unproductive because all the listener is really doing is biding her time, planning her next remark, and waiting for a chance to interrupt. Active listening requires a much higher and more sustained level of interaction between speaker and listener, not

> **active listening** listening that demands close attention to the literal and emotional meaning of a message and a level of responsiveness that shows the speaker the message was both heard and understood.

> **cognitive dissonance** the tendency to reject messages based on personal value systems.

to mention concentration and openness. Asking questions, anticipating what will be said next, reviewing and paraphrasing points that have already been made, and tuning in to non-verbal cues are active listening techniques that let you focus on the speaker's main idea and essential message. For more on active listening, take a look at the tips in "Participating in a Meeting" in Chapter 12. The following chapters will also provide suggestions and strategies for improving skills mastery and proficiency in these four basic areas—speaking, writing, listening, and reading.

INFORMAL AND FORMAL CHANNELS

Formal and informal pathways of communication operate both inside and outside the organization. Generally, the more an organization grows and expands, the greater its need for instituted systems that formalize and regulate its communications. With the purpose of enhancing efficiency, productivity, and overall performance, a **formal communications network** defines the manner in which messages such as letters, memos, reports, and proposals are sent according to a company's organizational structure or chain of command. This hierarchical structure is often laid out in the form of a chart. Once mapped out, an effective communication system establishes lines of communication—how certain types of messages flow within the company hierarchy and at what level each message should be aimed.

Managers whose objective is to achieve business goals by putting these systems in place may also recognize that communication can be channelled through an **informal oral network**. These informal internal communication channels are known as *grapevines*. They develop when individuals socialize by talking about work—chatting around the water cooler, trading unofficial news in the coffee room, or exchanging gossip over lunch. Passed from one person to the next, according to a pattern of serial communication, a message that travels through the grapevine spreads quickly but may not be entirely accurate or reliable. Despite this, the grapevine is still a major source of information in most workplaces, helping to alert managers to problems with morale, allowing them to test opinion, and letting employees in on upcoming changes such as layoffs or restructuring. Though most employees prefer to learn important information through formal channels, astute managers may choose to use the grapevine to their advantage by placing someone with reliable information within the network or issuing the official version first, before a dangerous rumour has a chance to spread.

THE FLOW OF INFORMATION

Among workers within an organization, information flows through **formal communication channels** in three directions: upward, downward, and horizontally.

Upward communication flow. Communication that takes this route, from subordinates to superiors, can be enormously beneficial to organizations that take it seriously enough to foster a climate of openness and trust in which opinions and ideas can be voiced freely. Whether in the form of solicited feedback or unsolicited suggestions, this kind of communication can help insulated upper management to stay in touch with workplace realities and give subordinates a valuable opportunity to provide input. While subordinates may feel they are part of a company team, they may also find that differences in status make it more difficult to communicate.

formal communications network a system of communication sanctioned by organizational management.

informal oral network unofficial internal communication pathways that carry gossip and rumours—sometimes accurate, sometimes not (also known as a *grapevine*).

formal communication channels facilitate the flow of information through an organization's hierarchy.

upward communication flow channels information from subordinates to superiors.

DIVERSITY IN THE WORKPLACE

The communications hurdles associated with the rise of a global economy are equally part of another significant trend—the internationalization of the workforce here in Canada. It is common to work with people of many different ethnic, national, and religious backgrounds. Because culture has the power to influence behaviour, it also has the potential to create clashes and misunderstandings in the workplace. It is now essential for everyday work that we learn to resolve differences and close cultural gaps. Successful businesses are adept at capitalizing on the strengths of a diverse multinational workforce and reducing misunderstanding in order to benefit consumers, promote harmony, and forge high-performance work teams.

UNDERSTANDING CULTURAL DIFFERENCES

Culture—the shared system of values, beliefs, attitudes, norms, and practices—is, like language, something that we learn. It is not part of our genetic code. What we value and how we behave, even how we communicate, is determined by the culture in which we grow up and by which we continue to live into adulthood. How we learn and what we learn can be, and frequently are, culturally determined. Sometimes it is only when we come in contact with other cultures and are made aware of differences in our efforts to communicate that our own ever-evolving cultures come sharply into focus. Because people from different cultures encode and decode messages differently, there is always the potential for misunderstanding across cultural boundaries and for that misunderstanding to boil over into antagonisms. Part of the challenge in communicating interculturally is to defy **ethnocentrism**, or the belief that one's own culture is superior, which serves only to intensify cultural misunderstanding.

culture the shared customs and patterns of behaviour of a particular group or society, including its language, rules, beliefs, and structures.

INTERCULTURAL COMMUNICATION DEFINED

Cross-cultural or intercultural communication is guided by principles for understanding those cultural differences and for exchanging meaningful information in a clear and unambiguous way that upholds mutual respect. In today's globalized business environments and diverse workplaces, achieving competence as an intercultural communicator is a skill for all business practitioners to aim for and live by.

ethnocentrism the tendency to make false assumptions, based on limited experience, that one's own cultural or ethnic group is superior to other cultural or ethnic groups.

The global nature of business and growing diversity of most cities and nations has created connections and mutual interdependencies among people and groups of varying cultural, ethnic, and religious backgrounds. Differences in attitudes, values, and beliefs are many, but communication must still go on despite them—across cultures. *Intercultural communication* is defined as the management of messages for the making of meaning among peoples and groups of different cultural and ethnic backgrounds.

Research on intercultural communication. Intercultural communication, as a specific branch of communication, developed in the 1950s and 1960s as multinational businesses looked for ways to overcome miscommunication and resolve the difficulties that resulted from the ways different cultures perceived reality. The distinction between high-context cultures, where most of the information of a message is inferred from the message's context, and low-context cultures, which depend on explicit verbal and written messages, sheds light on cultural differences according to the beliefs, practices, and communication styles of each particular group. Developed by Edward T. Hall, this system, with its general categorizations of complex cultures, is not meant to—nor should it ever be misapplied in order to—create or reinforce stereotypes or to distort the truth about individuals, who may in fact act independently of their cultural group. Instead, it simply serves as a useful analytical tool in preparing for cross-cultural interactions and as a means of making broad assessments of national styles of communication and negotiation. As such, Hall's model has special relevance to any dialogue and correspondence you conduct with international vendors, suppliers, and operators.[21]

Cultures tend to differ in several important respects:

- in attitudes to individualism and collectivity;
- in reliance on logic and feeling;
- in the relative directness of their communication styles;
- in attitudes to the relational role of communication in business transactions;
- in attitudes to the elderly, life partnerships, and gender roles;
- in time orientation;
- in their propensity for risk and uncertainty;
- in the degree of formality and protocol that governs social interactions; and
- in their interpretations of non-verbal communication and body language.

HIGH- AND LOW-CONTEXT COMMUNICATION STYLES

High- and low-context cultures value different styles of communication. This applies not only to the words and nuances of verbal communication but also to the facial expressions and gestures of non-verbal communication. Knowing about high- and low-context cultures can help you adapt your perspective and keep up with the demands of communicating in multicultural and cross-cultural environments.

low-context cultures
cultures that favour direct communication and depend on explicit verbal and written messages exclusive of context.

Low-context cultures. Communicators in low-context cultures (such as those in Germany, Scandinavia, and North America) convey their meaning exclusive of the context of a situation. Meaning depends on what is said—the literal content of the message—rather than how it is said. Information has to be explicit and detailed for the message to be conveyed without distortion. Low-context communicators can say "no" directly. They don't need to be provided with much background information, but they do expect messages to be professional, efficient, and linear in their logic. Low-context cultures value individualism and the self-assertion that they regard as the means to achievement and success.

high-context cultures
cultures in which communication depends not only on the explicit wording of a message but on its surrounding context.

High-context cultures. In high-context cultures (such as Japan, China, Korea, and Arab countries) communication relies heavily on non-verbal, contextual, and shared cultural meanings. In other words, high-context communicators attach great importance to everything that surrounds the explicit message, including interpersonal relationships, non-verbal cues, and physical and social settings. Information is transmitted not through words alone but through non-verbal cues such as gestures, voice inflection, and facial expression, which can have different meanings in different cultures. Eye contact, for example, which is encouraged in North America, may have ambiguous meaning or be considered disrespectful in another culture. Meaning is determined not by what is said but by how it is said and by how social implications such as the communicator's status and position come into play. For high-context cultures, language is a kind of social lubricant, easing and harmonizing relations, relations that are defined according to a group or collectivist orientation where "we" rather than "I" is the key to identity. Because directness may be thought of as disrespectful, discussions in high-context cultures can be circuitous, circling key issues rather than addressing them head-on. Communicating with high-context cultures can require you to focus on politeness strategies that demonstrate your respect for readers and listeners. Doing business internationally can also involve a higher degree of formality and strict adherence to rules of social etiquette.

COMMUNICATING INTERCULTURALLY

Communicating with an international audience—whether by writing or speaking—can require you to rethink the ingrained habits that govern how you express yourself. Showing respect for your readers and listeners, and learning whatever you can about their cultural expectations are the first steps in achieving clarity and mutual understanding in your communication.

Oral Messages: Speaking

1. **Pay attention to non-verbal behaviours**. "Listen" to what is not being said and interpret what silences communicate. Look for eye messages—raised eyebrows, loss of eye contact—and facial gestures indicating that listeners are confused or not following what you say.

2. **Use simple English and speak slowly enough to enunciate clearly**. Opt for familiar, unpretentious words and avoid idiomatic expressions (*up to my ears, two cents' worth*), slang, and colloquialisms. Deliver your message at a slower pace than you would normally use for an audience of first-language English speakers.

3. **Adjust the level of formality to what is considered culturally acceptable**. Addressing someone on a first-name basis and being direct may be acceptable in certain cultures but undesirable in others, where reserve, deference, ceremony, and social rules play a bigger role in business communication.

4. **Excuse misunderstanding**. Don't play the blame game with your audience. If they don't understand, take the time to make your message clear without causing embarrassment.

5. **Encourage feedback and test your audience's comprehension**. You will want to know if your message is getting across. Pause from time to time to ask if your listeners would like you to clarify any points. Confirm their comprehension by inviting them to sum up your message in their own words.

> **non-verbal behaviours** communication that takes place through gestures, facial expressions, eye contact, and posture.

Oral Messages: Listening

1. **Don't interrupt**. Be patient and allow the speaker to finish a thought. Don't be too ready to jump in and offer to elaborate.

2. **Practise active listening**. Concentrate on the speaker's message. If necessary, ask questions or restate the message to focus your listening.

3. **Be sensitive and patient**. Don't assume that a person who can speak English will automatically comprehend every word you say. Recognize the challenges the speaker may face communicating in an adopted language.

Writing for Culturally Diverse Audiences

1. **Adopt formats that are used in the reader's country**. Study the communication you receive and, as much as possible, adapt your own correspondence to the formatting preferences of your audience. Use appropriate diacritical marks (the symbols added to letters to indicate their pronunciation), especially for proper names (*Dubé, Müller, Curaçao*).

2. **Address readers using their professional titles, not their first names**. Direct address is usually too informal for international correspondence, especially in an initial contact.

3. **Use only those terms that can be found in English-language dictionaries**. Words classed as slang or colloquialisms are usually specific to one context or country and don't necessarily translate well to others. Readers whose first language is not English—and even English-speakers in another country—may not know what you mean by "suits" (referring to business executives) or "the 411" (referring to information). Similarly, it is best to avoid unnecessary jargon, idioms (*blue moon, fruits of your labours*), unusual figures of speech, abbreviations, and sports references (*it's a slam dunk, a ballpark figure*). If possible, try to avoid words with double meanings.

4. **Keep sentences as direct and simple as possible**. Communicate using complete but not complex sentences, arranging your thoughts in short, coherent paragraphs. Add relative pronouns (*that, which*) for clarity and check for correct pronoun reference (readers should be able to judge what *this* or *that* refers to). Avoid contractions.

5. **Use correct grammar**. Never insult your reader's intelligence by writing in second-rate or babyish English. An overly simplified style can offend readers. Instead use language that is literal and specific.

6. **Include politeness strategies where they are required**. Show courtesy by thanking the reader when it makes sense to do so and by using the words *please* and *thank you* where required. An indirect approach, which delays a direct request, gives you the chance to establish goodwill and build a business relationship.

7. **Avoid humour, irony, and sarcasm**. These rarely translate well to other contexts and can be easily misunderstood.

8. **Use international measurement standards** (such as the metric system).

●● Privacy and a Changing Workplace

Doing business, in fact any commercial activity, involves the collection and retention of the personal information of customers, clients, patients, and employees. According to the Personal Information Protection and Electronic Documents Act of Canada, better known as PIPEDA, "personal information" includes information about an identifiable individual, such as

- name, age, ID numbers such as a Social Insurance Number (SIN), income, ethnic origin;

Checklist for Improving Intercultural Communication and Supporting Workplace Diversity

There are several ways to bridge the gap between different cultures, whether you are writing for an international audience or just helping to make diversity work for everyone in your workplace.

☐ **Show respect**. Acknowledge respect for each other's languages, values, and behaviours. Be yourself without having to be defensive in justifying your culture. Realize that differences do not inevitably lead to conflict. View them simply as differences, not as a matter of right or wrong.

☐ **Develop awareness**. Become aware of your own thinking and assumptions. Educate yourself and seek information about other cultures as a means to overcoming prejudice and stereotypes, and take advantage of the diversity-training program your company may offer. Recognize the richness available to you through other cultures and the synergy of different viewpoints.

☐ **Avoid negative judgments**. Do not express damaging assumptions or views based on your own cultural heritage. Instead attempt to understand how your own cultural conditioning or ethnocentrism has the potential to influence your behaviour. Curb any impulse to let negative perceptions or defensive attitudes dictate your conduct and communication. Aim for objectivity.

☐ **Cultivate a work environment that values diversity**. Make sure the diverse voices, cultures, and expertise in your workplace are heard and capitalized on. Values of tolerance and sensitivity, if given enough emphasis, can allow your organization to foster harmony among employees and build high-performance international and multicultural teams.

☐ **Ask questions**. Foster openness in your communications and encourage feedback and constructive dialogue. Exercise sensitivity in the way you ask others about themselves. When communicating globally, consult with someone from your intended audience's culture to determine acceptable usage and style elements.

☐ **Prepare to be flexible and seek common ground**. Where there is potential for cultural conflict, look to what you share by emphasizing compromise and solutions. Being adept at cultural understanding does not mean that you have to adopt the entire cultural style of others, but that you are open to meeting others halfway and making some necessary adjustments.

☐ **Tolerate ambiguity and uncertainty**. Communicating with someone from another culture can create uncertainty and sometimes make you uncomfortable. Accept that you may face difficulties in communicating and overcome uncertainty by facing it rather than avoiding it.

☐ **Listen to others, not to the voice of your ethnocentrism.**

☐ **Bridge cultural gaps**. Demonstrate your culture's positive characteristics and speak positively for the strengths of other cultures. Rather than simply memorizing facts about other cultures, *live* the values of greatest importance to you and those you share with others through consideration and sensitivity. Think of your communication as a dialogue between equals.

☐ **Encourage your employer to commit to a harassment- and discrimination-free workplace**. If such a commitment has not been made, a human rights policy and set of procedures can be instituted to quickly and fairly resolve problems related to diversity issues.

- bank account number, credit records, loan records, transaction histories, tax returns; and
- medical records, employee personnel files, and even voiceprints and fingerprints.

With technology now affecting almost all aspects of business activity and posing unwarranted intrusions and techno-threats, concerns about privacy—and the protection of personal or privileged information, and the best way of ensuring it—have never been greater. Despite the best efforts of most companies to safeguard the personal information of customers and employees, privacy breaches are becoming more common.

- In 2007, discount clothing retailer TJX Company, the parent company of Winners and HomeSense, revealed that up to two million Canadian credit cards had possibly been accessed by computer hackers.
- In 2004, top officials at CIBC went into damage control after the confidential information of hundreds of customers in Canada was mistakenly faxed to a junkyard in West Virginia. The foul-up resulted in a review of the company's communication strategy. In 2007, CIBC again disclosed a security breach, this time involving the loss of account information of 470,000 customers as the result of a computer file that went missing in transit between company offices.

To combat problems of this kind, privacy legislation in the form of PIPEDA, which applies to the private sector, and the Privacy Act, as it applies in the federal public sector, set down rules for the management of personal information. Under the law, personal information should be collected, used, and disclosed only for the legitimate purposes for which it is intended and with an individual's knowledge (and sometimes consent). The 10 privacy principles of PIPEDA form the cornerstone of most corporate privacy agreements: organizations must provide accountability, identify their reason for collecting personal information, gain consent, only collect necessary information, only use the information for the intended purpose, maintain accuracy of the information, provide safeguards, inform individuals of what the information will be used for, give individuals access to their own information, and develop straightforward procedures for complaints. Because governments and businesses collect such a wide array of information, compliance with PIPEDA has implications for communications practices at every level. Adopting new protocols is a step in the right direction, and problems—such as the one CIBC experienced in 2004—can be minimized or avoided altogether with a few simple safeguards:

- faxing personal information only when it must be transmitted immediately,
- taking steps to prevent unauthorized individuals from seeing a document that contains personal information,
- checking the recipient's number and verifying it in the fax machine's display window before you send the document,
- identifying the sender and receiver on the fax cover sheet and including a warning or disclaimer that the document is intended for the recipient only, and
- calling the recipient to verify successful transmission of the document.

There are several steps you can follow, as an employee, to help ensure your organization meets privacy standards:

- learn about the federal privacy laws and provincial privacy legislation that apply to you and your organization;

- identify what constitutes "personal information" in your workplace—what can be legitimately collected, used, and disclosed by fair and lawful means—many organizations, such as TD Financial Group (www.td.com/privacy/agreement.jsp), have their own privacy agreements;
- obtain written, verbal, electronic, or, in some circumstances, implied consent from customers for the collection, use, and disclosure of any of their personal information; and
- be accountable for the personal information you collect, use, and disclose and be proactive in protecting it with security safeguards to prevent unwarranted intrusion, release, or misuse.

Giving up some privacy is something you can expect on the job because the premises and equipment you use belong to your employer, because your employer's human resources department needs your personal information to manage your pay and benefits, and because your employer needs to ensure that work is being done properly. Infringements on employee privacy, however, are becoming much more common. Video surveillance, on-the-job drug testing, web-browsing records, and keystroke monitoring are part of an employer's need to know, but this need must be balanced with respect for employees' rights to privacy.[22] Fair employers have clear policies in place that tell their employees exactly what personal information can be collected and how it will be used. Employees should be well advised of web and e-mail policies, random surveillance, and any monitoring of their Internet.

WORKSHOPS AND DISCUSSION FORUMS

1. **Elements of Effective Communication: Brainstorming a Checklist**. As a class, or in small groups, discuss the skills and characteristics essential to effective business communication and, from your discussion, devise a list of words that accurately describe it. Rate each skill on a scale of 1 to 10, with 10 being most important, and provide examples to support each characteristic.

2. **Analyzing Barriers to Communication**. Working in large groups, play a variation of the game broken telephone. Nominate a group leader to compose a message of no more than 12 words. The group leader will then whisper this message to the person seated to her immediate left or right, who will in turn pass it on to his neighbour, and so on. Anyone who is uncomfortable with the process may opt out at any time. Once the message has made its way through the entire group, ask the last person to say the message aloud. Repeat the process, only this time circulate a longer/shorter message or write the message down on a scrap of paper and ask each member of the group to re-copy it, pass it on, re-copy it, and so on. Once again, ask the last person to read the final copied message aloud. What happens to each message in the course of its transmission? Does the message transmit most successfully in oral or written form? Discuss what you have learned about the nature of serial communication.

3. **Taking Stock of Non-Verbal Communication**. Working in a small group, discuss examples of non-verbal communication (gestures, facial expressions, paralanguage) that typically express each of the following emotions, sentiments, or actions:
   - happiness or celebration,
   - anger,
   - sadness,
   - shame,
   - hailing a cab,
   - showing respect,
   - "come here,"

- "over there,"
- "this one,"
- friendship or warmth,
- love or flirtation,
- showing sympathy,
- showing praise,
- "saying" hello or goodbye,
- disbelief,
- "good luck,"
- agreement,
- disagreement,
- like, and
- dislike.

Identify at least one example in each case and compile a list. To what extent do group members agree on the meaning of each gesture or expression? Is there a universal language of gestures, or is the meaning of a gesture culturally determined?

4. **Comparing the Meaning of Gestures**. In a small group, have each person work on his or her own to assign a meaning to each of the following gestures, and then discuss and compare the meanings that have been assigned in each case:
   - shaking one's head (side-to-side),
   - nodding one's head (up and down),
   - winking,
   - waving,
   - looking down or averting one's eyes (gaze aversion),
   - raising one's thumb,
   - handshake,
   - turning one's back on another,
   - rolling one's eyes,
   - shaking one's fist or finger,
   - finger pointing,
   - patting someone's back,
   - tapping one's shoulder,

   Can gestures serve as signals of group membership? Can they have secret meanings?

5. **Observing and Analyzing Non-Verbal Cues**. (This exercise requires video-recording equipment.) Videotape a five-minute conversation between you and a partner. During video playback, note the use of non-verbal cues that repeat, contradict, substitute for, complement, or accent each partner's spoken message. Note any discrepancies between your verbal and non-verbal communication. (If video-recording is not possible, use a classroom or lab computer to watch a 5–10 minute speech or business presentation downloaded from a video-sharing platform such as YouTube or Google Videos. Note the speaker's use of non-verbal cues and discuss the ways in which that contradicts or enriches his or her message.)

6. **Experimenting with Proxemics**. In a classroom with moveable furniture, work in a small group and rearrange the furniture in the following positions:
   - in a circle and half-circle;
   - in standard classroom style, with all chairs facing one direction; and
   - in a random formation.

   How do the dynamics of the group change according to the seating arrangement?

7. **Experimenting with Eye Contact**. For this pair-share activity, work with a partner and note and compare your reactions to the length and intensity of eye contact. Begin by maintaining eye contact for two seconds, increasing by increments of two seconds up to an interval of twenty seconds. At what point does your partner's gaze become unsettling and intrusive? Try the experiment again, this time by looking away (for up to fifteen seconds) before you hold and increase your gaze. What is the effect of interrupting your gaze or increasing its frequency?

8. **Experimenting with Personal Space**. For this activity, first work with a partner and then take part in a small group session. Determine the dividing line between comfortable and uncomfortable distance by saying "continue" or "stop" as your partner or group members move toward you, starting from a distance of three metres. Vary the experiment by pretending that your partner and group members are (a) friends and family members and (b) business colleagues. Keep a log of your reactions, according to what is an allowable distance between you and your group members. At what point did you begin to feel uncomfortable?

9. **Improving Your Active Listening Skills**. In small groups, have each person perform a one- or two-minute introduction that covers such subjects as that person's program of study, career goals, school- or job-related interests, and technological proficiencies. When every group member has spoken, take a few minutes to record what you can remember of each person's introduction. Compare your observations and recollections with those of other group members.

Discuss what makes the difference between poor and effective listening. Variation: Choose a partner to interview about his or her program of study and interests. Based on what you have learned, deliver a one-minute introduction to members of the class.

10. **Establishing Guidelines for Ethical Workplace Communication**. Working in a small group, assume that you and your fellow group members are the co-CEOs of a new business. You are meeting to establish an ethical framework for your company's internal and external communication. Draw up a concise list of guidelines, or code, for ethical communication in your workplace. If you need help in starting your discussion, refer to "Five Questions that Corporate Directors Should Ask" at www.ethics.ubc.ca/papers/invited/5questions.html.

11. **Cross-Cultural Round-Table Discussion**. In small groups, invite members who have lived in other countries, or who have first-hand experience of another culture, to share their knowledge. Compare what you know of North American business culture with the degree of formality, time orientation, communication styles, and typical business greetings that are considered acceptable elsewhere. Prepare the findings of your discussion in a short report.

12. **Round-Table Discussion: The Facebook Phenomenon and You**. In a small group, discuss your answers to the following questionnaire about Facebook:
    - How long have you used Facebook?
    - How long do you spend per day on the site, and how many times per day do you log on?
    - What is in your profile?
    - Who has access to your profile?
    - What privacy settings do you use?
    - What are your online interactions?
    - What positive outcomes have resulted from your use of Facebook?

    Share your findings with your instructor and compare them with findings and viewpoints from the rest of the class. What conclusions can you draw about Facebook and social networking platforms in general?

13. **Ethics Assessment: Facing Ethical Challenges**. In a group, discuss the following situations and decide whether they are permissible under any circumstances:
    a) using a company phone to make long-distance calls to friends and relatives,

    b) not informing consumers about weaknesses in the side-door impact panels of your company's best-selling SUV,

    c) exaggerating qualifications and experiences on resumés and in job interviews,

    d) leaking the results of a drug trial for an important new cancer medication developed by a major pharmaceutical company,

    e) revealing details of a patient's medical history to a prospective employer without the consent of the patient,

    f) falsifying one or two figures on an expense report, and

    g) lying on a performance review to protect a colleague who is also a friend.

14. **Privacy Challenge: A Day at the Bank**. In small groups, review each of the following scenarios and discuss whether they constitute breaches of privacy according to the 10 principles set out in PIPEDA (see p. 28).
    - Scenario 1: You work at the reception desk in a local bank branch. A customer rushes in and says that her boyfriend needs to review his financial transactions and desperately needs a monthly statement that was issued to him last month but which he has now lost. The woman explains that her boyfriend is attending a two-day conference out of town and the bank will be closed on Sunday, when he returns. You ask her for her boyfriend's name, access and print the monthly statement she has requested, and hand it to her.
    - Scenario 2: You are a financial representative about to go on your lunch break. You remember that you have to make an important phone call before leaving, so you immediately phone your client to provide her with the account information to set up her pay for direct deposit. You are not able to reach her directly, but leave a detailed voice-mail message for her, which includes the account information, despite the fact that her outgoing message does not include her name. Realizing that you have only 45 minutes left for lunch, you rush out—without logging off your computer—and leave files and loose documents on your desk.
    - Scenario 3: You are a bank teller who processes a transaction for a casual labourer-tradesman who does not have an account at your bank but who

frequently comes in to cash cheques from his clients. As you finish the transaction and count out his cash payment, he asks if he may open an account, since your branch is located in the neighbourhood where most of his clients live. You tell him that he needs only two pieces of ID to open an account and you direct him to a financial service representative who asks for his Social Insurance Number. He returns to your service area a few minutes later, angrily questioning the need to show his SIN and taking exception to the financial service representative's insistence that this information is required by law. Hint: Refer to the fact sheet on Social Insurance Numbers from the Office of the Privacy Commissioner of Canada at www.priv.gc.ca/resource/fs-fi/02_05_d_02_e.asp.

WRITING IMPROVEMENT EXERCISES

1. **Establishing Your Goals in Business Communication**. Write an introductory memo to your instructor in which you explain your reasons for taking the course, the outcomes you hope to achieve, your strengths and weaknesses as a writer, the role communication will play in your chosen occupation or profession, and the type of writing you currently do or expect to do on the job.

2. **Identifying Your Communication Channels and Choices: Always On**. Linguistics professor Naomi S. Baron claims that online and mobile technologies including instant messaging, cellphones, Facebook, blogs, and wikis are transforming how we communicate, creating an environment in which we are "always on" one technology or another.[23] These technologies offer users the power to control who they communicate with—with the option of blocking incoming IMs, creating alter egos in virtual worlds, and screening cellphone calls. On your own, analyze the percentage of your day you devote to communications and estimate the amount of time you devote to each of the following:
   - face-to-face and telephone conversations, e-mail, and IM (communicating with individuals); and
   - social networking through blogs, Facebook, and micro-blogs such as Twitter (presenting yourself to others).

   In a few paragraphs or as a brief e-mail to your instructor, outline your communication preferences and describe how your communication style, behaviour, and self-presentation change according to the technology or channel you use.

3. **Analyzing Your On-the-Job Communication**. If you currently have a job or have recently been employed, analyze your on-the-job communication by answering the following questions:
   a) What channel(s) do you principally use to communicate on the job?
   b) How important is communication to the duties you must perform?
   c) In what direction does your communication primarily flow—upward, downward, or horizontally? With whom do you primarily communicate internally and externally?
   d) What types of messages/documents do you typically create or generate? What types of messages/documents do you receive?
   e) What barriers to communication exist on the job?
   f) How does your organization facilitate communication in the workplace?
   g) How formal or informal is it necessary to be when communicating on the job?
   h) How easy it is to communicate on the job?
   i) Is the grapevine in your organization accurate?
   When you have answered these questions, draw a diagram that illustrates the flow of communication in your workplace.

4. **Assessing Communication Needs for Employment**. Refer to the classified or careers section of any daily newspaper or a job site, such as www.monster.ca. Review several advertisements and note the communications skills that are required for each position. Write a memo or e-mail to your instructor summarizing the skills employers want most. Variation: Create a word table (or matrix) in which you provide examples from your own work history and experience that correspond to the skills employers seek.

CHAPTER 1 | GETTING THE MESSAGE ACROSS

5. **Assessing Barriers to Communication**. Recall a recent event or situation that made you very angry (e.g., a parking ticket, a missed transit connection, an incident of road rage, an unfair grade, or a ruling or school/government policy with which you strongly disagreed). Write two messages, each seeking restitution or settlement of the problem. In the first message, vent your grievance and sense of frustration according to what you felt in the heat of the moment. Allow at least several hours to elapse—enough time for you to gain perspective on the situation—before you write your second message. Compare the messages you have written on the basis of their tone, content, and coherence. Discuss how emotional barriers affect the communication process.

6. **Assessing the Flow of Communication**. In each of the following situations, consider whether communication is channelled through an upward, downward, or horizontal flow:
   a) an e-mail message to a co-worker in your department asking for clarification of the latest sales figures,
   b) a recommendation report to the president of your company suggesting the development of a staff incentive or awards program,
   c) instructions to new hires in your department on the operation of the photocopier,
   d) discussions with co-workers over revisions to a report written collaboratively, and
   e) a policy statement outlining the firm's position on client privacy issues.
   Discuss the special demands of each message.

7. **Identifying Forms of Internal and External Communication**. Distinguish between the following types of communication according to whether the message remains inside the organization or goes outside of the organization:
   a) a response to a request for proposals (RFP) that tenders a bid on a plumbing contract for a municipal housing project,
   b) a group e-mail to staff members who have signed up for a series of telecommuting training sessions,
   c) an announcement of changes to the company pension plan,
   d) a press release announcing the hiring of a corporate legal representative,
   e) an annual report for shareholders,

f) an adjustment letter settling a claim against your company, and
g) a formal report on the outsourcing of human resources functions.

8. **Analyzing Non-Verbal Cues** Although it is sometimes difficult to interpret gestures, body language, and other non-verbal signals, consider what each of the following scenarios communicates:
   a) Olivia Visconti, human resources director, places visitors' chairs across the room from her desk and arranges a coffee table in front of the chairs;
   b) Paul O'Donnell averts his eyes when his team leader asks him if he has finished his part of the report;
   c) Bev Saunders places her hands on her hips as she conducts a training session; and
   d) Goran Garabedian, while being interviewed for a job, crosses his arms over his torso and looks at the floor.

9. **Improving Intercultural Communication**. The following message is intended for a reader in another country. Make it more reader-friendly by eliminating any colloquial expressions and slang, inflated language, and acronyms. Simplify sentence structures that are too complex and add pronouns where they are needed for clarity.

Ms. Masako Ito
Honshu Imports

Dear Masako:

I am sure you know slip-ups are bound to happen from time to time. Since we always play by the rules, we thought we'd make it up to you by sending you ASAP another shipment of our premium maple syrup pro bono. This is our gift to you.

Phone me or give my assistant a ring if the product isn't up to snuff.

Sincerely,

Jill

10. **Understanding the Challenges of International Communication**. On your own, or with a partner, interview a company manager who buys, supplies, or sells to customers outside the country and who must communicate instructions to customers whose first language is not English. Ask your interview subject about the problems and challenges she has encountered. Present your findings in a memo to your instructor.

11. **By-Country Web Pages for Multinational Companies: Noting Cultural Differences**. Large multinational corporations, such as McDonald's, create web pages for every country or region in which they operate. Log on to the following web pages and note the similarities and differences in language, content, and site design. Write a memo, accompanied by URLs or a printout of the applicable sites, that summarizes and analyzes those similarities and differences.

www.mcdonalds.ca	McDonald's Canada
www.mcdonalds.com	McDonald's USA
www.mcdonalds.com.cn	McDonald's China
www.mcdonalds.it	McDonald's Italy
www.mcdonalds.ru	McDonald's Russia
www.mcdonalds.com.br	McDonald's Brazil

ONLINE ACTIVITIES

http://www.

1. **Identifying Elements of the Communication Process**. Log on to Brian Brown's page *Introduction to Communications* and scroll down to the photographs featured in the first exercise. Apply Shannon and Weaver's communication model to each. Next, scroll down to "Modes of Communication" and identify the type of communication represented in each photograph.
   http://uva.ulb.ac.be/cit_courseware/ datacomm/dc_001.htm

2. **Body Language Activities**. These exercises are designed to help you tune in to the subtleties of body language. Along with warm-up exercises, you will find activities that involve mirroring the body language of others.
   www.rider.edu/%7Esuler/bodylang.html

3. **Active Listening Games and Exercises**. *Test Quest: Active Listening* is a web page maintained by Northeastern Educational Television of Ohio. On it, you will find quick-reference listening tips as well as links to online listening games and exercises.
   http://westernreservepublicmedia.org/ testquest/listen.htm

4. **Listening Skills: Self-Evaluations**. Visit the following web page for *Psychology Today* and take the Active Listening Skills Test by examining a number of statements and choosing the option that applies to you. A snapshot report will be created for you when you finish your test.
   http://psychologytoday.tests.psychtests.com/ take_test.php?idRegTest=3206

5. **Improving Your Listening Skills**. Read the *Marketing Matters* article on how to improve your listening skills, then try the 25-question self-scoring quiz to find out how your listening skills measure up.
   www.basis.com/advantage/v10n4/marketing_ matters.html

6. **Doing Business in Other Countries**. Log on to Foreign Affairs and International Trade Canada's web page for the Centre for Intercultural Learning. Select a country from the scroll-down menu, and note the political, economic, and cultural considerations for doing business in that country.
   www.intercultures.ca/cil-cai/ countryinsights-apercuspays-eng.asp

7. **Analyzing Privacy Issues**. Log on to the following website for the Office of the Privacy Commissioner of Canada to watch a video or read the print version of an overview of the Personal Information Protection and Electronic Documents Act as discussed by Privacy Commissioner Jennifer Stoddart. When you are done, write a two- or three-paragraph summary.
   www.priv.gc.ca/media/sp-d/2004/vs/ index_e.asp

8. **Privacy Quiz: How Well Do You Know Your Privacy Rights?** Log on to the following web page maintained by the Office of the Privacy Commissioner of Canada and try the five-question true/false

interactive quiz covering issues such as e-mail privacy and the tracking of your travels on the World Wide Web. Click on an answer and receive an explanation of the question-related issue.
www.youthprivacy.ca/en/myprivacyquiz.html

9. **Researching Company Ethics Codes**. Read ethics codes for several companies, available on the following websites, and look for similarities among them. Summarize your findings on the fundamental standards of most organizational ethics codes.

Company Codes   www.ethicsweb.ca/
                 resources/business/
                 codes.html
Lululemon   http://investor.lululemon.
                 com/documentdisplay.cfm?
                 documentid=2420

Motorola   www.motorola.com/code/
                 code.html
Merck & Co. Inc. www.merck.com/about/
                 conduct.html

10. **Privacy and Your Workplace**. Individually, or as a group, watch the following video summarizing privacy principles as outlined in PIPEDA:
www.youtube.com/watch?v=kwoN8e9stEI

11. **Facebook as a Business Tool**. Find a company that has a profile on Facebook. How does this company use this social networking tool to promote its products and services or to put forth its mission statement and increase its market share?

Getting Started: Planning and Writing Business Messages

2

In this chapter you will learn to

1. Identify steps in the writing process.

2. Plan a message according to its purpose, scope, audience, content, and most appropriate channel.

3. Use prewriting techniques such as brainstorming, mapping, and questioning to generate content and gather ideas.

4. Organize business documents by creating informal and formal outlines.

5. Apply strategies for overcoming writer's block and writing under pressure.

6. Apply strategies for revising and editing your messages.

7. Apply strategies for effective group communication, including collaborative writing.

⬤⬤ Steps in the Writing Process

In the future, perhaps, we can imagine business communication that is entirely spontaneous and completely effortless, resulting in a perfect finished product every time without the need for forethought, shaping, or polishing. For now, though, the most reliable route to a successful finished product is a process that involves several stages:

- **Prewriting**—assessing the purpose, audience, and most appropriate channel for the communication;
- **Organizing and outlining**—mapping out the most strategic and logical arrangement of ideas and details;
- **Drafting**—composing the actual message by choosing the precise wording and the style of organization that delivers information most strategically; and
- **Revising and editing**—evaluating your draft from the point of view of your readers to check for completeness, coherence, accuracy, consistency, conciseness and appropriateness of language, and organization. Revising and editing represent a last chance for improvement.

Leaving out any one of these steps or taking too many shortcuts can lead to communication that causes misunderstandings, frayed tempers, and poor results. Effective documents come about through a gradual refinement that doesn't necessarily involve a great deal of time. In fact, the more you follow this process, the easier and more natural good writing becomes until it is simply second nature. Your written message will be less susceptible to misinterpretation, more readable, and more relevant to its audience.

Making the practice of this four-step process part of your regular writing routines can simplify communication tasks and reduce the time it takes to complete them. After all, there is more to writing than just keying in a document or jotting down whatever crosses your mind. While all writing involves the making of decisions, effective writing involves the making of *informed* decisions. Thinking ahead allows you to catch problems before they become insurmountable and to size up the context in which your communication will be received so it is more likely to have an impact, receive the response you desire, and accomplish what it is meant to do. Taking one last look and reviewing what you have written before a document leaves your hands enables you to check that your communication meets the requirements you originally set out for it and maintains the standards of professionalism demanded by you and your firm. This final step ensures that your mistakes don't become someone else's problem. Perhaps the best part of learning this process is that the skills you acquire can be applied to other forms of communication, such as oral presentations and deliverables (see Chapter 12).

MESSAGE PLANNING

In writing a document or making a presentation, you usually have only one chance to get your message across accurately and with impact. There are no second chances to correct mistakes or misunderstandings, no opportunities to "get it right" the second time. Planning and preparation are forms of risk prevention—your best insurance against miscommunication. In helping you get it right the first time, these steps ensure that your communication achieves its intended purpose and meets the needs of its audience while conveying information clearly, accurately, and concisely. Planning contributes to business communication that is

- **Purpose-driven.** Effective business communication is carried out for a reason, to fulfill a specific purpose—whether it be to convey information or to solve a problem.
- **Audience-focused.** Skilled communicators profile their audiences and shape each message according to the needs, interests, and knowledge of a particular individual or group. They know that relevance can depend on looking at information or a problem from the audience's perspective rather than their own.
- **Concise.** Only freelance journalists are paid by the word—business communicators practise word economy and understand that making a document or presentation longer will not necessarily improve it. A message should consist of only the number of words needed to present ideas clearly and courteously.

PREWRITING

prewriting the process of gathering ideas and establishing the purpose, audience, and channel for a message.

Thinking a message through is the best thing you can do to simplify the communication process. The longer and more complex a message, the more that can be gained from proper preparation and planning and the less you can afford to simply say or write whatever comes to mind. Thinking critically about your subject, the reason for your communication, and its intended audience brings the greatest benefits to written correspondence and reports, but it applies as well to any sizable oral presentation. Planning or prewriting involves analyzing the writing task and its context. Each time you write, take a few seconds to analyze the context in which your message will be received by performing the following actions:

- Identify the primary purpose of the document.
- Estimate the scope of the subject you must cover.
- Determine your receiver's needs.
- Select the channel that is most appropriate for your message.
- Collect the information you plan to exchange.

Doing these things will help you adapt your message to the situation and tailor it to the needs of its readers.

Purpose

Business communication is purposeful and results-oriented. For every message you write you must first understand your reason for sending it and what it is meant to achieve. Once the goal you need to accomplish is clear, you will have an easier time organizing and composing your message. Forgetting the reason for writing increases the chance that a message will fail—for example, the writer of a claim letter may describe a faulty product but neglect to ask for an adjustment, or a congratulatory e-mail may fail to foster goodwill.

Most business communication has only one of two purposes: to *inform*, which is the most common purpose, or to *persuade*. Commonly, messages may have multiple purposes—a primary purpose and a secondary one as well. A letter informing customers of new store hours, for example, can also be used as an opportunity to convey goodwill and encourage future business. In business, people communicate with each other for one or more of the following reasons:

- to request or provide information,
- to create a record,
- to explain a policy or procedure,
- to give instructions,
- to persuade or encourage action, and
- to convey good wishes and promote goodwill.

In defining the reason for writing or speaking, also consider what you want your receiver to know and believe when they have read the document or heard you speak. Keep in mind the particular result you are you seeking from the receiver—a general response, a specific action, approval for an initiative, or a decision.

Scope

Scope refers to the breadth and depth of detail in a document relative to the subject that must be covered. Understanding the scope of your message can help you weed out irrelevancies that can otherwise bore receivers and bury your most important information. After all, why write a three-screen e-mail when all the receiver really expects is a few compact but informative sentences? Too little detail, on the other hand, can make for a trivial or pointless message. Before you begin to compose your document or launch your oral presentation, consider how detailed or technical it must be to achieve its purpose, answer readers' questions and concerns, and enable them to act on your message. Familiarize yourself with the level of detail that is normally considered acceptable for similar documents or deliverables in your workplace. Carefully follow through on instructions and be mindful of corporate and industry standards while taking into account the receiver's expectations about length, format, and visual elements.

scope the breadth or limitations of a document's coverage.

Audience Profile

Most messages aren't just communicated: they are sent with a specific audience in mind, even if that audience is a large or dispersed one. In business today it is not uncommon to communicate with people you may never meet face to face and about whom you can only make a series of informed assumptions. Even so, it is useful to focus your message by thinking about the members of your audience beforehand and evaluating their needs within the context of their organizational culture (what they do and where they work) and cultural environment (what their backgrounds are).

You may be lucky enough to have communicated with a particular audience before or to have gained knowledge through your organization's previous dealings with an individual. If your contact with the receiver has been limited, however, it is still possible to learn a great deal from an initial contact. While you should guard against false assumptions, you can also make a few educated guesses based on the receiver's professional position and responsibilities relative to your own. Applying this analysis through audience adaptation can influence how a message is received and increase its chances for success, especially if you are able to put yourself in the receiver's place and see beyond your own perspective. An audience-focused message has immediate and unmistakable relevance and works toward reversing the mass-produced, rubber-stamped boilerplate quality for which routine business communication often gets a bad reputation.

audience analysis the process of assessing the needs and knowledge of readers and listeners and adapting messages accordingly.

Audience analysis and adaptation is sometimes done unconsciously, almost out of habit, but in other cases it may require serious consideration to determine what your receiver is like. Asking the following questions may help:

1. **What are the receiver's responsibilities and position?** Understanding the receiver's responsibilities will help you determine how the information you pass on will be used. Also ask yourself if you are communicating with a superior (for instance, a supervisor), a subordinate, or a co-worker. Considering the receiver's position relative to your own can help you select the appropriate level of formality and cultivate a tone that balances deference and authority. A message to a long-time business associate may be more easy-going and familiar in its tone and language, but using the same style in a memo to your supervisor may risk offence through the lack of respect it conveys.

2. **What are the receiver's attitudes, interests, and questions?** Think about the level of importance the receiver will assign to the message. A lack of interest on the receiver's part may require you to compensate by giving additional emphasis to key points highlighting its relevance in a subject line or by making the action the receiver is supposed to take that much easier. Shaping a message to the receiver's needs can also involve anticipating the questions that the person might ask.

3. **What is your experience with the receiver?** Based on personal or professional experience you or your colleagues may have had with the receiver, you can predict possible areas of need or conflict that you should take into account when shaping your message. When you must communicate with someone who views you or your organization negatively, it may require extra effort on your part—and careful control of tone and emphasis—not to let reciprocal hostility or defensiveness interfere with your ability to get the message across tactfully and professionally.

4. **How much does the receiver know about the subject?** The reader's level of knowledge will determine the amount and type of detail included in the message. Estimating exactly what to include can be difficult, as it carries the risk of patronizing, confusing, or annoying the receiver. Refrain from telling receivers with technical expertise or specialized knowledge too much of what they already know by defining key terms they use each day. The same applies to managers, who may have a low tolerance for technical details but a general concern for findings and recommendations. On the other hand, avoid overestimating the knowledge receivers may have by failing to define key terms or concepts or neglecting to interpret specialized information they will need to follow instructions. Build on the knowledge the receiver may already have by linking it with new facts.

5. **What is the receiver's likely response?** Anticipate what the receiver's reaction to your message will be—neutral, receptive, or resistant. If the receiver is unlikely to agree with you, be prepared to use persuasive strategies or structure your message according to an indirect pattern that presents an explanation before the main message.

6. **What words define your relationship with the receiver?** Be deliberate in your choice of pronouns (*I, you, we*), as these words can define or change your

relationship with the receiver. Pronouns can also make a significant difference to your tone. Consider the point of view that represents the most effective way of addressing or appealing to the receiver.

7. **Is there more than one receiver?** Receivers with whom you must communicate to achieve your purpose are your **primary audience**. Anyone else who may, indirectly, happen to read or listen to your message forms your **secondary audience**. Because electronic messages can be forwarded and documents can be called as evidence in legal cases, there is no way to know for certain where the messages you send may end up. For this reason, it makes good sense to uphold ethical and legal standards in all communication.

8. **Do you need to adapt your message for an international receiver?** Consider what you need to take into account about the receiver's background, environment, and beliefs.

9. **Does the receiver have particular expectations?** The receiver may intend to use the document in a particular way, which will influence her expectations about the document's length and form.

To make the task of answering these questions easier, try to envision your reader by imagining that the person is sitting across from you as you write. Performing audience analysis can also help you define reader benefits for informative and persuasive messages by uncovering factors that will motivate readers. **Reader benefits** are the advantages the receiver stands to gain by complying with your policy, supporting your idea, buying your product, or using your service.

Medium or Channel

The **medium** or **channel** for a message is its vehicle of transmission. Given that more than one channel may often do, choosing the best channel depends on its appropriateness to the messaging situation and your purpose in communicating—to solve a problem, collaborate, pass on information, or establish rapport. It also has to do with how well you understand the receiver's preferences. You have a choice of traditional means such as memos and letters, face-to-face meetings, and telephone calls, or more recent technologies such as fax, e-mail, voice mail, text messaging, and video conferencing. To assess which channel is best for your purpose, consider the following factors:

- **Accuracy of transmission required.** Is the channel susceptible to technical difficulties or can you count on its reliability? Think back to your most recent bad cellphone connection for an example of how misunderstandings can result from channel barriers.
- **Speed of transmission required.** Does the message have to reach someone quickly? Telephone, text messaging, e-mail, and voice mail are good options in time-sensitive situations.
- **Cost of the channel.** You should be able to justify the cost of transmitting a message according to its importance and urgency.
- **Need for a permanent record.** Instructions, policies, and legally binding agreements have more than a passing importance and must be recorded and archived for future reference.

primary audience the intended receiver of a message—the person or persons who will use or act on a message's information.

secondary audience anyone, other than the primary audience, who will read a document and be affected by the action or decision it calls for.

reader benefits the advantages the reader gains by complying with what the writer proposes in buying products, following policies, or endorsing ideas.

medium or **channel** the physical means by which an oral or written message is transmitted.

- **Detail of the message.** If your message is complex or highly detailed, you should avoid channels such as telephone or voice mail that cannot accommodate a high level of detail or precise wording. Written communication is better for this purpose.
- **Importance of the message.** Certain channels project more authority and command more respect than others. For an initial contact, a formal business letter may communicate a company's professionalism in a way that an e-mail message does not.
- **Privacy required.** E-mail is an unsuitable means to transmit confidential information or private messages.
- **Size and location of the audience.** Channels such as e-mail are effective for communicating with a large, dispersed audience. When travel is impractical, video conferencing can bring together people who are spread out geographically and allow them to both see and hear one another.
- **Level of formality required.** The decision of whether to write a formal business letter or simply pick up the phone depends on your relationship to the receiver and your purpose.
- **Immediacy of the feedback required.** Some channels, such as the telephone or a face-to-face conversation, allow for immediate feedback. If you use other channels, such as voice mail, a hard-copy letter, or e-mail, feedback will be delayed, so be prepared to wait for it.
- **Level of control over how the message is composed.** If you must word your message carefully, your best channel choices are hard-copy letter, e-mail, and voice mail. On the telephone and in face-to-face conversations, you will have to think on your feet.
- **Richness of the channel. Richness** refers to the different types of cues—verbal and visual—from which meaning can be inferred. A rich medium is better for building rapport. If you have to deliver bad news, the tone of voice and facial expressions you use in a face-to-face conversation convey an empathy and sensitivity that cannot be so easily expressed in an e-mail message, where visual cues are absent and tonal cues can be misleading.
- **Preferences of your organization.** An organization may have preferences about which channel you use for certain types of communication.

The medium or channel you choose has the power to influence how your message is interpreted. Each channel has its own specific advantages and drawbacks.

Content Generation

Good content contributes to effective communication. Collecting all the information you need before you start to write, whether by researching data or simply generating ideas, is essential. Keep in mind that the facts you gather should warrant your efforts and your readers' attention. Formal research methods, required for formal reports and presentations, are detailed in Chapter 11. Many types of business messages, for example routine memos and e-mails, require only informal idea-generation strategies, such as the following:

1. **Brainstorming.** Brainstorming is a free-association exercise that helps to stimulate creative thinking, unlock ideas, and reveal hidden connections. If you have reached a point of stalemate in planning your document, brainstorming can put a fresh perspective on a stubborn topic. Start with a blank computer screen or a fresh

richness a quality of the types of cues by which meaning can be derived from a message.

brainstorming a method of generating content by listing ideas as they come to mind.

TABLE 2.1   Channels and Their Benefits

Channel	Benefit
Report or proposal	For delivering extensive data internally or externally
Letter on company stationery	For initial contacts with customers, suppliers, and outside associates, or when you need a written record of subsequent correspondence with them
Memos	For internal communication, when you need a written record to issue reminders, outline policies, explain procedures, or gather information
E-mail	For less formal communication replacing letters and memos; when you ask for feedback, solicit opinions, start discussions, collect data, or send information with or without an attachment; useful for communicating with large, decentralized groups; not appropriate for sending private or emotionally charged information
Fax	For recipients who do not have access to e-mail, when information must be received quickly and viewed in its original form
Telephone call	For gathering or sharing information quickly, or for negotiating and clarifying contracts when it is impossible to meet in person; for meeting with three or more participants via conference call as a less expensive alternative to a face-to-face meeting
Voice-mail message	For leaving a brief, uncomplicated message—a question, answer, request, or confirmation—to which the receiver can respond when it is convenient
Text message	For brief messages containing important or routine information; only when your organization authorizes the use of instant messaging
Face-to-face meeting	For establishing initial contact and rapport with clients, customers, and associates; for negotiating, brainstorming, problem-solving, or any other group communication where consensus is required
Face-to-face conversation	For delivering a personal message or negative news, or for communicating persuasively
Video conferencing	For meeting when travel is impractical; like a face-to-face meeting, it allows participants to both see and hear each other

sheet of paper and write down your topic keyword. Set aside ten uninterrupted minutes and, while suspending judgment about how good or bad your ideas are and without stopping, jot down any thoughts that come to mind. When the ten minutes have elapsed, sort through and analyze what you have recorded, saving only your best ideas and discarding the rest. If a single attempt doesn't yield enough ideas, repeat the process. Next, group the items that are related or arrange them in logical order according to the purpose of your document and the needs of your reader. This process will yield a preliminary outline. A further brainstorming session can help you fill in any omissions and correct any weaknesses.

Problems of office e-mail communication:

— overstuffed inboxes
— shouting
— flaming—angry messages

— rampant cc-ing of bosses and colleagues
— poorly written messages
— overly telegraphic style
— grammar mistakes
— spam
— lack of e-mail protocol
— inappropriate and/or offensive messages
— unnecessary/irrelevant messages
— rambling messages
— misleading/inaccurate subject lines
— incorrectly addressed messages
— lack of formatting
— incomplete information

Grouped items:
— poorly written messages
   — mistakes in grammar, spelling, and punctuation
   — rambling, poorly formatted messages
   — incorrect address
   — overly telegraphic style
   — misleading/inaccurate subject lines
— overstuffed inboxes
   — rampant cc-ing of bosses and colleagues
   — spam
   — unnecessary/irrelevant messages
— lack of e-mail protocol
   — flaming—angry messages
   — shouting
   — inappropriate and/or offensive messages

mapping or **clustering**
a method of generating content by visualizing the main topic and its subcategories.

2. **Mapping or clustering.** Mapping, also known as clustering, is a form of brainstorming that involves a visualization of the main topic and its related classifications and subtopics. A cluster diagram is useful for defining the relationship between ideas. Start with a fresh sheet of paper and put a keyword that best characterizes your topic in a circle at the centre of the page. Draw lines, like spokes radiating from the hub of a wheel, to connect your topic word with related ideas that come to mind. Circle each new idea you generate and allow each subtopic to stimulate additional subtopics. Continue the process, without stopping to critique yourself, until you have exhausted the many possibilities of the topic. The resulting map will show clusters and subclusters of ideas grouped around the central concept.

journalistic questions
the essential questions (*who, what, why, when, where,* and *how*) that frame journalists' inquiries as they focus and prepare their stories.

3. **Asking questions.** The five *Ws*—*who, what, why, when,* and *where*—not to mention *how,* are productive **journalistic questions** to ask about your topic and its major ideas, especially if you intend to write a clear and compelling document.

Prewriting exercises supply you with the raw material for the next stage of the composition process—outlining.

FIGURE 2.1 Defining Terms of Part-Time Contracts

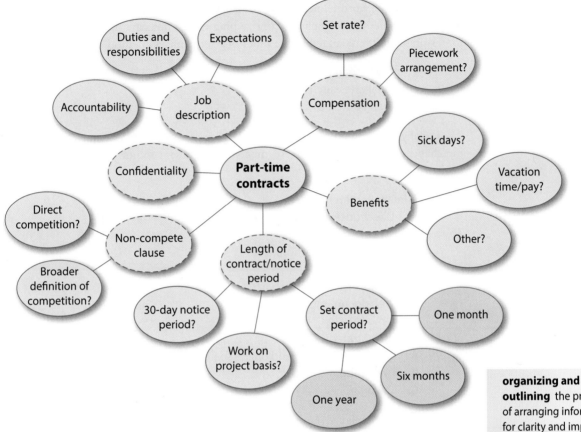

ORGANIZING AND OUTLINING

Once you have gathered your material, it needs to be structured in a coherent way so readers will understand it. Based on your purpose and your readers' needs, select a method of development that orders your subject from beginning to end. There are four methods:

- the **sequential method of development**—mapping the steps in a process;
- the **chronological method of development**—tracing an event from the beginning to the present;
- the general to specific method of development; and
- the **cause-and-effect method of development**.

Not all business documents require **outlines**, but those of any length, importance, or complexity do. An outline is a skeleton or framework of the document you are going to write. Preparing an outline helps to ensure your document is complete and also helps you detect errors in logic and coherence. It plots out your document from beginning to end and gives you the opportunity to experiment with the arrangement of ideas before

organizing and outlining the process of arranging information for clarity and impact.

sequential development a method of organization describing the arrangement of steps in a process.

chronological development a method of organization that describes events in the order in which they occurred.

cause-and-effect development a method of organization that links events with the reasons for them.

outline a framework for a document, showing its divisions and elements.

you commit them to the written page. Once you begin to write, the work of deciding how to organize your document will have already been done, leaving you to concentrate on tone, word choice, sentence structure, and the accuracy of your content. A short, basic topic outline includes concise phrases that describe the breakdown of your topic's presentation, arranged in the order of your primary method of development.

I.   Primary Research
II. Secondary Research
III. Research Strategies

Usually an outline breaks the topic down into three to five major categories that can then be divided into smaller segments that represent minor points and supporting evidence.

I.   Primary Research
    A. Direct observations
    B. Interviews
    C. Surveys and questionnaires
II. Secondary Research
    A. Books, articles, and reports
    B. Web documents   } Classification
    C. E-mail discussions
III. Research Strategies
    A. Conducting library and online searches
    B. Evaluating resources   } Sequential
    C. Taking notes

For more complex documents, use alphanumeric and decimal outline templates, which can be found in most word-processing software. You can find examples of these outlining systems in Chapter 10. In Chapters 5, 6, 7, and 8, which cover the most frequently written types of messages, you will be introduced to basic writing patterns for receptive and unreceptive audiences—sometimes known as good-news and bad-news patterns for business correspondence.

DRAFTING

drafting the preliminary writing of a document.

When you write for business, you cannot always wait for inspiration. In fact, **drafting** a message is a task best viewed as a necessary means to an end, like any other business function. Rely on good preparation to get the job done and begin by expanding your outline without worrying too much about creating a perfect copy on your first try. Remember, you can usually refine your language and make corrections later. With practice, writing and revision can become simultaneous activities. Write continuously, not stopping once you have gained some momentum. You may want to begin with the part of the message or document that seems easiest to write. If you are writing a sizable document, such as a report, you may want to write your introduction last so it will more accurately reflect the overall contents. In longer documents, an introduction will serve as a lens to focus the detailed information that follows. In shorter routine messages, the opening may either reveal the primary purpose for writing or prepare the reader for the details to come.

Overcoming Writer's Block

Eventually, even the best and most confident writer will experience a bout of **writer's block**—the temporary inability to fully formulate and express one's thoughts due to a lack of inspiration. The good thing about writer's block, if anything, is that it usually doesn't last; it is just a short-term halt in the writing process. The bad thing about writer's block is that it can strike at any time, when you least expect it, and—worst of all—when you are up against a deadline. Feeling rushed can intensify feelings of communication anxiety and turn procrastination into paralysis. The end results can be missed deadlines, a breakdown in the communication process, and decreased productivity. Though potentially serious, writer's block is entirely curable. With proper intervention, it doesn't have to become chronic. Experimenting with a few simple strategies may be all you need to do to banish writer's block:

1. **Start early.** Give yourself enough time to think through a writing task and complete it according to your goals. Remember that good writing is easier to produce when you are relaxed. Stress is only beneficial when it gives you that extra push to get the job done.

2. **Work on a computer.** Drafting is considerably easier when you have the ability to add, delete, and move passages of text. From a rough draft produced on a computer, you will have a fairly good idea what your finished document will look like.

3. **Talk it out.** Many people are more experienced talkers than writers and may be able to articulate their thoughts more fluently in spoken as opposed to written language. Verbalizing your ideas or dictating them into a tape recorder can help you get your thoughts down in some form. Ask yourself *what am I trying to say here?* and answer the question as directly as possible. Ease up on self-criticism for the time being—there will be time to polish and perfect your draft later. What you want to do at this stage is capture the essence of what you mean. If you worry that you might earn a reputation for talking to yourself, especially if you work in a crowded office, you can internalize your verbalizations and make this strategy work for you in silence. Just write down your thoughts once they are fully formed.

4. **Skip around.** The advantage of working with word-processing software is that sections of a document can be prepared in any order and then cut and pasted according to an outline. Don't feel you have to start at the beginning and work your way through to the end of the document. Capitalize on your inspiration by starting with the section you feel most comfortable about. Leave the section you are unsure about until you've had a chance to build your confidence.

5. **Take a break.** Obviously, if you are at work, you won't want to fritter away company time, but switching to another activity—filing, tidying up your desk, answering a telephone call, listening to voice mail—can give you the objectivity you need to return to the writing task refreshed.

6. **Practice freewriting.** Freewriting is an exercise in dedicated, non-stop writing. Basically, it involves forcing yourself to write on a particular subject for a period of ten uninterrupted minutes so that ideas can be unlocked and translated to the page. Not everything you write will be useful, but you may want to keep some parts

writer's block a psychological state of being unable to begin the process of composition out of fear or anxiety over the communication task.

freewriting a method of generating content based on unstructured writing and the recording of ideas as they come to mind.

of the draft. Repeat the process until you have accumulated enough material on which to base your document.

7. **Adopt a positive attitude to writing.** Practise writing regularly and ask colleagues and bosses for feedback. Through interaction you can learn about the corporate culture in which you are writing and determine exactly what readers expect and what certain situations demand. Think of writing as a means toward achieving your professional goals and be positive in thinking that those goals are achievable.

Writing Under Pressure

Business documents are usually produced quickly in response to demands and deadlines. It can be difficult to keep up with the volume of daily messaging let alone generate formal reports and documents on which the bottom line depends. Producing error-free, results-oriented documents in time-sensitive situations requires a cool head and a little preparation. The following process can help busy communicators cope under pressure:

1. **Allocate your time.** Consider how much time and energy you need to invest in writing your message relative to its purpose and importance. Spending an hour drafting a brief e-mail may not make sense if you have fifty more messages to write that day. Develop a mental timetable for accomplishing your writing tasks.

2. **Keep distractions to a minimum.** Tune out office banter and organize your writing area by setting out all the tools and resources you will need.

3. **Get the most from word-processing software.** Use the outline feature to brainstorm and organize an outline, then cut and paste to organize alternative ways of presenting information

4. **Take a few seconds to plan the structure.** Every document has a beginning, a middle, and an end. Quickly select a method of development to keep your information under control: sequential, chronological, general to specific, or cause and effect.

5. **Remember your reader.** Visualize your reader. Explain difficult concepts by relating them to what is familiar and already known to your reader.

6. **Go with the flow.** Start with the section of your document that is easiest to write and resist the temptation to take a break once you have momentum. Plan to reward yourself in some way—with a break or a cup of coffee—once you have finished your task.

7. **Leave refinements for revision.** Your copy doesn't have to be perfect until it is time to send it.

REVISING AND EDITING

revising or **revision** the process of reviewing and making changes in a draft document—adding, deleting, reorganizing, or substituting—to transform it into a finished document.

editing the process of checking a writing draft to ensure it conforms to standards of good English, style, and accepted business-writing practice.

Revising a document involves adding, deleting, reorganizing, and replacing the words, sentences, or paragraphs of a final draft. **Editing** is the fine-tuning of the revised draft—a final correction of spelling, grammar, punctuation, and consistency problems. Together, revising and editing represent the now-or-never phase of document production—the point at which final changes and refinements can make or break a piece of writing. Even a document that looks fine at first glance can usually do with a few last-minute adjustments, some gentle tweaking, or even some major rethinking. At this stage, you become your own impartial critic, deciding if your document measures up to the goals you set out for it, correcting potential weaknesses and spotting improvements that have to be made. Always keep your prewriting goals in mind so you won't be tempted either to ignore the revision process altogether or, at the other extreme, to be too hard on yourself and feel you must start again from scratch. Your goal should be to make the document better, continuing until the document is satisfactory.

Before you start the revision process, take a break to ensure that you can look objectively at the document you have written. Clear your head by doing something different for a few minutes or a few hours—whatever the time frame for your document and its deadline allow for. A cooling period is essential to the revision of any important document—without it you will be too close to the draft to evaluate it effectively. For brief, routine letters or e-mails, you can usually carry out a quick but careful proofreading on the spot or revise onscreen as you go, checking for the effectiveness of organization, appropriateness of style and tone, and the accuracy of both language and content.

For all other documents, especially for important external or upwardly directed communication, the revision process needs to be taken very seriously. Follow a few basic strategies:

1. **Work from a paper copy of your draft.** Print out your document rather than first making changes onscreen. You will want to have a record of what you originally wrote in case you decide that the first version was preferable. Mark up the copy (which is best double-spaced to make room for comments) using standard proofreaders' symbols (see Figure 2.2).

2. **Reduce your reading speed.** It is unlikely you will find any errors if you speed-read. Take your time.

3. **Look at your document from the reader's perspective.** Because a shift in perspective is essential to good revision, put pride aside and pretend you didn't author your document, remembering that it is always easier to find errors in someone else's copy. Give yourself credit when you find an error. It means you are doing your job well and performing a valuable service for your reader.

4. **Make several passes over the draft.** No matter how careful and scrupulous a reader you are, you won't be able to spot every error or analyze every need for global revision on a single reading. Simplify the revision task by reading for one specific set of problems at a time.

5. **Read your draft aloud.** Errors and instances of awkwardness are detected more easily when you hear them rather than read them silently. Making a recording and playing it back is sometimes a useful method for clearing up problems with sentence structure, tone, and fogginess in documents that have to be perfect.

6. **Use spell- and grammar-checkers, but respect their limitations.** Diagnostic software has great capabilities, but it may not flag every error. Sometimes, it may isolate a proper noun and suggest an incorrect spelling for it or fail to detect a misspelled technical term, so look carefully at each highlighted word and be prepared to use your own judgment. There is no substitute for reading the document yourself—even if you have to do it two or three times.

FIGURE 2.2 Proofreaders' Symbols

Mark in Margin	Instruction
∧	Insert
ℓ	Delete
(stet)	Let stand
⌣	Close space
(cap)	Capitalize
(lc)	Make lowercase
(ital)	Italicize
(bf)	Set in boldface
(rom)	Set in roman type
(sp)	Correct spelling/Spell out
¶	Start paragraph
run-in	No paragraph
⊙	Insert period
⌄	Insert comma
⌄/⌄	Insert quotation marks

A critical read-through requires that you pay close attention to the following factors, many of which are discussed in Chapters 3 and 4:

- **Accuracy.** You must be able to verify the accuracy of the information you present. Look for inaccuracies and ensure your information is free of distortion. Compare names and numbers with their sources.
- **Conciseness.** Prune deadwood phrases and redundancies and tighten your style to create a lean, reader-friendly document.
- **Completeness.** Ensure that your document achieves its purpose and meets readers' needs. Adequate information should be provided without causing information overload. Check that essential material enables readers to take action, make a decision, or know what do to when they are finished reading the document.

- **Structure and coherence.** The elements that make up your document should be organized logically according to the rhetorical purpose you wish to achieve. Related ideas should be linked through logic and appropriate transitional devices.
- **Sentence and paragraph construction.** Look for awkwardness in sentence construction. Give impact and directness to your writing by using the active voice and replacing weak verbs and noun phrases with precise, forceful verbs.
- **Consistency and format.** The use of language, style of visuals, and overall design should be consistent. Check for lopsided formatting by making sure your document is balanced on the page. Look for possible problems with lettered items, headings, bulleted and numbered lists, capitalization, underlining, bold print, and italics.
- **Readability, word choice, and ethics.** Decide if the document's level of difficulty is appropriate for the reader(s). Replace vague or pretentious words with specific and familiar ones. Keep biased language out of your document and ask yourself whether you would mind if someone other than the intended receiver read your document.
- **Grammar, spelling, and punctuation.** Check for possible grammar errors—unbalanced sentences and verbs that might not agree with their subjects—that can undermine the professionalism and readability of your document. Scan for spelling mistakes and punctuation errors that can make your document look sloppy.
- **Typographical errors.** Check for any inadvertent errors—transposed letters and misplaced punctuation, for example—that may have crept into your draft. Most spell-checkers can tag these errors, but they are no replacement for a careful line-by-line reading. Unless your organization tells you to do otherwise, ensure that your spell-check program is set for Canadian English. If you opt for U.S. English, be sure to use its distinctive spellings consistently.

Revision becomes easier with practice. Make the most of the constructive feedback you receive from instructors, and always use it to help you evaluate the success of your communication relative to your goals. Review the advice and comments you receive and assess the types of faults and errors most common to your writing. From this assessment, devise a customized checklist you can refer to when revising and proofreading your documents. The end of Chapter 4 offers additional tips on proofreading.

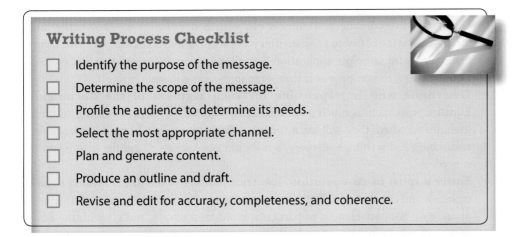

Writing Process Checklist

- ☐ Identify the purpose of the message.
- ☐ Determine the scope of the message.
- ☐ Profile the audience to determine its needs.
- ☐ Select the most appropriate channel.
- ☐ Plan and generate content.
- ☐ Produce an outline and draft.
- ☐ Revise and edit for accuracy, completeness, and coherence.

Collaborative Writing

Most successful businesses rely on teamwork to bring their projects and initiatives to fruition. Teamwork, though, is only possible when a spirit of co-operation exists in the workplace and when individuals are willing to collaborate in the give-and-take of shared responsibilities and decision-making. Employers today screen applicants partly on the basis of their ability to work collaboratively. This important skill has increasing application to writing **collaborative writing** projects, whose size or time constraints may demand that two or more writers work together to produce a single document. A project may involve multiple areas of expertise that no single person is able to supply on her own. Responsibility for the success of the project doesn't rest on one person, but on the ability of the group to communicate, build loyalty, and both accept and give criticism objectively.

> **collaborative writing**
> the process of writers working together to create finished reports, proposals, and other important documents.

Here are some key points to keep in mind when working and writing collaboratively:

- **Practice active listening.** Take other viewpoints seriously and consider them impartially and open-mindedly. Be attentive to the nuances and inferences of discussions. Make sure you understand what you've heard before responding to it.
- **Designate a team coordinator.** This person may not have authority over the entire project but can coordinate planning and activities. The team coordinator keeps track of progress on the document and consolidates draft segments of the document into a master copy.
- **Do up-front planning.** Meet to discuss the document before anyone begins to write. Brainstorm ideas for the project, conceptualize the document, evaluate its content, and create an outline, documenting the planning process as you go. Create a schedule that accommodates all group members' work commitments and notes due dates for drafts, revisions, and final versions.
- **Agree on writing-style standards.** Establish the style points and formats writers are expected to follow. This will help to diminish differences in individual writing styles.
- **Use technology to overcome constraints of physical location.** An initial face-to-face meeting can help group members get to know each other and build group loyalty. After that, planning and virtual meeting software can help members collaborate over distances. Members can e-mail documents to each other, use instant messaging software to share files and carry on live text chats, or share a virtual whiteboard (a helper application that allows a document to be shared by two or more users) to compose as if they were in the same room.
- **Determine who is responsible for each segment of the document.** Equalize workloads as much as possible. Allow others to work according to their strengths or where they will learn the most. Each group member is responsible for researching and writing a segment, but should not hesitate to ask for help when it is needed.
- **Foster a spirit of co-operation.** Everyone should feel that she is making a contribution and can be heard. To do this, you may have to be flexible enough to compromise on your attachment to particular words and phrases and go with the flow of the project. Even when you check your ego at the door, expect a certain level of

disharmony. Creative differences can be a good thing, however, as under the right conditions divergent viewpoints gradually meld in productive consensus.

- **Harmonize writing styles.** Exchange and review writing segments while remaining diplomatic in your criticism of others. Leave it to the group's best writer or editor to do a final check for consistency and integration of writing styles. The final copy should read in one voice, have a continuous style, and not look as though sections have simply been pasted together. Ask several people to check the document to make sure all the parts are properly integrated and error-free.

WORKSHOPS AND DISCUSSION FORUMS

1. **Multiple Choice: Selecting the Most Effective Channel.** Decide which communication channel would be most effective in each of the following situations. Be prepared to defend your choice in each case and discuss why the options you rejected would be ineffective.

   a) Your manager has just rewarded you for a job well done with two tickets to the ballpark for tonight's game. The first pitch is in just over three hours and you would like to invite a colleague in another department to attend with you. To contact him, you

      i. send a fax to his department and hope he will read it in time.

      ii. telephone him and leave a brief message in his voice-mail box.

      iii. write a detailed e-mail message although you know he checks his e-mail only twice a day, once when he arrives at work and again after lunch.

      iv. send a text message because you know he is never without his Blackberry.

   b) As a departmental manager, you have just received a directive from the company CEO advising you of a new and very detailed sexual harassment policy that will go into effect shortly. To explain the terms of this policy to members of your department, you

      i. call a fifteen-minute meeting and tell all staff members that they are responsible for recording details of the policy.

      ii. write a detailed departmental memo clarifying every aspect of the policy and offering to address potential questions and concerns.

      iii. post an announcement of the new policy on the departmental message board and tell department members to read it when they have a chance.

      iv. talk the new policy over when you meet department members in the coffee room.

   c) Although you hold a junior position in your company, you have a few suggestions to improve the efficiency of operation and would like to run your ideas by the COO. You decide the best way to present your ideas would be to

      i. prepare an informal recommendation report in which you outline your ideas based on evidence you have gathered from company documents.

      ii. tap him on the shoulder in the hallway, as he's rushing to a meeting, and ask if you can bend his ear.

      iii. book an appointment with him to discuss your ideas in a face-to-face meeting.

2. **Collaborative Writing Workshop.** Assemble a group of up to eight classmates and appoint a team leader. Assume that you have been asked to design three new college or university courses for programs in which you are now studying. Meet to brainstorm ideas, establish style preferences, and assign responsibilities (for example, researching current courses, identifying potential needs, establishing course outcomes

and outlines, writing course descriptions, revising and polishing draft material). Once each member has completed her portion of the draft, meet again to discuss problems and harmonize writing styles. When you are satisfied with the finalized version, submit it to your instructor for feedback. Each team member should then write a brief one-paragraph assessment of the collaborative writing process. What were its benefits and advantages? What were its drawbacks?

3. **Revision Workshop.** Working together as a group, read the text of the following extract from a press release and consider how it can be improved through editing and revision. Keep in mind the factors for successful revision summarized on pages 50–1.

FOR IMMEDIATE RELEASE

For More Information Call
Susan Sullivan

WINNIPEG, MANITOBA, MAY 10, 2009 . . . Gordon Wong has joined Superior Plastics as vice president—marketing. Superior Plastics, headquartered in Winipeg, produces polymer tubing and coils. Since 1991 Superior also been producing tubing for U.S. distribution through the firm of Reliable Plastics, Chicagoe. Wong will coordinate overseas distribution through, the company's Jakarta office. Wong will travel extensively in the Far East while developing marketing channels. For Superior.

Formerly, Wong was director of services at Big Name Marketing Associates, a consulting group n Montreal. While at Big Name, he develop a computer-based marketing centre that link textile firms in Hong Kong, Poland and Portugal. He graduate from the Rotman School of Business. Wong was chosen out of a pool of 350 applicants that included well-known marketing executives such as Peter Farnsworth and Livy Cohen.

WRITING IMPROVEMENT EXERCISES

1. **Identifying the Purpose.** For each of the following examples, identify the primary purpose—to inform, persuade, or convey goodwill.
   a) a newspaper editorial
   b) a corporate year-end report
   c) a request to a charitable organization for a grant/donation
   d) a set of operating instructions for the departmental photocopier
   e) a congratulatory e-mail
   f) a sales letter for a low-interest-rate credit card

2. **Assessing the Receiver.** Assume that you must write to each of the following individuals to ask for a favour:
   a) your bank manager
   b) your course instructor
   c) a friend, sibling, or other close family member
   d) a former employer
   e) a company vice-president

   Consider the receiver's needs in each case and draw up a reader profile based on your assessment. Indicate what your approach might be in each case.

3. **Messages and Their Audiences.** For each of the following writing situations, devise an audience analysis.

   a) an unsolicited sales letter promoting life insurance to university alumni

   b) a letter of application for a job posted on an employment website (your qualifications are a close match for the position)

   c) a letter from the municipal waste department explaining the introduction of a mandatory composting program

   d) a letter to a fellow electrical engineer outlining the technical specifications for a new circuitry panel

   e) an e-mail to your departmental manager suggesting the introduction of an internship program

   f) a letter to members of a municipal board asking for the lifting of height restrictions on a multi-storey condominium project your company is currently developing

   g) your letter to a supplier in Hong Kong requesting textile samples to be used in your new clothing line

4. **Choosing Functional and Appropriate Communication Channels.** Analyze each of the following situations and select the most appropriate communication channel: face-to-face conversation, telephone call, voice-mail message, e-mail message, hard-copy memo, text message, or formal letter. Also consider the channels that are least suited to the situation.

   a) cancelling a business lunch appointment at the last minute

   b) announcing an important policy change to employees

   c) confirming attendance at an upcoming meeting

   d) informing a claimant of the advantageous terms of a claim's settlement

   e) notifying a long-time, soon-to-be terminated employee of the company's decision to downsize

   f) convincing a potential customer to purchase a line of software your company manufactures

   g) presenting findings and recommendations related to your organization's need for a new health insurance provider

   h) notifying five department members of a training seminar scheduled for two weeks from now

5. **Freewriting Exercise.** Select one of the following tasks and write about it for ten minutes, without stopping.

   a) Explain the registration procedure at your college.

   b) Describe the skills requirements for your current job.

   c) Describe the communication skills required in your current job or in your program of study.

   When the time has elapsed, stop and analyze what you have written. If the exercise has not helped you uncover at least three to five major ideas, repeat the process and use the points you generate as the basis for an outline. Has the process helped you uncover new ideas?

6. **Cluster Diagram Exercise.** Assess a problem you have encountered on campus or at your workplace—inadequate or faulty equipment, inefficient or under-staffed services, or inconvenient scheduling. Prepare a cluster diagram to explore the problem and analyze possible solutions. Use the diagram as the basis for a three- to five-point outline.

7. **Creating an Outline.** Assume that a friend is interested in the degree or diploma program in which you are currently enrolled and has asked you to write a letter or e-mail describing its prerequisites, annual cost, and course requirements. Create an outline for your message.

ONLINE ACTIVITIES

http://www.

1. **Business and Professional Writing Quiz.** This online quiz, from the University College of the Cariboo, tests your knowledge of business writing by asking you to answer a series of questions as if you were a member of the business community. Enter your numeric choice, then click to check your answer. **www.tru.ca/disciplines/biz.html**

2. **Brainstorming and Drafting Online.** Although this Application Essays web page from the Writing Centre at the University of Wisconsin-Madison is intended for writers of expository essays, it offers useful practice in brainstorming and composing online, so fill in each field but pretend that your task is to compose an e-mail message. At any point in the writing process, you can send the writing you've done to yourself in an e-mail by filling out and submitting the form at the bottom of the page. **www.wisc.edu/writing/Handbook/apessay_tutorial.html**

3

Business Style: Word Choice, Conciseness, and Tone

In this chapter you will learn to

1. Use plain, precise, and familiar language to get to the point, prevent misunderstanding, and write with impact.

2. Identify and eliminate problem words that do not convey your meaning clearly and directly.

3. Choose accurate and appropriate words to create constructive, inclusive, reader-oriented messages.

4. Identify strategies for concise messaging.

5. Develop a conversational and confident tone and adjust it to suit a range of writing purposes, professional situations, and readerships.

6. Differentiate between personal and impersonal style.

Good writing is a matter of how well you reach your readers and how well you get your message across in the way you intend. Developing an effective business style is the key to achieving these goals in the workplace. By definition, style comprises the rules, conventions, and options you need to consider whenever you write. These are rules that apply to the words you choose and combine to form sentences: how correct they are, how well they support the substance of your information and ideas, and how right they are for particular situations and audiences.

Effective business style is more than a matter of adhering to the rules of grammar, though these too are vital in ensuring that what you write makes sense to your readers. Good business style involves thinking about how words "sound" and how your readers are affected by the words you use. With practice, you can learn to vary your style to suit a variety of situations.

Your writing style is a reflection of who you are in the workplace, how you think, what you think of your readers, and how you and your company do business. Good style creates a good impression, not just of you but of the company you represent. Each time you have something important to say or a task to carry out that involves written communication, your business style will be key to getting the job done properly, ethically, and on time. By paying attention to the language you use, you can help to build and sustain business relationships by eliminating the frustration that can result from communication that is hard to read, confusing, or uninformative. After all, readers on the job are busy enough without having to deal with messages full of word clutter, ambiguous double meanings, offensive language, or message-obscuring jargon.

Savvy communicators know that a clear, crisp, adaptable style, kept as tight and lean and factual as possible, can simplify everyday tasks and make information manageable. In the long term, good writing backed up by an effective business style is a major contributor to career growth and a vital factor in building personal and corporate credibility.

◖◗ Word Choice

PLAIN STYLE

plain style or **plain language** a style of writing that places value on simplicity, directness, and clarity.

The need for clear, understandable, concrete language is not unique to the age of high-speed communication. In fact centuries ago, when people first began to write for science and business and industry, demands were heard for the kind of simplicity and economy that is now the hallmark of **plain style** or **plain language**. Plain style makes it acceptable for you to write in the same everyday language that you use when you speak. It helps you reach your readers instead of putting your audience at a distance. One of the aims of plain style is to banish dead and empty words in favour of lively, expressive ones that readers connect with immediately and remember easily. Because it saves time, puts readers first, and makes ideas and information meaningful, plain language is good for business. For a sense of the impact plain language can have, note the difference in the following sentences:

- I will be responsible for actioning and undertake a prioritization of my commitments in terms of my daily scheduling.

- I will arrange my daily schedule.

The case for putting plain language into wider practice continues to gain momentum. In recent decades the international plain-language movement—dedicated to presenting information so it makes sense to most people and can be acted upon after a single reading—has gained the endorsement of government agencies, businesses, professions, and industries that value comprehensibility over management-speak and the bureaucratic bluster of legalese. Plain style, with its pared-down, keep-it-simple approach, is characterized by a few common-sense principles:

- **Use common, everyday words, except for necessary technical terms.** Language should be familiar and accessible, not pretentious.
- **Use reasonable sentence lengths.** Aim for twenty words or fewer to avoid padding or needlessly overloading sentences.
- **Use active-voice verbs and phrasal verbs.** Active voice verbs show who or what performs an action. Phrasal verbs are simple and informal, combining verbs and prepositions to deliver their meaning (for example *work out* instead of *devise*). (See also Chapter 4, "Applying Active and Passive Voice," pp. 99–100.)
- **Use personal pronouns: *I, you,*** and ***we*.** Personal pronouns, used in moderation in all documents except formal reports, give you the fluency to say what you need to say with as little awkwardness as possible.
- **Use unambiguous language. Ambiguity** refers to an inexact expression that has a double meaning and is therefore open to interpretation (for example, does *Ricardo likes boring classmates* mean that Ricardo likes to bore classmates or that he likes classmates who are boring?). Good communicators do their best to prevent ambiguity from creeping into their writing.
- **Place the subject as close as possible to the verb.** The meaning of a sentence relies on the clear relationship of its subject and verb. Tangled sentences result when long modifying phrases separate these all-important elements.

Some writers have a hard time accepting plain style because they think it will make their writing dull, simplistic, or boring, but such fears are unfounded. Communicating in a plain style won't require you to oversimplify or "dumb down" your content. In fact, an effective plain style gives daily communication energy, impact, and precision that sustains readers' interest and enables them to easily grasp complicated ideas and activities.

WORD CHOICE STEP 1: USE FAMILIAR WORDS

A plain style relies on familiar, accessible language—common, everyday words of one or two syllables. Difficult, overstated words tend to be longer, with three or more syllables. In long sentences they can make even the most routine message dense and unreadable. Writers usually resort to long, pretentious, important-sounding words for the wrong reasons—out of inexperience, to intimidate, to impress, or to express authority. Pretentious words can be tempting status symbols and smokescreens, dressing up or hiding your intended meaning, but in the end they usually alienate readers instead of impressing them. Readers often skip over unfamiliar words or only partly grasp their

voice a term that describes a verb's ability to show whether the subject of a sentence acts or is acted upon.

phrasal verb a verb that combines with one or more prepositions to deliver its meaning.

pronouns words that replace or refer to nouns.

ambiguity a term that describes an obscure or inexact meaning.

meaning. The consequences of not opting for plain and familiar language can be seen in the following "translation" of a well-known saying:

Pretentious: It is preferable to effect the adoption and implementation of precautionary measures than to embark on a regrettable course of action.

Plain: It's better to be safe than sorry.

If you suspect your own writing is more pretentious than plain, use a readability index (such as Robert Gunning's fog formula) to measure its level of difficulty.

The following tips will help you avoid common word traps:

1. **Curb Your Use of Words Ending in *-ize* and *–ization*.** Verbs ending in *-ize* and nouns ending in *-ization* may sound rich and sophisticated, but they can also lead to an inflated, heavy-handed style that grinds comprehension to a frustrating halt. Some words that fit this category (such as *privatize, hospitalize, authorization, unionize, maximize,* and *specialization*) are common and irreplaceable enough to be used without compromising readability. However, many other words ending in *-tion, -ment, -ate,* and *-ism* can boggle the mind with their obscurity and obfuscation, so it is important to remember that bigger isn't always better, especially when it comes to these so-called Latinisims that owe their origins to the ancient language of the Roman Empire. The chart below offers some simpler substitutes for bigger, more difficult words:

Plain English	*-ize* Verb	*-ion* Noun
make communal	communalize	communalization
use	utilize	utilization
make best use of	optimize	optimization
make real	actualize	actualization
develop a business	corporatize	corporatization
finish	finalize	finalization

2. **Use words derived from French sparingly.** Words the English language has borrowed from French can sound prestigious and distinctive when used sparingly, adding formality to your writing. When overused, though, they can sound contrived and affected when compared with simpler English alternatives.

Plain English	French Derivative
talk, have a conversation	converse
tell, inform	apprise
begin, start	commence

3. **Avoid foreign words and phrases.** Phrases such as *ad hoc* (for a particular purpose), and *pro bono* (for free) are used in legal documents and formal writing, where they are part of an established idiom. Otherwise, use foreign expressions only when absolutely necessary.

Plain English	Foreign Word/Phrase
reason for being	raison d'être
genuine	bona fide
a day	per diem
substitute, compensate	quid pro quo

4. **Use only job-related jargon.** Jargon is the special vocabulary for a group, trade, profession, or sphere of activity. Terminology of this kind is essential for conducting business and describing sophisticated concepts and activities accurately and concisely. Certain types of jargon once thought of as specialized—such as computer jargon—are now the stuff of common knowledge. Once-ordinary words such as *import*, *export*, and *cookie* have taken on meanings unique to computing, which in turn have come to be understood by almost everyone. Similarly, many business-related terms, such as *fixed rate*, *intangible assets*, *scalable technology*, *delist*, and *buyback* describe actions and concepts that cannot be summed up easily in any other way.

   Jargon is permissible when it is purposeful and transparent. Because jargon is a private language of the "inner circle," anyone who uses it must be sure that its special terms, abbreviations, and acronyms will be mutually understood. To ensure that one person's jargon won't be another person's gobbledegook, size up your audience first and define any special terms you may have used in documents intended for a broad readership.

> **jargon** a term that describes (1) the specialized terminology of a technical field or (2) outdated, unnecessary words used in a business context.

5. **Bypass buzzwords.** Buzzwords are fashionable, often technical-sounding pieces of jargon. Known as trendy attention-getters, buzzwords sound fresh, current, and suitably corporate. Their trendiness is part of their appeal, but it is also a large part of their drawback because they tend to go out of style quite quickly, often through overuse. Some better-known buzzwords include

synergy	co-operative or combined action
globalize	make or become global
paradigm shift	a fundamental change in approach or philosophy

> **buzzwords** fashionable, technical, or computer jargon.

   Communications professionals are split on whether buzzwords are a feature of good writing. Clunky corporate "double-speak" can kill meaning and be a smoke-screen, camouflaging financial problems or poor performance—that is why readers distrust it. In fact, "straight-talking companies" have been shown to outperform "non-straight-talking companies."[1] Screening documents, especially external ones, for buzzwords demonstrates reader awareness and concern for fair dealing that helps build confidence in your firm or organization.

   A final thought about familiar words: use simple language for getting simple, time-sensitive messages across. Keep in mind that you won't have to shelve your more sophisticated vocabulary completely, just re-evaluate and save it for types of writing that require greater finesse or formality. On the job, pay attention to and learn about language preferences in co-workers' documents and consult your organization's style guidelines, if available, to help you make effective vocabulary choices.

WORD CHOICE STEP 2: USE LANGUAGE THAT IS FRESH AND CURRENT

To stay competitive, today's businesses make an effort to explore and implement progressive approaches and technologies. It makes sense, then, for them to do business by using contemporary language that reflects and reinforces those aims and creates a corporate image that is modern and up to date.

clichés overused, tired expressions that have lost their ability to communicate effectively.

1. **Replace clichés.** Clichés are descriptive expressions that have been drained of meaning through overuse. Once vibrant and full of impact, they are now trite and hackneyed. Unless a cliché adds uniqueness or, by way of analogy, sums up something that is otherwise impossible to describe, replace it with fresh and direct language. Some better-known business clichés include

tighten our belts	needless to say
on an annual basis	make ends meet
true to form	address the bottom line
all over the map	explore every avenue
rest assured	with all due respect
a big value	protect the bottom line
a change for the better	get your fiscal house in order
at this moment in time	to be perfectly honest
without further delay	a different ballgame
fit the bill	push the envelope
outside the box	

2. **Retire outdated business expressions.** Many commonly used business expressions have outlasted their usefulness. As holdovers from a centuries-old tradition of business protocol, stock phrases of business jargon have slowly lost their meaning for modern readers, who see them more as artifacts than as communicative tools. Unless your organization recommends a very formal or traditional style, substitute modern phrases for stiff, outmoded business expressions, especially if you want to project a modern, contemporary image for your organization and yourself.

Old Style	New Style
as per your request/ in accordance with your request	as you requested
comments duly noted	I read your comments
enclosed herewith please find	enclosed is/are
please	kindly
I wish to acknowledge receipt of	thank you for; I have received
pursuant to	according to, as follow-up to
pursuant to your request	as you requested
receipt is acknowledged	we received, we have received
thanking you in advance	thank you
under separate cover	separately

3. **Eliminate slang.** *Slang* is the term for colourful, highly informal words or figures of speech that have meaning specific to a particular era, locality, or occupation. Words that fit this category may be new words or familiar words used in new and sometimes humorous ways (for example *pony up*, which means "to hand over a sum of money"). Most slang has a short shelf life and may have meaning only for a small audience.

Slang	Translation
greenback	US dollar
schlepp	carry, haul
suit	a business executive
serious coin	a large sum of money
blow off	disregard, ignore
confab	a conversation
slugfest	an intense quarrel
SINK	single, independent, no kids

Because slang is extravagant and street-smart in its appeal, it has the power to shock readers who are unprepared for it, making it unsuitable for most professional communication. An exception is slang that is specific to business and management, including widely accepted terms such as *telephone tag*, *team player*, *walk* (resign from a job), and *spot* (a radio or TV commercial). Slangier terms such as *tire kicker* (a prospective customer who demands a lot of attention but doesn't buy anything) are fun and unique but may be too informal for general use.

4. **Avoid instant messaging abbreviations and emoticons.** The popularity of chat rooms and personal e-mail has brought about a new lexicon special to high-speed communicators. At the same time, the popularity of *instant messaging* (IM) and its adoption by businesses as a productivity tool is having implications for business style. Features of IM style—smiley-face icons, deliberately misspelled words, and e-friendly **acronyms**—make typing dialogue in real time quicker and easier; however, anyone unfamiliar with this cyber-shorthand may view it as an unwelcome secret language.

Abbreviation	Plain English
JTLYK	just to let you know
b4	before
any1	anyone
UW	you are welcome
BTW	by the way
LOL	laughing out loud

Limit your use of Internet abbreviations and **emoticons** (punctuation used to create sideways faces conveying emotions: ☺, ☹, :-<, :-D, and so on) to the channel for which they are intended—IM communication—and leave them out of office e-mail and formal correspondence. (Appendix A, under the heading "Abbreviations and Acronyms," covers abbreviations and acronyms suitable in professional communication.)

slang coined words or existing words that are informal and have meanings specific to particular groups or localities.

acronym a pronounceable word formed from the initial letters of other words (NATO).

emoticon a symbol consisting of a sequence of keystrokes that produce a sideways image of a face conveying any one of a range of emotions.

WORD CHOICE STEP 3: KEEP LANGUAGE SPECIFIC, PRECISE, AND FUNCTIONAL

Novelist Mark Twain once wrote, "the difference between the right word and almost the right word is the difference between lightning and the lightning bug." Words that are almost right tantalize but ultimately frustrate readers by hinting at an intended meaning without actually delivering it. When reading involves guesswork, readers cannot be expected to act on instructions, accept decisions, or give new ideas serious thought. Imprecise wording puts writers in a bad light, too, because poor word choice can be mistaken for fuzzy logic or unclear thinking. It is worth keeping in mind that the more exact your word choice is, the more persuasive and informative your message will be. Every word you write should be clear and purposeful. Here are some tips for writing with precision:

1. **Provide specific details that help readers act on information and requests.** **Concrete nouns** (things knowable by the senses—*computer, annual report, resumé*) are easier to grasp than **abstract nouns** (intangible things knowable only through the intellect—*integrity, loyalty, justice*). Use concrete language as much as possible to support and explain abstract words and show readers exactly what you mean. Because the language of business is full of intangible abstracts—*security, prestige, profitability, leadership*—hard data can be used to make concepts that are difficult to pin down meaningful to readers.

> **concrete nouns** things knowable through the senses.

> **abstract nouns** things not knowable through the senses.

Abstract:	Our company demands loyalty.
Abstract/Concrete:	Our company demands employee loyalty to corporate policy.

2. **Quantify facts and avoid vague qualitative statements.** Tell readers how much, how many, or what type you mean, specify when something happened or happens, and identify by title or name the agents and recipients of particular actions.

Vague:	They received some complaints about it some time ago.
Specific:	Our customer service representatives received 36 complaints about Model G500 in 2009.

Readers, though we might wish otherwise, are not mind readers. They may not understand what descriptive omnibus terms such as *soon, later, good, bad, nice, numerous, substantially,* or *a majority* really mean. These are terms that are often used out of politeness, as hedging devices that sound less harsh and demanding than specific words.

Vague:	A majority of employees indicated they would sign the agreement soon.
Specific:	Close to 75 per cent of employees indicated they would sign the agreement by Friday.
Vague:	The stock is performing poorly. (*Which* stock? Performing *how* poorly?)
Specific:	Shares of Grocerynet.com lost 15 per cent of their market value in 2009.

3. **Avoid ambiguous and non-idiomatic expressions.** Ambiguous statements—statements that are open to interpretation—can be confusing for readers. For instance, a sentence such as *She said on Thursday she would drop by the office* can mean two things—either that the statement was made on Thursday or that the visit would occur that day. As you compose your draft or write your message, check for potential double meanings and keep in mind that readers like consistency, thus making it important to avoid using two or more names for the same thing.

Using idiomatic expressions can also reduce confusion. **Idioms** are word groupings that "sound right" to a typical reader and have special meaning distinct from their literal meaning: *hand in* (submit), *look up* (search for information), and *find out* (determine *or* discover information). Used correctly, these phrasal verbs add punch to your writing, but they can also be difficult for anyone new to English to remember or decipher. Idiomatic usage also applies to the pairing of prepositions with adjectives (*different from*) and nouns (*use for*). For instance, the phrase "to have confidence *in*" is correct but "to have confidence *on*" is not. When you need to know which preposition to pair with a particular word, it is always wise to refer to a college-level dictionary or an idiomatic dictionary, such as the *Oxford Advanced Learner's Dictionary*.

> **idiom** a word or phrase that has a meaning different from its literal meaning.

4. **Use comparisons and analogies to clarify.** Likening an unfamiliar or complex concept to a familiar one is a common form of explanation. In fact, the business world is full of descriptive **analogies**, such as *brain drain* (a general term used by management for the cross-border or overseas migration of specialists), which make fuzzy concepts clear and tangible. When there is no other way to explain a concept, a comparison can help to bring it into sharper focus. (See also Appendix A, under the heading "Usage: Differentiating Commonly Confused Words.")

> **analogy** an explanation of the unfamiliar in terms of the familiar.

WORD CHOICE STEP 4: PRACTISE FACTUAL AND ETHICAL COMMUNICATION

How you communicate on the job is a reflection of your ethical standards and those of your organization. With this in mind, it is important to follow ethical practices in your workplace communication. Here is a recap of tips for ethical business communication already discussed in Chapter 1.

1. **Be reasoned, factual, and moderate in your judgments.** Keep personal biases out of your workplace communication and use only inclusive, non-discriminatory language (see the following sections).

2. **Consider the impact your communication has on others as well as yourself.** Make sure the actions you endorse are legal and that your communication would reflect well on you if it were disclosed publicly. Bending the rules, even for a trusted colleague, might compromise your integrity.

3. **Consult qualified colleagues.** If you suspect that what you are writing is contentious or incriminating, seek out experienced co-workers to help you navigate ethical minefields and find feasible solutions to the wording of important messages and documents.

4. **Avoid libellous language.** Libellous words arouse hatred, contempt, or ridicule toward the individuals to whom those words are applied. Libel is printed defamation characterized by false, malicious, derogatory remarks. Common law protects

every person against this sort of unmotivated character assassination.[2] Words that are harmful and potentially libellous include *drunk*, *lazy*, *crazy*, *crooked*, *corrupt*, *incompetent*, *stupid*, *maniac*, *drug addict*, *junkie*, *thief*, and *crippled*.

5. **Be timely and accurate in your communication.** Avoid unjustified delays in replying or processing information. Retain print or electronic copies of important documents.

6. **Avoid untrue, deceptive, or misleading statements.** There are stiff penalties for all forms of misrepresentation, including false advertising. It is a good policy to back up any generalization qualified by *entirely*, *completely*, or *always* with supportable facts and evidence.

7. **Know what you can and cannot disclose to certain parties.** Familiarize yourself with corporate disclosure practices and confidentiality agreements, and handle your organization's intellectual property with care. Follow proper channels of communication, know what you can or must communicate, and carefully weigh both sides of an issue before you act or comment on it.

8. **Distinguish between fact and opinion.** Let readers know the difference between unsubstantiated belief or conjecture and verifiable fact. Passing off an opinion as a fact is misleading and unethical.

9. **Don't claim authorship of documents you have not written.** The consequences of plagiarism—not giving credit where credit is due—are serious. Always acknowledge your sources through notes or citations, and never take credit for ideas not your own.

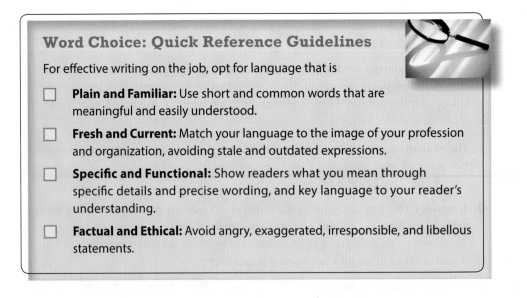

Word Choice: Quick Reference Guidelines

For effective writing on the job, opt for language that is

☐ **Plain and Familiar:** Use short and common words that are meaningful and easily understood.

☐ **Fresh and Current:** Match your language to the image of your profession and organization, avoiding stale and outdated expressions.

☐ **Specific and Functional:** Show readers what you mean through specific details and precise wording, and key language to your reader's understanding.

☐ **Factual and Ethical:** Avoid angry, exaggerated, irresponsible, and libellous statements.

Achieving Conciseness

It may come as no surprise that the origin of the term *business* is *busy-ness*. Time constraints and pressing deadlines are the norm for most business people. Because of this, they expect to receive workplace documents that get to the point directly, with an economy of words and a minimum of clutter. A modest amount of time spent in craft-ing a concise, easy-to-read, well-organized message is time saved for your reader(s). In turn, time saved translates not just into money earned or saved but into goodwill from the busy people you communicate with on a regular basis. Compare the following mes-sages—think about how long it takes to read each one and how the choice of words affects coherence and readability:

Original: This is a just a very brief memo to inform you that it is the opinion of the employee council that at the present time it is expedient to undertake an investigation of the possible institution of a proposed on-site fitness centre. Kindly be advised that anytime up to August 31 you should make your views known to your employee council representative.

Revised: The employee council invites your input on the proposed creation of an on-site fitness centre. Please contact your employee council representative before August 31.

Long, indirect ways of expressing things are a major source of wordiness. While con-ciseness is a virtue in business communication, the same cannot be said for conciseness that is overdone, leading to messages that sound uneven and choppy, too blunt, or too rude. A little terseness or abruptness—like the kind that occurs naturally in a quick e-mail as you move from one thought to the next—can be expected from time to time and is usually excusable. Readers may begin to have problems, though, when they encounter a writing style that is so telegraphic that there is not enough detail or devel-opment to make a message lucid, understandable, and complete. After all, readers should not be expected to supply or mentally fill in missing words.

Conciseness means using the fewest words to say what you need to say accu-rately and completely. Weighing the need for conciseness against similar concerns for completeness and politeness is important once you pass the draft phase, where word-iness is understandable. Understanding what you can eliminate without sacrificing your intended meaning or ignoring your reader's needs is key to answering the triple demands of conciseness, completeness, and politeness.

Wordy: Please note that you are requested to read and offer your comments on the attached file.

Terse: Read this. Get back to me.

Concise and polite: Please review the attached file.

Politeness strategies sometimes work at cross-purposes to editing techniques, but it is still relatively easy to write concise messages that have the right level of courtesy. Editing documents for conciseness is really a form of precision revision. You can start by easily eliminating anything that does not add meaning to your message: long lead-ins, noun conversions, padded and redundant expressions, needless relative pronouns, and excess modifiers. Getting rid of sentence padding and achieving conciseness requires only a little extra time, so avoid falling into the same trap as French mathematician Blaise Pascal, who once admitted to a friend, "I made this letter longer than usual because I lack the time to make it short." Here are nine ways to keep your messages concise:

1. **Eliminate long lead-ins.** Baseball pitchers warm up in the bullpen before they head to the mound and start pitching to batters. Many writers prefer to "limber up" in the same way by starting their sentences with an introductory phrase or two before they get to the point. While softening a message in this way is a common politeness strategy, lead-ins are mostly unnecessary because they add nothing to a sentence except for information that is already obvious (e.g., *This message is to inform you that* . . .). Readers in a hurry want information conveyed to them as directly as possible. Unless extreme politeness is required, delete any opening phrases ending in *that* or *because*. In brief messages, such as routine e-mail, make sure you get to the point before a count of three.

> **Wordy:** I am writing to inform you *that* parking lot C will be closed for maintenance Monday, September 28.
>
> **Concise:** Parking lot C will be closed for maintenance Monday, September 28.

verbs words that describe actions, occurrences, or states of being.

nouns words that name people, places, things, and abstract concepts.

2. **Revise noun conversions.** Each type of word has a different purpose. **Verbs** are "doing" words that convey actions, conditions, and states of being. **Nouns** name people, places, things, and abstract concepts. When verbs are converted into nouns, often with the addition of a *-tion* or *-ment* ending, they lose their power and agency, like an engine running on empty, and in turn require weak supporting verbs to fully convey their actions. All the attention is then focused on the converted noun—words such as *establishment*, *approval*, *decision*—instead of on the primary action of the sentence, which is hidden in the long noun phrase. As you review the chart below, note how affected and formal noun conversion phrases sound when compared with the verbs from which they are derived:

Noun Conversion Phrase	Verb
reach a conclusion	conclude
make the assumption	assume
make a decision	decide
conduct an investigation	investigate
engage in consultation with	consult
give consideration to	consider
give authorization for	authorize

noun conversions or **nominalizations** verbs that have been converted into nouns with the addition of *-ment* or *-tion* endings.

Noun conversions (or **nominalizations**, as they are sometimes known) may sound impressive and can even slow down the pace of your writing, but they will also make your writing weak and wordy, so it is best to avoid using them.

> **Wordy:** CanPac **undertook a revision** of its full-year earnings forecast.
>
> **Concise:** CanPac **revised** its full-year earnings forecast.
>
> **Wordy:** Leading economists **made a prediction of** a stronger Canadian dollar.
>
> **Concise:** Leading economists **predicted** a stronger Canadian dollar.

Wordy: City council **brought about an amendment** to the bylaw.

Concise: City council **amended** the bylaw.

3. **Eliminate redundancies.** Redundancies are unplanned repetitions—word pairs that express the same meaning twice. Avoid the following "doubled-up" expressions by eliminating the italicized word:

> **redundancies**
> unplanned repetitions.

absolutely essential	enter *into*
past experience	*necessary* imperative
each and every (use each or every)	*mutual* co-operation
reiterate *again*	*exactly* identical
refer *back*	

4. **Eliminate or revise empty words and phrases.** Rid your sentences of imprecise, inexact language. Clear away the deadwood—words that lack meaning—and trim padded expressions.

Replace	With
am of the opinion that	believe
as a matter of fact	actually (or nothing at all)
at a later date	later
at this point in time	now, currently, at present
by an act of coincidence	coincidentally
despite the fact that	although, though
due to the fact that	because (of), since
during the course of	during, in
during the time that	when, while
for the purpose of	to
for the reason that	because, since
in addition to the above	also
in light of the fact that	because
in the amount of	for
in the event that	if
in the process of	now, currently
in view of the fact that	because (of), since, as
in spite of the fact that	even though
it is probable that	probably
it has been brought to our attention	we have learned
I wish to call your attention to	note, please note
make the necessary inquiries	look into, investigate
notwithstanding the fact that	even though, although
the point I am trying to make	————
the question as to whether	whether
to all intents and purposes	in effect, really
with the exception of	except, except for

Articles such as *the*, *a*, and *an* are sometimes over-applied. Omit *the* before plural nouns expressing generalizatons.

Unnecessary Article:	The human resources specialists review the applications.
Articles Omitted:	Human resources specialists review applications.

5. **Use strong, precise, accurate verbs.** Opt for clear, precise, instructive verbs rather than extended verb phrases.

Wordy:	The learning centre **placed an order for** materials for the courses.
Concise:	The learning centre **ordered** course materials.

Eliminate the need for intensifiers and qualifiers—words such as *really*, *extremely*, *incredibly*, *definitely*, *rather*—by finding a verb that is an exact fit for the meaning you wish to deliver.

Wordy:	We were **really incredibly thrilled** to hear of the partnership.
Concise:	We were **delighted** to hear of the partnership.

Avoid poorly defined, ambiguous verbs whose meanings are open to interpretation. Substitute strong verbs for *-sion* and *-tion* words.

Weak Verb:	Buying market share in foreign markets **affected** profits. (*affected* how?)
Precise:	Buying market share in foreign markets **increased** profits **by 10 per cent**.

Replace weak verbs, such as *have* and *be* (*am*, *is*, *are*, *was*, *were*) when they occur alone, with strong ones.

Weak Verb:	The CEO **is of the opinion** that the company will survive the current crisis that **has to do with** dot-com instability.
Precise:	The CEO **believes** the company will survive the current crisis **caused by** dot-com instability.
Weak Verb:	It **is necessary** for him to complete the application.
Precise:	He **needs to** (or **must**) complete the application.

Replace *could/would/should* with strong verbs when you do not need to show that an action is conditional.

Weak Verb:	In her previous job, she **would write** to charitable foundations.
Precise:	In her previous job, she **wrote** to charitable foundations.

As much as possible, write in the **active voice** (as opposed to the **passive voice**), which is usually the most concise way to convey an action (see Chapter 4).

Passive Voice:	The script of the speech should be edited and double-spaced.
Active Voice:	Edit and double-space the script of the speech.

6. **Revise prepositional phrases.** Prepositions—common words such as *in*, *to*, *at*, *of*, *after*, *with*, *between*—combine with other words to form **prepositional phrases**. These modifying phrases show relationships in time and space, indicating how, when, where, or how long something happens. The wordiness of some prepositional phrases can make sentences sound awkward and overwritten. Usually the phrase can be replaced with a single-word modifier.

Wordy:	An **error in computation** was discovered in **the report from last spring**.
Concise:	A **computational error** was discovered in **last spring's report**.

Prepositions are useful in breaking up long chains of nouns used as adjectives. They clarify relationships so readers can tell which nouns are modifiers and which nouns are being modified.

growth management executive training → growth management training for executives

petroleum diesel replacement fuel → replacement fuel for petroleum diesel

climate change mitigation technologies → technologies to mitigate climate change

7. **Eliminate fillers.** Avoid beginning sentences with empty filler words such as *there is/are* and *it is/was* (when *it* has not been defined) that force readers to wait for the subject that the entire sentence hinges on. **Expletive constructions**, as they are called, act as a common delaying tactic that makes sense only when extreme politeness or emphasis is called for. Otherwise, delete the expletive and craft a straightforward sentence that begins with the subject, followed closely by verb and object.

Wordy:	**There are** three bids **that** the board is considering.
Concise:	The board is considering three bids.
Wordy:	**It is** paying down debt **that** is our priority.
Concise:	Paying down debt is our priority.

8. **Shorten multiple *that/which/who* clauses.** Used to excess, clauses introduced by *that*, *which*, and *who* create a clumsy stop-and-go sentence flow. In most cases, you can drop *that*, *which*, or *who* as well as the verb that immediately follows it.

active voice a writing style in which the grammatical subject of a sentence performs the action.

passive voice a writing style in which the grammatical subject of a sentence is acted upon.

prepositional phrase a phrase beginning with a preposition and functioning as a modifier.

expletive construction a phrase such as *there is/are* or *it is/was* at the beginning of a clause, delaying the introduction of the subject.

Sometimes an entire clause can be reduced to a single word by making this simple change.

Wordy: His company, **which is reputed to be a leader in employee satisfaction**, hosts regular events for employees **who have retired**.

Concise: His company, **a reputed leader in employee satisfaction**, hosts regular events for **retirees**.

Wordy: We offer prices **that are competitive**.

Concise: We offer **competitive prices**.

9. **Combine shorter sentences, reduce clauses and phrases.** Use pronouns (*that, which, who,* as well as personal pronouns) to combine shorter *related* sentences and eliminate monotonous repetition. Reduce sentences to clauses, clauses to phrases, and phrases to single words.

Wordy: She is a sales representative. She specializes in commercial real estate.

Concise: She is a sales representative who specializes in commercial real estate.
(second sentence reduced to a clause)

Concise: She is a sales representative specializing in commercial real estate.
(second sentence reduced to a phrase)

Concise: She is a commercial real estate sales specialist.
(second sentence reduced to descriptive words)

Conciseness: Quick-Reference Checklist

☐ Have you used as few words as possible to make your point?

☐ Have you eliminated long lead-ins and sentence fillers?

☐ Have you replaced noun conversions (and *-ize* words) with strong verbs?

☐ Have you eliminated redundancies, empty words, and empty phrases?

☐ Have you replaced prepositional phrases with single-word modifiers?

☐ Have you shortened clumsy *that/which/who* clauses and combined short, related sentences?

Tone

Read between the lines of almost any business message and it is possible to detect the writer's frame of mind, inklings of demand or respect, arrogance or modesty, indifference or concern. This impression is a product of its **tone**. Tone refers to the mood of a message—the implied attitude of the writer to the subject and his reader. In the absence of vocal inflection and visual cues such as body language, tone in written communication creates an impression based purely on the words that are used and the length and structure of sentences the writer happens to choose.

> **tone** the implied attitude of the author to the reader, as reflected by word choice.

The tone of a message should support its content and remain fairly consistent from beginning to end. A wide range of tone is possible in workplace communication, meaning that a casual tone appropriate for an e-mail message to an associate will not be acceptable in a formal report, which demands a more serious and professional tone. Ultimately, much depends on the writing situation, purpose, and channel of communication. Once you have determined the tone you want to use, it should remain consistent throughout a document, mainly because erratic, "Jekyll and Hyde" shifts in tone give mixed messages that unsettle readers and leave them confused about your attitude and intentions. Make sure the tone you establish supports your content and creates the right impression.

TUNE IN TO WORD CONNOTATIONS

Words with similar or overlapping meanings, like the synonyms in a typical thesaurus entry, rarely mean exactly the same thing. While a word's **denotation**—its literal, dictionary definition—is something it may share with many synonyms, its **connotation**—its implied, associative meaning—is distinct in terms of the positive or negative emotional response the word provokes. The way a word affects the reader helps to differentiate it, even subtly, from other words with similar or overlapping meanings. Consider the connotation or emotional overtone of each word in the following series:

> **denotation** a word's literal or dictionary definition.

> **connotation** a word's implied or associative meaning, often coloured by emotion.

- cheap/inexpensive/cost-effective/low priced/thrifty/economical
- artificial/faux/synthetic/sham/fake/man-made/imitation/mock
- flexible/changeable/fickle/adaptable/compliant/resilient

Implied meaning has the power to shape perceptions, which accounts for why a "pre-owned vehicle" may sound like a better investment than a "used"' or "second-hand" car, even though the products theses terms label may be virtually the same. Tuning in to the connotations of words can help you anticipate your reader's reaction to the words you choose. The right words may not just be the ones with the more accurate denotations, but the ones with the most appropriate connotations.

KEEP YOUR STYLE CONVERSATIONAL

Formality involves the observance of style rules and conventions. Levels of formality depend mostly on word choice, sentence length, and sentence structure. Most business writing, with the exception of formal reports, meets the needs of a wide audience with a mid-level style that is fairly conversational and moderately informal. Writing

> **formality** the level of writing; whether the writer is using the appropriate register based on an observance of the rules and conventions of writing.

conversationally is as easy as imagining yourself sitting across from your reader and expressing yourself as you would in an ordinary face-to-face discussion or meeting. In writing your message as you would say it, try to resist the temptation to be overly chatty or to repeat yourself. The result should be unforced and natural, not stiff or stuffy. Naturalness, however, should never be confused with sloppiness, so keep sentence length manageable, use correct grammar, and edit to eliminate awkwardness. A written style that is too informal or casual—with noticeable slang, colloquialisms, and grammar abuses—can give the impression of carelessness and even suggest poor work habits. Writers have some freedom to vary their level of formality from document to document, but a mid-level style is typical of business letters, memos, informal reports, and most print journalism. Its elements are summed up in the checklist below:

- ☑ even-handed, efficient, conversational tone
- ☑ mix of familiar words and business terms
- ☑ correct grammar and standard punctuation
- ☑ manageable sentence structure (one to three clauses per sentence)
- ☑ single-word verbs and phrasal verbs (*look into* instead of *investigate*; *throw out* instead of *discard*)
- ☑ occasional contractions (*I'm, she's, we're, it's, can't, isn't, who's*)
- ☑ personal pronouns and limited forms of personal address
- ☒ slang, legalisms, long words, outdated language

Examples: I am pleased to submit the enclosed report.

Please have a look at the enclosed report.

SELECT THE RIGHT LEVEL OF FORMALITY: PERSONAL AND IMPERSONAL STYLE

personal style a style of writing that seems warm and friendly based on its use of first- and second-person pronouns.

Within the acceptable range of business style, it is possible to be more or less formal and more or less personal. A **personal style** puts you and/or your readers into your sentences through the free use of first- and second-person pronouns (*I, me, we, us, you*). The impression it gives is one of warmth, friendliness, and candour, helping to build rapport and engage readers. Because facts are either delivered from the writer's perspective or targeted specifically at readers, it sometimes seems that personal style is biased or slanted, even when it is not. Personal style is characterized by the following elements:

- short sentences,
- personal pronouns,
- first names and personal references, and
- active voice used throughout.

impersonal style a style of writing that seems objective and detached based on its use of third-person pronouns.

An **impersonal style** uses only third-person pronouns (*he, she, it, one, they*). It sounds detached yet objective, emphasizing facts and concepts rather than the perspective of the writer. For this reason, impersonal style is commonly used for announcements and policy statements. Warmth gives way to efficiency, but the result is not necessarily stuffy or pretentious. Impersonal style is characterized by the following elements:

- a mix of sentence lengths, including long sentences,
- no personal pronouns,
- no first names or personal references, and
- legitimate use of the passive voice.

Personal Style	Impersonal Style
I recommend that the company reschedule its annual general meeting.	The company should reschedule its annual general meeting.
Please let me know if you have any questions.	Employees should submit all inquiries to their supervisors.

BE POSITIVE

Is the glass half empty or half full? The answer to this question separates the optimists from the pessimists. Readers usually like to think of their glasses as half full, which means they are more receptive to good news or neutral news that is free of negativity. Although you should never knowingly distort facts or ideas just for the sake of putting a positive spin on them, it is worth remembering that positive wording makes messages reader-friendly and inviting. Unless you are issuing a warning meant to stop or deter certain actions, it is useful to emphasize what the reader can do instead of what the reader can't.

Negative attitude: You cannot use your new Verified by Vista service until you have been issued a password.

Positive attitude: You may begin using your new Verified by Vista service once you receive your password.

Avoid negative wording for positive or neutral ideas:

Negative wording: You will never be sorry you purchased a three-year extended warranty.

Positive wording: Your three-year extended warranty covers all parts and on-site repairs.

Weigh the impact of blatant or hidden negatives such as *unfortunately*, *allege*, *careless*, *regret*, *mistake*, *oversight*, *overlook*, *negligence*, *neglect*, *unable*, *reject*, *deny*, and *fail(ure)* before you use them. Used the wrong way, these can be harsh, inflexible words that antagonize readers by painting them as adversaries or inferiors.

- ☒ By failing to park in your assigned space, you caused our visitors a terrible inconvenience.
- ☑ Parking spaces adjacent to the entrance are reserved for visitors.

Rely on the subordinating power of grammatical structures such as dependent clauses and the passive voice (see Chapter 4) to reduce negativity and depersonalize unfavourable facts.

Negative:	We cannot extend credit to you at this time.
Less negative:	Although credit cannot be extended to you at this time, we look forward to serving you on a cash basis.

STRESS READER BENEFITS AND RELEVANCE

reader benefits the benefits or advantages a reader can gain by complying with the action the writer endorses.

Everyone, from time to time, reads a message only to ask, "what does this have to do with me?" Relevant, reader-focused messages never provoke this reaction. Instead readers can easily see how information concerns them or how they stand to benefit.

When readers feel that their opinions matter and have been taken into consideration, they are more likely to follow instructions and comply with requests. To write in a reader-focused style, edit your messages with the following suggestions in mind:

1. **Present meaningful content.** Avoid sending trivial or unnecessary messages, as they might cause your reader to overlook the seriousness of future, more important messages.

you-attitude a writing style that focuses on the reader rather than the writer.

2. **Develop a positive you-attitude.** Make the reader part of your message by presenting your information from her point of view rather than your own whenever possible. An exclusively writer-centred approach can sound egotistical, but it is possible to inject you-attitude into your messages by switching from first-person pronouns (*I, me, my, we, us, our*) to more inviting second-person pronouns (*you, your, yourself*).

Writer-centred:	I am hosting a private reception at the Royal York Hotel on December 15 and am inviting all senior managers to attend.
Reader-focused:	As a senior manager, you are cordially invited to a private reception at the Royal York Hotel on December 15.
Writer-centred:	We offer our repeat customers substantial discounts.
Reader-focused:	As a repeat customer, you will enjoy substantial discounts.

A sincere you-attitude is one that doesn't overuse second-person pronouns to the point where readers feel uncomfortable or manipulated. Do not use the you-attitude negatively, as readers could feel singled out, criticized, or accused:

Negative you-attitude:	Your failure to observe safety guidelines will result in a mechanical shutdown.
Neutral attitude:	The machine automatically shuts down whenever a safety infraction occurs.

A good way to involve readers is by using a compliance-boosting **we-attitude**—a common feature of managerial communications—that breaks down authority and unites writer and reader in common "we're-all-in-this-together" values, goals, and initiatives.

> **we-attitude** a writing style that focuses on the shared goals and values of the writer and reader(s).

3. **Emphasize benefits to readers.** Put yourself in your reader's place. Appeal to readers and their interests by indicating what they stand to gain. This may be all the incentive or motivation necessary to encourage a favourable, action-oriented response. This technique is especially well suited to service-oriented messages.

Writer-centred:	We ask that all customers complete the enclosed questionnaire by April 30 so that we may assess the effectiveness of our technical support services.
Reader-focused:	To ensure you receive the highest standard of technical support, please assist us by completing the enclosed quality-control questionnaire.

BE POLITE

A little common courtesy can make readers feel uncommonly good. Politeness creates a humane environment of mutual respect and consideration where work gets done more easily. Rudeness, pushiness, sarcasm, and abruptness—whether actual or perceived—can alienate readers. Being courteous involves more than just adding a simple *please* or *thank you* to brief or routine messages: courtesy is a mindset with zero tolerance for sarcasm, condescension, presumptuousness, or anger. Emotional language can provoke hostile reactions, so avoid phrases of demand or advisement that belittle or talk down to readers.

Rude:	Obviously, if you had the slightest idea of our policies you would have known that unless you want to be fired you should never use company-issued cellphones for personal calls.
Polite:	Please reserve your company-issued cellphone for business calls so that customers and associates may contact you without delay.

Extreme politeness, on the other hand, can be mistaken for coldness or insincerity. It can also undermine your assertiveness or authority, especially if you suppress or censor what you need to say for fear of sounding impolite. Do your best to strive for a courteous tone that sounds natural, friendly, and unforced.

Too Polite:	Kindly be advised that if even the smallest question arises we will be only too happy to help.
Polite:	Please contact us if you have any questions or concerns.

USE INCLUSIVE LANGUAGE

No one likes being unfairly singled out on the basis of sex, ethnicity, age, disability, or group membership—but this is exactly what happens in cases of discrimination. Not only unacceptable but against the law, discrimination involves the making of unjust and prejudicial distinctions about individuals. The Canadian Human Rights Commission

(CHRC) defines discriminatory treatment on eleven prohibited grounds: age, sex (including pregnancy and childbirth), sexual orientation, religion, race, colour, national or ethnic origin, marital status, family status, physical or mental disability (including past/present alcohol dependence), or pardoned criminal conviction. Discriminatory and gender-biased language, even when it is unintentional, demeans and offends readers, leaving them hurt and unreceptive. Such language is actionable, opening the way for harassment suits and legal proceedings. Using inclusive, bias-free language that treats all groups equally and fairly shows sensitivity, consideration, and respect, all of which build goodwill and better business relations.

1. **Don't make discriminatory comments.** Avoid prohibited references when writing about groups and individuals. Such information, even when it is offered in a positive spirit, is irrelevant and can contribute to negative stereotypes.

   - ☒ Hassan, who fasts throughout the day during this month's observance of Ramadan, will nevertheless be available to answer your questions.
   - ☑ Hassan will be available to answer your questions.
   - ☒ Please contact Piotr, who has a nice Polish accent but speaks English well.
   - ☑ Please contact Piotr, our director of marketing services.

2. **Use only gender-neutral job titles and salutations.** Substitute correct and neutral job titles—ones that do not suggest that only men or only women can hold a particular job—for traditional, gender-specific ones:

Gender-Biased	Gender-Neutral
salesman	salesperson, sales representative
spokesman	spokesperson, company representative
businessman	business person
chairman	chair, chairperson
workman	worker
man-hours	working hours
female manager, male nurse	manager, nurse
man and wife	husband and wife, spouses
deliveryman	courier

Sexist salutations such as *Dear Sirs* and *Gentlemen* are likewise considered outdated, because they exclude a female audience. Revise any sentences containing sexist terms and automatic gender assumptions about jobs:

- Account managers are invited to bring their ~~wives~~ spouses/partners.

- The ~~girls in bookkeeping~~ bookkeepers will correct the error in your account. *or* Aruna Sharma and Joyce Fitzgerald in bookkeeping will correct the error in your account. (Whenever possible, refer to men and women by their specific names.)

salutation a greeting at the beginning of a letter: "Dear Ms. Gill."

- ~~Each secretary reports to her supervisor.~~ → Secretaries report to their supervisors.

3. **Use Masculine Pronouns Reasonably.** Avoid using masculine pronouns (*he, his, him, himself*) to refer to groups or individuals of unknown gender. The old grammatical rule of "common gender"—with its blanket use of masculine pronouns to refer to men as well as women—no longer applies and now comes across as sexist. Consider the exclusionary nature of the following sentence, in which all executives are assumed to be male: *Each executive has his own parking space.* There are several ways to make your writing gender-neutral when it comes to pronoun use:

   ☑ **Replace the offending pronoun with an indefinite article (*a, an*):** *Every executive has a parking space.*

   ☑ **Recast the sentence, making the singular pronoun plural:** *All executives have their own parking spaces.*

   ☑ **Use both masculine and feminine pronouns** when they do not recur throughout the sentence: *Every executive has his/her own parking space.* Multiple pronoun pairs can be awkward and impractical when revised this way.

   ☑ **Choose plural pronouns:** *They* and *their* are non-standard replacements for *he* and *his*—common in spoken English and increasingly acceptable in written English but still not necessarily the best choice, especially in formal documents: *Every lawyer has their own parking space.*

WRITE WITH CONFIDENCE

A confident tone encourages readers to accept your decisions and opinions rather than question them. When you need to express yourself firmly and decisively, apply the following strategies:

1. **Use definite, forward-looking language.** Give priority to strong, deliberate verbs, precise nouns, and vivid adjectives.

   ☒ Although I might not have as much experience as the other applicants, I did take a few courses in risk management while trying to complete the requirements of my MBA.

   ☑ Two courses in risk management for my recently completed MBA degree will allow me to contribute to your mutual funds division.

   Use helping verbs of qualification, such as *seems*, *could*, *might*, and *may*, only when you need to express conjecture, doubt, or uncertainty.

2. **Don't make unnecessary apologies.** Apologies weaken your perceived authority, especially if you find yourself apologizing for routine requests you must make

to do your job effectively. Understand when apologies are needed—when something has gone wrong—and when they are not.

> ☒ I am so sorry to have to ask you to confirm the time and location of our next meeting.

> ☑ Please confirm the time and location of our next meeting.

3. **Use strong, assertive phrasing rather than "weasel words."**[3] Deferential and well-intentioned phrases such as *I hope* and *I trust* can sometimes sound weak and tentative. With overuse, phrases such as *perhaps if you have time*, *maybe if it's not too much trouble*, *if you could possibly*, or *I find it probable that* can slowly drain the power and assertiveness from your writing. Other hedging words to watch for and use selectively include *tend*, *in some ways*, *perhaps*, *seems*, *seemingly*, *possibly*.

4. **Be knowledgeable and informative.** Know your subject well enough to make it intelligible to the reader. A command of the facts is a natural credibility booster. Well-presented data and meaningful information help reduce readers' uncertainty and allow them to take action and make sound decisions.

5. **Guard against overconfidence.** Too much confidence can make you sound egotistical. Try not to cross the line between firmness and blatant arrogance. Remember that bragging and boasting not only affect credibility, but also turn readers off.

> **Boastful:** You will undoubtedly agree that my marketing genius makes me more than qualified for the job.

> **Confident:** My experience in marketing and additional background in public relations have prepared me for this challenging position.

Tone: Quick Reference Guidelines

To achieve a professional and businesslike tone,

☐ **Select the right level of formality:** Decide how formal or personal you want to be and choose words in the right register for your reader.

☐ **Be positive:** Use constructive language and avoid dwelling on negatives.

☐ **Stress reader benefits and relevance:** Cultivate a sincere you-attitude and interpret facts and information to appeal to the reader's point of view.

☐ **Be polite:** Show courtesy and consideration.

☐ **Use inclusive language:** Don't discriminate. Use only bias-free terms.

☐ **Write with confidence:** Be firm and decisive, but never arrogant.

Chapter Review Checklist

Define your business style by following a few basic principles of word choice, conciseness, and tone:

☐ Use plain, precise, and current language to make your message clear and meaningful to your reader.

☐ Be ethical and purposeful in your choice of words to reflect good public relations for your company and good human relations with colleagues.

☐ Be brief and use as few words as possible to express your thoughts and pass on information.

☐ Make your messages constructive, relevant, reader-focused, and inclusive.

☐ Use a personal or impersonal style that's appropriate to the type of message you write.

☐ Adopt a tone that's conversational, confident, and courteous.

WORKSHOPS AND DISCUSSION FORUMS

Tuning in to Word Choice and Tone. In each of the following exercises, compare the sentence options and identify the factors that make one sentence preferable to the other(s).

a) Which style is more readable?
- The March 1 effectuation of amended plant employee safety measures institutes a requirement applicable to all machine operators who will be expected to wear protective eyewear devices whether or not they are engaged in machine operation in the assembly facility.
- When new safety measures for plant employees go into effect March 1, machine operators will be required to wear protective goggles at all times in the assembly facility.

b) Which writing style is more decipherable?
- A prestigious consulting firm reached the conclusion that a specially formed committee should undertake an investigation of corporate asset mismanagement.
- A prestigious consulting firm concluded that a special committee should investigate the mismanagement of corporate assets.

c) Which sentence conveys its information more positively?
- Our systems will be down until 4:00 p.m. today.
- Our systems will be operational as of 4:00 p.m. today.

d) Which sentence makes a better impression on the reader? How would you describe the tone in each case?
- If you fail to notify head office of your travel plans, you will cause terrible inconvenience for all concerned.
- Please let head office know of your travel plans in advance so that suitable arrangements can be made for you.

e) Which writing style is more likely to win over a potential customer?
- We are proud to be opening our new location, with the largest square footage of any of our five stores.
- You are invited to our convenient new location in Bonaventure Mall.
- Come celebrate the opening of our new location in Bonaventure Mall and enjoy GST-free shopping on Friday, October 15.

f) Which writing style is more likely to attract the favourable attention of an HR job specialist?

- Notwithstanding my lack of any full-time work experience and the fact that I am still trying to get my college diploma, I probably could be the "dynamic and progressive individual" for which your company advertised.

- With five years of part-time work experience in a related field and a soon-to-be-completed diploma in logistics management, I would like to be considered for the position of inventory specialist offered by your company.

WRITING IMPROVEMENT EXERCISES

Recognize the Need for Plain, Precise, and Current Language

1. **Using Familiar Words.** "Translate" the following sentences by replacing long, unfamiliar words, jargon, and noun phrases with plain English equivalents.

   Sample: Please ascertain labour costs pertaining to the Corbin project.

   Revision: Please estimate labour costs for the Corbin project.

   a) It is incumbent on our organization to pursue radical debt reduction through the implementation of a corporate asset divestment program.
   b) Please acquaint yourself with the plans for the optimization of plant-level information systems.
   c) In lieu of a full refund, might we suggest a suitable quid pro quo or a complimentary pro bono service.
   d) By formulating a timeline, we will facilitate production and accomplish our goals more expeditiously.
   e) We provide assistance consistent with your requirements.

2. **Using Fresh and Current Language: Eliminating Slang and Clichés.** Revise the following sentences by replacing slang and updating old-fashioned business expressions.

   Sample: Here's the 411 coming down the pike on our latest corporate meltdown: everyone's gonna be sacked unless the top guns upstairs pony up and come up with some megabucks.

   Revision: The workforce will be downsized unless management secures new funding.

   a) Don't knock the head honcho: he may not have deep pockets but he never blows his cool.
   b) Hey, office dudes and fellow paper pushers, check out this most excellent report.
   c) Please rest assured that if we tighten our belts and stay true to form, we should see a change for the better.
   d) As per your request and for your perusal, please find enclosed our newest home ownership saving plan brochure.
   e) FYI: a directorship is up for grabs but apparently the job pays peanuts.

3. **Using Specific and Functional Language.** Revise the following sentences by replacing vague words and abstract nouns with purposeful, concrete details.

   Sample: Please contact me sometime soon.
   Revision: Please phone me tomorrow.

   a) Past performance reviews show that Vanessa is a good employee.
   b) Five of our current top salespeople are young.
   c) Our real estate brokerage firm has low commission rates.
   d) A majority of shareholders think a hostile takeover bid will affect share prices substantially.
   e) Our high-speed Internet service is really fast.

Identify Strategies for Concise Messaging

4. **Achieving Conciseness by Eliminating Clutter.** Edit and revise the following sentences by eliminating noun phrases, long lead-ins, expletive constructions, prepositional phrases, and relative clauses.

Sample: The company undertook action that was decisive despite the fact that the resources it had were limited.

Revision: The company acted decisively despite its limited resources.

a) It was a clerk from accounting who located the spreadsheets that had been missing.

b) This is to fully apprise you of the fact that there are only six more working days in which to submit your claim for reimbursement for travel expenses for 2009.

c) By and large, it is our assumption that share prices have been sagging due to the fact that there is by all accounts weakness in this particular sector.

d) In response to your letter of August 16 that was received August 18, we cannot act in accordance with your express wishes in making a refund due to the fact that the warranty of the product you purchased from us has expired.

e) For each and every customer who is dissatisfied, there isn't only a sale that is lost, there is a lifetime value of that customer that is lost as well.

5. **Achieving Conciseness by Eliminating Noun Conversions.** Revise noun conversions and imprecise verbs in the following sentences.

Sample: The budget chief endeavoured to make an elimination of expenditures that were unnecessary.

Revision: The budget chief tried to eliminate unnecessary expenditures.

a) A senior engineer will make an assessment of the safety requirements and, if necessary, make changes to them.

b) Our claims specialists are responsible for giving assessments of coverage, liability, and damages.

c) We gave consideration to how the company would be affected before we made the decision to undergo conversion to clicks-and-mortar retailing.

d) The marketing team saw to the finalization of the branding agreement.

e) Many analysts have a preference for a layered approach to security.

6. **Achieving Conciseness by Eliminating Redundancies and Repetition.** Revise the following sentences to eliminate obvious statements and unnecessary repetition.

Sample: Her sister is a woman who works as an investment adviser at Forest Financial.

Revision: Her sister is an investment adviser at Forest Financial.

a) If you refer back to the final section of the report, you will see that the recommendations suggest we should continue on with the current profit-sharing plan.

b) In view of the fact that your freight has not arrived as scheduled, we have asked our supervisor of shipping to make the necessary inquiries.

c) During the course of the meeting, the need for mutual co-operation was brought to our attention.

Differentiate between Personal and Impersonal Style

7. **Writing Conversationally and Informally.** Rewrite the following sentences in a less formal, impersonal style.

Sample: Subscription rates have increased by less than 5 per cent.

Revision: I am sorry to tell you that subscription rates have increased by less than 5 per cent.

a) Those interested in volunteering for the United Way fundraising committee should inform human resources at their earliest convenience.

b) Supervisors should discipline brokers who use discriminatory language when communicating with clients and co-workers.

c) The customer service department should continue to monitor all calls for purposes of quality control.

8. **Writing Informally.** Lessen the formality of the following e-mail message.

It is most important to note that, as of today, advertisements for departmental job openings must be routed through the human resources department. This improvement is made in accordance with the company's commitment to efficiency and operating expenditure reduction.

Following this new procedure will save employees work and enable human resources to help employees fill their openings more quickly.

Create Constructive, Inclusive, and Reader-Oriented Messages

9. **Recognizing Positive and Negative Connotations.** For each of the following sentences, select the word(s) with the most positive connotations. Which words are too negative or colloquial for business use?

   a) Our senior analyst was (instructed/indoctrinated/trained/educated/brainwashed) at Algonquin College.

   b) His gradual concession to salary demands shows that he is (careful/cautious/wary/calculating).

   c) Jim is a(n) (productive/Type-A/hard-working/diligent/industrious) member of our staff who is a(n) (creative/imaginative/gonzo/innovative/inventive/original) problem-solver.

10. **Being Positive.** Revise the following sentences to create a positive impression.

Sample:	Because you failed to provide us with your postal code, we could not send you the estate-planning package you requested.
Revision:	Please tell us your postal code so that we may send you your estate-planning package.

    a) We never fail to offer our GIC investors the most highly competitive rates.

    b) In your e-mail message to our customer service department, you allege that our Dependability-Plus model printer is defective.

    c) Aren't you being unreasonable in asking for your vacation at this time of year?

    d) It is categorically impossible for us to obtain model A311, which is no longer in production. Only model A312 is available.

    e) In your initial letter of January 10, your failure to mention your concern over our billing procedures showed great carelessness. You were negligent in failing to mention your concern over our billing procedures.

11. **Stressing Reader Benefits and Relevance.** Revise the following sentences so that they reflect the reader's viewpoint.

Sample:	We charge our guests only $175 per person for one night's accommodation at our deluxe resort, a full spa treatment, and dinner at our award-winning restaurant.
Revision:	For only $175 (per person), you can enjoy a night's accommodation at our deluxe resort, a full spa treatment, and dinner at our award-winning restaurant.

    a) I will allow you to take your vacation during the last two weeks of August.

    b) We are currently seeking individuals to be part of our highly focused and dedicated team.

    c) We are pleased to announce a new rewards program that guarantees discounts on future purchases.

    d) I am enclosing Form C52, which must be completed before we can reimburse you for your educational expenses.

    e) Because we won't assume responsibility for personal injuries that occur on our premises, we ask that you refrain from using the front lobby while it undergoes renovation.

12. **Being Polite.** Revise the following sentences to reduce their harshness and hostility and improve courtesy.

Sample:	You had better get moving on that draft proposal.
Revision:	Please begin work on the draft proposal as soon as possible.

    a) If you honestly expect me to meet the November 21 deadline, I need the latest sales figures and I need them now, so hand them over!

    b) If you had been paying attention, you would undoubtedly have known that without exception all requests for temporary personnel must be made through the Human Resources Department.

    c) We have far better things to do here at Apex Industries than speak with customers who could easily find the same information on our website.

d) Have the decency to let me know how the meeting went.

e) Since you're the team leader, motivating team members is your problem, not mine.

13. Using Inclusive Language. Revise the following sentences so that they are bias-free, gender-neutral, and non-discriminatory.

Sample: John is the best handicapped IT specialist we've ever had.

Revision: John is one of the best IT specialists we've ever had.

a) Although she's just a young thing, barely out of business school, Jessica has shown considerable leadership and acumen in her eight months as a junior analyst.

b) The suspension of mandatory retirement means that old folks can stay in their jobs as long as they like.

c) Jennifer suffers from bouts of clinical depression, but her mood never seems to adversely affect her job performance.

d) All executives and their wives are invited to our annual Christmas party. Every executive will have his choice of seating arrangement.

e) Although Mei Lin came to Canada from China only a few years ago, she is an able spokesman for the agency.

Develop a Conversational and Confident Tone

14. Writing with Confidence. Revise the following sentences to eliminate any doubtful tone and tentativeness.

Sample: I'm sorry to have to ask you when we might receive our new software.

Revision: Please tell us the delivery date of our new software.

a) Perhaps you could send me the latest figures sometime, that is, if it's not too much trouble for you.

b) Although I don't have much related work experience, I'm attempting to complete an MBA degree.

c) I hope you won't find fault with my investigation.

d) Apparently, the missing laptop you asked about doesn't seem to be on our premises.

e) In some ways, decentralization is possibly the best thing we have ever tried to do.

ONLINE ACTIVITIES   http://www.

Recognize the Need for Plain, Precise, and Current Language

1. Writing in Plain Style. Visit the site of the Plain Language Association International and click on "Business." Read the original excerpts from an insurance company form letter and travel agent correspondence. Without peeking at the suggested revisions, rewrite each message in plain style. Afterward, cross-check your revisions with those provided by the site.
www.plainlanguagenetwork.org/Samples

2. Learning about Plain Style. Go to the "Plain Language in the News" link at the Plain Language Association International website. Select three recent articles, share what you've learned with your class, and summarize your findings in a short memo to your instructor.
www.plainlanguage.gov/examples/index.cfm

3. Identifying Greek and Latin Roots. Visit the following site, which includes a printable Roots Dictionary, and complete the six-section quiz and multiple-choice review.
http://english.glendale.cc.ca.us/roots.html

4. Revising Abbreviations for Readability. Visit Better-English.com and complete the interactive abbreviation exercises by correctly identifying the abbreviation in each case. In a small group, discuss how recognizable each abbreviation is and consider its suitability for professional communication.
www.better-english.com/vocabulary/abbreviations.htm

5. **Eliminating Slang and Clichés.** Visit Better-English.com and complete the interactive online exercise on business idioms by filling in the blanks for each of the twenty questions. The results will feature business slang and clichés. Suggest fresher, more professional alternatives to the words provided in the online activity and discuss your choices with other members of your class.
www.better-english.com/vocabulary/busids.htm

6. **Avoiding Clichés in Writing.** Visit the Writing Center at the University of Richmond and rework the exercise's two paragraphs to eliminate trite, overused, and tired expressions. Compare your revision with those of several of your classmates.
http://writing2.richmond.edu/writing/wweb/cliche.html

Identify Strategies for Concise Messaging

7. **Writing Concise Sentences.** Visit the Online Writing Lab at Purdue University and examine the "Eliminating Words" examples. Revise each "wordy" sentence or phrase, then compare your revision with the "concise" version on the web page. Bring your revisions to class and compare and discuss your revisions with other members of your group.
http://owl.english.purdue.edu/owl/resource/572/02

Create Constructive, Inclusive, Reader-Oriented Messages

8. **Accentuating the Positives.** Read the online tutorial from Purdue University and then scroll down to "Effective Use of Space" and evaluate examples 1–6 to determine whether they present negative information favourably.
http://owl.english.purdue.edu/owl/resource/654/01

9. **Recognizing Word Connotations.** Go to Thesaurus.com and enter three of the following words: *ambitious, intelligent, careless, advanced, aggressive.* Compare the synonyms and, in groups of three or four, discuss their connotations and suitably for business messages.
http://thesaurus.reference.com

4 Business Style: Sentences and Paragraphs

In this chapter you will learn to

1. Recognize basic types of sentences and the building blocks of sentences.

2. Improve sentence variety by matching sentence style and length to purpose.

3. Phrase basic types of questions effectively.

4. Improve sentence clarity.

5. Emphasize important facts and ideas; minimize less important ones.

6. Use parallelism to write with consistency and impact.

7. Distinguish between active and passive voice.

8. Eliminate sentence errors that impair clarity and unity: sentence fragments, run-ons, misplaced and dangling modifiers, mixed constructions.

9. Develop logical, coherent, and focused paragraphs.

10. Apply strategies for proofreading different kinds of messages.

For better or for worse, readers form an impression of you based on how you write. A mastery of sentence structure—combining fluency, variety, and impact—gives you a strategic edge that reinforces your other professional skills. Clear, error-free, context-specific sentences and coherent paragraphs speed up the exchange of information and win kudos from readers who know you by the precision of your words and the ease of your communication.

◗◗ Effective Sentences

Is there a formula for effective written communication? How well you express your thoughts depends largely on how well you can craft sentences and use their building blocks to your advantage. While not exactly a formula in a scientific sense, there is a simple logic to sentence construction. The next few sections explore the phrase, clause, and sentence types that give you the versatility to write effectively.

THE BUILDING BLOCKS OF COMPLETE SENTENCES— PHRASES AND CLAUSES

As a writer, the tools of your trade are groups of related words—better known as phrases and clauses. Understanding what they are and how to put them together helps you write in complete sentences and adds to your range of expression and versatility as a communicator.

A **phrase** is a group of words containing a subject or a verb, but not both. Phrases function as parts of speech—as nouns, verbs, and modifiers—but they do not express complete thoughts, so pay attention to how they're used. A phrase punctuated like a complete sentence is a sentence fragment, a potential source of confusion.

> **After negotiations**, the company offered a new bonus plan **to its employees**.
> **By contacting our customer service representative**, you may learn more **about this program**.

A **clause** is a group of words containing a subject and a verb. Depending on what category they fall into, certain types of clauses are complete sentences while others are not:

1. **Independent clauses** are grammatically complete and can stand on their own as sentences:

   > The program cost more than we expected.

2. **Dependent clauses** are grammatically incomplete and reliant on independent clauses for their meaning. Dependent clauses begin in one of two ways: with a dependent marker (a word such as *if*, *as*, *because*, *since*, or *although*) or with a relative pronoun (*that*, *which*, or *who*). Any combination of subject and verb loses its grammatical completeness with the addition of one of these simple words.

   > **Although the program cost more than we expected**, it has improved company morale.

   > The program, **which cost more than we expected**, has improved company morale.

phrase a group of words containing either a subject *or* verb, which cannot stand on its own as a complete sentence.

clause a group of related words containing a subject and a complete verb; when it delivers full meaning it is called an *independent clause*; when it doesn't deliver full meaning by itself, it is called a *dependent clause*.

independent clause a clause, containing a subject and complete verb, that functions on its own as an independent grammatical unit.

dependent clause (or subordinate clause) a clause that cannot function on its own as an independent grammatical unit.

Clauses and phrases are the building blocks of sentences. Treat them with the respect they deserve by combining and punctuating them carefully.

TYPES OF SENTENCES

A sentence is not just a group of words but a formula for full and accurate communication. A sentence, to be complete and effective, must have two things: a **subject** and a complete **verb**, which carry the core of your meaning. For a group of words to qualify as a sentence, these elements must make sense together and express a complete thought.

The way ideas are linked affects your reader's understanding of the relationship between and among those ideas and their relative importance. There are four types of sentences, each with its own distinctive quality and purpose.

Sentence Type	Consisting of	Example
1. Simple sentence	one independent clause	We will vote on the issue.
2. Compound sentence	two independent clauses	John will present his report, and we will vote on the issue.
3. Complex sentence	one dependent clause and one independent clause	When we meet Thursday, we will vote on the issue.
4. Compound-complex sentence	one dependent clause and two independent clauses	When we meet Thursday, John will present his report, and we will vote on the issue.

Simple sentences are straightforward and emphatic. The shorter they are, the more emphasis they have, although simple sentences may have up to twenty words. There are two potential drawbacks. Without the connecting words typical of other sentence types, a simple sentence may not fully show relationships among ideas. A string of simple sentences can be flat, boring, and monotonous:

> Tax season is approaching. I would like to update you on some details. These details relate to allowable deductions.

Compound sentences join related sentences with coordinate conjunctions such as *for*, *and*, *nor*, *but*, *or*, *yet*, and *so*. Compound sentences stress the equivalence or equal value of the ideas they express. It is important to use this connecting technique—known as coordination—only for related sentences. Over-coordinated sentences skew logic and lack unity:

Over-coordinated sentence:	You may choose from a number of investment options and I look forward to our next appointment.
As two sentences:	You may choose from a number of investment options. I look forward to our next appointment.
As related clauses:	I look forward to our next appointment, when you may choose from a number of investment options.

subject the word or group of words in a sentence that acts or is acted upon.

verb the word or group of words in a sentence that describes an action, occurrence, or state of being.

simple sentence a sentence containing one main or independent clause.

compound sentence a sentence containing two or more independent clauses joined by one or more coordinating conjunctions.

complex sentence a sentence containing one independent clause and one or more dependent clauses.

Complex and **compound–complex sentences** are best at showing the relative importance of ideas and encompassing details. Any of the following subordinate markers lessen the grammatical value of the word groupings they're added to:

although	even if	though
as	even though	unless
as if	if	until
as soon as	if only	when
because	in spite of	where
before	rather than	whereas
despite	since	whether
even	that	while

A clause introduced by a subordinate marker won't make sense on its own and must rely for its meaning on an independent (or stand-alone) clause that is part of the same sentence. Remember this grammatical principle when you need to de-emphasize unpleasant news.

Dependent clause:	**Although** tomorrow's e-business seminar has been cancelled.
Complex sentence:	**Although** the e-business seminar has been cancelled, you will have another opportunity to learn about e-business issues at a series of lectures scheduled for April.

Keep in mind that the longer your sentences are and the more clauses they have, the harder it is to find the subjects and verbs essential for delivering meaning. Sentences with more than three clauses can be difficult and confusing to read.

Quick Review Checklist for Sentence Completeness

Make sure every sentence you write passes the "completeness" test.

- ☐ Is there a verb?
- ☐ Does the verb have a subject?
- ☐ Do the subject and verb make sense together and express a complete thought?
- ☐ If the sentence contains subordinating words—relative pronouns (*that*, *which*, *who*) or subordinate markers—does the sentence also contain an independent clause?

If the answer to every question is yes, the sentence is complete.

IMPROVING SENTENCE VARIETY AND LENGTH

Good writing relies on a natural mix of sentence styles and lengths; however, you do not need to be a "sentence contortionist," constantly shaping and reshaping sentences just for the sake of variety. Let the patterns of normal, everyday speech be your guide to fresh and energetic writing. The following tips will help you break sentence monotony and create useful distinctions among ideas:

1. **Vary the rhythm by alternating short and long sentences**.

   > Please complete and return the enclosed survey [short sentence]. Your answers to our questions will help us review our current practices so that we may provide the highest standard of customer service [long sentence]. By completing the entire survey, you will also receive a 25 per cent discount coupon that you can apply to your next purchase from Software Plus [long sentence].

   Sentences of up to twenty words have a high rate of reader comprehension. Beyond that point, the reader's ability to easily grasp a sentence's meaning falls off sharply. Your word-processing software will usually flag sentences that are too long to be comprehensible. Sentences of ten or fewer words naturally have greater impact and readability, but strings of short sentences can be dull and monotonous and fail to show relationships among ideas.

2. **Turn a clause into a prepositional phrase**. A **prepositional phrase** is a group of words beginning with a preposition (a word such as *with*, *at*, *to*, *of*, *by*, *against*, *toward*, *from*, *above*, *on*, or *in* that relates a noun—a naming word—or pronoun to another word in the sentence).

Two independent clauses:	The plan has the support of upper-level management. It will include extended health benefits.
Sentence with prepositional phrase:	**With recent support from upper-level management**, the plan will include extended health benefits.

   > **prepositional phrase** a phrase beginning with a preposition that sets out a relationship in time or space.

   Another way to convert two or more sentences into one is to use a sentence builder known as a relative clause (a clause beginning with *that*, *which*, or *who*). The new clause, which replaces an entire sentence, acts like an adjective by adding information to define or describe a particular word or group of words.

Sentence with relative clause:	The plan, **which has the support of upper-level management**, will include extended health benefits.

   A modifying phrase—sometimes called a participial phrase—can also be used to streamline sentences. A participial phrase is easy to spot, as it contains a verbal—a present participle (*working*), infinitive (*to work*), or past participle (*worked*). These are words that look like verbs but don't actually qualify as verbs.

appositive a word or group of words that renames a preceding noun.

| **Sentence with modifying phrase:** | **Supported by upper-level management**, the plan will include extended health benefits. |

3. **Convert a sentence defining or describing something into a phrase or clause.** Use commas to set off the descriptive phrase or clause—called an **appositive**—from whatever it follows and renames.

| **Two sentences:** | Frederica Schmidt is an investment consultant. She is a frequent speaker at trade shows and conferences. |
| **Single sentence:** | Frederica Schmidt, **an investment consultant**, is a frequent speaker at trade shows and conferences. |

PHRASING BASIC TYPES OF QUESTIONS

declarative sentence a sentence that makes a statement.

Declarative sentences—sentences that make statements—are useful for relaying facts and decisions, but what if your goal is to get information? Asking questions is an important part of doing business, but there is, of course, more than one way to ask a question. The type of question you ask depends on the type of response you seek—a quick confirmation, a probing analysis, or a creative breakthrough. Asking the right type of question is the first step in getting the information you seek. Here are three types of questions you can ask:

closed question a question with a limited number of possible responses.

1. **Closed questions** can be answered with a simple yes or no or, when you are fact-checking or seeking verification, one or two words. Closed questions follow inverted word order and do not feature question-forming words such as *why*, *what*, and *how*.

   - Can you ship our order today?
   - Are the new sales figures ready?
   - Will you attend tomorrow's meeting?

open question a question with an unlimited number of possible responses.

2. **Open questions** call for a fuller, more thoughtful response than is possible with just a single word.

   - How can we reduce production costs?
   - In what way will deregulation affect the industry?
   - Why do you support this initiative?

hypothetical question a question that poses a supposition.

3. **Hypothetical questions** ask readers to suppose that circumstances are different from what they actually are. These "what if" scenarios are useful for brainstorming and contingency planning.

   If you were given creative control of this project, what would you do?

A well-phrased question will elicit a useful response without putting readers on the defensive or causing confusion.

IMPROVING SENTENCE CLARITY

From time to time, sentences may need a sharper focus for their exact meaning to be clear to readers. Here are a few tips for revising fuzzy, ambiguous sentences:

1. **Avoid broad references using *this, that,* and *it*.** When you use *this, that,* and *it* by themselves, make sure the reader fully understands what the pronoun renames and replaces. Check that the **pronoun reference** isn't ambiguous (i.e., that the pronoun doesn't refer to more than one thing). If necessary, repeat the noun after the pronoun that renames it.

> **pronoun reference** the relationship between a pronoun and the antecedent to which it refers.

Vague pronoun reference:	She helped to negotiate the recent settlement and **this** makes her an asset to the organization. [*This* can refer to both the negotiations and the settlement.]
Clear pronoun reference:	She helped to negotiate the recent settlement and this experience makes her an asset to the organization.

(See also Appendix B, under the heading "Using Pronouns with Precision.")

2. **Avoid embedding dependent clauses.** Put dependent clauses at the beginning or end of a sentence, not in the middle where they can come between the all-important subject and verb. Choppy, stop-and-go sentences formed in this way are difficult to read. They can seem tangled, with too much squeezed into them. Opt for more fluid sentence patterns that mimic natural thought processes.

Embedded clause:	The recycling facility, **although it was originally intended for use by only one municipality**, is now shared with neighbouring townships.
Revision:	**Although the recycling facility was originally intended for use by only one municipality**, it is now shared with neighbouring townships.

3. **Limit multiple negatives.** Multiple negatives are sometimes used for rhetorical effect or as euphemisms (bland terms substituted for blunt ones), but the range of meaning a multiple negative may have sometimes results in confusion.

Unclear:	He was **not un**happy about **not failing** to meet the criteria.
Clearer:	He was pleased he met the criteria.

WRITING WITH CONSISTENCY

Observing the rules of consistency—by sticking to certain grammatical principles and patterns that shape your writing—is another good way to banish awkward, unreadable sentences. Readers like the predictability of sentences that follow through with their initial promises by staying consistent in the following ways:

number a term that refers to whether a word is singular (one) or plural (more than one).

1. **Number.** Don't switch from singular to plural when referring to a particular thing.

   > **Women** have made considerable strides in **their** [not **her**] chosen fields.

person a term that describes who or what is performing or experiencing an action in terms of the noun or pronoun that is used: first person (*I, we*), second person (*you*), and third person (*he, she, it, they*).

2. **Person.** Don't shift the frame of reference from first person *I* to second person *you* or third person *he/she/one*.

   > Before **you** apply for a permit, **you** [not **one**] must show proof of Canadian citizenship or landed immigrant status.

3. **Verb tense.** Show time changes only when logic requires them.

   > When the CEO **entered** the auditorium, the crowd **applauded** [not **applaud**] wildly.

verb tense the form of a verb that shows time (past, present, or future).

4. **Voice.** Don't shift unnecessarily from active to passive voice.

   > Financial analysts expect continued growth in the third quarter <u>but anticipate weakness in the tourism sector</u> [not **<u>weakness in the tourism sector is anticipated</u>**].

WRITING BALANCED SENTENCES: PARALLEL STRUCTURE

parallelism the use of the same grammatical forms or matching sentence structures to express equivalent ideas.

Parallelism involves delivering similar content in a similar way. The consistency of a repeated pattern helps readers absorb and remember information more easily. Balanced constructions—matching nouns with nouns, verbs with verbs, and phrases with phrases—have a rhythmic appeal that makes sentences more forceful and compelling.

Unbalanced:	Britannia Capital's chief analyst proposes three strategies for debt servicing: **slowing** spending, **issuing** equity to pay down debt, and **to sell** assets.
Parallel:	Britannia Capital's chief analyst proposes three strategies for debt servicing: **slowing** capital spending, **issuing** equity to pay down debt, and **selling** assets. [parallel construction matches *-ing* nouns]
Unbalanced:	We anticipate expansion into **underserved regions, border areas**, and **markets that are located overseas**.
Parallel:	We anticipate expansion into **underserved regions, border areas**, and **overseas markets**. [parallel construction matches nouns]

Unbalanced:	Our priorities are to **improve** employee morale, **reduce** absenteeism, and **encouraging** professional development.
Parallel:	Our priorities are to **improve** employee morale, **reduce** absenteeism, and **encourage** professional development. [parallel construction matches verb infinitives]
Unbalanced:	To qualify for funding you must submit an application and **three letters of reference must also be provided**. [switches from active to passive voice]
Parallel:	To qualify for funding you must submit an application and provide three letters of reference. [active voice matched with active voice]

Parallelism also applies to statements of comparison. It is important to balance these constructions for readability and rhetorical force.

Unbalanced:	This is a time not for restraint, but boldness.
Parallel:	This is a time not for restraint, but for boldness.

WRITING FOR EMPHASIS

Office information is often exchanged and processed quickly, not always leaving time for methodical word-for-word readings. Make sure your most important information gets the attention it deserves by adding special emphasis. **Emphasis**—the act of making facts stand out—is a matter of mechanics and style. These approaches can be used on their own or in combination.

emphasis in writing, the practice of making facts and ideas stand out from surrounding text.

Use Eye-Catching Mechanical Devices, Punctuation, and Formatting

These strategies can enhance the visual appeal of the written word. The most common of these simple strategies include

<u>underlining</u>

boldface

italics

modified font sizes

ALL CAPS

text boxes

colour

Use dashes—the most emphatic of all punctuation marks—in place of commas and parentheses when introducing or enclosing facts that demand special attention. Another way to make important details stand out is to format them in lists that run horizontally or vertically. These mechanical devices are effective as long as they are used in moderation. Overused, the device itself can be distracting. A message typed in all caps, for example, is hard to read and "shouts" its information. **Shouting** is the name given to

shouting the largely unacceptable practice of typing a message in block letters.

this heavy-handed practice. In addition, too many bolded letters, italics, and font sizes and styles can make a serious document look crude and amateurish, much like a cut-and-paste ransom note.

Add Emphasis through Style

Style adaptations for emphasis require more planning but are generally worth the extra effort in terms of their impact on readers. Techniques for creating emphasis through style involve three basic principles:

- placement,
- sentence length and structure, and
- word choice.

Here is a closer look at techniques that give power to your writing through emphasis:

1. **For maximum impact, put important facts first or last.** The most emphatic, "high-wattage" placements are first and last in a sentence. Avoid creating an "information sandwich" that embeds crucial facts and details in the middle of a sentence or paragraph where surrounding words may cloud or lessen their impact.

Unemphatic:	A new deadline of **March 15** has been set for all funding applications.
Emphatic:	**March 15** is the new deadline for all funding applications.
Unemphatic:	**No one can deny** that the bear market has had a substantial impact **on pension funds**. ["No one can deny" is an empty phrase given emphatic initial placement. The most important idea, "the bear market has had a substantial impact," is slotted in the middle where it is less noticeable.]
Emphatic:	Undeniably, the bear market's impact on pension funds has been substantial.

   Generally, the subject word at the beginning establishes a focus for the remainder of the sentence. Changing the subject allows you to change the intended emphasis of a sentence.

Focus on *survey*:	The survey indicated that most employees support the adoption of staggered work hours.
Focus on *employees*:	Most employees support the adoption of staggered work hours, according to the survey.
Focus on *adoption*:	The adoption of staggered work hours is supported by most employees, according to the survey.

2. **Use short, simple sentences to spotlight key ideas**. The fewer words there are in a sentence, the more impact each of its words has. A short, uncluttered

sentence, consisting of a single independent clause, rewards readers instantly with information.

Readers also like simple sentences because the "start-with-the-subject" word order allows information to accumulate in a way that mimics human thought processes. A short sentence after several long ones has even greater impact because it breaks the pattern and adds an element of surprise.

> **Short and emphatic:** The on-site fitness centre opens next Wednesday.
>
> **Long and unemphatic:** The on-site fitness centre opens next Wednesday, at which time all employees will be invited to try out top-quality equipment that includes exercise bikes and rowing machines.

3. **Use tags and labels to flag important ideas.** Simple word-markers such as *most importantly*, *most of all*, *above all*, *particularly*, *crucially*, or *most important* alert readers to an idea's significance.

4. **Present important ideas in list form.** Horizontal and vertical lists give extra emphasis through their distinct formatting. Horizontal lists that number items within a sentence are less emphatic than vertical lists that tabulate items.

> The newly created Employee Integrity Website has links to several vital resources:
> - Haskell Networks Employee Code of Conduct
> - Professional development seminar information
> - Citation guides

5. **Use precise and specific words to identify the main point.** Avoid generalization and obfuscation. If something is *good*, describe the way in which it is good. Specifics are more involving because they show rather than tell.

> **Vague:** The conference was good.
>
> **Specific:** The conference was lively and informative.

6. **Repeat key words in a series for rhetorical effect.** Advertisers and marketing specialists sometimes rely on repetition to persuade customers of the value of a product, concept, or service. Because this technique can easily induce boredom instead of acceptance, it does not necessarily work well in other, more subtle forms of writing:

> Look how far **we've** come. **We were the first** Canadian company to receive the Gold Award from the International Customer Service Association. **We were among the first** in the world to introduce service breakthroughs like voice dialling, Internet access from your cellphone, and 1X technology. **We simplified** the prepaid world by making minutes available at bank machines, and **we simplified** the banking world by facilitating cellphone transactions. **We're working hard** to continue to earn your business.

Apply Opposite Rules for De-emphasis

News that is unfavourable to your readers or merely less significant can be de-emphasized by applying principles opposite to those used for emphasis. Here are a few simple tips to follow:

1. **Use complex sentences to de-emphasize bad news.** Complex sentences have a dual advantage: their independent clauses emphasize while their subordinate clauses de-emphasize. Capitalize on these strengths by putting the bad news in the opening subordinate clause and using the independent clause that follows for better news.

Bad news emphasized:	We must reject your credit application at this time.
Bad news de-emphasized:	Although credit cannot be extended to you at this time, we would look forward to serving you on a cash basis.
Bad news emphasized:	Although the quality of the applications has never been higher, the number of applications is down.
Good news emphasized:	Although the number of applications is down, the quality of the applications has never been higher.

2. **De-emphasize unpleasant facts by embedding them.** Unfavourable information seems less harsh and less noticeable when buried mid-sentence or mid-paragraph.

Mid-sentence de-emphasis:	Our bestselling global positioning device, **though currently out of stock**, will be reissued in a new deluxe model next month.

Flash Review EMPHASIS CHART

For Emphasis	For De-emphasis
mechanical devices	no mechanical devices
short sentences	long sentences
simple sentences (independent clauses)	complex sentences (dependent clauses)
precise, vivid words	general words
labels	no labels
placement first or last	middle placement

APPLYING ACTIVE AND PASSIVE VOICE

The voice of a verb tells you whether a sentence's subject acts (active voice) or receives an action (passive voice). Voice often accounts for why one message or document can sound lively and direct, while another can seem impersonal or flat. The active voice should be your first choice for business messages, but you should also make room for legitimate uses of passive-voice constructions.

The *active voice*, a staple of good writing, is energetic, forceful, and direct. In the active voice, the question of "whodunit" is always clear because the grammatical subject "acts" by performing the action of the sentence: *The supervisor* [ACTOR] *approved* [ACTION] *the changes* [RECEIVER]. Use the active voice in the following situations:

1. **To state good and neutral news clearly and directly.** By comparison, the passive voice can result in awkward, convoluted constructions.

   Active: John completed his expense report before the April 1 deadline.

   Passive: John's expense report was completed by John before the April 1 deadline.

2. **To emphasize the doer of an action.** The active voice tells the reader in no uncertain terms where actions originate and who is responsible for them.

   Active: Belinda authorized the purchase.

   Passive: The purchase was authorized (by Belinda).

The *passive voice* is less vigorous and forthright. To some readers, it sounds flat, weak, and evasive because it is not always clear who or what performs the action of the sentence, only that the action is done to the subject. Passive constructions invert the order of the active voice: *The changes* [RECEIVER] *were approved* [ACTION] *by the supervisor* [ACTOR]. Emphasis falls on the action itself, not on who or what performs it. Look for three common elements to check for passive constructions:

> **the verb TO BE** (*am, is, are, was, were, be, been*) **+ past participle +** *by . . .*

The term *institutional passive* refers to the practice of concealing the performer of an action (by omitting the word or words after *by*), especially when the performer is unknown or unimportant. Use the passive voice in the following situations:

1. **To conceal the doer of an action when that information is unimportant, unknown, or harmful.** The active voice assigns responsibility for actions; the passive voice does not, which in certain cases can seem evasive or even dishonest. The passive voice should not be used in a blatant attempt to cover up facts, weasel out of agreements, or manipulate readers.

   Active: The executive committee delivered the development plan on schedule.

   Passive: The development plan was delivered on schedule.

2. **To de-emphasize negative news.** The passive voice depersonalizes sentences by taking people and personalities, as expressed through names and personal pronouns, out of the picture. It is therefore useful in situations where you need to soften negatives or avoid accusations. The passive voice puts the emphasis matter-of-factly on a refusal or denial, not on the individual(s) responsible for that decision.

> **Active:**   We cannot release specific salary information.
>
> **Passive:**   Specific salary information cannot be released.

3. **To show tact and sensitivity.** The passive voice is one of many "politeness strategies" in business writing. Its natural "weakness" is an alternative to the bluntness of the active voice and allows you to pass on information without allocating blame, finding fault, or making readers feel needlessly singled out.

> **Active:**   You must return all materials to the resource centre.
>
> **Passive:**   All materials must be returned to the resource centre.

4. **To reduce intrusive first-person pronouns.** Writing in the passive voice is a way of avoiding the egotism of the active voice and eliminating its multiple *I*'s and personal pronouns. The passive voice is appropriate when it is already clear from the context that you are responsible for an action. Use this technique sparingly.

> **Active:**   I based this study on extensive market research.
>
> **Passive:**   This study is based on extensive market research.

The passive voice in this case allows you to emphasize the study rather than who authored it.

5. **To maintain consistency or avoid awkward shifts in focus.** Stick with the passive voice if a shift to the active voice results in awkwardness.

> **Active:**   When the new shipment arrived, the sales associates unpacked it.
>
> **Passive:**   When the new shipment arrived, it was unpacked by the sales associates.

Diagnostic grammar-checking software is programmed to flag passive-voice constructions, but keep in mind that not all instances of the passive voice make for ineffective writing.

Flash Review   ACTIVE AND PASSIVE VOICE CHART

Use the Active Voice to	Use the Passive Voice to
• State good/neutral news clearly	• De-emphasize negative news
• Be direct	• Show tact and sensitivity
• Emphasize the doer of an action	• De-emphasize or conceal the doer of an action

ELIMINATING GRAMMAR ERRORS AND AWKWARDNESS

Sentence errors detract from the professionalism of your messages and reduce readers' confidence in what you have to say. Writing under pressure can increase the likelihood that errors will occur, but recognizing the types of errors you tend to make is the first line of defence against a finished product that fails to communicate thoughts and ideas in the way you intended. Here is a guide to some of the most common grammatical errors:

1. **Sentence fragments.** These incomplete portions of sentences—phrases or dependent clauses—are punctuated like complete sentences. As a result they create ambiguity and distortion. To detect them easily, work backward, proofreading from last sentence to first in order to separate the fragment from the grammatical unit that completes it.

> **sentence fragment**
> a portion of a sentence that is punctuated like a complete sentence but does not deliver full meaning.

Fragment:	We will discuss the Orkin account. **Which has been experiencing problems lately.** [relative clause punctuated as a complete sentence]
Revision:	We will discuss the Orkin account, which has been experiencing problems lately.
Fragment:	Sales figures for the year were strong. **Even though there was weakness in the third quarter.** [subordinate clause punctuated as a complete sentence]
Revision:	Sales figures for the year were strong even though there was weakness in the third quarter.
Fragment:	The company has experienced numerous setbacks. **For example, the failure of its light industrial division.** [The example cannot stand on its own as a sentence.]
Revision:	The company has experienced numerous setbacks— for example, the failure of its light industrial division.

2. **Run-on (fused) sentences.** Run-ons, or **fused sentences**, are marathon sentences—two or more independent clauses that are combined without an adequate full stop (semicolon or period) or connecting element (comma and conjunction). To put a stop to the run-on, opt for one of these forms of correction:

> **fused sentence** two or more independent clauses erroneously run together without the use of required punctuation or coordinating conjunctions.

Run-on:	Most companies reported moderate growth this year some anticipate similar growth next year.
Revision:	Most companies reported moderate growth this year, **and** some anticipate similar growth next year.
Revision:	Most companies reported moderate growth this year. Some anticipate similar growth next year.

comma splice the error that occurs when two independent clauses are connected with nothing more than a comma.

3. **Comma splices.** In a comma splice, independent clauses are strung together with nothing more than a comma to separate them. To eliminate the splice, add a conjunction or change the comma to a period or semicolon.

Comma splice:	I decided against purchasing an extended warranty, however when my credit card statement arrived this month I noticed an extra $149 charge from Info Service, Inc.
Revision:	I decided against purchasing an extended warranty; however, when my credit card statement arrived this month, I noticed an extra $149 charge from Info Service, Inc.

modifier a word or group of words that describes or gives more information about another word in a sentence.

misplaced modifier an incorrectly placed descriptive word or phrase that attaches its meaning illogically to another word in a sentence.

4. **Misplaced modifiers.** A **modifier** is a word or word group that describes another word or words. Modifiers that end up where they do not belong can be unintentionally funny and make your meaning ambiguous. To eliminate the **misplaced modifier** and its potential for embarrassment, position modifiers as close as possible to the word or words they describe. Do this by asking yourself, "What goes with what?"

Misplaced modifier:	The changes in personnel taking place recently affected productivity. [In this case, *recently* could refer to the changes in personnel or when those changes affected productivity.]
Revision:	Recent personnel changes affected productivity.
Revision:	Changes in personnel recently affected productivity.

dangling modifier a phrase that describes something that is implied rather than actually stated in a sentence.

5. **Dangling modifiers.** A phrase is said to dangle when its descriptive words do not clearly apply to another word in the sentence. This problem often occurs with introductory verbal phrases containing a past participle (*informed*), an infinitive (*to inform*), or a present participle (*informing*) but no subject. Verbal phrases can enhance the flow of your writing, but to use them effectively, make sure the subject being described in the introductory phrase comes immediately after the phrase itself. Otherwise, convert the dangling phrase into a dependent clause using the technique shown in the second revision below.

Dangling phrase:	Sent by overnight courier, you will receive your package by 9:00 a.m. the next day. [This sentence says *you are sent by overnight courier.*]
Revision:	Sent by overnight courier, your package will arrive by 9:00 a.m. the next day.
Revision:	When a package is sent by overnight courier, you will receive it by 9:00 a.m. the next day. [In this case, the dangling phrase has been converted to an initial dependent clause.]

Tolerance for dangling modifiers is sometimes higher in e-mail communication, as long as a message is still understandable. The more formal the document, the less excusable dangling modifiers are. Sometimes a dangling modifier results from misuse of the passive voice, as in the following example:

Dangling phrase:	To qualify for our points program, your mother's maiden name must be provided. [This sentence says *your mother's maiden name will qualify for the program.*]
Revision:	To qualify for our points program, you must provide your mother's maiden name.
Revision:	To qualify for our points program, please provide your mother's maiden name.

6. **Elliptical constructions.** *Ellipsis* means "omission." An **elliptical construction** leaves out words that have already appeared in a sentence because their meaning is inferred from the context: *Private-sector administrators earned on average $80,000 a year, their public-sector counterparts significantly less.* Don't automatically assume that a word appearing elsewhere in the sentence will stand in for the omitted word in the elliptical construction. The implied word has to be exactly the same as the one already used for the construction to be correct:

> **elliptical construction** a sentence structure that deliberately omits words that can be inferred from the context.

Word omitted:	The new treatment was intended and administered to patients who had not responded to conventional therapies.
Word added:	The new treatment was intended **for** and administered to patients who had not responded to conventional therapies.

7. **Faulty predication and mixed constructions.** Mixed-construction sentences pair mismatched elements that do not logically fit together and must be untangled in order to make sense. In a sentence with faulty predication, there is sometimes an illogical pairing of subject and verb.

> **faulty predication** an error involving the illogical combination of subject and verb.

Faulty predication:	The solution to this problem was remedied when Johnson proposed a splitting of company stock. [Solutions don't need to be remedied, but problems do.]
Revision:	This problem was remedied when Johnson proposed a splitting of company stock.

Is when or *is where* combination

To fix a sentence featuring an *is when* or *is where* construction, drop *when* or *where*, add a classifying word, or substitute another verb for the verb *to be*:

Faulty predication:	Direct channel is when you sell and distribute products directly to customers.
Revision:	*Direct channel* is a marketing term for selling and distributing products directly to customers.
Revision:	Direct channel refers to selling and distributing products directly to customers.

Reason ... is because combination

The expression *the reason ... is because* is redundant (akin to saying *because ... because*); replace it with *the reason is that*:

Faulty predication:	**The reason** he can't travel overseas **is because** he has family obligations.
Revision:	The reason he can't travel overseas is that he has family obligations.
Revision:	He can't travel overseas because he has family obligations.

mixed construction the error of substituting an incompatible grammatical structure for one that is correct, resulting in unclear or illogical meaning.

In a sentence of **mixed construction**, the sentence starts in one grammatical form, then shifts to another. Common culprits in mixed construction sentences are introductory phrases such as the following:

The fact that

Mixed construction:	The fact that more job seekers submit their resumés electronically than they do by more traditional methods.
Revision:	The fact **is** that more job seekers submit their resumés electronically than they do by more traditional methods.
Revision:	More job seekers submit their resumés electronically than they do by more traditional methods. [drops troublesome opening phrase]

An illogical sentence subject

Sentences sometimes feature an illogical sentence subject:

Mixed construction:	By reviewing job performance on a semi-annual basis was how we aimed to increase productivity. [*By reviewing* cannot be the subject of a sentence. The same applies to any phrase made up of a preposition and an *-ing* verbal.]
Revision:	By reviewing job performance on a semi-annual basis, we aimed to increase productivity.
Revision:	Reviewing job performance on a semi-annual basis was aimed at increasing productivity.

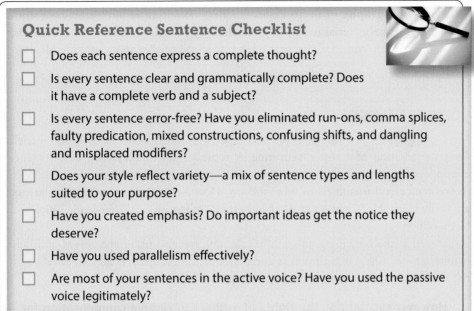

Quick Reference Sentence Checklist

- [ ] Does each sentence express a complete thought?
- [ ] Is every sentence clear and grammatically complete? Does it have a complete verb and a subject?
- [ ] Is every sentence error-free? Have you eliminated run-ons, comma splices, faulty predication, mixed constructions, confusing shifts, and dangling and misplaced modifiers?
- [ ] Does your style reflect variety—a mix of sentence types and lengths suited to your purpose?
- [ ] Have you created emphasis? Do important ideas get the notice they deserve?
- [ ] Have you used parallelism effectively?
- [ ] Are most of your sentences in the active voice? Have you used the passive voice legitimately?

Effective Paragraphs

A **paragraph** is a unit of meaningful thought—a group of sentences that introduces a subject and makes one or more points about it. Paragraphs are the building blocks of effective writing: tidy information packages held together by a controlling idea and a clear sense of development. The white space that separates paragraphs alerts the reader to a change in subject, paving the way for new ideas and mapping out information so it is easier to understand and remember.

paragraph a group of sentences that develops one main idea.

PARAGRAPH LENGTH

There is no ideal paragraph length. The length of a paragraph is regulated by what you need to say and how you need to say it. For most types of business messages, though, short paragraphs are usually best. Short paragraphs promise easier reading and retention. Long, overloaded paragraphs form uninviting blocks of text that are visually intimidating. A series of them, just by their dense appearance, can lessen readers' receptivity even before they begin to read. Choose from a range of short, moderate, and long paragraphs to match your purpose and support your content:

- **Single-sentence paragraphs** (or paragraphs of up to two sentences) are common message openers and closers. Brief and serviceable, they are also useful for lending emphasis to especially important facts or ideas and have a special place in e-mail. A series of single-sentence paragraphs, however, can be mistaken for point form, robbing your message of coherence and development.
- **Short paragraphs** of up to five or six sentences (or eight lines of text) are standard in most types of business messages.

- **Long paragraphs** of up to eight sentences belong in reports, where the complexity of the material merits full and thorough development. Beyond the eight-sentence limit, consider regrouping sentences into smaller, more manageable units.

A well-constructed message usually relies on a natural mix of paragraph lengths.

TOPIC SENTENCES

topic sentence a sentence that summarizes the main idea in a paragraph.

Most paragraphs—not just ones with complicated information to pass on—benefit from the addition of a **topic sentence**. A topic sentence, usually the first sentence, announces the paragraph's purpose. It previews the paragraph so readers can decide on the relevance and usefulness of what follows. Documents that feature topic sentences are easily scannable because the most important information is front-loaded into each block of text.

Placed at the beginning, the controlling idea prevents paragraph sprawl and helps maintain focus. Once it is clear that a sentence in the grouping is no longer related to the first one, it is time to start a new paragraph.

> **However substantial, the rights of authors to receive compensation for their efforts are limited by the doctrine of fair use.** According to law, fair use gives writers a limited right to use brief sections of copyrighted material without asking for permission. For instance, quoting a single sentence from a magazine article is considered fair use, whereas quoting a page or more is not.

Topic sentences are recommended for paragraphs that define, describe, classify, or illustrate.[1] They are less suited to paragraphs that reveal bad news, where it is important to first establish a rationale or justification for a negative decision. Revealing the bad news first risks alienating readers, who are less likely to accept unexpected and unwelcome news. In paragraphs of comparison or persuasive purpose, the topic sentence may be delayed or embedded to allow for an opening statement of contrast or concession.

PARAGRAPH DEVELOPMENT

The form a paragraph takes depends on how you develop the main idea introduced at the beginning. Typically, your purpose may be to do one of the following:

- describe a chronological sequence of events,
- compare or contrast one idea with another,
- evaluate causes or relate them to effects,
- analyze a topic or offer a solution to a problem,
- classify the parts of a whole,
- illustrate an idea or support a claim with examples/data, or
- define terms.

Identifying your subject and purpose are the first steps in writing a clear, effective paragraph. While it may not be possible to get your whole message across in a single paragraph, these methods of development can be sustained over as many paragraphs as it takes to thoroughly accomplish your purpose.

All except the shortest paragraphs of one or two sentences require supporting sentences that explain and amplify. A typical paragraph should follow a logical pattern that builds and expands on the topic sentence in a relevant and meaningful way.

PARAGRAPH COHERENCE

Good "flow"—the free and continuous movement of sentences from one to the next—is a quality many writers strive for. Flow is really a matter of coherence. **Coherence** refers to the logical and semantic links between sentences. In other words, the sentences in a group have to make sense in sequence and sound as though they belong together. Coherence is lost when logical gaps and unrelated sentences appear within a sentence group. Lack of flow is tolerated only in very short e-mail messages. To make your sentences fit together seamlessly, focus on linking and bridging techniques that enable you to guide your readers through a paragraph from beginning to end.

coherence the logical and semantic links between sentences.

Creating Logical Coherence

Develop a paragraph game plan: know your line of reasoning and order your ideas accordingly. Anticipate where your sentences will lead and what readers will expect next. Consider if a sentence is meant to show a cause-and-effect relationship or consequence.

> Despite an increase in revenue, the company showed a decline in profit.

The climactic order of this sentence leads to the main idea—decline in profit—at the end. If the paragraph were to continue, the next sentence, according to logic, would offer reasons for the decline or a statement of its degree.

Creating Coherence through Word Choice

Fluid, unified writing is easily achieved through a few simple techniques.

1. **Carry over a topic from sentence to sentence.** To prevent redundancy, use synonyms to stand in for the sentence subject or put a phrase or clause in front of the sentence subject to reduce its impact. An especially effective technique is to connect an idea at the end of one sentence to an idea at the beginning of the next.

2. **Use pronouns to carry over a thought from a previous sentence.** For clarity, combine *this*, *that*, *these*, and *those* with the single word to which each refers. Other pronouns, such as *some*, *they*, and *it*, can be used alone when they clearly refer to the nouns they replace. The following paragraph combines methods 1 and 2 to improve coherence:

> Their company offers an outstanding **flexible payment plan**. **This plan** permits deferred payments of up to two years. **Its** payment schedule can be customized to suit the needs of individual **clients**. **Customers** can choose from a range of payment options. **Some** may even decide to make their payments online with just a few simple keystrokes.

3. Use transitional words and phrases to segue from sentence to sentence.
Because **transitional expressions** show logical, temporal, and spatial relationships, they act as helpful signposts, preparing readers for what comes next and guiding them with precision through the twists and turns of your train of thought. For every relationship—contrast, contradiction, consequence, development, illustration, concession, conclusion—there are expressions that reinforce that particular meaning. Some are more workable than others, so choose the word or phrase that fits the exact context. Use them in moderation as aids to comprehension instead of predictable and unwelcome distractions from your message. Adding them where they don't belong can lead to logical gaffes and odd non-sequiturs. Transitional expressions can play a number of roles:

transitional expressions
words and phrases that show logical, temporal, and spatial relationships and connect ideas to create coherence.

- **To add a point**
  also, and, as well, besides, for the same reason, furthermore, in addition, likewise, moreover, similarly

- **To illustrate**
  for example, for instance, in fact, in particular, namely, to be specific

- **To show cause and effect (or explain a previous point)**
  as a result, because, in this way, in view of, since

- **To show contrast or reversal**
  although, at the same time, by contrast, but, conversely, despite, however, in contrast, in spite of, instead, nonetheless, on the contrary, on the other hand, still, whereas, while

- **To show similarity**
  in the same way, likewise, similarly

- **To summarize or conclude**
  accordingly, consequently, for this reason, in short, hence, so, therefore, thus

- **To concede a point**
  certainly, granted, naturally, of course

- **To show time sequence**
  first, second, third, last, during, currently, concurrently, finally, at this point, now, meanwhile, to begin, then

The following paragraph highlights some of these transitional expressions:

> **Once** a drug patent expires, generic competitors usually introduce copies that retail at a fraction of the price, **meaning that** brand-name manufacturers' share prices can be hit hard. **For example**, Biotex Corp. has declined from over $55 (U.S.) a share in early 2001 to less than $20 (U.S.) recently **because** its patent on the blood pressure drug Ambutroxin expired last May. **Altogether**, patents on brand-name drugs with about $40 billion (U.S.) a year in sales will expire over the next three years. **As a result**, even fund managers have trouble picking pharmaceutical stock.

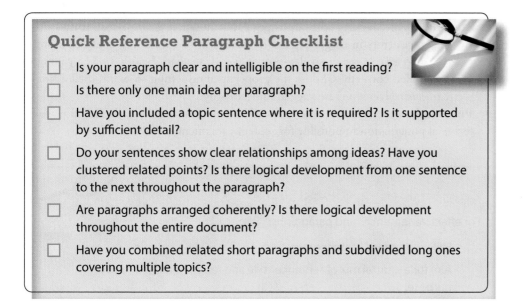

Quick Reference Paragraph Checklist

- [ ] Is your paragraph clear and intelligible on the first reading?
- [ ] Is there only one main idea per paragraph?
- [ ] Have you included a topic sentence where it is required? Is it supported by sufficient detail?
- [ ] Do your sentences show clear relationships among ideas? Have you clustered related points? Is there logical development from one sentence to the next throughout the paragraph?
- [ ] Are paragraphs arranged coherently? Is there logical development throughout the entire document?
- [ ] Have you combined related short paragraphs and subdivided long ones covering multiple topics?

Proofreading

Accurate documents are ones that writers have taken the trouble to read and review. It is important to get in the habit of **proofreading** messages before sending them, even if it means just casting your eye over a quick e-mail on screen or a printout of a routine message. Effective proofreading is reading with a difference. It involves reducing your reading speed, reading word for word, and gaining the objectivity you need to spot errors before they cause you embarrassment. The point is to read what is actually written on the page or screen, not what you think you have written. To give you the objectivity you need to read impartially and analytically, it always helps to have a "cooling period" between the composing and proofreading steps—as little as a few seconds for a brief e-mail or considerably longer for a formal report. If a careful, silent reading isn't enough to help you catch all your errors, try reading your messages aloud—even taping yourself as you read. The time and energy you devote to proofreading depends on the length and importance of the document. It may be necessary to make several passes over an especially significant document or message, each time reading for two or three potential problems:

- **Accuracy of names, facts, and figures:** Double-check important facts for accuracy; compare figures with source material to eliminate typographical errors; transcribe names and addresses correctly.
- **Appropriateness of format:** View page-layout options or print a document out to see if it appears balanced and uncluttered and conforms to style guidelines.
- **Correctness of grammar:** Use the "Quick Review Checklist for Sentence Completeness" that we saw earlier in this chapter. Remember that diagnostic software often flags passive-voice constructions, sometimes unnecessarily. It may also underscore clauses beginning with *that* or *which*. Try substituting one for the other until the problem corrects itself. Consult Appendix B for more on grammar and usage.

proofreading a process of checking the final copy of a document for errors and inconsistencies.

format a term for the parts of the document and the way they are arranged on a page.

- **Spelling:** Spell-checking software is good, but nowhere near perfect. It may not always detect errors in usage, like the transposition of commonly confused words (*accepted/excepted*). It may also flag proper (i.e., Canadian, British, or U.S.) nouns that are spelled correctly. Choose the proper spelling setting so words spelled correctly (*cheque/check*) won't be flagged unnecessarily.
- **Punctuation:** Follow the basic rules of comma usage and watch for misplaced terminal punctuation responsible for sentence fragments.

Chapter Review Checklist

For effective sentences and paragraphs:

- ☐ Follow standard sentence structure.
- ☐ Aim for a natural mix of sentence style and length matched to your purpose.
- ☐ Emphasize important facts and ideas with visual devices, punctuation marks, and the order of words and phrases.
- ☐ Use parallelism and other techniques to write with consistency.
- ☐ Stay in the active voice as much as possible.
- ☐ Eliminate grammar errors and awkward constructions.
- ☐ Rely on coherence-building techniques that show relationships between ideas.
- ☐ Limit paragraph length.
- ☐ Develop proofreading strategies for different kinds of messages and documents.

WORKSHOPS AND DISCUSSION FORUMS

1. **Grammar-Checking Software: Help or Hindrance?** The following message contains multiple faults and errors. Work together in a group as editors, first of all flagging and counting up the total number of errors, then correcting them to improve the message's overall accuracy and precision. Once you are satisfied with the finished product, retype the original and your revision on a computer equipped with grammar and spell-checking software. What errors did you miss that the software has flagged? Has the software inadvertently labelled correct usage as incorrect? Discuss how useful diagnostic software can be in improving your writing proficiency.

   During the last several months. Our company, after we undertook extensive market research and considered many different diversification options, had a new gourmet food category launched. The reason we are embarking on this new cross-merchandising venture is because the annual turn rate for food is far above the industry average of two times a year.

Wanting you to attend an information session and see the new line of products, the information session will be next Monday from 7:00 in the evening to 9:30 at our downtown location. Come and sample such delicacies as caribou pate, pepper jelly, chili-infused olive oil, and cherries that have been infused with amaretto. From several gourmet food purveyors, we will have representatives on hand to answer questions about their products. A product and price list on line.

WRITING IMPROVEMENT EXERCISES

Recognize the Building Blocks of Sentences

1. **Building Sentences.** Combine each list of words to create a logical sentence, inserting punctuation where necessary.
   a) turned
      into
      the merger
      two companies with two specialty channels each
      one company with four
   b) studied
      business school
      Connie
      the
      risk management
      CFO
      at

Improve Sentence Variety by Matching Sentence Style and Length to Purpose

2. **Improving Sentence Variety.** Revise the following paragraphs by varying the sentence structure and reducing the prominence of personal pronouns.

   a) I joined R.H. Rayburn's marketing team in 1997. I provide marketing information for companies that make consumer-packaged goods. I have had several responsibilities. I collected point-of-sale data from stores, analyzed the data, and then passed the information on to corporate clients. I have learned that employees are key to strong revenue growth.

   b) We maintain an ongoing relationship with our clients. We train one or two client staff members. They train the rest of the staff. They provide immediate on-site assistance on routine matters. They can contact us when they need help with more complicated matters.

Phrase Basic Types of Questions Effectively

3. **Types of Questions.** Identify the following questions according to type: open, closed, or hypothetical.
   a) How must we improve our product so that it meets CSA specifications?
   b) If we were to improve our product, what modifications would you suggest?
   c) Will CSA approve our newest model before production is scheduled to begin?
   d) In what way is our competitor's product better than our own?
   e) How many similar products has CSA approved in the past five years?
   f) Have you considered seeking approval from Underwriter's Laboratories in the United States?

4. **Asking Questions.** Imagine that you are a team member who must do research for an upcoming report. With your research task 80 per cent complete, you must make an unscheduled out-of-town business trip related to another high priority project, leaving you no time to complete the research as promised. Draft several types of questions—closed, open, and hypothetical—to determine the best way to ask your fellow team members for the favour of helping to complete your research.

Improve Sentence Clarity

5. **Improving Sentence Clarity.** In the following sentences, correct problems such as vague pronoun

reference, embedded dependent clauses, and multiple negatives that interfere with clarity.

a) The proposed changes, while they do not entirely solve our personnel shortage, will help to improve morale.

b) We do not doubt that borrowing from home equity is not an unrealistic way for seniors to source extra cash.

c) Courtney is familiar with debt-reduction initiatives. That is her primary focus.

d) The committee recommended the adoption of a cost-cutting plan, but this has not been implemented.

e) The plan, when he first opened his doors six years ago, was to, in part, pitch their services to small businesses.

Emphasize Important Facts and Ideas; Minimize Less Important Ones

6. **Writing with Emphasis.** Assess the following sentences.

a) Which sentence is more emphatic?
   i) Our banking services are good for your business.
   ii) We offer highly competitive commercial rates and 24–hour online services to meet all your business needs.

b) Which sentence is more emphatic?
   i) We reduced inventory by 40 per cent.
   ii) We reduced inventory substantially.

c) Which sentence is more emphatic?
   i) Alberta's workforce is smaller than Ontario's.
   ii) Alberta's workforce is half the size of Ontario's.

d) Which sentence is more emphatic?
   i) His supervisor was able to take decisive action.
   ii) His supervisor acted decisively.

e) Which sentence puts greatest emphasis on the date of the meeting?
   i) On August 30, a meeting will be held to discuss stock options.
   ii) A meeting will be held on August 30 to discuss stock options.

f) Which sentence places more emphasis on risk management?

   i) Risk management is a primary concern for investors.
   ii) Investors are primarily concerned about risk management, although other concerns may enter into their choice of funds.

g) Which sentence de-emphasizes the job refusal?
   i) We filled this position months ago. Our company cannot offer you employment at this time.
   ii) Although our company cannot make an offer of employment at this time, we wish you success in your future career.

7. **Adding Emphasis.** Revise the following sentences to emphasize key facts and concepts.

a) Emphasize the date:
   The deadline is March 31 for requesting transfers to the Toronto sales office.

b) Emphasize individual departments:
   Three departments, namely Marketing, Sales, and Distribution, are participating in the pilot project.

c) Emphasize the appointee:
   Our current operations manager, John O'Reilly, will now head up our Montreal office.

Use Parallelism and Other Techniques to Write with Consistency and Impact

8. **Writing Balanced Sentences: Parallelism.** Revise the following sentences to improve parallel structure.

Sample: I believe that employee satisfaction drives client satisfaction, which the satisfaction of shareholders is in turn driven by.

Revision: I believe that employee satisfaction drives client satisfaction, which in turn drives shareholder satisfaction.

a) Renovating our current location is less expensive than to buy or rent a new property.

b) Japanese and Korean carmakers are gaining in every market segment with products that offer reliability, performance, designs that are alluring, and prices that are competitive.

c) Fabiola Cortez, of our R&D division, will now head our Regina facility; and our head office in Toronto will now be managed by Lu Huang, former chief of our consulting department.

d) Good security is based on a combination of three types of identifying information: something you know, usually a password or PIN, something you have, such as a plastic card, key, or security token, and what you have on your person.

e) Most biometric systems are expensive to buy and using them is awkward.

f) A radio spot will air contest details, where promotional events will be held, and what products are new.

Distinguish between Active and Passive Voice

9. **Using the Active Voice.** Convert the following sentences to the active voice. Add subject words if necessary.

Sample: Substantial career rewards are provided by this challenging position.

Revision: This challenging position provides substantial career rewards.

a) It was found by the committee that profits had been affected by the new industry guidelines.

b) Credit derivatives are used by banks to offload troubled loans.

c) The pack is led by heavy-parts manufacturers who show innovation.

d) A recommendation was made that all advertising and promotion must be handled by senior marketing specialists.

e) After approval was sought, the new site was approved by city building inspectors.

f) Your personal information is not sold or otherwise marketed to third parties.

10. **Using the Passive Voice.** Convert the following sentences to the passive voice. Decide whether to omit the doer of the action.

Sample: Last year, the township issued an advisory on the illegal disposal of yard waste.

Revision: Last year, an advisory was issued on the illegal disposal of yard waste.

a) When the hiring committee has concluded its search, we will notify you.

b) Tiffany over-budgeted for the team-building retreat in Muskoka.

c) If you do not remit your full term premium by July 25, we will cancel your insurance coverage.

d) Marjorie, Tom Chrysler's assistant, has rescheduled tomorrow's meeting to Friday.

e) We have added the following exclusions to your policy.

Eliminate Sentence Errors that Impair Clarity and Unity

11. **Eliminating Sentence Fragments and Run-Ons.** Fix fragments, comma splices, and run-ons in the following sentences.

Sample: Our new line of high-resolution copiers is affordably priced it will be introduced in the fall.

Revision: Our new line of high-resolution copiers is affordably priced. It will be introduced in the fall.

a) All our branches have extended hours, some even offer weekend banking.

b) Before the Internet was developed and before it began to have such an impact on market research. One of the most effective techniques for building mailing lists was sweepstakes.

c) The president and CEO embarked on a spending spree. Resulting in a higher debt load.

12. **Eliminating Mixed Constructions, Faulty Predication, and Over-Coordination.** Correct the following sentences.

Sample: One reason spam e-mail is unpopular is because most people find it time-wasting.

Revision: One reason spam e-mail is unpopular is that most people find it time-wasting.

a) The purpose of the program was established to reduce job dissatisfaction.

b) When the demand for industrial goods increased was an indication to expand our operation.

c) We look forward to speaking with you and you'll find additional information in the enclosed booklet.

d) We're proud of our services and you should call when you need help.

e) The main reason that supervisors are concerned that staff members consider the request to be an invasion of privacy.

13. **Correcting Misplaced and Dangling Modifiers.** Correct dangling and misplaced modifiers in the following sentences.

Sample: Her co-worker told her on the first day no one eats in the cafeteria.

Revision: On the first day, her co-worker told her no one eats in the cafeteria.

a) A shipment was forwarded from the warehouse that cost more than $12,000.

b) Mouse pads were given to conventioneers featuring the company logo.

c) The computer was returned to the manufacturer that was defective.

d) To apply for this position, an updated resumé and the names of three referees must be submitted.

e) Outsourcing its printing jobs, substantial amounts of money were saved by the company.

f) Complaints from customers must be taken seriously by all sales associates, regardless of their triviality.

Develop Logical, Coherent, and Focused Paragraphs

14. **Adjusting Paragraph Length.** Revise the following memo by dividing it into several manageable paragraphs.

Please answer the questions below about the possibility of instituting an in-house daycare at Resource Management Plus. Many employees and some managers have inquired about the possibility of providing company-sponsored daycare services on the premises. In my opinion, on-site facilities, similar to the recently opened fitness centre, increase job productivity, morale, and job satisfaction. Employees are at ease knowing their toddlers and preschoolers are close at hand and well cared for in a fully accredited and supervised facility. They enjoy the convenience of dropping off and picking up their children with no additional commuting time. On the other hand, an on-site daycare facility might be a distraction from business. Your answers to the following questions will help us make an informed decision on the issue.

15. **Paragraph Coherence: Transitional Expressions.** Add transitional words and phrases to improve the coherence of the following paragraphs.

a) Our Small Parts Division needs to improve its quality control. Complaints so far have been few. Spot inspections revealed serious defects that could have an impact on long-term contracts and result in legal liability. We need to hire more quality control specialists. We need to foster better work habits.

b) We will soon introduce a new procedure that will allow us to project resource costs more accurately. Team members will be required to complete weekly time sheets and submit them to the project manager. The time sheets will be used to update the forecasts. A monthly, consolidated report will be presented to the directors for review. The new procedure will not improve efficiency immediately. It will allow us to take advantage of current methods in project management.

16. **Paragraph Coherence: Transitional Expressions.** In a newspaper, magazine, or trade-related publication, find a sample passage of approximately two hundred words and make a photocopy. Highlight and list the transitional expressions used. Would the article still make sense with the transitional expressions removed?

Apply Strategies for Proofreading Different Kinds of Messages

17. **Correcting Sentence Errors: Proofreading Checklist.** Draft a list of your ten most frequent writing errors (look for feedback on your previously graded assignments). Before handing in your next three messages or assignments, refer to your customized checklist as you proofread. When your graded assignments are returned to you, see if using a checklist has helped you achieve greater writing proficiency. Work toward the goal of gradually reducing the number of items on your list.

ONLINE ACTIVITIES

http://www.

Recognize Types of Sentences and the Building Blocks of Sentences

1. **Recognizing Dependent Clauses and Types of Sentences.** Before you try this interactive quiz from Capital Community College, click on the link for a review of dependent clauses. Then, go back to the quiz and make your choice for each question. You will receive immediate feedback on the accuracy of your answer.
   http://grammar.ccc.commnet.edu/
   grammar/quizzes/niu/niu5.htm

2. **Understanding Sentence Structure.** Visit Hyper-Grammar at the University of Ottawa to sharpen your skills in identifying different types of sentences.
   www.arts.uottawa.ca/writcent/
   hypergrammar/rvsntstr.html

Use Parallelism to Write with Consistency and Impact

3. **Writing Balanced Sentences: Parallel Structure.** Try the Big Dog's Self-Test on Parallel Structure. For each of the eight sentences, submit your revision online to receive feedback.
   http://aliscot.com/bigdog/
   parallel_exercise.htm
   For additional practice, complete this parallel structure quiz from Capital Community College.
   http://grammar.ccc.commnet.edu/grammar/
   cgi-shl/quiz.pl/parallelism_quiz.htm

Eliminate Sentence Errors that Impair Sentence Clarity and Unity

4. **Eliminating Sentence Fragments.** Test your knowledge of complete sentences by logging on to this exercise from Purdue University's Online Writing Lab. Act as editor of these real-life examples from student papers, then check your answers using the address at the bottom of the page.
   http://owl.english.purdue.edu/
   exercises/5/18/38

5. **Improving Modifier Placement.** Try this interactive exercise from Capital Community College for practice in identifying sentences with effective modifier placement. In groups of three or four, discuss your answers and compare results.
   http://grammar.ccc.commnet.edu/grammar/
   cgi-shl/quiz.pl/modifier_quiz.htm
   For more practice, visit the following site and check for dangling and misplaced modifiers in the sentences in the exercises.
   www.aliscot.com/bigdog/dmmm_exercise.htm

6. **Combining Sentences.** Complete these quizzes from Capital Community College by combining groups of sentences into effective single sentences containing only one independent clause each.
   http://grammar.ccc.commnet.edu/grammar/
   quizzes/combining_quiz1.htm
   http://grammar.ccc.commnet.edu/grammar/
   quizzes/combining_quiz2.htm

Develop Logical, Coherent, and Focused Paragraphs

7. **Improving Logical Coherence in Paragraphs.** Visit the following page from UEfAP.com (Using English for Academic Purposes: A Guide to Students in Higher Education) and complete the four interactive exercises that require you to reorganize sentences for logic and coherence.
   www.uefap.com/writing/exercise/parag/
   paragex5.htm

5

Memorandums, E-mail, and Routine Messages

In this chapter you will learn to

1. Recognize the nature and characteristics of memorandums and e-mail.

2. Apply formatting rules and writing plans for memorandums and e-mail.

3. Format horizontal and vertical lists for clarity and conciseness.

4. Develop correct e-mail style and tone.

5. Eliminate common e-mail problems, dubious practices, and etiquette gaffes.

6. Recognize steps in processing and managing e-mail.

7. Write memorandums and e-mail that inform, request, respond, follow up, and convey goodwill.

Memorandums

Memos can be many things—reminders, instructions, records of actions and decisions, data-gathering tools, and aids to problem-solving. Sent to people inside your organization, they are a fast, efficient way of putting information in the hands of people who need it and getting answers from the people who can provide them. Once the primary means of inter-office communication, the hard-copy paper memo, with its distinctive style and structure, has left its mark on **e-mail** communication, the channel for both internal and external messaging that has largely taken its place. E-mail in fact brings the best of memo style to internal and external communication, adhering to the time-saving format and straightforward approach of a hard-copy memo but eliminating its wasteful paper trail. Even a quick glance at the guide word information at the top of the screen or page can tell a reader what the message is about, who it is from, for whom it is intended, who else received it, and when it was written.

Together memos and e-mail are the workhorses of business communication, indispensable aids to the tasks of gathering, sharing, and analyzing information about products, day-to-day operations, services, stakeholders, and personnel. Bringing corporate levels together, the paper memo and its electronic counterpart are the most common ways for managers to inform employees of policies and decisions, and for employees to stay informed and offer their input. Everyone from upper management down uses memos and e-mail. Writing them not just competently but well can win kudos for employees eyeing the road to advancement. It pays to take some time perfecting the e-mail style through which your managers and co-workers will come to know you—and to always review your messages before you send them. Learning about your receivers' e-mail preferences and deciding when it is appropriate to use e-mail can help you become a more effective communicator.

The advantage of a typical memo is its simplicity. It is designed to be read quickly, even when it is organized like a report or conveys vital information. Usually less formal than a standard letter, a well-written memo opens with its purpose—the main idea or primary action—and is presented so that it makes sense even to secondary readers. Any hard-copy memo or electronic message should be clear, concise, and informative, sharing the following common traits:

1. single-topic focus,
2. brevity, and
3. two-part structure: **header** (*To, From, Subject, Date* guide words) and message (divided into an opening, body, and closing).

Because corporate e-mail systems vary and style guidelines are constantly evolving, there is some variation in the way writers treat e-mail and in the form some messages may take. Some writers use salutations; others don't. In some instances, a complex or critically important memo might be more than a page, or an e-mail message might fill more than a single screen; however, the longer or more complicated a message happens to be, the more it requires additional formatting techniques such as **headings**, subheadings, **boldfaced** elements, **bulleted** items, and lists.

memo a specially formatted document that is sent to readers within an organization.

e-mail (electronic mail) messages distributed by a computerized mail service.

header a block of text appearing at the top of a document.

headings visual markers consisting of words or short phrases that indicate the parts of a document and signpost its organization.

boldface a thick, black typeface used for emphasis.

bullets visual cues, usually large round dots or squares, that set off items in a vertical list or emphasize lines.

MEMO FORMAT

A memo has a no-fuss, two-part structure. The *To*, *From*, *Subject*, and *Date* headings or fields tell readers exactly what they need to know about a message's content and distribution. In replacing standard letter elements such as the inside address, salutation, and complimentary close, these guide words save time and make formatting easy. They can appear in horizontal or vertical format; their standard order can be altered to suit a company's needs. It is common practice to type guide words in capitals, leaving a double space between headings and three lines before the body of the memo. The fill-in information following each guide word should be aligned, usually two to three spaces following the longest guide word (SUBJECT). Many companies provide memo templates, as do "wizards" in most word-processing programs; these templates simplify the task of formatting and alignment.

<table>
<tr><td>

DATE:
</td><td>

Provides the complete and current date. To reduce confusion, follow company practice in choosing between North American (March 1, 2010) and European (1 March 2010) dateline styles.
</td></tr>
<tr><td>

TO:
</td><td>

Identifies the destination or the person(s) to whom the message is addressed. The job title of the addressee is optional, except when the name alone isn't enough to ensure that the message reaches its destination. Courtesy titles (Ms., Mr.) and professional titles (Rev., Dr.) may also be omitted unless you are addressing a superior. Dispense with surnames only if you are on a first-name basis with the addressee. If your memo is directed to several people, list their names alphabetically or in descending order of importance in the company hierarchy. Crowded address lines can be avoided by simply using a group designation ("Claims Processors," "Marketing Group," etc.).
</td></tr>
<tr><td>

FROM:
</td><td>

Identifies the author or origin of the message. Job titles and the department name can be used if a name alone is not sufficient to identify the writer. Courtesy titles generally aren't used because they're too formal to suit this relatively informal mode of communication. The practice of initialling the end of the line applies to hard-copy memos only.
</td></tr>
<tr><td>

SUBJECT:
</td><td>

Identifies the topic and/or purpose of the message for reading and filing. The more old-fashioned "RE" (from the Latin for "about" or "concerning") is sometimes also used to designate the content of the message. Ideally, the subject description should not exceed one line. It does not have to be a complete sentence and can be abbreviated (leaving out articles—*the*, *a*, and *an*). Nevertheless, it must be specific enough to give readers a full and accurate idea of what follows (i.e., instead of "Estimate" write "Cost Reduction Estimate"). Optionally, tell readers how they are to act on your information ("Cost Reduction Estimate for Review").
</td></tr>
<tr><td>

CC:
</td><td>

This stands for "carbon copy," an obsolete term for the generic "copy." Insert the name(s) of anyone who will receive a copy of the message. In the case of e-mail, avoid unnecessary copying that will clog receivers' inboxes and e-mail systems. Learn what others want to be copied on.
</td></tr>
</table>

subject line indicates the title, topic, or purpose of a document, used to file and retrieve the document; it tells readers what is important about the document.

MEMO ORGANIZATION

Even though print and electronic memos tend to be short and sometimes fairly informal, they still require forethought and planning. Before you begin to write, consider the facts and issues you must cover and anticipate your readers' needs. Then choose a writing plan that meets those requirements. Observing the principles of good writing will help make your memo focused and informative. Most positive and neutral messages conveying routine or non-sensitive information can be organized in the way demonstrated in the memo below:

> To write an effective memo, use the **opening** for your most important information, purpose for writing, or required action. Don't waste time mechanically restating the subject line. Instead amplify it by filling in the *who, what, where, when,* and *how* that can't be supplied by the subject line alone. Get to the point as quickly as possible. As an option, include a few words of context, giving a reason for your request or telling readers why they need to know the information you're sharing: "To maintain productivity levels during power outages, our company has leased an on-site power system from Energy Now." One to three sentences are usually sufficient to summarize your central idea.
>
> In the **body** of the memo, move on to particulars and more detailed information. Expand on, discuss, or explain the problem, assignment, request, or action you wish the reader to take. Pare down details to include only the ones your readers must know to act on your information. If you are relaying a sequence of actions or several requests, put them in a grammatically parallel list prefaced by a summary statement that first allows readers an overview or glimpse of the "big picture." Points may be presented in the following ways:
>
> 1. chronologically, sequenced from beginning to end or start to finish;
>
> 2. in order of specificity, from most to least specific or vice versa; or
>
> 3. in order of importance, from most to least or vice versa.
>
> Make sure the middle paragraph(s) provide sufficient background, bringing readers up to speed on preliminaries and clearly identifying deadlines and people involved.
>
> In **closing**, summarize your request or call for action, clearly indicating who should do what, by when, and for how long. If compliance isn't assured, point out alternatives or benefits to readers. It may be appropriate to end-date requests, cite reasons for them, invite feedback, provide contact information, tell readers where they can get more information, or state what happens next. Avoid canned or mechanical phrases that do not suit the situation. Show courtesy and appreciation as the situation merits.

Double-spacing between paragraphs marks off one topic from another and reinforces good organization. Graphic highlighting techniques can help emphasize key information, but be aware that some e-mail systems may not allow you to use boldface or **italics** or other more sophisticated typographical features, only plain text. For memos longer than a page, open with a summary statement—a condensed version of the

italics sloping letters used for emphasis or to distinguish foreign words.

memo highlighting purpose and action sought. Organize the rest of your information under headings—even ones as basic as "problem," "situation," and "solution"—so ideas and initiatives can be understood and easily acted on. To simplify messaging and ensure uniformity, some companies provide templates for different kinds of memos—ones delivering information, asking for action, or demanding urgent action.

When you must deliver bad news, or convince people to do what you want, or write persuasively, use an indirect start-with-the-evidence strategy. Readers are more likely to accept a decision, even a negative one, when they are prepared for it and know it is logical and well justified.

FORMATTING LISTS FOR MEMOS AND E-MAIL

list a group of three or more logically related items presented consecutively to form a record or aid to memory.

A **list** is a group of at least three logically related items. Its purpose is to give order and emphasis to important information—breaking up solid blocks of text, sequencing events and actions, and making concepts easier to understand, remember, and reference. It puts into practice the principles of balanced, parallel construction and in doing so helps improve readability. Similar phrasing for each item, where every item begins with the same part of speech, reinforces the similarity of the list's content.

Any list, to be effective, must have the following:

- a lead-in introducing, explaining, and putting in context the items that follow,
- at least three and, ideally, not more than eight items,
- parallel phrasing for every item,
- semantic and grammatical continuity between the lead-in and items (in other words, every item must read grammatically with the lead-in), and
- adequate transition to the sentences that follow after the list.

Lists are formatted in two ways: *horizontally* (or in-sentence) and *vertically* (tabulated). *Horizontal lists*, like the one below, give minimal emphasis but are also less intrusive:

> We will discuss the following items at next Monday's meeting: the need for new quality control measures, the performance of our customer service hotline, and the proposed switch to voice-recognition phone technology.

> As director of commercial real estate finance, you will monitor market trends, provide information and support on our lending programs, and recommend refinements to existing programs.

A colon is required before a list if the lead-in forms a complete sentence (as in the first example above). For additional impact, individual items can be introduced with a bracketed letter or number.

> Please bring the following items with you on retreat: (1) walking shoes, (2) a raincoat, and (3) sunblock.

Restrict yourself to a maximum of four or five in-sentence items per list. If items exceed that limit, a vertical list is your best choice.

Vertical lists, whether they're bulleted or numbered, are among the best-known and most frequently used design elements. With their high visual impact, vertical lists break up imposing blocks of texts into manageable, "bite-sized" segments.

To begin, create a strong explanatory lead-in that reads logically and grammatically with each point that follows. If your introduction is complete, you will not need to repeat explanatory details in each point. Punctuate the lead-in with a colon if the lead-in can be read as a complete sentence; use no punctuation at the end of the lead-in if the lead-in depends on the point that follows to complete its meaning.

☒ Our company

- has one segment that deals with investing
- has another segment that takes care of mortgages
- also has leasing operations

☑ Our company has three key business segments:

- investing,
- mortgage operations, and
- leasing operations.

Use numbers or letters to indicate chronological sequence or importance, especially if you plan on referring to an item later. Numbers are useful for indicating priority. Bullets, on the other hand, are much more democratic. They suggest that all items are of equal importance.

When each point forms a complete sentence, capitalize and punctuate each item as you would a sentence. If you are giving instructions or issuing directives or polite commands, begin each item with an action verb:

To ensure fairness in the evaluation process, please follow these instructions:

- Distribute evaluation forms to seminar participants.
- Remind participants that their responses will remain confidential.
- Ask for a volunteer to collect and mail completed forms.
- Leave the room.

Among listed items, try not to mix clauses and sentences that require different terminal punctuation. Any item expressed as a complete sentence or as a phrase that completes the lead-in requires terminal punctuation, as does any item consisting of two or more sentences.

Apply the principles of **chunking**—a yardstick for list design—to determine the number of items that a list can accommodate. The average person's short-term memory

chunking the grouping of items of information together to be remembered as a unit.

Flash Review EFFECTIVE LISTS

- Begin with a strong lead-in summing up purpose or context.
- Make sure the lead-in makes sense with each item.
- Don't overload lists. Limit the number of items. If necessary, subdivide or consolidate points.
- Use parallel phrasing. Keep verb forms and tenses consistent.
- Punctuate in a consistent way.
- Choose the type of list—horizontal or vertical—based on the emphasis or sequencing you need to show.
- Use similar types of lists for similar purposes throughout a document.
- Don't use lists so much that they lose their effectiveness.

can store seven pieces of data, plus or minus two, depending on the complexity of the data. The more complex each item, the fewer items a reader can reasonably be expected to remember. Ideally, a list should be brief and kept to a maximum of seven or eight items. More than that and the list can lose its focus and purpose, at which point it is best to find a way to subdivide points and consolidate them under appropriate lead-ins.

PAPER MEMO VS. E-MAIL

Faced with a choice of communication channels, you do not have to opt for electronic transmission instead of paper-based messaging every single time. There are instances where a hard-copy memo is preferable, when legality, confidentiality, or document integrity (preserving the layout or formatting features that e-mail systems cannot accommodate) are primary concerns. Traditional paper memos do without the informal salutations and complimentary closes sometimes used in e-mails.

The following memo functions as a letter of transmittal, accompanying and explaining other hard-copy documents.

FIGURE 5.1 Sample Paper-Based Memo

TO: Tomas Simic, Campus Planning

FROM: Arley Simpson, Registrar

RE: Fall Registration for Continuing Education Courses

DATE: July 20, 2009

Opens directly with a polite command and uses active-voice sentence →
Please distribute the enclosed calendars and remind your staff that the Department of Continuing Education is now accepting registration for its fall courses, beginning September 10.

Explains the opening request, offers details, and supplies end date for action →
College staff members are eligible to enrol tuition-free in up to five full courses per year. A $25 processing fee is applicable to each course registration. Please note that the registration closes September 5.

Explains enclosed material, cites reader benefits, and offers additional information →
Enclosed are five copies of the fall 2009–summer 2010 calendar listing over 200 personal enrichment and professional development courses. Courses in areas such as IT management and computer applications offer staff the opportunity to upgrade work-related skills for professional success. For detailed course descriptions and easy online registration, visit our new website at http://omnistudies.manitou.ca. Please call me if you have questions about our range of programs or require additional calendars.

Expresses appreciation for action →
Thank you for your help in distributing the calendars.

AS: ml

Enc. 5

Quick Reference Guidelines for Memos

- Fill in appropriate information, including a strong subject line, after headers.
- Be as brief as your message allows you to be.
- Follow the style guidelines of your organization.
- Be direct and begin with your most important point when relaying routine news or information.
- Provide only as much background or evidence as your reader needs to act on your instructions or information.
- Itemize supporting details, related questions, and additional requests in bulleted or numbered lists in parallel form.
- End courteously with a request for specific action, reason for the request, and deadline.

E-mail

Few technologies have had such dramatic impact on the business world as e-mail has in recent years. Few are as loved and hated as this essential medium of communication has come to be. E-mail is now an unavoidable fact of business life; it is an indispensable, multi-use tool of management work and the most common means of transmitting workplace documents and files. Its advantage—and ironically its disadvantage—is that messages can be produced easily and quickly and transmitted instantaneously. E-mail's versatile capabilities and wide availability make it an ideal productivity tool—a cheap and convenient way to access, exchange, and process information. Collaborative work can be carried out more easily than before, due in no small part to the interaction and more equal participation that e-mail fosters. E-mail has revolutionized the workplace in other ways too, helping to improve customer service, boosting the quality and quantity of ideas employees share with their colleagues, and giving managers an effective way of dealing with people who report and are accountable to them.

Only recently has e-mail become a source of corporate embarrassment—a smoking gun that can offer incriminating and permanent proof of companies' wrongdoing. Because e-mail can end up anywhere and compromise confidential and classified information, many organizations have been forced to clamp down on e-mail use and to regulate and monitor it closely, even going as far as requiring employees to save their messages for several years as proof of ethical conduct.

While e-mail has certainly changed the way companies do business, many of the e-mail practices that are meant to boost efficiency can result in poor, lazy behaviours that waste time and energy and leave recipients frustrated and vexed by unwanted messages. Not surprisingly, e-mail has its own special set of problems: clogged inboxes; indiscriminate distribution lists; serious privacy violations; uncooperative servers; unsolicited, sloppy, inflammatory, or undeliverable messages; and difficult-to-follow "thread" e-mails. The urge to check for incoming messages or to hit the "Send" button without first reviewing a message can strike even the most disciplined e-mail user. An ever-increasing portion of a typical day at or even away from the office involves the necessary but sometimes tedious work that e-mail demands. The fact that it is possible to access e-mail almost anywhere at any time has created a round-the-clock virtual work-day. E-mail is now inescapable. Some people are compulsively preoccupied by their e-mail and can't live without it, while others consider it a ball and chain, a source of anger and stress.

Part of the problem is that e-mail is a relatively new technological frontier, an evolving medium with practices that still haven't been fully standardized. Although users may love the technology, they should also stop to consider e-mail's relevance and suitability to a given task. Because e-mail is a hybrid form of speaking and writing, users also sometimes have trouble deciding exactly what it replaces—an informal chat or a formal hard-copy letter—and this accounts for the range of e-mail styles and quirky tonal variations that characterize today's e-mail traffic.

Some organizations have come to the rescue by instituting e-mail guidelines—rules about what their employees can say and how to format that information. Though these guidelines vary from organization to organization and though e-mail style varies from document to document, savvy communicators recognize the value of smart e-mail practices. Knowing your **netiquette** and being proactive in managing your messaging makes e-mail a channel that is fast, functional, and efficient.

netiquette the informal code of conduct governing polite, efficient, and effective use of the Internet.

GENERAL E-MAIL GUIDELINES

Keep in mind some general considerations for successful electronic communication:

1. **Keep it brief.** A short message (one screen or less) stands the best chance of being read fully. Long messages may end up skimmed in recipients' inboxes, marked to be read later or simply forgotten. Scrolling down to the end of a long message can be time-consuming, so make sure each message merits its word count and consider using attachments. Include only as much information as is needed for recipients to take action and make decisions.

2. **Remember that e-mail is not your only option.** Strive for a balance between the convenience of technology and the rapport of human contact. Don't use e-mail simply to avoid face-to-face contact, especially if you only wish to distance yourself from conflicts, arguments, or bad news. Match the situation to the correct communication channel.

3. **Compose crucial messages offline.** This allows you to review them and reduce the chance they will be lost as a result of a technical glitch.

4. **Follow organizational rules for e-mail.** Some companies have standardized procedures for e-mail; some have only unwritten or loosely applied guidelines. If guidelines haven't been established, allow the most effective messages you receive to guide you to e-mail preferences and practices.

5. **Don't use company e-mail systems for personal communication.** Your organization's resources shouldn't be used recreationally, to swap personal photos, shop, or send personal messages. Some companies allow their employees "reasonable personal use" of e-mail while others prohibit it. Sending personal e-mails and

using the Internet for matters unrelated to business is risky and may have profes-sional repercussions for you. Protect your inbox from spammers by having your address removed from **spam** and junk lists that can expose you and your company to racist, sexist, or sexually explicit messages.

6. **Aim for a balance of speed and accuracy.** Speedy e-mail writing and the errors it can cause make for slower e-mail reading. E-mail readers are generally more tolerant of writing errors, but there are limits to allowances for incorrect spellings, poor grammar, and misused punctuation. Careless messages can result in lost credibility and clients. Glance over your messages to catch errors in spelling, grammar, and punctuation before you hit "Send." Give important, non-routine documents close and careful reading, and employ the same kinds of strategic planning and range of writing skills as you would for non-electronic documents. Because e-mail involves the rapid exchange of information, let your readers' needs be your guide, but don't double or triple your composition time by putting every single word under the microscope. After all, e-mail should boost your productivity, not reduce it.

7. **Avoid emoticons.** Think of your credibility and professionalism before using emoticons—such as ☺ (the smiley symbol), ☹, and :-)—that are intended to com-municate the tone of a message. Their charm and whimsy may go over well with close friends, but not with business contacts, who may take their cuteness for a lack of professionalism. Instead, state your business plainly in standard English. Use *please* and *thank you* for the sake of politeness, and adjust your tone if you want to sound friendlier.

8. **Understand that e-mail is not guaranteed to be private.** E-mail is easily deleted, but even deleted e-mail can be retrieved, providing a permanent record of actions and decisions. It can be saved, archived, forwarded, and even used as legal evidence. Some companies make a practice of monitoring employee e-mail or instruct that it not be used for certain types of communication. While "big-brother" may not necessarily be watching you, avoid sending gossipy, incriminating, disparaging, or inflammatory messages. Refrain from making jokes, sarcastic jabs, or facetious remarks. Don't write anything in an e-mail message that you wouldn't be comfortable writing on a postcard or seeing published in the company newsletter.

9. **Don't "write angry".** Avoid **flaming**—the act of firing back and venting emo-tion via e-mail. No matter how good letting off steam feels at the time, it can have serious repercussions. Quick, angry responses flare tempers and usually resolve nothing. Instead, communicate contentious matters and sensitive issues through other channels, preferably ones with visual or tonal cues. If you have to deal with an angry e-mail, give yourself enough time to cool down and consider your response before you respond and hit "Send." If an immediate response is not required, save the draft overnight, review the document the next day, and then decide whether to trash or revise it.

10. **Don't send unnecessary messages.** The more you bombard readers with unnecessary e-mails, the less attention they'll pay to the ones that really count. Don't send trivial messages or ones that say merely "thank you" or "you're wel-come." Respect your fellow e-mail users by putting a stop to the nuisance of

spam an advertising message—electronic junk mail—sent widely and indiscriminately.

flaming the act of sending out an angry e-mail message in haste without considering the implications of airing such emotions.

time-wasting spam or bulk junk mail from cyberspace. You can fight spam by using anti-spam software that blocks unwanted messages and by not posting your e-mail addresses on web pages, where they can be easily copied into the mailing lists and databases of bulk e-mail companies.

11. **Protect yourself and your company.** Be aware of ownership and copyright issues and safeguard your organization's intellectual property. Add a copyright (©) symbol to all corporate material intended for Internet posting. Keep your password and user ID confidential to ensure secure applications aren't compromised.

READING AND PROCESSING INCOMING MESSAGES

Manage your e-mail and maintain professionalism by following a few common-sense principles:

1. **Schedule time for reading and writing e-mail.** E-mail can be intrusive and distracting, but don't allow it to rule your workday. Urgent messages excepted, set aside a few times a day to read and respond. Be systematic, first scanning for important messages from stakeholders and superiors and leaving personal messages for last. Check for incoming messages regularly, especially before sending out anything significant, just in case a new incoming message necessitates a reply different from the one you had in mind. After long absences, open your most recent mail first, then scan for earlier messages from critical stakeholders and superiors.

2. **Do regular inbox clean-ups.** Learn what your company expects you to file or archive, then get rid of the clutter by deleting unwanted, irrelevant, or outdated messages and checking for ones that may have escaped your attention. Assign messages you want to save to project files. Update your e-mail address book.

3. **Scan the entire list of new messages in your inbox.** Read all current messages before writing follow-up responses.

4. **Use filtering options and anti-spam software.** Ensure the mail you get is the mail you want. Most companies make ample provision for this in their e-mail systems.

5. **Capture your e-mail in a recognizable records system.** Follow your organization's guidelines for the secure management and storage of your messages.

FORMATTING AND WRITING E-MAIL

As you prepare to write, follow these tips to ensure your message stays on target and gets the inbox attention it deserves:

1. **Type the e-mail address correctly.** Ensure your message won't be lost in cyberspace. Rely on your electronic address book if you routinely leave out or mistype characters. As an option, include <the recipient's name> in angle brackets. Determine **distribution lists** and mailing lists beforehand so you can tailor messages to recipients' specific needs. Add CC (copy feature) and BCC (blind copy feature) addresses accordingly. Send copies only to people who have a legitimate need for your information and keep some e-mail addresses anonymous if recipients are likely to object to their circulation. Your program will usually insert your e-mail address and the date automatically.

distribution list a group of e-mail recipients addressed as a single recipient, allowing the sender to e-mail many users without entering their individual addresses.

2. **Compose an action-specific subject line.** Subject lines help readers decide how relevant, important, and urgent a message is. Together, the sender's name and the subject line help recipients prioritize their reading. Labels such as "URGENT" can be used from time to time when companies approve of them. The best way to command attention for your message is to create a descriptive subject line, like a newspaper headline that tells readers what the message is about in as few words as possible. Be specific—for example, instead of "New Statement" (too general) write "Revised Quality Assurance Statement." If an action is needed, use a verb (e.g., "Complete Attached Survey"). Be sure to revise RE: (reply) subject lines when they no longer reflect the content of the message. E-mails without subject lines stand the greatest chance of being deleted without being read.

3. **Wrap text after 70 characters.** Short lines can look ragged and disjointed. Line length settings are found in the preferences option of your e-mail program's toolbar.

4. **Use a regular mix of upper- and lowercase letters.** Text-messagers use all lowercase, but this is a practice business writers should avoid. Capitalize the first letter in each sentence and use correct punctuation. THE PRACTICE OF WRITING MESSAGES IN ALL CAPS (**SHOUTING**) IS FORBIDDEN BY MANY ORGANIZATIONS. Not only is it considered rude and oppressive, it is also difficult to read. Headings and subheadings may be useful in organizing long messages. If you use bold and italics, be aware that some platforms won't accommodate them. Use ★asterisks★ around a word to show italics and _underscores_ to show underlining.

> **shouting** the practice—often considered rude—of typing e-mail messages in upper-case letters.

5. **Keep paragraphs and sentences short.** You should aim to keep text shorter than in regular word-processing documents. Use double-spaced paragraph breaks for emphasis and readability. Design your message so readers can skim it easily, noting shifts in topic with each new paragraph. Smart organization means less reading time per message, helping readers cope with the ever-increasing volume of inbound e-mail.

As you begin to compose your message, keep in mind the following strategies for shaping its content:

1. **Use appropriate greetings to soften messages.** Common informal **salutations** to use when you know the recipient well include *Hello*, *Hi*, and *Greetings* used on their own or followed by the recipient's first name. Memos omit greetings, and quick, routine messages may not require a greeting at all but can sound impolite or abrupt without one. In some cases you may simply incorporate the recipient's name in the first line of the body of your message. For external e-mail, salutations are recommended, but avoid the "one-size-fits-all" approach and make sure the greeting you choose fits the context. Use *Dear Ms.* or *Mr.* (plus the recipient's last name) when you aren't on a first-name basis with the recipient and *Dear* (followed by the recipient's first name) when you know the person well.

> **salutation** the greeting in a letter, used to address the person being written to.

2. **Get to the point immediately.** Begin by asking for action, information, or a reply—or provide an overview if your message runs longer than one screen. A strong opening that identifies issues, people, products, or services is vital to a message's success.

3. **Use lists without overloading them.** Divide material into short, manageable segments or into lists with bullet points or numbers. Limit lists to between three and eight points. Use formatting strategies to make your e-mail visually appealing and quickly scannable because only the most important messages are read word for word.

complimentary close a formulaic closing, usually a word found after the body of a letter and before the signature.

4. **Sign off with a complimentary close and your name.** Your closing should maintain the tone of your greeting and of your message as a whole. If nothing too formal is required, a simple *Regards* or *Thanks* will do. Reserve *Sincerely* for messages where you need to show deference. Use *Cheers* only if the message is cheerful. Drop the closing in quick routine messages where politeness isn't a concern or in messages that function as memos.

5. **Tell people who you are.** For external e-mails in particular, set up an automatic signature through your e-mail program. Recipients will then know your professional title, telephone number, regular address, and full name.

6. **Edit your text and run a spell-check.** Readers won't expect absolute perfection, but the more correct your e-mail is, the more professional and credible you will seem.

attachment an independent computer file sent with a regular e-mail message.

7. **Follow common sense rules for attachments.** Attachments are independent computer files sent with a regular e-mail message. Before you create an attachment, consider if its contents could be put in the text of the message. Label attachment documents so they can be easily recognized and summarize their contents in your e-mail. Also be certain to identify the application you are running as well as its version. Ask permission first when sending large attachments to make sure your recipient's system can handle them, and avoid sending too many attachments with a single message.

REPLYING TO E-MAIL

1. **Reply as promptly as possible.** Develop a response game plan, deciding how best to juggle this and other tasks. If you can't reply immediately, write a quick message indicating you will send a full reply later (e.g., "Will reply Friday").

2. **Modify your distribution list.** If you receive a group e-mail, you may need to send your response to the entire group. On the other hand, think twice before you automatically hit "Reply All." Prune the distribution list so that only individuals who have a legitimate need for your message receive it. Indiscriminate use of "CC" and "Reply All" tops the list of e-mail users' biggest complaints, so take a few seconds to decide who needs the contents of your reply and who doesn't.

3. **Don't automatically include the sender's original message with your reply.** How much of the original message to incorporate in a reply is a common e-mail dilemma, so consider the context in which your own reply should be placed. For short, routine messages, the original message can be included with your reply, but be sure to put your reply at the top to save readers the trouble of scrolling down. If you decide not to return the sender's message, provide a reply full enough (not just "OK" or "No problem") for readers to know exactly what you're referring to. For lengthy or complex messages, cut and paste your response—copy into it relevant portions of the original message, but always make sure the distinction between your words and those of the original is clear. Choosing the right reply

style can help reduce major irritants, such as chain e-mails, now banned by some organizations.

4. **Avoid indiscriminately forwarding e-mails.** First consider whom the message is relevant to and who really needs the information.

5. **Don't be impatient for a reply.** Wait for a response instead of jumping to conclusions—that the message has been misdirected, left unopened, or overlooked—and sending out a duplicate message. People do not always answer their mail the same day they get it, so be patient and allow a reasonable amount of time for a response. If you need an immediate answer on a pressing matter, make a quick telephone call instead.

6. **Make provision for your absences from the office.** Let people who are trying to reach you know you are out of the office. Arrange for automatic receipt of incoming messages and out-of-office outgoing messages that let readers know when you will return and whom they can contact in your absence.

7. **Protect and respect authorship.** Select a *read-only* status for critical documents that could subsequently be altered without your knowledge, and retain a time-stamped copy of the original. Always credit the original author of forwarded documents. The rules of plagiarism apply equally to electronic communication.

E-MAIL STYLE AND TONE

E-mail is not just a technology, but also a matter of style. It becomes a statement of your personal and professional image. That's why some users are dissatisfied when their "e-mail voice" doesn't match their speaking voice. If you keep in mind what your e-mail replaces—a face-to-face conversation, a telephone call, a hard-copy letter, a traditional proposal—you will begin to understand how informal or formal your style should be. E-mail is so flexible and adaptable that it accommodates a range of styles.

Semi-formal or *conversational style* applies to most e-mail messages, especially routine communication. It resembles the proceedings of a well-conducted meeting transcribed without the pauses and, hopefully, without any errors. Personal pronouns, contractions, and active-voice constructions are what make this style crisp and accessible. E-mail tends to be somewhat more *informal* when it replaces a phone call, face-to-face conversation, or casual note; however, a telegraphic style marked by abrupt shifts in topic and omitted subject words is not recommended for most e-mail messages.

Formal style is reserved for documents that are e-mail only by virtue of their transmission—reports, policy statements, and proposals. Any document meant to be printed out should conform to style conventions for its type.

Tone is hard to control in e-mail because of the rapid and informal way most messages are written. For many e-mail users, the prime concern is simply getting their point across clearly and not how a message sounds. Users who are not by nature cold, impersonal, or rude may sound that way to fellow users who know them only through their e-mail. Anger, resentment, or impatience may be inferred where none was intended. To avoid this, think of your recipients and their needs. Visualize the recipient and consider how she might respond in a conversation. Then read your message back to detect tonal miscues; proofread important and compliance-gaining messages with a critical eye.

ROUTINE MESSAGES: POSITIVE AND INFORMATIVE MEMOS AND E-MAIL

informative memo
a message to which the reader will react neutrally.

Informative memos and e-mail convey announcements, company policies, guidelines, instructions, and procedures. Informative messages must be clear and direct in order for readers to put directives into practice and carry through on initiatives. A clearly worded subject line, direct opening, clear explanation, and follow-up instructions (often in an enumerated list), good closing, and positive emphasis support the message's informative aim.

Figures 5.2 and 5.3 are two versions of a message explaining the adoption of new order procedures for office catering services. Numerous faults reduce the effectiveness of the message in Figure 5.2, which begins with a vague subject line that doesn't accurately describe the purpose or content of the message. A sloppy, weak, and negative opening puts a complaint first, well before important information. It isn't immediately clear what the message is about. Random, out-of-sequence steps aren't itemized, making the instructions difficult to follow. The tone is alternately breezy and accusatory, creating incoherence, and many key details are left out—the effective date of the new ordering procedure, the time and location of the tasting session, and contact information.

Figure 5.3 creates a focus for the message with a specific and descriptive subject line. The direct opening tells readers exactly what the message is about, and the explanation in the paragraph that follows indicates why the new procedure must be

FIGURE 5.2 INEFFECTIVE Informative E-mail Draft

Subject line is vague and uninformative →

Slow opening paragraph makes it unclear what message is about →

Uneven tone affects readability →

Random order and lack of details contribute to fuzzy or unclear focus →

Subject:	Food, Glorious Food
Date:	Mon., April 13, 2009, 9:45 AM
From:	Tyler Fisk <Tyler.Fisk@clicksnmortar.ca>
To:	Ella.Bridges@clicksnmortar.ca, Pho.Nguyen@clicksnmortar.ca, Dora.Juarez@clicksnmortar.ca

Arranging for catering has always been a major headache. Remember those meetings where all we had to eat was a box of soda crackers and a few cubes of cheese? Well, those days are over and we have our new partnership with Gusto Fine Foods to thank for it. Now we'll have tasty low-cal and low-carb snacks for all our boardroom meetings, on-site seminars, and receptions. There will be a tasting session on April 15 so you can try some of these unbelievable sandwiches and hors d'oeuvre.

Soon it will be possible to order food like this online. Ordering is easy—just remember to specify quantities and dates required. There are so many food choices it's hard not to order every single thing.

Of course, it's possible to over-indulge even in healthy food, so forget about ordering catered lunches and snacks every day.

And don't forget to order at least 24 hours in advance, otherwise you might be out of luck (and hungry). By the way, you can find Gusto Fine Foods online at www.gustofinefoods.com. Bon appétit!

FIGURE 5.3 EFFECTIVE Informative E-mail

Subject:	New Catering Requisition Procedures	Accurate and descriptive subject line creates focus for message
Date:	Mon., April 13, 2009, 10:15 AM	
From:	Farah Aswan <Farah.Aswan@clicksnmortar.ca>	
To:	Ella.Bridges@clicksnmortar.ca, Pho.Nguyen@clicksnmortar.ca, Dora.Juarez@clicksnmortar.ca	

Effective April 30, all requests for office and event catering should be made online through the Gusto Fine Foods website. → *Opening paragraph focuses on action to be taken*

As you know, Clicks 'n' Mortar, Inc. recently awarded Gusto Fine Foods, Inc. a contract to cater all board meetings, on-site training sessions, client consultations, and receptions. Gusto Fine Foods specializes in offering health-conscious businesses low-carbohydrate and low-calorie alternatives to traditional office fare. During the six-month introductory period ending October 30, you may choose from a specially priced product line that includes fruit platters, hot and cold hors d'oeuvre, light lunches, fresh juices, specialty coffees, and VQA Ontario wines. → *Explanation highlights benefits*

You can ensure prompt and efficient delivery of your order by placing it 24 hours in advance and following this procedure:

1. Log on to the Gusto Fine Foods website: www.gustofinefoods.com. → *Hotlink makes additional information available*
2. Click on "Orders."
3. Enter your department number and password.
4. Make your menu selection.
5. Fill in the time, date, location, and guest-number fields. → *Procedure outlined in list form*
6. Submit your order and print out a hard copy of the requisition.

The cost of each order, plus applicable taxes, will be automatically deducted from your departmental hospitality allotment, up to a maximum of $400 per month.

To learn more about Gusto's extensive catering services, you and members of your department are invited to an information session on **April 15, from 5:00–7:00 p.m.** in the Central Atrium. Giorgio Delmonico, president of Gusto Fine Foods, will be on hand to answer your questions and offer you the best from his tasting menu.

Following the order guidelines established through this new partnership will improve the quality and efficiency of our in-house amenities and client hosting. Call me at ext. 211 if you have any questions about the new procedure. → *Reader benefits emphasized*

implemented and what its advantages are. The numbered list shows the steps in the new procedure in sequence, simplifying instructions for easy reference. To encourage compliance, the writer, in the final paragraph, reminds readers of the benefits of the new procedure and invites their questions by offering contact information. Readers are left knowing when the new procedures go into effect and what they are supposed to do. Hotlinks (also known as hyperlinks) are a way for readers to access information that can't be provided in a short message.

The purpose of an informative message can also be to confirm a change in plans or schedule or to acknowledge receipt of materials. Writing an acknowledgement is usually a matter of courtesy and requires no more than one or two sentences.

ROUTINE MESSAGES: REQUEST MEMOS

request memo a message that asks the reader to perform a routine action.

If you seek routine information or action, always use the direct approach. **Request memos** stand a greater chance of gaining compliance when readers know by the end of the first paragraph what you are asking for and what action they must take. This directive is usually expressed as a polite command (*Please explain the procedure for ordering a transcript of one of your broadcasts*) or a direct question (*What is the procedure for ordering a transcript of one of your broadcasts? How may I obtain a transcript of one of your broadcasts?*). Multiple requests can be introduced by a summary statement, and then listed as numbered or bulleted questions. For ease of response, readers can be invited to reply within the original message. Explanations and justifications belong in the body of the message. While politeness is key to gaining compliance, citing a reason for the request, reader benefits, and an end date can build goodwill and help to ensure a useful and timely response. A consistent tone that's not too apologetic or demanding reduces the chance readers will overlook or be resistant to your request.

Requests that make sizable demands on the reader's time and resources should follow the indirect plan that puts a reason for the request before the request itself. If you think the reader may not readily comply with your request, reduce resistance by persuading with reasons and justifications.

FIGURE 5.4 E-mail that Requests

Subject clearly indicates that a response is required

Opening combines statement of benefits with polite command

Multiple requests presented in a numbered list

Explanation establishes the necessity for the request

You-attitude, active-voice verbs, and reason for end date help to encourage action

Subject:	Your Reaction to Proposed Power Conservation Plan
Date:	Fri., July 17, 2009 8:30 AM
From:	Derwin Waters <dwaters@aerosport.com>
To:	Sandy McPhee <smcphee@aerosport.com>

To help us meet new government guidelines for workplace power conservation, please answer the following questions regarding your energy consumption and preferences on the job.

1. Would raising summer office temperature to a maximum 24 degrees Celsius be acceptable?
2. Could overhead lighting be reduced in well-lit work areas?
3. Based on your use of office kitchen equipment, could you do without the refrigerators and automatic coffee makers located on each floor?

The recent blackouts and power outages have put the issue of energy conservation high on our agenda. Our aim is to create an environmentally responsible yet still comfortable workplace by reducing power consumption by as much as 15 per cent.

Your answers to these questions will assist us in establishing new recommendations to reduce power consumption and related costs. Please respond by August 15 so we may compile data and act on your input when the Health and Safety Committee meets on August 20.

ROUTINE MESSAGES: REPLY MEMOS AND E-MAIL

Like requests, **responses** are crucial to the day-to-day operation of organizations. Response messages deliver specific information itemized in the order that the requests were made. Using the direct approach, you can write an effective response that is complete, focused, and well organized. Open by announcing the most important fact or answer (often by referring to the previous message), sharing good news, or introducing multiple responses by way of a summary statement. Arranging these responses according to the order of the original requests saves time and increases coherence. Boldfaced

> **response** a message that answers a request or query.

FIGURE 5.5 E-mail that Responds

Subject:	Reaction to Proposed Power Conservation Plan
Date:	Mon., July 20, 2009, 9:42 AM
From:	Sandy McPhee <smcphee@aerosport.com>
To:	Derwin Waters <dwaters@aerosport.com>

Here are my reactions to the proposed power conservation plan you inquired about in your message of July 17.   *← Opening refers to the previous message and provides a summary statement to introduce responses to individual questions*

- **Raise summer office temperature?** Yes, this would be a welcome change. Staff members have complained that the overly efficient air conditioning system leaves them in a "deep freeze" throughout the summer. Many people bring extra clothing with them to wear at their desks. Raising the office temperature would improve our overall comfort level.

- **Reduce overhead lighting?** Possibly. Most workstations have more than ample lighting, especially the outside offices that have a good supply of sunlight. After the 2003 blackout, overhead lighting was temporarily reduced by one third with no ill effects on safety or productivity. I think we should proceed cautiously with this recommendation and explore potential health and safety concerns.   *← Responses arranged as bulleted points in order of original requests; boldfaced catchphrases summarize original questions*

- **Remove unused office kitchen equipment?** Yes, only a few department members use the refrigerator and coffee maker on a regular basis, especially since the specialty coffee franchise opened on our premises. I think we should keep the coffee maker, which was purchased only a year ago and requires little power. The 25-year-old refrigerator, however, could be scrapped or replaced with a smaller, more energy-efficient model. Instead of having one refrigerator per floor, we could make do with one or two for the entire building.

I agree that most of the proposed changes could be implemented with minimal disruption to operations and little inconvenience to staff. Let me know if I can provide further assistance in making our organization more energy efficient.   *← Final paragraph summarizes overall response and offers assistance*

headings or catchphrases can be used to summarize the focus of each response. It may be appropriate to provide additional information relevant to the original request. The closing sums up your response or offers further assistance. A prompt reply indicates both efficiency and a willingness to help. The memo in Figure 5.5 replies to the request for feedback on the power reduction plan proposed in Figure 5.4.

GOODWILL E-MAIL MESSAGES

Messages that you send saying thank you or offering congratulations are a matter of courtesy and make good business sense. In putting good wishes ahead of business transactions, **goodwill messages** help reinforce the professional and personal bonds between writer and reader. Thank-you messages express appreciation for help, invitations, hospitality, interviews, recommendations, past business, favours, emergency services, and special duties performed. Congratulatory messages recognize special achievements or milestones—career promotions, job appointments, awards, or special honours. These types of messages use the direct approach, first identifying the situation, then including a few reader-focused details, and ending pleasantly, often with a forward-looking remark. Avoiding trite, wooden expressions allows you to give the impression of spontaneity and sincerity. The goodwill e-mail message shown in Figure 5.6 conveys appreciation for participation in a business-related charity event.

goodwill message a message that enhances the value of a business beyond its tangible assets by creating a bond of friendship and establishing trust and mutual understanding between the writer and recipient.

FIGURE 5.6 Thank-You E-mail Message

Opening paragraph conveys thanks to the recipient for services provided and describes those services in detail

Second paragraph describes the benefit derived from that service

Closes pleasantly with further thanks and recognition of the positive effort recipient has made

Subject:	Thanks for Making a Difference
Date:	Tuesday, September 15, 2009, 9:23 AM
From:	Greg Stockwood <gwstockwood@baxtercable.com>
To:	Trish Corelli <tcorelli@baxtercable.com>

Trish, thanks for helping to make last Sunday's Run for the Cure a runaway success. By completing the 20-km course, you and your Baxter Cable teammates helped raise over $5,000 for breast cancer research.

Your commitment to the community is something to be proud of. In recognition of your achievement, Baxter Cable will match the money raised last Sunday by making a $5,000 donation to the Canadian Cancer Society.

Thanks again for so generously giving your time and devoting your energies to such a worthy cause.

Because e-mail is informal and spontaneous, it has become a common means of transmitting quick or impromptu goodwill messages. But bear in mind, the more deferential and reserved you need to be, the more you should consider sending a typed or handwritten letter.

FOLLOW-UP MEMOS AND E-MAIL

A **follow-up** is a more specialized type of informative message, one that reflects good business practices. As the memory of a conversation or meeting fades, a follow-up message serves as a record for future reference confirming the time, place, and purpose of a meeting. The follow-up also serves as a reminder of the names and titles of participants, and sometimes even the terms of a verbal agreement or the roles of a working relationship. Restating basic facts and major directives, decisions, and issues ensures that each person's version of what took place is the same. Because others may not remember a conversation exactly as you do, make allowances for differing accounts by using phrases such as "As I recall" or by inviting feedback that verifies the information you have passed on ("Please reply if you agree that this message accurately reflects our conversation"). Writing follow-up messages protects you and your reader, lessening the chance of later retractions, falsifications, or broken commitments. The more important an oral agreement is, the more vital it is to have proof in the form of written confirmation. For especially crucial or sensitive agreements, print out a copy of your follow-up e-mail or send a hard-copy letter.

> **follow-up message** provides a record of a meeting—its time, place, purpose, and any agreements that may have been made.

FIGURE 5.7 Follow-Up E-mail Message

Subject:	Confirmation of Conversation about Seminar Details
Date:	Wednesday, December 2, 2009, 16:53
From:	Jo Costello <jcostello@solutionsplus.ca>
To:	Rebecca Cohen <rcohen@solutionsplus.ca>

Thanks, Rebecca, for talking with me yesterday about how to assist in upgrading the writing skills of your department members. This message confirms the details of the on-site course we agreed on in our conversation. *[← Opening identifies the date and subject of the meeting]*

- A three-session course for 20 accounting personnel will be held from 4:00–6:00 p.m. on January 11, 18, and 25.

- Ryan Mackenzie of Stylus Writing Services will conduct the course. Mr. Mackenzie, who is under contract to our company, has presented similar courses to customer service and marketing personnel. Feedback on the two previous courses was very positive. *[← Major details and points agreed upon are listed as bulleted items]*

- The course will include grammar review but will focus primarily on how to write letters and e-mails in a plain-language style. A full course outline will be distributed to registrants by December 20.

- Each registrant will receive a 30-page learning guide. Individualized feedback is available on request.

I am confident that this six-hour intensive course will help members of your department achieve their writing goals and improve communication with internal and external stakeholders. If this message accurately reflects the details of yesterday's conversation, please confirm your agreement by return e-mail. *[← Uses positive tone and forward-looking approach; message ends with allowance for correction of details]*

Instant Messaging (IM)

instant messaging (IM)
the exchange of messages over the Internet between two or more users who are online simultaneously.

Some organizations support the adoption and integration of **instant messaging (IM)** into their businesses; some take steps to ban it. Like many new technologies, IM has trouble being taken seriously and used productively. While there is no consensus among IT managers that instant messaging is the way of the future for maximizing productivity and profitability, many users claim they can't do business without it. IM combines features of synchronous, real-time communication (face-to-face meetings, telephone calls) with traits more commonly identified with e-mail. Many of the guidelines for using e-mail also apply to IM:

1. **Limit the use of abbreviations.** The IM lexicon is a specialized language, often strongly identified with its teenaged users. Abbreviations such as *ttfn* ("ta ta for now"), *imo* ("in my opinion"), and *btw* ("by the way") may confuse individuals who are unfamiliar with these terms.

2. **Use a natural mix of upper- and lowercase.** Although small key pads, rapid information exchange, and other factors account for the spareness of text messaging style, try to make your messages as readable as possible by avoiding practices such as *shouting*.

3. **Keep conversations to a few people at a time**. More than four or five participants in a conversation can make for an interactive free-for-all. Notify participants before distributing the contents of a thread conversation.

4. **Set status flags to "away" or "busy" if you don't wish to be engaged.**

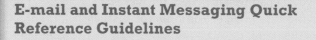

E-mail and Instant Messaging Quick Reference Guidelines

Netiquette

- Be an effective e-mail manager, checking your inbox at regular intervals, responding promptly, and filing messages for easy reference.
- Adopt good e-mail practices (pruning distribution lists, using anti-spam software, resisting the urge to "flame," and using company e-mail only for business purposes).
- Use e-mail as a primary means, but not your only means, of communication.
- Make every message count by avoiding unnecessary replies, gratuitous forwarded messages, and blanket messages.
- Create a functional and descriptive subject line for every message you write.

Composition

- Be brief, putting your main message in a strong opening so readers won't have to scroll down through multiple screens to find it.
- Remember that e-mail is permanent and public—be careful what you write.
- Write with speed and accuracy by obeying the rules of good writing but not agonizing over every character or line.
- Be conversational by writing "talking" messages.
- Cut and paste responses whenever possible to avoid creating chain e-mails.

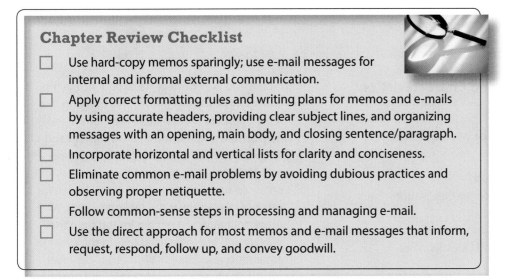

Chapter Review Checklist

- ☐ Use hard-copy memos sparingly; use e-mail messages for internal and informal external communication.
- ☐ Apply correct formatting rules and writing plans for memos and e-mails by using accurate headers, providing clear subject lines, and organizing messages with an opening, main body, and closing sentence/paragraph.
- ☐ Incorporate horizontal and vertical lists for clarity and conciseness.
- ☐ Eliminate common e-mail problems by avoiding dubious practices and observing proper netiquette.
- ☐ Follow common-sense steps in processing and managing e-mail.
- ☐ Use the direct approach for most memos and e-mail messages that inform, request, respond, follow up, and convey goodwill.

WORKSHOPS AND DISCUSSION FORUMS

1. **E-mail Round-Table Discussion:** In groups or as a class, answer the following questions, then propose solutions to some of the most pressing problems and dubious practices.

   a) How many e-mail messages do you receive daily?
   i) fewer than 10
   ii) 10–25
   iii) 26–50
   iv) more than 50
   Is your inbound e-mail manageable or do you suffer from e-mail overload?

   b) How many e-mail messages do you write each day?
   i) 5 or fewer
   ii) 6–10
   iii) 11–25
   iv) 26–50
   v) more than 50

   c) If you use e-mail to communicate at work, how much of your workday is spent writing or answering e-mail? Does e-mail create more work or help you do work?

   d) How long is your average message?
   i) one or two sentences
   ii) one or two paragraphs
   iii) one screen
   iv) more than one screen

   e) How does e-mail make you feel? What types of messages do you most dislike or look forward to, and why?

   f) What bothers you most about communicating by e-mail?
   Record your responses and draw up a list of general e-mail guidelines based on your discussion. Decide which ones would help you the most in communicating effectively in your current or future occupation.

2. **E-mail Style: Bending the Rules of Usage.** Identify faults and weaknesses in the following routine message. Discuss to what extent its flaws reduce readability. Are errors in spelling, grammar, usage, and punctuation ever permissible in e-mail?

   Subject: Meeting
   Date: June 18, 2009
   To: All Concerned

   FYI, we have alot of problems with our shipping proceedurs, its making me really L. May be it'd be a good idea to discuss it. hoping to work out some solutions, a meeting will be held. A meeting to discuss shipping proceedures will take place next Tuesday, if that's o.k. with yous. Their three items we need to discuss. . . . see yous at the meeting ☺. TTFN.

WRITING IMPROVEMENT EXERCISES

Recognize the Nature and Characteristics of Memos and E-mail

1. **Specific Subject Lines for Memos.** Mark each of the following as *V* for vague or *S* for specific.

   a) Holiday Celebration
   b) Cancellation of Holiday Celebration
   c) Casual Dress
   d) Proposed Casual Dress Day Program
   e) Complete Attached Questionnaire
   f) Questionnaire
   g) Your Request for Information on Corporate Media Relations
   h) Media Article
   i) Customer Service
   j) Introduction of Customer Service Hotline

2. **Writing Subject Lines for Memos and E-mail.** For each of the following scenarios, write a focused and action-specific subject line.

   a) You are writing to all employees to ask them to complete an attached questionnaire on proposed changes to the pension plan.

   b) To promote a more positive and inclusive work environment, your company will be holding a diversity awareness seminar on June 8. Attendance is mandatory.

   c) Because many staff members wear clothing inappropriate for the workplace, including midriff-baring tops, micro minis, and T-shirts with offensive slogans, your company will introduce a dress code to take effect on October 9.

3. **Getting to the Point.** Unscramble the following memo so that it starts with the main message and reserves the explanation for the body. Eliminate unnecessary details.

   Trespassing and vandalism have become increasingly serious problems for our organization. Following three reported security violations in the past month, we have hired Garrison Safety Consultant Services to redesign building access and entry procedures. Garrison Safety Consultant Services has a proven track record and over forty years' experience in the industry. The altered procedures Garrison has recommended will go into effect June 8 and help ensure a safe working environment and the protection of company property. Please access the building by the Wilcox Street entrance and present your photo ID badge for security inspection at the reception desk. All other doorways will remain locked from the outside and are to be used only in the event of emergency evacuation. Visitors will be issued security badges and must sign in and out at reception. While on premises, all personnel must wear their photo ID badges.

4. **Composing Strong Memo Openings**. Revise the following paragraphs to front-load and summarize the main message.

   a) Many of our employees have indicated that they favour adjusted work hours throughout the summer. After careful consideration, we have decided that new hours will go into effect from May 30 to September 2. The new hours are 8:30 a.m.–4:30 p.m.

   b) Our association holds its annual conference in March and we are interested in your hotel and conference centre as a possible venue for next year's event. We require a hosting facility to accommodate our five hundred members from March 15–18, 2009 and need information about cost and availability.

   c) We have recently received numerous complaints from points program members indicating that they have been prevented from applying their accumulated bonus points for discounts on recent purchases. I am asking customer relations to conduct a study of and make recommendations on the efficiency of the points program.

   d) We have noticed recently a steady decline in the quality of our high-speed Internet service. As our contract with our current provider expires next month, I am asking you to investigate the rates and service records of its chief competitors.

Format Horizontal and Vertical Lists for Clarity and Conciseness

5. **Effective Lists.** Reorganize the following information into list form, tabulating steps and supporting points. Compose a lead-in that "reads" with each item.

   a) Please follow these packaging procedures to ensure that all shipped items arrive undamaged. First of all, ensure that the item does not exceed weight restrictions for the type of packaging used. Fragile items should be shipped in special protective packaging. Larger items should be shipped in customized crates and containers. Always ensure that the package is properly sealed.

   b) Setting up your new HT printer involves only a few steps. You should start by plugging the unit in and making sure the printer cable is connected to your computer. Then you should follow printing software instructions and align print settings, but before you commence your first print job, you should run a test sample in case settings need adjustment.

   c) The new direct-deposit payroll system has several advantages. Employees will no longer have to wait in bank lineups to deposit their cheques and there is less risk that paycheques will be lost or stolen. Employees can enjoy the added security of

knowing that their salaries go directly into their bank accounts on bi-monthly paydays.

Eliminate Common Problems and Dubious Practices in E-mails

6. **Extinguishing "flaming."** Revise the following message to neutralize its angry tone and improve its professionalism.

   I absolutely have to have the latest sales figures by Friday—no ifs, ands, or buts. I find it difficult to understand why so simple a request goes unnoticed until the deadline has passed, especially when the survival of our retail clothing division depends on ongoing analysis of this important data.

Develop Correct E-mail Style and Tone

7. **Adopting a conversational e-mail style.** Revise the following message between two long-time co-workers to eliminate stiffness and undue formality.

   Dear Mr. Harry Singh:

   Please be advised that you are instructed to review the revised procedures for sending courier packages to the United States. Please find attached a copy of the revised procedures for your perusal. Substantial savings will be realized if all personnel comply with the new procedures and I would be most grateful if you complied with them as well.

   Respectfully,
   Paula Wittington

CASE STUDY EXERCISES

Write Memos and E-mails that Inform, Request and Respond, Follow Up, and Convey Goodwill

Analyze the following writing cases and select relevant details to include in your message.

1. **E-mail that Informs—Design-Show Trends:** As Marc Paradis, assistant buyer for Space One, a new Vancouver-area furniture and home accessories store, write a message to Marcella Ponti, proprietor and chief buyer, summarizing the top trends at the Interior Design Show. Marcella is currently on a

buying trip in Italy and has sent you to the show in her place. The Interior Design Show in Toronto is Canada's largest resident design show, attended by 8,500 design professionals and over 50,000 visitors every year. Its exhibits and presentations by designers from around the world showcase innovative products and trends in furniture, textile and home accessories design, residential interior design, and landscape architecture. In your three days at the show, beginning with Trade Day, you noted many new trends but were most impressed by the innovative use of materials in furniture design. Standouts included a collection of ottomans and chairs in leather, fur, and chrome priced in the $1,000–$2,000 range from the Montreal design team Verité. "Clear" was another hot trend in furniture and accessory design, seen in an array of glass, Lucite, and acrylic products and best exemplified by Philippe Starck's interpretation of a classic Louis XV armchair and the use of glass tile and countertops in kitchens and bathrooms. In textile design, the most noticeable trend was toward textural and richly embellished fabrics in silk and synthetic blends, notably in a colour palate of golds, browns, and corals. Having carefully reviewed product literature and pricing information, you believe a strong case could be made for stocking several Canadian items that reflect Space One's design sensibility.

2. **E-mail that Informs—Counterfeit Internet Coupons:** As François Durant, director of loss prevention for a small chain of grocery stores, write an e-mail to store managers advising them of a surge in the use of counterfeit Internet discount coupons. In recent months, the problem has grown more serious. In July, for example, retailers were hit with a flood of bogus coupons promising free ice cream bars from Häagen-Dazs, a brand represented in Canada by Nestlé. With this in mind, advise store managers to monitor the situation closely and warn cashiers to closely inspect coupons offering free or heavily discounted items and to decline coupons without bar codes and expiry dates. Of course, you realize that some bogus coupons are difficult to detect because technophiles can easily alter manufacturers' coupons or create their own from scratch with the right tools. The Food Marketing Institute, an international association based in Washington, D.C., estimates that frauds cost the sector up to $800 million (U.S.) annually. Make it clear to your readers that the cost of these downloaded forgeries is a cost you prefer to avoid.

3. **E-mail that Informs—Retirement Dinner:** As Vicki Wu, office events coordinator, write an e-mail to all employees informing them of a retirement dinner party for Gerald Dwyer. Gerald joined the company in 1967, first working as a mail clerk and steadily earning promotions to become manager of operations. Known as a team player, he spearheaded the company United Way fundraising drive for five record-breaking years and streamlined office procedures for greater efficiency. Retirement parties are usually dreary affairs but you'd like this one to be different. Include information about when and where the party will be held, how formal it will be, what type of food will be served, whom to contact for tickets, cost per ticket, whether guests are permitted, additional charges for a gift presentation, and venue parking and accessibility details (consider a hotlink for this final item). Use appropriate formatting techniques for easy readability.

4. **Goodwill E-mail—Congratulations on Your Retirement:** As Tracy Nagada, write a congratulatory e-mail to Gerald Dwyer (see Case 3 above) conveying your best wishes on his retirement. Gerald was your supervisor when you first joined the company ten years ago. Although you found his attitude toward you somewhat paternalistic, especially when he referred to you and your female coworkers as "my best gals," you appreciated his fairness and guidance, both of which contributed to your career advancement. A longstanding family commitment prevents you from attending his retirement dinner. Write to Gerald and offer your good wishes.

5. **E-mail that Requests—Reaction to Proposed WLAN on Campus:** As Ted Brenner, associate vice-president for information technologies at Kelso Community College, compose an e-mail to faculty asking them for their feedback on a proposed WLAN (wireless local area network), part of the college's comprehensive e-strategy. For you, the advantages of "going wireless" are obvious. Instructors will be able to manage their course workload, schedules, and student needs online, leaving more time for them

to be actively engaged in research. Students will be able to more easily access grades, e-mail assignments to instructors, and interact with fellow classmates. You would like to know if faculty members agree that wireless technology will create a more effective way of teaching and a more efficient way of learning. Will it make their work easier? Do they have the skills—for example, knowledge of computer troubleshooting—to make good use of the new technology? Can students be relied upon to bring their laptops to class and use them consistently? Do they have other concerns?

6. **E-mail that Responds—Reaction to Proposed WLAN on Campus:** As Monica Chan, chair of the Early Childhood Education Program at Kelso Community College, respond to Ted Brenner (see Case 5 above). Having heard that most other academic institutions have adopted wireless technologies, you would like to see Kelso gain a similar "electronic edge," though you still have a few reservations. Primarily, you are concerned about online anti-virus security and related privacy issues. Would students' marks be secure? What would happen if the system crashed? Another issue that concerns you is student access to laptops and available funding for those unable to meet the technological requirements. Many of your students cannot afford to buy a laptop computer, so you would like to see funding set up before such a program could be implemented.

7. **E-mail that Informs—Relocation of Scheduled Retreat:** The sudden closure of Cedarcrest Resort and Conference Facility due to a health alert has left your marketing division without a venue for its summer meeting and team-building retreat, scheduled for August 8–10, two weeks hence. Rather than cancel the event, you have negotiated with the resort operator, Riverwood Inc., to move the event to Huntingwood, a nearby luxury resort in the Riverwood chain. The health alert has not affected Huntingwood, nor is it expected to. The aim of the retreat remains the same: to foster better relations among your sometimes-combative marketing team members. The program of events is also unchanged. From 8:30 a.m. to noon each day, the group will make presentations and discuss marketing strategy. From 1:00 to 4:00 p.m., the group will participate in fun and challenging team-building exercises such as three-legged races and obstacle courses. As Gus Agnopolis, marketing coordinator, write to members of the marketing division advising them of the change of venue.

8. **E-mail that Follows Up—Confirming Details of Intramural Office Teams:** As Siobhan Cunningham, coordinator of your organization's newly established intramural sports program, write a message to Garinder Singh, vice-president of human resources, confirming the details worked out in a meeting several days ago. Since it is your responsibility to organize events for the upcoming winter–spring season, you want to be sure that you and Garinder agree on the terms of participation and the structure and membership of the teams. The program has been established to promote friendship, co-operation, and healthy lifestyles among employees. Six co-ed teams will be open to employees only and will offer them the opportunity to participate in non–body-contact hockey, soccer, and softball. Everyone is welcome to participate in more than one sport and will be notified by e-mail of game dates and cancellations. Registration will commence immediately and end one week prior to the season-opening games. You will be responsible for notifying team members of game dates and cancellations and for booking arenas and diamond times. To ensure employee safety, Garinder has asked you to arrange for volunteers with refereeing experience who in turn could be offered a small gift or honorarium for their services. A $20-per-person rink fee applies to hockey participants to cover booking and rental charges. Hockey players are expected to provide their own equipment, including sticks, skates, helmets, and mouthguards. Softball players must come to games equipped with gloves and appropriate footwear. All other softball and soccer equipment will be provided. During the program's inaugural season, teams will play every two weeks. There will be prizes for winning teams and certificates for players who attend throughout the season.

ONLINE ACTIVITIES

Recognize the Nature and Characteristics of Memos

1. **Revising Poorly Written Memos:** Visit the following website and revise the poorly written memos. In a small group, share your revision with your classmates and compare the strategies you have applied.
   www.writing.engr.psu.edu/exercises/correspondence.html

2. **Memo-Writing Exercises:** Visit the "Challenges" section. For each of the four "Challenges" exercises, add a subject line, introductory statement, and bullets. Form a discussion group with three or four of your classmates and compare your results. Next, click the "Answers" link beside each exercise and check your results.
   www.webwritingthatworks.com/eGuideScan2dChallenges.htm

Recognize Steps in Processing and Managing E-mail

3. **Writing E-mail Subject Lines:** Visit the following site and click on the box that corresponds to the most appropriate subject line for the message that follows.
   https://www.dlsweb.rmit.edu.au/lsu/content/4_WritingSkills/writing_tuts/business_%20english_LL/emails/subject_line.html

4. **Reducing Spam:** Review the spam you receive over a two- or three-day period, then visit the Spamhaus Project, a database on the history and methods of spammers. Discuss ways to reduce and eliminate spam.
   www.spamhaus.org

5. **Analyzing Websites:** Read the "How to Recognize a Business/Marketing Web Page" section (www.widener.edu/about/campus_resources/wolfgram_library/evaluate/busmarketing.aspx) on the Wolfram Memorial Library web page, then use the checklist to evaluate one or more of the following Canadian retail websites:
   http://canada.roots.com
   www.chapters.indigo.ca
   www.leevalley.com
   www.danier.com
   www.canadiantire.ca
   www.hbc.com
   www.marks.com

7. **Tracking E-mail Use:** Visit Statistics Canada's *The Daily* from Wednesday, May 25, 2011 for a review of the 2010 Canadian Internet Use Survey (CIUS), outlining personal computer access according to public- and private-sector industries.
   http://www.statcan.gc.ca/daily-quotidien/110525/dq110525b-eng.htm
   Then, refer to the following analysis of the data:
   http://www.convurgency.com/blog/2011-canadian-internet-usage-statistics.html
   Write a brief summary about what you have learned about personal computer access in Canada, then e-mail your assignment to your instructor.

6

Routine and Goodwill Messages

In this chapter you will learn to

1. Use a direct writing plan for routine business messages.

2. Request general information and claims adjustments.

3. Order services and merchandise.

4. Respond positively to requests for information, claims adjustments, and purchase orders.

5. Compose messages of appreciation, sympathy, and congratulation that answer basic human needs.

6. Write follow-up letters, announcements, and acknowledgements.

7. Format formal letters in a variety of ways.

◗◗ Direct Writing Plan

Good news messages, which inspire positive reaction from readers, establish rapport all on their own. Readers are always receptive to good news and they are usually anxious to learn key information immediately, without first having to read a preamble or explanation. The same applies to routine and informative messages, to which readers react neutrally. Together, good news and informative messages are the mainstays of business correspondence. When it comes to communicating good news, handling routine information, or even making a simple inquiry, don't make readers wait. Take the direct approach and make your point right away. Not only will you be getting your message off to a good start, your readers might even thank you for your directness.

> **direct-approach message** a message that presents the main point in the first paragraph.

A **direct-approach message** makes your purpose clear from the start, stating the main point in the first sentence before moving on to details. At first glance, readers can tell if you are asking for or supplying information, requesting or granting credit, or making or settling a claim. You can count on the direct approach to speed the flow of information and expedite purchase orders, credit applications, and claims adjustments.

Direct-approach messages save time and carry impact, but not every culture responds to direct correspondence in exactly the same way. While straightforwardness is the norm in North America, it does not translate well to all cultures. In high-context cultures—such as those in China, Japan, and Arab nations—directness is considered rude and may actually prevent you from getting your message across properly. In such cases, it is important to establish rapport before citing a problem or making a request, and even then to suggest or ask rather than demand. In Japan, where formality is important, it is customary to embed a request, no matter how routine, and to soften it with preliminaries and other politeness strategies. On the other hand, people in Western cultures consider a lack of directness to be a waste of their time. When you are communicating cross-culturally, weigh your reader's tolerance for directness first, before you launch into your request or begin your response. Plan ahead and familiarize yourself with local styles, protocols, and preferences. Making directness work for you means avoiding a *one-size-fits-all* approach to messaging.

THREE-STEP WRITING PLAN FOR DIRECT-APPROACH MESSAGES

A three-part structure helps to guide readers, navigating them through a message from beginning to end. Each part has its own specific function:

- **Opening**—delivers the main message first. It answers your reader's most important questions; states the good news; makes a direct, specific request; or provides the most important information, whenever possible from the reader's perspective.
- **Middle**—explains details of the news or inquiry and supplies background and clarification when needed. If there are further points or questions, they are presented in parallel form in a bulleted or numbered list (maximum five or six items).
- **Closing**—ends pleasantly in one or more of the following ways: provides contact information; asks for action, input, or a response, often by a deadline; tells the reader what happens next; communicates goodwill; or shows appreciation.

Straightforward and versatile, this writing plan is one that can be used for most routine correspondence, including requests and responses.

Requests

The first step in getting something you need—data, merchandise, a product replacement, refund, action, or assistance—is knowing how to ask for it. The direct approach puts your request (often in the form of a **request memo**) before the reader right away and helps to speed the exchange of information and pace of transactions. Keep in mind the following tips as you draft your direct-approach message:

> **request memo**
> a message that asks the reader to perform a routine action.

- **Put the main idea first.** Embedded requests are easy to overlook. Phrase your request as a question (*Will you please provide recommendations on technology purchases that would help reduce turnaround time on document production?*) or a polite command (*Please provide recommendations on technology purchases*). State exactly what you want—vague requests only encourage vague responses.

- **Give a reason for the request or state its benefit in the second paragraph,** unless you can incorporate this information into the opening paragraph in one sentence or less: *Please assist me in preparing an article for* Accountants Monthly *by answering the following questions about your CPA work-study program.*

- **Introduce multiple requests or questions with a summary statement.** Phrase your request as a polite question that requires no question mark: *Will* (or *Would*) *you please answer the following questions about your executive search services.* Another option is to phrase it as a polite request: *Please answer the following questions about your executive search services.*

- **Anticipate details** the reader will need in order to process or act on your request.

- **Strike a tone that is right for your reader**—firm but still respectful. Don't apologize or be afraid to ask for something to which you are entitled, but at the same time don't browbeat the reader to do as you say. Show courtesy, especially in an externally directed message.

- **Keep minor points to a minimum.** Unnecessary information blunts the impact of your request. Edit out unrelated facts. If you want to give your reader additional information, enclose supporting documents.

- **Use a layout that focuses attention on your request.** Incorporate bulleted or numbered lists, surround specifics with white space, and boldface or italicize key points for emphasis.

- **Close in a courteous and efficient way.** Focus on the action you want the reader to take and use positive language to communicate goodwill and show appreciation. Avoid closing with canned expressions, such as *Thanking you in advance,* or ones that make your request sound unfocused, such as *Thank you for any information you can provide.* Opt for something that is fresh and relevant to your particular message.

ASKING FOR INFORMATION, CREDIT, AND ACTION

An effective request for information or action lets the reader know at the beginning exactly what is required, what should be done, or what compliance you seek. A common fault of information and action requests is that they are either too abrupt and demanding or too apologetic and deferential, so aim for a tone that is firm yet still polite. To elicit as much relevant information as possible, pose opened-ended questions (ones impossible to answer with a simple *yes* or *no*). If appropriate, explain how you will use the information you obtain or whom it may benefit. If the reader is expected

FIGURE 6.1   INEFFECTIVE Information Request (extract)

Dear Ms. O'Connor:

Begins with an explanation rather than a direct request →

The recent relocation of our company offices to smaller premises has forced us to consider off-site document storage and upgrades to our filing and records system. I have been entrusted with the important task of researching options and finding a solution to our current document storage and retrieval crisis. Your company was recommended to us by one of our suppliers, but we could not locate your website, hence the necessity of writing to you now. I hope you will be able to answer some questions I have about the services you provide.

Rambling second paragraph makes it difficult to identify individual questions →

Our chief interest is cost. We are interested in finding the safest and most cost-effective way to store documents that have been on file more than two years. First of all, we need to know how expensive your services are. Perhaps you offer discounts based on volume. Can we retrieve documents immediately or would it take several days to process a request? What sort of security does your company guarantee for our most confidential documents? We also need to know what sort of support you provide your customers. We have many other questions, but this should be enough to give us a rough idea of whether your company is the right fit for us. What other services do you offer?

Closing makes request less specific, inviting response not tailored to the inquiry →

I need any information and recommendations you can provide regarding the storage and retrieval of documents.

Sincerely,

Ross Camrose

Ross Camrose, Manager
Operations

to perform an action, citing the benefits can sometimes encourage a more favourable reply. End with a paragraph—even a short sentence—specific to the reader and the request. Make a point of refocusing your request, end-dating it if necessary and expressing appreciation for compliance.

ORDER REQUESTS

order request a request for merchandise that includes a purchase authorization and shipping instructions.

You may decide to write an order request for merchandise (1) when it isn't possible to order merchandise by catalogue order form, telephone, fax, or through a website, or (2) when you need a record of having placed an order. This type of letter should supply all details needed for the order to be filled: specific product names and descriptions, quantities, order numbers, units and total prices, desired method of shipment, preferred

FIGURE 6.2 IMPROVED Information Request

ASHANTI ACCOUNTING ASSOCIATES

418 Grafton Street, Brampton, ON N9C 2G8

905-681-2045

January 5, 2010

Ms. Melanie O'Connor, Manager
Simplified Document Storage Services
1100 Terra Cotta Road
Toronto, ON M5W 1Z4

Dear Ms. O'Connor:

Please answer the following questions regarding the document storage and
retrieval services your company provides.

1. What are your billing rates?
2. Are discounts based on volume available?
3. How long does it take to process a document retrieval request?
4. Would the security of our documents, especially our most confidential
    ones, be guaranteed?
5. What support do you provide to your customers?

Our company must find a suitable document storage solution before June 30,
when we will move to smaller premises while our permanent offices undergo
a year-long renovation. We would appreciate answers to these questions and
any other information you can provide on your document services by May 15.

Sincerely,

Sasha Mistry

Sasha Mistry
Manager, Operations

Opens with a direct request for information in the form of a summary statement

Phrases questions in parallel form and organizes them in an easy-to-read list

Makes reason for the request secondary to the request itself

Refocuses request at the end, bettering the chances of obtaining quality information

End-dates request to motivate prompt response

FIGURE 6.3 Sample Order Request (in simplified style)

Subject line identifies purpose of the message and emphasizes shipping instructions

Simplified style uses no salutation

Opening authorizes purchase and indicates method of shipment

Itemized list clearly identifies and quantifies order purchase

Preferred method of payment included with special instructions

No complimentary close is used in simplified style letters

ASHANTI ACCOUNTING ASSOCIATES

418 Grafton Street, Brampton, ON N9C 2G8

January 5, 2010

Practically Everything Office Supply
6315 Haliburton Boulevard
Oshawa, ON L4K 2M9

RE: RUSH PURCHASE ORDER

Please send by overnight courier the following items from your Fall 2009 catalogue.

Quantity	Catalogue Number	Description	Price
10	X88900	Deluxe staplers	$215.00
15	X82270	Tape dispensers	150.00
50	X85540	60W fluorescent tubes	500.00
		Subtotal	$865.00
		Estimated taxes	60.55
		Shipping	$ 36.00
		Total	$961.55

Our newly expanded tax preparation centre is scheduled to open January 18 and we would appreciate receiving these items promptly in preparation for that event. Please charge this order to our account no. 590 837 428. Should you need to discuss any of these items, please call me at 905-751-2240.

Ashanti Achebe

Ashanti Achebe, CA

FIGURE 6.5 EFFECTIVE Claim

4 Runcible Lane
Winnipeg, MB R6N 1U3
February 5, 2010

Mr. Richard Doherty, Manager
Atlas Fitness
24 Industrial Park Drive
Winnipeg, MB R6R 2Y7

Subject: Refund of Processing and Card Fees for Cancelled Membership 00583 ◄——— Neutral subject line creates focus for message

Dear Mr. Doherty:

Please honour your service agreement and refund the $50 processing fee and ◄——— Opens with appeal to company to stand by its agreements to do the right thing
$19 card fee that were deducted from my account in error following the
cancellation of my membership on January 15.

I first visited Atlas Fitness on January 12 and signed up for a $789 one-year
membership. After touring your facility and consulting fitness experts on ◄——— Provides a coherent, unemotional explanation
January 14, I realized that your programs are geared to advanced fitness
enthusiasts rather than beginners like myself. Because the contract I signed
followed provincial guidelines that allow for a 10-day cooling-off period, I
understood that I would be entitled to a full refund if I backed out of the
agreement within the trial period. Enclosed is a copy of the letter sent to you ◄——— Supplies supporting documentation
by courier on January 15 in which I give official notification of the cancellation
of my membership.

When I received a statement from your company at the end of January, I was
surprised to find that processing and card fees totalling $69 had been charged to
me under the prepaid agreement that is now void. These unauthorized charges
also appeared on my monthly bank statement. According to the cancellation
terms in the contract I signed, members who withdraw within the 10-day period
are not liable for processing and card fees.

I joined Atlas Fitness on the basis of its fine reputation and standards in the ◄——— Ends courteously with request for specific action
fitness industry. I am confident that this billing error can be corrected and that
you will honour my request for a refund without delay.

Sincerely,

Sean Acheson

Sean Acheson

Enc.

Request Letter Checklist

- ☐ Have you phrased the request so the reader views it positively?
- ☐ Is your request straightforward and specific? Have you stated your purpose at the beginning rather than embedding it?
- ☐ If there are multiple requests, are they introduced with a summary statement and then presented individually in a numbered or bulleted list?
- ☐ Have you kept the number of questions to a minimum?
- ☐ Are the questions specific, concise, and phrased so the reader will know immediately what you are seeking?
- ☐ Have you selected details that will help the reader respond more promptly and completely?
- ☐ Have you told the reader how to and by when to respond? Will the reader know what to do? Have you provided contact information?
- ☐ Have you expressed appreciation to the reader for taking the trouble to respond?

Responses

response a message that answers a request or query.

A **response** is usually most effective when it is prompt, informative, and gets to the point. When you can respond favourably to a request for information or action, you should waste no time conveying the news and building goodwill when it is necessary to shape readers' attitudes to policies or business practices. A routine response provides focused details of a decision, answer, or action so readers can make informed decisions, follow through, or know what happens next. Here are a few tips for writing a good response:

- **Determine if you are the right person to handle the response.** If you do not have the knowledge or authority to process a request, refer it to someone who does.
- **Reply as soon as you possibly can.** A prompt response shows that you have taken a request seriously, and that you uphold good service standards. Delays, especially when they are unexplained, test the patience of readers and strain business relationships.
- **Begin with good news or the most important piece of information.** When you can provide what the reader has requested, you should say so in the first sentence.
- **Design your response to be useful.** Anticipate information your reader may need.
- **Respond within your company's ethical guidelines.** Disclose only information your reader has a right to know. Don't share legally sensitive, potentially

contentious details in an effort to make your response absolutely complete. Your letter is, in effect, a legal contract, and all facts and figures contained within it must be accurate.

- **Make your closing work for you.** Avoid clichés and expressions such as "I hope" or "I trust" that might convey a lack of confidence. View your closing remarks as an opportunity to cement relationships if they are in need of reinforcement.

INFORMATION RESPONSE

A response to an inquiry (or information request) should supply requested information first without the need for an introduction. It is unnecessary to confirm the receipt of a request—which is evident from the response itself—or to begin by thanking the reader for having written or having made an **inquiry**. Instead, include words of thanks after the main response or at the end, where they help to build goodwill.

> **inquiry** a message that asks for or seeks information. (An inquiry or information response is a message that supplies information.)

Cluttered:	Thank you for your letter of July 14, received July 17, in which you requested information on day trading.
Better:	Here is a copy of our brochure, *Day Trading: A Beginner's Guide*.

When replying to multiple requests, answer questions in the order they were asked and use headings, bulleted or numbered lists, or other graphic highlighting techniques to arrange information logically for maximum readability. Introduce your answers with a summary statement. Writing a complete and useful response may require you to interpret hard-to-grasp facts and statistics and to anticipate questions your readers still might have once their original inquiries are answered.

FIGURE 6.6 INEFFECTIVE Information Response (extract)

Thank you for your letter of inquiry dated March 12. This is to advise you that we are now in receipt of this message. We are always glad to receive requests of this kind and are happy to assist you with the research for your article on employee recognition programs. I believe your specific questions relate to the impact of our program on employee morale. There are many issues to be addressed, but we will try to answer what questions we can.

Our program is good for our employees. We give rewards—some nominal, others quite substantial—for all kinds of initiatives, including good ideas and leadership. Since the program was established, many employees have seen their good work rewarded.

We are glad to have helped. Good luck with your research.

Annotations:

Opens with obvious information—that the request has been received. Language is stiff and formal

First paragraph padded with irrelevant details

Second paragraph fails to provide concrete details. No evidence is offered to prove why the program is "good"

Closing remarks sound insincere because little information has been offered

FIGURE 6.7 EFFECTIVE Information Response

Opens directly, with a summary statement to introduce the specific answers that follow

Answers each inquiry logically and fully in list form

Builds goodwill with offer of other resources and assistance

Crystal Communications Systems

702 Commercial Drive, Mississauga, ON M8N 2B4 | 905-553-8800 | www.CCS.ca

August 27, 2009

Ms. Maxine Sharpe
Mississauga Dispatch
77 Anglesey Avenue
Mississauga, ON M3N 2P1

Dear Ms. Sharpe:

Here are answers to your questions about our employee recognition program. We are pleased to supply you with details of a program that we believe has been an unqualified success.

1. **Why did we introduce the program?** Employees appreciate being noticed for a job well done and for an idea that saves time or money. Like many organizations today, we realized we could improve business and boost team spirit by giving employees a public pat on the back. Our program was instituted to attract, retain, and motivate people.

2. **For what types of achievements do we give rewards?** We give rewards for effective management, visionary leadership, outstanding creative ideas, and initiatives that lead to cost savings.

3. **What is the scope of our recognition program?** Over the past year, we awarded more than $65,000 to 76 winners, ranging from $450 to an employee who noticed misleading wording in one of our brochures to a top award of $25,000 to a team of eight employees who designed an automated transaction system. Roughly three hundred ideas are submitted each month, with awards given monthly and annually. In the three years of the program's existence, there have been close to four hundred award winners.

4. **Do we anticipate any changes to our program in the future?** Companies such as GGI Technologies Inc. in Markham, Ontario, link rewards to company performance, with engineers receiving public recognition in the form of stock options. Expanding the program to include this type of reward merits our consideration.

Our recognition program is part of our commitment to maintaining a positive work experience for our employees. For additional information on our program, please see the enclosed fact sheet or speak with me at 905-553-8840. We wish you the best for your article and look forward to seeing our company represented in it.

Sincerely,

Audrey Bryant

Audrey Bryant
Vice President

PERSONALIZED FORM LETTERS

Personalized form letters allow you to deliver the same routine information without the inconvenience of keying in a message again and again. Once composed, a message can be sent in response to a recurring situation—as long as the message remains appropriate for the situation for which it is used and answers questions the reader has asked. Word processing software enables you to customize a message so it applies to the reader. Simply merge your document with your mailing list and use variable data fields to insert names, dates, addresses, balances—whatever information is specific to the message. A well-written form letter provides a way to save time and money when sending order acknowledgements, requesting action from customers and suppliers, and supplying answers to frequently asked questions (FAQs).

ORDER ACKNOWLEDGEMENT

The ability to order by telephone, online, or by e-mail has increased expectations for prompt replies to requests for goods and services. Customers are eager to know when and how their transactions will be completed. An effective **order acknowledgement** answers this need with a message that is upbeat, efficient, and as concise as possible. The following template can be modified if you need to send an acknowledgement or confirmation as a matter of courtesy, letting readers know that information or materials have been received.

1. **Acknowledge when and how a shipment will be sent.** There is no need to mention that you received an order. Readers are most interested in knowing that a shipment is on its way. Preface the first paragraph with a personal salutation:

   Dear Mr. Vukovic:

   Your industrial air conditioning unit and invoice forms have been shipped to you by air freight and should arrive by April 2.

2. **Give details of the shipment and convince readers they have made a wise purchase.** As you specify individual items, build confidence in them by referring to their features or confirming their popularity. Mention any irregularities in the order (i.e., products currently unavailable or to be shipped later):

   The air conditioning unit you ordered features a humidity-control mechanism that allows you to regulate the amount of moisture in the air. Customers say that this dehumidifying feature has kept their offices and residences comfortably cool while helping them to reduce their summer energy costs.

3. **Use discretion in pushing additional products.** Gently suggest similar or related products and emphasize their benefits, but avoid aggressive sales tactics—avoid the hard sell:

   For your interest, we are enclosing a price list of Northwind Air Conditioning filter attachments. Customers who have already purchased a customized Northwind Air Conditioning unit from us receive an automatic 20 per cent discount on the purchase of any anti-allergen or aromatherapy attachment.

4. **Close pleasantly.** Express appreciation for the reader's business and include a forward-looking, personalized remark:

   We genuinely appreciate your order, Mr. Proctor, and we look forward to serving you again.

personalized form letter a letter in which the identical message is sent to more than one person; it is adapted to the individual reader with the inclusion of the reader's name, address, and perhaps other information, all of which may be stored in a database and merged with the form letter.

order acknowledgement an informative letter that confirms the details of a merchandise purchase and shipment.

FIGURE 6.8 Sample Form Letter

TOP FOOD

99 St. Elizabeth Avenue East
Toronto, ON M2A 8G5

{Current date}

{Title} {First name} {Last name}
{Street address}
{City}, {Province} {Postal code}

Dear {Title} {Last name}:

We appreciate your interest in the construction of our new Top Food Lakeview superstore. The enclosed brochure highlights the superior shopping experience that begins with our grand opening in June 2010.

Our new 5,500-square-metre facility will be our flagship store, offering customers the best in quality produce and the largest selection of brands in the Greater Toronto Area. Among the many amenities and conveniences you will find are a pharmacy, shoe-repair, hot-meals take-away counter, flower shop, dry cleaners, and coffee bar. Our new location will be equipped with two hundred underground parking spaces and an express checkout.

Please drop by for our open house on {date} to tour the store, sample our newest product lines, and see for yourself the many ways in which we are committed to making your shopping experience enjoyable.

In the meantime, we invite you to continue shopping with us at our nearby Duchess Park location. Shuttle service from our Lakeview store departs daily at {time}.

We appreciate your patronage and look forward to offering you the best at our expanded superstores and our Lakeview location.

Sincerely,

TOP FOOD SUPERSTORES

Suzanne Wong

Suzanne Wong
Customer Service Specialist

Enclosure

MESSAGES CONFIRMING CONTRACTS AND ARRANGEMENTS

A message of confirmation summarizes and clarifies any of the following:

- the terms of an agreement;
- an action or transaction that has taken place, including receipt of an invitation, resumé, or report;
- a decision; or
- arrangements for a future event.

The goal of a confirmation message is to confirm and explain details already established in a related document or to put an oral agreement into writing. A message confirming a contract helps to ensure that the meaning of an agreement is shared by all parties who enter into it, so that there is no confusion between the parties or any misunderstanding that could lead to disputes. Confirmation of an arrangement, including time-specific events such as travel, meetings, conferences, and appointments, keeps planners and participants onside so that they can properly coordinate their activities and ensure that those activities have the outcome they intend.

A message of confirmation has several key functions:

- highlighting the key terms and conditions of a contract, including the offer, obligations, rules for acceptance, and effective date, or the details of arrangement, including date, time, place, the nature or purpose of the event, and the length of the event;
- showing appreciation to the reader for agreeing to participate in or helping to set up the event or arrangement;
- specifying and delegating tasks to be completed and identifying administrative tasks;
- providing clear wording that allows the reader to point out anything in the agreement that is contrary to what he or she thought it should be; and
- setting out actions the reader must take, such as signing and returning an agreement.

Some letter agreements, in which the recipient's signature is required on the letter itself to show agreement to the stated terms, can have the legal effect of contracts, so it is always best to check with a lawyer to determine whether to use a contract or a letter of agreement.

FIGURE 6.9 Sample Letter Confirming Arrangements

Lakeside Polytechnic Institute
School of Communication
270 Albert Street, Toronto, Ontario, Canada M5W 1D9
Tel: 416-920-5990 Fax: 416-920-5940 www.lakeside.ca

December 1, 2009

Mr. Ray Choudhary
Business Development Analyst
Fitzroy-McCormack Technology Ltd.
867 Millway Boulevard
Toronto, Ontario M9W 1E6

Dear Mr. Choudhary,

Thank you for agreeing to take part in "Communicating for Engineering Success: Industry Standards, Practices, and Licensing," a five-member panel session to take place at Lakeside Polytechnic, S353 Richardson Hall, on Wednesday, January 6, from 10:00 a.m. to 12:00 p.m.

As we discussed over the telephone this morning, this session will introduce the 350 undergraduate students enrolled in "Perspectives in Technical Communication" to Professional Engineers of Ontario's licensing standards and collaborative approaches to engineering communication. This letter confirms that you will speak for 20 minutes, beginning at 10:30 a.m., on the topic "Globalized Communications in the Engineering Industry." A full program for the event is attached.

Please arrive at the southeast entrance to Richardson Hall, 80 Temple Street, by 9:50 a.m. so that we may escort you to the lecture hall and set up your technology for you. The hall is equipped with a podium and full visual and sound systems for the screening of PowerPoint presentations and videos.

A luncheon for all participants will follow at 12:30 p.m. at Verdi's Restaurant, located at 54 Elm Street, between Dundas and Gerrard Streets.

I am enclosing a map of the Lakeside Polytechnic campus and a parking voucher redeemable at any of the Lakeside campus parkades. I look forward to meeting you in person on January 6.

Sincerely,

Dima Al Said

Dima Al Said
Coordinator, School of Communication

CLAIMS ADJUSTMENT

Consumer protection laws and the need to retain customers prompt most businesses to grant claims and make swift adjustments in all but those cases where claims are fraudulent. Claimants typically want to learn the good news about a refund, replacement, or other compensation at the beginning of your message. From the start, a claim response rights a wrong resulting from poor service, poor product performance, or a billing error. Its purpose is threefold: (1) to inform a customer that her claim has been successful, (2) to show how you intend to rectify the problem or resolve the complaint, and (3) to repair customer relations, rebuild goodwill, and restore confidence. A prompt response that reflects a thorough investigation of the problem and sounds happy about making the adjustment helps to repair the relationship with the customer and promote favourable attitudes to your company. A **claim adjustment** is damage control in action. The reader should be left with a sense of having been dealt with fairly—and have every reason to want to do business with your company again.

> **claim adjustment**
> a response to a claim letter telling the customer what your company intends to do to correct the problem.

1. **Grant the adjustment.** Open with news of the favourable adjustment, using positive and reader-focused language. Apologize for any significant error or problem that has cost the reader time or money. Avoid alibis, excuses, and especially admissions of negligence that could be used against your company in court.

2. **Explain how you intend to make the adjustment.** Give details of how you will comply—worded carefully to take into account legal issues and company policy. Consider how the language you use will affect the reader. Acknowledge that customer feedback, like the kind you just received, helps your company improve its

FIGURE 6.10 INEFFECTIVE Claim Response (extract)

Dear Alexis:

The failure of our sales staff to honour our famous price-matching policy is a common occurrence. Nevertheless, we are extremely sorry for the inconvenience you must have suffered when you requested a discount at our Northridge Mall outlet. As a result of past abuses of this policy, our staff is sometimes over-scrupulous in demanding proof of our competitors' retail prices. Apparently, the advertisement you presented did not seem to meet standards that would qualify you for an in-store discount.

Despite the weakness of your claim—and because we want to keep you satisfied—we will allow you a refund of the price difference in this case. Incidentally, if you are in the market for a printer capable of meeting the needs of your small business, may we suggest the HP Deskjet 5150.

Let us say again how very sorry we are for this problem. We sincerely hope it doesn't happen again.

- Addresses claimant on a first-name basis—too personal
- Begins with admission of negligence—pointing to a chronic problem that has gone unchecked
- Fails to reveal good news immediately
- Questions the validity of the claim and sounds grudging in granting the claim
- Introduces promotional information at the wrong time
- Apologizes excessively and ends with a reminder of difficulty

products and service. Identify how you will prevent a recurrence of the problem, but do not admit fault or liability.

3. **Close pleasantly.** Don't remind the reader of the problem or refer to unpleasantness. Instead, look forward to a continuing business relationship and build on the goodwill your explanation has already helped to re-establish.

FIGURE 6.11 **EFFECTIVE** Claim Response

Announces good news immediately

Regains customer's confidence with positive language and an explanation of the claim investigation, resulting improvements, and claim settlement

Closes by conveying respect for the reader and expressing confidence in a renewed business relationship

Computer Central Ltd.

124 Queen Street East, Suite 601
Toronto, ON M5R 2T8
1-888-764-3333
www.computer_central.com

January 11, 2006

Ms. Amelia Sorensen
525 Gosling Lane
Toronto, ON M4G 2K7

Subject: Enclosed Price-Matching Refund

Dear Ms. Sorensen:

The enclosed cheque for $158.85 demonstrates our commitment to our price-matching policy and our desire to offer our customers quality brand-name products at the lowest possible prices.

When we received your letter, we immediately contacted our store managers and asked them to review our price-matching policy with their sales associates. A few of our sales trainees, it seems, were not fully acquainted with our refund requirements, so we instituted a special training session and redesigned this portion of our website to make it easier for both our employees and our customers to find this information. We invite you to have a look the next time you visit us at www.computercentral.ca.

According to our guidelines, the advertisement you presented at the point of purchase should have immediately qualified you for a discount. We are of course happy to meet Computer Country's price of $2,199 for an Apatel XG package.

Please accept the enclosed cheque and our appreciation for bringing this important matter to our attention. We look forward to offering you continued discount pricing in the future.

Sincerely,

Meredith Anderson

Meredith Anderson
Manager, Customer Service

Enc.

Checklist for Response Letters

- [ ] Do you have the knowledge and authorization to handle the response?

- [ ] If you are the right person to answer a request, have you responded as promptly as possible?

- [ ] If a request was referred to you to answer, have you notified the letter writer that the request has been forwarded? Does the first paragraph clearly state why someone else—not the original addressee—is answering the inquiry?

- [ ] Does the first paragraph give the good news or answer the reader's most important question?

- [ ] Is your response complete enough to meet the reader's needs? Have clarifying details been included?

- [ ] Have you disclosed only what the reader has a right to know?

- [ ] As much as possible, have you answered questions in the order they were asked?

- [ ] As required, have you shaped the reader's attitude to the information or the organization by citing reader benefits?

- [ ] Does your message reflect goodwill and good business practices?

Goodwill Messages

The saying "it's the thought that counts" is true of **goodwill messages**. They show you are thinking of the reader and care about more than just your profit margin. Goodwill messages aren't all business—they have a social function. They can say "thank you" to readers or show that you share their sorrow in loss and happiness in personal milestones and achievements. With just a few words, they satisfy basic human needs and recognize what it is to be human, even in the workplace. Goodwill messages put you in a positive light, enhance your visibility, and make people more willing to help you in the future. Sending them is not so much a matter of business but of good business etiquette. Such messages have the power to improve and solidify relationships with customers and co-workers. To be effective, goodwill messages should be

> **goodwill message** a message that enhances the value of a business beyond its tangible assets by creating a bond of friendship and establishing trust and mutual understanding between the writer and recipient.

1. **Personal.** Specific details make the difference between an impersonal, store-bought greeting and a message that is meaningful because it is individualized. Handwritten messages can convey genuine warmth better than computer-generated ones, although letters set on company letterhead are always acceptable. Address the reader by first name if you know the person well.

2. **Prompt.** Send goodwill messages immediately, while the news and events that inspired them are still fresh in the reader's memory. The longer you wait, the less it can seem that you care.

3. **Spontaneous, short, and sincere.** Goodwill messages don't have to be long, but they should sound sincere, as though you truly mean what you say. Avoid canned, clichéd expressions that suggest you are going through the motions just to win favour. Instead, imagine what your reader would like to hear.

THANK-YOU LETTERS

thank-you letter (or **letter of appreciation**) a message thanking someone for helping you, extending hospitality to you, or doing business with your company.

If you or your company has benefited from what another person or organization has provided, it is important to express your gratitude—for hospitality, business, a gift, or a favour—with a brief but sincere letter. A good **thank-you letter** doesn't overplay or

FIGURE 6.12 Appreciation for Business

Opening identifies relationship and length of association and expresses gratitude

Reminds recipient of pledge to customer service and service details and makes this relevant by use of you-attitude

Closes with personalized gratitude and forward-looking statement

Highland Cleaning Services

165 Albany Avenue, Halifax, NS B2H 6B1
(902) 555-1717
www.HCS.ca

March 20, 2009

Mr. Henry Sutherland, Office Manager
Carlyle Information Systems
471 Water Street, Suite 400
Halifax, NS B2P 4C7

Dear Mr. Sutherland:

Providing cleaning and maintenance services to your corporate headquarters has been our pleasure for the past 10 years, and we sincerely appreciate your business.

With a new year ahead, you can continue to rely on us for careful, fully bonded and insured cleaning services guaranteed to keep your premises spotless. Our specialized 24-hour janitorial services come with our commitment to quality, affordability, and customer satisfaction. As a long-time customer, you know how cost-effective it is to outsource commercial office maintenance and post-construction cleanup.

Thank you for the confidence you have shown in our company. We look forward to serving you for many years to come.

Sincerely,

Susan MacDonald

Susan MacDonald
President

underplay expressions of gratitude. Its words of thanks are honest and meaningful—not just part of a hollow exercise. Skip generic statements and canned phrases and instead focus on the reader.

1. **Thank the reader for what she has done, given, or provided.** Recall what it consisted of by identifying the situation or your purpose in writing.

2. **Include a few details.** Show that you are not just standing on formality. Detail the benefits you derived and why you are grateful. If you are expressing thanks for hospitality, compliment your host on the food, company, or surroundings. If you are sending thanks for a gift, tell why you appreciate it and how you will use it. Express thanks for a favour by stating plainly what the favour means to you.

3. **Close with goodwill or a forward-looking remark.** Consider ending with a compliment, further thanks, or good wishes.

FIGURE 6.13 Appreciation for Hospitality

Fiona Dubois
14½ Brock Street
Guelph, Ontario
N2Y 2K9

May 15, 2009

Josephine Camarelli
128 Maplewood Avenue
Guelph, ON N1L 6V4

Dear Josephine:

Paul and I want you to know how much we enjoyed the dinner you hosted for apprentice CAs last Saturday. The evening was a welcome break from our exam preparations, and we were especially touched by the warm reception you gave us. Your superb Italian cookery and great dinnertime conversation definitely succeeded in taking our minds off our studies for the entire evening, just as you had planned.

We are grateful for your kind hospitality and the chance to get to know you better. Thank you again for making the evening such a special one.

Yours truly,

Fiona

Handwritten on personal stationery

Opening identifies the situation and describes it, using personalized details enhanced by you-attitude

Closing expresses warm appreciation for hospitality

FIGURE 6.14 Appreciation for Service or Favour

4400–27 Pacific Way
Victoria, BC V6W 2L7
November 30, 2009

Ms. Naomi Perkins, Reference Librarian
Simon Andrews Memorial Library
Blackstone University
Victoria, BC V9C 0Z9

Dear Ms. Perkins:

Opening thanks the recipient for what she provided → We appreciated the chance to learn about your impressive collection of business-related books, periodicals, and electronic resources when we toured your library last week.

Next paragraph specifically recalls what the service/favour consisted of → The visit was the highlight of our introductory business course and gave us much insight into the kinds of resources available to us as we pursue more specialized studies. Your explanation of how to use the Information Commons Resource Centre left us with an in-depth understanding of how to locate and retrieve the types of materials we are most likely to need. We especially appreciated your thorough introduction to the business-related e-journals and your expert demonstration of how to use the online databases. These research tools will be

Tells recipient of benefit derived from service/favour → very helpful to us in our business studies. We very much appreciated learning about the special corporate partnerships sponsored by your library and look forward to tapping into this key resource for future research projects. Your library is a state-of-the-art facility.

Closes with final expression of appreciation → We are very grateful for the care you took in answering our questions and organizing a tour geared to our academic interests. Under your guidance, we are now well prepared to make the best possible use of the resources in your library. On behalf of our entire group, I thank you.

Sincerely yours,

Aaron Grey

Aaron Grey

LETTER OF CONGRATULATIONS

letter of congratulations
a message conveying pleasure at someone's happiness or good wishes on someone's accomplishment.

A **letter of congratulations** expresses happiness at a reader's good fortune. Because your good wishes should seem genuine, it is important to avoid language that might sound patronizing—such as a put-down masquerading as praise (e.g., *it seems only yesterday you were a struggling young writer from the wilds of Yukon, hungry for that elusive byline*)— or anything to suggest an honour isn't deserved. Show that you share in the reader's

FIGURE 6.15 Letter of Congratulations

Krasner and Associates Advertising Agency

1025 Wilson Drive
Winnipeg, MB R2E 0G3
(204) 555-3376 telephone
(204) 555-3388 fax
www.Krasner.ca

August 15, 2009

Vincent Martin
VinMart Advertisements
437 Sinclair Street
Winnipeg, MB R2E 2F6

Dear Vincent:

Your Creativity in Advertising Award is long overdue and well deserved. I can think of few individuals who have contributed as much as you have to the advertising industry. With their unique combination of humour and brand enhancement, the campaigns you spearheaded always reflected the ingenuity for which you are now being recognized. Members of the department join me in expressing our heartiest congratulations upon your achievement.   ◄——— Commends recipient on well-deserved honour, using its exact title, and reflects on its meaning and the activities that merited it

You were greatly missed when you left to establish your own agency, but we take much pleasure in offering our good wishes for your continued success.   ◄——— Closing reiterates personal good wishes

Cordially,

Sonia Vargas

Sonia Vargas
Vice President, Creative Division

---

happiness by using words that correspond to the occasion—not ones that sound falsely effusive or hollow.

LETTER OF SYMPATHY

Responding to loss is always difficult. A **letter of sympathy** lets your reader know you care and are ready to offer help and support, if required. The message should be hand-written and sent as soon as possible after you learn of the bereavement. Your purpose in writing is to express your sadness at learning of the reader's loss and to offer sympathy. Your first sentence should refer to the loss—and your reaction to it—in a tactful and

letter of sympathy (or **condolence**) a message expressing sadness at someone's bereavement and offering words of comfort.

FIGURE 6.16 Letter of Sympathy

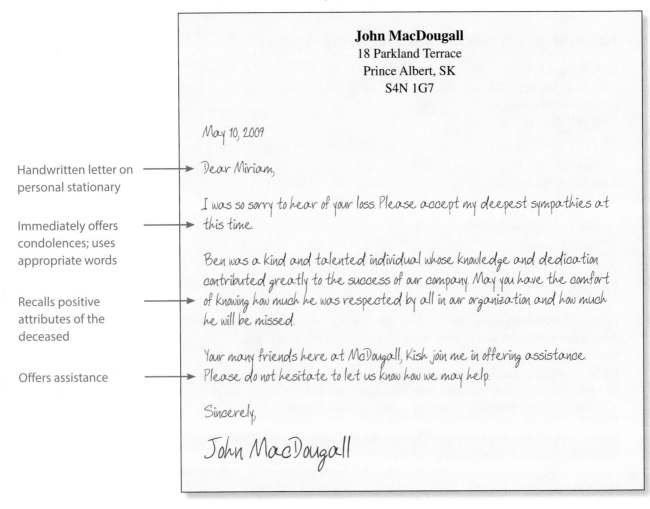

Handwritten letter on personal stationary

Immediately offers condolences; uses appropriate words

Recalls positive attributes of the deceased

Offers assistance

> **John MacDougall**
> 18 Parkland Terrace
> Prince Albert, SK
> S4N 1G7
>
> May 10, 2009
>
> Dear Miriam,
>
> I was so sorry to hear of your loss. Please accept my deepest sympathies at this time.
>
> Ben was a kind and talented individual whose knowledge and dedication contributed greatly to the success of our company. May you have the comfort of knowing how much he was respected by all in our organization and how much he will be missed.
>
> Your many friends here at McDougall, Kish join me in offering assistance. Please do not hesitate to let us know how we may help.
>
> Sincerely,
>
> John MacDougall

sensitive way. If you knew the deceased as an acquaintance or personal friend, recall positive attributes for which that person will be remembered. Offer something you can do—personal help or business-related assistance. The reader may find it difficult to absorb more than a few paragraphs, so keep the message brief and its sentiments sincere. After all, a sympathy letter should be a source of comfort and support.

informative letters
messages that provide important/relevant information and to which the reader will react neutrally.

Informative Letters

Some types of **informative letters** are neither requests nor responses. Their purpose is explanatory—to simply let readers know what something is or to keep them up to date on changing policies, personnel, or circumstances.

announcement a
message that makes something known about a company policy, event, or personnel change.

ANNOUNCEMENTS

Announcements keep readers informed of company policies, events, and personnel changes—something as simple as a change of address or as major as a company merger.

When the news you have to deliver is positive or neutral, use the direct approach and keep in mind that announcement letters are opportunities not only to pass on information but also to promote goodwill. A typical announcement gives its most important news first and then moves on to clarify details that answer questions readers are likely to have. If there are negatives, make them clear but try to present them as positively as possible. Explain any reader benefits, pointing out how a product, policy, or dealing with the company is good for the reader.

> Goldsmith Press is pleased to announce the appointment of Jocelyn Harwood as its director of marketing. Ms. Harwood has more than ten years' experience in the publishing industry and most recently worked as Assistant Marketing Director at Manticore Publishing. She joins us as we expand our business publishing division and brings with her extensive experience in marketing texts to colleges and universities.

COVER OR TRANSMITTAL LETTERS

A **cover or transmittal letter** accompanies something you are sending to someone inside or outside your organization—a report, proposal, or shipment of materials. It identifies what is being sent and the reason for sending it. The message serves as a permanent record of the exchange of goods or information. The more important your document or material is, the more essential it is to type a transmittal letter to accompany it, rather than try to squeeze handwritten information on a sticky note or piece of paper.

> **cover or transmittal letter** an informative letter that accompanies materials sent from one person to another explaining why those materials are being sent.

1. **Identify what you are sending.** Your phrasing depends on how friendly or formal you want to be:

   - *Enclosed is a proof copy of the article you recently wrote for us.*
   - *I am pleased to enclose a proof copy of the article you recently wrote for us.*
   - *Here is a proof copy of the article you recently wrote for us.*

2. **Briefly summarize the attached document** or describe the enclosed materials. Call attention to sections of particular interest: *"Minding Your Periods and Commas" is a welcome addition to Vol. 7 of* Resources for Business Writers.

3. **Point out important details** that will help the reader understand the document or give instructions on how to use the materials. Have all the items the reader requested been sent as promised? Is the document a draft or a final version? Will other documents or materials be forwarded later? Are there recommendations or findings the reader is likely to support? *The proof copy you received reflects minor editorial changes, including the abbreviation of some subheadings.*

4. **Offer further assistance or tell the reader what happens next.** State what you will do or tell the reader what to do if you expect action or a response. If needed, give a deadline, then close in a friendly or helpful way, perhaps by expressing hope that the material will fulfill its purpose. *Please examine your copy carefully to make sure it contains no typographical or factual errors. If you have changes to suggest, please call my office by May 4 so that we can be begin production on May 6. You should expect to receive a copy of* Resources for Business Writers *in early June.*

INSTRUCTIONAL LETTER/MEMO

Instructions systematically explain a process, activity, or operation and make it doable for the average reader. Directives share important information about what employees must do as a result of changes in regulations, policies, or day-to-day procedures. Anyone who works and works responsibly will read and/or write instructions and directions on a regular basis. Because staying competitive and working responsibly involve keeping pace with new technologies and regulations, instructions and directives help organizations ensure that those technologies can be used effectively and that new rules and procedures are complied with. Written as e-mail messages, memos, or letters, these types of routine messages enable work to be carried out legally, ethically, and safely, without costly mistakes. It is generally understood that readers have no trouble accepting instructions and directives, so use a direct approach when writing instructions.

Without instructions, it would be impossible to learn how to use or operate office equipment, industrial machinery, or any other device; it would be difficult to learn a new task, for example how to use a new software application or hold a web conference. Good instructions display the following characteristics:

- **Clear and accurate**: There should be no ambiguity or guesswork involved in following the instructions. Because instructions are used on the spot and lead to immediate action, there is no margin for error. The logically ordered steps into which a procedure is divided should be obvious and self-explanatory.
- **Precise:** Instructions should include no more and no less than what readers need to know. Attention to phrasing is essential. Positive phrasing, emphasizing what readers should do, rather than negative phrasing, emphasizing what readers must not do, is easier to follow and understand than negative phrasing. Exact times, amounts, and measurements should be used to quantify details.
- **Complete**: Missing or out-of-sequence steps can lead to non-performance, damage, or injury. Any warning or caution should be previewed at the beginning or highlighted in the step to which it applies. Specialized terms must be defined. Effective instructions are self-sufficient, with no need for the reader to seek information from another source.
- **User-friendly**: Audience analysis is important, so take nothing for granted and include basic information that a reader with no knowledge of the procedure would need to achieve the desired result. List-form and numbering make the steps easier to follow and make information easier to find.
- **Action-oriented**: The active voice and imperative (command) mood give instructions clarity and authority. Each step in the sequence should begin with an action verb. Parallel phrasing and similar structures focus attention on the actions readers must take, while transitions (*next, before*) help to mark the time sequence and keep steps in order.

Writing instructions that meet these guidelines involves a systematical approach:

1. Be sure you understand the procedure well enough to explain it, either from having performed it yourself or having seen an expert demonstrate it.
2. Assess your audience's familiarity with the procedure and determine the right levels of technicality and explanation. Think about how and in what circumstances the instructions will be used and whether you must persuade readers that the instructions are beneficial or necessary.

3. Include an introduction, a list of equipment and materials, a description of the steps, and a conclusion.

4. Provide warnings if there is a risk of damage or injury.

5. Explain the purpose (the *what* and the *why*) of the procedure or activity in the introduction.

6. Organize your information in short, manageable numbered steps, each beginning with an action verb and arranged in chronological sequence, or in paragraph form, using transitional words and signal phrases. Note the relationship or impact of one step on another.

7. Use headings to divide long lists of steps into shorter sections.

8. Give warnings, but only when necessary, to show how mistakes can lead to damage or injury. Note the consequences of missing a step or performing a step incorrectly.

9. Use visuals to repeat or reinforce prose descriptions.

10. Put the procedure in perspective by commenting on the result or outcome it is meant to achieve.

Directives let employees know what to do—when an activity or requirement takes effect, what it involves, and where it takes place. Figure 6.17 is an example of a group e-mail message that combines features of directives (telling readers what they must do) and instructions (telling them how they must do it).

FIGURE 6.17 Sample Directive/Instructional Message (E-mail)

Subject:	New Scheduling Procedure for Project Planning Meetings
From:	Ella Hanczyk <ehanczyk@intellasource.ca>
Sent:	Wed., April 14, 2010 10:33 AM
To:	Ross Jacobs <rjacobs@intellasource.ca>, Amil Mohammed <amohammed@intellasource.ca>, Jessica Bourke <jbourke@intellasource.ca>, Amy Chan <achan@intellasource.ca>, Anna-Maria Casareno <mcasareno@intellasource.ca>, Chantal Provost <cprovost@intellasource.ca>

Hello everyone,

To help us in selecting dates and times that can accommodate the most people in attending all future project planning meetings, you will now be asked to vote using the free online scheduling tool Doodle. Doodle makes it easier for groups to find the right day and time for a meeting by enabling users to vote democratically and transparently for their preferred meeting times and activities. No registration or software installation is required.

Please follow these instructions to participate in the poll for the May project planning session:

1) Click on the following link: http://rollins.doodle.com/bwa9jpw5cf2ed9np. (Please note: You do not need to log in at the top.)
2) Scroll down to type your name into the box marked "Your Name".
3) Click the boxes that correspond to the times and dates you are available to attend the next project-planning session.
4) Click the save button.

The poll will be closed on Monday, April 26, and at that point we will choose the date and time that works best for most of you.

Thanks,
Ella

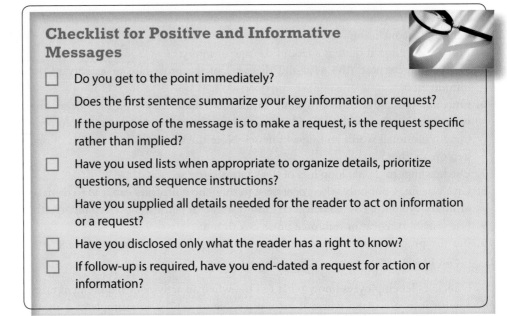

Checklist for Positive and Informative Messages

- ☐ Do you get to the point immediately?
- ☐ Does the first sentence summarize your key information or request?
- ☐ If the purpose of the message is to make a request, is the request specific rather than implied?
- ☐ Have you used lists when appropriate to organize details, prioritize questions, and sequence instructions?
- ☐ Have you supplied all details needed for the reader to act on information or a request?
- ☐ Have you disclosed only what the reader has a right to know?
- ☐ If follow-up is required, have you end-dated a request for action or information?

Letter Formats

The appearance of a document is a reflection of the professional standards of the writer and the organization to which that person belongs. Well-prepared letters are accurately keyboarded and use standardized formats that make them appear attractive, well proportioned, and balanced on the page. They follow standard practices and conventions—many of them centuries old—according to how their elements are arranged and styled.

LETTER BALANCE AND PLACEMENT

A professional-looking letter is centred vertically and horizontally on the page, like a picture formed by blocks of text surrounded by an even frame of blank space. Word-processing software provides templates for correspondence that make it relatively easy to centre a letter on a page. In these programs, the standard default setting for margins—which create the blank frame—is 1 inch (2.54 centimetres), but you may have to adjust your margins to balance and give a fuller appearance to very short letters. For letters of this length (two hundred words or less) increase margins to 1½ inches (3.81 centimetres) and leave four to ten lines blank after the dateline instead of the usual two or three. Letters with "**ragged**," or **unjustified**, **right margins** are easier to read, so turn off the justification feature on your word-processing program. Before you print, check for proportion and make sure your letter is pleasing to the eye by using the preview or full-page feature.

ragged right margins unjustified margins that end unevenly on the right side of the page.

LETTER STYLES AND LAYOUTS

The most common formats or styles for business letters are *full block*, *modified block*, and *simplified*. The choice of letter format is usually determined by the company, but it is important to be familiar with all styles so you may use them accurately when special circumstances call for them.

FIGURE 6.18 Letter Formats

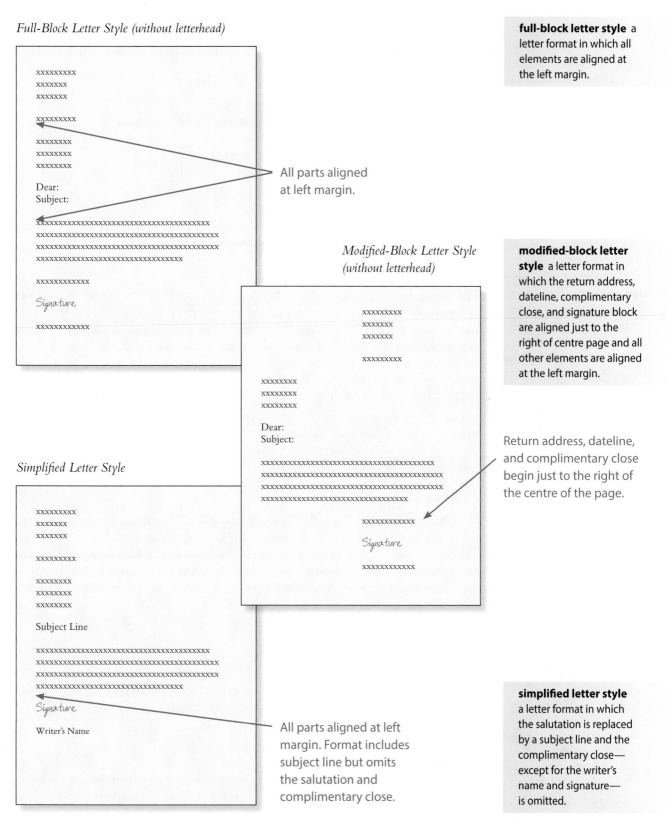

Full-Block Letter Style (without letterhead)

full-block letter style a letter format in which all elements are aligned at the left margin.

All parts aligned at left margin.

Modified-Block Letter Style (without letterhead)

modified-block letter style a letter format in which the return address, dateline, complimentary close, and signature block are aligned just to the right of centre page and all other elements are aligned at the left margin.

Return address, dateline, and complimentary close begin just to the right of the centre of the page.

Simplified Letter Style

All parts aligned at left margin. Format includes subject line but omits the salutation and complimentary close.

simplified letter style a letter format in which the salutation is replaced by a subject line and the complimentary close—except for the writer's name and signature—is omitted.

LETTER ELEMENTS

Professional-looking business letters have multiple parts that are arranged in a conventional sequence. Each part, properly used, has a specific function. For a letter that is balanced and easy to read, double space between elements, single space within:

Standard Elements	**Optional Elements**
Heading/return address	Reference line
Dateline	Delivery or confidential notation
Inside address	Attention line
Salutation	Subject line
Message	Identification initials
Complimentary close	Enclosure notation
Signature block	Copy notation
	Postscript
	Continuation page heading

Letterhead/Return Address

letterhead a printed heading on company stationery, containing the address of an organization or individual, but not the individual's name.

The 8½ by 11–inch stationery used by most businesses is usually printed with a **letterhead** that features the following information: company name, full address, telephone and fax numbers, and, if applicable, a website address and company logo. When a letter extends beyond one page, use a plain sheet, not letterhead, for the subsequent pages. For personal letters—when it isn't possible to use printed letterhead—type your return address immediately above the date, avoiding abbreviations except for the two-letter provincial code. In full-block style letters, the return address is aligned at the left margin and no line of the address should extend beyond the centre of the page. In modified-block style letters, the return address block starts just to the right of the centre of the page and aligns with the complimentary close. Never include your name as part of the return address—it is typed at the end of the letter.

Dateline

dateline identifies the date on which a message was written.

On company letterhead, the **dateline** appears at the left margin two to three lines below the last printed line of the letterhead. Usually, this corresponds to line 13, 5 centimetres from the top of the page. In modified-block style letters, the date appears on the next line after the return address, aligned with it at the centre of the page. The most common date style is as follows: *February 22, 2010* (Month Day, Year). Ordinals (1st, 3rd, 14th, etc.) should not be used, and the months should not be represented as abbreviations. In European correspondence, the dateline assumes the following format: *22 February 2010* (Day Month Year).

Delivery/Confidential Notation

delivery/confidential notation an optional letter element identifying how a message is transmitted and who is authorized to open and read it.

Notations identifying the method of transmission—SPECIAL DELIVERY, FAX TRANSMISSION—and who is authorized to open the letter—PERSONAL, CONFIDENTIAL—are typed in capital letters or italics two lines above the inside address.

Inside Address

inside address a standard letter element supplying the name and full address of the recipient.

The **inside address** identifies the person and/or company to whom the letter is being sent. Placed flush with the left margin, it consists of two to five single-spaced lines that use both upper- and lower-case letters. Depending on the length of the letter, leave anywhere from two to ten blank lines between the dateline and the inside address (two to three is usually standard). No line of the address should end with a comma or extend beyond the centre of the page. If an item is long, continue it on the next line and indent two spaces. Obtain accurate information for the inside address from the addressee's company letterhead or the receiving company's human resources department. Copy this information exactly, spell it correctly, and avoid abbreviations. The first line begins with the person's courtesy title—*Mr.*, *Ms.* (applies to women unless a preference for *Mrs.* or *Miss* is known), *Dr.*, *the Honourable*. Omit the courtesy title only if the addressee's gender is unclear or unknown. A business or professional title—*Chair*, *Treasurer*—may follow the surname on the same line or on the next line if the title is long. Abbreviate the names of provinces and territories (AB, BC, YT, etc.). Leave two spaces, then type the postal code (e.g. Toronto, ON M5S 3K7):

> Ms. Elenor Rutherford
> Director of Sales
> Boditree Inc.
> 2700 Broad Street
> Victoria, BC V9A 7N2

Attention Line

An **attention line** is used when you are directing your correspondence to a department within an organization or to the holder of a particular position rather than to a specific person. It helps to ensure that someone in that department—not necessarily the person to whom the letter is directed—will open the letter and deal with it immediately. An attention line should be placed flush with the left margin, two blank lines above or below the salutation:

> Web Hosting Enterprises
> 50 Rossiter Avenue
> Toronto, ON M4L 3G9
> ATTENTION: MARKETING DIRECTOR

attention line an optional letter element identifying the individual, officer, or department to whom or which the letter should be directed.

Reference Line

This identifies a file number or policy number. It appears two lines above the salutation.

reference line an optional letter element identifying a file or policy number.

Salutation

The **salutation**—a greeting that is used with all letter styles except the simplified style—is typed flush with the left margin one blank line below the inside address or attention line. It can take the following forms:

Dear Mr. Chisolm:	(courtesy title, surname, and colon are standard)
Dear Ms. Vasari:	(courtesy title for women regardless of marital status)
Dear Francesca:	(when you are on a first-name basis with the recipient)

salutation a letter greeting identifying the individual for whom the letter is intended, including the recipient's personal title and surname (e.g., "Dear Ms. Gill").

Dear T. Sutherland:	(when you are unsure of the recipient's gender, use an initial and surname or first name and surname)
Dear Sir or Madam:	(when you don't know the name of the recipient and have used an attention line)
Ladies and Gentlemen:	(when you don't know the names of the recipients and have used an attention line)
Dear Sales Representatives: Dear IT Professionals:	(when addressing a group)
Dear Customer: Dear Colleague:	(when addressing a member of a group)

Generally, the salutation is followed by a colon; in less traditional open-punctuation style, the colon is omitted.

Subject Line

subject line an optional letter element that identifies the content or focus of a message.

The **subject line** can be placed flush left two lines above or two lines below the salutation, depending on your employer's letter-formatting preferences. Written in capital letters, regular font or italics, this optional element briefly identifies the content or focus of a message and rarely exceeds one line. A good subject line is specific and concise, like a well-written headline. It summarizes information that is neutral and highlights news that is good:

SUBJECT: IMPROVED HEALTH BENEFITS PACKAGE

RE: SPEAKERS FOR RETIREMENT PLANNING SERIES

Subject: Request for Updated Schedule

Message Body

The body of the message begins two lines below the salutation. The message is single-spaced within paragraphs and double-spaced between them. It should occupy the middle of the page, not the top or bottom. With the exception of modified-block style, which allows you the option of indenting paragraphs, begin each new paragraph at the left margin.

Complimentary Close

complimentary close the word of formal closing (often "Sincerely") after the body of the letter and before the signature.

Typed two lines below the last line of the letter, the ending *Sincerely* (followed by a comma) is standard. Some employers prefer *Yours sincerely* or *Yours truly*. Less formal expressions, such as *Cordially*, *Best wishes*, and *Regards*, are also common, especially if the recipient is a friend. Only the first letter of a complimentary close is capitalized. The simplified style letter omits the **complimentary close**. Generally, the complimentary close is followed by a comma, but this punctuation is omitted in open-punctuation style.

Signature Block

After the complimentary close, leave four blank lines (room for your signature) and type your name. Your title may appear on the same line, separated from your name by a comma, or be placed on the next line. Add a courtesy title in parentheses before your name if it is not readily distinguishable as male or female:

Sincerely,   Yours truly,   Sincerely,

Pat Quinn   *Harry Takamoto*   *Sue Roth*

PL INDUSTRIES   Harry Takamoto,   Sue Roth, Manager
                                  Project Manager   Technical Services

(Ms.) Pat Quinn
Executive Assistant

> **signature block** includes the writer's name, title, and organization in a neatly formatted arrangement.

Identification Initials

Capitalized initials, followed by a colon, indicate who wrote the letter; lower-case initials indicate who keyed it. When a personal signature is shown in the signature block, the writer's initials are omitted:

> GB: hw

> hw

> **identification initials** indicate the writer (capital letters) and typist (lower-case letters) of a message.

Enclosure Notation

An **enclosure notation** (abbreviated *Enc.* or *Encs.* or spelled out as *Enclosure* or *Enclosures*) indicates enclosed or attached material—a brochure, invoice, article, etc.—accompanying a letter. It may tell the reader something about the enclosed item(s) or specify the number of enclosures:

> Enclosure: Claim Form 523

> Enclosures (3)

> **enclosure notation** indicates enclosed or attached material that accompanies a document.

Copy Notation

A **copy notation** (*c* or *cc*) indicates that copies of the letter have been sent to individuals other than the addressee. When several individuals receive the letter, their names are stacked one on top of the other:

> c   R. Pettigrew
>   J. Espinet

> **copy notation** indicates that copies of a letter have been sent to individuals other than the addressee.

Continuation Page Heading

At least three lines of the message should be carried over to any continuation sheet. Each new sheet should have a header with the recipient's name, the page number, and the date. This information can go in the upper left-hand corner or can run across the page 1.25 to 2.5 centimetres below the top edge.

> **continuation page heading** identifies the second and succeeding pages of a letter with a heading that includes the name of the addressee, date, and page number.

FIGURE 6.19 Putting the Elements Together

The following full-block style information-request letter features many of the elements just mentioned.

Letterhead

Align elements at left margin (2.5 cm)

Dateline (line thirteen, or two to three lines below letterhead)

Inside address (two to ten blank lines below dateline)

Salutation

Double spacing between paragraphs

Signature block (identifies author and title)

Identification initials (indicate author and typist)

3–6 spaces at the bottom of the page

Magnatel

465 Hastings Avenue, Hamilton, ON L9S 4L3
(905) 743-8129 • www.magnatel.ca

January 27, 2010

Ms. Justine Ducette, Manager
Canadienne Language School
533 Rue St. Germaine
Quebec City, QC G1C 2H4

Dear Ms. Ducette:

Can the Frontenac Language School provide intensive language training and accommodations for 20 Magnatel employees from April 18 through April 22?

Your language school was recommended by several of our suppliers. Our company is currently expanding its operations in Quebec and New Brunswick and must be able to ensure that our regional sales and customer service representatives possess a high level of speaking, reading, and writing proficiency in French. Employees who have been selected for our Quebec and New Brunswick operations have a minimum six years of French-language training but require a "refresher" so they may communicate with confidence. Will you please answer the following questions regarding the Frontenac Language School.

- Do you offer pre-course assessments to determine each student's conversational fluency?
- Do you have a one-on-one program for students requiring more intensive training?
- Can you adapt your training sessions to help our group acquire the technical and business terminology they will need to deliver quality service to our French-speaking customers?
- If you cannot provide accommodations for all group members, can you recommend hotels and guesthouses located nearby?

I would be grateful for answers to these questions by February 15. Our Quebec operations committee meets at the end of February to finalize our start-up details.

Sincerely,

Harry Ferguson

Harry Ferguson
Manager, Human Resources

HF:sr

ADDRESSING ENVELOPES

Follow Canada Post guidelines for formatting envelopes:

- On envelopes without a pre-printed return address, the return address should be formatted in the same way as the destination address and located in the upper left-hand corner.
- In both the return address and the address block, the municipality, province or territory, and postal code should appear on the same line.
- Postal codes should be printed in uppercase, and the first three elements should be separated from the last three by one space.
- Affix the stamp(s) in the upper right-hand corner.

WORKSHOPS AND DISCUSSION FORUMS

1. **Letter of Congratulations.** What mistakes does the writer of the following letter make? How would you feel if you received this message?

Dear Imogen:

Talk about overnight success! I find it hard to believe that someone who has been with the company for as little time as you have could rise through the ranks so quickly, putting us all to shame. It seems that only yesterday you were our eager office assistant, fetching us coffee from the local Starbucks. Well, times have changed—and it couldn't have happened to a nicer person. No doubt your pleasant smile and excellent telephone manner will help you with the many challenges that lie ahead in your new job as assistant district manager. I would like to know what a person has to do to climb the corporate ladder as fast as you have.

Cheers,

Larry, et. al.

Larry and the gang

2. **Letter Style.** Rewrite the following full-block style letter in simplified style. When would a simplified style be appropriate?

Salmon Run Tackle and Fishing Supply
4 Timberline Avenue
Carlyle, BC W9G 2B1

July 28, 2009

North by Northwest Supply
28 Timberline Avenue
Prince George, BC W5L 2K9

ATTENTION ORDER DEPARTMENT SPECIALIST

Ladies and Gentlemen:

SUBJECT: ORDER FOR GAS GENERATOR

Enclosed is a cheque for $1,682.98 in payment for the Deluxe Genron Gas Generator, item #7753 in your Fall 2008 catalogue.

As arranged, I will pick up this item at your Selkirk Road service depot when I am in Prince George on August 5.

Please enclose an updated price list with my order.

Sincerely,

Brad Hutchinson

Brad Hutchinson

Enc.

Phone: 304-590-8831   salmonrun@ccre.net   Fax: 304-590-8824

3. **Applying the Direct Approach.** Rearrange paragraphs in the following extract from a request letter according to the direct–approach writing plan.

My supervisor at KDS Laboratories has asked me to investigate car-fleet leasing options. Our sales representatives require reliable, low-maintenance, fuel-efficient sedans for servicing their territories throughout Ontario and Quebec. Our current lease expires August 31. We will require twenty vehicles.

I would be grateful for answers to these questions by July 15, when our transportation committee must meet to decide.

Please answer the following questions about car leasing options and vehicle features:

1.   What leasing packages does your dealership offer?

2.   What level of servicing do you provide?

3.   Do you offer flexible leasing payments?

4.   What model sedan provides the greatest fuel economy?

4. **Analyzing a Request.** How well does the following extract meet the guidelines for an information request? How easy would it be to respond to this inquiry?

What you can tell me about your banquet facilities? A few weeks ago, my boss asked me to find out as much as I could about upscale banquet facilities in the GTA. Our company is hosting an event to celebrate its twentieth anniversary. We expect that the event will be held the week of June 6–10, although June 10 is our preferred date. Any other week would be unsuitable. Of course, we are only interested in booking a facility if it is air-conditioned. Is your banquet hall air-conditioned? We anticipate having two hundred guests. Do you have a banquet room that would accommodate two hundred guests? I would also like to know if your banquet centre is wheelchair-accessible. Because our workforce is quite diversified, we would like to offer menu selections that appeal to many different tastes. Do you offer international menus? Thank you for any information you can provide.

5. **Revising an Announcement for Clarity.** What common errors make the message below ineffective? Focusing on clarity, rewrite the following announcement—a call for papers for an upcoming business conference.

Announcement

WRITE ON BUSINESS COMMUNICATIONS CONFERENCE

The National Write On Association herewith wishes to inform you that it is seeking presentations concerning the impact of electronic communication on business writing efforts for its annual national conference scheduled for March 18th to 21st, 2010, in Halifax, Nova Scotia.

Joining the NWOA in sponsoring the conference are the Canadian Jargon Association, the National Society for the Prevention of Obfuscation, the Stop Flaming Now League, and the Canadian Anti-Spam Federation. The last conference, held in 2008 under the sponsorship of the National Save the Comma Society, drew over 750 participants from every province with the exception of PEI and saw representation from various branches of industry, business, government, academia, industry, and business from across the country.

Conference coordinators desire presentations that deal with documented cases histories of e-mail abuse in business and industry. According to Dr. Lyle Mudd, the NWOA executive coordinator, "We are most interested in the impact of e-mail on standards of grammar and the corporate measures that have been implemented to redress existing problems. We are also seeking presentations on acceptable e-mail length and the introduction of corporate e-mail guidelines." Members wishing to give presentations on any of the aforementioned topics are advised to submit a two-hundred-and-fifty (250) word proposal.

All proposals must be postmarked no later than November 1, 2009, and directed to the attention of Dr. Lyle Mudd, NWOA Executive, St. Sebastian University, Halifax, NS D4A 2E1.

---

6. **Arranging Letter Elements.** Retype the following letter using your computer software's letter wizard and note the resulting changes in style and formatting.

Subject: Summer Outreach Tours

FAX TRANSMISSION

July 15, 2009
Mr. Jordan Fisher, Marketing Director
College Life Tours
1515 Aubrey Avenue
Toronto, ON M5S 2K1

18 Belgrave Street
Toronto, ON M9M 3H7

Dear Mr. Jordan Fisher:

Please answer the following questions about the student outreach tour packages offered by your company this summer.

1. Can you recommend a tour of Central America that combines volunteer work with adventure vacationing?

2. Could such a tour accommodate a group of five travellers in June or July?

3. What is the approximate cost per person for a three-week package?

Along with a group of friends, I plan to tour Central America this summer. While there, my friends and I would like to contribute what we can to the communities we visit. We are therefore looking for a tour that would allow us to do volunteer work, similar to our past work for Habitat for Humanity, while also giving us the chance to pursue extreme sports and explore some of region's best-known ecological preserves.

I would appreciate answers to these questions by March 30, when my friends and I will meet to discuss our summer travel destination.

Yours very sincerely,

Justin Littleton

Justin Littleton

WRITING IMPROVEMENT EXERCISES

1. **Writing Subject Lines:** Below are opening sentences from request and response messages. Write a concise and specific subject line that corresponds to each.

   a) The enclosed cheque for $365 represents our quality commitment to our customers and our desire to earn their confidence.

   b) Please answer the following questions about the role of mediation service companies in the labour–management relationship. I am writing an article on this topic for *Business Weekly*.

   c) Here are answers to your questions about our corporate gift services.

2. **Itemizing Parts of a Request or Response:** The following request has several parts. Revise the message using a list to improve readability.

   > Please answer the following questions about your new line of high-nutrition sports snacks.
   >
   > First, I would like to know if individual food items are vacuum sealed. I conduct guided cycling tours of Prince Edward County and I need assurances that the products I supply to tour members will be fresh and appetizing, even at the end of a hot summer day. How long do products remain fresh after they have been opened? Is dietary information for each item printed on the packaging? I am also interested in finding out if you have any gluten-free and organic products. And are your snacks suitable for diabetics and people with food allergies? Of course, I would like to sample products from your new line before I commit to purchasing them. Can you send me some samples to try? I already have your price list.
   >
   > As an operator of tours for experienced cycling enthusiasts, I would like to offer complimentary premium sports snacks on my one- and two-day excursions.
   >
   > I would appreciate answers—in fact all the information you can provide—by April 15, when our tour planning committee meets to finalize purchasing details.

3. **Direct-Approach Openings:** Revise the following openings to make them direct, professional, and specific.

   a) Hello! My name is Wayne Dumont. I am a junior accountant at Hammond Financial and I have a number of questions for you to answer. Let me first explain that all of these questions have to do with import and excise taxes.

   b) It is my pleasure and privilege to write to you today to ask about your retirement planning education programs. I am most interested in finding out if your educational package includes a focus section on financial planning for early retirement.

   c) Give me any information you can on your conference-hosting services. I need to know how much it costs to hold a half-day conference for thirty people at your conference facility.

   d) We always appreciate hearing from customers who have experienced problems with products under warranty and have the courage to ask for a refund. While your claim seems valid, and there doesn't seem to be a strong reason why we should not do as you request, let me first explain company policy on this issue.

   e) In response to your letter of inquiry, received September 29, in which you asked about the availability of price discounts on our web hosting services, I am pleased to tell you that the answer is yes.

   f) Pursuant to your letter dated August 30, we would like to advise you that you can take the PowerPoint projector with which you have apparently had so much trouble to Prism Servicing for inspection and, if necessary, free repair.

4. **Letter Closings:** Rewrite the following closings to make them more specific and polite.

   a) Please get back to me soon. My boss really needs this information and I don't want to get into trouble for missing our April 5 deadline.

   b) Because we want to keep you satisfied and because we would like to resolve this problem once and for all, we are offering you a complimentary repair on your automatic door. We hope the inconvenience and minor injuries your customers experienced as a result of our malfunctioning door will not discourage you from doing business with us in the future.

c) I trust that I have provided the information you require. If you need information in the future, I recommend that you direct your inquiry to my assistant, who has time to handle minor requests of this kind.

CASE STUDY EXERCISES

1. **Transmittal Letter:** As Liam Kelly, president of an architectural firm specializing in historical restoration, you have been asked by real estate developer Jay Delmonico to develop a proposal for restoring a heritage building his company is thinking of buying. Mr. Delmonico plans to convert the four-storey heritage property to a multi-purpose commercial space that will still retain its historical designation. Write a letter of transmittal to accompany the draft version of your proposal.

2. **Information Request:** As Sujata Bhatt, assistant to the vice-president of Excelon Investments, you have been asked to research business etiquette agencies. Your boss, Francesca Franca, has noticed that many of your company's top managers and investment counsellors are conscious of the etiquette gaffes they make while attending corporate functions and formal dinners. Entertaining important clients is customary, but it is a part of the job that many talented senior personnel seem reluctant and at times unwilling to do. Which fork is used for the fish course? Why is it wrong to whistle for the cheque? Ms. Franca would like to ensure that senior personnel know the answers to these questions and, without causing them embarrassment, see to it that company representatives have good table manners and can do business with savvy while eating a meal. She has proposed that an etiquette course be made available to interested personnel. You have heard that Decorum Business Etiquette Services offers a one-day seminar on telephone manners, dining etiquette and interpersonal skills for client retention. You are wondering if Decorum could accommodate a group of up to twenty. Because the social functions your employees attend include casual lunches and formal dinners, you would also like to know if students have the opportunity to test their new skills in a supervised restaurant-style meal. Will students, for example, learn to use each piece of cutlery properly? You would prefer that the training take place within the next three weeks because senior employees are set to attend the premier fundraising dinner next month, an event for which Ms. Franca has already booked two $10,000 tables.

3. **Order Request:** Rewrite the following order request so that details of each item are formatted for quick-and-easy reference. Clearly indicate the products you intend to buy, your planned method of payment, and how you would like your order shipped. Eliminate parts of the letter that detract from the effectiveness of the request.

> My small home-decorating business has an account with your company. I am interested in several items that were featured on your website last week. Because your website is currently down, I have chosen to send my order by conventional mail. I hope this is acceptable.
>
> I am most interested in the deluxe paint sprayer that was advertised as your monthly special. I believe it was manufactured by Craftline. Its unit price was around $175. I would need two of them. You also advertised a cordless sander manufactured by Precision Master. Its unit price was approximately $80. Please send me three sanders. Another item caught my eye—a virtual decor software program that would allow my customers to preview a room in a variety of colours and finishes. I would require the version for Windows XP. I believe it cost $95 and went under the name of Samtex Color Options.
>
> By the way, my company's account number is 551H27. Please notify me if the prices you

advertised are no longer in effect. Because we have many contracts to complete in the next few weeks, please ship my order as fast as you can.

4. **Order Request:** As Jackie Lao, marketing director of Ambiant, a new lighting design firm and retailer of electrical fixtures, you have been appointed to represent the company at a number of upcoming design and trade shows. Because the market for lighting products and services is extremely competitive, you would like prospective customers to keep your company in mind for their next lighting project. To help your fledgling business gain a foothold in the marketplace, you plan to distribute novelties bearing your company name and logo at the upcoming trade shows. You have heard that Your Name Here, a supplier of corporate gifts and novelties, can customize any item from a product line that includes LED flashlights, glow-in-the-dark pens, pen lights, and illuminated pens. Because your instructions are more detailed and specific than what Your Name Here's website allows for, you have decided to fax an order request. You would like fifty mini LED flashlights, item No. 62-J, in red if possible, listed at $9. You also want two hundred glow-in-the-dark pens, item No. 98-K, with black ink, listed at $2 per unit. Finally, you would like one hundred pen lights, item No. 55-R, again in red, listed at $4 per unit. You would like the company logo to be reproduced as accurately as possible, so you are attaching an enlarged sample. Each item should also be stamped with the slogan "Ambiant—Lighting the Way" together with the web address, www.ambiantlighting.com. You would like to be invoiced for this purchase. Because you need these items for a trade show to be held in ten days, you want this to be a rush order, with shipment by overnight courier. You would like immediate notification if, for any reason, Your Name Here is unable to process the order as stipulated. Write to Your Name Here, 215 Grand Prairie Boulevard, Moose Jaw, SK S6H 3L8.

5. **Claim Request:** Write a claim letter based on a problem you may have experienced with a product or service that was under guarantee or covered by a warranty.

6. **Claim Request:** As Gus Hampshire, office manager of Inukshuk Mining and Exploration in Yellowknife, NWT, you have received a shipment of mismatched modular office components from Cubicle Junction of Vancouver. When you telephoned Cubicle Junction's customer service hotline to complain, you were told that the faulty components could be replaced, on condition that they be returned to the warehouse. However, Cubicle Junction could not promise to cover shipping costs—the charges for which would be passed on to you. You feel these charges are unwarranted and unfair, as Cubicle Junction was at fault for the irregularities in the original shipment. Write to Maya Sutcliffe, manager of customer service at Cubicle Junction, asking that the company cover the estimated $300 in shipping charges.

7. **Follow-up Letter:** As Cassandra Fogerty, owner of Get It Write, an editorial and tutoring service, write to Giacomo Giancarlo confirming the details of yesterday's telephone conversation. Mr. Giancarlo, a marketing expert with a high profile in the business community, is writing a series of articles for a business publication and is also working on a book-length manuscript that he plans to submit to publishers in Canada and the United States. He has asked you to review his writing and make necessary changes so his academic style will have broader popular appeal. You agreed on an hourly rate of $80 and discussed the type of style for which he is aiming. You also agreed to meet next week to discuss his projects in greater detail.

8. **Information Response:** When you graduated from high school, you volunteered for a mentorship program designed to help students in the next graduating class choose colleges and universities best suited to their needs and career objectives. You agreed to write briefly to your former guidance counsellor with details of academic programs, standards of instruction, student services, residence accommodations, extracurricular activities, and overall college life at the academic institution you attend. Although you prefer not to include personal information, you would like to record your impressions and provide helpful details that supplement what prospective students can find on your college's or university's website. Write to your guidance counsellor with brief comments on the topics listed above. Offer to greet a small group of students from your former high school when they tour your college/university next month.

9. **Order Response:** As Brett Chetkovic, sales director of Your Name Here, you have just received Jackie Lao's order by fax (see Case 4). The only negative element you must include in your message is that the mini LED flashlights she ordered are available in black only due to high demand. A new shipment of red mini LED flashlights is expected in one week. Although you cannot guarantee that the red LED flashlights will be ready for her first trade show, you would like to offer to fill the order partially or fully with black LED flashlights, available at a substantially discounted price of $5 per unit. All other items on order can be customized as requested and shipped immediately. Write a customer order response to Jackie Lao, Marketing Director, Ambiant Lighting, 218 Harbourview Avenue, Vancouver, BC V6C 2R1.

10. **Claim Response:** As Maya Sutcliffe, manager of customer service at Cubicle Junction, write to Gus Hampshire of Inukshuk Mining and Exploration (see Case 6 above) granting his request to have $300 in shipping costs waived. In reviewing the records of his telephone calls to customer service, you immediately determined that the problem with his prefabricated office system resulted from the inclusion of five mismatched panels in his shipment. The bolts provided were compatible only with the panels he ordered, not with those shipped in error, making it impossible for the parts to be assembled correctly. When only a few components require replacement, your company policy is to simply ship the replacement parts free of charge, not to demand the return of the entire order at the customer's expense. In investigating the cause of the problem with Mr. Hampshire's shipment, you discovered that a changeover to new software had temporarily disrupted inventory control at the time Mr. Hampshire's order was processed. By bringing the matter to your attention, Mr. Hampshire has allowed you implement a backup system so problems of this kind will not recur. Advise him when he can expect to receive his new shipment and offer him technical support through your website www.cubiclejunction.com and 1-800 number.

11. **Letter of Appreciation:** As Peter Ricco, a junior accounts executive for an asset-management firm, you and a small group of your colleagues were invited to an afternoon of golf and dinner at a private country club. The host was your division manager, Rob Stockwell. Although you had to miss your daughter's first ballet recital, the day produced some impressive golf scores and gave you the opportunity to bounce around some creative strategic planning ideas. The meal itself was outstanding—far more than you had expected. Write to Mr. Stockwell expressing your appreciation for his hospitality.

ONLINE ACTIVITIES

1. **Applying the Direct Approach to a Claim Request:** Visit the web link below and take a look at the sample complaint letter featured on the Writing Business Letters site. Using the information provided, rewrite the letter so it follows the direct writing plan. **www.writing-business-letters.com/ complain-letter.html**

7

Delivering Unfavourable News

In this chapter you will learn to

1. Identify the special demands and characteristics of bad news messages.

2. Apply direct and indirect writing plans for bad news messages.

3. Organize bad news messages with a direct plan.

4. Organize bad news messages with an indirect plan: writing buffers, citing reasons, and de-emphasizing the bad news.

5. Politely refuse requests, claims, and credit; follow up on problems; decline invitations; turn down job applicants; and announce bad news to customers and employees.

Delivering bad news is an unavoidable fact of doing business—and a task that is often more difficult than just saying no. Breaking bad news can make even confident writers uneasy while leaving recipients defensive, disappointed, or shocked. No one enjoys provoking these emotions, let alone experiencing them. When readers first detect negativity in the form of a problem, refusal, or criticism, it is usually enough to make them stop reading, especially when they haven't been prepared for unpleasant information and have no way to adjust to it. Often, the anger provoked by a message can spill over into antagonism toward the person who wrote it, especially if the bad news has been trivialized, exaggerated, or stated too bluntly. Writers who routinely antagonize their readers when they must deliver bad news get reputations for being thoughtless and insensitive, a perception that can erode goodwill and damage relationships with business colleagues, suppliers, and customers.

However, communicating unfavourable news or saying no doesn't have to result in bad feelings. Strategic **negative messages** are unique in their special attention to content, structure, context, and tone. These elements work together to preserve goodwill and ensure the recipient finishes reading the message and accepts the bad news without feeling bitter, hostile, or resentful. The following are some important goals to keep in mind when communicating bad news:

> **negative message**
> a message that communicates negative information that may upset or disappoint the reader.

Primary Goals

- To give the bad news in a clear, brief, and respectful way, and state it only once.
- To help readers accept the bad news by showing the fairness and logic of the decision, offering an explanation when it is possible to do so, and eliminating unnecessarily negative language.
- To maintain and build goodwill toward the reader and the reader's organization despite the unpleasant facts the message must communicate.
- To get your purpose across the first time, without ambiguities that may create a need for clarification, follow-up correspondence, or ongoing dispute resolution.

Secondary Goals

- To balance business decisions with sensitivity to readers by putting yourself in their position.
- To reflect promptness, accountability, and due consideration—factors that reduce impatience and potential hostility—by delivering the bad news at the right time.
- To protect yourself and your organization from legal liability.

Bad news messages fall into several categories:

- **Refusals** turn down invitations, suggestions, proposals, and requests for information, action, employment, and credit
- **Announcements** disclose price increases, policy changes, delivery delays, cancellation of services, and product defects or recalls
- **Assessments or appraisals** offer negative assessments of employee job performance or personnel issues

Tone in Bad News Messages

Tone is important in bad news messages. A tactful, neutral tone tailored to the situation puts readers in a receptive frame of mind and lowers their psychological resistance to a refusal or denial. It is especially important to avoid phrasing that is harsh, defensive, and accusatory—wording that can intensify readers' feelings of anger and inadequacy. The following are a few tips for maintaining an even, reader-friendly tone:

- Don't plead with the reader (*please understand*) or resort to name-calling.
- Beware of mixed messages, for example, by expressing an unwillingness to comply when it is within your power to do so (*I am sorry that we have chosen not to*).
- Avoid statements based on assumptions that the reader will accept the bad news (*you will certainly agree/understand/appreciate*).
- Stick to facts and keep your language jargon-free.
- Avoid statements of opinion that can expose you and your company to legal liability.
- Edit timid or overly apologetic statements that may weaken the reader's confidence in your decision (*I am afraid that we cannot*).
- Avoid unnecessarily writer-centred remarks (*we cannot afford to/we must refuse/disappoint/reject your*).
- Use expressions of sympathy (*sorry/I regret/unfortunately*) carefully to avoid hinting at the bad news.

A positive emphasis, as long as it doesn't mislead readers into expecting good news, can compensate for the sense of limitation a reader may feel in being told you cannot do what he wants. Sincerity and politeness are the best ways to let readers down gently and help them adjust to negative information.

SUBJECT LINES AND COMPLIMENTARY CLOSES

The subject line sets the tone for a message. For negative responses, you can simply add "Re:" to the original subject line. You will need to type a new subject line only if the negative information you pass on is crucial to action-taking and decision-making. It is possible to drop the subject line altogether from a letter if it states the bad news too bluntly. If you decide to use a subject line, select the type that best suits your purpose:

- **Positive subject lines** highlight solutions in problem-oriented messages and persuade readers of the benefits of potentially unpopular policies or changes. However, a subject line should never overstate positives to the point of misleading readers. The following subject line is from a message announcing an increase in monthly deductions for employee benefits:

    Subject: Upgrading Employee Benefits Package

- **Neutral subject lines** signal the topic but without referring to the bad news. Use them in routine memos to peers and subordinates, especially when the bad news is minor or expected.

    Subject: Water Shut Off Sunday, October 5
    Subject: Subscription Rate Increase, Effective March 31

- **Negative subject lines** are uncommon but can be used to command attention for serious internal problems and issues that might otherwise be ignored. They sometimes headline brief e-mails alerting readers to situations for which the readers are not at fault.

> Subject: Error in Q3 Sales Data [when the error is your own]
> Subject: Downgrade to AA Credit Rating

Closings, too, should be in keeping with the balance of your message. Readers who have just been let down can be easily upset by an upbeat complimentary close such as *Cheers*, mistaking its friendliness for sarcasm or flippancy.

Organizing Bad News Messages

There are two writing plans—direct and indirect—for structuring negative messages. Knowing which plan to use is a matter of analyzing the context and the message's anticipated effect on the reader. There are several important factors to consider before you write:

- how well you know the reader,
- what position the reader holds relative to you in the company hierarchy,
- how much information you can safely disclose to the reader,
- how prepared the reader is for the bad news,
- how much resistance you anticipate,
- how adversely the refusal or denial will affect the reader, and
- what readers, especially of internal messages, are accustomed to.

By carefully examining these factors, you will be able to decide how to compose your bad news message. Several useful plans are discussed in the following sections.

Direct Writing Plan for Bad News Messages

USING THE DIRECT WRITING PLAN

Some readers prefer directness. Some messages demand it. It is not always necessary to break the bad news gently by using the special delaying strategies that characterize the indirect writing plan, which reveals the bad news only after an explanation has prepared the reader for it. In many situations it is possible to level with the reader and begin with the main message. Use the direct approach to deliver bad news in the following situations:

- when you know the reader well enough to understand her preference for directness (readers who expect conciseness and immediacy in their messages may not have the time or patience to read a lengthy lead-in);
- when the bad news is expected or related to a known problem or minor delay;
- when critical information might otherwise escape notice (organizations commonly use the direct approach to announce price increases, disruptions in service, or changes in policy; if you embed this information somewhere in the middle of the message, you may not succeed in bringing it to the reader's attention);

- when the bad news is not serious, significant, or detrimental to the reader;
- when it is company practice to write all internal messages straightforwardly; or
- when you intend to terminate a business relationship.

The direct writing plan for delivering bad news is similar to that used for good news messages with one notable difference: it follows up the explanation with the offer of an alternative. Use the following four-part approach when writing a direct bad news message:

1. **Begin with a simple, well-phrased statement of the bad news.** Give the bad news only once.

2. **Provide an explanation for it—one that the reader can reasonably accept.** Keep the explanation brief and make it clear. Tell readers only what they need to know and what you need to say to justify a decision or relay basic facts.

3. **Offer an alternative if it is possible to do so.** You cannot do as the reader asked, but perhaps you can offer the next best thing. Promise only what is legally and realistically allowable for you or your company to do.

4. **Close with a goodwill statement that doesn't refer to the bad news.** Avoid words and phrases such as *difficulty*, *mistake*, *problem*, or *regrettable error*.

The sample direct approach messages in Figures 7.1 and 7.2 inform registrants of the cancellation of an on-site course.

LIMITATIONS OF THE DIRECT APPROACH

The direct, up-front approach is all business. The impression it gives is of no-nonsense decisiveness. However, an overly brief message constructed according to this plan can sometimes seem cold and brusque. To make your message polite without adding to its length, focus on using a tone that conveys respect and courtesy.

FIGURE 7.1 **INEFFECTIVE** Direct Approach Message (extract)

Opening expression of sympathy also announces the bad news

Gives no reason for the cancellation and does not identify the cancelled course

Offers no alternative —another course or possible rescheduling

Closing an afterthought that reminds readers, somewhat facetiously, of their disappointment

Dear Registrants:

Unfortunately, the course you registered for has been cancelled.

It looks like we may not be able to make this course available to employees for at least another few months.

We hate to disappoint our registrants, but I am sure you understand our budgetary constraints.

FIGURE 7.2 EFFECTIVE Direct Approach Message

Page 1 of 1

FROM: Ahmed Khan <akhan@eureka.ca>

SENT: February 1, 2010

TO: learning@eureka.ca

SUBJECT: Outlook 2007 Level 2 Course Cancellation

Dear Registrant:

The Outlook 2007 Level 2 course, originally scheduled to begin on March 22, has been cancelled due to insufficient registration levels.
   — Delivers and explains the bad news directly in the first paragraph

In its place, please consider one of several self-directed e-learning courses available through the Learning and Employee Development Centre. Rooms in the Development Centre can be booked for up to two hours at a time, and each course takes four to eight hours to complete. Staff members who have opted for our e-learning program say the experience compares favourably to traditional classroom instruction.
   — Quickly moves on to an alternative and tells readers how to act on this information

Please let me know if you are interested in self-directed learning so that suitable training times can be arranged for you.
   — Closes with a final reminder of the alternative, which is reader-centred and phrased politely

Thanks,

Ahmed

Ahmed Khan
Learning Centre Coordinator
Tel: 416-631-7710
Fax: 416-631-7785
Email: akhan@eureka.ca

Indirect Writing Plan for Bad News Messages

USING THE INDIRECT APPROACH

The indirect strategy is a more traditional way of delivering unfavourable news. It allows you greater tact and diplomacy, and you should use it in the following situations:

- when you don't know the reader well,
- when the bad news isn't anticipated by the reader, or
- when you anticipate a strong negative reaction from the reader.

indirect writing plan
a method of organizing
a document so that the
main message is delayed
and presented toward
the end.

Instead of beginning with a blunt announcement of the bad news, the approach of an **indirect writing plan** gradually eases the reader into the news and thereby reduces its impact. The main message is embedded—delayed until the reader has been prepared for it. This unique organization makes the message readable—and easy to tolerate—from beginning to end. The advantage of such a plan is clear: a reader who grasps the reasons for a negative decision or assessment is less likely to react negatively, toss the message aside, or take the bad news personally. The following simple four-part formula can be modified depending on the specific type of message and how sensitive you need to be:

1. **Begin with a buffer**—a short statement that grabs attention, cushions the bad news, and guides the reader to the explanation.

2. **Provide a solid, reasonable explanation.** A crucial part of any bad news message, the explanation establishes background and reasons that will later help the reader understand, adjust to, and accept the bad news.

3. **State the bad news,** phrased to minimize its impact and, if possible, balanced by an alternative.

4. **Close with a goodwill statement** to end the message pleasantly, showing consideration for the reader.

The following sections offer a closer look at each of these four elements.

BAD NEWS BUFFERS

buffer a meaningful,
neutral statement that
cushions the shock of
bad news.

The **buffer** (one to three sentences) is a first defence against toxic messaging. It is a meaningful, neutral statement that establishes rapport with the reader without forecasting the bad news. It reduces the shock or surprise a reader might otherwise experience upon suddenly learning unpleasant news. With its conciliatory tone, the buffer puts the reader in a more agreeable frame of mind, helping to neutralize the bad news when it is finally revealed. A buffer can be an expression of agreement, appreciation, or general principle, or a chronology of past communications (see Table 7.1 "Types of Bad News Buffers"). It is usually worded to avoid connotatively negative language (for example *no*, *not*, *cannot*, *refuse*, *deny*, *unfortunately*, *regrettably*, and the prefixes *un-* and *non-*). An effective buffer never misleads the reader into thinking that positive news will follow. Instead it guides the reader toward the explanation, often by planting a keyword that carries over to the next paragraph. Internal messages on routine matters may not require buffers, but messages intended for superiors, customers, or job applicants benefit from the sensitivity this device helps to show. Writing a good buffer can be difficult, so let the situation govern the type of buffer you use.

EXPLAINING THE BAD NEWS

An explanation of the bad news is the most important part of a negative message because it prepares the reader for the refusal or denial. Whether you choose to justify or explain negative information, you need to let readers see that the negative decision is based on valid, legitimate reasons, not snap judgements or weak excuses. It is important to be objective and reveal only what the reader rightfully needs to know to understand your decision.

1. **Stick to the facts and avoid editorializing.** Focus on your strongest reason or reasons for saying no, being careful not to divulge confidential, legally sensitive

TABLE 7.1	Types of Bad News Buffers
Appreciation	Thanks readers for their inquiries, contributions, applications, business, feedback, or interest: *Thank you for allowing us to review your application for the position of accounts executive at Pendleton Management.* It is best to avoid expressions of gratitude that might seem illogical, especially if the opening remark is connected to a request you are about to refuse. Saying *we were very pleased to receive your request* sounds insincere if you have no intention of complying with the request.
Good or neutral news	The "first the good news, now the bad news" approach that begins with positive elements wins over readers, but only if the good news is relevant and meaningful. Don't struggle to find something pleasant to say unless it is related to the main message.
General principle or fact	Outlines organizational policies or practices. For example, a memo announcing a reduction in paid release time for corporate fundraising events can open by reminding readers of the "big picture" that won't change as a result of the bad news: *Our company has shown a long tradition of support for employees in their fundraising activities for local charities.* A message announcing the cancellation of an employee service can be buffered by a statistic illustrating that the service is under-subscribed: *Consumption of coffee in our complimentary Grab-a-Java program has dropped in the past year. More than 90 per cent of the staff now say they prefer to purchase their coffee off the premises.*
Chronology of past communications	Retraces events or correspondence relevant to the current situation. In responding to a claim that must be refused, for instance, you may begin by recapping what has happened so far: *When we last spoke on October 7, I agreed to review our shipping procedures for perishable goods.*
Statement of agreement or common ground	Refers to a relevant view shared by the writer and reader. In rejecting a proposed method of expenditure reduction, you could begin with an endorsement of the general principle that inspired the plan in the first place: *We both agree on the importance of operational expenditure reduction.*
Apology or statement of understanding	Expresses sympathy or regret for what has happened or what the reader has experienced as a result of a decision made. An apology may be necessary in cases where the reader suffered severe or unreasonable difficulty, inconvenience, or financial loss. Otherwise, apologies can lead to legal liability, so they should be issued with care. It is important not to overdramatize an error. If you are in doubt about what to say, consult your organization's legal department. Tailor the apology to the situation and make sure it is sincere and genuine, not half-hearted. *Please accept our apologies for any inconvenience caused by the temporary malfunction of our automatic transit turnstiles.*
Compliment	Praises the reader's efforts and contributions without resorting to false flattery. Avoid beginning with an ego-booster so big that it raises hopes for good news to follow or builds a reader up only to let the person down. The compliment should take into consideration noteworthy achievements, actions, conduct, or overall performance, but not trivialities such as attire and appearance: *Your attention to detail and your thorough research are commendable. Once again, you have prepared a complete and cogent proposal.*

information that may be damaging to you or your company. It is also important to avoid expressing a personal opinion that might be mistaken for the view of your organization or criticism of its policies (e.g., *I know how senseless this policy must seem, but it must be enforced*). Your goal is to clarify your or the company's decision and put it in perspective, briefly and tactfully, without taxing a reader's patience or making the situation worse with accusations. Statements that imply you doubt a reader's honesty (*you claim that, you state that, we are surprised at your request*) should likewise be avoided.

2. **Refer to company policy as needed but don't hide behind it.** Unless you want to distance yourself from negative information by using an official tone, avoid

mechanically restating company policy to justify your decision: *Our company policy forbids the conversion of lease payments to purchases.* Instead, tactfully point to the reason why the policy is reasonable, fair, or beneficial: *As our company is committed to keeping rates low, conversion of payments toward a purchase is not an available option.*

3. **Use positive or neutral words** to present your explanation and make the reader more receptive to its facts. Your explanation should sound humane and helpful, not as though you are passing the buck or using technical language to evade the real issue. Edit out words that are known to create resistance: *impossible, unable, unacceptable, unwise, unwilling, difficulty, inconvenience, unwarranted, unreasonable.* Also avoid phrases such as *please understand* and *you surely understand* that beg the reader to agree with you. Show respect by taking the matter seriously.

REVEALING THE BAD NEWS

Withholding the bad news until after the explanation is fundamental to the indirect strategy. However, delaying tactics alone may not make disappointing or upsetting news any easier to accept. It helps to remember that saying no or revealing disappointing information doesn't necessarily mean being negative. You can take the sting out of unfavourable news by using one or more de-emphasizing techniques that lessen its grammatical presence and impact. Even with these techniques, it is still essential to state the bad news clearly and unequivocally, so readers will understand it the first time and won't need to ask for clarification.

1. **Put the bad news in a dependent clause.** Dependent clauses de-emphasize what they convey because of their grammatical incompleteness. Readers are less likely to linger over clauses beginning with *although, as, because, if, since, while,* or *whereas* and more likely to focus on the independent clause in a complex sentence.

2. **Suggest a compromise or alternative.** Readers like solutions. Alternatives emphasize what you or your company *can* do and show you are focused on solving the problem. Such conciliation can ease the sense of limitation a reader may feel upon receiving a bad news message. Give the alternative maximum impact by putting it in an independent clause in a complex sentence or in an independent clause on its own. Provide enough information for the reader to be able to act on the suggestion.

   • *Although your printer could not be repaired, we would like to offer you a 15 per cent discount and free extended warranty on your next purchase of a printer in our Laser-best 5000 series.*

   • *Although we cannot disclose individual salaries, we can provide you with a fact sheet listing the salary range of our senior managers.*

3. **Use the passive voice.** Passive-voice verbs allow you to describe an action without identifying who performed it. Facts stand out; personalities and their conflicts fade into the background. Use passive-voice constructions alone or as part of a dependent clause: *Although credit cannot be extended at this time, we look forward to serving you on a cash basis.*

4. **Use long sentences rather than short ones.** Put the bad news in a sentence containing more than 15 words—long sentences tend to de-emphasize content.

5. **Use positive language.** Readers are usually more receptive when you present the glass as being half full rather than half empty. While it is never advisable to make unrealistic promises or use overly effusive language, it makes sense to avoid words and phrases that readers may perceive as harshly negative or antagonistic: *we must refuse/reject/deny your request/disappoint you.* The statement *we refuse to accept applications after March 15* is less severe when rephrased as *applications will be accepted until March 15.*

6. **Avoid spotlighting the bad news.** Embed the bad news in the middle of a sentence or paragraph where it is less noticeable. Beginning with the bad news increases its shock value; ending with it adds to the possibility that readers will dwell on it. Try to combine the bad news with a reasonable explanation or good news alternative. Don't let it sit by itself in a single, high-emphasis paragraph.

7. **Imply the refusal.** For this technique to be effective, the explanation must be clear and thorough. Here is an implied refusal for a request for software training for a group of thirty people: *Our onsite training facility can accommodate a group of up to twenty.* Implied refusals backfire if readers don't grasp the negative information, putting you in the awkward position of having to say no in a second letter that states the news more directly.

GOODWILL CLOSING

The closing is the last chance to repair goodwill and normalize relationships so that business can continue. A **goodwill closing** must be consistent with the overall tone and content of your message—never so canned or mechanical that it seems unrelated or sounds insincere. At the same time, it must refocus business relationships and, as required, express confidence that those relationships will continue. Positive, you-centred remarks work well in closing as long as their cheerfulness doesn't encourage the reader to think you are happy about delivering bad news.

goodwill closing draws attention away from the message to a positive and continuing relationship with the reader.

1. **Don't repeat the bad news, remind the reader of past problems, or hint at future difficulty.** Words and phrases such as *problem, difficulty, error, mistake, trouble, unfortunate situation,* or *inconvenience* renew the bad feelings you have worked so hard to dispel. Instead focus on the problem's resolution and look ahead to a continuing business relationship.

2. **Do offer your good wishes to the reader.** Obviously, this is more important when declining job applications and invitations or writing to customers. Your comments should sound genuine and conciliatory, not overdone: *Thank you for the interest you have shown in our research and development program. I wish you every success in your future career.*

3. **Don't invite further correspondence unless you sincerely want contact.** If the matter isn't open to debate or discussion, don't encourage the reader to believe your decision isn't final by signing off with a suggestion of further contact: *please feel free to contact me if you would like to discuss this matter.* Readers who won't take no for an answer will interpret such a statement as an invitation to pursue the matter further. A goodwill closing should be the final step in encouraging the reader to accept the bad news and closing the door on further correspondence.

4. **Don't apologize for having to say no, especially at the end of your message.** A brief, sincere apology may be appropriate at the outset if the situation merits it, but unnecessary apologies later on can undermine your perceived authority and weaken your explanation. Apologies can sometimes expose organizations to legal liability, so exercise caution or seek legal counsel before issuing them.

5. **Don't take credit for helping the reader unless you have actually provided assistance.** Even brief statements that are meant to boost the reader's mood—such as *I hope this information has been useful to you*—ring false if you have done nothing for the reader.

INDIRECT APPROACH MESSAGE

The following message announces a substantial increase in dues for membership in a professional association. Because higher dues could mean a substantial drop in membership, the message has a strong persuasive component. It begins by expressing appreciation to members for their contributions and by stressing, through the keyword "services," the benefits of membership. News of the increase is minimized by the helpful suggestion to pay immediately and save. The closing conveys goodwill with a forward-looking emphasis. Typical of some bad news messages, the purpose of this letter is also persuasive in encouraging readers not just to note but also to accept the bad news.

The Canadian Association of Business Management values the ground-breaking initiatives and active participation of its members. Thanks to a strong collective effort, the array of services and events now available to members has helped make our group the fastest-growing professional association in Canada.

Our mentorship program matches young members with those possessing years of experience in the industry. This program has been a success. Membership now includes a quarterly publication with the latest trade information and access to websites and online resources, including hundreds of trade publications. Although the cost of these services has led to an unavoidable increase in annual dues, we now offer a three-year membership for only $230—a $50 saving over the one-year membership rate.

To take advantage of this special rate, please complete and send in the attached renewal form before December 31. We thank you for your past support and look forward to your continued participation in our organization.

LIMITATIONS OF THE INDIRECT STRATEGY

The indirect strategy does have its drawbacks. When readers fail to find good or neutral news in the first few sentences, they may see through the delaying or "hedging" tactics of the buffered opening and explanation and suspect the true purpose of the message. When this happens, readers may see the lack of directness as manipulative rather than polite. Messages organized according to this pattern also tend to be longer, making greater demands on the reader's time and patience.

Quick Reference Chart: Direct vs. Indirect Approach

Use the Direct Strategy

- To deliver bad news to someone you know well
- For internal communication on matters already familiar to the reader
- To announce routine rate increases to customers
- To deliver bad news policy statements to employees
- To refuse to write letters of recommendation

Use the Indirect Strategy

- For tactful, explanatory *in-house* communication with superiors and co-workers and *external* communication with customers, job applicants, and vendors
- To refuse requests, claim adjustments, and credit
- To decline invitations
- To deliver bad news about products or orders
- For negative performance reviews

Checklist for Indirect Strategy Messages

- ☐ Have you buffered the bad news with an opening that is relevant, focused, and neutral?
- ☐ Have you explained the circumstances of the situation or the facts leading to the refusal or bad news?
- ☐ Have you presented reasons that will help the reader understand and accept the negative information as a logical conclusion?
- ☐ Have you stated the bad news as clearly and tactfully as possible? Have you used appropriate techniques to de-emphasize it?
- ☐ Have you closed by re-establishing goodwill?

APOLOGIES IN BAD NEWS MESSAGES

Apologies are not necessarily part of every bad news message. Knowing when and how to apologize, though, is fundamental to business interests. Saying sorry shows you care, rights wrongs, and helps to fix problems. A poorly worded apology, however, can be misinterpreted as an admission of fault or liability—all the more reason to handle apologies with care.

- **Don't apologize for minor errors** that have been promptly corrected or when there is nothing to apologize for. When you have done your absolute best to correct a problem or delay resulting from circumstances beyond your control, provide an explanation in place of an apology. Unnecessary apologies weaken your perceived authority and erode confidence in your decisions.

Unnecessary Apology:	I am so sorry to have to tell you that our Get It Fresh or It's Free policy does not apply to reduced-for-quick-sale items.
Positive Explanation:	To guarantee our customers a high standard of food quality and freshness, our Get It Fresh or It's Free policy applies only to regularly priced or nationally advertised sale items.

- **Do apologize for any serious trouble** or inconvenience for which you or your company is responsible. Issue a brief, sincere apology as early in the message as you possibly can, without overdramatizing. An apology left to the end can seem like an afterthought and remind readers of their difficulty. Acknowledge the wrong done to the injured party. Be aware, however, that apologies not only convey regret or sympathy, they can also be taken as admissions of responsibility or negligence. If you think an apology could admit liability, refer the matter to an experienced colleague or company-affiliated legal expert.

Apologetic:	I'm sorry that the order for five hundred embossed folders won't be ready by September 14.
Explanatory:	Due to shipping delays related to customs inspections, the embossed folders you ordered will not be ready by September 14. Would you like to keep this order or would you prefer to look at the enclosed samples of comparable products from other suppliers?

⬤⬤ Types of Bad News Messages

REFUSING REQUESTS FOR INFORMATION, ACTIONS, AND FAVOURS

When refusing requests from people outside your organization, you can say no tactfully by using the indirect writing plan that buffers, explains, and softens the bad news. Putting reasons before the refusal shows you are sensitive to the reader's concerns. It also prepares the reader for unwanted news—namely that a request for information, action, credit, or a favour must be turned down. A direct writing plan is workable only when you know the reader well or when politeness is not absolutely essential to maintaining a business relationship.

1. **Buffer the opening.** Writing a buffer can be difficult, so concentrate on information that is relevant to the message as a whole but isn't so positive that it misleads the reader.

2. **Give reason(s) for the refusal.** Limit your explanation to the main reason for refusing the request, focusing on what you can rightfully disclose in order to help the reader accept your decision. Be brief and make it plausible.

3. **Soften or subordinate the bad news.** Avoid harsh, negative phrasing and use one or several de-emphasizing techniques to cushion the bad news. Your refusal should be unequivocal—not open to interpretation or so subtle that readers miss the point. Implied refusals, however tactful they may be, may not say *no* clearly enough.

4. **Offer an alternative or compromise if a good one is available.** You have just stated what you cannot do. Is there something that you *can* do in response to the reader's request? Provide an alternative or compromise only if it's a viable one.

5. **Renew goodwill in closing.** A sincere, forward-looking ending can renew good feelings, but it is unlikely to succeed if it sounds sarcastic or clichéd, or if it doesn't fit the circumstances. Ending with *we are happy to have helped in this matter and look forward to providing more information whenever we can* is illogical if a company has just refused to help. Keep the closing pleasant and focused on the reader by maintaining a sincere you-attitude or making a comment that reduces the sense of limitation imposed by the bad news.

The message in Figure 7.3 politely turns down a request for volunteers to participate in a fundraising event for a local charity. It opens by offering praise for the event but also sets the stage for a refusal by setting limits on participation. The policy on which the refusal will ultimately be based is explained, rather than simply stated, so that readers can understand how it is beneficial and fair. Rather than hiding behind policy, the writer shows that the refusal is based on legal obstacles, not on an unwillingness of staff to participate. A good news alternative helps to balance the refusal, and the message ends with good wishes and a forward-looking remark.

REFUSING CLAIMS

Not all claims are valid or reasonable. Some are the result of an honest mistake or misinformation on the part of the claimant. A rare few are fraudulent. Saying no to someone who is already dissatisfied enough to make a claim can be difficult. In refusing a claim, you may find yourself in the middle of an upsetting or hostile situation that can easily deteriorate. Using the indirect approach allows you the tact to let the reader down gently. Its emphasis on an explanation helps you communicate the desire to be fair and encourages the reader to believe that the claim has been given thorough and serious consideration. The dual purpose of a claim response, even a negative one, is to put the matter to rest while retaining the goodwill and patronage of current customers.

1. **Begin with a statement of appreciation, common ground, or understanding.** Opening with a refusal is enough to shock an unprepared reader. Instead, open neutrally, even if it is just to thank the reader for bringing the matter to the company's attention:
   - *We appreciate your taking the time to write to us regarding your purchase and we welcome the opportunity to explain our price-matching policy.*

FIGURE 7.3 Refusing Requests for Information, Actions, and Favours

Edmonton Public Television

14 Media Street | Edmonton, AB T9C 2G8 | (780) 555-3399 | www.ept.ca

August 4, 2009

Ms. Sasha Ibrahim
Fundraising Administrator
Alliance for Living Standards
400 Telner Road
Edmonton, AB B3W 1Z4

Dear Ms. Ibrahim:

[Opens neutrally on relevant topic but without reference to the bad news →] The premier event of your Alliance for Living Standards' upcoming fundraising drive, Race against Poverty, is recognized throughout Edmonton for its success in raising awareness of local community issues and providing much-needed assistance to families in crisis. Edmonton Public Television supports the commitment of volunteers whose terms of employment allow them to take part in such worthy events.

[Second paragraph establishes logical basis for refusal through its explanation →] As you are perhaps aware, our organization is publicly funded. Its mandate is to provide fair, unbiased, non-partisan coverage of local and national news events. This commitment is made so that our reports accurately reflect the greater Edmonton community and the issues that affect it. Although, as employees of a Crown corporation, our on-air personalities, journalists, and technicians are not [Announcement of bad news de-emphasized by dependent clause placement, passive voice construction, and offer of alternative →] permitted to represent our organization at charitable or fundraising events, we would like to invite your spokesperson to take part in a three-member panel discussion on fall fundraising events that will be televised live locally on September 15. Our lineup editor will provide you with the full details once you've indicated your willingness to take part.

[Concludes with good wishes and forward-looking remark →] We wish you every success in your fundraising drive and look forward to seeing the Alliance for Living Standards represented in our panel discussion.

Sincerely,

Rita Shelley

Rita Shelley
Communications Manager

- *We can understand your concern when you received an invoice for an amount substantially higher than what you had anticipated.*
- *Your purchase of an Exacta product comes with a twenty-year record of quality assurance.*
- *The XBJ software you purchased recently is the only software in its price range with superior graphics capability.*
- *I can appreciate your need for a dependable air-conditioning system, especially during the summer months.*

Don't raise false hopes or mislead readers into believing they're entitled to something they're not with a statement such as *you were absolutely right in bringing your problem to our immediate attention.*

2. **Provide a concise, factual explanation.** Use emotionally neutral, objective language to review facts of a sale or dispute and explain why a claim must be refused. To show a desire to be fair, acknowledge any correct assertion by the claimant and avoid assigning blame (e.g., avoid phrases such as *if you had read the instructions carefully you would have realized your claim is invalid.*). Remind the claimant pleasantly about a stated or unstated company policy—don't use it as a smokescreen. Briefly show how the policy is reasonable by emphasizing its purpose or benefits in the current circumstances. Avoid negative language that conveys distrust—*you claim that, you state that, you failed to*—and edit long-winded explanations that can leave readers feeling patronized or hoodwinked.

3. **Don't apologize for saying no.** Apologize only if the situation truly warrants it. Even then, a brief *I'm sorry* early in your letter does the job. Unnecessary apologies can weaken your perceived authority. Hedging your refusal can give readers the false impression that your decision isn't final. A firm yet helpful refusal tells a potentially persistent claimant that the matter isn't open to further discussion. Implied refusals are workable, but only if the claimant can fully grasp that the answer is *no*.

4. **End in a friendly, confident, conciliatory way.** Don't close by reminding the claimant of the refusal or by using language that implies the claimant will be dissatisfied with your decision and, therefore, stop being your customer. Assume the role of problem-solver. When a full adjustment is not possible, consider if you can offer the claimant the next best thing—an alternative or compromise, perhaps in the form of a substitute service, minor repair, or replacement product. If it is in your company's best interest to do so, provide information about where the claimant can seek help with the problem or go for servicing on a product. If a claim has been denied only for lack of supporting documentation, suggest that the claimant resubmit the request for adjustment. Otherwise, do not invite the claimant to try again.

REFUSING CREDIT

Refusing credit can cause hard feelings, with consequences for future business. Given the sensitive nature of this type of message, most companies prepare carefully worded, lawyer-reviewed credit refusals, often as templates, for use by credit managers and their departments. These letters can vary in content depending on the source of negative information.

FIGURE 7.4 INEFFECTIVE Claim Refusal (extract)

Dear Mr. D'Agostino:

We cannot refund the price difference on your recent purchase of an 80-gigabyte Western Digital hard drive unit because you are mistaken about our price-protection guarantee. This guarantee applies to boxed products only. If you had read the fine print of our price-guarantee agreement, as posted on our website, I am sure you would have realized that you do not qualify under the terms of your purchase. It is impossible for us to match the price of $107 advertised by Megabyte Computers.

The extra $73 you have paid reflects our assurances that your quality purchase is supported by the best warranty in the business. If we were to make adjustments in all cases such as yours, we could no longer promise to stand behind the products we sell.

I know that you must be very upset that your claim has been denied, but I am sure you can understand our desire to be fair in these situations. It is our pleasure to have served you and we look forward to your future business.

Annotations:

- Opens with a direct refusal—the reader may never get to the explanation
- Only partially explains why the price-protection guarantee doesn't apply
- Rephrases the refusal several times and constantly reminds the reader of the price difference that cannot be refunded
- Mechanical closing does nothing to renew goodwill

In all cases, the goal is to draft a sensitive, respectful refusal that says *no* without criticizing applicants for their low cash reserves, debts, or poor credit records—and without raising false expectations of future credit. Being careful in handling third-party information from credit agencies about an applicant's record reduces the chance of litigation. It is sometimes in a company's best interest to give no reason for the denial, but to simply refer the applicant to the credit agency on whose information the decision is based. A courteous, respectful tone and, if appropriate, a cheerful reminder that orders can still be filled on a cash basis helps keep the letter as positive as possible despite current circumstances.

1. **Buffer the opening.** Begin by referring to the credit application and expressing appreciation for the customer's business.

2. **Use discretion in explaining the reason for the refusal.** Be careful in disclosing third-party information from credit agencies. Business clients often provide financial information directly to suppliers. Only in these circumstances are you free to state your reasons straightforwardly, and even then you must exercise tact to avoid offending anyone.

3. **Soften the refusal with a passive-voice construction.** A refusal such as *credit cannot be extended to you at this time* is less likely to cause bad feelings than *we cannot extend credit to you* or *your credit application has failed*.

4. **Offer incentives to sustain business.** Point out the advantages of doing business on a cash basis.

FIGURE 7.5 EFFECTIVE Claim Refusal

Computer Giant

41 Tech Street, Markham, ON M4C 6K8
1-888-234-5555 www.CompuGiant.com

March 26, 2009

Mr. Don D'Agostino
154 Confederation Road
Toronto, ON M2W 4C8

Dear Mr. D'Agostino:

For top-quality computer merchandise at the lowest possible price, thousands like you have come to rely on Computer Giant. Our confidence in the computer products we sell prompted us to establish our price-protection guarantee.

Opens neutrally with a statement of company policy and philosophy; last sentence foregrounds main topic of the claim response

This guarantee applies to all factory-sealed equipment and entitles our customers to the lowest advertised price on identical items. In other words, we'll match the price as long as the model number matches. To qualify for an immediate point-of-purchase discount or a refund within thirty days, a customer need only produce verified proof of purchase or a copy of an advertised price listing.

Because we not only sell for less but also promise to stand behind everything we sell, we must be able to back each product's warranty. When an item comes to us unsealed from the factory, it is sold as an OEM (original equipment manufacturer) product. The lack of packaging means an OEM product is more susceptible to damage during shipping. The extra care Computer Giant takes in bringing OEM products to you is reflected in a slightly different cost structure when compared with retail boxed products. Because we wanted our customers to be aware of this important difference, we adopted the slogan "Packaged Products, Better Prices."

Offers factual explanation in neutral language and makes important distinctions that lead to a logical conclusion

The 80-gigabyte Western Digital hard drive unit you purchased from us for $180 is an OEM product. It comes with a three-year warranty and our pledge to you of high performance and reliability. This hard drive unit is, as you rightly pointed out, available for less elsewhere. The Computer Giant price reflects our assurances to you that your quality product comes with the best warranty in the business. Although our price-protection guarantee does not apply in this case, we would like you to accept the enclosed coupon redeemable for a 20 per cent discount on your next retail boxed purchase at Computer Giant. This coupon can be used in conjunction with our price-protection guarantee.

Refusal de-emphasized by dependent clause and conciliatory offer of next-best alternative

We value your business and look forward to offering you packaged products at better prices.

Closes by expressing confidence in a continued business relationship

Sincerely,

Ryan Tan

Ryan Tan
Communications Manager

FIGURE 7.6 INEFFECTIVE Credit Refusal (extract)

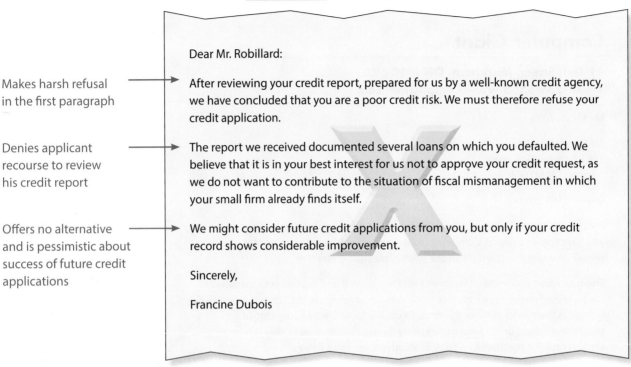

Makes harsh refusal in the first paragraph

Denies applicant recourse to review his credit report

Offers no alternative and is pessimistic about success of future credit applications

Dear Mr. Robillard:

After reviewing your credit report, prepared for us by a well-known credit agency, we have concluded that you are a poor credit risk. We must therefore refuse your credit application.

The report we received documented several loans on which you defaulted. We believe that it is in your best interest for us not to approve your credit request, as we do not want to contribute to the situation of fiscal mismanagement in which your small firm already finds itself.

We might consider future credit applications from you, but only if your credit record shows considerable improvement.

Sincerely,

Francine Dubois

TURNING DOWN JOB APPLICANTS

A single job advertisement can net hundreds of applications, but out of this applicant pool only one person will eventually land the job. A sad fact of the hiring process is that many applicants must be turned down. Sending written notification to every unsuccessful candidate is often impossible, so many job advertisements now state that only candidates selected for an interview will be contacted.

Companies that do have the resources to inform applicants may draft a rejection letter based on the indirect approach, which is still widely preferred for communicating bad news to job applicants, or the direct approach, which is increasingly common. In either case, a job rejection has to be courteous and respectful, subordinating the bad news to a message of good luck and encouragement. Ignoring these general principles comes at a cost. Insensitive rejection letters aren't only damaging to applicants' egos but to the corporate image, earning a company a reputation for treating its applicants badly. Effective employment refusals, on the other hand, preserve a company's good name and leave the applicant's self-esteem intact, so the rejection is less likely to be taken personally. This helps to ensure there are ready applicants for the next job opening.

Because time and resources are often at a premium, form letters are a common way of notifying a sizable applicant pool. The "merge" feature in word processing software can be used to personalize a standard letter, allowing each applicant to be addressed individually. A form letter is an acceptable way to decline unsolicited applications and to inform applicants eliminated from the candidate pool prior to interview. A personal letter is a must for applicants selected for interview but not hired, because these individuals have already spent much time and effort pursuing a position.

FIGURE 7.7 EFFECTIVE Credit Refusal

Megabyte Computers

42 Telemark Street, Toronto, ON N9K 1J8
416-322-4481
www.megabyte.com

September 28, 2009

Dr. Frank Robillard
RobTek Enterprises
11 Livingstone Road
Toronto, ON M1K 1Z4

Dear Mr. Robillard:

Thank you for the order for one hundred flat-screen PC monitors that you placed with us last week. You can find no better monitors on the market today than our G-3000 series. We appreciate your patronage and hope to continue serving you in the future.

According to our standard practice, we submitted your credit application to Equifax Canada. After carefully reviewing their report, we find that credit cannot be extended to you at this time. If you would like to learn more about your record, you may speak with an Equifax representative at (416) 731-8863. In due course, when your firm's financial situation improves, we look forward to serving you on a credit basis.

In the meantime, we will be happy to fill your current order on a cash basis, with our customary 4 per cent cash discount.

When you need high-quality computer monitors, we're glad that you think of us. If we can do business with you now or in the future, please call us at 1-800-992-2921.

Sincerely,

Francine Dubois

Francine Dubois
Communications Manager

Opens neutrally, expressing appreciation for business without referring to the bad news

Offers tactful explanation of the processing of the credit request

Refusal softened through use of passive voice and offer of alternative

Closes with forward-looking expression of confidence in current or future business

Here are a few things to remember as you prepare to communicate bad news to job applicants:

1. **Open by cushioning the refusal.** To avoid breaking the bad news too harshly, thank the applicant for applying or politely express appreciation for his interest. A general comment on the overall standard of applications is another common way to begin—*we were very impressed by the applications we received*. A well-intentioned opening should never mislead the applicant into thinking she got the job.

2. **Give reasons for the company's selection, if it is possible to do so.** Without going into specifics or mentioning an applicant's personal deficiencies, briefly explain the basis for your selection. Take care to protect the confidentiality of decision-makers. Never disclose details of the selection process or legally sensitive information that could embarrass your organization or invite litigation. Volunteering too much information or expressing a personal opinion (for example, *if it were up to me, I'd hire you*) can be risky and hurtful.

3. **Quickly move on to the bad news.** State the bad news only once, using appropriate de-emphasizing techniques and a personal, humane tone.

4. **Gently encourage the applicant.** Offer a positive message of good luck expressed with sincerity, not false flattery. Point to future employment possibilities if you are interested in hiring the applicant when there is a suitable opening (for example, mention that the application will be kept on file.)

FIGURE 7.8 INEFFECTIVE Employment Refusal (extract)

Applicant not addressed by name; bad news doubly stated at beginning

Writer-centred explanation discloses confidential information, giving the impression that the outcome of the job competition was predetermined

Intended compliment weakens confidence in the refusal and patronizes the applicant

Good wishes incorporate reminder of the difficulty of finding suitable work

Dear Applicant:

I regret to inform you that your application for the position of IT specialist has been unsuccessful and we will not be hiring you.

I trust you will understand this was a most difficult decision for us. Our hiring committee was split on whether to give external applicants equal consideration with those who have worked for us for many years. After much disagreement, we realized we would face legal challenges unless we hired from within. In the end, we offered a promotion to Anna Maria di Marco from her former position as junior IT specialist. The final acceptance of our offer was delayed, hence the lateness of our notification to you.

Personally, I would have liked to have had you on staff. You are a bright young thing and we can certainly use people with talents such as yours.

We wish you success in finding an equally good position in this most competitive field.

FIGURE 7.9 **EFFECTIVE** Employment Refusal

JavaTech Inc.

83 Industry Street
Toronto, ON M9K 4G7
www.JTI.com

November 13, 2009

Ms. Jody McAllister
11 Wellington Road
Toronto, ON M5N 1Z6

Dear Ms. McAllister:

On behalf of the members of our hiring committee, I want to thank you for
your interest in joining our IT specialist team and for your impressive application.
We received a great number of applications, all of which were of extremely
high quality.

After conducting a careful review in light of the needs of the team, our hiring
committee has now completed its search for a senior IT specialist. Although
we are unable to offer you a position at this time, our decision is in no way a
reflection of your potential in the IT field. We will keep your credentials in our
confidential file for one year should you wish to apply for another advertised
position with our company.

Members of the committee join me in extending best wishes for you in your
future career.

Sincerely,

Paolo Ciardullo

Paolo Ciardullo
Human Resources Coordinator

Opens with appreciation for expression of interest in the company and general comment on overall quality of applications

Refusal softened by use of the passive voice and the prospect of future consideration

Closes with good wishes for applicant

ANNOUNCING BAD NEWS TO EMPLOYEES

Bad news is often handled differently when the audience in question is within an organization rather than outside it. Announcements of setbacks (e.g., lost contracts, rising
benefit costs, declining profits, and public relations crises) and reminders of unpopular
policies or altered procedures (e.g., reduced benefits, cutbacks, and reductions in raises)
have the potential to affect employee morale and performance. Information on these
issues has to be communicated skilfully—in a way that motivates employees to comply
with new measures and accept less advantageous circumstances. From a managerial
standpoint in particular, it helps to be able to explain why a change is necessary and
how it relates to business objectives.

Individual organizations pass on unfavourable news to their employees in different ways. Some organizations use a direct approach for all internal messages, no matter if the news is good or bad. Others use the indirect approach if the negative information is new or surprising. Usually, the more serious the bad news is, the more readers benefit from an explanation that helps them take stock of the situation and put it in perspective. Your knowledge of your organization—based on its size, values, goals, and openness of communication—can help you communicate bad news more effectively. Before you write, you should have firm answers to the following questions:

- Why has the decision forcing the announcement of bad news been made?
- What is the purpose of the change?
- How does the bad news affect employees?

The e-mail in Figure 7.10 announces an increase in employee premiums for long-term disability.

FIGURE 7.10 Announcing Bad News to Employees

Opens with brief statement of benefits and direct statement of bad news and when new measure goes into effect

Details and purpose of the change help to reduce resistance; language is factual and unapologetic

Directs recipients to additional resources offering information and further interpretation of the change

Subject: Changes to Insurance Benefits Plan
Date: Wednesday, April 1, 2009 8:31 AM
From: Marlene Tsang
To: Insurance Benefits Plan Employees

To maintain the quality of disability coverage, effective May 1 all employees who are currently covered under Ridgeway Realty's insurance benefits plan will see an increase in their long-term disability (LTD) premium. Since this is an employee-paid benefit, the premium increase will be deducted from paycheques commencing with the May 15 pay period.

Ridgeway Realty, as part of the Ridgeway Group of Companies, is on an annual renewal schedule with Great North Provident, our LTD provider. Our rate will be increasing by $0.20 per $100 of monthly benefit, an increase of approximately 11 per cent.

The reason for this increase is based on the fact that all LTD providers are experiencing significant increases in claims, many of which are for "new" disabilities that were not previously deemed as such. On average, rates in the industry are up by between 20 and 30 per cent.

Please refer to the LTD policy found on our intranet site under the heading "Benefits" for information on how to calculate your semi-monthly LTD premium.

If you have any questions, please contact me at extension 531.

Marlene Tsang
Benefits Administrator
Ridgeway Realty
250 Granite Street
Toronto, ON M5W 2P1
Tel: 416-971-4329, ext. 531
Fax: 416-971-9320

DECLINING INVITATIONS

Invitations are an integral part of business life. They offer valuable opportunities to network, learn, and promote your organization. When you must decline an invitation to speak at or attend an event, how you communicate your regrets depends on how well you know the reader and how much your attendance is expected. For large-scale events where your absence is unlikely to cause disappointment, it is possible to send brief regrets, along with an expression of thanks for the invitation. When turning down an invitation from an important client or superior, you must ensure your refusal won't seem like a personal rebuff. Though your refusal can still be brief, make a special effort to maintain goodwill by adopting a warm tone and focusing on something positive about the situation.

1. **Express appreciation for the invitation or pay the reader a compliment.** Recognize the significance of the event, event sponsor, or organization.

2. **Express your regret at not being able to attend and, if appropriate, explain why you are unavailable.** Briefly offer a valid reason for not accepting—not a weak or trivial excuse that might belittle the event or its hosts or organizers. Use the passive voice or keep the reason vague if you need to soften a refusal that might be taken too personally.

3. **Propose a constructive alternative if one is available.** Name someone to speak in your place or express interest in attending a future event.

4. **End by renewing goodwill.** Close on a friendly note with good wishes for success, a word of thanks or praise, or a forward-looking remark. Don't backtrack to the refusal. Tact and courtesy will earn your readers' respect and keep you on their guest lists.

FIGURE 7.11   INEFFECTIVE Refusal of Invitation (extract)

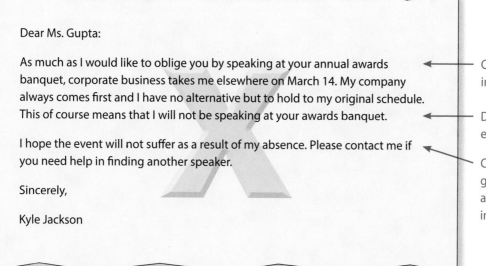

Dear Ms. Gupta:

As much as I would like to oblige you by speaking at your annual awards banquet, corporate business takes me elsewhere on March 14. My company always comes first and I have no alternative but to hold to my original schedule. This of course means that I will not be speaking at your awards banquet.

I hope the event will not suffer as a result of my absence. Please contact me if you need help in finding another speaker.

Sincerely,

Kyle Jackson

— Condescending, self-important tone

— Delivers the bad news early and repeatedly

— Closing fails to convey good wishes or to show appreciation for the invitation

FIGURE 7.12 EFFECTIVE Refusal of Invitation

Stonehall Productions

314 Cherry Street, Toronto, ON M5A 1A9
416•928•8950
www.stonehallprod.com

April 17, 2009

Ms. Neelam Gupta
Communications Coordinator
SPN! – Stop Poverty Now!
130 Wellington Road
Ottawa, ON K1A 0N4

Dear Ms. Gupta:

You have good reason to be proud of your organization's impressive achievements this year. There is perhaps no greater gift to the community than the elimination of child poverty, and I am honoured to have been asked to speak at your annual awards banquet. That you would consider me as a potential keynote speaker at such a gathering is genuinely flattering.

On checking my schedule, I was sorry to find that I will be attending the annual general meeting of our parent company in Geneva on that date. Although your generous invitation must be declined, I will see to it that our program of corporate sponsorship for your fundraising events continues in the year ahead.

As I fully support your initiatives, I would welcome the opportunity to speak at a future event. I wish you well with what is sure to be a splendid evening.

Sincerely,

Kyle Jackson

Kyle Jackson
Vice President, Finance

Annotations (left margin):

Opening compliments the reader and expresses appreciation for the invitation

Offers a plausible but not overly detailed reason for not being available

Uses the passive voice to decline the invitation and attempts to compensate by offering an alternative

Closes with a forward-looking remark and good wishes, reinforced by a friendly tone

Chapter Review Checklist

- [ ] Apply the direct or indirect approach according to the type of bad news and its audience.

- [ ] Never mislead the reader by implying that the purpose of the message is to deliver good news.

- [ ] Use an appropriate subject line.

- [ ] If you use a buffer, make sure it is neutral and relevant—not simply a delaying tactic.

- [ ] Limit the explanation of the bad news to relevant facts and details arranged in a logical order. Make sure your reason is clear, complete, and airtight.

- [ ] Avoid hiding behind company policy; instead, show how the policy is reasonable by explaining its purpose or benefits.

- [ ] State the bad news only once, clearly.

- [ ] For direct approach messages, begin with a concise statement of the bad news, followed by a brief explanation, alternative, and goodwill closing.

- [ ] For indirect approach messages, buffer, explain, and de-emphasize the bad news, and close with expressions of goodwill.

- [ ] Offer a counter-proposal or alternative if a good one is available, and provide enough information for the reader to act on that alternative. Taking this step shows that you care.

- [ ] Use neutral, respectful, and non-accusatory language to maintain goodwill. Avoid a condescending, patronizing, know-it-all tone.

- [ ] End positively with a goodwill-building statement not related to the bad news while avoiding clichés or remarks that suggest your decision isn't final.

- [ ] Don't invite further correspondence unless you truly want it.

WORKSHOPS AND DISCUSSION FORUMS

Analyze the following excerpt from a letter. List its faults and weaknesses. Using the Chapter Review Checklist as your guide, decide how to revise it.

> I regret to inform you that it is impossible for us to admit children under the age of 6 to our Junior Trekker summer camp program. Our camp policy does not allow us to make any such exceptions, no matter how precocious or mature a child may seem. To allow children of that age to participate in full-day activities that even a 10-year-old might find challenging would endanger all campers and put our operation at risk.
>
> Thank you for understanding our position. Call us when your child is older. We take pride in offering safe and fun activities for children of many ages.

WRITING IMPROVEMENT EXERCISES

1. **Writing Plans for Bad News Messages:** Identify which writing plan—direct or indirect—you would use for the following messages.
   a) A memo to employees announcing the cancellation of a lunchtime lecture series.
   b) A letter informing a customer of a six-week postponement of on-site software training.
   c) A memo to an immediate subordinate denying him a requested two-day leave to participate in a square-dancing competition. It is company practice to write all internal messages straightforwardly.
   d) A memo from an executive rejecting a manager's phased retirement plan.
   e) A letter from a roofing company denying a customer's request to repair a roof for which the warranty expired five months ago.

2. **Evaluating Buffer Statements:** Analyze the strengths and weaknesses of the following openings for bad news messages.
   a) We were very happy to receive your recent request for a refund of the purchase price of your new XJL copier, the model *Consumers Annual* ranked tops for efficiency and customer satisfaction.
   b) We are so sorry that we won't be repairing your poorly functioning air conditioning system.
   c) Thank you for contacting Amitron about a marketing position. I receive hundreds of applications from qualified college graduates just like you.
   d) You honestly can't expect us to investigate a claim for a product that is no longer under warranty.
   e) We at Timberline Tire and Auto make every effort to provide our customers with high-quality products at the lowest possible prices. We are committed to finding ways to make shopping at our stores more convenient for you.
   f) Each year, our company sponsors a holiday dinner for employees to show our appreciation for their hard work and commitment, but this year severe budget cuts prevent us from hosting such an event.
   g) You are surely our best-dressed sales representative. I always look forward to receiving proposals from well-attired staff members.

3. **Softening the Bad News with Subordinate Clauses and the Passive Voice:** Use dependent clauses and/or passive-voice constructions to de-emphasize the bad news in each of the following statements.
    a) We cannot extend credit to you at this time but we invite you to fill your order on a cash basis.
    b) We cannot waive service charges on chequing accounts.
    c) It is impossible for us to send you the information you requested. We can provide you only with an updated price list.
    d) We cannot substitute a more expensive item for the one you purchased, but we are sending you a complimentary upgrade kit.

4. **Evaluating Bad News Statements:** Discuss the weaknesses of the following statements and revise them as needed.
    a) It is utterly impossible for us to ship your order before November 1.
    b) How can you honestly expect us to act on your complaint more than three years after your purchase?
    c) Since you failed to include the sales receipt, we refuse to give you a refund.
    d) Although we cannot offer you a position at this time, we wish you the best in finding employment equal to your fine qualifications.
    e) We cannot grant your request, but we can assure you that your next visit to our conference facility will not be so unpleasant.
    f) To be honest, we like your resumé, but we find we must hire from within or face legal action from our current employees.

    g) We cannot provide you with the information you requested because doing so would violate agreements with our employees and expose us to legal action.
    h) We don't accept credit cards.

5. **Evaluating closings:** Analyze the weaknesses of the following letter closings and revise them as needed.
    a) We thank you for understanding our position and hope to see you in our store very soon.
    b) I am sorry that we were forced to refuse your application, but I wish you the best of luck in finding employment when there is so much competition for the few jobs that are available.
    c) Please accept our apologies for discontinuing this popular service. We hope you will still shop with us despite this added inconvenience.
    d) Although we must turn down your request for a refund, we usually do issue refunds if merchandise is undamaged and returned within ten days of the date of purchase.
    e) If we knew the answer to your question, we would be only too happy to provide you with the information that you are seeking. Perhaps we will able to help you with a future inquiry.

6. **Evaluating Subject Lines:** revise the following subject lines from negative messages to make them more reader-centred and neutral.
    a) Insurance Premiums Going Up
    b) Layoffs Possible
    c) Suspected Theft of Equipment
    d) No More Personal Use of Photocopiers

CASE STUDY EXERCISES

1. **Refusing a Request:** Editors of the monthly publication *National Business* have asked you, a consultant with Brandwise Solutions, to write a brief case-study article for their magazine. In particular they are interested in your response to the rebranding of Goliath Groceries, Canada's fourth-largest supermarket chain, which commands a 14 per cent market share. Goliath has recently merged its distribution network, switched over to large-format stores, and repositioned itself as a whole foods and express foods retailer in order to gain a market niche distinct from recently arrived U.S. rivals such as Stars and Stripes of Arkansas. Although you would like to offer your opinions on the subject, you fear a possible conflict of interest since your consulting firm advised on the branding and redesign of Goliath's low-price chain,

Save-a-Buck. You are also scheduled to leave this evening for a three-month overseas consulting job. Write to the editors declining their request but leaving the door open for future writing opportunities.

2. **Claim Refusal—No Return Policy on Opened CDs:** As Gus Traynor, owner and proprietor of Audiophile CDs and Multimedia, you must refuse the claim of Jason Yee. Mr. Yee recently purchased CDs valued at $750 from your downtown Vancouver store. A few days later, he brought them back with opened packaging and asked for a refund, saying that he was disappointed with their sound quality. When he was refused, Mr. Yee decided to write to you in person to complain, angrily. Although you don't want to accuse Mr. Yee of wrongdoing, you realize that the practice of copying CDs and then returning them is well documented and widespread. In fact, your profits have suffered as a result of it. A year ago, out of respect for copyright law as it applies to the recording industry, you revoked your no-questions-asked return policy. You still offer refunds, but only on items that haven't been opened. Write to Mr. Yee refusing his request.

3. **Claim Refusal—Not Covered for Additional Moving Expenses:** As Lilly Gao, manager of human resources, you must refuse a request for reimbursement for additional moving expenses from Roger Laramie, the new assistant manager of Information Systems. When Roger transferred divisions last month from Montreal to Calgary, he was promised the standard relocation allowance of $5,000 to cover cartage and insurance costs for a long-distance move, based on estimates for the contents of a three-bedroom home. As soon as Roger received news of his transfer, he was informed that out-of-province moves for your company are handled by Express Movers, a corporate moving specialist offering discounted rates. Despite the existing agreement with Express Movers, Roger instead signed a contract with Elite Movers, a company whose rates are substantially higher because of their experience in shipping fragile short-wave radio equipment such as his. As a result, the claim for moving expenses he submitted exceeded $9,000. Write to Roger Laramie explaining your reasons for the refusal while attempting to retain his goodwill.

4. **Credit Refusal—Office Furniture Purchase:** As Melissa Shim, credit manager at Concept Office Furniture, you must turn down a credit application from Alan Medwell of Discount Realty. Mr. Medwell has placed a sizable order for modular office furniture, asking for 120-day credit terms. Though Discount Realty has been a good customer in the past, a review of their financial statement and information supplied by credit references has led you to conclude that the firm is in financial difficulty. Refuse Mr. Medwell's request for credit while encouraging his business now or in the future.

5. **Announcing Bad News to Employees—Changes to Office Catering:** As head of the occupational health and safety committee at your workplace, you are concerned about the practice of stocking employee kitchenettes with free coffee and cookies. Lately you have begun to notice that harried employees routinely skip lunch and instead grab handfuls of cookies to eat at their desks. While you understand the necessity for these makeshift meals, you feel that there is room in the budget to provide healthier alternatives to these high-fat, carbohydrate-laden snacks. In fact, the health and safety committee voted with you in favour of such a motion at a recent meeting, but you anticipate a high level of resistance from employees for whom the cookies are a dietary staple. Write a memo to all staff announcing that, effective next month, kitchenettes will be stocked with a selection of fresh fruits, whole-grain snacks, and spring water instead of the usual coffee and cookies. Consider which approach would be most appropriate.

6. **Announcing Bad News to Employees—On-Site Fitness Program for Employees Only:** When you established an on-site fitness program a year ago, you had no idea how popular it would be. Employees at your small packaging plant quickly signed up for free lunch-hour and after-work yoga sessions and Pilates classes. Enrolment soon reached capacity, prompting you to expand the program at additional cost to you. After a few inquiries, however, you were upset to discover that non-employees routinely breech security and take part in classes meant solely for the benefit of employees. You would prefer not to cancel the program because it has helped to reduce absenteeism and indirectly boost productivity, but you must enforce limits on participation in order to keep costs down. E-mail the staff reminding people of the restrictions on participation in the program.

7. **Announcing Bad News to Employees—Indefinite Postponement of Holiday Party:** In past years, your company has hosted a premier corporate entertainment event for all employees and their spouses/partners in early December. The celebration has always featured a cocktail reception, three-course dinner, live entertainment, charity raffle, and dancing. Only days before this year's event was to take place, however, there has been a serious outbreak of salmonella at the planned venue, forcing a shutdown of the hotel's food services by the regional board of health. Because the hotel's facilities are booked until February, it will not be possible to reschedule the event in the immediate future. As events coordinator for your organization, you doubt that most people would be happy with a rebooking at this venue, given the recent health alert. Write a group e-mail message to employees informing them of the postponement and possible cancellation of the holiday party. Suggest an alternative that would still allow employees to socialize and celebrate the holiday season.

8. **Announcing Bad News to Customers—Virus Problem for Internet Customers:** As chief of the services team for a small Internet provider, it is your responsibility to issue a virus alert to customers. Your team recently detected a virus affecting several computers in your network. Although the virus has affected only a limited number of members, you feel it is appropriate to assume a proactive role in controlling viruses by contacting members and helping them upgrade their operating systems and providing them with regular virus updates. Compose an e-mail message to customers, drawing appropriate attention to this important problem.

9. **Announcing Bad News to Employees—Office Relocation:** As Garth Thomas, president of a small insurance brokerage firm, it is your task to inform employees of the upcoming expropriation of your office premises for a new condominium development. The news of the expropriation was sudden and you have had to move quickly to find a new location. This task has not been easy. High property taxes and corporate rental rates in downtown Toronto have forced you to relocate your insurance brokerage to Pickering, many kilometres from the downtown core. You know that many employees may be inconvenienced by this

change, as many live within walking distance of your current location. Some staffers do not even own cars for the fifty-kilometre commute. On the plus side, the new low-rise building to which you are relocating is a state-of-the-art facility, with ample parking and easy access to public transit. The increase in square footage and money saved in rental fees means there will be no layoffs as a result of the relocation. Compose an e-mail message to employees informing them of the changes. Remember to include a schedule of the proposed changes.

10. **Claim Refusal—Damaged Cedar Deck:** As Vikram Vassanji, owner of Cedar Country Decks and Fences, you must refuse the following request. Josh Starowicz, president of Animatronix Computer Animation, has asked you to repair his office's rooftop deck, which you installed eight years ago when the century-old building was owned by Caption Advertising. On completion of the carpentry, you applied a generous coat of Thompson's Water Seal and advised Gord McNamara, Caption's president, that the sealant should be reapplied regularly. To help him maintain the deck cheaply, you even offered him a low-cost annual maintenance contract, which he refused. When Animatronix purchased the property and moved in a year ago, staff members were alarmed at the condition of the deck—boards were warped and rotten, sections of the security railing were missing, and stair treads were loose. Apparently, Gord McNamara's cousin, a general contractor, had been called in to do repairs, but he had ceased work after sanding away the sealant that remained, hastening the deck's deterioration. Although you normally guarantee your work, you do not feel justified in repairing it at no cost, according to Josh Starowicz's request. The damage clearly resulted from poor maintenance and shoddy workmanship by other contractors. In addition, the cost of materials alone for such a job would exceed $5,000, an expense your small business simply can't absorb. Although you firmly believe that fault does not rest with you, you would like to retain the goodwill of the building's new owner, in part because neighbouring businesses have recently been accepting bids for deck projects. Write to Josh Starowicz refusing his claim but offering a solution, perhaps in the form of a free inspection or a discount on repairs.

ONLINE ACTIVITIES

Identify the Special Demands and Characteristics of Bad News Messages

Read "The 10 Commandments for Delivering Bad News" from *Forbes* online:

http://www.forbes.com/sites/forbesleadership
forum/2012/05/30/10-commandments-for-
delivering-bad-news/

Then watch the following video of Maple Leaf Foods CEO Michael McCain as he spoke in the wake of the listeria outbreak in 2008:

http://www.youtube.com/watch?v=
zIsN5AkJ1AI

To what extent does McCain's speech uphold the principles outlined in the *Forbes* article?

8

Persuasive Messages

In this chapter you will learn to

1. Identify the need for persuasive communication.

2. Use the indirect writing plan to persuade.

3. Apply persuasive appeals.

4. Ask for favours and action persuasively.

5. Make contestable claims successfully.

6. Gain support for new ideas in persuasive memos.

7. Convince debtors to pay their bills promptly.

8. Compose effective sales letters and fundraising messages.

Writing Persuasively

How do you encourage the people you work and conduct business with to agree with you or do what you ask? When you ask for a favour, present new ideas, promote a product, or explain how to solve a problem, you can sometimes meet with resistance. People may hesitate to do as you say if it involves time, money, effort, or change. When you have to convince the reader to adopt your point of view or take a particular action, however, you can rely on special persuasive strategies and an indirect approach to help you gain compliance, minimize objections, and get the results you seek.

Persuasion—the attempt to influence opinion—works at changing attitudes, beliefs, and behaviours. It involves a skilful use of words that help put ideas into action and make things happen. Persuasive communication motivates readers to accept recommendations and act on requests. It gradually breaks down resistance and establishes rapport with readers by appealing to their needs, interests, values, and powers of reason. The value of persuasive messaging is that it achieves its purpose without threats or manipulation. It doesn't coerce or *make* readers do something; it makes them *want* to do it, in part by respecting their views and intelligence.

The ability to write persuasively is a valued workplace skill, and those who master it earn kudos for themselves and their companies through their ability to sell products and ideas. Needless to say, persuasion is a skill with endless applications. Any message that encourages action requires persuasion: favour requests, job application letters (see Chapter 9), contestable claims, sales and fundraising letters, and collection letters.

PREPARING TO WRITE PERSUASIVELY

The following are some points to remember that will help you write effective persuasive messages:

- **Know your purpose and what you want your reader to do.** Your goal is not only to make your request, but also to make it seem reasonable, appealing, and beneficial to the reader. It is easier to convince your audience when you know exactly what your purpose is—before you begin to write. A good persuasive message must be informative, so collect data that will help you overcome resistance and allow readers to follow up easily.
- **Understand what motivates your reader.** Analyze your audience in terms of its perceived goals and needs. Organizational psychologist Abraham Maslow defined these motivating factors in terms of an ascending **hierarchy of needs**, from the most basic needs at the bottom to the abstract needs at the top (see Figure 8.1).

  Once basic needs, which take priority, have been met, individuals move on to fulfill needs at higher levels. Persuasive writing taps into those motivational needs, so it is important to show how your request satisfies one or more of these needs—how a product or policy benefits readers by saving them money, solving a problem, or helping them achieve a work objective.

persuasion the process of gradually influencing attitudes and behaviours and motivating the audience to act.

Maslow's hierarchy of needs a specific order of needs identified by Abraham Maslow—physical needs, the need for safety, social needs, the need for self-esteem, and the need for self-actualization—all of which motivate humans.

FIGURE 8.1 Maslow's Hierarchy of Needs

Self-actualization is the highest level of need, met when people use their talents and problem-solving skills to serve humanity and live up to their potential.

Esteem is first among what Maslow termed "growth needs." The need for status, appreciation, and recognition leads people to strive for status symbols, work promotions, positions of authority, or good reputations.

Love and a sense of belonging are at a slightly higher level of need. Most people seek acceptance, companionship, and group identity. They don't want to be alone—they need to be needed.

Safety and security represent the next level of need. People are often motivated by the fear of not having a comfortable standard of living, a good health insurance or pension plan, reliable investments, job security, home security, or a pleasant work environment. They want to hold onto the money and resources that give them a sense of security.

Physiological needs include basics such as food, shelter, clothing, medical care, and a safe working environment.

- **Consider design and layout.** Opinions are often formed before a message is read, based on its appearance alone. A proper layout—one that conveys non-verbal messages through proportioning, typography, and use of white space—puts a document in a positive light and makes it look both attractive and professional.
- **Be positive and accurate.** Plan on adopting a sincere, confident tone and using positive, you-centred language. Match your phrasing to your relationship with the reader and avoid giving the impression that you are handing out orders. Stick to the facts—don't distort information just to get your way.
- **Anticipate objections and plan how to deal with them.** Persuasion is necessary whenever you expect resistance or when you think readers would prefer to keep things as they are. It is important to consider why readers might object to what you have to say and to be prepared to offer clear and compelling counter-arguments to refute the opposing view. Overcoming opposition is a delicate matter best done in a non-threatening and balanced way. Readers are naturally more receptive and more likely to change their minds when their views have been respected, taken into account, and not simply labelled wrong. Try to frame your persuasive request as a win-win proposition. A concession statement can let you acknowledge those objections in a non-judgmental way before you offer a rebuttal that proves that what you are asking for makes sense and needs to be acted on: *although the new system may cause some disruptions at first, it will speed processing dramatically and give us access to all relevant company-wide databases.*

To counter resistance and encourage readers to say yes, present your request in light of one of the following arguments:

- Short-term pain for long-term gain: small sacrifices or inconveniences now will result in the achievement of greater long-term objectives.
- The advantages outweigh the disadvantages.
- Money spent is money or time saved in the long run.
- Investment of time or money will bring other benefits.

Deal with serious objections early. However, don't let trivial objections sidetrack you, and don't give these objections a false importance by spending time on them at the expense of your own arguments.

PERSUASIVE APPEALS

Persuasive messages appeal to the reader's reasoning, emotions, or sense of what is right and credible. The success of your communication depends on the strength of the case you build. Because not all audiences or persuasive tasks are alike, messages that must convince can rely on single or combined **appeals**.

appeal an attempt to persuade.

- **Appeal to Reason:** Because people in business must be able to justify the decisions they make, they usually respond best to logical presentations of evidence—non-numerical facts, expert opinions, statistics, examples, and analogies. Effective reasoning based on evidence, in one or more of these forms, leads the reader to a conclusion—and to accept that the writer is right and knows what she is talking about. For a reader to accept a claim or opinion as reasonable, the persuasion that supports it must show clear, logical development, with facts adding up like numbers in an equation. A cause–effect, problem–solution, or chronological pattern can help an appeal make more sense. In addition to proving your point, you should also answer questions the reader is likely to raise and eliminate errors in logic—flaws that can rob your appeal of its persuasive power. Among the most common **logical fallacies** are *post hoc ergo propter hoc* (mistaking coincidence for cause), *circular arguments* (restating an opinion instead of backing it up), *begging the question* (sidetracking the reader from an important issue), and *false analogy* (making a comparison that doesn't apply).

logical fallacy an error in logic that weakens a persuasive argument— for example, a personal attack, a mistaken assumption that one event causes another, or reliance on testimony of someone who isn't an expert.

- **Appeal to Emotion:** Emotions are powerful persuasive tools. When facts alone fail to convince, an emotional appeal can motivate people to act and respond. A play on emotions can create a desire to act on a request. The reader doesn't only see the logic of doing something, but actually *wants* to do it. It is worth remembering, however, that tapping into emotions such as pride, hope, honour, pleasure, respect, and fear can be risky and seem manipulative to a reader who is not entirely on your side. For this reason, emotional appeals have only the most limited application to business messages and work only when they rest on a strong logical foundation. Emotional power comes from language—the use of words that evoke certain responses—*deserve, special, safe, new, free*. Stories, concrete examples, and descriptions based on sense impressions (what the reader can see, feel, hear, taste, and smell) can all help you to persuade with emotion. The following are two examples of appeals to emotion:
  1. A memo that asks for safer working conditions may play on a sense of responsibility and pride in a company's reputation: *our company has always maintained a level of safety above industry standards.*

2. The final letter in a series of collection letters or payment-past-due notices may arouse fear at the consequences of not paying immediately: *if we do not receive payment immediately, we will be forced to turn your account over to an attorney for collection. Such action will damage your previously good credit rating.*

- **Appeal to Ethics.** If you want to influence people, it is important to establish your credibility beforehand or to create it during a message. Credibility has to do with the image you cultivate. It refers to how believable, responsible, and ethical you, your company, and your statements are perceived to be. Personal credibility is based on your knowledge, reputation, position of authority, and familiarity with your reader. Credibility has several sources:

  1. **Specialized knowledge.** Demonstrating your expertise earns your reader's confidence, especially when the reader doesn't already know you. Readers will evaluate you and your message on the strength of your evidence and the logic of its presentation. You can compensate for a lack of expertise by citing expert opinions or the views of someone the reader trusts.

  2. **Reputation.** The better your reputation—how you are thought of according to your character and past conduct—the more likely readers are to trust you.

  3. **Authority.** The built-in authority that comes with your business title can give you added leverage and command respect as long as it isn't perceived as bullying or coercion. It is fine to project your authority, but not to abuse it.

  4. **Familiarity.** Relationships build trust, but if you don't know the reader you can still forge a connection by finding common ground—for example, by identifying a mutual interest, shared problem, or common goal.

Finally, if you want people to trust you, avoid image-damaging sarcasm and hostility. Your credibility can be further enhanced when you focus on reader benefits, not on what you have to gain personally.

INDIRECT WRITING PLAN FOR PERSUASIVE MESSAGES

The purpose of an indirect persuasive strategy is to break down resistance and prepare readers for a request or proposal that could easily fail if made directly. A gradual, deliberate approach allows you to first earn trust and reason with readers, making it easier for them to understand how they will benefit from what you ask them to do at the end of the message. An indirect message may take more time to write, but following the three-step plan outlined below is worth the effort if you need to overcome resistance and indifference:

1. **Obtain interest.** In a short paragraph, make a good first impression and provide incentive for the reader to pay attention to the rest of your message: define a problem, identify common ground, cite reader benefits, ask a pertinent question, or state a related fact that stimulates interest. Use an attention-getting technique that is relevant to your audience and purpose.

2. **Prove your proposal or product can benefit the reader.** Capitalize on the interest you have generated by explaining how what you propose or sell meets a particular need. Benefits may be direct, coming automatically from doing something (e.g., receiving an income tax deduction as a result of making a charitable donation) or indirect (e.g., the satisfaction of knowing that your donation will help

someone else). Give readers the information they need to act on your request, and deal with any objections readers might have.

3. **Ask for action and link it to reader benefits.** Even a request that makes a positive impression doesn't succeed unless readers act on it. An effective persuasive appeal ends with a specific and confident request linked to incentives that motivate readers to act immediately and decisively, sometimes by a set deadline chosen for a particular reason.

This basic pattern is multi-purpose and can be modified to deliver a variety of persuasive messages.

Types of Persuasive Messages

FAVOUR AND ACTION REQUESTS

Small favours are easy to ask for. However, when you make greater demands on readers by asking them to donate money or volunteer their time and expertise—with the promise of little or nothing in return—you can expect resistance, so persuasive strategies are vital. An indirect strategy allows you to gain acceptance for invitations, requests for volunteer services, and appeals for any kind of unpaid help. The direct benefits of performing such favours are usually small and sometimes non-existent. An explanation focusing on the indirect benefits of complying (see the second point below) reassures readers that they are doing the right thing.

1. **Gain favourable attention.** Because you need to entice the reader to comply, don't begin by phrasing your request as a question that can be answered with a *yes* or *no*. Instead catch readers' attention with a genuine compliment or a fact that awakens their social conscience. Don't encourage readers to decline your request by providing them with a convenient excuse or making an apology. You need to make a positive first impression.

2. **Persuade the reader to accept.** Readers won't feel obliged to help you unless they know background details of the request and understand what they have to gain. Help readers view the request positively by associating it with one of the following:

   - the chance to assume a leadership role or showcase talents,
   - the opportunity to network, develop professional contacts, or gain exposure for their views, or
   - the chance to help others or bring about positive change in their workplace or community.

   Specify exactly what the favour involves by referring to dates, times, and locations.

3. **Ask for action.** Express your request with confidence and courtesy to encourage acceptance. Provide the information (telephone numbers, contact names) the reader will need to follow up. End with a reminder that you are looking forward to a response.

The letter in Figure 8.3 is an effective favour request from a municipal councillor to employees and selected constituents requesting a ticket purchase for a fundraising event.

FIGURE 8.2 INEFFECTIVE Favour Request (extract)

Please consider supporting the Children's Aid Foundation by purchasing a $250 family package for our "Be a Kid Again" fundraising event, which will be held at Paramount Canada's Wonderland on Friday, April 30, 2010.

We guarantee that this money will be put to good use. The amount we raised last year certainly was.

If you have any questions about this event, you should phone me at 416-331-8693. Remember to buy your tickets—the kids are counting on you. Don't make them suffer.

Hoping you'll get back to me,

Fiona Walsh

Regional Councillor

Begins with a direct and expensive request

Fails to build interest in the event and doesn't provide readers with details of how the money raised will be spent and who will benefit

Offers no details about the fundraising event and doesn't mention direct and indirect benefits (e.g., the chance to have fun and help others)

Bullies readers into buying tickets and doesn't mention how the tickets can be ordered

PERSUASIVE MEMOS

How can you successfully lobby for safer working conditions, persuade staff to accept a new computer system, or justify the expense of a new program? A persuasive memo describes a problem to management or colleagues, then presents a solution that ends in a related proposal or request. Its indirect problem–solution strategy gains attention and gradual support for an action required of employees or an idea that needs approval prior to implementation. Because a persuasive memo communicates facts and benefits before it pushes for action, there is less chance the initiative it endorses will be misunderstood or rejected prematurely. By building an honest and logical argument based on fact, not conjecture or false claims, an effective persuasive memo (Figures 8.5 and 8.6) overcomes resistance and convinces readers that a plan will work or that altered procedures are necessary. The memo ultimately succeeds when it puts words and ideas into action and wins support for a well-defined problem. Here are the steps to follow when writing a problem-solving memo that gives limited chance for readers to say no:

1. **Summarize the problem.** Identify the cause or source of a problem while suggesting that the problem is solvable. Keep readers interested by avoiding accusations and strongly negative language. To stimulate interest, begin with a subject line that focuses on positive results and benefits.

2. **Explain how the problem can be solved.** If a problem is relevant to them, readers will want to read on. Establish a logical foundation for your later request, citing statistical evidence, facts, and figures while also outlining benefits.

3. **Minimize resistance.** Anticipate objections readers might have (too expensive, too time-consuming, or a threat to someone's authority, professional status, or the status quo). Because you may have to acknowledge an alternative solution the

FIGURE 8.3 EFFECTIVE Favour Request

Town of Finsbury

164-A Blossom Petal Way, Finsbury, ON M5W 2X6

January 12, 2010

Dr. Elizabeth Rhynold
Finsbury Medical Centre
45 Main Street South
Finsbury, ON M5W 2X6

Dear Dr. Rhynold:

Last year our "Be a Kid Again" event in support of the Children's Aid Foundation of Lancaster Region raised over $20,000 for organizations serving children and youth in our community. Your support made a difference in the lives of children at risk, providing much-needed funds for sports equipment, music lessons, dental work, and summer camp programs.

The Children's Aid Foundation receives government funding for services that are directly related to protecting children throughout Lancaster Region from abuse, neglect, and abandonment. However, the CAF is not able to provide discretionary services within its budget. These are programs and services that are designed to offer children positive life experiences that they would not likely otherwise have.

Our second annual fundraising event is being held this year at Paramount Canada's Wonderland on **Friday, April 30, 2010,** from 4:00 to 10:00 p.m. The day promises a chance to "be a kid again" with fun-filled activities and surprises, including a deluxe theme-park dinner, admission to all rides and attractions, a souvenir package, special entertainment for children, and a lucky draw. The price for a four-ticket family package is $250. When you purchase this package you will receive a tax receipt for $210.

Please help this very worth cause by purchasing tickets for yourself and your employees. Simply complete and return the enclosed ticket order form along with your cheque, payable to The Children's Aid Foundation, marked to my attention at Town of Finsbury. Due to the popularity of this event, we recommend that you place your order by Friday, April 15 to avoid disappointment. For more details, please call me at 519-331-8693.

Annotations (left margin):

- Begins by praising readers for their social responsibility and generosity
- Explains why fundraising is necessary and who will benefit from the money raised
- Offers details of the event—time, date, location, cost
- Appeals to reason and emotions and highlights direct and indirect benefits: participants will have fun and help others

(continued)

FIGURE 8.3 (continued)

Dr. Elizabeth Rhynold
January 12, 2010
Page 2

If you would like to support this event but are unable to attend, we will be pleased to donate your tickets to a foster family from Lancaster Region Children's Aid Foundation—and you will still receive a tax receipt.

Join us on April 30 and be a kid again. The kids in our community will be glad you did. ← *Ends by summarizing the request and linking it to benefits*

Sincerely,

Fiona Walsh

Fiona Walsh
Regional Councillor

Enc.

---

reader may prefer, you should be prepared to offer convincing counter-arguments that show how your solution is superior to all others.

4. **Ask for a specific action.** Be firm but polite. Set a deadline for readers to act or respond as long as it won't seem aggressive and offer incentives (time or money saved) if you require action promptly.

FIGURE 8.4 INEFFECTIVE Persuasive Memo (extract)

Subject: Switching to Satellite Training ← *Vague subject line fails to highlight benefits or focus on positive results*

Lately, training costs have gone out of control. The real problem is covering the travel expenses of employees and trainers, who must travel between local branches and national headquarters. For this reason, I strongly urge you to meet with representatives from Finance Vision, operator of an interactive television network, and see their demonstration on satellite training. The cost for a half-day training session is just $10,000. I hope you will agree with me that this is the best possible solution. ← *Pushes for action before it fully communicates the reasons for that action; offers no statistical evidence to back up explanation of the problem*

Please get back to me as soon as possible. We will need to liase with Finance Vision soon if we hope to use this technology for our RRSP training season. ← *Aggressive closing*

FIGURE 8.5 EFFECTIVE Persuasive Memo

Bothwell and Associates, Inc.

Interoffice Memo

TO: Malcolm Reynolds, Human Resources Manager

FROM: River Simons, Training Coordinator

DATE: April 17, 2010

SUBJECT: Reducing Training Program Costs

Last year, the cost to send trainers on the road and to bring employees from across the country to training events at our national headquarters exceeded $1.2 million. Mounting travel costs accounted for the dramatic increase in training expenses. According to projections, by 2011 it will cost over $2.5 million to maintain training programs at current levels.

With advances in satellite delivery methods, however, it is now possible to conduct nationwide training more cost-effectively in virtual classrooms equipped with satellite dishes, television sets, and interactive handsets. Satellite presentations have several distinct advantages over conventional methods:

1. Everyone receives the same information at the same time from keynote speakers and slide and video presentations.

2. Employees can interact with each other and share ideas just as they would if they were sitting side by side. They can ask questions, take multiple-choice tests by keying responses into interactive handsets, and be polled by the presenter.

3. Nationwide training programs that normally take months can be conducted in a matter of days.

While computer-based training is an option, test groups often complain that this delivery method isn't engaging enough. Satellite training can be expensive, with the cost of in-house set-ups averaging $10,000 to $15,000 per site. However, by outsourcing the service to an interactive television network such as Finance Vision, it is possible to offer a half-day seminar to an unlimited number of sites at approximately the same price. Finance Vision operates from forty hotels across Canada, all fully equipped and staffed by technicians.

Please allow me to arrange for a demonstration from Finance Vision so that we can learn more about how a satellite training program can help us reduce our training costs.

Margin annotations:

Subject line focuses on positive results and benefits

Opening gains attention by describing problem and quantifying it with statistical evidence

Explains how the problem can be solved and lists advantages for greater emphasis

Minimizes resistance by acknowledging counter-arguments and potential drawbacks

Politely asks for action and connects action to benefits

FIGURE 8.6 Persuasive Memo II

Bothwell and Associates, Inc.

Interoffice Memo

TO: Simon Tam, Vice President, Sales

FROM: Winifred Burkle, Customer Service Manager

DATE: June 17, 2010

SUBJECT: Improving Customer Service ◄——— Subject line creates a positive focus on benefits

The majority of our sales associates currently rely on four computers at the payment desk whenever they need to provide customers with details of new products, warranties, and delivery dates. Retrieving information in this way has proven to be both awkward and time-consuming, often resulting in disgruntled customers and lost sales. ◄——— Opening describes the problem in detail, from both the employee's and the customer's perspective

I believe we could expedite sales transactions, eliminate in-store inconvenience to customers, and improve after-sales service if each of our eight sales associates was equipped with a hand-held personal digital assistant (PDA). Like desktops, PDAs can be used to record customer names, addresses, product information, purchases, dates of transactions, and sales bill numbers, plus any sales-related details revealed in conversation. ◄——— Explanation of solution highlights benefits and focuses on key facts

Once equipped with these hand-held units, sales staff will become walking databases of past and present transaction details, making it possible for them to deliver a higher level of personalized service. Sales associates can also program the devices to remind them to do important follow-up tasks such as sending a written thank-you note following a purchase. With additional software, the devices can be used to track inventory and write bills of sale. These factors help to make PDAs more customer-friendly than desktops. Most importantly, the improvements they promise to customer service will not add to overheads.

For these reasons, I recommend that we purchase 11 refurbished Palm M100 series PDAs for use by our sales associates, warehouse supervisor, and payroll clerks. Although Palm has discontinued this model in favour of producing more advanced smartphones, the basic, user-friendly design of the M100 is ideal for our needs. I have contacted a web-based distributor that has offered to sell us 11 models for $550; this offer includes a one-year repair warranty from the distributor. ◄——— Asks for action and minimizes possible objections

Attached are details of Palm's M100 series PDAs. Please give me authorization to submit a purchase order for 11 units by July 31 so that we may better serve our customers during the Kitchen Aid promotion that begins September 1. ◄——— Links action to positive outcomes and includes end date to encourage prompt response to proposed solution

Attachment

CLAIM REQUESTS

Straightforward, well-justified claims can be made directly. However, if a warranty has lapsed, if a term of a contract has been contravened, or if a product is no longer under guarantee, a claim may be judged questionable—and fail—unless persuasive strategies are used. This means you must first prove the legitimacy of your claim with a clear line of reasoning before you can ask for an adjustment. A weak or questionable claim can usually be strengthened with expressions of confidence in a company's integrity and fairness and appeals to its pride in its products and reputation—if only because successful businesses want customers to be satisfied. As with other types of claims, it is important to adopt a moderate tone—to make a complaint without sounding like a complainer. Your challenge is to show that the company or receiver is responsible for the problem, not you. However, if you succumb to anger or irrational threats and accusations, especially about a company's honesty, you lose respect and risk antagonizing the person handling your claim. The person in question is likely not at fault for your problem but a claims adjuster or customer service representative with no prior knowledge of the complaint or difficulty, someone whose job it is to help you. If you present yourself as fair and easy to deal with and show your disappointment without expressing anger, you will be taken seriously and your claim will stand a better chance of being granted—and granted promptly. Here are some steps to follow:

1. **Gain positive attention.** Establish rapport or common ground with the reader by beginning with a compliment, a point of shared interest, a review of action taken to solve the problem, or your original reason (if favourable) for buying the product or service.

FIGURE 8.7 INEFFECTIVE Persuasive Claim (extract)

Begins negatively and offers the reader a reason for not granting the adjustment →

Doesn't specify the type of membership, indicate when it was taken out, or refer to the terms of the contract →

Doesn't provide a chronology, supporting data, or a strong reason for granting the adjustment →

Ends angrily without asking for a refund →

Dear Manager,

The health club industry has a poor track record when it comes to responding to membership complaints. Now I hope you will prove this perception wrong by allowing me to cancel my membership even though the 10-day cooling-off period has now elapsed.

When I took out a membership, I thought it would guarantee me full access to every class and facility. As it turned out, all the classes I went to were full and I was turned away even though I had signed up in advance. I think this is a poor way to treat paying members, don't you?

If you don't do something about this situation, I will have no alternative but to contact the Canadian Council of Better Business Bureaus, the Ontario Ministry of Consumer Services, and my lawyer. Then we'll see what happens.

Angrily,

Signature

FIGURE 8.8 EFFECTIVE Persuasive Claim

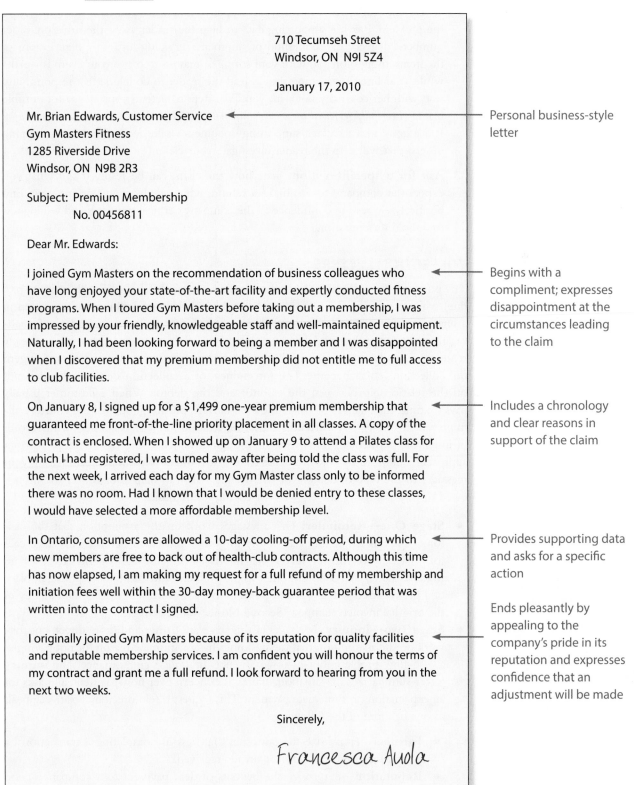

710 Tecumseh Street
Windsor, ON N9I 5Z4

January 17, 2010

Mr. Brian Edwards, Customer Service
Gym Masters Fitness
1285 Riverside Drive
Windsor, ON N9B 2R3

Subject: Premium Membership
No. 00456811

Dear Mr. Edwards:

I joined Gym Masters on the recommendation of business colleagues who have long enjoyed your state-of-the-art facility and expertly conducted fitness programs. When I toured Gym Masters before taking out a membership, I was impressed by your friendly, knowledgeable staff and well-maintained equipment. Naturally, I had been looking forward to being a member and I was disappointed when I discovered that my premium membership did not entitle me to full access to club facilities.

On January 8, I signed up for a $1,499 one-year premium membership that guaranteed me front-of-the-line priority placement in all classes. A copy of the contract is enclosed. When I showed up on January 9 to attend a Pilates class for which I had registered, I was turned away after being told the class was full. For the next week, I arrived each day for my Gym Master class only to be informed there was no room. Had I known that I would be denied entry to these classes, I would have selected a more affordable membership level.

In Ontario, consumers are allowed a 10-day cooling-off period, during which new members are free to back out of health-club contracts. Although this time has now elapsed, I am making my request for a full refund of my membership and initiation fees well within the 30-day money-back guarantee period that was written into the contract I signed.

I originally joined Gym Masters because of its reputation for quality facilities and reputable membership services. I am confident you will honour the terms of my contract and grant me a full refund. I look forward to hearing from you in the next two weeks.

Sincerely,

Francesca Auola

Personal business-style letter

Begins with a compliment; expresses disappointment at the circumstances leading to the claim

Includes a chronology and clear reasons in support of the claim

Provides supporting data and asks for a specific action

Ends pleasantly by appealing to the company's pride in its reputation and expresses confidence that an adjustment will be made

2. **Prove your claim is valid.** Describe the problem in a calm and credible way. Give a chronology to explain what happened and what you have done to resolve the problem. Provide supporting data to help the reader assess the situation: order numbers, delivery dates, method of shipment, servicing locations, descriptions of the items in question. Go with your strongest reasons to prove your claim is worthwhile. Your line of reasoning should lead the reader to conclude that responsibility rests with her company, not with you. Take steps to defend yourself against possible blame (*I carefully reviewed the owner's manual before I attempted to install the new unit*). It is a good idea to attach supporting documents (sales receipts, invoices, shipping orders) that will help the reader investigate your claim.

3. **Ask for a specific action.** State how the claim can be resolved and what you expect the company to do (make a refund, offer a replacement or apology). End positively, expressing confidence in the company's ethical standards and willingness to uphold its reputation.

COLLECTION LETTERS

collection letters a series of increasingly persuasive appeals to a customer asking for payment for goods and services already received.

The purpose of a **collection letter** is to collect an overdue bill (a month or more past due) while preserving the customer relationship. Collections letters, usually written in a series of three to five letters, put polite yet persistent pressure on readers, persuading them to promptly pay debts owing for goods already received or services already rendered. Usually, the longer a bill remains unpaid, the more demanding and urgent the collection letters become. The forcefulness of a collection demand also depends on the relationship between the creditor and the debtor. When a customer usually pays on time, the chances of collecting on a current bill are good, making courtesy all-important to preserving a friendly customer relationship. For customers with records of unreliable payment or non-payment, though, it may be necessary to adopt a firmer approach, reinforced by a no-nonsense tone that is direct but still polite. Adapting your messages to the type of debtor you are dealing with can help you recover the money owed to your company faster—without risking future business.

reminder letter informs a customer in a friendly way that a payment has not been received and emphasizes the customer's good credit rating until now.

- **Stage One—Reminder:** First messages work on the assumption that the customer intends to pay but has simply forgotten and fallen behind. This stage calls for a friendly **reminder letter** that mentions the customer's good credit record (if there is one), alerts the customer to the problem, and asks for a response. In place of a personalized letter, it is also possible to use a form letter or to send a copy of the original invoice, stamped "Second Notice" or "Past Due."

inquiry letter attempts to determine the circumstances that are preventing payment and asks for payment.

- **Stage Two—Inquiry:** Messages at this stage are firmer and more direct, but they work on the assumption that the customer has a legitimate reason for not paying— a cash-flow problem, out-of-town absence, or similar circumstance. The **inquiry letter** summarizes the situation, expresses concern over non-payment, and asks for an explanation or immediate payment. This request is reinforced by positive appeals to one or more of the following:

  - **Fairness**—emphasize the customer's fairness in completing a transaction by paying for goods and services already received.
  - **Reputation**—emphasize the benefits of debt payment to a company's good name.

FIGURE 8.9 Sample Collection Reminder Letter

Portfolio Electronics

520 Wellington Street   www.portfolio.com
London, ON N6A 1J7   1-800-667-8384

February 4, 2010

Mr. Wesley Denisof
12 Adelaide Street East
London, ON N4S 7R9

Dear Mr. Denisof:

You have been sending your monthly instalments to us promptly for over
a year. However, we find that your payment of $3,558.77 for December has
not yet arrived. Please send us a cheque in this amount now to avoid the
buildup of interest charges and ensure uninterrupted service in the months
ahead. If you have already paid, please accept out thanks and disregard
this notice.

We value your business very much and look forward to serving you again
soon.

Sincerely,

Alexander Foster

Alexander Foster
Accounts Payable

Annotations (right margin):
- Opens politely, reminding customer of good credit record
- Mentions problem; uses neutral language
- Makes a polite request for payment in terms of benefits of paying on time
- Closes with appreciation for business

- **Sympathy**—express concern while reminding the customer that prompt payment is crucial to your operations.
- **Self-interest**—show that prompt payment removes risks to credit ratings and keeps interest charges low.

If the customer is unable to pay the whole bill immediately, you have the option of offering to negotiate an instalment payment plan. Make it easy for the customer to respond by including your toll-free phone or fax number, a postage-paid envelope, or web address for convenient credit card payment.

FIGURE 8.10 Sample Collection Inquiry Letter

Portfolio Electronics

520 Wellington Street
London, ON N6A 1J7

www.portfolio.com
1-800-667-8384

May 6, 2010

Mr. Wesley Denisof
12 Adelaide Street East
London, ON N4S 7R9

Dear Mr. Denisof:

Our records indicate that your account is now three months overdue. We are very concerned that we have not heard from you even though we have already sent you two reminder notices.

We are requesting that you pay your balance of $3,558.77 immediately so that you can preserve your excellent credit record with us and avoid further accumulation of interest charges. Because you are one of our best customers and have always paid your account promptly in the past, we are sure you will want to retain your good reputation by paying your bill now.

Please use the enclosed envelope to send your cheque today. If a problem is preventing you from making this payment, please call 1-800-667-8384, toll-free, to discuss your account or details of a mutually satisfactory payment plan.

Sincerely,

Alexander Foster

Alexander Foster
Accounts Payable

Annotations (left margin):

Opening summarizes facts of overdue account and expresses concern over non-payment; mentions previous correspondence

Makes direct request for payment and reminds customer of benefits of immediate compliance

Shows sympathy and fairness and appeals to customer's self-interest

Makes it easy for the customer to respond

Closes positively by expressing confidence in a solution

---

demand letter makes a firm and unequivocal request for immediate payment and attempts to convince the debtor to pay the bill within a stated time by raising the possibility of legal action.

- **Stage Three—Demand:** The last letters in a collection series are unequivocal demands for immediate payment. The **demand letter** usually takes the form of an ultimatum, urgently asking for payment and warning of the penalties for non-payment (including legal action, garnishment of wages, or referral of the account to a collection agency with consequent damage to the customer's credit rating). If you expect strong resistance, refer to previous collection notices that have been ignored or overlooked. This will show how reasonable you have been and will strengthen

FIGURE 8.11 Sample Collection Demand Letter

Portfolio Electronics

520 Wellington Street   www.portfolio.com
London, ON N6A 1J7   1-800-667-8384

June 10, 2010

Mr. Wesley Denisof
12 Adelaide Street East
London, ON N4S 7R9

Dear Mr. Denisof:

This is the fourth time we have called your attention to your long-overdue account. So far, we have received neither your payment nor the courtesy of an explanation. Because we value your business, you have already received a generous extension in time, but we cannot permit a further delay in payment. Now we are counting on you to meet your obligation.

Opening makes unequivocal demand for immediate payment

Unless you pay your balance of $3,558.77 by June 30, we will be forced to turn your account over to a collection agency, resulting in certain damage to your previously good credit rating.

Delivers an ultimatum, clearly stating the consequences of non-payment, and sets deadline for compliance with request

We would prefer to mark your account paid than to take this unpleasant action, so please send your cheque today.

Tone in closing is polite yet firm

Sincerely,

Alexander Foster

Alexander Foster
Accounts Payable

your case should you eventually launch legal proceedings. Although your tone should still be courteous, it should also express reluctance at having to take action but determination to do so if the customer doesn't pay. Impose a time limit for payment, usually 10 days, and be explicit about the follow-up action you intend to take.

Pre-authorized payment and the practice of phoning customers to notify them of overdue accounts have lessened the need for this type of communication.

⬤⬤ Sales Messages

Successful sales people are usually effective communicators.

- They know that sales messages help build a business by advertising a product or service directly to individual customers or business accounts.
- They rely on market research and use it to adapt their sales messages to the needs, preferences, and demographics of targeted groups. They use mailing lists based on this research to ensure sales messages reach the people most likely to be interested in particular products and services. This practice is known as direct-mail marketing. Direct-mail sales messages are reader-adapted, making them different from other types of promotion, such as brochures and catalogues, that are part of a direct-mail package.
- They realize that most sales messages are unsolicited and frequently ignored, so they avoid hard-sell pitches, empty hype, and deceptive product claims that turn readers off. Instead, they minimize risk for buyers by providing product information, indicating how buyers will benefit, and building confidence in the product's value and performance. Only at the end do they push for a sale.
- They use appropriate persuasive appeals and incentives to create desire for products and services. The aim is to translate that interest into sales and an ongoing relationship of trust with customers.

sales letter a letter that promotes a product, service, or business and seeks prospective customers or additional sales.

Among the types of persuasive messages, **sales letters** are unique. They tend to be longer than the average business letter because they are rich in details orchestrated to make readers want the product. Sales letters can be composed one by one or as form letters, sent out in mailings of hundreds or even thousands. In large organizations, specialists oversee market research and promotional writing. In smaller organizations, these areas are handled by individual employees or they're outsourced.

Even if your job doesn't involve sales and promotions, sales writing has broad applications. Knowing how to do it well can help you sell not just your company's products, mission, and values but also your own ideas and skills so you are better able to get the job you want, keep it, and build a reputation for your company. As you will see in Chapter 9, job application letters are closely related to sales letters.

AIMING TO MAKE A SALE: ANALYZING THE PRODUCT AND AUDIENCE

An effective sales message delivers specific facts to a specific audience. Careful planning is essential, so start with the following preliminary steps:

1. **Study the product or service.** One of your tasks will be to educate consumers about the product and to identify the problem the product helps to solve. To do this, you should be knowledgeable about its design, construction, composite materials, manufacturing process, and operation. Note the product's ease of use, performance, durability, efficiency, warranty, availability of colours and finishes, and arrangements for servicing. Analyze its special features, especially its central selling point—the thing that gives your product an edge over the competition—and compare its price with that of other products in its class.

2. **Learn as much as possible about the target audience.** Your message stands a better chance of being read and generating sales if it is adapted to a specific audience. Rely on market research to draw up a profile of intended readers based on their age, sex, education, income, lifestyle, and place of residence. Understanding potential buyers' needs will help you predict the desirability of your product.

3. **Aim for an ethical sales pitch.** There are severe penalties for false advertising. When describing your product's performance and capabilities, make sure you stick to the facts and use objective, concrete language.

4. **Consider other factors.** The timing, visual appeal (document design), personalization, and tone of sales messages also influence readers. Delivering your message at the right time, when interest is likely high, betters the odds of making sales. The same is true of messages that are visually appealing, so consider making strategic use of captions, headings, images, and typography, especially to emphasize a central selling feature. A personalized letter, instead of one addressed "Dear Occupant" or "Attention Householder," looks less like unwanted, mass-produced junk mail. Further, personalization can be achieved with a tone that conveys warmth and respect without sounding too chummy or informal.

WRITING PLAN FOR SALES LETTERS

A typical sales letter involves a four-step writing process:

1. **Gain attention.**

2. **Introduce the product.**

3. **Make the product desirable.**

4. **Ask for action and make responding simple.**

Step 1: Gain Attention

A strong, concise opening captures attention before the reader has a chance to lose interest. This is especially important when your sales message is unsolicited or uninvited. No matter what attention-getting device you use, it should not be just a gimmick but an honest and relevant lead-in. Choose from the following devices:

- **A thought-provoking fact or statement:** *Over 20,000 vehicles are stolen every year in the Greater Toronto Area.*
- **Good news that makes the reader feel important or unique:** *You're **pre-approved** for the Ultra Platinum Card. This exciting credit card is yours to help you achieve the best in life.*
- **A special offer or bargain:** *The cheque below is yours to cash toward your Ultra Card Registry service! It's a special way to introduce you to the protection and peace of mind that Ultra has provided to Canadians for over twenty years.*
- **A product feature:** Point to the standout feature that will make the greatest difference to the reader: *Ultra is the first platinum card that allows you up to 15 days of out-of-province travel medical insurance—absolutely free!*
- **A question:** *Have you ever wondered if you paid too much for an all-inclusive resort vacation?*

- **A story:** *I am pleased to write to you today to tell you an alumni success story about Janet and Steve, who may not be very different from you. They work hard and invest their money wisely to build a bright future for their family. Although they know they can't predict the future, they have protected it by investing in the Alumni Term Life Insurance Plan. With low rates for alumni, they protect themselves, their family, and everything they have worked so hard for.*

For extra emphasis, some of these devices can be bolded or underlined, in whole or in part, or incorporated as captions and headlines. Weak openings turn readers off, so avoid obvious statements, questions with obvious answers, and stories that take too long to get to the point.

Step 2: Introduce the Product

Once you have gained attention, the next step is to forge a link between the need you have identified and how the product you are selling meets that need. The following example ties a product to the sample story given above: *you too can take advantage of the Alumni Term Life Insurance Plan and provide the people you love with the same security that Janet and Steve did for their family.*

Step 3: Make the Product Desirable

Your challenge is to make readers want the product and understand the need it meets. They, in turn, want to feel confident that a purchase will live up to its promises and their expectations. Satisfy both goals by providing a carefully worded product description that combines concrete details with assurances of customer satisfaction.

Describe the product from the reader's point of view. Instead of listing flat details, suggest what it is like to use and benefit from the product. Rather than saying *our vacuum has a 6-metre cord*, interpret details so they are meaningful to readers: *the Power Vac's 6-metre cord allows you to vacuum even the largest rooms from a single outlet.* If necessary, balance and dispel possible doubts with clear reminders of product benefits: *if you ever worried that a home security system might mean a loss of privacy, we want to reassure you that our monitoring system is activated only when the alarm is triggered.*

Build product confidence by using hype-free language and risk-reducing inducements such as a warranty, money-back guarantee, special offer, free trial, or sample. Rely on statistics and testimonials—even stories about how the product was developed—to counter resistance and provide assurances of satisfaction.

Because price can make or break a sale, emphasize the price by mentioning it early if the product is affordable or a bargain. Otherwise, omit it or de-emphasize it in one of the following ways:

- Mention it only after you have created a desire for the product.
- Break the price down into smaller units (monthly instalment payments, cost per day or issue).
- Make the product a bargain by calculating the cost after discount or rebate.
- Show savings over a competitor's product or, for subscriptions, over the per-unit purchase price.
- Link the price with benefits.

The following example combines several of these approaches: *when you calculate what you could save with benefits such as Out-of-Province Travel Medical Insurance and Auto Rental*

Collision Insurance, you'll be pleasantly surprised that the fee for the Ultra Platinum Card is only $79 a year (with a current annual interest rate of 17.5%), which is actually less than $7 a month.

Step 4: Ask for a Simple Action

After you have created a desire for the product, tell readers how easy it is for them to purchase it and urge them to take action without delay. Use a positive emphasis combined with the imperative voice to discourage readers from procrastinating. Make the action simple by providing a toll-free order number, giving a website or e-mail address, or enclosing an order form or postage-paid envelope.

Say yes to your Pre-Approved Acceptance Certificate today! Simply complete and mail it to us in the postage-paid envelope provided or fax it to 1-877-553-0123.

Encourage the reader to act promptly with perks and incentives such as a time-limited offer, special offer, bonus, or rebate. If you cannot offer incentives, remind readers that the less they delay the sooner they will benefit from the product (*as quantities are limited, act now to avoid disappointment. Purchase your Zodiac watercraft today and enjoy it all summer long.*).

Postscripts

Postscript lines are more common in sales letters than in any other type of message. Postscripts are high-impact sentences, attracting attention as soon as the letter is opened. They are useful for spotlighting free offers, for summarizing the central selling point, or for making a final appeal to readers, urging them to act promptly.

P.S. Accept your Ultra Platinum Card today, so you can start enjoying its benefits right away!

*P.S. Remember to cash your cheque toward your **Ultra Card Registry Service** before the expiry date. You don't want to regret passing up card protection if your debit or credit cards are ever lost or stolen!*

FIGURE 8.12 INEFFECTIVE Sales Message (extract)

Dear Computer Owner,

If you think the computer system you're using now is good, you should see the desktop PCs and notebooks from Micro-Genius. We think you should check out our new A50 and R40 series. We think you'll be pleasantly surprised.

Our computers are fast, powerful, and affordable. Our customers say that overall they are quite satisfied with their performance. Now, for a limited time, you can get an additional 256MB of memory and no-charge shipping when you purchase any system included in our special promotion.

We have some real beauties in stock right now. If you think Micro-Genius might have a computer for you, give us a call. Micro-Genius computers aren't just good, they're very good.

Opening suggests the product already owned is satisfactory, making a replacement unnecessary

Does not specify how fast, powerful, and affordable the product is. Muted language ("quite satisfied") fails to create desire for the product

Closing action is conditional and doesn't provide enough information for easy follow-up

FIGURE 8.13 EFFECTIVE Sales Message

Gains attention with a question and limited-time and special offers

Product description links need and benefits to product features; builds confidence in product with documented assurances of customer satisfaction

Itemized list reduces resistances by highlighting advantages

Imperative voice and positive tone encourage immediate action; action is made easy

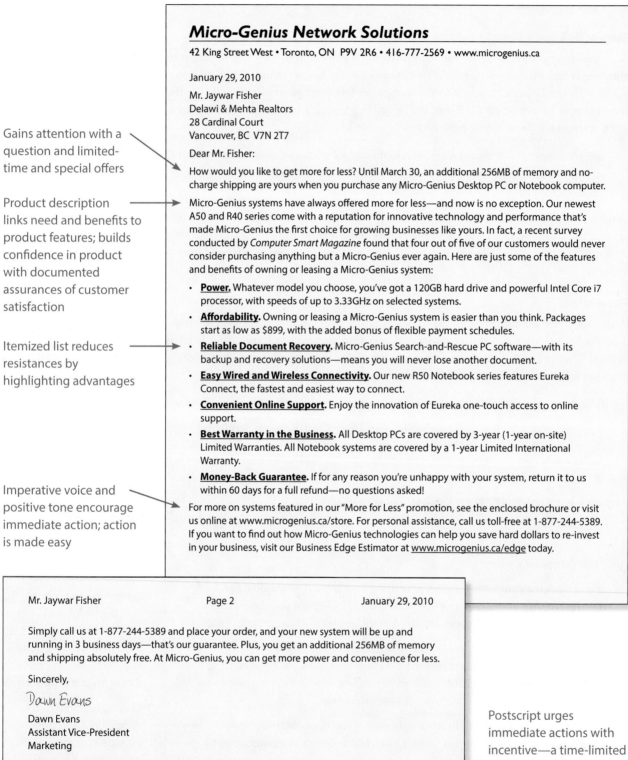

Micro-Genius Network Solutions

42 King Street West • Toronto, ON P9V 2R6 • 416-777-2569 • www.microgenius.ca

January 29, 2010

Mr. Jaywar Fisher
Delawi & Mehta Realtors
28 Cardinal Court
Vancouver, BC V7N 2T7

Dear Mr. Fisher:

How would you like to get more for less? Until March 30, an additional 256MB of memory and no-charge shipping are yours when you purchase any Micro-Genius Desktop PC or Notebook computer.

Micro-Genius systems have always offered more for less—and now is no exception. Our newest A50 and R40 series come with a reputation for innovative technology and performance that's made Micro-Genius the first choice for growing businesses like yours. In fact, a recent survey conducted by *Computer Smart Magazine* found that four out of five of our customers would never consider purchasing anything but a Micro-Genius ever again. Here are just some of the features and benefits of owning or leasing a Micro-Genius system:

- **Power.** Whatever model you choose, you've got a 120GB hard drive and powerful Intel Core i7 processor, with speeds of up to 3.33GHz on selected systems.
- **Affordability.** Owning or leasing a Micro-Genius system is easier than you think. Packages start as low as $899, with the added bonus of flexible payment schedules.
- **Reliable Document Recovery.** Micro-Genius Search-and-Rescue PC software—with its backup and recovery solutions—means you will never lose another document.
- **Easy Wired and Wireless Connectivity.** Our new R50 Notebook series features Eureka Connect, the fastest and easiest way to connect.
- **Convenient Online Support.** Enjoy the innovation of Eureka one-touch access to online support.
- **Best Warranty in the Business.** All Desktop PCs are covered by 3-year (1-year on-site) Limited Warranties. All Notebook systems are covered by a 1-year Limited International Warranty.
- **Money-Back Guarantee.** If for any reason you're unhappy with your system, return it to us within 60 days for a full refund—no questions asked!

For more on systems featured in our "More for Less" promotion, see the enclosed brochure or visit us online at www.microgenius.ca/store. For personal assistance, call us toll-free at 1-877-244-5389. If you want to find out how Micro-Genius technologies can help you save hard dollars to re-invest in your business, visit our Business Edge Estimator at www.microgenius.ca/edge today.

Mr. Jaywar Fisher   Page 2   January 29, 2010

Simply call us at 1-877-244-5389 and place your order, and your new system will be up and running in 3 business days—that's our guarantee. Plus, you get an additional 256MB of memory and shipping absolutely free. At Micro-Genius, you can get more power and convenience for less.

Sincerely,

Dawn Evans

Dawn Evans
Assistant Vice-President
Marketing

P.S. Place your order **by March 15** and you can add Microsoft Windows 7 Professional to your package for **only $199**. That's a saving of $100 over the retail price.

Postscript urges immediate actions with incentive—a time-limited special offer that makes product a bargain

FIGURE 8.14 EFFECTIVE Sales Message II

ICE BUSTERS
Snow and Ice Removal
101 Winter Drive
Edmonton, AB T4C 3B5
587-555-1357
www.ICEBUSTERS.ca

September 1, 2010

Mr. Albert Chin
1554 1st Avenue
Edmonton, AB T2F 5V6

Renew by September 30 and Save 15% ← Incentive highlighted in boldface at top of message to gain immediate attention

Dear Mr. Chin:

You wake up on a cold winter morning to find your street and yard heavily blanketed in snow. As you watch your neighbours lean wearily on their snow shovels, you relax and decide there's time for another cup of coffee. After all, you know your porch, front walk, and driveway will be clear and free of snow. Could you get used to another winter like this? ← Opening gains attention with story that encourages customer to imagine advantages of service

Ice Busters **Snow Removal Service** hopes you can. We specialize in residential snow removal, which means we make your property our highest priority. Unlike larger snow removal services, whose revenues depend on commercial contracts, we clear your ice and snow promptly, within four hours of the end of a snowfall. Plus, when conditions permit, we apply environmentally friendly ice-melter to ensure your home access stays safe. ← Second paragraph links need to services provided and introduces service in detail

You can expect the same reliable and fully insured services you've already experienced from Ice Busters, including

- Removal of snow accumulations of as little as 3 cm within four hours ← Bulleted list emphasizes features of service
- Careful plowing of entire driveway surface, not just a narrow path leading to your garage
- Hand-shovelling of steps and walkways, safeguarding your delicate shrubs and evergreens
- Service from first to last snowfall

For only $350, you can look forward to a trouble-free winter. Simply fill out the enclosed renewal form and send it to us. Renew by September 30 and **receive a 15% discount** on your snow removal contract. There's no beating winter, but Ice Busters sure beats shovelling. ← Introduction of price connected to customer benefits ← Closing request makes action easy; time-limited offer encourages prompt action

Sincerely,

Cam Stevenson

Cam Stevenson
President

Enc.

Sales Follow-Up

Although not specifically a persuasive message, a sales follow-up confirms to customers the fact that they have made the right decision by purchasing a product. Its expressions of appreciation for an order reinforce goodwill and promote future business. A follow-up may also confirm details of a sale or offer further services.

FIGURE 8.15 Sales Follow-Up

AUDIOTRAX TECHNOLOGIES INC.

2300 Laneway Drive, Unit 200
Scarborough, ON M4W 2T9
1-888-555-7711
www.AudioTrax.com

May 6, 2010

Ms. Yasmin Jafari
IT Manager
Vanguard Industries
67 Westincreek Drive
Mississauga, ON N5G 2T2

Dear Ms. Jafari:

Expresses appreciation for order →
Congratulations on your decision to purchase an Audiotrax voice-recognition system. We appreciate the confidence you have shown in us and hope you will benefit from the added security that only voice-recognition technology can provide.

Confirms details of sales/ service agreement and provides schedule for delivery of services →
It will be our pleasure to install your new system and train your staff the week of May 24. Our expert trainers will be on site to oversee this project and answer your questions. The system should be fully operational by May 30.

Sarah Anderson, our customer service specialist, will be contacting you next week to arrange a training schedule that is convenient for you. She will be available throughout the installation process to answer your questions and concerns. We also invite you to call our product support hotline, which is open 24 hours a day to answer your technical questions and assist you in maximizing the features of your new voice-recognition system.

Offers further assistance →

Closes in friendly but professional manner →
If we can be of help now or in the future, please call on us.

Sincerely,

Nick Papadakis

Nick Papadakis
Audiotrax Sales Team

Checklist for Effective Sales Messages

Ask yourself the following questions to see how effective your sales message is.

☐ **Opening:** Does the opening command attention? Is the attention-getting technique suited to the product, audience, and type of appeal? Does the opening provide a strong and logical lead-in for the rest of the message?

☐ **Product Description:** How is the product introduced? Have you used only concrete language to describe the product? Does the description help the reader picture what it is like to use and benefit from the product? Have you offered proof to back up your claims about the product?

☐ **Selling Points:** Does the message identify and emphasize the product's central selling points?

☐ **Persuasive Appeals:** What type of appeal have you used? Does it respond to the reader's needs? Have you created a desire for the product?

☐ **Resistance:** Have you dealt with questions and objections the reader might have?

☐ **Price:** Have you introduced the price strategically?

☐ **Closing:** Does the closing tell the reader exactly what to do? Does it motivate the reader to take action quickly? Does it make the action easy?

☐ **Postscript:** If a postscript is included, does it recap and give extra emphasis to a special offer or product feature, or spur to action?

FUNDRAISING MESSAGES

A variation on a sales letter is the fundraising appeal. Readers in this case are asked not to spend money but to donate it to a worthy cause. Their support and generosity depends on how well you show how a problem could be solved or alleviated with a donation that will be put to good use. A fundraising letter should make readers feel good about giving.

1. **Identify an important problem.** Explain why the reader should care about it.

2. **Show that the problem is solvable.** If a problem seems insurmountable, readers will naturally feel incapable of doing anything to help. Hold out hope for even a partial, short-term solution. Link a need to your organization's ability to respond to it.

3. **Explain what your organization is doing to solve the problem.** Prove that funds will be going to a good cause, not just to the cost of fundraising. Outline past accomplishments and future goals, citing facts and statistics. If readers might find it difficult to grasp the enormity of a problem, describe the difference your group or charity can make in the life of one individual or a community. An enclosure—a brochure or reprint of an article about your organization—can supply potential donors with useful background information.

4. **Ask for a donation.** Explain deficiencies in public funding that make private donations necessary. If appropriate, suggest amounts in descending order or propose a monthly pledge. Put the gift in terms the reader will understand by indicating what it will buy. Broaden the scope of your message by suggesting other ways (volunteering, writing letters) readers can lend their support.

The sample favour request (see Figure 8.3 on pages 224–5) shares certain characteristics with a typical fundraising letter. A fundraising package will usually include an appeal for a donation, a reply form, and a postage-paid envelope.

Checklist for Persuasive Messages

☐ Have you begun by capturing the favourable interest of the reader? Have you made the message immediately relevant to the reader's concerns? Have you put the request in a positive light? Have you provided enough incentive for the reader to read on?

☐ Have you chosen the right appeal or persuasive strategy to help you connect with your reader? Is the persuasive strategy an ethical one your company condones?

☐ Have you overcome the reader's resistance?

☐ Have you built credibility with your audience?

☐ Have you justified the request with a clear explanation of its reasons, details, and benefits?

☐ Have you inspired the reader to act? When necessary, have you provided incentive for the reader to act promptly? Have you provided sufficient information so that the reader will know what to do next?

WORKSHOPS AND DISCUSSION FORUMS

1. **Analyzing a Sales Message:** Using the "Checklist for Effective Sales Messages" on page 241 as a guide, analyze the strengths and weaknesses of a sales message you or a friend received recently. Did the message grab your attention? Did it make you want to buy the product?

2. **Evaluating Fundraising Appeals:** As a group, collect three or four fundraising messages you have received and compare the types of appeals and approaches they use. Evaluate opening and closing statements and decide if each message has provided you with enough information to encourage you to make a donation. Write a brief report on your analysis of the letters.

3. **Fundraising Challenge:** Select a registered Canadian charity; for listings, go to the CharityVillage website at **https://charityvillage.com/directories/organizations-a-h.aspx**. Individually or in a group, plan a strategy to convince your classmates to make a donation.

4. **Analyzing persuasive messages:** Working in small groups, discuss weaknesses in the following messages and share ideas on how to revise them. Make an overhead transparency or PowerPoint slide of one of your revised messages and discuss the changes you have made with the rest of your class.

a) **Persuasive Request (Follow-Up)**

Let me first apologize for the delay. In sending this letter. We have had a number of staff changes and personnel problems recently and I realize now that we have not yet followed up on the meeting we had three months ago. Please be rest assured your interest in supporting our organization is really appreciated, and our response to subsequent discussions will probably be timelier in the future.

Gordon, as you are an extremely wealthy alumnus of our university, I believe that a strong case exists for your law firm to provide financial support at a leadership level. By making a leadership gift, your firm will realize significant reputational benefits. We propose a pace-setting gift of $500,000. In recognition of your support for our organization at the $500,000 level, we would be delighted to include your firm's name on a small plaque in the lobby of our offices.

I strongly urge you to consider donating $500,000 to our well-deserving university. We need this money desperately and will put it to good use. Thank you for your consideration. Once I settle our personnel problems, I will be in touch with you again to remind you of this important opportunity to donate $500,000 to such a worthy cause.

b) **Persuasive Memo**

I propose that our company sponsor a contest in order promote our new line of low-carbohydrate products. Administering a contest can be expensive, but the benefits are obvious. If you don't agree with me, I think you will be missing out on a valuable opportunity. I will need your authorization in order to proceed.

5. **Identifying Types of Appeals:** Review recent magazines and newspapers and find advertisements that fit each of the following categories:
a) banking and investment
b) travel and leisure
c) computers and technology

What types of appeals are used in each case? Is there a correspondence between the type of product and the appeal that is used?

WRITING IMPROVEMENT EXERCISES

1. **Openings for Persuasive Messages:** How persuasive are the following openings?
   a) **Sales letter:** A free leather carry-on is yours with your next return-airfare booking on Travelwell.com.
   b) **Sales letter:** Have I got a deal for you! For **only $699** per person (+ GST), an amazing, all-inclusive, one-night getaway to the absolutely fabulous Muskox Inn can be yours!
   c) **Sales letter:** Are you tired of waiting precious minutes to download Internet files via your dial-up connection?
   d) **Sales letter:** We take such great pride in our engineering that we know you won't be able to resist our new line of digital cameras.
   e) **Sales letter:** How would you like to get more for less? An additional 356MB of memory and no-charge shipping are yours when you purchase any Micro-Genius Notebook PC.
   f) **Sales letter:** Hi! My name is Kevin. Maybe you haven't heard of my company, Picture Perfect, but I think you'd be amazed by our new line of digital cameras.
   g) **Favour request:** Hi! My name is Joey (Josephine) Jones and I have been entrusted with the important job of finding someone to speak before a large gathering of our sales representatives. I realize that three days is very short notice for this kind of request, but would you perhaps be interested in this speaking engagement?

h) **Favour request:** While I understand how busy you must be, I have no choice but to ask you for a really big favour.

i) **Favour request:** With the support of businesses like your own, Project Outreach has counselled over 2,500 at-risk high school students and helped them realize their dreams of post-secondary education.

j) **Collection letter:** You owe us $5,048.00—so pay up!

2. **Closings for Persuasive Messages:** Do the following action closings motivate readers to act quickly? Is the action made clear and easy in each case?

a) **Sales letter:** Unless you act quickly and phone us now, you'll be out of luck and won't qualify for the 10% discount.

b) **Claim request:** If I don't hear from you by May 15, I will assume you have rejected my claim and I will have no alternative but to seek legal action.

c) **Favour request:** We really must have our list of speakers finalized, so try to respond by June 3, if not sooner.

d) **Sales letter:** I cannot urge you strongly enough to place an order now by calling 1-800-625-8771 and, when prompted, asking for Donald. To qualify for a 5% discount, you must quote this reference number: 9312866B. Discounts do not apply to all products. For a list of exclusions, please see our website: www.easy_order.com.

3. **Clear and Concrete Descriptions:** Revise each of the following product descriptions by making the language more positive, concrete, appealing to the senses, and reader-focused.

a) **Sales letter:** Our chocolate products, which sell for as little as $5 a box, are made from cocoa imported from Europe and they taste good.

b) **Sales letter:** Our Wind-Turbo Vacuum has a 12-amp motor and an 8-metre cord.

c) **Sales letter:** We think discerning customers, like you, will be pleasantly surprised by the luxurious selection of imported linens on which we pride ourselves.

d) **Sales letter:** Although our products aren't maintenance-free, they require less maintenance because they feature self-cleaning mechanisms that prevent the buildup of unsightly lime and mineral deposits.

e) **Sales letter:** Just because our cookware costs less doesn't mean it isn't durable.

4. **Citing Benefits:** For each requested action, cite one or more potential benefits.

a) Call us today and for just $25 a month you can equip your home with a voice-activated security monitoring system.

b) Please give me authorization to purchase hands-free telephone headsets for each of our 20 customer service representatives.

c) Please respond by June 1 so I may add your name to the list of distinguished speakers for the Vancouver Young Business Associates summit on September 14.

d) Visit us soon at one of our five convenient Calgary-area locations to book your mid-winter getaway to sunny Barbados for as little as $899 a week.

5. **Analyzing Subject Lines:** Identify the most persuasive subject line in each case.

a) Subject: Donations Required
   Subject: Can You Spare $10 for a Good Cause?
   Subject: Meeting Our Target for the United Way Campaign

b) Subject: Suggestion
   Subject: Improving Security with Better Passwords
   Subject: Have You Changed Your Password Lately?

c) Subject: Reducing Absenteeism and Low Morale
   Subject: On-Site Fitness Centre Required
   Subject: Couldn't You Use Some Time on a Treadmill?

6. **Adding Postscripts:** Compose postscripts for the following sales messages.

a) A letter that offers readers a premium for taking out a membership in an automobile association.

b) A letter that offers readers a 25% discount if they renew their magazine subscriptions right away.

c) A letter that advertises a quality home-security system.

CASE STUDY EXERCISES

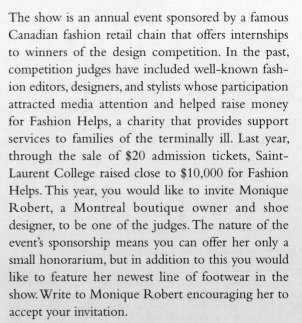

1. **Sales Letter—Peddling a Bicycle Courier Service:** As Mike Reid, owner of Swiftcycle Courier Services, write a sales message to prospective customer Florian Heinz, president of Frontier Equity Mutual. Your 10-year-old company provides bicycle courier services at highly competitive rates to a large number of businesses, including six other tenants of First Canadian Place in downtown Toronto's financial district, where the head office of Frontier Equity Mutual is located. For the next three months, you are offering an introductory special to new clients, which entitles them to a 15 per cent discount on all envelope and small-package courier services. Your radio-dispatched delivery personnel are fully bonded and are experts at time-critical delivery. Online ordering is also one of the services you offer. Size up your prospect, then write a letter to Florian Heinz (make up any additional details you require).

2. **Favour Request—Seeking Volunteers for a Good Cause:** As Tanya Jacobs of Canmuir Industries, you are responsible for organizing a golf tournament fundraising event, with proceeds going to the Heart and Stroke Foundation. Last year, at a similar event, your company raised over $50,000—money that went toward research and educational programs. This year the event will be hosted at Northland Golf and Country Club. In addition to a day's golfing on the award-winning links, there will be a draw to win lessons with a golf pro, special promotional kiosks, and a putting competition, followed by a four-course dinner. You have already secured the support of local retail businesses, which have donated items to be sold at kiosks at each of the course's eighteen holes. Now you need 36 committed individuals from your organization to oversee the kiosks from 10:00 a.m. to 4:00 p.m. the day of the event. Compose a memo to all employees, asking for their assistance.

3. **Favour Request—Seeking a Judge for a Fashion Show Benefit:** As Lilly Chow, a student in the Fashion Design and Technology program at Saint-Laurent College in Montreal, you have been appointed chair of a committee that must organize a fashion show and competition featuring the designs of students in the program's graduating class.

The show is an annual event sponsored by a famous Canadian fashion retail chain that offers internships to winners of the design competition. In the past, competition judges have included well-known fashion editors, designers, and stylists whose participation attracted media attention and helped raise money for Fashion Helps, a charity that provides support services to families of the terminally ill. Last year, through the sale of $20 admission tickets, Saint-Laurent College raised close to $10,000 for Fashion Helps. This year, you would like to invite Monique Robert, a Montreal boutique owner and shoe designer, to be one of the judges. The nature of the event's sponsorship means you can offer her only a small honorarium, but in addition to this you would like to feature her newest line of footwear in the show. Write to Monique Robert encouraging her to accept your invitation.

4. **Favour Request—Seeking Volunteers for an Outreach Program:** Your company has recently responded to a request from Project Protégé, an educational mentorship program designed to help promising high school students at risk of dropping out achieve their goals of post-secondary education. Because you hire only college graduates and give preference to those with post-graduate degrees, you understand the importance of keeping teenagers in school. You would like your company to participate, but you realize this will require three volunteers from your firm to give up an entire Saturday to speak with students about career opportunities in the aerospace industry. As far as you know, mentors will receive no fee but all will be invited to a year-end banquet in return for donating their time and services. Write a memo to staff asking for their help.

5. **Sales Letter—Promoting a Catering Business:** As Glenn Maitland, a graduate of the Culinary Arts Program at Foothills College in Calgary, you and fellow graduate Tatiana Melnikov are launching your own low-carb catering business, Smart Food. You have two years' experience as head chef at Food for Life, a highly rated local restaurant, and have worked as a sous-chef at restaurants in Vancouver and Halifax. Tatiana has previously worked as a registered dietitian.

Together you plan to fine-cater intimate, casual, and formal events, especially business-related functions. Direct office-delivery of affordable, low-carb lunch specials, ordered through your website, is another service that you will offer. You think busy professionals will be impressed by your extensive repertoire of healthy, low-carb specialties, a full listing of which also appears on your website. To promote your new business, you have considered hosting a tasting event that would allow potential clientele to sample the best of your menu. Compose a promotional letter suitable for a direct-mail campaign aimed at local businesses.

6. **Claim Letter—Unexpected Service Charges:** As Vikram Das, co-owner of a small graphics design firm, you recently hosted a one-day business retreat for all staff at the Ocean View Inn, a conference facility you have long counted on for its excellent catering and technical services. One month in advance, you made an $800 deposit on the room booking and catering costs. The remainder of the total $4,000 cost (which includes all applicable taxes) was to be paid after the event. The retreat was a success, but you were surprised when you later received a new invoice for $3,550, when you were expecting to pay $3,200. The additional charges were for a $100 user's fee and a $250 booking fee. You feel these charges, because they were not part of the original agreement, are either unwarranted or erroneous. The Ocean View Inn, you have just discovered, is under new management, which may account for the discrepancies. Write to manager Kaleigh Smith requesting an adjustment.

7. **Claim Request—Waive Inactivity Fee:** You recently received a $250 gift card from your department manager as a reward for work well done on an important contract. However, when you tried to use it at Folio, the bookstore that issued the card, you were told that it had expired and you would have to pay an inactivity fee before you could make your purchase. At the time you felt there must have been some mistake. The card was issued only three months ago and not stamped with an expiration date. Although the reactivation charge was only $15, you believed that in principle you shouldn't have been penalized and the unreasonable fee should have been waived. You left the store disappointed, without redeeming the gift certificate. After some research, you discovered that, under provincial guidelines, retailers are not allowed to issue gift cards that have expiry dates, nor

are they allowed to charge reactivation fees. You don't believe that the staff at Folio are intentionally breaking the law, but you want to make them aware of their obligations and for them to revise their practices in the future. Make your case in a persuasive claim to Folio's customer service division.

8. **Persuasive Memo:** Write a persuasive memo on one of the following topics:

   a) Colleagues have complained that the office environment you share is drab and depressing. Lighting is poor, filing systems are disorganized, and office furniture is in disrepair. Visitors complain that your office looks downright unprofessional. Write a memo presenting a plan to perk up your office environment.

   b) Three years ago, your business introduced extended hours. Although the new hours do not force employees to work more than the number of hours per week set out by labour laws, there have been some negative repercussions. Absenteeism is up, payroll costs have soared, and the evening work hours have posed a challenge to employees with children, especially those who must pick up preschoolers from daycare facilities. Write a persuasive memo asking for the cancellation of extended hours.

   c) A number of your colleagues are considering switching to part-time hours as an alternative to retirement. You have developed a plan for a mentorship program that would allow these individuals to provide invaluable support to trainees. Write a memo to the chief operating officer suggesting this idea.

   d) Your company is currently without an e-mail policy. This has led to widespread abuses of the technology and a lack of uniformity in messaging. Based on your knowledge of e-mail problems and abuses, write a persuasive memo asking for the creation of corporate e-mail guidelines.

   e) You work at the Toronto head office of a large Canadian investment house. You and most of your colleagues put in exceptionally long hours. Recently you read an article reporting that almost half of *Fortune* magazine's top one hundred companies provide take-home meals for their employees. Your office already has a well-staffed, state-of-the-art catering and kitchen facility. Compose a persuasive memo suggesting that take-home dinners be made available at a reasonable cost.

f) You believe employees appreciate being noticed for a job well done or for an idea that saves time or money. That's why you agree with the 2003 Work Experience Study, conducted by consulting firms Towers Perrin and Gang & Gang, which reported that what employees really want is to feel good about their abilities and to be recognized for the contributions they make. Companies such as BBDO Canada have put this theory into practice by offering an annual $500 award to the employee with the best overall creative idea, insight, or strategy. Motivation among your colleagues is currently at an all-time low. Write a memo suggesting the introduction of a similar innovation reward program in your company.

g) With recent cuts to the funding of public education, you have noticed that, increasingly, your staff members are taking on their children's school fundraising efforts at work. Every day, it seems, someone is selling chocolate-covered almonds, magazine subscriptions, or garbage bags. Although money is being raised for a good cause—public education—you feel you must respond to serious complaints about this practice. Since your brokerage firm requires staff to give customers and other stakeholders their undivided attention, you feel such fundraising activities should be restricted to lunch hours and break times. Write a persuasive memo to all staff establishing limits on office fundraising.

9. **Persuasive Memo—Lobbying for Change:** Identify a problem in need of a solution or a situation in need of improvement in your school or place of employment. Write a well-researched memo identifying the benefits of what you propose and make a compelling case for change.

10. **Collection Letter Series—Reminder, Inquiry, and Demand:** You are the owner of a general contracting business that undertook extensive renovations on a property owned by Arnold Levitt. Work valued at $17,000 was completed on schedule three months ago. The property subsequently passed inspection. Because Mr. Levitt has always paid you on time for all previous contracts, you are somewhat surprised that all but the original $1,700 deposit remains unpaid. There is some urgency to your request for payment because you must settle your own accounts with electrical and plumbing subcontractors who worked for you on the project. Mr. Levitt travels frequently, so you have been unable to reach him by phone. Your voice-mail messages have gone unanswered. Write a collection series.

ONLINE ACTIVITIES

http://www.

1. **Eliminating Fuzzy Logic:** Read the following article on logical fallacies from the Online Writing Lab at Purdue University:
http://owl.english.purdue.edu/owl/resource/659/01
Then, log onto the following pages and identify weaknesses in logic in each of the examples:
http://www.writing.engr.psu.edu/exercises/fallacies.html
http://faculty.stevenson.edu/jsalvucci/WritingHelp/log_exer.htm

2. **Writing a Product Description:** Log on to this site and select a product you think would appeal to members of your class. Read the accompanying product overview and note its features, then write your own product description so that it clearly outlines benefits to the reader and creates a desire for the product. Present the description to your classmates as though it were an actual sales letter and ask for their reaction. Print out the corresponding page from the website and hand it in with your product description.
www.sonystyle.com

3. **Improving You-Attitude and Reader Benefits:** Log on to this archived site from Washburn University, entitled "Persuasive Communications: Using You-Attitude and Reader Benefit," and read the article outlining the benefits of using *you* instead of *I* and *we*. Then move on to the exercise and revise sentences to improve their you-attitude.
http://web.archive.org/web/20100731062800/
http://www.washburn.edu/services/zzcwwctr/you-attitude.txt

9

Communicating for Employment

In this chapter you will learn to

1. Prepare for employment by assessing your career objectives, interests, and professional strengths.

2. Use resources to network and find out about jobs and employers.

3. Compose chronological and skills-based resumés that provide overviews of your professional background and capabilities.

4. Create online and scannable resumés.

5. Write solicited and unsolicited job application letters that strategically target and sell your skills to prospective employers.

6. Prepare for and follow up on the job interview.

7. Write a range of messages related to job-seeking, including requests for recommendation.

⬤⬤ Analyzing Your Career Goals and Qualifications

Finding a job you can grow and succeed in starts with knowing your values, goals, preferences, qualifications, and aptitudes. Some professional stock-taking and personal soul-searching can guide you to the right career path and point the way to employment options that are likely to fulfill your needs. Self-assessment involves considering what you enjoy doing, identifying personality traits that apply to your work style, and learning from earlier work experiences. Answering questions in the following categories can help you decide what type of work is best for you.

ASSESSING YOUR SKILLS AND VALUES

- Who are you? What are your values, interests, and marketable skills? How have you demonstrated those skills? Will your skills allow you to capitalize on employment trends?
- What drew you to your career path or program of study? Does your work allow you to realize your original desires and intentions?
- What are you good at? What are you most interested in doing? Resolving troubled situations? Developing ideas? Helping people? Making things happen?
- Are you willing to acquire new skills or retrain for the sake of advancement?
- Where, realistically, do you see yourself in five or ten years?
- What trade-offs are you willing to make for your job (i.e., reduced salary and/or benefits for job satisfaction; less personal time due to travel, commuting, or over-time work)? Do you live to work or work to live?

ASSESSING YOUR WORK PREFERENCES AND PERSONALITY

- Are you an introvert or an extrovert? Do you most enjoy socializing, directing, or thinking?
- In what work setting are you most comfortable? Do you prefer to work in a large organization (with a big hierarchy or chain of command) or a small one (involving direct, informal, one-to-one contacts)?
- Do you enjoy working with people, materials, ideas, or data? Do you best succeed when working in a group or alone? What level of interaction is right for you?
- Are you decisive? Do you enjoy making decisions?
- Do you prefer to take a leading role or a supporting one? How much say do you like to have in the workplace? How much freedom do you need? How important is it to be your own boss?
- Do you appreciate and apply feedback? Is it necessary to your success on the job?
- Do you like work that is fast-paced or slow-paced? Are you looking for excitement and variety from your job? Do you find certain tasks boring? What type of work do you find most stimulating?
- Are you looking for challenges and risks, even if they make your job less secure? Are you looking for a secure and stable job with a regular routine?
- Would you rather be a specialist or a generalist?
- What do you want from your job in terms of rewards (money, creative opportunities, status, travel, security, the chance to build something lasting)?
- How important are colleagues, working conditions, and job stimulation?

ASSESSING YOUR WORK HISTORY

- What accomplishments are you most proud of? Where have you gone right in your career so far?
- What work experiences have you found most satisfying? What was your motivation in that job? What qualities or features did the work have (learned on the job, worked with intelligent/creative people, applied skills successfully, believed in product or company mission)?
- What work experiences have you most disliked? What qualities or features did the work have? What turned you off most about the jobs you have had?
- How well do you communicate and learn on the job?
- On the basis of work you have already done, what hard and soft skills can you offer a prospective employer?

Having a successful and fulfilling career is not just a matter of finding a job where you *fit in*, but of finding a career area that fits your personality and qualifications. Look for a position that allows you to play to your strengths and develop skills in those areas. Be prepared to change jobs every few years to learn from experience, and adapt to fluctuations in the job market and economy by building your marketable skills.

⬤⬤ Job-Hunting

Very few job offers materialize as if by magic. Job-hunting requires time, effort, and perseverance, but the payoffs of a successful search can be enormous. It is usually wise to work on the assumption that the more information you have about employment opportunities, the greater the chance is of getting the job you want. A successful search campaign begins by studying the job market, identifying sources of employment, learning about the organizations you would most like to work for, and matching your skills and training to the most suitable positions.

1. **Read the career pages, classified ads, and financial sections** of newspapers, trade and professional journals, and business magazines. To monitor these publications for free, check out the periodical section of your local or school library. Join professional and trade associations that put you in line to receive regular listings and announcements of job openings. Study trends in the labour market by reading articles on expanding companies and business sectors. This will help you to predict where new jobs will be created based on need.

2. **Master electronic job-search techniques.** Employers often post positions on job-bank websites and on their own company websites. Many job-bank websites allow you to post your resumé online and browse through thousands of help-wanted ads by occupation or geographic area. You can also participate in newsgroups to get industry-specific job listings. A list of online job banks and career resources can be found at the end of this chapter.

3. **Learn to network.** Networking is an essential business tool. It involves meeting new contacts and cultivating relationships that could lead to personal and business success. You can develop a good network of contacts in the industry by becoming involved in community activities and by attending networking events

or professional conferences regularly or by becoming involved in mentorship programs offered by your college or university. Doing so will increase your number of potential contacts and give you the opportunity to promote yourself and your accomplishments. Don't be afraid to ask your personal and professional contacts for advice, especially people who are knowledgeable about your field—professors, instructors, career service advisors, co-workers, college mentors, family friends, and alumni. Networking may not work for everyone, but it can produce unexpected opportunities for those who take the trouble to follow leads.

4. **Tap into the hidden job market.** Only a small percentage of jobs are advertised. Unadvertised jobs are part of a hidden job market that can be accessed via cold-call inquiries and networking with personal contacts. To find out if a company in which your are interested might have an opening for someone with your qualifications or might be motivated to create such a position, you can write an unsolicited letter of application, otherwise known as a **job-prospecting letter**, and send it to the company along with your resume. You can also make **cold calls** to companies and set up information interviews. Such interviews put you in touch with individuals who are prepared to talk with you, even for a few minutes, about skill requirements, job duties, and hiring prospects. These individuals may very well have the power to hire you. Have several specific questions in mind when you call so you won't waste the prospective employer's time or make a nuisance of yourself. Another way to scout for unadvertised jobs is to sign up for interviews when company recruiters visit your school. Job recruitment fairs, including online job fairs, may also yield the big break you have been looking for. When attending recruitment events, go with a stack of resumés in hand.

5. **Visit employment agencies.** Take advantage of the job placement services at your school, college, or government agencies by registering early. Check out job notice boards and ask about counselling services offered by the centres.

6. **Think ahead.** Look into the possibility of getting a summer internship or co-op job while you are still a student. Non-salaried employment can help you gain valuable experience that gives you an edge once you graduate. Plan to devote as much time as you can to your job search—and be persistent.

7. **Polish your interpersonal and communication skills.** Brush up on telephone manners and make sure your oral and written communication skills are first-rate. Your ability to communicate can make or break your first contact with a company.

◖◗ Writing Persuasive Resumés

A **resumé** is a one- to two-page document—a personal marketing tool—that tells prospective employers about your education, employment experience, and skill sets. It itemizes this information as specific blocks of information organized under easy-reference headings, arranged strategically to play up your strengths. At the top of the page, it supplies contact information (full mailing address, telephone number, fax number, and e-mail address) so that interested employers can reach you. A resumé represents you and your best work on paper, providing evidence that will help prospective

job-prospecting letter an unsolicited letter in which a job-seeker introduces herself and asks about job openings.

cold call an unsolicited telephone call in which a job-seeker introduces himself and asks about job openings.

employment agency an organization that matches job candidates with jobs, sometimes for a fee.

resumé a persuasive written document in which a job applicant summarizes her qualifications and relates her education, work experience, and personal accomplishments to the needs of a prospective employer.

employers decide whether you qualify for interviewing. It may not tell an employer everything about you—non-essentials are best excluded—but it provides a summary of your qualifications for a specific job and shows the results you have achieved in past work ex-periences. An effective resumé enables you to get your foot in the door, giving you the chance to win over prospective employers in person. Because your resumé is the first proof employers may have of your ability to communicate in writing, it should reflect your professionalism in its neatness, accuracy, and careful formatting.

HOW EMPLOYERS USE RESUMÉS

Resumés help employers gather standardized data about applicants. Employers use resumés to screen out applicants, though few resumés are read word for word. Faced with the huge task of reviewing hundreds of resumés for a single position, human resources specialists spend a minute or less perusing each one. To simplify and speed up the sorting and screening process, they may scan resumés into an electronic job-tracking system. Only applicants whose resumés contain keywords matched to job requirements may pass to the next stage of the job competition. To ensure you remain a candidate for the job you seek, prepare your resumé for easy skimmability and scannability (see "Preparing a Scannable Resumé" on page 262).

RESUMÉ WRITING STYLE

Because resumés deliver information quickly through lists and phrases, resumé writing requires a tight, clipped, action-oriented style that focuses on results. The reader will already understand that details in the document pertain to you, so there is no need to use *I*. Telegraphic phrases that begin with action verbs take the place of complete sentences.

Conventional style:	I designed and coordinated two marketing campaigns that resulted in a 15 per cent increase in sales over one year.
Resumé style:	• Designed and coordinated two marketing campaigns. • Increased annual sales by 15 per cent.

As much as possible, these phrases should quantify details and incorporate keywords that relate your qualifications to those being sought. Here are a few more tips to help you produce a perfect final copy.

- **Use capitals and/or boldface for headings.** Avoid hard-to-read capitals and italics for other parts of your resumé.
- **Use consistent indenting.** If you use columns to arrange information, make sure they are regular. Be consistent in setting off details in each section.
- **Leave space between sections.** Think of your resumé as a work of art, not a crowded house or crib sheet. Use wide margins to make information stand out.
- **Proofread to catch errors** (misspellings, typos, errors in mechanics, and poor grammar) that might disqualify you from consideration. Accuracy can make or break a resumé. If you routinely miss errors, ask a knowledgeable friend to give your resumé an objective reading.

PARTS OF A STANDARD RESUMÉ

Resumés commonly contain the following sections, usually in the order given. Categories marked with asterisks (*) are optional.

> Name and Contact Information (do not use a heading)
> *Objective/Career Profile
> *Summary of Qualifications
> Education
> Experience
> *Skills and Capabilities
> *Awards and Activities
> *References

Alternate headings may also be used, depending on your field of expertise:

> Publications
> Advanced Career Training
> Licences and Accreditations
> Language Proficiency/Foreign Languages
> Presentations
> Professional Affiliations/Memberships

You have some flexibility in how you arrange this information. Without distorting facts, you can shape your resumé to relate your education, work experience, and personal accomplishments to the needs of prospective employers. You can also emphasize your most impressive selling point—for instance, specialized training, an advanced degree, or strong work experience—by customizing the standard resumé templates supplied by your word-processing software. Simply vary the standard order and put important material near the beginning—just after the objective statement—where it commands the most attention. Your most noteworthy qualification should come first. Any weaknesses can be de-emphasized by their placement.

Contact Information

No heading is needed for the contact information section. Type your full name at the top of the page, making it stand out by centring it and setting it in boldface; you could also set it in a slightly larger point size. Below it, type your permanent address (and/or your local campus address), phone number(s), e-mail address, and, if applicable, your web address and fax number. Your contact information has to be correct; the difference of one digit in a telephone number can cost you an interview, maybe more.

First Name R. Last Name

Address until May 14, 2010	Address after May 14, 2010
Pitman Hall	52 Hawkswell Drive
160 Mutual Street	Orillia, ON
Ryerson University	LV3 2J1
Toronto, ON M5B 2M2	
	(705) 733-1211
(416) 979-5000	

Career Objective

An optional section, your career objective is a short, assertive summary (containing one to three lines of text) that identifies your main qualifications and anticipated career path. It helps you target a specific job by enabling you to match your qualifications with key requirements. If you decide to make your career objective part of your resumé, you should revise it for each new application. It will not help you unless it is relevant. Use descriptive phrases and minimal punctuation. Depending on your strategy, you can highlight the position you desire, a professional goal, the type of field you want to work in, your main qualifications—or all of these combined.

- To utilize my [qualifications] as a [position title]: To utilize my working knowledge of maintenance techniques as a maintenance reliability supervisor.

- [Position title]: Marketing position with opportunity for growth and development.

- To [professional goal]: To assist low-income families in finding housing and support services.

Summary of Qualifications/Profile

As an alternative to the career objective section, a summary of your qualifications is a high-impact statement—consisting of one or two sentences—that provides an overall picture of you and your qualifications as they relate to the job you are applying for. This section is useful if your experience has been varied or accumulated over a number of years.

Education

The education section—always of interest to employers—supplies information about your schooling and academic training, providing proof of your ability to do the job effectively. You should list all undergraduate and graduate degrees, diplomas, and certificates you have earned or are about to earn. Begin with your most recent or most relevant degree. Using commas to separate elements, list the following details:

- the degree, diploma, or certificate;
- academic honours you graduated with (for any degree earned *with distinction*, *magna cum laude*, *summa cum laude*, or *with high distinction*, italicize or bracket this information);
- the name of the institution that granted the degree;
- the location of the school;
- your major field of study, concentration, or specialization; and
- dates of attendance and/or date of graduation.

Use the same style for every degree or diploma you list. Some job applicants also choose to list courses they have taken that are relevant to a current application. If you decide to do this, you should list courses by short descriptive title (not course code) and organize them under a subheading such as "Courses Related to Major" or "Courses Related to [position for which you are applying]." If you have an exceptionally high GPA (a grade point average of 3.5 or better), you might want to mention it; otherwise withhold this information.

Work Experience

Information about work experience is key, especially for recent graduates new to the job market. Employment history is given in reverse chronological order (beginning with your present or most recent job). In addition to listing full-time and part-time jobs, you should include unpaid jobs, internships, volunteer work, and self-employment if these work experiences contributed to your set of relevant skills. Provide only minimal details of high school jobs, but do indicate if you earned a substantial portion of your educational expenses through jobs concurrent with your college studies. For each position, list the following:

- job title(s) (indicating promotions),
- the company and its location (city and province),
- dates of employment (including month and year), and
- significant duties, activities, achievements, and promotions (use phrases introduced by strong action verbs to describe these details).

Use the present tense for the job you are in now; use the past tense for a job you no longer hold. Because each description serves as an advertisement for your skills, deal in specifics rather than generalities—quantifying accomplishments and activities—and incorporate dynamic verbs that help to portray you in a positive light and accent your most impressive qualifications.

Vague: Responsible for direct-mailings.

Specific: Supervised over 40 direct-mail marketing campaigns.

If there are gaps in your work history or frequent job changes, consider using a format that de-emphasizes employment dates. For example, you could place these dates after the job title, rather than tabulating them or setting them in boldface. In functional resumés, work can be organized according to the type of work or skill, rather than by positions held.

Skills and Capabilities

The skills section outlines the abilities and proficiencies that make you more employable. It gives you the opportunity to spotlight your technical training—your mastery of computer programs, interfaces, applications, special communications skills, or operating procedures for office equipment—as well as your fluency in foreign languages.

- Experienced with e-mail, Microsoft Office, MS Word 2007, Lotus, Excel.
- Proficient in PowerPoint, Internet research.
- Keyboard 80 wpm accurately.
- Trained in technical writing, including proposals and documentation.
- Fluent in French.

Awards/Honours and Activities

If you are a recent graduate or are re-entering the workforce, you can benefit from including an awards and activities section, reserved for academic awards and scholarships, volunteer experiences, special projects, leadership positions, professional memberships, and university and community service positions. This information shows you are a well-rounded person, with commitment, initiative, team spirit, or problem-solving ability—qualities that are important, especially when your interests or activities are relevant to the job. Include the date of involvement in an activity or the date of an award.

FIGURE 9.1 Action Verbs for Resumés

acted	estimated	prepared
adapted	expanded	presented
advised	facilitated	processed
analyzed	formulated	produced
arranged	founded	programmed
assembled	guided	promoted
assisted	handled	provided
built	harmonized	purchased
carried out	headed	raised
catalogued	identified	recommended
collaborated	implemented	recorded
collected	improved	redesigned
completed	increased	reorganized
computed	initiated	repaired
conducted	inspected	represented
conserved	installed	reviewed
constructed	instituted	revised
consulted	instructed	saved
controlled	introduced	scheduled
co-operated	investigated	selected
coordinated	launched	serviced
counselled	led	set up
created	made	sold
dealt	maintained	started
decided	managed	streamlined
decreased	monitored	supervised
delivered	negotiated	supplied
designed	operated	supported
determined	ordered	trained
developed	organized	unified
directed	performed	upgraded
distributed	pioneered	
established	planned	

Personal Information

A resumé is not the place for personal information. By law, employers are not allowed to ask for personal information relating to country of origin or religious affiliation. Human rights legislation protects job applicants from discrimination. Your resumé should not include details about your age, marital status, or health.

References

As a job candidate you can wait until a recruiter shows interest before you give the names of references, since such information is not vital to securing an interview. Simply stating "references will be supplied on request" should be sufficient, and it saves space on your resumé. The alternative is to prepare a separate reference list (entitled "Reference

Sheet for [Your Name]"), which can then be submitted to employers at the time of your interview. However, if you do include references on your resumé, give each person's full name and title, professional affiliation or company, address, phone number, and e-mail address. List this information in parallel form and put e-mail addresses in angle brackets. Always contact references in advance and ask permission to use their names. This will ensure they are prepared to discuss your qualifications.

RESUMÉ LENGTH

The debate over resumé length is never-ending. Many companies insist on one page; others find a two-page resumé perfectly acceptable. The general rule is to keep it to one page as long as there is enough white space and room for formatting to ensure the resumé is readable and well balanced. Resumés that look crowded are hard to read. Recent graduates can easily stay within the one-page limit if they eliminate filler and consolidate headings; applicants with extensive work history and advanced training may require a second page to adequately represent their qualifications. Before you elect to use a longer resumé, you may want to check the job advertisement for application instructions and details on resumé preferences.

RESUMÉ STYLES AND LAYOUTS

There is a resumé style to suit every applicant, from the rookie job-seeker with little experience to the seasoned veteran with an armload of honours and achievements. Because writing a resumé allows for some flexibility, you can choose a style that will help you look as good on paper as you are in person. The most widely used resumé styles are the *chronological*, the *functional*, and the *combination*. Each style has its own distinctive character, ranging from the fairly conservative and conventional to the more flexible and innovative. Opt for a style that allows you to (1) showcase who you are as a potential employee, and (2) project an image of yourself that is right for the company.

Chronological Resumé

This style (see Figure 9.2, "Chronological Resumé," on page 259) has been popular with employers and recruiters for a long time and is considered the standard resumé style. It tells employers what you have done professionally and when you did it, organizing details in chronological order. It presents information under categories that recruiters have come to expect and can review quickly: "Objective," "Education," "Work Experience," "Special Skills," "Honours and Activities," and "References." The chronological style works well for applicants who have work experience in their field of employment and show sustained career growth and continuity. Because it emphasizes the jobs you have held rather than the skills you possess, the chronological style is less suited to younger applicants with limited experience. For anyone with a negative or irregular work history, its arrangement by employment dates has the added disadvantage of making gaps in employment more obvious.

chronological resumé a document in which a job applicant's work experience, education, and personal achievements are presented in reverse time sequence, with the most recent experience in each category listed first.

Functional Resumé

This skills-based resumé style (see Figure 9.3, "Functional Resumé," on page 260) emphasizes work-related skills and competencies rather than work history. It markets relevant attributes, accomplishments, and achievements, and demonstrates capabilities

functional resumé a document in which a job applicant's qualifications are presented in terms of notable achievements and abilities rather than work experience.

that will be of value to the company. It works well for applicants who are about to redirect their careers or for anyone who has limited work experience but untold ability. The functional resumé is a good choice for accenting skills gained through volunteer experience. Its customizable categories allow for greater flexibility: "Objective," "Summary of Qualifications/Profile," "[Type of Work] Experience," "[Type of] Skills/ Areas of Expertise," "References." Skills can be arranged according to several types, bringing to light hidden strengths. Some recruiters may view the omission of job history as a weakness.

Combination Resumé

combination resumé
a document that combines characteristics of chronological and functional resumes.

This cross between the chronological and functional resumé draws together the best of each style (see Figure 9.4, "Combination Resumé," on page 261). It highlights capabilities at the same time as it provides a complete record of employment. This style works well for recent graduates who may or may not have experience, but do have the skills to gain employment. Its headings are borrowed from chronological and functional styles: "Objective," "Skills and Capabilities/Special Skills," "Experience," "Education," "Honours and Activities," "References." Because this style is less traditional, it is a more risky choice for anyone applying for jobs in traditional fields such as accounting, law, or banking. The formatting should be strategic and methodical, so that the combination of styles is not confusing to readers.

General Tips

1. **Tell the truth.** A resumé is a legal document and purports to be the truth. It is fraudulent to lie on a resumé and unethical to tell half-truths. Companies routinely do background checks and can easily detect applicants engaging in these practices, which are grounds for dismissal. Resist the temptation to inflate your academic honours, embellish your job titles, exaggerate your accomplishments, or alter employment dates.

2. **Keep your resumé up to date.** Make sure your resumé is fresh and reflects recent accomplishments and current responsibilities and activities. When your dream job is advertised, you want to be ready to seize the opportunity, so schedule regular resumé updates. Last-minute efforts at revision can result in sloppy formatting and job-limiting typos.

3. **Create different versions of your resumé**—one that can be scanned into a resumé database and one that you can e-mail to company contacts. Keep in mind that companies and recruiters often have specific preferences regarding the way your resumé should be transmitted.

4. **Fine-tune your resumé for each new application.** Revise your career objective statement to link it to the job for which you are currently applying.

5. **Avoid gimmicks.** Your resumé should invite further reading by looking well prepared and professional, but not necessarily flashy. Print your resumé on good quality, standard 8½ by 11–inch white paper. Pale-coloured paper is also acceptable, but save your supply of Day-Glo paper for craft projects. Use enough white space to make your resumé easy to read, and resist the temptation to decorate with clip art.

FIGURE 9.2 Chronological Resumé

MITRA DAS
253 Elderwood Crescent
Brampton, ON N5L 2S9
(905) 862-5540
mdas@rogers.ca

OBJECTIVE

To assist a fashion retail chain in providing superior customer service while managing merchandise efficiently and maximizing store sales in an entry-level management position

Statement emphasizes professional goal in relation to the advertisement for the position being sought

EDUCATION

Ryerson University, Toronto, Ontario
Working toward a Bachelor of Commerce in Retail Management
Degree expected June 2010
Major courses: • Managerial Accounting
                • Advanced Retail Management
                • Organizational Behaviour

Places education first for emphasis, as degrees and diplomas of this young candidate relate directly to position being sought

Seneca College, Toronto, Ontario
Diploma in Fashion Merchandising (Co-op Education Program), 2008
Major courses: • Fashion Retail Entrepreneurship
                • Retail Organizational Management
                • Retail Human Resources Management

EXPERIENCE

Assistant Manager (part-time), Skylark Fashions, Vaughn, Ontario
May 2008 to present
• Assisted in directing, training, and motivating store sales team of eight in order to provide a high level of customer service and increase profits by 15 per cent
• Improved inventory-control procedures to reduce stock surpluses by 20 per cent

Describes work experience, quantifies specific achievements, and uses action verbs

Fashion Intern (work term), Shoe Depot Inc., Toronto, Ontario
January 2008 to March 2008
• Assisted district manager in coordinating store programs and events
• Created and managed seminars and team-building exercises to enhance customer service
• Maintained and updated client mailing lists

Visual Merchandiser, Suzy Shier, Square One, Mississauga, Ontario
September 2007 to December 2007
• Responsible for store signage, pricing, visual displays, and replenishing stock

Sales Associate, Roots Canada Inc., Toronto, Ontario
May 2006 to September 2006
• Handled cash and credit transactions
• Worked with sales team to deliver excellent customer service

SKILLS

• Proficient with MS Word, Lotus, Excel, PowerPoint, and Internet research
• Superior time-management and organizational skills

Mentions some skills commonly requested by employers

FIGURE 9.3 Functional Resumé

Includes profile statement to summarize strengths and capabilities

Highlights skills mentioned in advertisement by listing them first; uses strong action verbs to describe achievements and market capabilities

Mentions experience last to de-emphasize limited work history

Troy Ng   109 Ludlow Avenue, Brampton, ON K2L 3B5

905-555-2241 (home)
905-567-7783 (cell)
tjng@hotmail.com

OBJECTIVE

Position as assistant manager of front desk operations with opportunity for growth and development

PROFILE

College graduate with Travel and Tourism Diploma and co-operative experience in the hotel industry

RELEVANT SKILLS AND QUALIFICATIONS

Computer and Office Skills
- Knowledge of Sabre, Fidelio, and Opera
- Proficient with Windows, Word, Acrobat, and e-mail applications
- Keyboard 60 wpm with accuracy
- Able to perform general office duties, including photocopying, filing, and faxing

Organizational and Marketing Skills
- Scheduled events and arranged catering plans for groups of up to 300
- Provided concierge services to guests, including tours of hotel facilities
- Prepared advertising copy for summer resort
- Trained and supervised three desk clerks at Big Trout Lodge
- Responsible for individual reservations through telephone and central reservation system

Communicaton Skills
- Demonstrated friendly and courteous telephone etiquette in answering guest inquiries regarding rates, special packages, and general information
- Performed test calls to competition and Global Reservation Centre
- Polished speaking skills by giving talks to class
- Completed college communication courses with an A grade
- Fluent in Japanese and Mandarin

Interpersonal Skills
- Demonstrated ability to work independently with minimal supervision and to work co-operatively in the interest of better guest satisfaction
- Assisted front desk manager in conducting team-building activities

EDUCATION

Seneca College, Toronto, ON
Diploma in Travel and Tourism (Co-operative Education Program), 2008

Troy Ng   Page 2

RELEVANT EXPERIENCE

Reservations Agent (co-op position), Royal York Hotel, Toronto, ON
January 2008 to March 2008

Front Desk Clerk, Big Trout Lodge, Bracebridge, ON
May 2007 to August 2007

OTHER EXPERIENCE

Sales Clerk, Holinger Hardware, Brampton, ON
Summers, 2004 to 2006

FIGURE 9.4 Combination Resumé

KELLY MARACLE
21 Rockycrest Drive
North Bay, ON P1A 2H7
Home: (705) 495-9035 Cell: (705) 490-1166
E-mail: kjmaracle@gmail.com

SKILLS AND CAPABILITIES	• Type 90 wpm with accuracy • Take symbol shorthand at 80 wpm with accurate transcription • Produce effective legal documents in fast-paced environment • Experienced with MS Office, Word, and Internet • Comprehensive knowledge of legal procedures as they apply to the commercial real estate business • Able to communicate in a professional manner with clients and lawyers

← Highlights skills named in advertisement

EXPERIENCE	**Legal Assistant**, Real Estate Group, Ball LLP, Sudbury, Ontario May 2007 to August 2010 • Performed clerical, administrative, and general office duties, including accounting, closing files, docketing, and billing • Transcribed and typed legal documents, confidential letters, and reports in detail-oriented environment • Scheduled meetings and initiated follow-up with clients **Office Assistant** (part-time), Horizon Realty, North Bay, Ontario Summer 2006 • Routed and answered routine correspondence • Typed and proofread documents • Produced advertising copy and coordinated 15 mass mailings

← Experience reinforces skills already described for impact and emphasis

EDUCATION	**Seneca College**, Toronto, Ontario Diploma in Office Administration (Legal), 2007 Major courses • Legal Procedures–Real Estate/Corporate • Legal Word Processing • Communications and Machine Transcription • Spreadsheets

← Education emphasizes major courses relevant to the job applied for

ACTIVITIES AND HONOURS	• Volunteer, Daily Bread Food Bank, 2004–present • Student Council Representative, Seneca College, Fall 2006 • Silver Medallist, 400m Hurdles, Ontario Junior Track and Field Championships, 2002

← Mentions activities that show leadership, achievement, and community involvement

References are available on a separate sheet to be left, if required, after interview →

REFERENCES

KELLY MARACLE
21 Rockycrest Drive
North Bay, ON P1A 2H7
Home: (705) 495-9035 Cell: (705) 490-1166
E-mail: kjmaracle@gmail.com

Professor Anya Giles Office Administration Program Seneca College 2581 Finch Avenue East Toronto, ON M3L 2E9 (416) 250-8641	Mr. Bill Yan President Horizon Realty Ltd. 880 North Shore Avenue North Bay, ON P1C 7R7 (705) 641-3328	Mr. Jeff Ball, QC Chief Partner Ball LLP 80 Brady Street Sudbury, ON P3A 2B2 (705) 555-2948

PREPARING A SCANNABLE RESUMÉ

A **scannable resumé** is one that has high visibility in an electronic resumé-tracking system or electronic resumé database. Unlike a traditional resumé, which emphasizes action verbs, a scannable resumé spotlights an applicant's pertinent experience with keywords that correspond to ones used to describe the ideal candidate in the job posting or advertisement. Placed after the main heading of your resumé or near the end and entitled "Keywords," this pool of up to fifty relevant, attention-getting words may include current and previous job titles, job-specific professional jargon and its synonyms, titles of software programs, marketable skills, and adjectives describing interpersonal traits. Here are a few examples:

accurate	efficient	planning ability
active	experienced	positive
adaptable	flexible	problem-solving
communication skills	innovative	productive
creative	leadership	results-oriented
customer-oriented	motivated	takes initiative
detail-oriented	organizational skills	willing to travel

Applicants with the highest percentage of matches are identified as good candidates for the job and stand the best chance of being interviewed.

A scannable resumé must have a plain, crisp, uncluttered appearance to guarantee its acceptance by electronic scanning systems that cannot handle graphics and symbols. To create a scannable resumé,

DO

- List your name and address at the top of every page of your resumé.
- Use white space as your main formatting tool, leaving blank lines around headings.
- Use as many pages as necessary to list your skills and experience—in the absence of other formatting tools use plenty of white space.
- Inspect your resumé for letters that overlap to reduce the chances your information will be misread; use a font in which letters do not touch.
- Send a crisp copy of your resumé—preferably one printed on a laser printer.

DON'T

- Use horizontal or vertical lines.
- Use hollow bullets.
- Use italics, underlines, boxes, columns, graphics, borders, or shading.
- Use unusual fonts and typefaces—instead use sans serif fonts such as Arial in ten- to twelve-point size.
- Print your resumé on coloured or textured paper.
- Fold, staple, or fax your resumé.

Before you send your resumé, it is a good idea to first find out if the recipient uses scanning software. You may wish to prepare two versions of your resumé—one traditional and one that is computer-friendly—and ask if it is acceptable to send both.

FIGURE 9.5 Scannable, Computer-Friendly Resumé

CAMERON TUCKER
158 Gardenview Blvd.
Barrie, ON L4M 6J1
Phone: 705-231-9976
Email: cameron.tucker@sympatico.ca

KEYWORDS

Public Relations. Marketing Communications. Event Marketing. Media Advertising. Sales
Promotion. Advertising Research. Visual Communication. Telemarketing. Advertising Sales.
MS Office Suite. Excel. Quark. Photoshop. Communication Skills. Organizational Skills.
Persuasive Presentation Skills. Bilingual. Ontario College Diploma in Progress. Georgian College.

OBJECTIVE

Motivated, fast-learning individual seeks advertising/marketing position utilizing communication
and organizational skills.

EDUCATION

Georgian College, Barrie, ON
Ontario College Diploma in Advertising, 2009

RELEVANT COURSEWORK

Advertising Computer Applications
Professional Writing
Marketing on the Web
Copywriting
Media Planning Computer Applications

CAMERON TUCKER
158 Gardenview Blvd.
Barrie, ON L4M 6J1
Phone: 705-231-9976
Email: cameron.tucker@sympatico.ca

Page 2

EXPERIENCE

Bradford Community Gazette
June 2008 to present
Part-Time Advertising Sales Representative

    Represent the *Bradford Community Gazette* to assigned and potential advertisers.
    Handle incoming advertiser calls.
    Increase advertising revenue and expand client base by 15% annually through cold calls and
    outbound sales.
    Provide clients with creative advertising solutions and implement sales strategies for existing
    clients.

Part-Time Sales Associate
    Greeted customers, demonstrated products, successfully served more than 50 customers daily.
    Answered questions and solved customer problems.

SKILLS

Computer: Macintosh Applications, Microsoft Office, Web Publishing.
Interpersonal: Communicative, persuasive, team-oriented, fluent in English and French.
                 Able to follow through in fast-paced, deadline-driven environment.

FURTHER INFORMATION

References, university transcripts, and a portfolio of computer programs are available upon request.

PREPARING AN E-MAIL RESUMÉ

Most companies now solicit resumés via e-mail as a way of cutting human resources costs and avoiding human contact. However, not every resumé transmitted by e-mail ends up in the right hands. There is always the risk that recruiter inboxes may be flooded by e-mails after a job is posted online or that junk–e-mail filters may keep resumés from reaching their destination. Here are a few tips to help ensure your e-mailed resumé isn't ignored or lost:

1. **Read instructions for job ads carefully.** Some companies advertise positions online but do not accept resumés via e-mail. If companies want the resumé in plain text, they will usually specify "a plain-text document sent in the body of the message."

2. **Attach a resumé or cover letter to your e-mail only when specifically requested.** Employers may delete e-mails with attached resumés rather than risk exposing their computer systems to viruses hidden in attachments. Unless you are absolutely certain the employer is using a compatible e-mail program, put your cover letter and resumé as text within the body of your e-mail message.

3. **Use keywords.** Your document may end up on a resumé database essential to the screening process. Study keywords specific to the job ad and your field and incorporate ones that match your qualifications and background.

4. **Include a cover letter** and send both your letter and resumé in one e-mail message.

5. **Put the job title and/or reference number in the subject line of your message** if you are responding to an advertisement or job posting.

6. **Use formatting methods that make your resumé more computer-friendly.** You can easily convert a resumé formatted in MSWord or WordPerfect to plain text. Avoid fancy formatting (no graphics, lines, italics, bullets, or special characters). When writing your resumé, simplify the editing work you will have to do by keeping your resumé conversion-friendly:

   DON'T

   - Use special characters (characters not on your keyboard).
   - Use a word-wrap feature (lines can end up wrapping at awkward spots).
   - Use bullets, italics, underlined text, graphics, slashes (e.g., "Supervisor/ Administrator"), and page numbers (you have no way of knowing where page breaks will fall).
   - Use non-proportional typefaces such as Times New Roman that have different widths for different characters—instead use a fixed-width typeface such as Courier that will produce a true sixty-five-character line, as accepted by most e-mail programs.

FIGURE 9.6 Sample Plain-Text Resumé

Joshua Cheechoo
jcheechoo@sympatico.ca

CAREER PROFILE

— eBusiness specialist with relevant degree and background in supply-chain
  processes and website development and management.
— Emphasis on IT and pharmaceutical industries.
— Recent supervisory experience, with developed interpersonal, decision-
  making, and communication skills.
— Strong capabilities in a DOS, Windows, and Internet Explorer environment.
— Fluent in French.

EXERIENCE

WEBULTIMA INC.
January 2009 to present
Toronto, ON
eMarketing Manager

— Develop strategy and execute demand generation programs using interactive
  media and search engine marketing in order to maximize marketing objectives.
— Plan and buy interactive and digital media, including Internet, Wireless,
  iTV, etc.
— Lead initial kickoff preparation on all new demand-generation projects.
— Act as Account Manager, interfacing with the client as the single point
  of contact.

MARKSON PHARMACEUTICALS
July 2005 to December 2008
Mississauga, ON
eBusiness Deployment Specialist

— Maximized e-ordering utilization between Markson Pharmaceuticals and its
  pharmacy and retail sales, increasing sales by 15 per cent.
— Served as outside trainer and resources provider for the Ontario
  marketplace, conducting over thirty seminars annually.
— Developed POV documents on new trends.
— Evaluated, built, and maintained relationships in the local and national
  online sales and vendor community.

EDUCATION

Humber College Institute of Advanced Learning
Toronto,ON
Bachelor of Applied Business-eBusiness, June 2005
Major Courses: Management Support Systems, eStrategy, Marketing and eBusiness,
Information Technology Management

Preparing a Persuasive Application Letter

cover letter (or
application letter)
a letter that accompanies a
resumé to summarize a job
applicant's qualifications
and value to a prospective
employer.

An **application letter**—also called a **cover letter**—is essentially a sales letter. Its persuasion is aimed at advancing a candidate to the interview phase of the job-screening process and beyond. Usually no more than a page in length but never skimpy, an application letter introduces you to a prospective employer and helps to make a good first impression. It offers a quick snapshot of your qualifications—introducing your resumé and extracting key information from it. A cover letter interprets raw data from your resumé so readers may better understand how your skills and experience fit the requirements of a specific job. An application letter can do what a resumé on its own cannot—tell prospective employers what you are prepared to do for their company and convince them you are qualified for the job. Its sales pitch highlights the benefits of hiring you as well as your interest in the company. While not every application may require this kind of introduction, a cover letter must be written accurately and skilfully. You have just a few paragraphs to grab the reader's attention and leave a strong impression—leaving no room for errors in grammar, spelling, and typography that can easily eliminate you from consideration.

- **Opening**—gets attention and clearly identifies the position for which you are applying
- **Body**—builds interest with a summary of your qualifications, as much as possible matching your strengths to the requirements of the job
- **Closing**—asks for an interview and provides a contact number

GENERAL TIPS FOR COVER LETTERS

1. **Camouflage *I*, *me*, and *mine*.** It is almost impossible to write an application letter without using *I*, but some people worry that overusing first-person pronouns may make them sound egotistical or boastful. To make *I* less noticeable, avoid placing it at the beginning of consecutive sentences. Vary your style by occasionally embedding *I* in the middle of sentences. This has the added benefit of keeping your style from becoming monotonous. By showing and interpreting what you have done rather than praising your own efforts, you can convince the reader of the benefits your employment can bring.

2. **Get the company name right.** Because most companies seek employees who are detail-oriented and efficient, small things, like good typography and accurate spelling, mean a lot to the success of a cover letter.

3. **Use keywords from the job ad or posting.** Show that your skills are transferable and relevant to the job you are applying for.

4. **Use the same font that you used for your resumé.** This gives a unified look to your application. Print on high-quality bond paper.

5. **Avoid dense, overloaded paragraphs.** Your letter should be designed for ease of readability. Long paragraphs can bury your reason for writing, blur facts, and diminish the strength of your qualifications. Shorter paragraphs make your letter quick to review.

6. **Don't plead, apologize, or exaggerate.** Desperation usually weakens a message's persuasive impact, especially when employers are seeking positive and self-confident personnel.

7. **Avoid a cookie-cutter approach.** A generic, multi-purpose letter is less likely to gain interest, so work from a bulleted list of your qualifications, achievements, and educational credentials to prepare a new cover letter targeted to each job opening. Make your letter relevant to the job you are applying for, keeping in mind the requirements outlined by the employer in the job ad.

8. **Strive for a tight, clear writing style.** Use your letter to introduce yourself and identify your strongest selling points—no more than a page but no less than half a page.

9. **Keep a copy of your letter**, and keep a record of jobs you have applied for. How you capture attention at the beginning of your letter depends on the hiring situation—whether the position for which you are applying is solicited (an ad response) or unsolicited (a cold call).

SOLICITED APPLICATION LETTERS

When you know a company is hiring, you can respond to an advertisement by writing a **solicited application letter**. Its purpose is to ask for an interview, not for the actual job. By putting your interview request at the end—in line with the indirect approach—you can first demonstrate and persuade screeners that your experience and preparation fill the requirements of the job. The goal is to convince prospective employers that you are not only qualified for the job, but are better than other candidates.

FIGURE 9.7 INEFFECTIVE Letter of Application (Solicited) (extract)

This letter is an application for a position that was advertised in yesterday's careers section.

→ Does not clearly identify the job being sought or refer to the resumé

I have worked part-time for R.J. McCormack for a few months. I am looking for a full-time position, preferably as a senior legal assistant. I think you will agree that my qualifications are a good match for the requirements of the job. I have strong practical skills that will benefit your company. I will receive my diploma soon.

→ Description of work experience is vague and does not specify skills or educational credentials

I think this job was made for me. If you agree that I could be the right person for the job you advertised, I could find time to meet with you to discuss my qualifications. To arrange an interview, just leave a message for me on my voice mail, but try not to call early in the day.

→ Writer-centred approach reinforces what the company is supposed to do for the applicant, not what the applicant can do for the company

1. **Introductory paragraph: Gain attention.** Name the specific job for which you are applying and indicate where you learned about the job. Include job competition or reference numbers to ensure your application ends up in the right hands. Clearly state that you are applying for the job. There are several approaches that you can use and combine in order to do this and at the same time gain attention for your application. Briefly show that you possess the major qualifications listed as requirements in the posting.

   - **Summary + Request Opening**

     With five years' experience as an industrial designer, I would like to be considered for the position of Design Team Leader advertised by your company in the June 20 edition of *The Globe and Mail*.

   - **Shared Values/Interest in the Company Opening**

     A recent survey of the Canadian industrial sector ranked Weir Services first in the repair and refurbishing of mechanical equipment. I am interested in joining the expert, customer-focused Weir sales team because I share your company's belief in quality and dependability. With a soon-to-be-completed degree in sales management and two years' experience in industrial service sales, I am prepared to be an immediately productive member of your sales team.

   - **Request Opening**

     I wish to apply for the position of Regional Sales Manager, as advertised in yesterday's *National Post* (competition #4368). As the attached resumé suggests, my experience in fashion retail has prepared me for the challenging and dynamic work environment offered by this position.

   - **Name Opening**

     At the suggestion of Mr. Farouk Aziz of your Accounting Department, I submit my qualifications for the position of Human Resources Specialist posted at globeandmail.workopolis.com.

2. **Middle paragraphs: Show that you are qualified by relating your skills to what the company requires.** Using action verbs (*managed*, *designed*, *organized*, *upgraded*), describe the skills, schooling, achievements, and experience that would make you valuable to the company. Rather than trying to mention everything you have done, summarize aspects of your background that will help you get an interview. Emphasize your strongest skills, especially the kinds that employers generally seek—the ability to communicate well, take responsibility, learn quickly, and work as part of a team. You can use bullet style to highlight your qualifications and bring them to the forefront quickly and easily. Give one or two examples that relate what you have done to the ways you can benefit the company.

   > Three years as a sous-chef at Chez Tom taught me how to work under pressure and maintain high standards of food presentation and menu selection on a limited budget.

FIGURE 9.8 **EFFECTIVE** Letter of Application (Solicited)

62 Robin Street
Toronto, ON M4D 2P3
August 24, 2010

Ms. Patrizia Chernienko
Rossiter, Fleet, and Lee, LLP
1220 Yonge Street, Suite 230
Toronto, ON L4T 5S7

Dear Ms. Chernienko:

Subject: Legal Assistant Position (Ref. No. 68146) ◄——— Clearly identifies the position applied for

With a soon-to-be-completed diploma in legal office administration and high-level skills, I wish to apply for the position of Legal Assistant, as advertised in the March 5 edition of *The Globe and Mail*. As the enclosed resumé suggests, my intensive internship training has given me the necessary practical experience to be immediately productive in a prestigious legal firm such as Rossiter, Fleet, and Lee, LLP.

◄——— Gains attention with a concise summary of qualifications

◄——— Refers to accompanying resumé

My courses in the legal office administration curriculum at Great Huron College have provided me with background in all aspects of legal assistance, including legal transcription, word processing, legal procedures (real estate), and spreadsheets. Over six semesters I transcribed and processed more than 300 legal documents and mastered the proofreading skills necessary to ensure the kind of accuracy Rossiter, Fleet, and Lee would expect.

During my six-month internship in the offices of R.J. McCormack, I learned to manage time effectively in a detail-oriented environment and to perform and prioritize office duties such as docketing and closing files while maintaining flexibility. Assisting the chief legal assistant with additional duties, including the reorganization of client files and overhaul of billing procedures, allowed me to demonstrate my knowledge of office procedures and commitment to expediting the flow of work within the firm. My recent internship experience and participation in school organizations have helped me develop my ability to communicate in a professional manner with clients and lawyers and build the interpersonal skills needed to work effectively as part of a team.

◄——— Relates skills and background to requirements of position, incorporating keywords from the job ad and quantifying achievements

After you have reviewed my resumé for details of my qualifications, please call me at (905) 661-9865 to arrange an interview at your convenience. I look forward to discussing with you ways in which I can contribute to Rossiter, Fleet, and Lee, LLP.

◄——— Asks for action courteously and provides information necessary for follow-up

Sincerely,

Amy Fulton

Amy Fulton

Enclosure

Show what separates you from the other applicants—your course work, summer jobs and internships, knowledge and experience gained from skills and leadership-building activities. Refer the reader to your resumé—a good cover letter will make the reader want to know more about you.

> As you will notice from my resumé, I hold a certificate in cosmetology from Pioneer College.

> Please refer to the attached resumé for a complete list of references.

3. **Closing paragraph: Ask for action.** A call for action takes the form of asking the recruiter to call you to arrange an interview or telling the employer that you will take the initiative to call. Your request should sound courteous, appreciative, and respectful. Make it easy for the reader to contact you by supplying a telephone number and, if you are hard to reach, suggesting the best time to call. Here are a few suggestions for ending your letter:

> I would like the opportunity to discuss my background and qualifications with you in a personal interview. I look forward to hearing from you and to arranging a meeting in the near future.

> I hope that this brief summary of my qualifications and the additional information on my resumé indicate my interest in putting my skills to work for Goldcrest Investments. At your convenience, please call me at (905) 881-9776 to arrange an interview so that we may discuss the ways in which my experience can contribute to your company.

> After you have examined the details on the attached resumé, please call me to arrange an interview at your convenience.

UNSOLICITED APPLICATION LETTERS

unsolicited application letter (or **job-prospecting letter**) an employment letter written when the applicant does not know that a company is hiring.

Unsolicited letters of application—also called **job-prospecting letters**—are written on the chance that employers may have an opening for someone with your skills and qualifications in the foreseeable future—even though no such position has been advertised. Writing an unsolicited letter of application can be more difficult because you do not have a list of job requirements on which to base your pitch for employment. Because there is no way to predict that a tailor-made position with the company will ever materialize or if anyone will even want to read your letter, you have the added challenge of catching the reader's attention right from the start and encouraging her to read on. Among the best ways to do this are the following:

- show some enthusiasm,
- use the indirect approach (for persuasive messages), and
- do research that enables you to demonstrate your interest in and knowledge of the company—the products it manufactures, the personnel it seeks, and the challenges it faces.

From your letter, it should be clear why you want to work for the company, what you are prepared to do for it, and how your assets and qualifications can bring benefits. An unsolicited letter of application attempts to create an opportunity where it might not yet exist—putting you in line for future consideration or inspiring the creation of a position tailor-made to your talents.

FIGURE 9.9 INEFFECTIVE Letter of Application (Unsolicited) (extract)

Dear Human Resources Director:

Can you tell me when there might be an opening for an HR recruiter like me? I have read about your company and it sounds like an organization I would like to work for. I have many skills I feel you could use. In fact, hiring me would be good for your company.

Shall I drop by your office for an interview sometime next week?

Warmest regards,

Sheila Finch

Does not demonstrate knowledge of the company

Fails to mention why job-seeker wants to work for the company

Tone fails to communicate interest and enthusiasm

Overly brief message leaves out details about background and qualifications, making a request for a job without building interest in the job-seeker's capabilities

Salutation too general (if possible, research the name of the individual to whom inquiry should be sent); complimentary close too familiar

Closing question (and lack of contact/follow-up information) makes it easy for hiring manager to say no

E-MAIL COVER LETTERS

Many employers and hiring managers now state a preference for e-mail resumés. You can still introduce your online resumé with a cover letter, using the same strategy as for a solicited application letter. The main difference is that an e-mail cover letter is briefer, more like a cover note. An electronic cover letter may improve your chances of obtaining interview offers more than a resumé submitted alone and is an essential component of an online application. Using the same technical guidelines as for your e-mail resumé, you can lead off with your cover note, and then cut and paste the text of both your note and resumé into the body of your e-mail message.

- **Include a specific and meaningful subject line.** Instead of the generic "Resumé," indicate that this is *your* resumé by making the subject line "Resume—Your Name." Alternatively, identify the job you are applying for or highlight a key point of your background. Use abbreviations so you can fit in a detail that will motivate the reader to open your e-mail.
- **Keep it short and succinct.** It may be a challenge to showcase all your significant qualifications in a one-paragraph or brief multiple-paragraph message, but strive to include your top two or three. Clearly identify the position for which you

FIGURE 9.10 EFFECTIVE Letter of Application (Unsolicited)

Rob Milton
115 Verity Drive
Mississauga, ON M8T 5Y3

March 15, 2010

Mr. Bertie Kwinter,
Director of Human Resources
Braintrust Solutions
240 Richmond Street West
Toronto, ON M4C 3H5

Dear Mr. Kwinter

Gains attention by demonstrating knowledge of and interest in the company →

In a recent article on Canada's top emerging growth companies, *Profit Magazine* ranked Braintrust Solutions as number 1. As your company continues to attract new clients with its innovative web-based workforce management software, you are likely in need of experienced HR recruiters with strong networking skills and proven records of recruiting and resourcing ERP and J2EE consultants.

Links potential employment needs to the job-seeker's assets and skills →

Here are three significant qualifications, summarized from the enclosed resumé, that I believe you will find of interest:

Refers to resumé; relates job-seeker's accomplishments to potential contributions →

- Five years of formal training in business administration and HR recruitment, including a BA from Queen's University and a diploma in Business Administration HR from Seneca College, with specialized courses in strategic marketing, recruitment and selection techniques, and negotiation strategies.

- Four years of practical experience as a Recruitment Partner at JSM Software, where my responsibilities included conducting initial meetings with managers, developing and executing sourcing strategies, overseeing our reference and offer processes, and conducting salary negotiations.

- Strong networking skills and a knowledge of HR resources and applicant tracking technology, with an ability to work and apply problem-solving skills in a fast-paced environment.

Takes initiative for follow-up →

At your convenience, I would like to have the opportunity to meet with you to discuss how my track record and skills could be of value to your company. I will contact your office next week to schedule an interview.

Sincerely,

Rob Milton

Rob Milton

Enc.

are applying and make an attempt at communicating your value to the employer. Remember to ask for an interview.

- **Limit yourself to the characters on a standard keyboard.** A no-frills approach to formatting—no bullets, boldface, lines, or italics—helps to eliminate potential glitches. Send the message to yourself to see how well it transmits before you submit your document to an employer.

JOB APPLICATION ROUND-UP—SOME ADDITIONAL TIPS

1. **Keep track of the companies to which you have applied.** Conducting a job search means you may be applying to many companies at once. Having to ask a prospective employer "what job am I interviewing for?" can make you seem badly organized.

2. **Ensure future contacts remain professional.** Make sure your e-mail address and voice-mail greeting are acceptable by professional standards. Maintaining an unusual e-mail address such as leggysupermodel@hotmail.com or greeting callers with an outgoing voice-mail message such as, "Hey, dudes, the beer's chillin'!" can be a career-limiting move. If necessary, open an e-mail account specifically for the purpose of your job search—you can close it when your search is done. Using your work e-mail address may alert your current employer to your desire for better prospects—not to mention the fact that you are putting company resources to personal use.

3. **Consider privacy and confidentiality.** Be selective about where you post your resumé, sticking to sites that are password-protected and accessible only to legitimate employers. To reduce the risk of identify theft, give only an initial and surname and limit information to only those details an employer rightfully needs to know. Omit your street address and phone number when posting your resumé on the web.

4. **Ensure your application is delivered on time, in the appropriate way.** Follow instructions and submit exactly what the advertisement asks for. Check for further instructions on the company's employment opportunities web page, if the posting supplies the web address.

⬤◗ Job Interviews

A good cover letter and resumé can open the door to a **job interview**, but they cannot ensure your success in the meeting. Being granted an interview is a sign of interest and encouragement. It is now up to you to meet the employer or recruiter face-to-face and talk about the skills, experience, and other qualifications that make you right for the job.

BEFORE THE INTERVIEW

1. **Prepare in order to minimize job interview anxiety.** Do advance research on the potential employer and what the job entails. Spend an hour or so on the Internet gathering intelligence on the company and how it is doing. Focus on the

job interview
a structured, face-to-face conversation between one or more recruiters and a job candidate, in which the job candidate's qualifications for a position and potential performance are assessed.

department or division in which you are interested and learn about its products, people, culture, issues, and customers. Check out the websites of company competitors to gain an understanding of the industry in general. Find out about the challenges each company faces.

2. **Become familiar with your non-verbal communication habits.** Presentation style and appearance are important at interviews. Closed body language—the tendency to cross your arms, for example—can send a message that you are cold or nervous. Fidgeting—nail-biting, hair-twisting, finger-drumming, and knuckle-cracking—can be a sign of nervousness that draws attention away from what you have to say, robbing the interviewer of the chance to see your full potential. Be aware of your posture, facial expressions, and gestures so you can work on controlling them.

3. **Dress for the job.** Match your attire to the type and style of organization you are applying to—dressing in a conservative manner, keeping jewellery to a minimum, and using perfume or cologne sparingly, if at all. Wear clothes that look professional—slightly more formal than what you would wear on the job—but comfortable enough to keep you from being distracted and self-conscious, so you are free to devote your full attention to the interview. A case in point: a too-short skirt may look fine when you are standing, but it may be a source of embarrassment and concern when you sit down. The way you dress should show that you understand the corporate culture, so if you are interviewing for an office job, for example, wear a business suit. Also, don't forget that good grooming and personal hygiene are essential.

4. **Anticipate what questions you might be asked.** Plan a response strategy and take time to consider what your responses might be. Typical questions include (1) *What skills will you bring to the company that will help us meet our goals?* (2) *Describe your skills.* (3) *Why should we hire you when other applicants might have better credentials or more experience?* (4) *What attracted you to this position at our company?* (5) *Can you give me examples of where you have demonstrated the competencies you think will be key to performing well in this job?*

5. **Be prepared to talk about your experiences and how you handled problems.** Recall work experiences where you applied skills similar to those required for the job you are interviewing for. Keep significant work achievements and proven successes in mind. You can prepare a script that covers information you may want to convey, but do not memorize the script if you want to sound spontaneous.

6. **Prepare several good questions to ask the interviewer.** Use the information you have amassed to prepare insightful questions that will help you understand more about the company. If your Internet search left a question unanswered, plan to ask it at the interview. Job candidates are judged in part on the questions they ask. Preparing relevant questions can make you appear to be wise, interested, and informed.

7. **Practice.** Rehearse what you can. Find out if your campus has interview video-recording facilities where you can watch and assess your practice interview performance. Even recording a mock interview can guide you to a better interview

strategy. Nervousness is natural—fight it by reminding yourself of your enthusiasm for your work and having faith in your own self-worth. The more interviews you experience, the easier interviewing for a job becomes and the less nervous you will be.

AT THE INTERVIEW

1. **Arrive on time or a little early.** Consult digital maps on company sites or sites such as MapQuest or Google Maps to find out where you are going for the interview. Being late creates a bad impression and inconveniences the people who have the power to hire you.

2. **Go alone.** Although you may think you need moral support, leave family and friends at home. Unless you require physical assistance, you might become distracted or seem less confident if you bring someone else along.

3. **Bring an extra copy of your resumé and a reference list.** The interviewer will have your resumé on hand at the meeting, but bring a copy for your own reference, plus examples of your work (not school papers) as part of a portfolio. Avoid rattling or rumpling the documents. Be prepared to produce a writing sample during the interview as on-the-spot proof of your communication skills.

4. **Mind your manners.** Be congenial and courteous to everyone you meet before, during, and after the interview. From the time you enter the building until the time you leave, your conduct may be under scrutiny, so focus on being the best you can be.

5. **Make a poised and confident first impression.** Greet interviewers with a firm, but not crushing, handshake. Extend your hand, make eye contact, and introduce yourself: *I'm pleased to meet you, Ms. Radko. I'm [your name].* Smile in a genuine, unforced way. Be seated when a chair is offered to you, and if you make small talk before you begin, make sure it makes sense and stays away from controversial subjects.

6. **Listen carefully to the interviewer's questions—and don't interrupt.** You are not just telling the interviewer about yourself, you are taking part in a two-way dialogue—a job-specific conversation that requires you to use active listening skills. Let the interviewer finish asking a question before you begin.

7. **Use correct English.** Answer by expressing your thoughts as clearly as you can, using a pleasant tone and correct diction and grammar—and no slang or mumbling. Maintain good, but not unnerving, eye contact and speak in a well-modulated voice, with as few *uhm*s, *ahem*s, *yup*s, and *ah*s as possible. Try to project some life into your voice and avoid simple yes/no or one-word answers that might suggest you have little to say or have clammed up from nerves. The way you speak is evidence of your ability to communicate, deal with people, and build rapport.

8. **Concentrate.** It is a good idea to remember the interviewer's name and be attentive rather than appearing as though you are bored by the proceedings. Your body language should show interest.

9. **Avoid being negative.** Remember that you are trying to show you are bright, energetic, and capable. It is best to avoid negative comments about yourself and others, especially former employers, supervisors, and colleagues. Interviewers might assume from such remarks that you are a difficult employee with poor interpersonal skills. Keep your responses positive and informative and your mindset relaxed and focused.

10. **Make intelligent use of your research on the company.** Without showing off about the homework you have done, demonstrate you understand the business and its challenges by slipping relevant tidbits into the conversation. Make sure your comments fit the context. Show that you are knowledgeable and interested in the company.

11. **Don't obsess over salary or benefits.** An interview is not the place for excessive and unequivocal demands. Ask for information you require on these topics, but put your emphasis on what you can do for the company, not what you expect it to do for you.

12. **Don't expect an immediate response.** Avoid ending the interview by asking if you got the job. Most companies want to interview all candidates and review their resumés before making a final decision. You can ask the interviewer when you might expect a decision. Be sure to show courtesy by thanking the interviewer.

AFTER THE INTERVIEW

1. **Follow up with a letter.** Within 24 hours of the interview, write a brief, personalized letter thanking the interviewer (follow-up letters are discussed in the next section).

2. **Consider your options carefully.** Don't rush into accepting a job if you feel it is a bad fit for you and the employer. Express appreciation for the offer, then ask for a day or two to decide: *I'd like a little time to consider your offer. May I call you back tomorrow?* If you must decline the offer (because it does not offer the salary, benefits, and advancement opportunities you want), turn it down tactfully.

⬤⬤ Follow-Up Employment Messages

Follow-Up Letter

follow-up letter an informative letter that summarizes the key points of a job interview.

A follow-up letter can be sent if, within a reasonable time, you have not received a response to your resumé or have not heard from an employer following an interview. It lets the employer know you are still interested in the position and serious about working for the company. You can also use it to jog the employer's memory and give a quick recap of your selling points—but do not rehash your entire resumé. Briefly indicate the date you interviewed or first contacted the company and emphasize why you are interested in the position/company. Inquire if additional information is required or provide an update with new information.

Thank-You Letter

A thank-you letter shows good manners and is typically sent within 24 hours of an interview. It expresses appreciation to the interviewer for his time and the courtesy that was extended to you. By restating your interest in the position and your honest enthusiasm for the company, a thank-you letter can help you stand out from other applicants, especially those who may not bother to write. Begin by referring to the interview date and the exact position you interviewed for. You can personalize your message by mentioning anything that led you to believe you would fit the position well—a job-related topic that was of particular interest to you and the interviewer during your conversation or a skill or qualification that the interviewer was especially interested in. It is usually most appropriate to send a thank-you message via e-mail; you could also choose to send a printed letter via standard mail if you think your prospective employer would appreciate the formality. Also remember to send thank-you messages to anyone who has provided a reference for you.

Job-Offer Acknowledgement

An acknowledgement should be sent immediately on receipt of an offer, especially if you require time to make your decision. Briefly state the title of the job and salary, express your thanks for the offer, and reiterate your interest in the company. Indicate the date by which you will make your decision.

Job-Acceptance Letter

It is a good idea to put your acceptance in writing. Restate the title of the position, salary, and starting date, and clarify details or special conditions. If the employer has sent you forms to complete, indicate that they are enclosed. End by expressing appreciation and confirming your acceptance of the offer.

Job-Refusal Letter

Politely decline the position, thanking the employer for the offer and the organization's interest in you. Being courteous keeps goodwill intact and ensures that future job opportunities—for you and fellow graduates of your college—will not be adversely affected.

Reference-Request Letter

Always choose your referees with care from among people who have had sufficient opportunity to evaluate your academic, professional, or volunteer work. Seek out individuals who think well of you and can speak knowledgeably about your skills and capabilities. If you sense someone's hesitation to act as your reference, move on and ask another person who is more willing. Be sure to ask for permission before you list anyone as a reference. In your request, be sure to do the following:

- mention the job for which you are applying, its requirements, and the deadline for applications;
- update the reader on significant recent accomplishments;
- review good experiences the referee might remember you by; and
- include a copy of your resumé.

◑ Checklists for Resumés and Cover Letters

Resumé Checklist

☐ **Name and Address:** Does your resumé supply adequate contact information, including a daytime telephone number and a campus and/or permanent address?

☐ **Objective:** Does your resumé include an employment objective? Does the objective match the position you are applying for?

☐ **Education:** Are details of your education arranged in parallel form?

☐ **Experience:** Does your work experience start with your present or most recent employment? Do you use action verbs, specific details, and parallel form to describe your duties, activities, and achievements? Does your resumé show how you contributed to the workplace during previous employment? Is information about your work experience arranged strategically to show you are a reliable employee with a steady work history?

☐ **Skills and Activities:** Does the resumé include a section that describes your skills? Does it emphasize your mastery of software and computer applications?

☐ **Overall Content:** Do its skill headings and statements help to present you as well qualified? Is the content shaped to target a specific job?

☐ **Format:** Does your document look well balanced and tidy? Is the spacing attractive? Is the tabulated indentation consistent? Is the format consistent throughout? Does the resumé invite someone to read it? Does it fit on one or two pages?

☐ **Accuracy:** Is your resumé free of typographical errors, faulty punctuation, misspelled words, and incorrect capitalization? Has it been proofread by someone who gave you constructive feedback? Will it be submitted to the employer according to instructions posted in the advertisement or on the job site?

☐ **Persuasiveness:** Is your product persuasive? Does it market your skills and qualifications to human resources personnel? Does it accentuate positives and de-emphasize or eliminate negatives? Does it convince a prospective employer that you can make a strong contribution?

☐ **Edge-Factor:** Will your resumé stand out against the competition? Do its design and content give it an advantage?

Application Letter Checklist

1. Opening

- ☐ Does the letter gain attention and clearly identify the position for which you are applying?
- ☐ Is it free of clichéd, overworked expressions?
- ☐ Does it give a brief summary describing how your qualifications fit the job requirements?

2. Body

- ☐ Does the letter build interest by showing how your experience and preparation fill the requirements of the job?
- ☐ Does it emphasize reader benefits and give a brief summation of your selling points?
- ☐ Does it provide examples of your accomplishments and quantify them?
- ☐ Do action verbs accurately describe your skills?
- ☐ Does it refer the reader to your resumé?
- ☐ Does it vary sentence structure to reduce the dominance of *I*?

3. Closing

- ☐ Does it ask for an interview? Does it supply contact information that will make it easy for the employer to reach you?
- ☐ Does it briefly recap your main qualifications and link them to contributions you could make to the company?
- ☐ Does it include a forward-looking remark or mention how you will follow up?
- ☐ Does it end courteously?

4. Overall

- ☐ Is the letter brief enough to retain the reader's attention (not less than two paragraphs and not more than one substantial page)?
- ☐ Is it free of typographical errors as well as errors in grammar, spelling, and punctuation?
- ☐ Is it addressed correctly to the appropriate person or department?
- ☐ Is its layout neat and balanced?
- ☐ Is its tone pleasant, positive, and professional?
- ☐ Does the typography match that of the resumé in order to unify the application package?

Online Job Banks and Career Resources

CanadianCareers.com This site covers all facets of careers and employment. Check the "Internships" page for internship opportunities recommended for Canadians under 30.

Working.com This site features job leads from across Canada. Search for jobs by location or category, or use the advanced search to find the most recently posted positions.

eluta.ca This job search engine lists new job announcements posted on employers' websites across Canada.

Jobsect.ca This free human resources and skills development site is an interface offering assistance on job-seeking and career development. Job listings are also featured.

Monster.ca This site offers a full range of interactive career tools in addition to more than three thousand job listings. It offers advice on topics such as resumés and cover letters, job-hunt strategies, salaries and benefits, and career development.

National Job Bank (http://jb-ge.hrdc-drhc.gc.ca) This Service Canada site allows you to search by occupation or to search all jobs posted in the last 48 hours. You can create your resumé using their resumé-builder tool. The service is free.

The Riley Guide Job Listings—International Job Opportunities (www.rileyguide.com/internat.html) This site offers numerous links to international job-listing sites, including many for Canada. Included in its resources is information on resumés and cover letters, salary guides, and how to prepare a search and execute a campaign.

WorkinfoNET.ca As Canada's work information network, this site offers access to information on job vacancies, job searches, the labour market, and career information and profiles. Click on the link "Other WorkinfoNETS" to search job opportunities in your province.

workopolis.com Canada's biggest job site, this site allows you to search jobs by keyword, location, date, and job category. Its career resources centre features articles and advice. Registration is not required to search the jobs, but you can register for free to save searches and set up a career-alert e-mail service.

WorkopolisCampus.com This is Canada's biggest site for students and recent graduates. Registration is not required to view all of the job postings, but to take full advantage of the site's resources and to post your resume online, you will need to obtain an access code from your school in order to register on the site.

WORKSHOPS AND DISCUSSION FORUMS

1. **Research Employment Prospects.** Using library resources, the Internet, or your local white pages, compile a list of five companies that might present promising prospects for employment. Record basic contact information and instructions on how to apply. Take note of information (about corporate culture, size of the company, etc.) that might be used in a prospecting letter or help you compile a list of questions to ask at an informational interview.

2. **Prepare a Professional Data Record.** Evaluate your qualifications by compiling personal data relating to your education, work experience, skills, activities, awards, and references. Use action-oriented words to describe your skills and accomplishments.

3. **Revise Your Application Letter.** Working in groups of three or four, analyze the following application letters. How could their tone, professionalism, and overall expression be improved?

   a) What opinion do you form from reading the following extract from this applicant's letter? Collaborate on a revision that is less *I*-centred.

> I respectfully submit my strong application for the position of regional sales manager. I have attached my resumé. I have a great deal of experience in the fashion retail industry. I believe this position is tailor-made to my considerable skills and talents. I am more than ready to meet the challenges of this position. I believe I have earned the opportunity to work for a prestigious and well-respected employer such as Bryant McKay.
>
> I hold a degree in Business Administration from the University of Western Ontario, where I was an outstanding student. I completed all of my marketing courses with top honours. I am now a great salesperson. My communication skills are much better than those of my peers. I take pride in my ability to work well with others in a managerial capacity. Although I do not have any public-relations experience, I am a quick learner and should be able to master core public-relations skills in no time. My only regret in my short career is that my previous employers did not value the tremendous contributions I made to their organizations.
>
> It would be a shame if you were to miss out on the opportunity to hire me. I look forward to interviewing with you and to the possibility of earning $100,000 a year with your company.

b) What impression does the following letter make? How could it be improved? List and correct its faults and errors.

> Please be advised that this is an application for the job that was advertised recently. Although I have just part-time experience, I feel I could be the independent sales representative your looking for.
>
> I will graduate soon. I am sure you will recanize that my education qualifies me for this job. My communication skills are real good and people say I get along with them real well.
>
> Please telephone me and let me know when I should come in for an interview. Will I need to fill out an application?

4. **Revise Your Resumé.** The resumé on page 283 contains numerous faults. Analyze its strengths and weaknesses and suggest how it could be improved. Working in groups of three or four, collaborate on a revision that will help Nadia Salerno obtain an interview based on the qualifications she lists.

5. **Create a Standard Chronological Resumé.** Using the data you developed in activity number 2, create a standard chronological resumé.

6. **Create a Scannable Resumé.** Take your current resumé and use its information to prepare a scannable resumé.

7. **Create an E-mail Resumé.** Refer to "Preparing an E-mail Resumé" (page 264) and follow the instructions that cover preparing your resumé for transmission by e-mail or an online posting. Send messages containing your resumé to yourself and your instructor.

8. **Write Cover Letters.** Using details from your resumé, write solicited (ad-response) and unsolicited (prospecting) letters of application.
   a) From the classified section of a daily newspaper or an Internet job site, select an advertisement for a job related to your current training and studies. Write an application letter based on your qualifications to date.

   b) From the list of companies you have prospected (see activity number 1 above), select the one you are most interested in and write a prospecting letter.

9. **Practise Interview Role-Playing.** Working in pairs in groups of four, simulate the interview process. One person should play the role of the interviewer and another should take the role of the applicant while the other two members of the group evaluate the applicant's performance. Repeat the process until everyone has had a chance to be the applicant. Afterward, discuss the strengths and weaknesses of each applicant's interviewing skills.

10. **Compose a Thank-You Letter.** After completing the interview role-playing workshop (activity number 9), write a letter of appreciation to the interviewer. Exchange letters and discuss what makes a thank-you letter most effective.

11. **Identify Keywords.** From a newspaper careers page or online job bank, select an advertisement for a job you are or will soon be qualified for. Photocopy the ad or print it out. Make a list of its keywords and place an asterisk (★) beside the skills you possess. Are you currently missing skills that would make you more employable?

NADIA SALERNO

54 Big Nickle Lane   247 Dunlop Street
Sudbury, ON   Toronto, ON
P5K 1H7   M9A 2M1

(706) 555-9841   (416) 555-554

E-mail: soccergirl@hotmail.com

CAREER OBJECTIVE   Work in child daycare facility.

EXPERIENCE   **ECD Assistant**, Childcare Connection, Toronto, Ontario
May 2007 to present
- Play music for children.
- Write daily evaluations.
- Take care of children.

ECD Assistant (part-time), Play Well Daycare, Toronto

ECD Assistant (internship), Kids First Nursery, Toronto
September 2005 to May 2006

HONOURS AND   I enjoy playing soccer.
ACTIVITIES

EDUCATION

Humber College, Toronto, Ontario
Montessori Certificate

Seneca College, Toronto, Ontario
Diploma in Early Childhood Education, June 2006

Royal Conservatory of Music, Toronto, Ontario
ARTC (Piano), 2005

WRITING IMPROVEMENT EXERCISES

1. **Action Verbs for Resumés:** Rewrite the following descriptions of significant work duties and accomplishments in appropriate resumé style. Eliminate personal pronouns, begin points with strong and specific action verbs, make points concise, apply parallel structure, and quantify accomplishments where possible.

   a) Administrative Assistant Position:

   > I was responsible for the reorganization of procedures and implementation of cost-containment policies. I also monitored the production of all printed materials and ordered supplies and maintained on- and off-site inventories. I also did many mass mailings.

   b) Sales Manager/Production Assistant Position:

   > I did a study of automobile accessory needs of fifty car dealerships in the Greater Toronto Area. I was responsible for marketing and sales for a manufacturer of automobile accessories. I also developed new accounts and maintained existing customers. I headed a sales team that generated orders for sales of $3 million annually. In this capacity, I monitored and trained a sales staff of seven to augment a high standard of service and increase profitability. I also travel to off-road functions to promote products.

2. **Descriptive, Action-Oriented Language for Resumés:** Improve the following job descriptions by using more precise, action-oriented language.

   a) Gave advice to sales staff on meeting monthly sales quotas.

   b) Did all bookkeeping functions, including internal audits, once a month.

   c) Talked with regular clients all the time to do technical support.

   d) Did a study of cost–benefit to bring about the updating of PCs to make network integration for two hundred users a lot better.

   e) Got together a team to train staff in new safety procedures.

3. **Objective Statements:** From a job site or the careers pages of a newspaper, select three advertisements for jobs that closely match your qualifications. For each one, write a one- to three-line objective statement targeted to the position.

4. **Writing a Letter of Application:** Using information from Mitra Das' resumé (Figure 9.2, "Chronological Resumé," on page 259), write a cover letter that answers the advertisement on page 285.

Redferns Limited

Area Sales Manager

Toronto, Ontario, Canada

Style. Sophistication. Elegance. It is what you expect from Redferns, one of Canada's leading fashion and lifestyle retailers.

This position will assist the Store Manager by providing team direction to ensure the execution and achievement of corporate initiatives, projected sales goals, and exceptional customer-service levels.

Responsibilities:

- Demonstrate visible leadership.

- Achieve targeted department sales goals through selling the Redferns way.

- Provide supervision, coaching/training, and mentoring to team members and participate in performance assessment of sales staff.

- Develop and maintain a high level of product knowledge pertaining to merchandise.

- Ensure ongoing department clientele development.

- Maintain high standards of accountability for department operation, budgets, and shortage control.

- Control and monitor proper stock-to-sales ratio.

- Follow all health-and-safety guidelines.

Required skills:

- Supervisory/management experience

- Strong demonstration of leadership skills

- Excellent organizational and follow-up skills

- Positive attitude

A career with Redferns is one of the most exciting opportunities in Canadian retail and includes a comprehensive benefits package.

Interested candidates are invited to submit their resumés to careers@ redferns.com.

ONLINE ACTIVITIES

1. **Online Career Tests:** For various online career tests, check out Job Star Central. Its "What Do I Want?" section features five tests, including the "Keirsey Temperament Sorter" and a personality-style test based on *The Platinum Rule* by Tony Alessandra.
http://jobstar.org/tools/career/career.php

2. **Government of Canada Online Training and Career Quizzes:** Log on to this site and complete up to six quizzes that will help you discover your work preferences, values, and learning style. You can save your quiz results by registering.
www.jobsetc.ca/toolbox/quizzes/quizzes_home.do

3. **Persuasive Communications.** Read the information about using "you attitudes" in your writing, then scroll down and complete the exercise at the bottom of the page.
http://web.archive.org/web/20100731062800/ http://www.washburn.edu/services/ zzcwwctr/you-attitude.txt

4. **Rate Your Resumé:** Try this quiz and find out if your resumé measures up by evaluating all its facets on a scale of 1 to 5.
www.provenresumes.com/quiz.html

5. **Research Companies Online:** What can you find out about a company through its website? Log on the following sites for Canadian companies and prepare a brief fact sheet on each. What distinguishes the companies in terms of size, corporate culture, products, etc.?

Research in Motion	**www.rim.net**
Schneider Foods	**www.schneiders.ca**
Bombardier	**www.bombardier.com**
Sobeys	**www.sobeys.com**

6. **eResumé Tutorial:** Visit the following site, where you can view a sample resumé, which will open in a separate window, as you work through this tutorial. Gain practice in listing job titles and responsibilities, choosing an appropriate resumé format, and creating a keyword summary.
http://eresumes.com/eresumes_practice.html

7. **Government of Canada Training and Careers Online Resumé Builder:** Click on "Resume Builder" and create a user account to be able to create resumés for your personal use or to apply online for federal government jobs.
www.jobbank.gc.ca

10

Informal Reports

In this chapter you will learn to

1. Identify the characteristics of an effective business report.

2. Differentiate between informal and formal reports and between informational and analytical reports.

3. Identify standard report formats.

4. Apply direct and indirect writing plans.

5. Identify steps in the report-writing process.

6. Describe types of reports according to their purpose.

7. Organize reports according to their purposes and apply informative headings.

8. Develop graphics that are meaningful and interesting.

Introduction to Report Writing

business report a document in which factual information is compiled and organized for a specific purpose and audience.

A **business report** is an essential form of corporate communication that helps other people—managers and co-workers—stay informed, review opinions, plan for the future, and make decisions. Over the years, the reports a company generates form an extended corporate log or journal, tracking trends, changing circumstances, and the status quo. They are permanent records of operations at every level of an organization, providing accounts of incidents, events, actions taken, decisions made, results achieved, and standards and policies met with, as well as interactions with employees, outside stakeholders, and the public.

Written with clear objectives in mind and designed for specific audiences, reports are based on reliable facts and evidence, always separating verifiable fact from opinion and substantiating any opinion that is expressed. Because they are legal documents that can be used as evidence in court, they must be accurate, complete, and objective, weighing both sides of an issue and demonstrating careful attention to detail. They play a major role in the day-to-day functioning of an organization and, as a result, must be clear, easy to read, and concise.

The larger an organization is, the more essential reports are to its successful operation and management. Reports help departments to coordinate initiatives and activities and help managers stay in touch with and on top of changing circumstances. They let management see the big picture so they can respond quickly and decisively to minor personnel, business, and technical difficulties before they become major problems. Managers generally have enough to do without having to sift through mountains of detail. They require reports that are selective in the information they present and structured to give impact to the most essential features.

Factors in Successful Reports

The quality of a report and its effectiveness depend on three things that you, as a writer, need to control: *content*, *clarity*, and *skimmability*.

CONTENT

- Write with your aims, objectives, and main message in mind.
- Weigh information according to what is going to be done with the report and what its future use will be.
- Include information the reader needs for action-taking and decision-making by extracting pertinent facts from reams of raw data and analyzing/interpreting those facts so that they make sense to readers and relate clearly to the problem you are solving, the question you are answering, and the conclusions that you draw. Never manipulate your facts and findings to arrive at a predetermined conclusion.
- Take readers' needs into account when selecting information and consider the background information readers may or may not already have.
- Help readers understand report information by organizing it in a logical way (chronologically, by level of importance, by the classifications into which a topic divides).

CLARITY

- Apply principles of good English—write in simple, straightforward, tightly constructed sentences with correct grammar, punctuation, and spelling.
- Guide the reader through your discussion—use overviews to forecast what you will discuss, use transitions to show how your discussion is continuing or changing, add headings of various levels to help readers find information, and use topic sentences to announce what each paragraph is about.
- Use text citations selectively; give formal credit to the sources you use or quote.
- Include visual elements that are explanatory, show the significance of your facts, match your objectives, and help the reader make an informed decision; introduce and label each visual you use.
- Ensure facts are introduced in the right place by editing your draft and deleting extraneous material.
- Use consistent evaluation criteria when you weigh options and draw conclusions.

SKIMMABILITY

- Select a readable font to reduce eye strain and lessen reading time.
- Use informative headings and lists to group similar data together, signpost significant facts, emphasize the main ideas, and show where your analysis is leading.
- Use white or neutral space effectively.

Reports should be reader-centred and user-friendly. For this reason, although reports usually follow standard structures or formats, it is really the content and your readers' needs that shape the structure of an informal report. Your ability to write good reports, by analyzing the writing situation and applying basic techniques, can win you favourable notice and increase your chances of promotion. This chapter deals with ways to give impact and professional polish to your informal reports.

Informal vs. Formal Reports

Depending on their complexity and depth, reports are termed either informal or formal. An **informal report** is usually under ten pages, and often under one or two. Its style is relatively informal, making it acceptable to use a personal tone and the occasional personal pronoun or contraction. Typically, it is written as a letter or memo divided into subsections that are marked off by headings and subheadings when they are required. The informal report is the most routine of all reports—and the type you will have to write most often.

Formal reports, by contrast, tackle more complex and difficult problems and typically require five or six pages to do so, sometimes as many as two hundred or more. Because formal reports must reflect the significance of their subject matter and the professionalism of the organizations they represent, their style is more formal and traditional, meaning that personal pronouns and contractions are not acceptable. Formal reports are typically organized into six basic parts and have to conform to standards of convention and layout so that extensive and detailed information—often coming from meticulous research—can be managed effectively. They may have some extra

informal report a report using a letter or memo format, usually ranging from a few paragraphs to ten pages in length.

formal report a business document of ten or more pages based on extensive research and following a prescribed format or pattern that includes elements such as a title page, transmittal or cover letter, table of contents, and abstract.

TABLE 10.1   Informal vs. Formal Reports: Quick Reference Chart

	Informal	Formal
Distribution	usually internal	external or for superiors internally
Style and Tone	some contractions personal tone and language	no contractions impersonal tone and language
Length	usually short	usually long
Structure	less structured several sections	more highly structured multiple sections and subsections
Transmittal	optional	memo (internal) or letter (external)
Title	in subject line	on separate title page
Table of Contents	none	on separate page for any report over five pages
Summary	within report (no heading)	on separate page
Introduction	first section (no heading)	on separate page with heading
Visual Aids	used infrequently	used extensively

supporting features—a separate title page, for instance, or a cover letter that briefly explains the purpose and contents of the report. Effective visual presentation—in the form of well-designed and well-integrated computer-generated graphics, tables, and illustrations—also plays a vital role in the way formal reports communicate information to readers by lending credibility and interest.

Distinguishing Features of Short Reports

Reports can be quite diverse in their content. They can vary in length, approach, and scope. They also differ according to their purpose, audience, and format (how they look and in what form their information is delivered). Here are a few ways of thinking of reports that will help to identify and differentiate them.

PURPOSE

A report may have one of several purposes or functions. It can pass on

- information (collecting data for the reader),
- information and analysis (interpreting data but not offering recommendations), or
- information, analysis, and recommendations (proposing a course of action, a solution to a problem, a new procedure, a new policy, or changing responsibilities).

Although there are as many kinds of reports as there are reasons for writing them, the purposes listed above define general kinds of informal reporting: informational reports and analytical/recommendation reports.

- **Informational reports** answer questions and provide information without analysis. Writers of informational reports gather and organize data relating to routine activities, providing readers with what they need most—the facts supported by relevant background details. Informational reports may look into options, outline performance, or investigate equipment, but they never go so far as to offer recommendations. Readers of this type of report are in a neutral or receptive frame of mind: they want to know certain facts without being persuaded of anything.

- **Analytical and recommendation reports** go a step further by interpreting data and offering recommendations that may aid in problem-solving and decision-making. Because persuasion may be required in convincing readers that the proposed recommendation or conclusion is appropriate, greater thought has to be given to how readers might respond and to how the pros and cons of each alternative should be weighed, presented, and discussed. Writers of analytical reports also need to present evidence in support of findings and establish criteria for any alternatives that are evaluated.

A full explanation of informational and analytical reports, with examples, is provided later in the chapter.

FREQUENCY OF SUBMISSION

Reports also differ in terms of how often they are submitted.

- **Periodic reports** are filed at regular intervals according to a schedule (weekly, biweekly, monthly, quarterly, semi-annually, or annually) and keep readers up to date on activities or operations, for instance the ongoing work on a project, the weekly activity of sales reps, or the status of monthly sales. The information supplied is fairly routine and may simply be filed as a matter of record.

- **One-time reports** deal with specific issues and take stock of special projects and non-recurrent situations. Often in the form of analytical or recommendation reports, they are designed to aid management decisions.

COMMON CATEGORIES

Later in the chapter, you will be introduced to common kinds of informal business reports, each designed to record the details of a particular situation, activity, or occurrence. In some cases, their characteristics may overlap just as their purposes do. Here are the best-known types or categories of informational and analytical business reports: periodic reports, situation reports (including trip reports and progress and activity reports), incident reports, investigative reports, compliance reports, recommendation reports, justification reports, feasibility reports, and summaries.

FORMATS AND DISTRIBUTION

Reported information can be prepared and distributed in several ways. The following options range from least to most formal:

- **Memorandum report:** This is an appropriate format for circulating data within an organization. Memorandum reports generally have no more than ten

---

informational report
a short report that collects data related to a routine activity without offering analysis or recommending action; it is organized in three parts: introduction, findings, and summary/conclusion.

analytical report
(or **recommendation report**) a report that interprets and analyzes information and offers recommendations based on findings.

periodic report an informational report that is filed at regular intervals.

one-time report a report that presents the results of a special or long-term project.

memorandum report
a short, internal report presented in memo format.

pages, use an informal, conversational style, and are typed like typical memos, with

- 1- to 1¼-inch (2.54- to 3.18-centimetre) side margins,
- the standard guidewords TO, FROM, DATE, and SUBJECT (usually the report's primary recommendation), and
- single-spaced paragraphs separated by two blank lines.

Descriptive headings can be added to arrange facts and mark each new section.

- **Prepared-form report:** Time-saving preprinted forms with standardized headings are useful for recording repetitive data or for describing routine activities within an organization.
- **Letter report:** Letter format is often used for short, informal reports prepared by one organization and sent to another. A letter report, prepared on company stationery, contains all the elements usually found in a letter (date, inside address, return address, salutation, complimentary close). Descriptive headings can be used.
- **Formal report:** Formal reports are usually prepared in manuscript format and printed on plain paper. They have headings and subheadings.

letter report a short, external report presented in letter format.

Direct and Indirect Approaches

As you learned in Chapters 6, 7, and 8, the choice of a direct or indirect writing plan depends on the content of your letter or memo and the expectations your reader may have about it. The same general approaches apply to the organization of reports. It is all a question of what should come first based on your need to persuade or simply inform your reader.

DIRECT APPROACH: INFORMATIONAL AND ANALYTICAL REPORTS

Routine, non-sensitive information related to recurring activities and one-time situations is delivered most effectively when it is presented directly. Organizing an informational report comes with the expectation that readers will support or be interested in what you have to say and won't have to be persuaded. Managers generally like this get-to-the-point approach. Because of its convenience, the direct approach is standard for most informational reports, where sections are found in the following order:

- Purpose/Introduction/Background
- Facts and Findings
- Summary

Writers of analytical reports do more than answer questions; they also present solutions to problems in the form of specific recommendations. You can use the direct approach when you expect that the reader will agree with your recommendations without any persuasion. A direct-approach analytical report, which includes conclusions and recommendations, presents its information in the following order:

- Introduction/Problem/Background
- Conclusions or Recommendations

- Facts and Findings
- Discussion and Analysis

INDIRECT APPROACH: ANALYTICAL REPORTS

In other cases, when you expect some resistance or displeasure on the part of the reader, an indirect approach works best. The more you need to persuade or educate your reader, the more you should consider using an indirect approach that builds gradual acceptance for the actions you endorse. The information is usually presented in the following order:

- Purpose/Introduction/Problem
- Facts and Findings
- Discussion and Analysis
- Conclusions or Recommendations

By mirroring the logical processes of problem-solving, this pattern works well when readers aren't familiar with the topic or problem.

Writing Style for Short Reports

Finding an appropriate style for a short report involves studying your audience and understanding their preferences and those of your organization. Short informal reports use more personal language than long reports and may include personal pronouns such as *I* and *we* and even contractions, but they still must project an air of objectivity and professionalism so that readers will accept their findings and conclusions.

When you know the reader fairly well, your tone can be somewhat relaxed. When the reader is a stranger or a top manager, it is better to err on the side of caution and use a more impersonal style, one that is neutral but not overly stuffy. You may not know what will happen to your report after it leaves your hands; therefore it is always best to avoid any kind of language that may offend, especially words that exaggerate or show bias.

Take care to write objectively and accurately, separating fact from opinion and backing up any opinion you do express with an explanation or sound evidence. Keep in mind that readers have to be able to decode the text when reading quickly. Your meaning must be clear. As you compose your report, it is worth the time it will take you to scrutinize for words and phrases that are ambiguous. What the word *you* means, for example, might be obvious to you but not to the reader, who may not be able to tell if the word refers to her specifically or to a larger organizational unit. If in doubt, spell it out in specifics and use the company name instead.

Headings

The longer a report and the more detailed its information, the more readers rely on **headings** to scan, skim, and navigate the document. Like signposts, headings guide readers through the text. On their own, headings provide an outline or overview, a way of showing that the structure you have chosen for your report is clear and cohesive. Headings break up text into meaningful and manageable segments, making information easier to find and creating breathing spaces where readers can pause to collect their thoughts and absorb what they have read. Different heading levels (distinguished by

heading title or subtitle, usually a word or short phrase, within the body of a document that identifies its parts and gives clues to its organization.

size, colour, weight, underlining, and italics) can show which parts of the report belong together and the relative importance of each part. Short reports usually feature headings of the appropriate level before every section and subsection. Each heading (consisting of a single word, a phrase, or a complete sentence) must describe all the material that appears beneath it. Here are seven tips for using headings effectively:

functional heading
each of a series of generic headings that, when taken together, show a report in outline.

descriptive head (or **talking head**) a heading that describes the actual content of a report and provides more information about it.

1. **Use either functional or descriptive headings. Functional headings** are basic, generic headings (*Introduction*, *Findings*, *Summary*) that can be used in almost any report but are found most commonly in routine reports. Because they are general, they also provide useful lead-offs to sensitive information to which the reader might react negatively. **Descriptive** or **talking heads** are high-information headings that reflect the actual content of a report, summarizing its key points, telling the reader what to expect, and making the report easy to skim (*Voice Mail Not an Appropriate Medium for Confidential Information*). Functional and descriptive headings can often be combined (*Recommendations: New Policy on Secure Messaging and Rights Management*).

2. **Keep headings short and clear.** Limit headings to eight words. Headings of more than a line are too long to be intelligible at a glance. Clarity is everything in a report. Keep in mind that a too-vague heading defeats the purpose of having a heading in the first place.

3. **Use parallel construction**. For the sake of consistency and readability, use balanced phrases and grammatical structures. Under a single main heading, subheads must be parallel to each other but not necessarily parallel to subheads listed under other main headings.

Not parallel:	Improved Transmission of Sensitive Information
	How can we end e-mail errors?
	Voice-mail problems
	Why we should change fax procedures
Parallel:	Improved Transmission of Sensitive Information
	Ending e-mail errors
	Eliminating voice-mail problems
	Changing fax procedures

4. **Ensure headings are clearly ranked.** Capitalize and underline headings consistently depending on what they introduce. Once you have chosen a style for each heading level, stick with it all the way through the report. Show the rank and relative importance of headings by formatting each level systematically. Here are a few suggestions on how to format three different levels of headings:

FIRST LEVEL

First-level headings can be typed in bold with all caps, centred. Text follows on a new line.

Second Level

Second-level headings can be typed in bold and run flush with the left margin. Only the first letter of each word is capitalized (this is also known as title case). Text follows on a new line.

Third level. Third-level headings can be typed in bold and run flush with the left margin. Only the first letter of the first word is capitalized. The heading is followed by a period and text follows on the same line.

5. **Put headings where they belong.** Don't use a subheading unless you plan to divide the material that follows into at least two subsections. Unless a heading or subheading will be followed by at least two lines of text at the bottom of a page, type it at the top of the next page.

6. **Don't enclose headings in quotation marks.** Quotation marks are unnecessary in headings. Bold type and capitalization are enough to distinguish a head from surrounding text.

7. **Don't use a heading as the antecedent for a pronoun.** The line of text after the heading or subheading should not begin with *this*, *that*, *these*, or *those* because the reader may not know what you are referring to; instead repeat the noun from the heading and add it to the pronoun *(This e-mail error . . .)*.

⬤⬤ Steps in the Writing Process

Reports, even short informal ones, can involve hours of work. Not only must data be generated, it must also be analyzed, evaluated, and compiled in a way that is meaningful to readers and adequately reinforces the answer to a question or the solutions to a problem. Like any task that involves time, effort, and resources, writing a report takes planning. Even before your planning begins, it may help to think of your report as a process involving several achievable steps: planning, researching/analyzing information, composing, and revising.

PLANNING

Your first job is to look at the situation, define the boundaries of the project, and think about any restrictions you may face in terms of time, finances, and personnel. While routine informational reports do not involve considerations of this kind, formal reports and reports offering recommendations benefit from the time you spend considering your deadline, for example, and what your budget will allow you to do in relation to the scope of the project. Ask yourself if you will require any special services or additional personnel to carry out your work. The more extensive a report is and the more people there are involved in its production, the more necessary it is to create a work plan that includes a timeline. A work plan sets out the scope of the project, outlines how work will be done, identifies the amount and type(s) of research, and divides responsibilities according to each phase of the project. It also schedules completion dates for each stage of research, writing, and production.

RESEARCHING/ANALYZING DATA AND INFORMATION

Before you launch an online search, head for the library, search company records, or check out pertinent databases, take some time to brainstorm your topic to grasp the big picture and the possibilities it presents to you. Once you have thought about the subject—its various aspects, how it can be divided into manageable sections, the larger issues related to it, and the changing trends or circumstances that may affect it—you will have a better idea about where to begin your search and where to find the data you need. Keep in mind that not all data is created equally. From whatever source it comes, the information you collect should be

- current,
- valid, and
- reliable.

Any data you use must meet these criteria, most of all statistics. For any figures you cite you must name their source, how they were derived, and how recent they are. Scrutinize survey results, paying close attention to the size of the sample group. Because any report is only as good as the information that backs it up, it is essential to evaluate data to decide what portion of it is usable in terms of supporting your document's specific purpose. From reams of raw data, it is possible to extract pertinent facts through a process of sorting and logical sequencing. In analytical reports, which go a step further, information gathering goes hand in hand with analysis and tabulation—spotting trends and relationships among the facts and numerical data you have gathered, identifying logical patterns, and being prepared to back them up with illustrations. If you are working from raw numerical data comprising a range of values, statistical terms for several important concepts may be of use to you as you attempt to describe and make sense of what you have assembled:

- **Mean** is the term for the arithmetic average calculated by dividing the total sum by the total number of units (e.g., the mean of 2, 5, 5, 5, and 13 is 6).
- **Median** is the term for the middle value of a series (e.g., the median of 2, 5, 5, 5, and 13 is 5).
- **Mode** is the term for the value that appears most frequently (e.g., the mode of 2, 5, 5, 5, and 13 is 5).
- **Range** describes the span between lowest and highest values.

No matter how compelling your data is, however, it won't have an impact unless it is first stored, tabulated, and managed effectively. Be sure to record information taken from documents carefully by developing good note-taking habits, scanning and photo-copying when you have (keeping copyright issues in mind). Always keep track of where your data comes from and establish a system for storing the information you collect. Individual file cards for each item or secure computer files are good for this purpose. For each source, record the bibliographic details you will need when compiling a list of resources. You need to note

- the title of the work/document/web page/article and the title of the periodical or book from which it was taken,
- the author's name,
- the publisher/web address, and
- the publication date/web access date.

COMPOSING AND REVISING

Once you finish collecting data and drawing conclusions from it, your task is to communicate your findings in a logical and methodical way. It is usually best to prepare your report on a word processor and safeguard against lost files and other mishaps by saving your document often, even printing out a provisional hard copy every now and then. Some writers—wary of writer's block, wanting their words to flow easily—find it helpful to draw up a quick first draft that can be revised and polished later. With less fuss over supplying every last detail, rapid writing is useful for recording ideas and establishing a coherent structure where ideas can flow well. Other writers may prefer a more deliberate approach that involves working from a detailed plan or outline or leaving more challenging sections for last, once the shape and rhythm of the report become clear.

Developing an outline, even a very brief one, can help you gain control over your material and smooth the flow of ideas and information. A working outline, using a numbering system found in most word-processing programs, can be written in point form or complete sentences. The template for your system may use an **alphanumeric outline** (based on a combination of numbers and letters) or a **decimal outline**. Whatever system you use, the number belongs before the heading with the benefit of making the heading easier to reference.

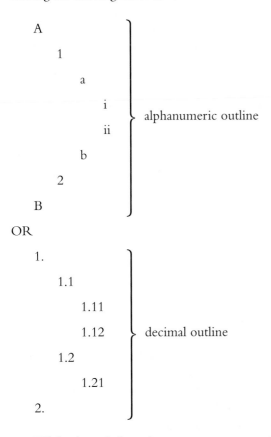

While short, informal reports may not require outlines, lengthy, formal reports do. Aside from an outline, you may also have to decide how to balance the text and visuals, if you happen to use the latter.

Until the final edited version is submitted, it is best to think of your report as a work-in-progress. Committing your facts and ideas to the printed page should not be a one-shot process and may in fact require up to three drafts as you move gradually from a rough idea of what you had in mind to something that resembles the shape of a finished report. From there, revising and editing your document may require cuts, additions,

alphanumeric outline an outlining system that combines numbers and letters to differentiate levels of headings.

decimal outline or **numeric outline** an outlining system that uses a combination of numbers and decimal points to differentiate levels of headings.

reorderings, and rewrites—cuts that can be made more efficiently if you put yourself in the reader's place and ask, *Is all this detail really necessary? Are items logically linked? Could entire sections be removed without harming the report?* Be prepared to make changes to any section containing so much detail that it might be difficult to read and interpret.

If you have been working collaboratively as a member of a team preparing the report, make sure each member of the group has read the report and is satisfied with the text of the final draft before you begin to have it edited. It is possible to solicit editorial suggestions by using a program such as Adobe Acrobat or MSWord, where annotations and changes can be made on screen, attached to the document, and signed.

Ideally, it is best to leave as much time as possible between completing the final draft and starting to edit. A day or two is optimal, but even an hour or so will give you the objectivity you need to read your document with a critical eye. Work from a printout so you have a record of what you wrote before you started to make changes, or use the "track changes" option available in many word processing programs. Once you are satisfied with the final version, leave time to proofread the document more than once, preferably making several passes over the document to read for content, spelling and grammar, tone, clarity, and coherence. Cast your eye over the report to check for formatting errors and problems with consistency.

⬤⬤ Elements of Informal Reports

Short, informal reports tell stories and share information in a logical and systematic way, grouping information in manageable, standardized elements from beginning to end. In general, any informal report has three major parts: an *Introduction* that includes a statement of purpose, a *Findings* section, and a *Closing Summary* or *Conclusion* (with or without recommendations). Because there is no single right way of organizing a report, the headings you use are largely up to you and depend on the type of report you are writing, what you have to say, and whether your report contains recommendations in addition to findings.

INTRODUCTORY STATEMENT

The introductory statement announces the report, indicating what it examines and providing any necessary background information. This section of the report is called the *Introduction* (or it can also be called *Background*). Sometimes it simply states the purpose of the report, often in just a sentence: *This report examines the disposal of documents in our workplace.* In other cases, it may link that purpose with report recommendations: *This report on document disposal suggests ways to protect our intellectual property and client privilege.* Whatever form the purpose statement takes, it should specify the problem or technical question you will deal with and indicate the rhetorical purpose your report is aimed at achieving. An introduction may also preview key points (in the sequence in which they will be presented) or establish the limits of the report. A preview of key points and a description of methods used to collect data can also be included in the introduction or under separate headings immediately following it.

FINDINGS

Also commonly called *Results* or *Facts*, the findings section is the most substantial part of a report. It offers details and relates results to circumstances. In a subsequent but

---

Introduction the first section in the body of a report, which provides readers with the information they need in order to understand and evaluate the report itself; it must include either the report's purpose or a statement of the problem the report addresses.

Findings the most substantial part of a report, in which qualitative and numeric data is presented and organized by time, convention, order of importance, or component.

related section called *Discussion/Analysis*, findings are explained and made meaningful through analysis. Overall these sections reinforce logical connections between relevant facts and any conclusions or recommendations that are ultimately made. Because the data presented in these sections may be extensive, it can be organized under several sub-headings (remember to use parallel form) devised to fit the subject and situation. Use an appropriate method of organization to guide the reader through your discussion: (1) present facts chronologically (when commenting on the progress of a project or the steps in a procedure), alphabetically, or in order of their importance (beginning with the most important item when you want to save the reader time or ending with the most important item when you want the reader to remember it); (2) draw comparisons, considering options one by one or developing point-by-point comparisons; and (3) divide or classify the topic, breaking it down into its component parts or applying consistent criteria in order to evaluate it.

SUMMARY/CONCLUSIONS/RECOMMENDATIONS

Optional in informational reports (where it is called *Summary*), the concluding section is crucial to analytical reports, where it is called *Conclusions and Recommendations*. The conclusions are the part of the report in which readers are often most interested. Though conclusions and recommendations are often found under the same heading and numbered for easy reference, they differ substantially in both purpose and phrasing. Conclusions present objective analysis directly related to the report's problem and findings (e.g., *Among forms of two-factor authentication, biometrics is the best method of ensuring secure online transactions.*), whereas recommendations make specific suggestions for actions that will solve the problem (e.g., *Explore the possibility of using biometric fingerprint readers as the primary means of two-factor authentication.*). These suggestions are typically phrased as commands, beginning with a strong action verb. It is appropriate to offer recommendations only when you have been asked to do so, in which case you may also choose to explain how those recommendations can be implemented. In an analytical report, the *Recommendations* section comes after the *Introduction* (in direct-approach reports) or toward the end (in indirect-approach reports). When chances are good that readers will be receptive to your recommendation, the recommendation itself can be included in the title of the report—*Recommendation to Limit Fax Transmissions of Client Information*—and then repeated in the body of the report itself. In cases where there is more than one recommendation, the recommendations can be listed in order of their importance (from most important to least important).

Designed for simplicity, most informal reports do not include front and back matter such as covers, title pages, tables of contents, or lists of illustrations; however appendices, though rare, can be used to incorporate charts, supporting data, diagrams, or other documents needed to understand the recommendations.

◖◗ Using Graphics and Visuals

Reports communicate complex and detailed data. A feature of this type of communication is the use of **visual aids**, which are designed not just to support the words you use but also, on some occasions, to replace words altogether. Visualizations reflect the analysis of data and plot out the patterns and relationships you have found through

Summary the closing or second-last section of a report that briefly restates its main points.

Conclusions and Recommendations the closing section of an analytical or recommendation report in which specific actions are proposed to solve a problem or aid decision-making.

visual aids (including **charts, graphs, tables,** and **illustrations**) materials that present information in visually appealing ways to show trends and relationships, represent numbers and quantities, and make abstract concepts concrete.

your observations and research. They make numerical information meaningful to readers and can speak in a dramatically persuasive and compact way. Above all, they clarify and simplify complex data, and by doing so give it extra emphasis. Easily created by computer and capable of presenting a wide range of data, visuals typically include tables, line graphs, flow charts, pie charts, bar/column charts, organization charts, and illustrations. To start creating professional-looking graphics, all you need is the assembled data and a computer graphics program such as Lotus 1-2-3, Excel, or PowerPoint. The finished graphic can then be printed on paper or inserted into your word-processing document.

Any graphic or visual is only as good as the data that goes into it and the thought that goes into its planning and matching of design with objectives. The most effective visuals are

- clearly titled and clearly labelled on each part or axis;
- uncluttered, intuitive, and easy to understand;
- accurate, functional, and ethical—with no made-up or skewed data;
- included for a purpose, to make a particular point and to add interest;
- integrated or placed where they make the most sense—near to where they are referred to in the text if they are important, in an appendix if they are supplemental; and
- supported by an explanation of the main point.

Edward R. Tufte, author of *The Visual Display of Quantitative Information* and expert in the presentation of informational graphics, has summed up how graphs and charts may best be used: "give the viewer the greatest number of ideas in the shortest space of time with the least ink in the smallest space."[1]

TABLES

table a chart that presents data, usually numerical, in a compact and systematic arrangement of rows and columns.

The most common type of visual, a **table**, is made up of rows and columns of cells that can be filled with exact figures and values. Concise and compact, tables consolidate a lot of data in a small space while retaining detail. They are useful for drawing attention to specific numbers and drawing comparisons between them. It is easy to create tables using your existing word-processing software. Here are a few tips for creating tables:

- Design your table so it fits on one page. If the table is too wide to fit this way, turn it sideways so the top of the table is next to the bound edge of the report. (In MS Word, you can do this by selecting "Landscape" rather than "Portrait" from the "Page Setup" tab.)
- Apply a heading that includes the table number and an appropriate title/caption. Number your tables sequentially as they appear in your report and number them separately from figures. Only when an explanation immediately precedes the table can the heading be omitted.
- Label all parts clearly and identify units in which figures are given. Numbers and titles/captions go above the table. Any other information, such as a source line identifying where the data originated from, goes below.

FIGURE 10.1   Simple Table

Canada's Most Counterfeited Bills in 2009

Denomination	Number of Fakes
$20	162,000
$10	159,000
$50	53,000
$100	51,000
$5	18,000
Total Value	$12.7 million

Source: RCMP, Interpol

FIGURE 10.2   Complex Table

Foreign Exchange Cross Rates

	Canadian dollar	U.S. dollar	Euro	Japanese yen	Swiss franc
Canadian dollar	—	1.2062	1.6431	0.0117	1.0661
U.S. dollar	0.4313	0.5203	0.7087	0.0050	0.4598
Euro	0.6086	0.7341	—	0.0071	0.6488
Japanese yen	85.4800	103.1100	140.4600	—	91.1400
Swiss franc	0.9380	1.1314	1.5412	0.0110	—

- For long tables with many rows, improve readability by shading alternate lines or by increasing the height of the cells.
- Use *N/A* (not available), a row of dots, or a dash to acknowledge missing data.

MATRIXES

A **matrix** is a word table that contains qualitative information rather than numerical data. Matrixes are used in reports and proposals to list instructional materials and consolidate complex information in a page or less. For example, a matrix could be used to describe the investment objectives and risks of different types of funds offered by a securities company.

matrix a word table containing qualitative information rather than numerical data.

FIGURE 10.3 Matrix

Aggressive-Growth Portfolio Balanced Funds

Canadian Equities	Target Weighing	Manager	Investment Objectives	Risk
Canstar True North Fund	11%	Canstar Investments Canada Limited	The fund aims to achieve long-term capital growth. It invests primarily in Canadian equity securities.	Main risk: • equity risk Additional risks: • credit risk • interest rate risk • small company risk
ACA Canadian Premier Fund	9%	ACA Exmark Investments Inc.	The fund seeks to generate long-term capital growth by investing in a diversified portfolio of Canadian equity securities.	• derivative risk • equity risk • liquidity risk • securities lending risk
St. Lawrence Enterprise Fund	6%	St. Lawrence Financial Corporation	The fund pursues long-term capital growth, while maintaining a commitment to protection of its capital by investing in Canadian small-capitalization equity securities.	• smaller companies risk • equity risk

PIE CHARTS

pie chart a circular diagram presenting data as wedge-shaped segments showing proportions or percentages of the whole.

A **pie chart** measures an area, showing different values as proportions of the whole. Each slice or wedge represents a percentage (usually identified with a horizontal label). The whole circle has to be equivalent to 100 per cent for the pie chart to make sense. Values in a typical pie chart start at twelve o'clock beginning with the largest percentage (or the percentage of greatest interest to your report). Wedges are then sequenced clockwise in progressively smaller slices. The pie slices (ideally, four to eight of them) are given visual separation by distinctive colour, shading, texture, or cross-hatching. Any slice can be set out from the rest to emphasize the value of a particular segment. Pie charts are most useful for comparing one segment to the whole, by demonstrating, for example, a product line revenue breakdown, how a municipal tax dollar is spent, or how one fund compares against all others in an aggressive–growth investment portfolio.

BAR CHARTS

bar chart a visual consisting of parallel horizontal or vertical bars of varying lengths, each representing a specific item for comparison.

The purpose of a **bar chart** is to show how items compare with one another, how they compare over time, and what the relationship is between or among them. As the name suggests, a bar chart presents data in a series of bars or columns, drawn

FIGURE 10.4 Pie Chart

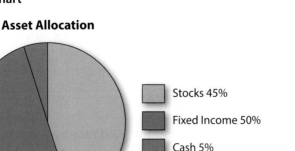

Asset Allocation

Stocks 45%

Fixed Income 50%

Cash 5%

FIGURE 10.5 Pie Chart

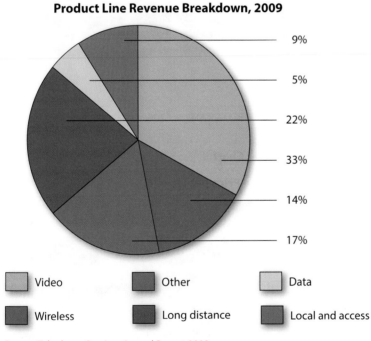

Product Line Revenue Breakdown, 2009

9%

5%

22%

33%

14%

17%

Video   Other   Data

Wireless   Long distance   Local and access

Source: Telephone Services Annual Report 2009

either **horizontally** (when labels are long) or **vertically** (when labels are short). The higher or longer the bar, the greater the value it represents. Bars have different meanings depending on their colour or shading, which also helps to distinguish them from the background. Arranged in logical or chronological order, bars can be **segmented**, **divided**, or **stacked** to show how the components of each add up (e.g., how a municipal tax dollar is budgeted or allocated). In this way, a **divided bar chart** (Figure 10.9) is much like a pie chart (Figures 10.4 and 10.5), but it can also be used to present complex quantitative information (Figure 10.10). A particular kind of bar chart called

segmented bar chart
(or **divided bar chart**)
a visual consisting of
a single bar divided
according to the different
portions that make up an
item as a whole.

deviation bar chart a specific type of bar chart that shows positive and negative values.

a **deviation bar chart** identifies positive and negative values, such as the year-by-year losses and gains of a dividend fund (see Figure 10.6). The data in all varieties of bar charts should be properly scaled to fill the entire chart, and not just squeezed into one corner. All bars should be the same width and close enough together to make comparison easy.

FIGURE 10.6 Vertical Bar Chart

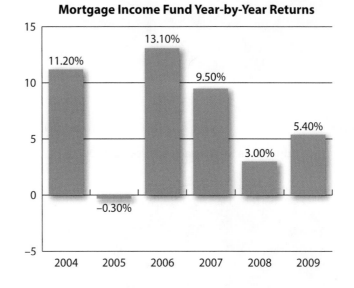

Mortgage Income Fund Year-by-Year Returns

FIGURE 10.7 Horizontal Bar Chart

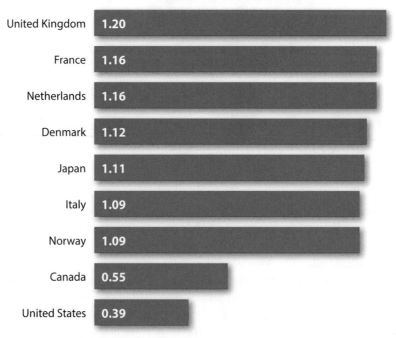

Gasoline Price per Litre (U.S. dollars)

Source: *National Post Business*

FIGURE 10.8 Bar Chart Showing Comparisons

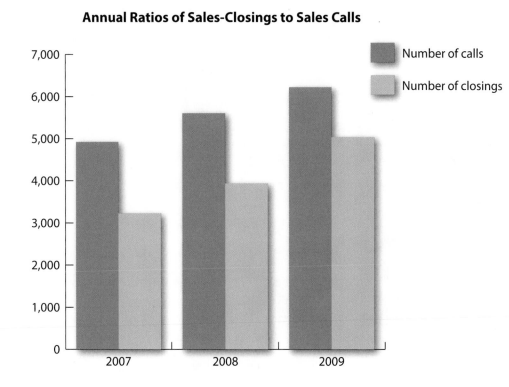

Annual Ratios of Sales-Closings to Sales Calls

Number of calls

Number of closings

FIGURE 10.9 Divided Bar Chart

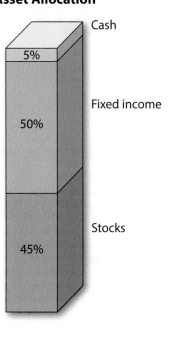

Asset Allocation

Cash

5%

Fixed income

50%

Stocks

45%

FIGURE 10.10 Divided Bar Chart

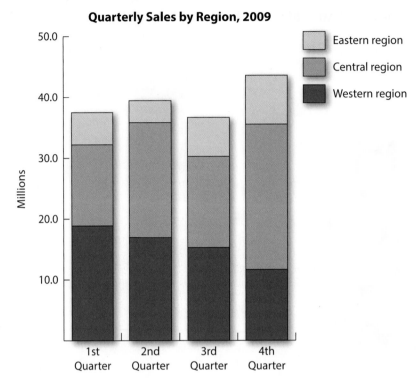

Quarterly Sales by Region, 2009

PICTURE GRAPHS

picture graph a visual that uses pictorial symbols to represent particular items.

Looking a lot like bar graphs, **pictures graphs** (or *histograms*) use pictorial symbols—for example, stick people, pine trees, or cars—to represent quantities of particular items. These symbols or images are then arranged in bars that can then be labelled with the total quantity.

FIGURE 10.11 Picture Graph

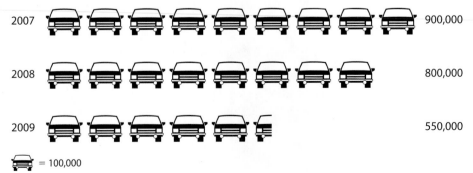

Automotive Sales by Year, 2007–2009

LINE GRAPHS

Line graphs show the relationship between two variables on a grid, plotted by connecting the dots to form a continuous line. They are useful for showing trends, fluctuations, or how things have progressed over a period of time. Below are some points to follow when devising a line graph or **grouped line graph**.

- Show the zero point of the graph where the two axes intersect. Insert a break in the scale if it is inconvenient to begin at zero.
- Quantities (litres, dollars, percentages) go on the vertical *y* axis; time goes on the horizontal *x* axis.
- Mark small dots at intersection points to draw attention to values.
- If you want to, shade between the lines to emphasize the difference between them.
- Handle the proportion of the horizontal and vertical scales carefully so that the presentation of data is free of distortion and all data is distributed equally over the graph.
- As needed, include a key that explains lines and symbols.
- If data comes from a secondary source, put a source line at the lower left corner of the figure.

line graph a visual that uses lines on a grid to show trends according to the relationship between two variables or sets of numbers.

grouped line graph a line graph that makes comparisons between two or more items.

FIGURE 10.12 Line Graph

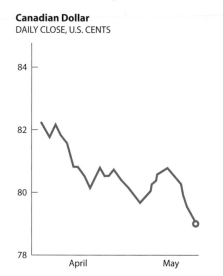

FIGURE 10.13 Grouped Line Graph

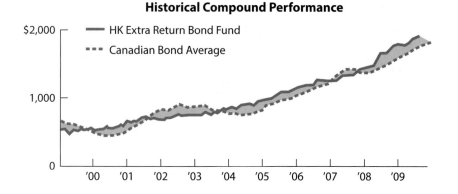

FIGURE 10.14 Line Graph—Distorted Scale

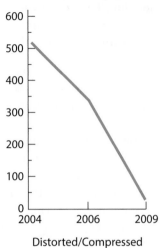

Customer Complaints

Distorted/Compressed

FIGURE 10.15 Line Graph—Distortion Free

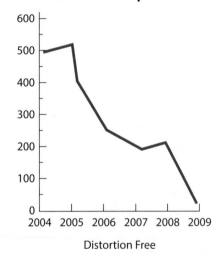

Customer Complaints

Distortion Free

GANTT CHARTS

Gantt chart a bar chart that is used to show a schedule.

Named for its inventor, Henry Laurence Gantt, a Gantt chart is used for planning and scheduling projects. Its most useful application is blocking out periods of time to show what stage a project has reached or when staff will be on vacation.

FIGURE 10.16 Gantt Chart

Project Development Schedule

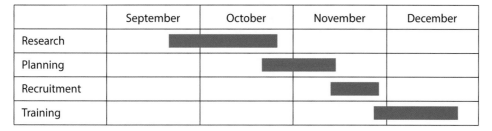

	September	October	November	December
Research				
Planning				
Recruitment				
Training				

FLOW CHARTS

A **flow chart** maps out a procedure, process, or sequence of movements diagrammatically using captioned symbols of different geometrical shapes (called ISO symbols) joined by lined arrows (for an explanation of these symbols, see Figure 10.18, "ISO Flow Chart Symbols"). Each shape represents a particular stage in the process. Flow charts, even ones that use simple labelled blocks as in Figure 10.17, help to clarify procedures and make complex systems understandable.

> **flow chart** a diagram that maps out procedures, processes, or sequences of movement.

FIGURE 10.17 Flow Chart

Claims Adjustment Process

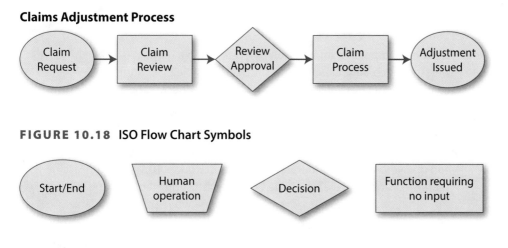

FIGURE 10.18 ISO Flow Chart Symbols

ORGANIZATIONAL CHARTS

Looking much like a family tree, an **organizational chart** maps out the structure of a company, showing chains of command and channels of communication within an organization and making it clear who reports to whom from front-line employees all the way up to senior managers.

> **organizational chart** a diagram that shows how various levels or sectors of an organization are related to one another.

FIGURE 10.19   Organizational Chart

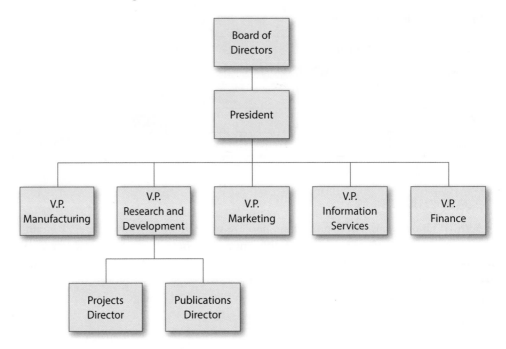

Quick Tips for Graphics

- Don't bury important information by overloading a graphic with too much data. De-clutter as much as possible by limiting the number of lines you use to what is absolutely necessary.

- Use a type of graphic that is appropriate to your message and objective.

- Use a scale that minimizes distortion (e.g., when points are too spread out or too close together). Equalize the distance between points so you don't end up overplaying or underplaying changes. Figures 10.14 and 10.15, "Line Graph—Distorted Scale" and "Line Graph—Distortion Free" on page 308, show that compressed data emphasizes change while spread out data de-emphasizes change.

- Unless you are expected to give exact figures, round off decimals to the nearest whole number (38 per cent or 38.2 per cent instead of 38.2431 per cent). Dollars in the millions can be simplified visually by adding *($ millions)* or *(in millions)* to a table or graph heading.

- Don't distort data by omitting relevant information.

- Apply consistent style for titles, numbers, and sizing of graphs and charts. Tables of equal importance should be of equal size.

FIGURE 10.20 Graphics Quick Reference Chart

Type	Example	Use
Table		to present exact figures concisely

	2008	2009
GR	403.1	395.9
AP	226.7	197.5

Type	Example	Use
Matrix		to present qualitative information concisely

Message	Plan
Good News	Direct
Bad News	Indirect

Pie Chart — to show a whole unit and the proportions of its components

Bar Chart — to show how one item compares with others

Line Graph — to show changes in numerical data over time

Flow Chart — to map out a procedure

Organizational Chart — to map out the structure or hierarchy of a company

⬤⬤ Commonly Used Short Reports: Informational and Analytical

Short reports can be either informational or analytical. Here is a brief look at some of the most frequently written categories of reports. Many of these categories are discussed in more depth later in the chapter.

INFORMATIONAL REPORTS

Informational reports have a specific purpose—to collect data and present it clearly and directly, without analysis, without conclusions, and without the need for writers to persuade their readers. These factual reports deliver routine information about different kinds of activities:

- **ongoing activities** (sales calls, for example) that need to be monitored at regular weekly, biweekly, or monthly intervals, and
- **non-routine, case-by-case situations** (such as business trips or major projects) that must be accounted for and reported to management.

The topics of informational reports are ones readers are familiar with and can understand without much background information. Instead of a lengthy introduction, a brief opening can provide the right degree of context. Because readers are usually receptive or neutral in their reaction to information about routine operations and activities, a direct, straightforward approach that gives results immediately is common for reports of this kind. A crisp, business-like style, pared-down paragraphs, bulleted lists, and graphic highlighting techniques, such as headings and white space, help to ensure that important facts are easy to find and comprehend. Informational reports can be prepared in letter, memo, and e-mail formats; for frequently recurring situations, standardized templates and fill-in forms are sometimes used.

General categories of informational reports include progress reports, activity reports, trip/conference reports, and investigative reports.

Periodic reports are informational reports written at regular intervals to describe periodic, recurring activities and record data and outcomes (monthly sales figures, the volume of customer service calls, etc.). Their purpose is to assist in the monitoring of operations and keep management informed on the status quo.

Situational reports are informational reports written in response to two specific types of non-recurring situations: (1) business trips or conferences (see Trip/Conference Reports, p. 314) and (2) the progress of a continuing project (see Progress Reports, p. 322; Job Completion Reports, p. 322, and Activity Reports, p. 320).

Incident reports are informational and document problems, unusual events, changes from routine, or unexpected occurrences that affect a company's day-to-day operations. This type of report provides complete and accurate details of an incident, answering the questions, *Who? What? Where? When? How?* and *Why?* It describes only what is known for certain happened, without speculation or inferences about supposed fault, cause, or liability. Viewed in the long term, incident reports spotlight areas of weakness in policy and procedure, helping to clear up trouble spots and prevent them from recurring.

Investigative reports evaluate problems or situations and present facts based on that evaluation. They are usually written in response to a one-time request for information.

incident report a short report that documents problems and unexpected occurrences that affect a company's day-to-day operations.

investigative report a report written in response to a request for information about a specific problem or situation.

Depending on their scope and topic, investigative reports can either simply supply the details that need to be collected or they can be more analytical and offer interpretation and recommendations. There are three basic parts in an investigative report:

- **Introduction:** states the purpose(s) of the report and defines its scope.
- **Body:** contains facts and findings arranged into several sections with descriptive headings. The topic can be divided into logical units according to importance, time, constituent elements, or criteria.
- **Summary:** may or may not offer conclusions and recommendations.

Compliance reports disclose information to governing bodies and government agencies in compliance with laws and regulations.

Recommendation reports present information but go a step further in evaluating options or existing situations and offering recommendations about them. Recommendation reports are commissioned—writers are asked to investigate situations or actions, express their professional opinions about them, and recommend appropriate actions or interventions.

Justification reports also have a problem-solving function, but unlike recommendation reports they are prepared on a voluntary basis, not in response to a commission or request. They are called justification reports because they justify a purchase, investment, policy change, or hiring, stating what is needed and why it is needed. Both recommendation and justification reports can be organized directly or indirectly (see below), depending on how receptive readers will be to the action or solution the report endorses.

> **recommendation report** an analytical report that recommends action, often in response to a specific problem.

> **justification report** an analytical report that justifies the need for a purchase, investment, policy change, or hiring.

- **Direct pattern:**
  - Introduce the problem briefly.
  - Present the recommendation, action, or solution.
  - Justify the recommendation by highlighting advantages and benefits and explaining it in more detail.
  - End with a summary that refers to the action to be taken.
- **Indirect pattern:**
  - Introduce the problem and provide details that convince readers of its seriousness—do not reveal the recommendation.
  - Discuss other measures or alternatives under descriptive headings, starting with the least likely and ending with your recommendation.
  - Show that the advantages of your solution outweigh the disadvantages.
  - Summarize the action to be taken and ask for authorization.

Feasibility reports evaluate projects or alternatives to determine if they are practical and advisable—in other words, to determine their worthiness and chances for success. They are necessary as a first step before any new project is launched. Typically, feasibility reports project costs, staffing needs, scheduling, and potential problems, and discuss benefits associated with a project so that readers have all the information they need to decide whether to accept it and proceed or opt for an alternative. The process of writing a feasibility report generally breaks down into the following steps:

> **feasibility report** an analytical report that evaluates whether a project or alternative is advisable and practical.

- Announce the decision to be made and list its alternatives.
- Describe the problem necessitating the decision.
- Evaluate positive and negative aspects of the project, including potential problems.
- Calculate costs and discuss the time frame.

Summaries compress longer information and condense it to what management needs to know: primary ideas, conclusions, and recommendations.

To-file reports provide a permanent written record of decisions, discussions, and directives. Left on file for future reference, they summarize decisions made and list the individuals involved in making them.

Proposals suggest the ways and means of solving problems. They present information about a plan or a project in order to persuade readers to accept the plan and you as the person to develop it and carry it out. Proposals may be competitive (competing to secure new business by seeking to sell goods and services to potential buyers and bidding for corporate or government contracts) or internal (suggesting changes in policy or spending to help change or improve the organization). Because they must not only sell ideas, products, or services but must first establish credibility, proposals are substantial documents. (Look for much more on proposals in Chapter 11.)

Trip/Conference Reports

Many jobs require travel to client, supplier, or branch locations, conferences and conventions, or training and professional development seminars. A trip or conference report is an internal document, prepared as an e-mail or memo and addressed to an immediate supervisor. It provides a permanent record of what an employee learned and accomplished on the trip. A trip report thus allows an entire organization to benefit from information one employee has gained about products, services, equipment, procedures, laws, or personnel and operations management. Trip and conference reports may be limited to this basic information or they may go a step further in recommending or suggesting actions based on trip events or conference participation. In this way, they may answer questions such as *Should our company consider purchasing equipment featured at the trade show? Should other employees attend this conference next year?*

Being selective is one of the keys to writing this type of report effectively. While the experience of work-related travel may be saturated with ideas and activities, its reporting should be brief and focused on major events, up to a maximum of five relevant and interesting topics. Use these topics to organize your report instead of a chronological pattern that can tempt writers to record everything that happened from beginning to end and leave readers without a clear sense of what the business traveller or conference attendee gained from his or her experiences. A writing plan for trip and conference reports includes the following elements:

- **Subject line**—identifies the event, destination, and dates of the trip.
- **Introduction**—gives the event/destination, specifies exact dates, explains the purpose of the trip, and previews main points.
- **Body**—devotes a section to each main topic, event, or highlight that will be summarized. Headings may be used for each section.
- **Conclusion**—expresses appreciation and may make a recommendation based on the information in the report.

Because business travel can be expensive, managers look for proof that company travel dollars have been wisely spent. For this reason, an expense report is often attached to the trip report.

The conference report in Figure 10.21 is incomplete. In place of specific information about events and accomplishments, it delivers non-essential details of little interest

proposal a document presenting plans and ideas for consideration and acceptance by the reader.

trip report (or **conference report**) a short report that summarizes the events of a business trip or conference.

FIGURE 10.21 INEFFECTIVE Conference Report

PITCH MARKETING
REACHING CUSTOMERS THE RIGHT WAY

DATE: May 28, 2010

TO: Natalie Forester

FROM: Ryan Sharma RS

SUBJECT: Conference

I was thrilled when you told me that I could attend a conference and even happier when you told me that the company would cover my expenses. Even though my flight to the conference was delayed for more than four hours and the airline lost my luggage, I think the trip was worthwhile. Now that I've returned, I have to tell you that I couldn't believe how much I learned in just three days. In the paragraphs below I will tell you about this event.

The conference agenda was as follows:

Day 1	Opening reception
Day 2	Conference presentations
Day 3	Discussion panels

The presentations I attended were very interesting and I learned a lot about branding. Perhaps in the future I will have the opportunity to share the highlights of the conference with you. I think other members of our team would benefit from knowing more about this worthwhile conference. I met some people and this could be of value to our organization. The registration fee was very high, but I would definitely recommend this conference to anyone who would like to know more about this fascinating subject.

Annotations:
- Subject line does not identify the event (name and date)
- Focuses on irrelevant details
- Provides only a generic program of events, not specific highlights
- Does not elaborate on details that would interest management

to management. What did the attendee learn? How can the knowledge he gained benefit the organization? What was the destination?

The trip report in Figure 10.22 was prepared by a junior design associate at K2 Design, a leading residential design and retail company based in Calgary. Her task in attending Professional Trade Day at the Residential Design Show in Toronto was to identify top trends and source new products that might complement the accessory and furniture collections already featured in her company's retail space. Professional Trade Day also gave her the opportunity to attend an accredited design seminar for which she can earn points toward her professional design designation. The report is presented in two optional formats, memo and abbreviated e-mail. The first report offers a recommendation based on the writer's view of the value of the event.

FIGURE 10.22A EFFECTIVE Trip Report (Memo)

K2 Design

Inter-office Memo

DATE: March 26, 2010

TO: Hilary Stanton, Retail Manager

FROM: Lisa Liu, Junior Design Associate *LL*

Subject line identifies event name and date → **SUBJECT:**   RDS Professional Trade Day, March 23

Provides event location and purpose → I was pleased to attend Professional Trade Day at the Residential Design Show (RDS), a premiere platform for contemporary interior design. Held in Toronto on March 23, this one-day event showcased the newest Canadian and international furnishings, fixtures, and accessories and featured trade presentations by renowned designers along with accredited ASID and IIDA seminars. Trade Day gave me the opportunity to discover and source new products, make useful

Previews major topics → contacts, and further my education towards ASID accreditation. This report summarizes details of my time spent at RDS Professional Trade Day.

Draws attention to major topics with centred headings → **Top Trends for 2010**

Many residential design trends were represented in the specially commissioned living spaces and exhibitor product lines. I have summarized three of the top trends:

Covers details of interest to management →

- **Eco-chic.** Organic shapes and materials from renewable resources inspired products such as a bamboo console from GreenFX Studio Works (www.greenfx.ca) and a stainless steel coil lamp by Ecobright Luminaries (www.ecobright.com).

- **Bold colour.** The trends towards bright colour and a palette that emphasized reds and oranges were represented by the Red Giacometti Chair from Swish Designs (www.swish.ca), the Orange Mosaic Console from Antic Design (www.anticdesign.com), and a red stool by SITT Designs (www.sitt.com).

- **Patterns and stripes.** Textiles in bold, variegated stripes and patterns reminiscent of Pucci print designs had a graphic appeal and were available at a variety of price points. Products such as the Summer of Love Chair by Ergo Designs (www.ergo.ca) and a striped stainless slipper sofa by Furniture Incubator (www.furnitureincubator.ca) were typical of this trend.

FIGURE 10.22A (continued)

The Orange Mosaic Console and coil lamp have touches of wit that would make them good additions to our Loft retail collection. Attached is a complete price list and source guide to over 100 new products, including the console and lamp, that may be of interest to you and senior buyers.

Keynote Addresses

The international speakers program was a great opportunity to learn first-hand about the design innovations and philosophies of Arcshop founder Yves Aubert and architect Felicia Urbano. Both keynotes stressed the need for simplicity in good design and the importance of industrial process in guiding design decisions.

Accredited Seminars

The accredited seminars focused on the practical dimensions of designing for clients. I attended "Colour 101" and received expert advice on key pigmentation factors and home colour trends from colour researcher Alexandra Fullerton. The attached certificate of completion confirms that I earned one ARIDO CE point ←——— Refers to attachments and enclosures
or 0.1 CEU towards my professional designation.

Sharing Trade-Day Resources

With its balance of design theory and practical product information, RDS ←——— Closes with synthesis of the value of the event and a suggestion for action
Professional Trade Day gave me insight into the residential design industry and offered me resources I can share with members of our team to help us source an exciting range of products for our retail space. The exposure RDS provides for new design firms like ours might make it beneficial for our company to be an exhibitor at next year's show.

Attachment

FIGURE 10.22B EFFECTIVE **Trip Report (Abbreviated E-mail)**

Greeting personalizes e-mail →

Introduces report with summary statement →

Heading style is simpler for e-mail

Lists facts of interest to readers →

Residential Design Show Professional Trade Day, March 23 ▢ ▢ ✕

From:	Lisa Liu <llui@k2design.ca>
Date:	March 26, 2010 4:52 p.m.
To:	<hstanton@k2design.ca>
Subject:	Residential Design Show Professional Trade Day, March 23
Attach:	RDS07 Source Guide.pdf; Colour101 Completion Certificate.pdf

Hello Hilary,

As you requested, here is a summary of my activities at Professional Trade Day at the Residential Design Show in Toronto.

Trending watching. After arriving in the evening of March 22, I spent the morning assessing and sourcing over 100 new products in the exhibition hall. I have attached a source guide that contains full product information and price lists. The furnishings, fixtures, and accessories on display reflected three top trends:

1. **Eco-chic.** Organic shapes and materials from renewable resources inspired products such as a bamboo console from GreenFX Studio Works (www.greenfx.ca) and a stainless steel coil lamp by Ecobright Luminaries (www.ecobright.com).

2. **Bold colour.** The trends towards bright colour and a palette that emphasized reds and oranges were represented by the Red Giacometti Chair from Swish Designs (www.swish.ca), the Orange Mosaic Console from Antic Design (www.anticdesign.ca), and a red stool by SITT Designs (www.sitt.com).

3. **Patterns and stripes.** Textiles in bold, variegated stripes and patterns reminiscent of Pucci print designs had a graphic appeal and were available at a variety of price points. Products such as the Summer of Love Chair by Ergo Designs (www.ergo.ca) and a striped stainless slipper sofa by Furniture Incubator (www.furnitureincubator.ca) were typical of this trend.

Learning from design innovators. At the International Speakers Program in the afternoon, keynotes Yves Aubert and Felicia Urbano stressed the need for simplicity in good design and the importance of industrial process in guiding design decisions. The residential design roundtable that followed offered good networking opportunities.

FIGURE 10.22B (continued)

Residential Design Show Professional Trade Day, March 23

From:	Lisa Liu <llui@k2design.ca>
Date:	March 26, 2010 4:52 p.m.
To:	<hstanton@k2design.ca>
Subject:	Residential Design Show Professional Trade Day, March 23
Attach:	RDS07 Source Guide.pdf; Colour101 Completion Certificate.pdf

Earning professional designation. I attended an accredited ASID/IIDA seminar on colour pigmentation factors and home colour trends. The attached certificate of completion confirms that I earned one ARIDO CE point or 0.1 CEU towards my professional designation.

Sharing Professional Trade-Day resources. With its balance of design theory and practical product information, RDS Professional Trade Day gave me the opportunity to discover and source new products, make useful contacts, and further my education towards ASID accreditation. Moreover, Professional Trade Day provided me with valuable industry resources I can share with members of our team to develop new designs and help us source an exciting range of products for our retail space.

Activity Reports

An activity report documents the ongoing activities or projects of a division or department. Because activity reports are written at regular weekly or monthly intervals, they are sometimes also called *periodic* or *status* reports. These routine, recurring reports, typically prepared by supervisors, help middle and senior managers stay informed of activities and alert to unusual events that might negatively affect operations and therefore require swift solutions or changes in strategy. Activity reports can contain a range of information, from numerical data on sales volume or product shipments to more detailed discussion of key activities. The story an activity report tells is developed through the following three categories or sections:

progress and activity report a short report that provides information on the status of a project, including current work, work done during the time since the previous report, and work to be completed in the next period.

FIGURE 10.23 Activity Report

Memo format used for internal report

Subject line identifies reporting period

Summarizes activities and events carried out during the reporting period

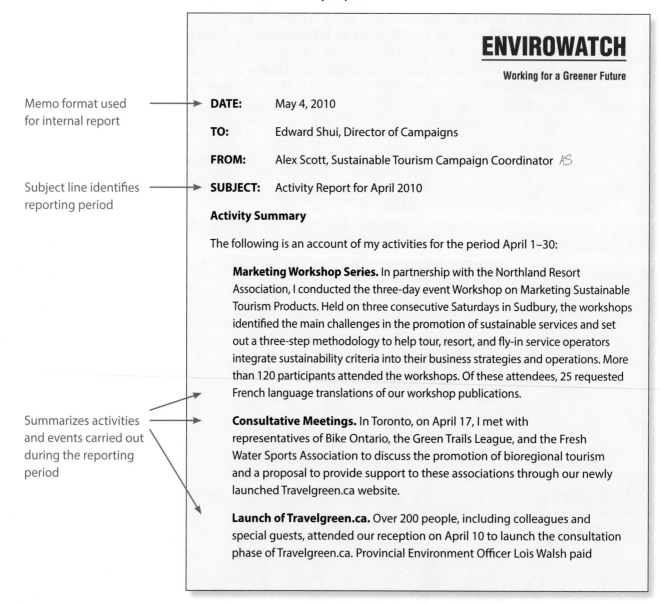

ENVIROWATCH

Working for a Greener Future

DATE: May 4, 2010

TO: Edward Shui, Director of Campaigns

FROM: Alex Scott, Sustainable Tourism Campaign Coordinator AS

SUBJECT: Activity Report for April 2010

Activity Summary

The following is an account of my activities for the period April 1–30:

Marketing Workshop Series. In partnership with the Northland Resort Association, I conducted the three-day event Workshop on Marketing Sustainable Tourism Products. Held on three consecutive Saturdays in Sudbury, the workshops identified the main challenges in the promotion of sustainable services and set out a three-step methodology to help tour, resort, and fly-in service operators integrate sustainability criteria into their business strategies and operations. More than 120 participants attended the workshops. Of these attendees, 25 requested French language translations of our workshop publications.

Consultative Meetings. In Toronto, on April 17, I met with representatives of Bike Ontario, the Green Trails League, and the Fresh Water Sports Association to discuss the promotion of bioregional tourism and a proposal to provide support to these associations through our newly launched Travelgreen.ca website.

Launch of Travelgreen.ca. Over 200 people, including colleagues and special guests, attended our reception on April 10 to launch the consultation phase of Travelgreen.ca. Provincial Environment Officer Lois Walsh paid

- a brief yet complete summary, listing highlights of activities and projects carried out during the reporting period,
- an update on current problems and irregularities, including competition news of interest to managers of for-profit businesses, and
- an overview of needs and forecast of plans for the next period.

An activity report should deliver a complete, accurate, and objective account of events—both good and bad—that have taken place during the reporting period. It should be honest and forthright in describing the state of regular activities, in noting problems that might affect operations, and in tracking the competition. This type of report represents

FIGURE 10.23 (continued)

Edward Shui   2   May 4, 2010

tribute to the site as a platform for promoting cooperation for conservation in the tourism industry. Travelgreen.ca has already attracted more than 300 visitors and averages 11 comments a day from tourist operators interested in reducing ecological impacts in their industry.

Funding News

In the latest funding round, Green Now received a $50,000 grant from the Simcoe Foundation to raise public awareness of the fight against climate change. Although this is good news for the local conservation movement, the awarding of this grant may minimize the impact of our own grant proposal to develop a training package on sustainable tourism. We may wish to re-evaluate our proposal or target other funding opportunities.

Problems

Eco Print, which produces our campaign literature on acid-free, recycled paper, will cease operation effective June 30. The closure means that the scheduled September release of our *Guide to Marine Impacts* may be delayed unless we find a cost-effective printer with a similar commitment to environmentally friendly practices.

Describes irregularities that require the attention of management

Needs

- Information on eco-friendly printing businesses in the GTA.
- French-language translation of Marketing Sustainable Tourism Products workshop literature.
- Identification of alterative foundation donors and funding sources.

Highlights special needs

a chance to check in with managers and inform them of problems that require their attention and perhaps corrective measures, so the project can continue.

The report in Figure 10.23 is from a non-profit environmental education organization. Among its mandates is a campaign to promote sustainability in the travel and tourism industry. This monthly activity report from the Sustainable Tourism Campaign coordinator highlights the status of projects and documents a problem that requires quick resolution to ensure the success of future commitments. Because this is a non-profit organization, the writer provides an update on funding initiatives instead of sales competition.

Progress Reports

Progress reports monitor headway on a project at various intervals from start-up to completion and summarize what has been done, what is currently underway, and what remains to be done. These reports indicate if a project is on schedule and if any measures need to be taken to correct problems or remove obstacles. Progress and activity reports help managers adjust schedules, allocate personnel and equipment, and revise budgets. They are typically arranged in the following pattern:

1. **Opening summary** (no heading)—comments on the status of the project in terms of the original schedule and goals and the progress that has been made to date.
2. **Under the heading "Work Completed"**—describes what has been done since the last report and notes any problems and solutions.
3. **Under the heading "Work in Progress"** (optional)—lists work currently being done.
4. **Under the heading "Work to be Completed"**—describes the work that remains and notes any foreseeable problems and likely solutions. A work schedule can be included in this section or under a separate heading.
5. **Closing/Forecast** (no heading)—looks ahead to the progress that will be made between this report and either expresses confidence that the project will be finished on time or discusses an extension of the project deadline. For an example, see Figure 10.24, "Sample Progress Report," on page 323.

Job Completion Reports

Job completion reports are typically last in a series of progress reports for a lengthy or substantial project. Sometimes they are one-time reports arising from a short or small-scale project. They provide closure, putting the project and what has been learned from it in perspective. A well-prepared project report ensures shared understanding about the work that has taken place and any actions that are required in response to it. While typically not more than three pages long, a project completion report can be longer if the scope and magnitude of the project require lengthy analysis and supporting material such as tables and charts. The bigger the budget, usually the more substantial and detailed the report will be. This short, informational report uses the direct approach:

1. **Opening**—provides a concise overview, naming the project and its client, confirming the completion of the project, briefly identifying major tasks or activities, and noting outcomes, successes, next steps, or special circumstances.
2. **Background**—describes the job's purpose, what necessitated the project, who authorized or supervised it, what the original contract called for, who was involved,

FIGURE 10.24 Sample Progress Report

The following progress report is designed to keep management of a publishing company informed of the arrangements for an author's promotional tour.

McAllen & Wallbridge Publishing

Inter-office Memo

DATE: January 11, 2010

TO: Suhanna Nair, Editor-in-Chief

FROM: Joanna Vickers, Promotions Manager

SUBJECT: Spring Promotional Tour for Penelope Seward's *North Road*   *Memo format includes concise, descriptive subject line that creates a focus for the report*

This memo describes the progress of plans and arrangements for Penelope Seward's first national book tour, following the launch of her third novel, *North Road*, on April 15 in Toronto. Details of the tour will by finalized on February 1, as you requested.   *Opens with a summary statement describing the project and its proposed deadline for completion*

Background: The launch of Penelope Seward's third novel, *North Road*, follows her recent longlist nomination for the prestigious IBISS Prize in the United Kingdom. Her enhanced media profile in recent months has resulted in a high level of interest from booksellers across Canada. I consulted Ms. Seward   *"Background" establishes purpose and special requirements* about her preferences regarding scheduling and venues and she told me that she was amenable to a three-week tour from April 15 to May 7, provided that no single day requires her to appear at more than two events. I have modelled Ms. Seward's spring tour on last fall's successful promotional series for John Sayer's *Wildfire Days*.

Work Completed: In the past ten days, I have contacted major print and   *"Work Completed" describes what has been done since the last report and mentions actions pending* broadcast media outlets, booksellers, and reading series coordinators across Canada and drawn up a preliminary program of events:

April 15	Toronto	Launch at the Blake Hotel, 8:00–11:00 p.m.
April 18	Toronto	Interview with Vivi Jones, *Good Morning Canada* (to air at 8:30 a.m.)
April 20	Toronto	Book signing at Vermilion Books, 1:00–3:00 p.m.
April 30	Halifax	Reading and book signing at Literati Books, 2:00 p.m.

(continued)

FIGURE 10.24 (continued)

Suhanna Nair, Editor-in-Chief Page 2 January 11, 2010

May 4	Saskatoon	Reading at Francis Morrison Library Theatre, 7:00 p.m.
May 6	Calgary	Book signing at Foothills Books, 4:00 p.m.
May 8	Vancouver	Books and Brunch, Pacific Hotel, 10 a.m.–noon

Other dates to be confirmed in the next week include a reading at Harbour Books in St. John's, tentatively scheduled for May 2, and a reading at Memorial University on May 3. I have forwarded advance copies of *North Road* to all editors and reviewers on our contact list to expedite the reviewing process in advance of the tour.

Work to be Completed: Airline and hotel bookings will be arranged pending finalization of the tour itinerary and schedule. I will prepare a press release and, upon your approval, have it distributed to all media contacts by February 15. I will also prepare ad copy, featuring advance praise for *North Road* and reading-tour dates, to appear in the April issue of *Books in Canada* and in *The Globe and Mail*'s Saturday books section in mid-April.

Anticipated Problems: If Ms. Seward's second novel, *Boneshop of the Heart*, is among the five IBISS Prize finalists to be announced next week, the Halifax reading on April 30 will have to be postponed until May 10 to allow her to travel to England to attend the awards dinner in London on April 29. I have discussed this eventuality with Alex Betts, manager of Literati Books, and he is agreeable to this scheduling change should it prove necessary.

By February 1, you'll receive my final report confirming all details, dates, and events for the tour.

Margin annotations:

"Work to be Completed" describes work that remains and mentions deadlines for anticipated completion

"Anticipated Problems" looks ahead to conditions and circumstances that may alter the proposed plan

Closes with confirmation of delivery time of next report

---

how much the project was budgeted at (optional), and who carried out the work. This section also identifies the start and completion dates (or schedule) outlined in the contract or original work plan.

3. **Project milestones**—identifies all major accomplishments (work done, targets reached, and results achieved).

4. **Variances**—notes deviations from the original plan, including problems encountered along the way that necessitated additional work outside the original scope of the project or work that had to be done differently in order for those problems to be solved. For each exception or revision to the original work plan, there should be an explanation of why it was necessary, how it addressed the problem, and how it affected the project overall.

5. **Action**—restates the outcome and asks the reader to review the project, respond, sign-off, or follow-up.

FIGURE 10.25 Sample Job Completion Report

Sky Garden Design

June 18, 2012

Audra Holt, Senior Project Manager
Arden Lofts Property Development Ltd.
301 University Avenue, Suite 502
Toronto, Ontario M5J 1K6

Subject: Completion of "Green Roof" Project at Arden Lofts

Dear Ms. Holt:

Installation of a "green roof" at the Arden Lofts condominium property at 105–107 Grenville Street in Toronto is now complete. Work that was scheduled to start on February 1 and end on June 1 was extended by four days due to the delays in project start-up caused by a severe early spring ice storm. The roof garden is now ready to provide outdoor recreational space for tenants due to take occupancy in mid-July and to offer enhanced energy efficiency and storm-water management to this 14-storey, 450-unit complex.

Background

The City of Toronto's Green Roof bylaw applies to all new residential developments with a GFA of 5,000 square metres or greater. In compliance with this bylaw and its commitment to sustainable design, Arden Lofts Property Development Ltd. commissioned my company, Sky Garden Design Landscape Architects, to design and install a 500-square-metre extensive "green roof" at the Arden Lofts property at 105-107 Grenville Street.

The decision to install an extensive green roof was made to maximize the planting area without having to adjust the structural loading capacity of the building. The plan called for the creation of three accessible pathways, a deck, a dog-run, and two green roof plots, surrounded by approximately 1,000 square metres of decorative hard-surface concrete pavers. Project partner Fortex Roofing accommodated the extra weight of the green roof and rooftop recreational facilities by reinforcing the entire roof with steel girders. We then proceeded to incorporate a drip drainage/filtering system, quality waterproofing, root-repellency, engineered growing media, and plants.

53 Borden Street, Toronto, Ontario M74 2M9   Tel. 416 244-1480   Fax 416 244-2311
www.skygardendesign.com

(*continued*)

FIGURE 10.25 (continued)

Ms. Audra Holt
June 18, 2012
Page 2

Project Highlights

The 500-square-metre green roof and corresponding 1,000-square-metre hard surface area were designed, supplied, and installed for just over $180,000, slightly below the $182,000 allocated for this project. Elements of Soprema's Sopranture green roofing system were used in the accessible extensive roof system. Sopraflor-X, the growing medium, was selected for its ability to cling to plants in windy conditions. A total of 27 different species of plants native to Ontario were included in the design, among them pale-purple coneflower, woodland sunflower, and sedum, a succulent plant tolerant to extremes in temperature. All plants are under warrantee for one year from the date of purchase. The plants are now irrigated with a drip irrigation system, installed at a nominal cost of $15,000. Total expenditures are detailed in the enclosed budget.

Installation and Technical Issues

Our team of landscape engineers encountered two technical problems that had to be overcome: (1) transporting materials onto the roof of the 14-storey structure and (2) selecting plants that could withstand rooftop winds of up to 100 km/hr. As the building was still under construction, Sky Garden Design worked with contractors to arrange for the hoisting of growing medium, concrete slabs, and plants using the crane that was already on site. The use of day lily and other plants less resistant to wind and sun exposure, which the plan originally called for, was curtailed in favour of hardier plants such as sedum and alpine grasses.

Action

The green roof at Arden Lofts, having now passed all inspections, supports vegetation that helps to manage storm water, improve air quality, increase energy efficiency, enhance biodiversity, and provide outdoor recreational space in a high-density urban area with limited parkland. At present, no monitoring of the green roof has been proposed. The condominium association has the option to create a budget for the replanting and maintenance of the green roof that will ensure tenants enjoy this urban oasis for many years to come.

Sincerely,

Tom Battleford

Tom Battleford
Chief Landscape Engineer & Owner

53 Borden Street, Toronto, Ontario M74 2M9   Tel. 416 244-1480   Fax 416 244-2311
www.skygardendesign.com

Incident Reports

Even the most caring and efficient workplaces, with the highest safety standards, are not always able to prevent the losses and harm that result from events such as onsite accidents, equipment failure, threats to personal safety, and health emergencies. When trouble occurs, and as soon as it is possible to assess the situation after it has stabilized, the event needs to be clearly and thoroughly documented. Fair and accountable business practices, not to mention occupational health and safety standards, demand it. An incident or accident report helps an organization assess the problem, correct it, and make the changes necessary to prevent the problem from happening again.

Incident and accident reporting serves a vital purpose in effective risk management in the workplace. It does this by capturing accidents and incidents, with the potential to become claims, as they happen. According to the Insurance Board of Canada, incident reports "serve as the basis for analyzing the causes of incidents and accidents and for recommending risk improvements to help prevent similar events in the future."[2] Workers' compensation claims, insurance claims, and lawsuits may hang in the balance, so it is important that reports of this kind be filed promptly, accurately, and with due diligence.

Most of the problems that incident and accident reports document are internal matters, so this type of report usually follows simple memo format. There is rarely the need for a document as long or as detailed as a formal report. More typically, forms or templates are used for this purpose so the reports can be filed quickly, with all the required information.

Incident reports are narratives, much like news stories, that present facts objectively and at the same time avoid assigning blame. There is usually a very short time frame for the completion and submission of an incident report (usually between 24 and 72 hours). Any delay in reporting the event must be disclosed and explained. At minimum, incident reports should contain the following information:

- names and contact information of the supervisor/reporter and any witnesses;
- a precise and detailed description of the event, including time, place, and names of individuals involved; and
- an objective assessment of the root cause of the event and recommendations to prevent a recurrence.

Providing answers to all of the questions that apply—using a direct writing plan, careful language, and factual details—will result in a complete and thorough report. When preparing an incident report, include the following information:

- **Subject line:** identifies the precise problem or event and the date it occurred.
- **Opening:** provides a brief summary statement noting the incident/accident, the date it took place, who it primarily affected, and what the result was.
- **Body:** gives a precise description of the problem:
  - What happened?
    - Where and when did it happen?
    - What was the exact sequence of events leading up to the incident?
    - What type of equipment, if any, was being used? What materials, if any, were involved?

FIGURE 10.26 Sample Incident/Accident Report

National Precast Concrete

Interoffice Memo

To: Lucinda Harvey, Chief Officer
             Environmental Health & Safety

From: Scott Lisgar, Site Supervisor

Date: February 10, 2010

Subject: Skid-Steer Loader Accident on February 9, 2010

The following report summarizes an accident that occurred on February 9, 2010, involving Joseph D'Alessandro (Employee #62651). The injuries he sustained resulted in three days of lost time and a one-hour work stoppage at a commercial construction site at 1119 Avery Boulevard, Oshawa.

Accident Summary

On February 9, 2010, 58-year-old Joseph D'Alessandro, a concrete truck driver employed for 12 years at National Precast Concrete's Oshawa facility, sustained injuries when he was struck and knocked down by a skid-steer loader. The accident occurred at 9:10 a.m. on a gravel section just outside the worksite trailer at the Maple Grove property development site.

Accident Details

On the day of the incident, it was windy, with intermittent freezing rain. Mr. D'Alessandro had taken shelter inside the trailer as he waited for the arrival of a contract worker he was assigned to train that day. Mr. D'Alessandro, who suffers from a disability on the left side of his body, had just descended a set of wooden stairs leading out of the trailer when he stepped into the path of the skid-steer loader as it was backing up at a speed of approximately 15 km/hr.

The contract worker, Jeremy Adams, who was just arriving at the site, shouted at Mr. D'Alessandro and waved his arms to warn him that the skid-steer loader was backing up. Mr. D'Alessandro, who was wearing a hood and a heavy woolen hat and who had turned his head back towards the trailer to avoid a heavy gust of wind, later told co-workers Jack Yip and Victor Plavzik that he thought Mr. Adams was greeting him. A few seconds before impact, the sound of the skid-steer loader's motor alerted Mr. D'Alessandro to the approaching danger, but his limited mobility prevented him from moving out of the way completely. He was struck of the left side and knocked to the ground. When his head struck the gravel

Skid-Steer Loader Accident Report, February 10, 2010

FIGURE 10.26 (continued)

pathway, Mr. D'Alessandro suffered facial lacerations, later requiring 20 stitches, and lost consciousness for several minutes. The skid-steer operator, Mr. Adams, immediately dialed 911 and Pete Wurlitzer, a foreman equipped with a first-aid kit and defibrillator, checked Mr. D'Alessandro's pulse and respiration. Emergency medical services arrived at 9:20 a.m., within minutes of the phone call, and Mr. D'Alessandro was taken to the hospital where he was kept for observation overnight after complaining of headache and dizziness. He was diagnosed by consulting physician Dr. Alexandra Cho at Oshawa General Hospital as having suffered a mild concussion; he was advised not to return to work for three days.

Of the 10 employees and contract workers on site at the time of the accident, Mr. Adams, Mr. Yip, and Mr. Plavzik, whose contact information can be found in the company registry, were standing on the gravel pathway within 10 metres of the accident when it occurred and had unobstructed views of the collision. The information contained in this report is based on on-site interviews conducted with the three witnesses in the hours following the accident.

The worksite trailer sustained minor damage to its aluminum siding when the skid-steer loader went out of control after hitting Mr. D'Alessandro. Damage is estimated at under $100. On brief inspection, the skid-steer loader did not appear to be damaged, but it will be taken out of service until a full mechanical evaluation can be conducted. The initial inspection of the vehicle revealed that its backup alarm and electronic sensor were not functioning.

The accident and its aftermath, during which time photographs were taken of the accident site, accounted for a work stoppage of one hour and ten minutes. During that time, all work at the site ceased and did not resume until 10:20 a.m., after police who were called to the scene and EMS personnel had left.

Recommendations

To prevent similar occurrences, our company should consider the following actions in the future:

- Conduct weekly inspections to ensure backup alarms and electronic sensors on all skid-steer loaders are functioning.
- Conduct monthly face-to-face reviews of reversing procedures with all drivers of skid-steer loaders rather than relying on a one-time viewing of a one-hour PowerPoint presentation.
- Erect barriers separating areas where heavy equipment, such as the skid-steer loader, is used from commonly used pathways.
- Institute a policy requiring workers-on-foot to maintain minimum clearance from skid-steer loaders.

Skid-Steer Loader Accident Report, February 10, 2010

- Was anybody hurt?
  - What type of injury occurred?
  - What body part and which side of the body were affected?
  - How severe was the injury? If known, what type of treatment was required?
  - Was first-aid administered? Was a physician required?
  - Did the injury result in lost time or a change/reduction in duties?
- Was there any property damage? What was the approximate value of material damage?
- Was there a work stoppage? How much time was lost?
- What were the contributing factors? While making it clear when you are speculating, what was the root cause of the event (e.g., unsafe equipment, lack of training)?
- **Conclusion:** follows through on the assessment by describing what can or will be done to correct the problem and alter conditions that led to its occurrence.
  - Was the accident or incident preventable? If so, how could it be prevented in future? What corrective measures are required? What has already been done to change the condition that led to the incident or accident?

Problem-Investigation Reports

Problem-investigation reports are written for two reasons: (1) to provide information or research that does not result in action or recommendation, as follow-up to a request, and (2) to document how a problem has been resolved. Investigation reports must clearly describe an issue that is up for study, whether that involves repairs, reorganization, the purchase and installation of new equipment to address old inefficiencies, the launching of a new project or initiative, or the allocation of people, space, or resources. The following plan outlines the organization of this type of direct approach informational report. Descriptive headings (applied to each section except the opening summary) are most effective in helping to preview the organization of this type of report:

- **Summary of Main Points:** defines the problem, notes its cause(s) and resolution, and notes any further steps that should be taken.
- **Background or History:** establishes the report's purpose and sets out the circumstances in which the problem was discovered and the causes of the problem the report investigates.
- **Approach and Findings:** describes the methods and approach taken and criteria applied in resolving the problem. It also reviews findings and discusses their significance.
- **Conclusion:** notes what has been or should be done—and by whom. It also briefly outlines any disadvantages of the proposed solution and states how the corrected problem makes for a better outcome.
- **Appendix or Attachment (optional):** supplies supporting data and evidence that cannot be easily included in the preceding sections.

FIGURE 10.27 Sample Problem-Investigation Report

Unitas Shoes

To: Jill Brody, President
From: Gustavo Suarez, IT Manager
Subject: Eliminating Loss Resulting from Data Mobility
Date: February 8, 2010

The purpose of this report is to explore the problem of data mobility and the risk it poses to our intellectual property (IP), proprietary personal information and customer data, and ultimately to revenue and profits at Unitas Shoes.

Background

As the maker of exclusive, high-end footware and luxury leathergoods, Unitas enjoys a unique position in the Canadian marketplace in competing with foreign brands such as Christian Louboutin and Jimmy Cho and in having secured a niche market of discriminating buyers throughout the country and more recently in select centres such as New York and London. Our unique designs are showcased at Toronto Fashion Week, Montreal Fashion Week, and other headline events in the fashion industry. Our beachhead into Canadian and foreign markets has been enhanced through extensive exposure in publications such as *Elle Canada* and *Fashion* and a print-ad campaign in *Vogue*. All of these factors contribute to Unitas' remarkable 20 per cent growth in sales in 2009, during the downturn of the recessionary economy; however, that growth cannot be sustained if the distinctness of our brand is not protected.

Instances of corporate theft are on the rise in all industries, and the fashion industry is no exception. Users find it relatively easy to take data away on a USB drive, by burning a DVD, or even by using e-mail for this purpose. The reality of present-day data mobility in an Internet- and network-connected world is that any data that resides on internal storage devices is at risk.

At Unitas, there has been one confirmed breach to date. The centerpiece of our Fall 2009 collection, John Ruddington's design for an aubergine suede stiletto, was leaked via email by an intern who had secured permanent employment with one of our competitors. The design was then copied and mass produced using quick-to-market manufacturing techniques and inferior materials and fabrication. The security breach was discovered by the intern's supervisor two days after the incident, but it was too late to reverse the damage that had been done. The shoe was featured in the window display of every Rock Bottom Shoes outlet weeks before our design made it to market. Although the discrepancy in quality was appreciable, especially to our discriminating customers, the design had lost much of its cache and sales were sluggish, with projected sales for the product falling flat by slightly over $18,000.

Findings

Companies in a similar position to Unitas' have several options for stemming the flow of data loss through data mobility. The first step is to conduct a loss-prevention audit. A data-protection

(continued)

FIGURE 10.27 (continued)

audit is a systematic and independent examination to determine whether activities involving the processing of personal data are carried out in accordance with an organization's data-protection policies and procedures.

To ensure this process runs smoothly, it will be necessary to encourage and secure the support of all staff. The two loss-prevention auditors I contacted, J & B Associates and Tucker-Bonwit IT Support, estimated that an audit of this kind in a company the size of Unitas would take approximately one week. Our company must also take steps to ensure that we are in full compliance with the Personal Information Protection and Electronic Documents Act (PIPEDA), which establishes laws that regulate the collection, use, and disclosure of personal information by private-sector organizations. For this purpose, we may need to revisit, review, and update our company privacy policy. The audit and any measures that result from it must be in full compliance with data-protection standards. Aims in this process are as follows:

- To assess the level of compliance with all data-protection acts.
- To assess gaps and weaknesses in the data-protection system.
- To provide information for data-protection system review.
- To verify that there is a documented and up-to-date data-protection system in place and that data are protected at rest, in transit, and in use.
- To verify that all staff are aware of the existence of the data-protection system, fully understand it, and know how to use it.

After an audit has been conducted, companies experiencing data loss have several options beyond this, including disabling USB ports and having diskless laptops. The inconvenience and severity of these measures, however, might create significant work-flow issues and cost us the goodwill and morale of Unitas employees.

Companies such as Ferrari have been able to avert losses by deploying the latest version of security software that offers multi-factor authentication, database encryption, a secure virtual perimeter, and disk and file encryption. In a well-publicized case, Ferrari was able to quickly detect a theft of IP when a former employee lifted designs for special gases to be used in the tires of the company's Formula One racing cars. New security software from Verdasys, as used by Ferrari, and other software leaders including McAfee and Digital WatchDog, provides a level of protection not offered by our current security software. To implement a Digital WatchDog 6 security system at Unitas would cost in the range of $10,000 to $15,000 a year, but those costs would be partially offset by a reduction in lost revenue that normally results from data loss.

Conclusion

Although conducting a data-loss audit can cause temporary disruption to workflow and raise concerns among employees that they are under suspicion, this routine activity, along with the upgrading of data-loss prevention software that secures data across the connected enterprise, significantly reduces the threat of data loss. At this time, I ask for your authorization to initiate this process by conducting a search for a data-loss prevention auditor.

Summary Reports

Managers and other decision-makers must have a full understanding of an issue before they can formulate a solution to the issued-related problem. To do this, they must have access to clear, credible, and concise information that can help them grasp the fundamentals of an issue quickly and easily. Without the time to review quantities of information on their own, busy managers rely on well-prepared summaries that put key facts and opinions at their fingertips.

Writing a summary report involves careful analysis of source documents, such as journal and newspaper articles, and the ability to distinguish essential information from amplifying material. To write a summary report that accurately reflects the organization and emphasis of the original article, follow these steps:

- **Scan, then carefully read, the source material.** Scan the article for its general topic and overall organization, then read it carefully and identify its central ideas. Underline significant facts. Studying keywords and headings can provide important clues to the information that may be most vital to your summary.
- **Decide what you can do without.** Eliminate amplifying material. Try to condense the material to one-third to one-fifth the length of the original—or less, if possible.
- **Use underlined points to create a draft of your summary.** Hold to the structure of the original material but use your own words and add transitional expressions to make the sentences in your draft fit together. Do not introduce new material that was not in the original article or document.
- **Add introductory and closing remarks that provide context.** Indicate the title and author of the source material and offer to provide further information as needed.

ANALYTICAL REPORTS

Learning to write informational reports is good preparation for the greater challenges of analytical reports. Whereas informational reports emphasize the presentation of facts, analytical reports pass on information with the intent of persuading readers to follow a specific course of action—or recommendation—that is supported by the reasoning of the report's findings and conclusions. Because analytical reports are persuasive, they must be organized strategically based on the reader's probable resistance or receptivity to the proposed plan. A good plan that is presented too quickly—before the reader can see the reasoning behind it—can spark a negative reaction. An indirect writing plan, with its more gradual approach to recommendation-making, can sometimes help readers see the logic of a recommendation they might have been ready to reject.

The "analysis" in an analytical report is focused on how to solve a specific organizational problem.

- Which health insurance package should our company choose?
- Should we open an overseas branch?
- Which brand and model of laser printer should our company purchase?

There are several different types of analytical reports—justification/recommendation reports, feasibility reports, and comparison/yardstick reports—each organized to answer a specific type of question.

Problem Statements, Problem Questions, and Purpose Statements

An effective business report, in its organized presentation of facts, functions in a very specific way: to answer questions and to solve one or more real and significant problems. Identifying the problem the report is meant to document and solve is a first step in approaching the writing task. This simple step allows you to

- understand what the real problem is (e.g., *Are a clothing retailer's declining profits due to high overhead, poor customer service or inventory control, or ineffective marketing?*);
- narrow the problem down so that it is solvable in the available time; and
- ensure that you have the right data and evidence to document the problem and make recommendations that lead to a solution.

Problem statements are most effective when they are unambiguous and precisely defined:

Problem Statement: A recent breach of online security has forced Ridgeway Products to move from one-factor authentication to two-factor authentication practices in order to ensure the greatest possible security of company and customer data. Ridgeway must decide on the safest and most convenient type of two-factor authentication.

Problem Question: What type of two-factor authentication should Ridgeway Products use to ensure the highest degree and most convenient form of online security?

Problem Statement: The cost of maintaining a fully-staffed human resources department at First Rate Financial has soared in the past five years. First Rate must determine if the outsourcing of some HR functions, such as payroll, would be a cost-effective solution.

Problem Question: Could First Rate Financial reduce HR functions by outsourcing functions such as payroll?

The type of problem question that is asked determines the type of analytical report (recommendation, feasibility, yardstick) that must be written in order to propose a solution.

- **Recommendation report:** *What should we do to increase efficiency of our printers?*
- **Feasibility report:** *Should we expand our customer base by introducing a line of products that appeals to teens?*
- **Yardstick report:** *Which of three proposed options would enable APL Technologies to upgrade its file servers?*

Once the problem has been analyzed and written down, it can be crafted into a concise purpose statement that helps to bring focus and perspective to the project or investigation and serves as a reminder of what the report is meant to accomplish. An effective purpose statement sets out clear action-specific objectives (for example, *to investigate, analyze, compare, evaluate,* or *recommend*) and notes organizational conflicts, challenges, and technical problems the report must address:

Purpose Statement: To investigate a possible reduction in HR costs through the outsourcing of certain functions, such as payroll, at First Rate Financial.

The more complex a report, the more elaborate a purpose statement can be in describing the scope, limitations, and importance of the investigation the report documents:

- **Scope**—What are the factors or issues to be explored? What is the amount of detail to be presented?
- **Limitations**—Do any special standards or conditions (budgetary, technical, geographical, or logistical difficulties, or limits on time or resources) apply to the investigation? How might those conditions affect the findings and how broadly they apply to the situation?
- **Importance**—Why is it important that this problem be solved right now? Can the problem be solved? How severe is the problem?

These additional factors, supported by specific, quantifiable facts (how much? when?), contribute to a more detailed purpose statement:

Detailed Purpose Statement: The purpose of this report is to investigate the outsourcing of certain HR functions, such as payroll, as a means of reducing HR costs at First Rate Financial. The report will compare costs for four human resources service providers. It will also poll employee reaction to proposed outsourcing of payroll services and determine the effect of HR downsizing on company morale. The study is significant, as contracts for four of the five current payroll specialists are due to expire at the end of the fiscal year and outsourcing payroll services could reduce costs, which increased by more than 25 per cent since 2007. The study is limited to payroll costs and outsourcing in the Central division.

The Justification/Recommendation Report

Justification and recommendation reports are persuasive documents, submitted within a company, that make suggestions for new or improved facilities, equipment, processes, capital appropriations or organizational change. Because their purpose, like that of proposals, is to advocate or argue for a specific course of action, justification and recommendation reports are sometimes known as internal proposals. Reports of this kind must first establish that a problem exists. Then they persuasively and objectively build a case based on complete, accurate, and relevant evidence to show how the proposed course of action represents a viable and beneficial solution to the report problem.

While some organizations have a prescribed form for recommendation reports, in most other cases writers can choose from two strategic writing plans depending on the sensitiveness of the topic and the receptiveness of the audience to the proposed plan. Topics that are unlikely to upset readers or raise objections can be approached directly. More sensitive topics and recommendations that readers might oppose require an indirect approach that minimizes resistance by persuading readers of the benefits of a plan before asking for action.

A direct writing plan frontloads both the report problem and the recommendation for a solution to that problem. Here are the steps in organizing a direct plan recommendation report:

- Describe the problem—and establish that it needs a solution; provide any background information the reader might need for decision-making.
- Offer a solution to the problem or announce the recommendation.
- Explain the benefits of the plan, supported by evidence.
- Discuss potential drawbacks and costs and justify expenditures. Compare possible alternatives.
- Summarize the benefits of the recommended action. Express willingness to provide additional information if it is required.

How far writers can go in making recommendations and expressing opinions depends on what their organizations have authorized them to do in preparing their reports.

An indirect writing plan can help writers win over cautious or reluctant audiences. Its strategic approach moves more gradually towards a well-supported recommendation—the strongest option that has first been shown to be logical and better than all the other alternatives:

- Indicate the problem but avoid referring to your recommendation in the subject line.
- Open with a clear, credible, and compelling description of the problem; persuasively establish that the problem is serious, significant, and in need of a solution; provide an overview of data-collection methods and report organization.
- Discuss alternative solutions strategically, from least to most effective. Weigh the pros and cons of each and provide cost comparisons when needed.
- Present the most viable alternative—the option you intend to recommend—last. Describe its benefits and show how its advantages outweigh its disadvantages. Evidence presented should support your conclusion and recommendation.
- Summarize your findings and announce your recommendation; if appropriate, ask for authorization to proceed.

Figure 10.28 contains a sample direct recommendation report based on the following situation. Chain-wide sales of cosmetics, grooming products, and over-the-counter medicines at Wellness Drug Mart have been sluggish over the past year, even during high-traffic periods. The assistant marketing manager proposes that a pilot-project be implemented at one of its under-performing pharmacies to test the use of an on-site paging system that would encourage customers who would otherwise remain in line at the dispensary to browse the store and make additional purchases. Because the plan is low cost and easy to implement, the writer expects little resistance and has decided to use a direct writing plan.

FIGURE 10.28 Recommendation Report: Direct Writing Plan

Wellness Drug-Mart

DATE: July 6, 2010   ←———— Applies memo format for internal report

TO: Julie Marco, Vice President

FROM: Havier Perez, Assistant Marketing Manager *HP*

SUBJECT: CONVERTING STORE TRAFFIC INTO RETAIL SALES

A busy store is usually a sign of healthy sales. Although traffic flow throughout ←———— Introduces report problem
our retail pharmacies continues to be high, in the past year the conversion of
browsing into sales has dropped by a rate of 12 per cent. Customers pass through
the doors of our stores and wait in line by the dispensary while their prescriptions
are filled but do not make purchases additional to their medicine orders.

In-store polls have indicated that customers standing in line are dissatisfied with
the amount of time spent waiting. Recent store performance reviews showed,
however, that Wellness Drug Mart customers wait no longer than 15 minutes on
average for their prescriptions to be filled. This misconception of external wait
times is a common one. A recent retail study found that people standing in line
perceive that they spend more time waiting than they actually do. To reduce the
perception of extended wait times and to encourage customers to buy as well as
browse or wait in line, I recommend that we do the following:

- Purchase 10 pagers as part of an on-site paging system.   ←———— Reveals recommendation immediately

- Conduct a six-month pilot test on pager use and its effect on sales in our
  underperforming Woodburn Avenue store.

How On-site Paging Systems Work

Pagers, including a range of models developed by market-leader Beckon Inc., ←———— Explains the product and its use
have been used in the restaurant industry for nearly 15 years. These compact,
battery-powered, rechargeable devices allow restaurant patrons the freedom
to step out of line and go outside or to the lounge area of the restaurant while
they wait for their tables. The device vibrates, flashes, or glows to alert patrons
that their table is ready. Loss of pagers due to theft or forgetfulness is minimal
because an anti-theft, auto-locate tracking mode pages continually until the
device is returned.

This technology has recently been adopted by Bargainers Drug Mart Inc. to
encourage customers to browse more throughout the store while they wait.
Pharmacy customers at Bargainers now have greater control over how they spend
their time in the store until their medicine order is ready.

(continued)

FIGURE 10.28 (continued)

An on-site paging system, similar to ones used by restaurants and our competitors, is a relatively low-cost and low-maintenance solution. The number of paging units required can be determined by dividing the average wait time in minutes by 1.5. A five-pack of pagers is priced at $279.72. Beckon specializes in pharmacy paging systems. Consumer guides rate its products as the most durable on the market. The devices operate on a UHF FM frequency (420-470 MHz) within a two-mile range. They are powered by low-cost nickel-metal hydride batteries and battery life is 48 hours on a single charge. Only a limited number of pagers would have to be purchased.

How an On-site Paging System Could Benefit Us

Lists benefits for readability and emphasis →

An on-site paging system, requiring 10 pagers, would help us improve customer service and encourage sales in three ways:

1. **Minimized wait times.** A paging system would allow customers the freedom to browse without the fear of losing their place in line. The time customers would have spent waiting they can spend the way they want to, with less potential for boredom. Time spent productively should help reduce the perception of long wait times.

2. **Increased customer conversion rates.** Customers can shop while they wait. In-store traffic should result in higher sales and a better browsing-to-buying conversion rate.

3. **Improved customer service.** Impatient customers waiting for their prescriptions to be filled frequently interrupt staff pharmacists to ask about the status of the medicine orders. These interruptions result in service errors and slowdowns and can compromise the privacy of other customers. A paging system would boost staff efficiency so that prescriptions could be filled faster and consultations about dosages, drug interactions, and side-effects could be conducted more privately once an order has been filled.

Summary and Action

I recommend that you do the following:

Gives specific details of the actions to be taken →

- Authorize the purchase of 10 Beckon pagers at $279.72 per five-pack, along with a transmitter and charger package priced at $345.97.

- Approve a six-month pilot test of the paging system in our downtown Calgary location that provides pharmacy customers with guest pagers and tracks the conversion rate of store traffic to sales.

Enclosure

Figure 10.29 contains a sample indirect recommendation report based on the following situation. The report is organized indirectly because its purchase recommendation requires employees to learn about and adapt to new technology—a colour digital press that lithographers at this mid-sized print shop might not have the training to be able to use. The writer of this report chooses to present a less effective alternative first in order to build support for an alternative that represents a superior solution to the problem of lost contracts for short-turnaround projects.

FIGURE 10.29 Recommendation Report: Indirect Writing Plan

BASKERVILLE Printing

Inter-office Memo

DATE: October 18, 2010

TO: Austin Wilson, Vice President

FROM: Mirella Herzig, Production Manager *MH*

SUBJECT: MEETING HIGH-VOLUME PRINTING DEMANDS ◄——————— Subject line highlights benefits without referring to the recommendation

At your request, I have examined methods of increasing printing output and ◄——— Identifies the report purpose and data collection methods
reducing turnaround time while maintaining current quality standards and colour printing capabilities. To carry out this study, I have consulted industry associations and reviewed professional publications; I also networked with industry contacts outside the GTA about their output systems.

This report presents data documenting the severity and significance of the ◄——— Previews report organization
problem, two alternative solutions, and a recommendation based on my analysis.

Significance of Problem: Lack of Speed and Flexibility Results in Losses

Until recently, our offset lithographic environment has been effective in ◄——— Establishes the scope and significance of the report problem
driving volume; however, since late 2009 our company has not been equipped to meet the increasing demand for short-run work, such as real estate books and stock prospectuses, which now accounts for 65 per cent of our business. Due to slow turnarounds on short-run rush jobs, many of our longtime customers are reluctantly turning to our competitors for quicker delivery and overnight service. Revenues for the first and second quarters of 2010 were down by 15 per cent from the same period in 2009, in part due to the loss of accounts for short-run business.

Another source of customer dissatisfaction is a lack of flexibility in the service we provide. Other print shops have the capability of updating large print runs on demand without having to commit to one version for the entire run. When one of our customers inspects advance copies and decides changes are needed, an entire press run, often in excess of 10,000 copies, has to be discarded. Below

(continued)

FIGURE 10.29 (continued)

Vice President Wilson	2	October 18, 2010

are two solutions other print shops have implemented to reduce turnaround times and eliminate waste.

Alternative 1: Purchase a Reconditioned Offset Press

The option that would present the fewest changes to workflow involves the purchase of an offset press, ideally one of a new generation of presses that use computer-plate systems and offer ease of operation, ergonomic design, and quality enhancements. Offset lithography continues to be the most common high-volume commercial printing technology. Offset presses, including the reliable Graumann models we currently use, deliver high image quality, offer the unsurpassed flexibility in the choice of printing medium, and are cost effective for high-volume printing jobs. The front-end cost load of offset printing reduces the unit cost as the size of the print run increases. As a result, customers are eligible for substantial volume-based discounts.

Other key advantages of offset technology include limited downtime and low costs for maintenance. Lithographic equipment rarely breaks down. Service calls are infrequent because veteran operators can usually troubleshoot and fix certain offset problems. A workforce like our own that is already accustomed to offset technology and familiar with the existing offset infrastructure could be quickly and easily trained, at minimal cost, to use a slightly more advanced lithographic press of similar design to ones already in the pressroom.

Although customers appreciate the quality and cost-effectiveness offset offers on high-volume jobs, they are generally dissatisfied with extended delivery time and high unit costs for short runs. The purchase of an offset press might help to drive up overall volume, but it would not address the shortfall in short-run capability we are currently experiencing. Although cheaper models are available, the most reliable offset presses offering the greatest flexibility are expensive. Purchasing a slightly older or reconditioned model would reduce costs. The price range listed below is typical.

Cost range: $65,000 to $110,00 for a one-colour to five-colour Graumann Printmeister GTO 52 offset press

Alternative 2: Purchase a Colour Digital Press

A less expensive, long-term solution is to purchase a colour digital press. A digital press is a computer-controlled device. Unlike an offset press, it is plateless and uses electrostatic toner instead of ink to image virtual printing forms (Henry, 2007, p. 1). In digital printing, many of the mechanical steps required for conventional printing, such as colour proofs and films, are eliminated, and less drying time is required. Digital presses have quick turnaround on short-run jobs, and as a result attract their own volumes.

Marginal annotations:

Desribes the less effective alternative first

Evaluates alternative objectively

Arranges alternatives strategically, with the most effective last

FIGURE 10.29 (continued)

Vice President Wilson   3   October 18, 2010

Digital capability allows commercial users to load a project file received via the Internet, print a proof, run the job, and trim the sheets in under an hour. The benefits for printers include reduced setup costs for small press runs and easy customization of pieces such as client brochures and letterhead. Electronic updating is possible on demand, even in the middle of a press run. Digital presses also take the guesswork and ambiguity out of achieving colour consistency and now offer an almost unrestricted selection of sheet sizes, including sheets as large as 14×20 inches.

Although digital presses may be offline more frequently for maintenance, good vendor support can minimize lost production time. The cost of consumable items such as image drums may add to operation and unit costs, but industry specialists advise that digital-press purchasers should negotiate an all-inclusive click rate that reflects the actual cost of maintenance, parts, labour, and supplies. Lithographers who make the transition to digital print production can expect to spend up to six months phasing in the new technology and integrating it with their current workflow (Henry, 2007, p. 4).

Cost: $10,000 for Xylon's GraphX digital press, with 36 ppm colour output and 40 ppm black-and-white output

Conclusions and Recommendations

Our print shop built its reputation on a guarantee of speedy delivery and quick turnarounds. The majority of our business, which comes from real estate and brokerage houses, depends on the continued capability of our shop to provide quality, cost-effective services for multi-format, high-volume print jobs and short-run work. If our goal is to genuinely do the most that we can for our customers, we should embrace a combination of technologies and integrate digital output systems into our offset environment. Done well, the work that digital capability would help to recapture could qualify our company for more offset jobs and make our business a one-stop source for the printing services that customers demand the most. Although the integration of digital technology will involve workflow adjustments and start-up training, it will help our business stay competitive and secure the last-minute jobs we might miss without the addition of this technology.

I recommend that we purchase a digital press within the next three months. With your approval, I will investigate possible printer options for our company based on brand name, cost, required features, run length, maintenance, and environmental factors.

Links need to recommended solution

Summarizes findings and gives reasons for making recommendation

Reveals recommendation based on logic of findings and conclusions

References

Henry, P. (2007, March). Going digital, staying lithographic. *American Printer*, 1–8.

The Feasibility Report

Any new project, from the purchase of new equipment and consolidation of departments to the development of products and services, involves risk and the possibility that the project may fail or not work out as expected. Before undertaking a new project, organizations must determine the project's chances for success based on whether it is possible or practical, economically wise and viable, and consistent with internal and public perception of the organization. Feasibility reports present evidence on the advisability of doing a project or proceeding with a specific course of action. Does it make good business sense? Is it right for the company? Is it practical and workable according to certain criteria? Can the company afford the costs involved? Feasibility reports answer these types of questions based on specific criteria and careful analysis. Managers rely on the evidence and advice feasibility reports present in order to make the decision about whether to commit resources and go ahead with a project. Because managers most want to know if a plan or project is do-able, feasibility reports use a direct writing plan to announce the decision first:

- **Opening paragraph:** identifies the plan and reveals your decision/recommendation about it; offers an overview of the report.
- **Introduction/Background:** describes the problem or circumstances that led to the report and discusses the scope, methods, and limitations of the study and the amount of data that could be collected to answer the feasibility question.
- **Discussion:** in logical sequence, presents a detailed analysis of the benefits and risks of the plan along with other positive and negatives factors, a calculation of costs, and a schedule for implementation; when appropriate, presents graphical elements to support data and interpret the results.
- **Conclusions:** summarizes data and significant findings.

The report in Figure 10.30 assesses the feasibility of converting an unused side-lot and an office storage room into space that employees of a publishing house could use for lounging and recreation. The recent construction of a large distribution centre at the same location has deprived employees of a grassy area they once used as a place to eat and relax in good weather. With additional staff returning from an offsite distribution centre and joining the workforce at head office, the lunchroom will no longer accommodate the full staff during the busy lunchtime period. The report is presented in e-mail format.

FIGURE 10.30 Feasibility Report

Feasibility of Side-lot and Storage Room Conversions

From:	Devon Andrews-Smith <andrewssmith@baskerville.ca>
Date:	January 12, 2010 1:15 p.m.
To:	<rdelgado@baskerville.ca>
Subject:	Feasibility of Side-lot and Storage Room Conversions
Attach:	General Contractor Assessment.doc

Hi Mr. Delgado,

The proposed conversion of a 200-square-metre side-lot and interior storage room to replace lost recreational and lunchroom space is workable. It is possible to fully execute the plan by the end of May, when the 15 full- and part-time staff members currently working at our leased off-site facility transfer to our Markham location. This report discusses the background, benefits, problems, costs, and time-frame associated with the implementation of this plan. *[Announces the decision immediately / Outlines report organization]*

Background: Inadequate Lounge Facilities and Loss of Lawn Space. The construction of our new on-site distribution centre has brought immediate and long-term benefits, including the single-site consolidation of shipping and receiving operations, improved inventory management, and a quadrupling of our storage capacity to 700,000 units. Because this 10,000-square-metre facility now occupies a former green space where employees gathered in good weather for lunch and coffee breaks, staff members are now without a designated outdoor recreational space and have no option but to eat and socialize inside. The result has been an overcrowding of our 30-seat lunchroom. The lunchroom simply cannot accommodate our 70-member staff during the peak noon to 2:00 p.m. period. *[Discusses the problem and background to the report]*

This problem of overcrowding will likely become more severe as the remaining 15 staff members at our leased Vaughn facility relocate to our main office and distribution centre over the next three months. These problems were factored in to an assessment carried out by outside general contracting consultants, who indicated that the structural soundness of our office building would permit relatively low-cost renovations.

Benefits of the Plan: The proposed plan calls for (1) the creation of a combined green space and patio space through the re-sodding and landscaping of a partially-paved, 200-square-metre side-lot currently used for overflow parking and (2) the enlargement of the staff lunchroom through the removal of a drywall partition that separates the lunchroom from Storage Room B, followed by the interior redecoration and lighting redesign of the 10 × 14 metre space. The plan proposes practical repurposing of under-utilized space on our premises. One of the objectives in bringing all staff on site, instead of having them in two locations, was *[Describes the advantages and disadvantages of the proposed plan]*

(continued)

FIGURE 10.30 (continued)

⌂ Feasibility of Side-lot and Storage Room Conversions   _ □ ✕

From:	Devon Andrews-Smith <andrewssmith@baskerville.ca>
Date:	January 12, 2010 1:15 p.m.
To:	<rdelgado@baskerville.ca>
Subject:	Feasibility of Side-lot and Storage Room Conversions
Attach:	General Contractor Assessment.doc

to promote collaboration and goodwill in the workplace by alleviating the malaise and isolation experienced by offsite workers. Providing attractive and functional indoor and outdoor spaces in which staff can socialize will help to improve morale and working conditions and contribute to the maintenance of good professional relationships between office and warehouse staff.

Problems of the Plan: Loss of Overflow Parking, Work Disruptions, and Safety Hazards.
A foreseeable problem will be compensating for the loss of three overflow parking spaces that are generally unused, but which may be needed as more staff members are brought on site. With the re-appropriation of ten of the current twenty spaces reserved for visitor parking, I expect that the shortage of staff parking could be eliminated with limited inconvenience to our customers, suppliers, and visiting authors.

Another problem is ensuring a safe and healthy working environment while the indoor remodelling is carried out. Noise from interior demolition and remodelling may disrupt employees in adjacent areas while they work; fumes from paint, drywall compound, and other chemical agents may present a hazard to office employees and result in downtime. In compliance with the Occupational Health and Safety Act, we expect to conduct periodic environmental assessments to monitor hazard levels and confine most construction activities to weekends and after-hours.

Presents costs and schedule →
Costs. Implementing this plan involves direct, one-time costs for landscape design, interior design, construction and landscaping material, fixtures and furnishings, building permits, and general contracting. Barring any structural weakness in our building, the costs involved are within the $80,000 estimate for the project.

Time Frame. Drafting a request for proposals and initiating the bidding on contracts for remodelling and landscaping projects should take us about one week. With time allowed for project development and the submission of bids, the review process will take another five weeks. Once construction begins, I expect that the remodelling and landscaping work will take at least two months. By July 1 the plan for expanded and upgraded indoor and outdoor recreational space will be fully implemented, with benefits for employee morale and work environment.

The Comparison/Yardstick Report

Yardstick is a term that describes a standard for comparison. A yardstick report compares and evaluates two or more solutions to a single problem to find the best solution or it weighs several options for acting on an opportunity. The report begins by establishing criteria—standards by which all options can be measured fairly and consistently. Criteria can take several forms: they can be dictated by management (for example, cost limits) or they can emerge from the study research. Some criteria are necessary (*need to have*) while other criteria are simply desirable (*nice to have*). Once identified, the criteria used for measuring the options can be followed by an explanation of how the criteria were selected. The criteria can also be used as bolded headings in the body of the report, where information for each category is weighed and presented. Conclusions are drawn about each option.

A report using a yardstick approach answers the question "Which option is best?" To make sure readers understand the reasons for choosing one option over another, writers can organize their information in the following order:

- Identify the problem, need, or opportunity that led to the report.
- Determine the options for solving the problem or alternatives for realizing the opportunity.
- Establish the criteria for the comparison of options; explain how the criteria were selected.
- Discuss each option according to the criteria; draw inferences from the data and make an evaluation of each option
- Draw conclusions by ranking all the options or classifying options into *acceptable/unacceptable* categories. Consider if the problem, company resources, or priorities have recently changed in a way that might affect the conclusions.
- Make recommendations based on the findings and conclusions.

Figure 10.31 presents a comparison report based on the following situation. An established telecommunications company, Instanet Inc., plans to hire an agency specializing in the management of corporate events. To showcase the organization to maximum effect and build relationships with employees and investors through its corporate functions, Instanet must first determine which among several well-respected firms can deliver the services it needs in a way that is appropriate to the company image.

FIGURE 10.31 Comparison Report

DATE: July 6, 2010

TO: Mike Vizcarra, Vice President

FROM: Manon Dupuis, Public Relations Director *MD*

SUBJECT: CHOICE OF CORPORATE EVENT PLANNING SERVICES

Introduces purpose and provides overview of report organization →

At your request, I have investigated the possibility of Instanet hiring full-service event planners to strategically develop and produce its corporate functions and new product launches. This report discusses current problems with the standard, planning and hosting of corporate events and sets out criteria for the selection of a corporate-event management company that would best enable Instanet to meet its marketing goals and build client and employee relationships. The report assesses three prospective corporate-event companies in the Greater Toronto Area and makes a recommendation based on that assessment.

Problem: Producing Memorable Corporate Functions and Events

Identifies problem and discusses background →

With the goal of increasing its profile and enhancing its relationship with stakeholders and the general public, Instanet initiated a program of unique and innovative corporate functions in 2006 that to date has included golf tournaments, merger events, and gala dinners. With our company's recent merger, the scale of these events will increase and demand a higher level of logistical support and coordination than can be provided by our current team of dedicated staff volunteers. Costs to produce these large events may be significantly higher. As a result, Instanet must ensure that its corporate events meet strategic goals, minimize potential liability, and bring expected returns on investments. Staging our events safely, successfully, and memorably will help us to attract investors and set us apart from the competition.

Solution and Alternatives: Corporate-Event Management Companies

Combines functional and descriptive headings →

Presents a solution and options for its implementation →

Event management firms provide strategic development and logistics services to corporations, non-profit associations, governments, and social groups in the hosting of events and activities that reward employees, celebrate milestones, facilitate communication with stakeholdlers, aid in fundraising, and increase an organization's profile. While some corporate-event management firms specialize in one specific type of event, such as conferences, others offer a wide range of services. Instanet requires a full-service management firm with the expertise, artistry, and precise logistical capabilities to produce many different kinds of events.

FIGURE 10.31 (continued)

Vice President Vizcarra   2   July 6, 2010

Our priority is to find an event management firm that will perform event strategy assessment specific to our company and tailor events to our company image. As our mission statement upholds a firm commitment to accountability, accessibility, and diversity, our company events and choice of an event management firm should reflect these standards. I have identified three prospective full-service event management companies in the GTA that can deliver services that meet our marketing and corporate culture needs: Boudreau & Hodges, The Unique Event Group, and Encore Events.

Determining Selection Criteria

The criteria I used to make my selection among the three firms is based on government publications, professional articles, a web search of event management sites, interviews with officials at certification agencies and at companies using event management services, and conversations with the prospective service providers. The following are three categories of criteria I used to evaluate the management firms:

Outlines criteria and explains how criteria were selected

1. Event management services—including catering and décor coordination; training of speakers and volunteers; accommodation, venue, and entertainment booking; VIP hosting; audio-visual production; development of substantive sessions for conferences; and media liaison, promotion, and public relations communications.

2. Reputation—as assessed according to professional association listings, professional certifications, testimonials from past and current clients, and telephone interviews with known clients.

3. Costs—for management and consultancy services.

Discussion: Criteria-Based Evaluation of Event Management Firms

The following table summarizes comparison data on the services and reputation of each of the three firms.

(continued)

FIGURE 10.31 (continued)

Vice President Vizcarra   3   July 6, 2010

Table 1

A COMPARISON OF SERVICES AND REPUTATION FOR THREE
TORONTO-AREA CORPORATE-EVENT MANAGEMENT FIRMS

	Boudreau & Hodges	The Unique Event Group	Encore Events
Event strategy assessment	Yes	Yes	Yes
Venue/entertainment selection	Yes	Yes	Yes
Training of volunteers	Yes	No	No
Catering coordination	Yes	No	No
Management of hosting activities	Yes	Yes	Yes
Marketing promotional assistance	Yes	Yes	Yes
Selection of promotional gifts	Yes	No	No
Coordination of A/V production	Yes	Yes	Yes
Media liaison	Yes	Yes	No
Canadian Special Events Society certification	Yes	Yes	No
Certified protocol officer	Yes	No	No
Reputation (by survey of clients)	Excellent	Good	Fair

Event Management Services

Services offered by all three firms were comparable, with the exception of the recently launched Encore Events. The companies differed in the way they outsourced essential services and employed part-time staff.

The Unique Event Group and Encore Events do not have resident hospitality and catering experts or protocol officers, and they typically outsource all catering functions to third parties. Companies that have used services of this kind report that this catering arrangement can bring inconsistent results, with hit-and-miss menu selections and cost-overruns. Without a protocol officer, whom etiquette experts agree is essential to the success of high-profile VIP functions, any of our company events that include dignitaries or participation from other countries or levels of government would be subject to embarrassing breaches of protocol in

---

Summarizes data for conciseness and readability

Compares and contrasts alternatives

FIGURE 10.31 (continued)

Vice President Vizcarra   4   July 6, 2010

the areas specified in Heritage Canada's Protocol Checklist: http://www.pch.gc.ca/
progs/cpsc-ccsp/pe/list_e.cfm. Boudreau & Hodges employs a graduate of the
Western School of Protocol and a Cordon Bleu chef who oversees menu theme
development.

Encore Events does not currently have the resources to employ full-time event
managers. Instanet would need assurances that Encore Events could provide a
consistent level of service and support with its part-time staff; otherwise, Encore
Events is better suited to producing small-scale conferences and seminars, which
it can support with its exceptional technical services including a dedicated
audio-visual department, on-site graphics department, and online conference
registration.

Reputation

To evaluate the reputation of each event management company, I consulted its
membership listing with the Canadian Special Events Society (CSES), a non-profit
organization that represents the interests of the Special Events Industry in Canada
and offers a certification program. Both Boudreau & Hodges and The Unique
Event Group are members but Encore Events is not. Boudreau & Hodges and The
Unique Event Group are also members of the Toronto Chamber of Commerce.

In surveying recent client feedback and summaries of event experience, I found
that each firm caters to a specific and decidedly different clientele. Encore Events
specializes in providing services to start-up companies defined by an urban,
under-40 demographic and chooses unconventional locations such as industrial
warehouses as event venues. The Unique Event Group has special expertise in
staging exhibits, shows, and awards galas in the arts community and fashion
industry. Boudreau & Hodges is a service provider to publicly listed corporations,
similar to Instanet, and has produced federal summits and dinners hosted by the
prime minister.

In assembling further evidence of each firm's reputation, I conducted telephone
surveys to determine the degree of client satisfaction with services received.
Client names and numbers were supplied to me on request by the event
planning firms. For the sake of consistency, I telephoned three former clients
of each firm and asked the same questions in each case. Most of the company
officials I spoke with were satisfied with the services they had received.

(continued)

FIGURE 10.31 (continued)

Costs

The fees schedules for all three firms are summarized in Table 2, which sets out a comparison of costs for planning and consultancy. Other fees, for catering and venue booking, are on a sliding scale based on the type of event, location, and number of guests or registrants.

While all three companies guarantee value-added services and respect for client budgets, Boudreau & Hodges has the highest fees but also offers the most flexible work arrangements, including the outsourcing of staff on a monthly retainer basis. Because Boudreau & Hodges and Encore Events pass on professional discounts to their clients, their somewhat higher consulting fees may not necessarily translate to higher overall budgets.

Refers to data from table →

Table 2

A COMPARISON OF COSTS FOR PLANNING SERVICES

	Boudreau & Hodges	The Unique Event Group	Encore Events
Event strategy assessment (one time)	$1,800/session	$1,400/session	$1,700/session
Project manager	$175/hr	$150/hr	$190/hr

Conclusions and Recommendations

Eliminates less effective alternatives from consideration →

Although Encore Events has a dedicated signage and graphics department that enables it to produce event signage at reduced costs, it does not offer flexible pricing options and is not listed as a member of the Canadian Special Events Society. These deficiencies make it a less viable option; therefore, the choice is between Boudreau & Hodges and The Unique Event Group. As both companies offer similar services and charge comparable management fees, the deciding factors are reputation and markups on third-party disbursements. Boudreau &

Narrows the choice →

Hodges has an experienced staff with protocol training and background in planning innovative, large-scale events on local and national levels for FP Top-100 companies. It stands by a commitment to pass on all professional discounts to clients. The Unique Event Group, on the other hand, has a younger, hipper image but a less business-oriented client list, and it may be more expensive because it does not disclose the discounts it receives on outsourced services. Therefore, I recommend that Instanet hire Boudreau & Hodges to plan and produce its corporate events.

Checklist for Informal Reports

Format and Design

☐ Is the format of your report appropriate to the purpose and audience?

☐ Are headings, white space, and graphic highlighting techniques used to enhance content and improve readability? Are headings consistently parallel?

☐ Does the subject line, if one is used, summarize the topic(s) of the report or encourage reader receptivity?

☐ Is information organized for easy comprehension and retention and adapted to meet readers' needs?

Informational Report

☐ Does your report answer a specific question? Is the purpose of your report made clear in the opening paragraph? Does your report begin directly? Does your report supply sufficient background information to bring the reader up to speed?

☐ Is information arranged logically and methodically? Is information divided into subtopics?

☐ Are the tone and style appropriate to the audience?

☐ Does your report include a summary or an offer of further information?

Analytical Report

☐ Is your report organized strategically, according to a direct or indirect writing plan? If you expect readers to be receptive, are the conclusions and recommendations summarized at the beginning? If you expect readers to be resistant, are the conclusions and recommendations reserved for the end?

☐ Is the purpose of your report clear? Has the problem you are attempting to solve been fully identified?

☐ Are findings presented in a thorough and logical way? Are findings supported with evidence? Do the findings lead logically to conclusions?

☐ Are the conclusions supported by facts and evidence? Do they relate to the problem identified at the beginning of the report?

☐ Are the recommendations, if they are required, action-specific?

WORKSHOPS AND DISCUSSION FORUMS

1. **Are All Graphics Created Equal?** Collect a sampling of graphs and charts. Good places to start include business publications—the financial pages of daily newspapers (*Report on Business* in the *Globe and Mail* or the *Financial Post* in the *National Post*) and business magazines (*Canadian Business*, *The Economist*, *Report on Business Magazine*, *National Post Business*). Try to find at least one example of each type of graphic. Determine if each graphic is well designed and appropriate for the explanation it supports. Critique the appeal of the graphic (does it add interest? does it make data speak?) and trade opinions on any unusual graphics you may have found.

2. **Match Graphics to Objectives.** In a group or individually, identify the type of graphic you would use to plot the following data. Consider if more than one type of graphic or illustration could be used:

a) figures showing the number of female students enrolled in university engineering programs nationwide over the last five years

b) figures showing an Internet auction company's share price between January 2008 and January 2010

c) figures showing the revenue and earnings for the same company in the years 2008 and 2009 (year ending December 31)

d) a comparison of the revenues of the three divisions of a company from 2004 to 2009

e) figures showing the income of a national doughnut franchise based on its three leading products

f) figures comparing the sales of those three products over the past ten years

g) data showing cities in Canada with the highest rates of obesity

WRITING IMPROVEMENT EXERCISES

1. **Distinguishing between Informational and Analytical Reports.** For each of the following situations, determine if you must write an informational or analytical report:

a) You have just returned from a conference you attended at the expense of your company. Write up the details for your supervisor.

b) As you do every month, you must inform management of the number of customer-service calls you have received and summarize activities and events performed during the report period. Note any irregular events.

c) You have been asked by your employer, Musicmission.com, to recommend three arts-related charities to which the company might consider donating money on an annual basis and to assess the relative merits and needs of each. Conclude your report with a recommendation on the charity your company should select.

d) You have been asked by your boss, the chief of product development, to investigate the feasibility of adding a Senomyx flavouring to your company's canned minestrone soup as a means of reducing salt by up to one-third and eliminating the use of MSG. Pending government approval of the flavour compound, you will examine its potential health effects.

2. **Matching Types of Reports to Situation Descriptions.** Identify the type of report you would write in each of the following cases:

a) A report addressed to your boss identifying a piece of equipment that should be upgraded or replaced.

b) A report requested by your manager providing an overview of smartphones, a subject she knows little about, and how they might be used by appliance sales associates.

c) A report requested by the head of your company's donations committee prospecting four new charities in the fields of education and community service.

3. **Identifying Types of Headings.** From the list of headings below, identify which are descriptive heads and which are functional heads.

a) Costs

b) Personnel

c) Richmond Hill Costs Less

d) Findings

e) The Manufacturing Process

f) Situation 1

g) Survey Shows Support for Software Upgrade

h) Parking Recommendations: Valet Service

4. **Making Subheads Parallel.** Revise the following subheads so that they all use the same grammatical structure.

> New Challenges for Human Resources Management
>> Providing Employees with Disabilities with the Tools to Succeed
>> We Must Adjust to Older Employees
>> Can We Accommodate Employees Involved in Family Care?
>> Dealing with Intermittent Absences Caused by Chronic Conditions

5. **Differentiating between Conclusions and Recommendations.** Indicate whether each of the following statements could be labelled as a conclusion or a recommendation.

a) Sites A and B are not viable because they are located in the suburbs and lack access to major highways.

b) Choose Site C, which offers direct access to major highways and a growing market in the downtown core.

c) Archway Company should review the current benefits package.

d) Develop an online marketing campaign.

e) A two-factor authentication system can be fully implemented by the end of 2011.

6. **Graphics: From Verbal to Visual.** For each of the following explanations, design a graphic or illustrations that conveys the data most effectively.

a) From 2004 to 2009 (year ending December 31), annual home-building-supply revenues were as follows: $150M in 2004, $155M in 2005, $187M in 2006, $191M in 2007, $196M in 2008, and $197M in 2009.

b) In preparing the report, your time in both hours and percentages will be used as follows: gathering information (10 hours, or 33.33 per cent of my time); analyzing information (4 hours, or 13.33 per cent); preparing a recommendation report (3 hours, or 10 per cent); writing a draft (5 hours, or 16.66 per cent); revising the draft (2 hours, or 6.66 per cent); typing and editing the report (6 hours, or 20 per cent).

c) Figure 1 shows the percentage of students, faculty, staff, and administrators who participated in the survey: students (63 per cent), faculty (22 per cent), staff (9 per cent), and administrators (6 per cent).

d) Figure 5 shows the annual ratio of sales closings to sales calls, by sales representative: Lauren McAllister (80:102); Rosa Santorini (76:105); Jorge Diaz (95:107).

7. **Graphics: From Visual to Verbal.** For each of the following graphics, write a brief explanation to support it.

a)

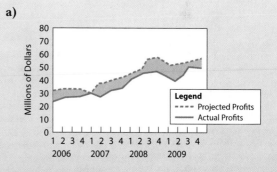

b) **Cellular Subscribers per Capita, 2009**

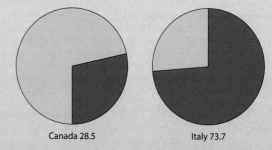

Canada 28.5   Italy 73.7

c) **Top 5 Companies for Loans to Executives and Directors**

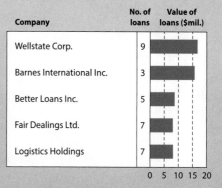

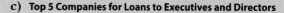

Source: *Canada's Business Magazine*

8. **Graphics: Spotting Design Flaws**. Each of the following graphics contains an error. Can you identify what is wrong in each case?

a) **Undergraduate Enrollment by Faculty**

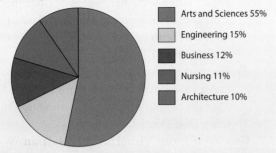

- Arts and Sciences 55%
- Engineering 15%
- Business 12%
- Nursing 11%
- Architecture 10%

b) **Loonie Dives**
DAILY CLOSE, U.S. CENTS

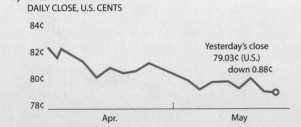

Yesterday's close
79.03¢ (U.S.)
down 0.88¢

84¢
82¢
80¢
78¢
Apr.   May

c) **Transport Truck Accidents**

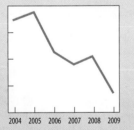

2004 2005 2006 2007 2008 2009

d) **Computer Sales and Leasing by Year**

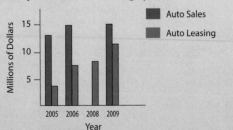

- Auto Sales
- Auto Leasing

Millions of Dollars
15
10
5
2005 2006 2008 2009
Year

9. **Informal Reports: Matching Reports to Situations.** For each of the following situations, identify the type of report you would write and discuss how to organize it.

a) Your team project is to provide an expanded database for the Information Management System (IMS). The IMS has been delayed. The original schedule was based on the assumption that the systems analyst responsible for the project would have no problem with the CNG software. An experienced systems analyst is now correcting the problem and is expected to complete the project within the next month.

b) Your team project is to provide an expanded database for the Information Management System (IMS). Before work on the project begins, you must seek authorization to hire two new engineers familiar with the system.

c) Your company's training manager has asked you to seek information about the basic english program that was adopted by Rix Technologies. You have been asked to assess whether some or all of the Rix program elements could be applied to the production of an employee manual at your company.

10. **Analyzing and revising problem questions.** Revise the following problem questions so that they are narrow enough and allow for solutions that can be investigated and implemented within a three-month time frame.

a) What new techniques can Edgeco Industries use to solve the problem of waste disposal?

b) How can Reverb Electronics market its products to teens?

c) What are the best businesses to invest in in developing countries?

d) How can the university improve student services?

e) What initiatives should the municipality undertake to build a greener, more sustainable community before next year's election?

11. **Writing problem statements and purpose statements.** Write a problem statement, purpose statement, and, if applicable, a detailed purpose statement for the following report situations:

a) Avatar Entertainment, which operates and has interest in 448 theatres across Canada, relies on timely access to information to make critical business decisions. Finding and sharing critical information, however, has become a complicated and difficult task. Without an integrated IT strategy, Avatar currently runs multiple back-end systems, each with different user interfaces. Employees looking for information often have to employ different search criteria based on the system they are searching within. Avatar wonders if having a single portal for its IT structure might help improve search functionality and make it easier for users to find, use, and share critical information.

b) Elegance Bridal Studio has been a retail clothing specialist offering a range of bridal gowns, veils, and accessories for over forty years in the competitive Toronto market. Elegance is concerned that its traditional fashion sensibility, modest online retail presence, and conservative store image have contributed to a gradual decline in sales since 2008. It is now September, with the highest volume of sales typically falling between January and June. Elegance Bridal Studio must act quickly if it hopes to win back sales during this important period.

c) Over the past year, operations at Arcan Investment Solutions have been compromised by the forced evacuation or physical lockdown of the building that houses its call centre and administrative offices. At one point, an overnight electrical fire in the building's heating system sent thick, acrid smoke billowing into most parts of the facility. The heavy concentration of smoke made the air unbreathable, leading to serious environmental and occupational health and safety concerns. While the company infrastructure was intact and the server rooms were operational, employees were forbidden from entering the building until a full health and safety assessment had been completed and problems caused by residual smoke damage had been corrected. The workforce, which included more than 200 call centre agents, could not be mobilized for two days. Arcan is worried that it will lose even more business if it does not take steps to put a data protection and disaster recovery plan (DRP) in place. Arcan wonders which type of web-based disaster recovery system might be right for the company: a bridging of primary phone lines with cellular phones, a remote access communication system provided by a disaster recovery specialist, or a solution that involves the use of virtual private networks or IP phones that could be quickly shipped to a temporary call centre. Due to the volume of customer complaints that followed the fire-related lockdown, Arcan has decided that it needs to act quickly and budget generously for the implementation of a disaster preparedness plan.

CASE STUDY EXERCISES

1. **Investigative Report—Team-Building Retreat Goes High-Tech:** As assistant coordinator of special events for Salk Pharmaceuticals Inc., you have been asked by the coordinator of special events, Tom Byington, to investigate three different models of GMRS (General Mobile Radio Service) two-way radios with which to equip the five team leaders during your annual three-day team-building wilderness retreat. The radios must be able to work within a range of 8 to 13 kilometres, the distance of many treks and canoe trips. Because teams may be outdoors and away from the conference centre for up to four hours at a time, the radios must have a long battery life. You have learned of three reliable brands: the Corsair PR3100-2D (unit price $120), which, according to consumer reports has dependable reception and easy operation but does not reach the rated range; the Unicall T6500 (unit price $120), which features good outdoor reception and funky styling but a short battery life and inadequate range; and the Unicall GM885 (unit price $125), an all-round good radio that fares well in different weather conditions and has excellent sound, despite the fact that it does not reach the rated range. The Unicall GM885 has a battery life of twenty-five hours compared with twelve hours for the Corsair and fourteen hours for the Unicall T6500 model. Prepare a report in which you present your findings to your supervisor.

2. **Investigative Report—Field-Trip Destinations:** For a course or program in which you are currently

enrolled, suggest three potential field-trip destinations that tie in with course content: businesses, industries, financial institutions, government agencies, museums, or resource centres. For each excursion, note the size of group the venue accommodates, discuss the allocation of time and resources as well as any special arrangements that may be required, and calculate the expenses involved in undertaking the field trip. Consider the purpose and educational value of each trip.

3. **Periodic Report—Work-Study Placement:** If you are currently enrolled in a work-study program at your college or university, prepare a periodic report for your course instructor or work-placement officer in which you document your work-related activities over the past month. Discuss any irregularities on the job and highlight solutions to problems you encountered and any special needs.

4. **Investigative Report:** Write a short investigative report that summarizes fact-finding you have done and makes recommendations toward the purchase of a car, a computer and/or office equipment, a camera, or a personal electronics item. Review the criteria you used and options you considered before making your purchase.

5. **Progress Report:** Using the plan outlined in this chapter, write a progress report that summarizes the status of a work, volunteer, or recreational project in which you are involved or a term report you are currently preparing.

6. **Progress Report:** As Fernando Sanchez, chief contractor for Grande Construction Company, prepare a progress report for Hilary Murdoch, owner of Best-Temp Employment Services, advising her on the status of renovations to her new downtown office, located in a heritage property. Work is progressing on schedule, perhaps even a little ahead of what you had expected. Although the cost of certain materials is higher than your original bid indicated, you expect to complete the project without exceeding the estimated costs because the speed with which the project is being completed will reduce labour expenses. Materials used to date have cost $90,850 and labour costs have been $217,000 (including some subcontracted electrical work). Your estimate for the remainder of the materials is $85,000; remaining labour costs should not exceed $73,000. As of April 15, you had finished all plumbing work, plus the installation of the circuit-breaker panels, meters, service outlets, and all sub-floor wiring. Replacement of the heating and air-conditioning system is in the preliminary stages. You have scheduled the upgrading of the central office and adjoining storage facilities to take place from April 30 to May 15. You expect the replacement of all drywall, resurfacing of all wood floors, and installation of lighting systems will take place from May 16 to June 1. You see no difficulty in completing all work by the scheduled date of June 15.

7. **Recommendation Report—Promotional Music Salon:** As the circulation manager of *Allegro*, a free monthly music magazine (circulation 35,000) covering the local classical music and jazz scene, you would like to gain a higher profile for your publication and increase the advertising revenue on which it depends. One way to achieve these goals is to host and sponsor a free lunchtime salon series of five jazz and classical concerts, held on consecutive Sundays in April and May at a local restaurant. You already know of several outstanding solo artists and ensembles that charge nominal performance fees and would be suitable additions to your program. The restaurant proprietor has previously let out space for free for similar events. Write a memo addressed to Hal Friedman, publisher and editor of *Allegro*. Although you know Mr. Friedman dislikes change of any kind, you feel the series could succeed based on similar initiatives taken by well-regarded music guilds and organizations in your area. Decide whether a direct or indirect strategy would be appropriate.

8. **Recommendation Report:** Could one of the services at your college—the computer lab, cafeteria, health services, campus bookstore, or parking system—be more efficient? Assess its quality and efficiency based on your own observations and experiences and suggest appropriate changes in a report to the president of your student council or the dean of students.

ONLINE ACTIVITIES

1. **Statistics Canada—Create Your Own Graph:** Follow the instructions given on this web page from Statistics Canada and use the graphing tool to create bar graphs, line graphs, or pie charts, all selected from the drop-down list. You can even select the colours for your data.

   www.statcan.gc.ca/edu/power-pouvoir/ch9/ create-creer/5214819-eng.htm

2. **Statistics Canada—Graph Type Exercise:** Complete the two exercises on this web page from Statistics Canada.

   www.statcan.gc.ca/edu/power-pouvoir/ch9/ exer/5214820-eng.htm

3. **Statistics Canada—Questionnaire Exercise:** First read the comprehensive StatsCan web page on important aspects of questionnaire design:

   www.statcan.gc.ca/edu/power-pouvoir/ch2/ questionnaires/5214775-eng.htm

   Next, log on to the accompanying exercise that requires you to see how many errors you can find in a sample questionnaire. When you are done, you can check the questionnaire answers.

   www.statcan.gc.ca/edu/power-pouvoir/ch2/ exer/5214910-eng.htm#link02

11

Proposals and Formal Reports

In this chapter you will learn to

1. Distinguish between formal reports and proposals.

2. Identify elements of informal and formal proposals.

3. Conduct research by generating primary data and collecting secondary data.

4. Apply standards for evaluating research material from a variety of sources.

5. Apply the writing process to formal reports.

6. Develop a report work plan for a formal report.

7. Write a report as part of a team.

8. Identify elements of formal reports and document sources.

9. Draw conclusions and develop recommendations from report data.

◗◗ Proposals

More than simply providing facts, **proposals** fill a need by suggesting the means for solving problems. Proposals, in other words, offer to do something—for example, to provide goods or services, or to assess, develop, and implement a plan. A proposal writer's ultimate goal is to persuade readers to follow or approve those plans or agree to their development. Depending on its type, a proposal may ask for action, business, or funding. It may stay within an organization (**internal proposal**), suggesting changes or improvements in much the same way that recommendation and justification reports do and addressing questions such as the following:

- How can this idea save money? When will the savings occur and how much does the company stand to save?
- How can this new procedure boost productivity or sales?
- How will this plan make the company more competitive?

More often, proposals are sent to potential clients or customers outside the organization (**external proposal**) as a means of generating income. External proposals can be solicited or unsolicited, competitive or non-competitive, though most are written in response to a **request for proposals** (**RFP**) issued by companies and government agencies. Essentially a sales presentation, a proposal formalizes the submission of a bid for a contract. Once entered in competition, a proposal goes up against proposals from other bidders vying for the same contract so that the best method and ultimately the most qualified contractor can be found. Unsolicited proposals involve a different challenge: convincing readers that a need or problem in fact exists.

Not all proposals look alike. Proposals may be informal—often just several pages prepared in memo form—or formal—dozens or even hundreds of pages divided into multiple parts and prepared by a team of writers whose goal is to secure a big contract, sometimes worth millions or hundreds of millions of dollars. Like other forms of persuasive writing, proposals stress reader benefits and offer both proof and assurances that whatever is promised can be delivered. The goal is to emphasize not how the project will make money for you, but how your project can help make money for the client and realize added benefits.

Most proposals, whether they are informal or formal, use a direct approach. Which elements are included, however, depends on whom the proposal is for and what its purpose and contents are.

ELEMENTS OF INFORMAL PROPOSALS

Introduction

The introduction should offer an overview of the proposal and its scope and highlight your qualifications to do the job. Refer here to start-up and completion dates and the cost of the project, if they are of special concern. For external, sales-driven proposals, mention previous positive associations your company has had with the client.

Background

The background section defines in some detail the problem you aim to solve or the opportunity you wish to address. In addition to identifying the purpose and goals of

proposal a business document that suggests a method for solving a problem or seeks approval for a plan.

internal proposal a persuasive document that attempts to convince management to spend money or implement plans to change or improve the organization.

external proposal a proposal issued to governmental or private industry clients outside an organization as a means of generating income.

request for proposals (**RFP**) a detailed document requesting proposals and bids on specific projects.

the project, it conveys your understanding of client needs and how the client stands to benefit from the implementation of the plan you propose.

Proposal, Method, Schedule

The proposal section details your solution to the problem. Explain (1) the products or services you are offering, (2) how the proposed method for solving the problem is feasible, (3) how your company intends to proceed with it and perform the work in the available time, (4) what special materials and resources you will use, and (5) when each phase of the project will be completed (create a timeline for this purpose). If the procedure you propose is complex or involves several steps, use headings to give each section impact and definition. You can also walk the client through the process.

Costs, Budget

The outline of costs and the budget are key. Give a carefully prepared breakdown of costs for the entire project and, if applicable, for each stage of the project process. The budget you submit is actually a legal contract that does not allow for later alterations, even if your expenses increase, so be realistic about the figures you submit and mention any costs that are impossible for you to factor in or estimate at the time of submission.

Staffing, Qualifications

The staffing section shows that you, your team, and your company are credible and have what it takes to do the job well. Instill confidence in readers by briefly mentioning the expertise and credentials of project leaders as well as special resources and facilities that equip them to outperform the competition. You can supply additional proof of the qualifications of project leaders by attaching privacy-sensitive generic (as opposed to actual) resumés at the end or in an appendix. As an option, you may also give references, but be sure to include only addresses and telephone numbers you have permission to disclose.

Benefits

The benefits section summarizes the reasons for accepting the proposal so that the client will be motivated to action. It helps to resell the proposed plan by highlighting the benefits of your solution, service, or product and the advantages of your plan over and above competing ideas and solutions. This approach shows that you are not just eager for business, but eager to assist the client in maximizing benefits.

Request for Authorization

Depending on the situation, the closing request—asking for authorization to proceed—can sometimes be made or negotiated after the client has received the proposal. Even without a request for authorization, this section is useful for stipulating the time period in which the proposal is valid and for expressing (1) confidence in the solution, (2) appreciation for the opportunity to submit the proposal, and (3) willingness to provide further information if required.

ELEMENTS OF FORMAL PROPOSALS

Formal proposals differ from informal proposals in format and length. The number of pages can vary from as few as five to as many as several hundred. Not surprisingly, formal proposals can contain additional elements that sort complex details into effective and easy-to-understand units that can be added or subtracted depending on the client and the contents of the proposal. Headings within the body can be customized to make the contents make more sense. Elements marked with an asterisk (★) are optional in an informal proposal.

Front Matter
    Copy of the request for proposals (if applicable)★
    Cover letter★
    Abstract or summary★
    Title page★
    Table of contents★
    List of figures★

Body of the Proposal
    Introduction
    Background or problem statement
    Detailed proposal, method
    Schedule
    Budget or cost analysis
    Staffing
    Authorization
    Benefits, conclusion

Back Matter
    Appendix
    References

> **front matter** the parts of a proposal or report that are included before the main body.

> **back matter** the parts containing supplemental information that may follow the main body of a proposal or report.

The following text provides is a closer look at some other important proposal elements.

Cover Letter, Letter of Transmittal

The cover or transmittal letter, bound inside the proposal as its first page, explains the proposal's purpose, major features, and tangible benefits; it expresses confidence that those benefits will satisfy the needs of the client. The letter should be addressed to the person responsible for making the final decision. It should either refer to the RFP or mention how you learned about the client needs to which your proposal responds. Because most proposals have a shelf life, the letter should mention when the bid expires but also offer assurances that your company is authorized to make a bid. The letter should end courteously by expressing appreciation for the opportunity to submit the proposal, for any assistance already provided, or for previous positive associations with the client.

Executive Summary or Abstract

The type of summary you write depends on whom the report is intended for. An **executive summary** (one-page maximum) is intended for decision-makers and gives the proposal's highlights in persuasive, non-technical language. An **abstract** (also one-page maximum) summarizes those highlights in specialized, technical language.

> **executive summary** (or **abstract**) a synopsis of the body of a proposal or report specifying its highlights and recommendations.

Title Page

The **title page** should include (1) the proposal title and subtitle in boldfaced type or upper-case letters, (2) the name of the client organization and/or the decision-maker to whom the proposal is directed, (3) the RFP reference number, (4) the name and title of the proposal writer and her company, and (5) the date of submission.

Table of Contents (TOC)

Best included with longer proposals, the **TOC** should list all main section headings used throughout the proposal with their corresponding page numbers.

List of Tables/Figures/Illustrations

If a proposal contains a combination of more than six tables and figures, the list of tables, figures, or illustrations is a guide, indicating the page number on which each table or figure can be found.

Introduction

If the plan you are about to describe is complex, you can use the introduction not just to offer an overview but also to tell a client how the proposal that follows is organized.

Appendix

An **appendix**, typically found after the body of a proposal, is used to archive specialized materials of interest to readers (e.g., graphics, statistical analyses, tables, generic resumés of project leaders, product photographs, and examples of previous projects). Creating an appendix allows you to de-clutter the body of the proposal so that its focus is purely on the selling of products, ideas, and services. Appendices labelled A, B, C, and so on can be set up for each type of material.

References

The references or works cited list identifies the source material for ideas and information you have mentioned in your proposal or consulted in its preparation. This section may be prepared in one of several referencing formats, each with its own distinguishing features and content requirements. Of the two most widely used systems, the documentation style of the American Psychological Association (APA style) is favoured by writers in the social and physical sciences and often in business as well. Its reference list is called *References*. The documentation system of the Modern Language Association (MLA style) is used in the humanities. Its reference list is called *Works Cited*. In each case, readers are guided to the reference list and its complete bibliographic information by short citations that have been inserted into the text of the proposal.

WRITING STYLE FOR PROPOSALS

Good proposals are persuasive and use words that communicate strength, confidence, know-how, and credibility. Unnecessarily tentative, doubtful, or defensive language can undermine the reader's perception of your ability to carry out the tasks you plan and get the job done.

---

title page a front-matter page of a proposal or formal report that includes the title of the document, the names of the intended recipient and the author, and the date of submission.

table of contents (TOC) a front-matter list of the first- and second-level headings that appear in a proposal or formal report, all of which constitute an overview of the material to follow.

list of tables/figures/ illustrations a front-matter list of the titles and page numbers for tables and figures included in a document.

appendix a section of the back matter of a proposal or formal report where specialized supplemental materials are archived.

references a section of the back matter of a proposal or formal report that lists the source material that has been cited in the text.

SAMPLE INFORMAL PROPOSAL

The following informal proposal (Figure 11.1), prepared in letter format, responds to a request for a twenty-hour on-site business-writing workshop. The request for proposals comes from Amanda Sullivan, coordinator of the learning centre at Vanguard Property Development, a company that has recently expanded through the acquisition of Goodwin Homes and Realty. Former Goodwin employees who were kept on after the merger have been experiencing difficulties in adapting to the demands of Vanguard's rigorous communication standards. Ordinarily, Vanguard staff members requiring remedial English assistance or a review of e-mail, letter-writing, and reporting procedures visit the learning centre and use its online, print, and CD-ROM resources to work on their own at their own pace by using self-teaching manuals and self-guided tutorials. Recent overbooking of the learning centre and complaints from departmental managers about the quality of in-house and external documents have prompted Ms. Sullivan to look for outside assistance. She has approached three writing-services consultancy firms Vanguard had previously contracted—with positive outcomes—and has asked each to submit a proposal.

COMMON MISTAKES IN WRITING PROPOSALS

A proposal may fail to secure reader interest for several reasons:

- it does not follow RFP instructions,
- it does not match project solution with purpose,
- it is writer-focused instead of client-focused,
- it is inaccurate or unrealistic with the budget,
- it does not establish credibility,
- it does not differentiate from competition, or
- it does not contain a clear plan or solution.

FIGURE 11.1 Sample Informal Proposal

Integra Communications Services

710 Conroy Street
Vancouver, BC V2A 1H5
(604) 603-8775
www.solutionscomm.com

November 15, 2010

Ms. Amanda Sullivan, Coordinator
Vanguard Property Development
1400 Oak Tree Way
Vancouver, BC V5S 2T1

Dear Ms. Sullivan:

It was a pleasure to talk with you several days ago and learn about the initiatives the City of Bristol has undertaken since its amalgamation. Integra Communications Services is pleased to submit the following proposal outlining our plan for a ten-week on-site workshop course aimed at improving the quality of document planning and business writing in your workplace.

Our company is prepared, upon receiving your approval, to immediately implement the plan outlined below and to modify it according to the needs determined through our preliminary assessment of writing samples submitted by your staff. We appreciate your interest in our suggestions and your ongoing support for our creative training solutions.

Background and Purposes

We understand that the individualized training modules and self-learning packages currently used by your employees to address weaknesses in their writing do not provide them with the level of ongoing support and suggestions for improvement they are seeking. A more effective means of training that meets those needs and delivers the desired learning outcomes involves a combination of classroom instruction, regular individual practice, and immediate constructive feedback that will allow employees to build on the strong basic-language skills they may already have and to polish, master, and apply those skills to the actual written materials they produce on the job. Our goal is to help your employees master the skills of writing the way they learn best—through supportive individualized workshops, consultations, and hands-on experience. Our proposed training program is designed to ensure your employees become more confident and efficient writers able not only to identify the qualities of good writing but to produce quality documents within allotted time frames.

Proposed Plan and Benefits

On the basis of our experience in conducting on-site workshops and writing training seminars, Integra Communications Services proposes the following plan to maximize benefits to your company:

> **On-Site Workshop.** Participants in a group of not more than twenty will receive ten hours of instruction through an intensive on-site workshop offered in five weekly two-hour sessions.

Working from your needs, our trainers will provide practical, interactive instruction and individualized attention in an environment that allows participants to learn from each other and share their knowledge and workplace experience. The 3:30–5:30 p.m. scheduling requires only one hour of release time per week. Trainers will remain on hand until 6:30 p.m. to take questions and conduct consultations. The ten hours of classroom time is significantly less than is now required for employees to complete a self-directed training module.

Consultation and Feedback. Each participant will undergo a preliminary skills assessment, based on work in progress, and receive continuous evaluation that focuses on her instructional needs. Through substantial written comments and three twenty-minute consultations, participants will also receive immediate and relevant feedback and information on topics ranging from remedial English to strategic document planning. On completing the course, each participant will also receive a one-page status report containing a final assessment and concrete suggestions for further skill development.

Course Materials. Each participant will receive a two-hundred-page manual containing learning modules, skill-building exercises, workshop guidelines and topics, printed copies of PowerPoint slides, and assignments specifically adapted to participants' workplace writing tasks.

Ongoing Support. Course participants have unlimited access to our comprehensive online writing resources website containing additional writing tips, links to business-writing resources, and self-correcting review exercises that participants can complete at their own pace and submit for immediate feedback. For one month after completing the course, participants may also telephone our Writers' Outreach Hotline and arrange a free one-hour consultation with a course trainer.

Course Outline. The following outline corresponds to five primary areas of interest and can be adapted and modified according to the needs of individual participants.

Week 1: Foundations of Effective Workplace Communication
        Adapting your message to your audience
        Organizing routine messages
        Legal responsibilities for writers

Week 2: Sharpening Your Style
        Determining tone and word choice
        Sentence style
        Editing techniques

Week 3: E-mail Composition and Management
        Netiquette
        Handling and processing e-mail
        Writing better e-mail messages

Week 4: Strategic Document Planning for Routine and Persuasive Messages
Applying standard approaches
Delivering bad news
Writing persuasively

Week 5: Reports and Collaborative Writing
Report planning
Types of reports
Writing proposals

Staffing and Qualifications

Integra Communications Services has earned a reputation as a local leader in the communications field by offering quality writing services and ongoing support to businesses and industries in the Greater Toronto Area. Our trainers, Dr. Gail Simpson; Ezra Nadel, M.A.; and Marie Brossard, M.A., hold graduate degrees in professional communication from the University of Waterloo, the University of Calgary, and the University of Western Ontario, respectively. All are members or the Association of Business Communication and have an understanding of government and corporate communications environments that comes from years of work with government agencies and businesses such as

- J.G. Hampson & Sons
- Elite Computers Inc.
- Blackwell Investments

Over 90 per cent of our clients report a significant improvement in the quality of their documents and a considerable reduction in the time it takes to process them. For a sampling of client comments and course evaluation surveys please refer to our website: www.solutionscomm.com. A full client satisfaction survey, administered by Dr. Simpson, will be conducted at the end of the course.

Cost

The total cost of the course, including a ten-hour workshop for twenty participants, consultations, all learning materials, and ongoing support services, is $3,500. All audiovisual equipment, including PowerPoint projectors and screens, will be supplied by Integra.

Authorization

Our unique approach to professional-writing training has been implemented to a high degree of client satisfaction and will enhance your efforts to improve the quality of written communication in your workplace. I look forward to discussing the details of this proposal with you and answering any questions you may have. The price in this offer is in effect until June 1, 2010.

Sincerely,

Elizabeth Rocca

Elizabeth Rocca
President

EPR:kl

Proposal Checklist

☐ If the proposal is a response to a request for proposals, does it follow the RFP exactly and meet all specifications and requirements for the job?

☐ Does the proposal include a summary of what you propose? Is it clear why the proposal is being made?

☐ Does the proposal show that you understand the significance of the problem or challenge the client faces? If the proposal is unsolicited, does it convince the client that the problem or need exists?

☐ Are details complete? Are the plan and its implementation fully explained? Does the proposal outline project completion dates, mention staffing needs and resources, include a cost breakdown, and provide evidence to support your ability to do the job?

☐ Does the proposal identify the client's competition and develop a customized solution that answers the client's needs? Does the proposal show how the project leader's qualifications, equipment, and resources are superior to those of competitors?

☐ Does the proposal outline potential benefits to the reader?

☐ Does the conclusion reinforce a positive perception of your company and its ideas? Does it include a date beyond which the bid figures are invalid?

☐ Is the proposal positive and forward-looking in its tone? Is its organization reader-friendly?

☐ If the proposal asks for authorization, can sign-off be attained easily?

☐ Does the proposal follow industry standards in its format and disclosures? For more information on this topic, visit the website of the Association of Proposal Management Professionals: www.apmp.org.

●● Researching and Collecting Data

Reports are based on evidence. How much data you need to gather and analyze—and how much research you need to do—will depend on the situation. Short, informal reports may require only minimal research since the facts may be already known to you or close at hand. Formal reports, however, often involve extensive research. Your research strategies—and the amount of time you spend gathering information—can also differ depending on whether you are working solo or as part of a group. In either case, your first job is to determine exactly what you are looking for, decide on the best way to find it, and weigh the time your research will take against its importance to the report.

There are a variety of types of information available: **paper**, **human**, and **electronic**. Where you search for information and what you use depends on the project and the sources that are available and affordable to you in your search. Access can depend on whether information is

- **in-house:** e.g., internal files, memos, reports, or company intranet or records;
- **publicly available:** e.g., consultants, experts, Internet, CD-ROMs, newspapers, books, or magazines; or
- **restricted:** e.g., members-only Internet sites, research by other companies and organizations.

Researching a report can be as straightforward as consulting a few second-hand sources—a computer printout or a published article—or it can be a matter of setting out and gathering new information first hand.

- **Secondary research** involves the retrieval of existing information based on what others have observed and experienced. This is the type of research you do when you conduct a library or online search.
- **Primary research** is a strategy that depends on first-hand sources where you do it yourself and generate the data you need, based on your own observations and experience. This is the type of research you do when you conduct interviews, carry out surveys, make your own observations, or rely on your own ideas.

Primary data can sometimes be collected informally, by talking with individuals who know about a particular topic or with the target audience to whom your report is most relevant. If, on the other hand, developing primary data entails the cost of interviewing large groups or sending out questionnaires, secondary research may prove a more cost-effective method—that is why it is where most research projects begin.

Because it is easy to be overwhelmed by the task of locating data and sifting through masses of material, you should begin by making a list of keyword-linked topics you need to investigate and the type of data you need to support your purpose and explore your topic. Your evidence can come in many forms: statistics, in-house organizational data, group opinions, expert opinions, even historical background. Not all searches will be the same, so keep in mind the options open to you:

1. **Look for information online.** Big search engines such as Google and Yahoo—convenient pathways to the World Wide Web—can find current articles on virtually any subject related to the search term you use, especially if you do an advanced search that combines keywords and alternatives. Besides article reprints, you can expect to find online databases, company news, mission statements and directories, company profiles (through www.hoovers.com), product facts, government information, scientific reports, sound and video files, library resources, online newspapers and magazines, press releases, job banks, and employment information. Some directories—and there are many of them—are specifically business related:

   AccountingNet: http://accounting.smartpros.com
   GlobalEDGE: www.globaledge.msu.edu/
   Louisiana State University, management and entrepreneurship:
     www.lib.lsu.edu/sp/subjects/management

When using web sources, evaluate each one carefully to determine its quality, relevance, and value. Much of what you find may not be right for your purposes. Look for the name of the site sponsor, note the last time the site was updated, scrutinize author credentials, and make sure the site gives evidence to support its claims. A less obvious online route to take is to access forums, newsgroups, and discussion lists. You may want to print out material gathered online, both for security and for convenience.

The rules of Boolean logic apply here. Refine your search using the following commands known as descriptors or Boolean operators:

- AND—using *and* between your search terms will give you titles of articles containing all of the specified words (e.g., organization AND communication AND systems);
- OR—linking search terms with *or* will yield documents containing at least one of the specified words (e.g., collaborative OR group OR communication);
- NOT—using *not* will exclude articles containing the specified term.

2. **Do a computer-based search.** Reference libraries and many businesses subscribe to comprehensive databases such as SilverPlatter, DIALOG, LEXIS/NEXIS Services, and ABI/Inform. Some databases are still offered on CD-ROM. Whatever type you use, it is up to you to select the focused search terms that will allow you to source material stored electronically—full-text documents, abstracts, bibliographies, and directories.

3. **Find information in print.** *Print* is a bit of a misnomer because so much print material is now available electronically. Enlist the help of a librarian in using library search tools: computerized periodical indexes (such as *The Readers' Guide to Periodical Literature* and *Business Periodicals Index*), book indexes, encyclopedias, directories, almanacs, and online catalogues. Expect sourced material to include academic articles, abstracts, newspaper articles, government documents, and specialty and reference books.

4. **Investigate primary, in-house sources.** It is possible that the information you are looking for is right under your own nose, or at least in the internal files and records of your company. Because the topic you are now researching may have been of ongoing concern to your company, there are likely previous documents and earlier reports on the same subject simply waiting to be retrieved. Such material, though not necessarily up to date, will still be useful and save you the trouble of starting your research from scratch. Just be sure to follow the proper channels for obtaining in-house data. Network within your company to find and consult with in-house experts who may have prepared earlier reports on the topic.

5. **Conduct interviews.** Chatting by phone or in person with an expert, authority, or seasoned corporate veteran can yield valuable information. Good interviews come about through good preparation.

- Locate experts by consulting articles, company directories, the membership lists of professional organizations, and faculty expert lists (e.g., the University of Toronto's Blue Book, www.library.utoronto.ca/bluebook).

- Familiarize yourself with the interviewee's professional background and achievements, so you can converse knowledgeably.
- Schedule interviews in advance, estimating how much time your conversation will take. Try not to exceed that limit. Consider providing the interviewee with a list of your questions in advance.
- At the very least, have several topics in mind that you wish to discuss. Otherwise, structure your interview more formally by preparing three or four major questions, but don't feel you have to stick to them rigidly. Let yourself "go with the flow" and seize the opportunity to ask important questions as they occur to you.
- If your aim is to probe the interviewee's opinions and obtain detailed answers, ask open questions (beginning with *Who? What? Where? When?* and *How?*) and hypothetical questions. You can elicit more information by asking the interviewee to explain. If you simply need to verify a story or check facts, ask closed questions that can be answered *yes* or *no*. You can keep the interview moving along by paraphrasing the content of the previous answer in your next question.
- Establish at the beginning what is on and off the record and what you are permitted to quote.
- Capture your conversation by using an audio-recorder or making decipherable notes. Write up the results of the interview as soon as possible after it has taken place.
- Be patient through temporary lapses and silences—the interviewee may just be formulating a response. Be friendly and objective, remembering that you are participating in a discussion, not a debate. Leave controversial questions for the end.
- End by expressing appreciation and asking permission to contact the informant for clarification of anything that was said.

6. **Quantify observations.** Information that comes from observation can be quite subjective and very open to interpretation. Observations that are reported in terms of measurable results and outcomes may be perceived as more objective and credible.

●● Formal Reports

formal report an account of a major project written according to a prescribed structure defined by formal elements such as a title page, letter of transmittal, table of contents, and executive summary or abstract.

Formal reports are accounts of major projects—the development of new products or services; reorganization at departmental, divisional, or company-wide levels; or analysis of competing products or alternative methods. Much like analytical business reports, except in length, formal reports present ordered information to decision-makers in government, business, and industry. Because the scope and complexity of long report topics is greater, however, there is also greater need for in-depth analysis and extensive research. Formal reports follow a more prescribed structure in order to accommodate this complexity and effectively deliver information and recommendations. The basic structure includes front matter, the body of the report, and back matter—segmented sections that together identify the significance and enhance the professionalism of the document. It is not uncommon for organizations to have a preferred "house style" where certain elements are treated a particular way or left in/out according to the guidelines established in a report-writer's manual. If your organization has no pre-scribed style, simply follow the writing plan outlined in this chapter, with the under-standing that there is wide variation in the ways to present a report.

PREPARING TO WRITE FORMAL REPORTS

Reports often require a detailed and technical type of writing. The most effective reports are the result of a process that involves thoughtful analysis and careful evaluation before the tasks of research and writing begin. Understanding the problem you must address, why you are writing, and whom you are writing for are key to the success of this process. As you begin to define the project, you should have a clear idea about the following things:

- Purpose: What is the report for?
- Content: What is it about?
- Audience: Who is it for?
- Status: Will other reports on the same subject follow?
- Length: How long should it be?
- Formality: How should it look and sound?

Thinking about these issues will save time in the long run by helping you gain control over your material in the time you have to develop it. One way to start planning is to review the questions in the following list.

Report-Planning Review List

Purpose

- What are you being asked to report on and why? What is the subject and situation?

- What is your main purpose? Are you expected to give information, information plus analysis, recommendations? Or is your task to persuade, solve a problem, initiate change, or just provide a record for future reference? Does your report have more than one purpose?

- What results do you hope to achieve by writing the report?

Content and Organization

- What details should you include and exclude in order to support your conclusions and recommendations?

- What information matters most? How can this information be presented so it is easy to follow?

- How detailed should your analysis be?

- To which plan, direct or indirect, will the reader best respond? Which plan is most convenient or persuasive?

- Could visual material enhance the reader's understanding of the subject?

- Do you have expertise in the subject you are reporting on?

- What research will the preparation of your content require? What sources are most credible? Whom should you consult? What are the most appropriate methods of collecting data? How long will information gathering take?

- If you are working with others, how will responsibilities be shared among you? How can team members best apply their skills?

Audience

- Whom is your report aimed at (small group, mixed readership)? Who else will read it?

- What are the reader's skills, concerns, and knowledge of the subject? How much of your knowledge does the reader share? How much background does the reader require?

- What objections might the reader have? How might the reader react?

Status

- Is your report a periodic/interim report (superseded by another report in a few weeks or months) or is it a special-projects report (a one-time analysis of a problem or situation written on request)?

Length

- How much are you expected to write?

- How much detail do readers expect?

- How much time do you have to prepare the report? What is the deadline for submission? When must each phase be completed?

Formality

- How formal does your report need to be? What is the setting and audience for your report?

- What will happen to the report afterward? Who else will read it?

- Is it for immediate, short-term use (less formal) or will it be presented to senior governing bodies of your organization (more formal)?

- If the report is short or informal, is it appropriate to prepare the report in a memo or letter or on a printed form?

- Based on preferences and previous reports, what tone is appropriate?

WRITING STYLE FOR FORMAL REPORTS

Serious matters deserve to be taken seriously. Formal reports reflect this in their tone and sentence style. Be prepared to adjust your style to convey objectivity and build credibility with readers who may be either external (outside your organization) or several rungs up on the organizational ladder. There are a few basic dos and don'ts to keep in mind:

- Use a more impersonal tone than you would for an informal report.
- Write using third-person pronouns, avoiding *I* and *we* as much as possible.
- Avoid the word *you*. Instead, supply the company name or department.
- Do not use contractions.
- Aim for a mix of sentence lengths and keep paragraphs to less than seven lines.
- Use verb tenses consistently—use the past tense for completed actions (*respondents were asked*) and for citing references, and use the present tense for current actions (*the purposes of this report are, recommendations include*).
- Put URLs in angle brackets (e.g., <http://canada.gc.ca>) to make them easier to read.
- Check organizational style guidelines before you begin to write to find out what style elements are permissible.

CREATING A WORK PLAN

Even though reports can require detailed and technical writing, writers of reports often have very little time to collect and analyze data, let alone compile findings and interpret them for readers in the form of meaningful conclusions and recommendations. Generating a proper report takes time. Exactly how long it takes will depend on the amount and type of research that needs to be done, the scope and complexity of the report, and the number of people involved in its production. The longer or more detailed a report is, the more you need to evaluate and define the project by creating a **work plan**, especially if success depends on working collaboratively, as part of a team. A work plan defines how work will be done, who will do it, and when each phase will be completed. It sketches out the project from beginning to end, making it easier to set priorities, allocate resources, and move forward. A work plan (see Figure 11.2, pp. 375–6) includes the following elements:

work plan a document that defines the approach, personnel responsibilities, resource needs, and scheduling for a major project.

- statements of problem and purpose,
- a strategy for conducting research—how you expect to find and generate data and who is responsible for information gathering,
- a preliminary outline, and
- work schedules for writing and submission.

TIME MANAGEMENT

In report writing, time is of the essence. Few reports are assigned without a deadline, so effective time-management skills and up-front planning are essential. The bigger the scale of the report, the more carefully you will have to set aside enough time to complete it.

Time-Management Quick Tips

- Learn how you work best—doing one task after the other or juggling several responsibilities at once. Design a system that works best for you by figuring out when you waste time and when you work most effectively.

- Set priorities (using a to-do list, or a daytimer if you have to) and try your best to ignore distractions. Give the task you are working on the attention it deserves.

- Start early. Don't procrastinate or leave an important task or project until the last minute. Leave room for unexpected occurrences—like computer trouble or power outages.

- Break tasks into component parts with time for each.

- Ask for additional information and resources if you need them.

- Let people know as soon as possible if you are running seriously behind. Work together to find solutions.

PEER-REVIEWING AND TEAM WRITING

team writing the practice of multiple writers working together to produce a single document.

More than any other type of business document, a report often has multiple authors, which means that writing a report can require collaboration, document cycling, and teamwork. Different sections of a team-written report can be strikingly unlike each other in tone, sentence and paragraph length, and word choice. Here are some ideas for collaborating successfully with co-workers:

- Agree on style points—the degree of formality and use of personal pronouns—before you start the drafting process.
- Tidy up the draft to minimize sharp contrasts in writing styles from section to section.
- Make sure all members of the team are satisfied with the final draft before you begin to edit it.
- Use a program such as MSWord that allows each member of the group to make signed annotations to the document onscreen.

FIGURE 11.2 Sample Work Plan

Statement of Problem

As a result of recent expansion, our company has outgrown its current human resources (HR) department. Inaccurately processed claims, increased benefit administration costs, out-of-control operating costs, and the need to reinvest in technology make the outsourcing of some or all of our HR services (HRO) a viable option in terms of realizing our commitment to cutting costs, improving service to employees, maximizing resource availability, and gaining efficiencies. Recent studies found that outsourcing is now firmly embedded as part of HR service delivery.

Statement of Purpose

The purpose of this report is to determine whether consolidation of HR services under one outsourcing provider can control operating costs and facilitate world-class delivery with respect to benefits, HR management, and payroll processing. The report will examine published studies, surveys, and accounts of how other companies achieved their HR objectives.

Sources and Methods of Data Collection

Magazine and newspaper accounts will be examined, as well as "HR Outsourcing: Benefits, Challenges, and Trends," the Conference Board's second study of the benefits of human resources outsourcing and changes in the HR marketplace. Our accounting department will conduct an internal audit to determine what we do well and what we need help with and will undertake cost–benefit analysis to estimate the strategic value of HR outsourcing (HRO) to our business and the cost savings over time. Our HR department will estimate growth in the number of employees in the next five years and the additional number of HR and IT staff required to support that growth using the current systems.

Working Outline

A. What is the scope of programs currently offered by our company?
    1. Who provides them?
    2. Are any programs already outsourced?
    3. Are packaged HR services right for our company?
B. What HR services should we outsource?
    1. Central HR functions?
    2. Technical or administrative functions?
C. What are the benefits and risks of outsourcing?
    1. Risk management
    2. Cost savings
    3. Impact on core functions
    4. Security issues
D. How do we choose a service provider?
    1. What are our selection criteria?
    2. How can we manage our outsourcing relationship?
E. Should we proceed with HR outsourcing?

SAMPLE

Work Schedule

Investigate newspaper and magazine articles	Mar. 15–20
Conduct an internal audit—What do we do best?	Mar. 21–25
Conduct cost–benefit analysis	Mar. 21–25
Investigate system options and service providers	Mar. 26–31
Interpret and evaluate findings	Apr. 3
Compose a draft of the first report	Apr. 6–10
Revise draft	Apr. 11–15
Submit final report	Apr. 16

Elements of Formal Reports

Below are the elements you can expect to find in a formal report. Elements marked with an asterisk (⋆) do not require headings.

Front Matter
Cover⋆
Title Page⋆
Letter of Transmittal⋆
Table of Contents
List of Figures
Executive Summary

Body of the Report
Introduction
Discussion of Findings
Conclusions
Recommendations

Back Matter
Appendices
References or Works Cited
Glossary

FRONT MATTER

The front matter gives report readers a general idea of the document's purpose and offers an overview of the types of information they can expect to find and the specific items that will be covered. Because scope and audience vary every time you write a report, it may not be necessary to include all the front-matter elements described here every single time you generate a report.

Cover

For protection and professionalism, formal reports should be presented in a durable cover of vinyl or heavy-stock paper that can be marked with the company name and logo. The title should be visible on the cover, either through a cut-out window or on a label. The cover does not have a page number.

Title Page

The title page includes the following items, centred on the page and formatted to cover most of it from top to bottom: (1) the full title of the report, typed in boldface or upper-case letters but not enclosed in quotation marks, (2) the name of the person and group or organization for which the report was prepared, prefaced by *Prepared for* or *Submitted to*, (3) the names of the writer(s) or compiler(s), along with their job titles and the name of their organization, prefaced by *Prepared by* or *Submitted by*, (4) the date of submission or the date the report is to be distributed. Items 2 to 4 are typed in a combination of upper- and lower-case letters (known as *title case*). The title page is unnumbered, but is considered page i.

Letter of Transmittal

A letter or memo of transmittal officially introduces the report and provides a permanent record of document delivery. It is written on company stationery and sent in memo form to insiders or in letter form to outsiders. It is usually formatted to allow for a 1¼- or 1½-inch (3.18- or 3.81-centimetre) top margin. A transmittal letter or memo (1) begins with a statement indicating the topic of the report and the fact that the report is being transmitted: *Here is the report on privacy issues you requested on November 3 . . .* (2) refers to the report's purpose and authorization under which it was written, (3) briefly describes the report and highlights its conclusions and recommendations, (4) expresses appreciation for the assignment and for special help received from others in its preparation, (5) closes with follow-up action and an offer of assistance in answering questions, or by looking forward to discussion of the report's details.

Table of Contents

A table of contents (or TOC) shows the report's overall structure, listing all the sections or headings of the report in order of appearance and giving an initial page number for each. Prepare your table of contents last, when the report has been completed. List sections in a column on the left and indent subsections a few spaces, using leaders (spaced dots) to direct the reader to the accurate page number. Use lower-case Roman numerals for front matter and do not list *Table of Contents* in your table of contents (keep in mind that the idea is to list every item coming after the TOC). Word-processing programs allow you to generate a table of contents automatically simply by keying in your report headings. Leave 1½ to 2 inches (3.81 to 5.08 centimetres) at the top of the page.

List of Figures/List of Tables/List of Illustrations

If your report contains more than five figures, they can be listed in a separate section at the bottom of your table of contents. If the report has many graphics and visuals, list them on a separate page immediately following the TOC. "List of Illustrations" is a label that can apply to both figures and tables. Be sure to number tables and figures independently and consecutively with Arabic numbers (meaning that there may be both a Table 1 and a Figure 1).

Executive Summary

Usually written after you have completed the report, an executive summary is roughly 10 per cent the length of the report it summarizes. It can be read independently of the report but accurately reflects the report's most important information without using any technical jargon. Like a well-written précis, an effective executive summary omits examples and instead highlights conclusions and recommendations. Sometimes it is the only part of the report management will read. Place it on a separate sheet of paper at the end of the front matter or at the very beginning of the body of the report.

BODY OF THE REPORT

The body of the report begins on page 1. This section, the heart of the report, describes methods and procedures that were used in generating the report, shows how results were obtained, and draws conclusions and recommendations from them. Not every report will follow the exact formula given below, so use either functional or descriptive headings according to what the project requires.

Introduction

The introduction is both a general guide and a road map that prepares readers for the rest of the report. An effective introduction covers the following topics, any of which may be assigned to a separate section.

- **Purpose or Problem:** The purpose statement, usually not more than one or two sentences, identifies the rhetorical purpose of the report (to explain, to recommend) as it applies to the problem the report addresses. Providing a clear statement of goals gives readers a basis for judging the findings and results.
- **Scope:** Sometimes combined with the purpose statement when both are relatively brief, the scope statement sets out the boundaries of your material and defines the limitations of the subject. It tells readers how broad or detailed your coverage is and defines what the report does and does not investigate. Readers may then evaluate the report purely on the terms you establish so it is less likely to be faulted for incompleteness or lack of thoroughness.
- **Background:** Background information puts the report in perspective and may help to fill in the blanks when a report is consulted years later. Avoid giving readers more background than they really need. Instead, give a brief review of events that led to the problem or a description of how other solutions have failed—information that allows readers to understand the design and purpose of the report they are about to read.
- **Organization:** This subsection maps out the structure of the report.
- **Sources and methods:** If you collected primary data by conducting interviews, surveys, or focus groups, outline the procedures you followed and any related details: who your subjects were; how you chose those subjects; what the survey-sample size was; when the collection of data took place; and whether the data you collected is open to dispute. You can also describe your secondary sources.

Besides covering these topics, you may also choose to say a few words about authorization (what the agreed-upon terms under which you are writing the report authorize you to do or suggest) or define key terms that clarify the subject. Almost unavoidably, an introduction will restate information from the executive summary and preview details from the discussion of findings, so use slightly different phrasing to reduce repetitiousness and redundancy.

Discussion of Findings

The discussion of findings is the most substantial section of the report. With careful interpretation and analysis of significant data and research findings, it presents a discussion of the results on which your conclusions and recommendations are based. Choose an appropriate way to arrange your findings (logically, chronologically, in order or importance, by region or topic) and then use structural guideposts such as functional or descriptive headings to move readers from one section to the next.

Conclusions

Carefully avoiding bias, use the conclusions section to tell readers what they have been waiting to learn—what the findings really mean and what the solution to the problem is. **Conclusions** repeat, infer from, and pull together points made in the report. In this they differ from recommendations, which are actions the readers are advised to take. Some reports present conclusions and recommendations in separate sections while others combine them, especially if the sections are short. Together or on their own, conclusions and recommendations are no place to introduce new material. In fact, every statement you make must be justified by a point already discussed, every result linked to the purpose and methods of the report. Conclusions make the most sense when they are given according to the order in which they are presented in the body and numbered or bulleted for ease of reference.

Recommendations

The recommendations section makes specific suggestions about what action to take as a result of the information you have presented. Your recommendations should be financially feasible and appropriate to the problem. Presented one at a time as numbered commands beginning with a verb, they should flow logically from findings and conclusions and be supported by the information found there. Number recommendations to make it easier for readers to discuss them, and use the imperative voice to emphasize actions to be taken, adding information as required to tell readers how those actions can be implemented. Some reports include timetables for putting recommendations into effect.

BACK MATTER

The back matter of a report contains supplementary material that

- identifies sources that were consulted in researching the report,
- provides any additional information that was too detailed or lengthy to include in the body of the report,
- defines unfamiliar technical terms used in the report, and
- makes individual topics discussed in the report easier to find by indexing them.

Each of the elements described below starts on a new page and should be given an appropriate label.

Works Cited/References

To (1) avoid charges of plagiarism, (2) support assertions, and (3) help readers access source material easily, cite and document as unobtrusively as possible the sources for any facts or figures you have quoted or referred to in the report. Even if you have summarized or paraphrased an idea, you must identify whose idea it is and where it comes from. The necessity of documenting your source material applies to any words, ideas, or data not your own—anything that is not common knowledge or which does not come from an internal source (such as company sales figures and financial statements). There are two common methods for documenting sources, each with its own style:

- **American Psychological Association (APA) style**—a system of citation used in the social sciences, and
- **Modern Language Association (MLA) style**—a system of citation used in the humanities.

Each method involves two elements:

- parenthetical citations in the body of the report, and
- a reference list (APA style) or list of works cited (MLA style) at the end.

Parenthetical in-text citations are placed within the text of your report. Whenever you quote, paraphrase, or summarize material from an external source, using either words or ideas that are not your own, you must add a citation to avoid the risk of plagiarism (meaning, literally, "to kidnap," plagiarism is the passing off of someone else's thoughts or words as your own). All you have to do to avoid plagiarizing material is to insert the right identifying details in parentheses before you close the sentence where the borrowed material appears. As you will see from the examples below, slightly different information goes within the parentheses, depending on whether you use APA or MLA style.

A **references** or **works cited** list includes all print, electronic, and media sources cited in the report. Source material is listed in alphabetical order by author surname. Entries for each work include author (or creator), title, and bibliographical details (including year of publication).

APA Documentation—Parenthetical In-Text Citations

An author–date method is used in creating citations in APA format. Items within the brackets are separated by commas.

APA In-Text Citation (single author)	(Author's last name, Date of publication) (Friedman, 2005)
APA In-Text Citation (two authors)	(Author & Author, Date) (Fluegelman & Hawes, 2004)
APA In-Text Citation (no date available)	(Author's last name, n.d.) (Bannerman, n.d.)
APA In-Text Citation (direct quotation)	(Author's last name, Date, Page) (Scardino, 2004, p. 8)
APA In-Text Citation (organization as author)	(Organization, Date) (Canadian e-Commerce Statistics, 2005)
APA In-Text Citation (website, no author)	(Shortened title, Date) ("Social Services in Canada," 2009)

Typically, in-text citations are inserted at the end of the clause or sentence in which the cited information or quotation appears. Punctuation is placed outside the citation. In the following example, the citation identifies the source of a direct quotation:

Financial Post Business reported that in 2005 "Toyota produced more than 8 million vehicles, compared to GM's 9.1 million" (Greenwood, 2005, p. 34).

American Psychological Association (APA) style a documentation system used by writers in the social and physical sciences.

Modern Language Association (MLA) style a documentation system used by writers in the humanities.

parenthetical in-text citations notations set within parentheses that identify sources of quotations or ideas that are cited in the body of a report.

references or **works cited** an alphabetically arranged list that identifies sources referred to in a report.

APA Documentation—References-Page Entries

Some general rules apply to the formatting of a references page:

- Arrange entries alphabetically by the author's last name or title of the work (if the author is unknown).
- Begin each entry flush left (at the left margin). Each additional line in an entry is indented five spaces.
- Place the date of publication in brackets following the author's name (if known).
- Capitalize (1) only the first letter of a work that is not a periodical (e.g., books, web documents, brochures); (2) only the first letter of the title of an article; (3) the first letter of a word that follows a colon; (4) the titles of periodicals (journals, newspapers, magazines).
- Italicize the titles of books, journals, newspapers, magazines, reports, media productions, and videos.
- For periodicals, italicize the volume number (do not use the abbreviation *Vol.*) and include the issue number in brackets immediately after it. Do not use the abbreviations *p.* or *pp.* for articles in scholarly journals or magazines: *15*(3), 49–58.
- For electronic sources, include a digital object identifier (DOI) or, if no DOI is available, the web address from which the material was retrieved: *Retrieved from http://strategis.ic.gc.ca.*

APA References Entry (book, one author)	Author's last name, Initial(s). (Year of publication). *Title of book.* Place of publication: Publisher. Friedman, T. (2005). *The world is flat: A brief history of the twenty-first century.* New York: Farrar, Strauss & Giroux.
APA References Entry (book by two authors)	Author, Initial(s), & Author Initial(s). (Year of publication). *Title of book.* Place of publication: Publisher. Fluegelman, A., & Hewes, J. (2004). *Strategies for business and technical writing.* New York: Random House.
APA References Entry (journal article)	Author's last name, Initial(s). (Date of publication). Title of article. *Journal, Volume number*(Issue), Pages. Limaye, M. (2002). Some reflections on explanation in bad news messages. *Journal of Business and Technical Communication, 15*(1), 100–111.
APA References Entry (online article)	Author's last name, Initial(s). (Date of publication). Title of article. *Title of Online Periodical.* Retrieved from URL. Pond, M. (2001, June 21). Sales letters for success. *Edmonton Small Business.* Retrieved from http://www.business-howto.com/articles/2001/13/index03.html

MLA Documentation—Parenthetical In-Text Citations

An author–page method is used in creating citations in MLA format. The author's last name and relevant page reference (with no *p.* or *pp.* abbreviation) appear in parentheses. In-text citations should be placed as close as possible to the content they cite, preferably within the same sentence. If the author's name already appears nearby within the text, then it is possible to include just the page reference in parentheses.

MLA In-Text Citation	(Author's last name Pages)
	(Watson 64)

Corporate leaders may intentionally obscure their meaning or they may do so out of habit (Watson 64).

Don Watson theorizes that "corporate leaders sometimes have good reason to obscure their meaning by twisting their language into knots, but more often they simply twist it out of habit" (64).

MLA Works Cited Entries

Some general rules apply to the formatting of a works cited list:

- Arrange entries alphabetically by the author's last name or by title (if the author's name is unknown). Single-space entries; double-space between them.
- Begin each entry flush left (at the left margin). Indent each additional line in the entry five spaces.
- Type the author's last name followed by a comma and his or her first name.
- Capitalize the first letter of each main word in the title of a book, article, web document, newspaper, report, magazine, media production, and video.
- Enclose the titles of articles in quotation marks.
- Italicize the titles of books, newspapers, magazines, government publications, online e-books, online magazines, brochures, and journals. In some cases, underscoring may be preferred for this, so ask your instructor.
- For journal articles, include the volume number and issue number, inserting a period between them and adding the date of publication (if needed) in parentheses: *Journal of Business Communication* 14.4 (2000): 444–98. Print.
- For newspaper and magazine articles, include the date of publication (the volume and issue numbers can be omitted).

MLA Works Cited Entry (book, one author)	Author's last name, First name. Title. Place of publication: Publisher, Year of publication. Format.
	Watson, Joe. *Death Sentences: How Clichés, Weasel Words, and Management-Speak Are Strangling Public Language.* Toronto: Viking Canada, 2005. Print.
MLA Works Cited Entry (journal article)	Author's last name, First name. "Title of Article." Journal Volume number (Year): Pages. Format.
	Mohan, R. Limaye. "Some Reflections on Explanation in Negative Messages." *Journal of Business and Technical Communication* 15.1 (2001): 100–11. Print.

**MLA Works Cited Entry
(online article)**

Author's last name, First name. "Title of Article."
Title of Online Periodical. Publisher or sponsor,
Date of publication. Format. Date of retrieval.
URL.

Pond, Meredith. "Sales Letters for Success."
Edmonton Small Business. Business Publishers,
21 June 2001. Web. 19 Apr. 2009.
<http:www.business-howto.com/
articles.2001/13/index03.html>.

Appendix

An optional element located at the end of a formal report, an appendix contains specialized, sometimes lengthy, information that clarifies and supplements the essential information in the body of the report. A report can have more than one appendix (labelled alphabetically as Appendix A, Appendix B, and so forth), but each appendix can contain only one type of information—tables, charts, diagrams, illustrations, raw data, computer printouts, interviews, questionnaires, statistical analyses, or technical support.

FIGURE 11.3 Sample Formal Report in APA Style

ANALYSIS OF THE CLAIRMONT COLLEGE SUMMER ARTS PROGRAM

Presented to Dr. Vivian Foster
Dean and Director of Programs

Clairmont College of Applied Arts and Technology

Prepared by Sebastian Marceau
Special Programs Development Officer

November 15, 2009

MEMORANDUM

TO: Dr. Vivian Foster, Dean and Director of Programs

FROM: Sebastian Marceau, Special Programs Development Officer

SUBJECT: Assessment of College Summer Arts Program

DATE: November 15, 2009

Here is the report, which you authorized on October 15, about the status of our Summer Arts Program in its first year of operation. The study involved a review of program enrolment figures, revenue variances, staff and classroom expenses, course curriculum design, class size, and student exit evaluations, as well as an assessment of the program mandate and the current and future educational needs of the greater Clairmont community.

Although response to the program has been and continues to be extremely positive, the information gathered shows that, as a result of substantial registration shortfalls in its first year of operation, we should in future expend considerable effort in marketing and refocusing the program to appeal to target audiences. The action plan outlined in this report reflects the results of research within the college and outside arts-in-education research.

I am grateful to summer staff instructors for their input and feedback and to members of the accounting department for their assistance in revenue analysis.

It is my hope that this report will provide you and the college board with the information needed to assess the effectiveness of the first year of the Clairmont College Summer Arts Program, to evaluate its implications, and to plan for the coming year. Please let me know if you have any questions about this report or if you need any further information. I may be reached at (705) 582-2119 and by e-mail at <smarceau@clairmontcollege.ca>. I look forward to discussing the report recommendations and action plan with you.

Enc.

TABLE OF CONTENTS

LIST OF FIGURES

SAMPLE

EXECUTIVE SUMMARY

A substantial shortfall in registration revenues has led to this review of the Summer Arts Program at Clairmont College. The purposes of this report are (1) to assess the continued financial and educational viability of the program based on findings related to its first year of operation and (2) to recommend modifications to curriculum, marketing, and financial structuring that would allow for its sustainability and future success.

The Summer Arts Program, encompassing the Summerworks, Danceworks, and Musicworks divisional programs, was launched in July 2009 after extensive market research indicated that the greater Clairmont community represented a ready market for arts-based educational programming where no comparable program existed. Based on such models as the Banff School of Fine Arts, the program was designed to respond to the needs of adult learners seeking cultural enrichment and personal development in a supportive and interactive learning environment. The program is aimed at enriching the cultural life of the community and at providing a segue to certificate, diploma, and degree courses at the college.

The results of this assessment show that a general restructuring of finances and curriculum are needed to reduce losses and build a market for the program, if in fact it is to continue.

As a result of our review and assessment, we recommend the following changes to the Summer Arts Program:

1. Reduce course overheads by implementing changes to course delivery and eliminating support-staff positions.

2. Increase class size and reduce the number of hours per course.

3. Apply strategies to encourage students not to withdraw from courses in which they are enrolled.

4. Restructure course curriculum and revise course descriptions to appeal to broader audiences.

5. Implement an aggressive new marketing strategy that would involve print and radio advertising campaigns. Gaining an audience for the program also demands a more proactive approach to community outreach.

6. Upgrade student services and improve campus efficiency during the summer months.

INTRODUCTION

The Clairmont College Summer Arts Program was established to promote standards of excellence in the fine and applied arts and to provide a community base for personal growth and cultural enrichment in the Greater Clairmont Area. According to its mandate, the Summer Arts Program encompasses three divisional programs: (1) modern and classical dance, including ballet; (2) jazz, orchestral, and choral music; and (3) a cross-section of special interest courses in drama and the visual and media arts.

Inspired by such renowned programs as the Banff Centre for the Arts (formerly the Banff School of Fine Arts), the Summer Arts Program at Clairmont College is designed as a "catalyst for creativity" ("About the Banff Centre," 2005). As an outgrowth of Clairmont College academic programs, the new arts programming is founded on established notions, voiced by visual artists such as Herbert Read, that "the aim of education ought to be concerned with the preparation of artists" (Eisner, 2004). The Special Programs Committee, which was entrusted with the task of developing programs to promote artists within the broader spectrum of liberal arts education, subscribes to the view that "there are no guarantees or easy solutions to the complex challenges in education, but an arts-rich curriculum can provide a vehicle to self-expression, self-understanding, self-confidence, creative problem-solving and motivation" (Elster, 2002).

Purpose of the Study

The Special Programs Committee (SPC) had projected that enrolment in the program would be substantially higher than the actual 2009 registration levels. In allowing for initial registration shortfalls, however, the SPC had also expected that the program would take several years to establish itself in the community and refine its curriculum to meet the needs of target audiences. The purpose of this study is to determine how well the Summer Arts Program fulfilled its mandate and to investigate underlying weaknesses in program funding and curriculum development as a basis for assessing possible changes and the long-term viability of the program. Recommendations for the increasing revenue and enrolment will be made based on the results of this study.

Scope of the Study

This review was intensive and extensive. It paid particular attention to the following concerns:

- Budgetary shortfall
- Underperforming course sectors and curriculum deficiencies
- Service deficiencies
- Customer satisfaction

Sources and Methods

Our assessment included

- Budgetary variance reports and revenue statements
- Student exit evaluations surveys
- Meetings with course instructors in all summer program sectors
- Discussions with students previously enrolled in the program

ASSESSMENT OF THE SUMMER 2009 PROGRAM

The findings of this study will be presented in four categories: (1) registration and revenue, (2) program structure and student appraisal; (3) program marketing; and (4) summer student services.

Program Registration and Revenue

The program had 808 registrants. The budgeted number of registrants was 937 (meaning the program was 129 registrants short of budgeted targets). The diversified Summerworks program accounted for the bulk of registration, at 89.2 per cent, with the smaller Danceworks and Musicworks divisions accounting for only 6.4 per cent and 4.3 per cent of registrations, respectively.

Figure 1 Registration by Program Division, Summer Program 2009

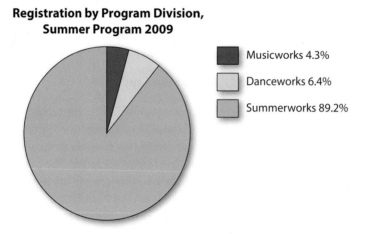

Registration by Program Division, Summer Program 2009

- Musicworks 4.3%
- Danceworks 6.4%
- Summerworks 89.2%

By division, the breakdown of Summer Arts Program registration was as follows:

- Summerworks had 721 registrants, well exceeding its projections of 600. Even with the popular demand for such courses as Canadian Gardening and Creativity in the Visual Arts that necessitated the creation of additional sections, many courses ran below their anticipated enrolment average that was budgeted at 12. The average enrolment per course was 10. This unexpected reduction in class size created good classroom circumstance, but weaker-than-anticipated fiscal returns.

- Danceworks had a registration level of 52 (52 @ $450 = $23,400) but still fell far short of the projected 80 students. This contributed to a revenue shortfall of $12,600.

- Musicworks performed below expectations. The budget registration for Musicworks was 251, but the program had in total 35 registrants @ $299 per registration, producing only $10,465 of revenue.

The figure below represents budgeted vs. actual registrations by divisional program.

Figure 2 Budgeted vs. Actual Registrations, Summer Program 2009

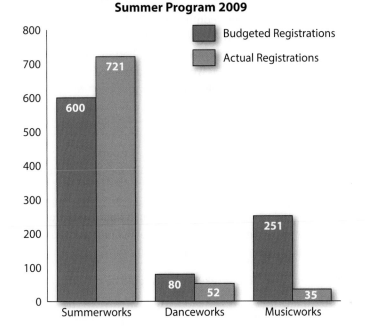

A variance analysis was undertaken to explain differences in revenue and expenses:

	Actual $	Budget $	Difference + (−)	
			$	%
Total Revenue	266,635	313,536	−46,901	−15
Total Expense	297,632	278,259	19,373	7
Net Revenue/Loss	−30,997	35,277	−66,274	−188

A full breakdown of revenue and expenses is provided in Appendix A. Total revenues for the Summer Arts Program amounted to $266,635, with a total shortfall for the program of $30,997. The most substantial expenses were incurred through casual and overtime labour—the casual fee paid to the individual who later converted to the Clerk A3 position ($23,011). It is possible to decrease expenses by eliminating this position and by making necessary adjustments to salaries and benefits, particularly by eliminating the $1,000 stipends paid to program guest speakers, for a total saving of $4,500. The cost of Marketing Services —including the production of brochures and a print advertising campaign—also exceeded projections. Instead of placing expensive ads in *Arts Monthly*, *Clairmont Life*, and *Arts Scene* at a total cost of $1,700, monies could be redirected for a single add in the *Globe and Mail*, a far more effective venue (@ $800 per ad), for a total saving of $900.

Program Structure and Student Appraisal

Student feedback was extremely positive, both in the formal exit evaluation surveys and in informal meetings convened at the college earlier this month. Appendix B provides a tabulation of the results from the evaluation survey issued at the close of the Summer Arts Program. Over 75 per cent of students who completed the survey ranked aspects of the program good or better than expected in all areas. This high approval rating was also reflected in discussions with selected members of the registrant body. Among former students, there was consensus on the following issues:

1. Course descriptions and outlines were too general. As a result, the descriptions in the brochure did not match course outlines, resulting in student withdrawals. Students complained of poor pre-registration counselling and an unwillingness on the part of registration staff to help them locate courses that reflected their interests. Where customer service is concerned, there is much room for improvement.

2. Courses were too long and too expensive. At 30 contact hours, most courses were too long for students simply studying for pleasure and personal enrichment, not to pass exams. Students agreed that 20 hours per course would be optimal.

3. Due to popular demand, the Danceworks program could be modified and expanded to allow for the intake of students aged 10–17. Since September, the Registration Office received over 100 requests for information on the Danceworks program. Most callers were seeking intensive training for younger students in this demographic range.

4. Course start-ups timed to coincide with long weekends discouraged potential registrants. This in turn led to course cancellations.

While many courses in the program met expectations, some did not. Under-subscribed courses included Make 'Em Laugh: Stand-Up Comedy Routines, Art II: German Expressionism, and the entire Musicworks program, which failed to attract sufficient numbers of registrants to make the intensive workshop format viable.

Program Marketing

Survey respondents and interview subjects commented that awareness of the program within the community is limited. Current marketing plans allow for (1) the production of a program brochure, (2) a limited direct-marketing campaign aimed at Clearwater College alumni, and (3) a modest print advertising campaign.

1. A substantial number of respondents suggested that the college increase its efforts to reach out to the community throughout the entire year by hosting open houses and arts-related events that would form a logical bridge to the Summer Arts Program.

2. Few registrants learned about the program through ads appearing in *Arts Monthly*, *Clairmont Life*, and *Arts Scene*.

Student Services Delivery

Although summer session degree and diploma courses run at the same time as the Summer Arts Program, fewer student services are available in June, July, and August. Food services are available on only a very limited basis, leaving students to depend on vending machines, most of which are located in the student commons area far from the summer program classroom locations. Neighbouring restaurants are located at some distance from the main campus.

Commuter students complained about the high cost of on-campus parking. Based on an hourly rate, parking fees for students enrolled in day-long intensive courses were prohibitive.

During the week of July 6–10, the physical plant received 12 complaints about the malfunctioning air conditioning and ventilation system, which forced the cancellation of a class in one documented case. Non-delivery of audiovisual equipment was also a problem, with five instructors filing complaints.

These factors contributed to the lowering of student satisfaction with the overall physical environment and created substantial dissatisfaction among course instructors.

CONCLUSIONS AND RECOMMENDATIONS

During its first year of operation, the Summer Arts Program fulfilled its mandate to provide quality non-credit arts programming to the greater Clairmont area. In exit surveys, students rated the program highly, with more than 85 per cent saying that, on the basis of their experience in the summer 2009 program, they would study in the Summer Arts Program again and recommend it to their friends. Based on this feedback and earlier market research, there is sufficient reason to conclude the program is sustainable and worth continuing.

Although the program succeeded in its delivery of quality educational services, it underperformed financially. Registration levels in certain course sectors fell significantly short of projections. The resulting budgetary shortfall may jeopardize the future of the program unless substantial changes are made within the next three months to address these losses. If the program is to be viable in the future, it will be necessary to (1) reduce overheads and (2) refocus and streamline program curriculum.

Supported by the findings and conclusions of this study, the following recommendations are offered in the form of an action plan to increase revenue and improve the marketability of the program.

Financial Actions

1. **Redistribute overhead allocations evenly across all summer program courses.** This would provide a more realistic picture of the profitability–loss status of each program.

2. **Raise the maximum number of students per Summerworks course to 20 from 16.** Although this may present challenges in the delivery of curriculum, with implications for customer satisfaction, it will save the direct expenses associated with opening another section (approximately $1,500).

3. **Consider reducing courses from 30 to 20 hours** (equivalently from 15 meetings to 8 meetings) to lower the price and make the courses more attractive to students. This would reduce revenue, but it would save on the direct expenses.

4. **Avoid scheduling course start-ups on or immediately before long holiday weekends.**

5. **Eliminate the Clerk A3 position from the Summer Arts Program office.** A downsizing of the Special Programs office would implement a saving of approximately $31,000 across the three program areas and reduce the program overhead load.

6. **Implement loss-prevention by devising ways to minimize the number of student withdrawals from the program.** This will entail several steps:

   a) Provide more effective customer service.

   b) Improve pre-registration counselling through a checklist of questions that can be asked over the telephone to help prospective students make appropriate course selections.

c) Revise course descriptions to reflect the specific content and learning outcomes of each course.

d) Hold a one-day instructors' workshop on teaching standards and interactive learning strategies to encourage excellence in pedagogical approaches and delivery methods.

Marketing Actions

1. **Develop a more aggressive marketing campaign.** Reconcentrate monies on the *Globe and Mail*, an effective venue (@$800 per ad), to save $900 over the previous year's advertising costs. Run a short-term series of strategically placed radio ads. Give the summer program prominence on the Clearwater College website or enlist graduating students from the COMM354 Web Design course to develop a related web page. Offer free arts-related events throughout the year to raise the profile and prestige of the summer program, especially at key times when registration drives are in progress.

2. **Become more proactive in terms of community outreach.** The success of the Canon-sponsored Clearwater Photography Contest and the positive reception of a series of free program-related summer concerts raised the profile of both the program and the college within the community. The launching of other initiatives, such as a spring open house, could increase awareness of the program during the crucial pre-registration period.

3. **Introduce a "flat rate" program for repeat registrants.** Close to 20 per cent of last summer's registrants enrolled in more than one course, but were not exempt from having to pay a registration fee for every course they took. A flat-rate program fee would allow students to take as many courses as they wished by paying a single registration fee of $550.

4. **Carry out further market research.** Test newly revised curriculum on focus groups drawn from the community and from among previous registrants.

Curriculum Development Actions

1. **Eliminate non-productive/non-profitable courses.** Replace these courses with more generic courses that could attract larger and more sustainable audiences. New, lecture-style courses such as Writing Your Autobiography and the History of Jazz could be offered, eliminating the cap on class size that is associated with workshop-delivered curriculum.

2. **Restructure the summer Danceworks program.** Refocus courses to appeal to a younger audience, aged 10–17, through the addition of jazz and hip-hop classes.

3. **Restructure the Drama workshop.** Dispense with the guest speakers at $150 per 90-minute session, for a saving of $1,200 on the afternoon curriculum of the event. We will dispense with the afternoon special guest speaker. This constitutes further savings of $2,000 on afternoon curriculum.

4. **Consider cutting the length of some courses from 30 hours to 20 hours.** Course-time reduction would also help to revitalize less popular courses with marginal enrolment that proved popular in our initial market research.

7

5. **Offer Saturday intensive courses and dance-drama workshops.** This move would attract a new audience, one comprising individuals whose schedules do not ordinarily allow them to take on-campus daytime courses.

Service-Delivery Actions

1. **Improve the physical environment of college facilities.** Begin by upgrading or repairing air conditioning and ventilation systems so that room temperatures do not exceed a comfortable 23 degrees Celsius.

2. **Upgrade student services during the summer months.** Issue parking passes to students enrolled in full-day courses and waive the system of hourly rates. Relocate vending machines so that they're adjacent to summer program classrooms and lecture halls for easy access.

3. **Review equipment-delivery procedures.** Implement measures to ensure A/V equipment and other resources reach classes on time to minimize inconvenience and loss of instruction time.

8

REFERENCES

"About the Banff Centre for the Arts." (2005). Retrieved from http://www.banffcentre.ca/about/history

Eisner, E.W. (2004, Oct. 14). What can education learn from the arts about the practice of education? *Journal of International Education and the Arts*, 5(4), Retrieved from http://ijea.asu.edu

Elster, A. (2002, Nov. 12). Learning through the arts program goals, features and pilot results. *Journal of International Education and the Arts,* 2(7), Retrieved from http://ijea.asu.edu/v2n7

APPENDIX A

Revenue Breakdown

A breakdown of the total revenue of $266,635 is set out below:

Summerworks (SW) Registration		
721 @ $337		$242,977
Musicworks (MW) Registration		
35 @ $299		10,465
Danceworks (DW) Registrations		
52 @ $450		23,400
Student withdrawals:		
Registrations		
129 @ $337	($43,473)	
Cancellation fee		
129 @ $32	4,128	
		(39,345)
Administration fee—$12		
Relating to SW — 721 × $12	$ 8,652	
Relating to MW — 35 × $12	420	
Relating to DW — 52 × $12	624	
Relating to other programs		
($23,701 – $8,652 – $420 – $624)	14,005	
		23,701
Other variables such as course-price range differential		
		5,437
		$266,635

A breakdown of the total revenue shortfall of $46,902 is set out below:

Musicworks Program		
(216) @ $299		($ 64,584)
Summerworks Registration Excess		
121 @ $337		40,777
Danceworks Registration Shortfall		
(28) @ $450		(12,600)
$12 Related Registration Fee Amounts		
(−216 + 93 − 28) = (151) × $12		(1,812)
Unexplained		(9,019)
	Total	($ 46,902)

Expenses

Summary of Indirect Expense Variance

Stipend & Benefits—negative variance	$ 5,874
Casual & Overtime—negative variance	23,011
Supplies—negative variance	335
Marketing Services—negative variance	4,802
Staff Expense—negative variance	1,831
Registration Costs—positive variance	(2,460)
Consulting—negative variance	67
Negative variance	$33,460

Summary of Direct Expense Variances

Stipend & Benefits—positive variance	$14,502
Teaching Aids—negative variance	(4,552)
Program Arrangements—positive variance	4,136
Positive variance	$14,086

11

APPENDIX B

Student Exit Evaluation Survey Results

Responses to this survey were provided in confidence to Clearwater College for purposes of program planning and instruction. This survey was administered to students upon course completion. Of a total of 820 students enrolled in the summer program, 760 completed the exit survey.

Criteria	Percentage of Respondents Ranking				
	Excellent	Very Good	Good	Poor	Not Applicable
Performance and enthusiasm of the instructor	34	38	28	10	—
Ability of the instructor to provide a supportive learning environment	25	20	40	5	—
Opportunity for input and feedback	32	48	14	5	1
Classroom materials	10	15	60	20	10
Physical environment	11	30	35	24	—
Overall satisfaction with the instructor and course	30	40	15	15	—
Innovation and appropriateness of instruction and delivery methods	28	54	12	6	—

Sampling of Comments and Suggestions on How Course/Program Could Be Improved:

- Offer weekend or evening instruction to accommodate students' work schedules and child-care responsibilities.

- Upgrade malfunctioning air conditioning system to ensure a comfortable learning environment for all students during the hottest month of the year.

- Assist course instructors through effective and efficient delivery of audiovisual equipment.

- Extend opening hours of food services or relocate vending machines close to classroom locations.

- Improve parking-fee system by issuing passes to students enrolled in full-day courses.

- Raise awareness of program within the community.

Report-Writing Checklist

The Whole Report

☐ Does the report fulfill your original intentions? Does it present a solution that is practical, financially feasible, and appropriate?

☐ Is the report professional in its presentation? Is the title complete and accurate? Does the transmittal letter tell readers what they need to know about the report? Does the table of contents offer an overview?

☐ Is the report shaped according to the needs of its primary and secondary audiences?

Introduction

☐ Has the problem or report situation been sufficiently analyzed? Does the purpose statement reflect this analysis?

☐ Does the introduction set the stage for the report? Does it supply information that brings readers up to speed and guide them through the report?

Findings

☐ Is the problem subdivided for investigation?

☐ Does each heading cover all the material under it? Are all subheads under a heading in parallel form?

☐ Is your analysis given in sufficient detail?

☐ Are facts and assertions supported by evidence?

☐ Have you used sources that are reliable and appropriate for the type of information you are expected to present?

☐ Do you cite your sources using appropriate documentation style?

☐ Is your language moderate and bias-free?

☐ Do visuals, if they are needed, support and clarify written material, without distortion? Are they straightforward and clearly labelled?

Conclusions and Recommendations

☐ Do facts and findings support conclusions and recommendations? Are recommendations linked to purpose?

☐ Have you achieved what you wanted to achieve in writing your report?

WORKSHOPS AND DISCUSSION FORUMS

Proposals and Their Criteria—Government-Subsidized Summer Business for Students: From a posting in a local employment office, you and your classmates have learned that the provincial government has created a special grants program to which students can apply for assistance in operating a summer business. The maximum grant available is $1,500. Now pretend that you and members of your group are responsible for establishing the criteria for awarding the grants—age restrictions and terms of eligibility, restrictions on what the money can be used for, and a protocol for reporting expenditures at the end of the summer. Exchange your application criteria with another group. On the basis of what is asked for, draft a proposal that pitches a winning project.

WRITING IMPROVEMENT EXERCISES

1. **Analyzing Requests for Proposals:** Search business classifieds, browse trade journals, or go online to company websites to find an example of an RFP. Note the specifications and requirements of the job. Include an outline of the proposal you would submit. Which heads would be appropriate for the proposal you would have to write?

2. **Identifying Conclusions and Recommendations:** Identify each of the following as either a conclusion or a recommendation:
   a) Begin an in-house daycare program operating from 8:00 a.m. to 6:00 p.m. five days a week.
   b) Disseminate this report in some form to employees to ensure their awareness of our company's commitment to uphold its ethics and procedures policy.
   c) Over half the respondents use public transit to commute to and from campus at least three days a week.
   d) Recruit student leaders to organize, implement, and staff a walk-safe program.
   e) The effectiveness of RPG's ethics program during the first year of implementation is most evidenced by the active participation of employees in the program and the 2,498 contacts employees made through the various channels available to them regarding ethics concerns.
   f) A safety-monitor program that relies solely on volunteers can be successful because of the availability of volunteer monitors and support for the initiative within the student body.

3. **Distinguishing Informal and Formal Reports:** Identify the following writing situations as requiring either informal reports or formal reports:
   a) You have been asked to investigate the automation of selected human resources functions, including technologies, training, resources, maintenance, and IT support. You must report your findings and make recommendations to the director of HR.
   b) You have attended the three-day general meeting and conference of Certified Management Accountants held in Edmonton, March 27–29. Your departmental manager has asked you to file a trip report to update him on your activities.
   c) Pit Stop, a chain of 1,900 convenience stores, is considering taking the fast-food trend a step further by incorporating several brands into its strategy. You have been asked by the chief of franchise and marketing operations to investigate and make recommendations on three quick-service restaurant franchises with potential to share space with your convenience-store outlets.

4. **Formatting Reference Entries:** On the basis of the following bibliographic information, create appropriate reference entries in APA style.
   a) Authors: James W. Steelman, Shirley Desmond, and LeGrand Johnson
   Title: *Facing Global Limitations*
   Publisher: New York, Rockford Press
   Date of publication: 2000
   b) Author: Virginia Galt

Title of Article: "Time for some new tips for older job seeks"
Title of journal: *Globe and Mail*
Date of publication: January 29, 2005
Page: B9

c) Author: Jerry Useem
Title of Article: "Conquering Vertical Limits"
Title of Journal: *Fortune*
Date: February 9, 2001

d) Title of Article: "The Case Against the Business Case"

Online Source: The Conference Board Review
Date of publication: Spring 2012
Date of retrieval: September 27, 2012
URL: <http://www.tcbreview.com/features/the-case-against-the-business-case.html>

5. **Creating a Work Plan:** For any of the following case study exercises, prepare a work plan that lists the problem/purpose of the report, outlines the method of conducting research, establishes a tentative outline, and sets out a work schedule.

CASE STUDY EXERCISES

1. **Formal Report—Customer Service Check-Up:** Imagine that a chain of clothing retailers has received complaints about the quality of its store maintenance and customer service. You have been asked to inspect one of the chain's stores and note your experiences and observations. Were you greeted when you arrived? Was the store clean and well maintained? Did a sales associate ask about your clothing needs? Did the associate suggest other items in which you might be interested? Was the sales associate polite, courteous, and helpful? Was the fitting room you used clean and well maintained? Did the sales associate return and offer to find other items or garment sizes for you? If you made a purchase, was it processed quickly and efficiently? Make several visits in order to arrive at a fair and proper assessment. Consider if previous complaints about customer service were justified and make recommendations based on your observations and experiences. Direct your report to Cindy Latimer, vice-president of in-store operations.

2. **Formal Research Report Requiring Secondary Research:** Select one of the following questions on which to base a report and draw up an outline that contains functional or descriptive headings.

a) Should online retailers compile customer profiles to help market their products?

b) Are on-site corporate daycare programs worth the cost?

c) Can mobile *telework*—working from home or car—increase productivity?

d) Do people over forty have trouble finding jobs in information technology? Is ageism rife in the IT industry?

e) What coaching and development should be provided to managers preparing performance reviews?

f) Outsourcing?

g) Can temporary pop-up stores play a role in the marketing of new products?

3. **Informal Internal Proposal—Improving Your Workplace:** Think of a problem or challenge you have observed or experienced at your workplace. Do you have an idea or solution that would help to save money, reduce costs, improve customer service, improve quality, or increase productivity? Consider the feasibility of what you want to propose so that you may justify expenditures in terms of the bottom line. Write up your idea in a brief informal proposal.

4. **Informal Internal Proposal—Working from Home:** What opportunities are there to work from home? Consider what tech tools would be needed at home (e.g., computers, Internet access) and who would pay for them. Make your case in an informal proposal to your current employer or instructor.

5. **Informal Internal Proposal—Mobile Devices:** As a textbook sales representative for a publisher of educational resources, you are away from the office for up to a week at a time as you make sales calls to the schools, colleges, and universities in your territory. Write a proposal in which you suggest that

you and other sales representatives be provided with wireless laptops and smartphones.

6. **Proposal—New Look for Sporting Goods Chain:** Sport Fundamentals, a retail sporting goods chain with 12 stores positioned in major malls and downtown locations, wants a new store image, one that will appeal to a younger, hipper demographic. Sports Fundamentals is looking for a creative design concept that will update store exteriors, improve ease of access, maximize retail space (which averages 370 square metres per store), and create an identifiable store brand based on design elements. Write a formal proposal for Omar Khan, president of Sports Fundamentals.

7. **Informal Proposal—Request for IT Services:** Roughly one-third of your staff now telecommute, working from home three to five days a week. You require ongoing on-site technical support and repair from a dependable mobile service able to make house calls within one business day. Your telecommuting employees live within a 100-kilometre radius of your office. Investigate the options within your area and make a case to the vice-president of operations in an informal proposal.

8. **Short Informal Proposal—Public Speakers Wanted:** Young At Heart, a local seniors organization, is looking for talented public speakers and entertainers to fill its thirty-hour program of events for the year ahead. It is scouting musicians, stand-up comedians, community outreach volunteers, experienced world travellers, and sports enthusiasts to give a series of three hour-long performances, lectures, demonstrations, travelogues, or talks about hobbies. Prepare a short proposal detailing a particular skill, talent, or public service experience and outlining the format and content of each hour-long presentation, with special mention of any audiovisual equipment or materials you will use or require. Explain why the program you propose would be of special interest to seniors.

ONLINE ACTIVITIES

1. **Practice Exercise in Avoiding Plagiarism:** Log on to this exercise from the Online Writing Lab at Purdue University to test your knowledge of plagiarism as it applies to a variety of resource usages. Identify potential risks of plagiarism and decide what to do in each situation.
http://owl.english.purdue.edu/owl/resource/589/04

2. **Exercise in Understanding the Problem of Plagiarism:** Read an article entitled "How Not to Plagiarize" from the Engineering Communication Centre at the University of Toronto, then try the plagiarism self-test—an online quiz consisting of various examples that must be rated from worst to best.
www.writing.utoronto.ca/advice/using-sources/how-not-to-plagiarize

3. **Report Structuring Exercise:** Log on to the site below, offered by the University of Surrey. Download the structuring exercise or work online, cutting and pasting sections of the report into their correct order.
www.surrey.ac.uk/Skills/pack/report.html

4. **Report Writing Exercise:** This exercise, from CILL Writing at Hong Kong Polytechnic University, presents a business situation involving a training course. Your task is to write a report on the course after first reading background documents and watching a series of interviews. You can submit your report for analysis and feedback, then modify it according to the instructions you receive.
http://elc.polyu.edu.hk/cill/reportvideo

5. **Using Formal Language in Reports:** Gain practice in formal writing by editing five boxes of text in which you replace informal words and phrases with formal ones. Submit your answers to check for results. Although somewhat formulaic, this exercise is useful practice for those suffering from writer's block.
http://elc.polyu.edu.hk/CILL/eiw/reportformality.aspx

6. **Report Correction Exercise:** Designed to help students improve their writing fluency, this exercise requires you to read a memo report and complete it by choosing the correct option from the drop-down list. You may check your answers at the end of the report, view explanations, and when finished read a corrected version.

   http://elc.polyu.edu.hk/CILL/eiw/ reportcorrection.aspx

7. **Abstract Writing Exercise:** Read "Abstracts and Executive Summaries" from the Faculty of Applied Science and Engineering at the University of Toronto, then follow the second link to try the abstract writing exercise from Mount Royal College.

   http://www.engineering.utoronto.ca/ Directory/students/ecp/handbook/ components/abstracts.htm

   http://uncgsoc301.wordpress.com/exercises/ exercise-6-writing-an-abstract/

8. **Organizing Your Report.** Complete these exercises from LearnHigher to gain practice in identifying standard report sections and arranging them in logical order. Scroll to the bottom of the page to check your answers.

   http://learnhigher.ac.uk/resources/files/ Report%20Writing/Reports_Organise_ Your_Report_Activity.pdf

12 Oral Communication

In this chapter you will learn to

1. Prepare for presentations and briefings by analyzing the occasion and profiling your audience.

2. Gather material, select content, and strategically structure your presentation.

3. Identify four methods of delivery.

4. Master effective public-speaking skills and apply strategies to increase confidence.

5. Incorporate visual and multimedia aids, including flip charts, handouts, overhead transparencies, and PowerPoint slides.

6. Handle questions and conduct follow-up.

7. Organize, manage, and participate in meetings effectively.

8. Communicate by telephone productively.

9. Deal with the media and get your message across.

Oral Presentations

The ability to speak well on the job is as important as the ability to write effectively. Because so much daily work activity is carried out through speech rather than the written word alone, oral communication and public-speaking skills can be critical to career advancement, whatever your job duties may happen to be. In fact, **oral presentations**, done well, can enhance your reputation within an organization. They represent valuable opportunities to sell your ideas and demonstrate both your competence and your value to your employers and co-workers.

The prospect of speaking in front of others, however, can be nerve-racking. It is good to remember that giving a presentation is in many ways similar to writing a document and draws on the same organizational strategies and audience adaptations with the same basic purposes to inform, persuade, and promote goodwill. There are also some distinct differences to keep in mind—as well as ones that differentiate live public speaking from a recorded performance. In public speaking, there are no pause or playback features. As far as the audience is concerned, a presenter has only one chance to make a positive impression and get the message across correctly and persuasively. Listeners, after all, don't have the luxury of being able to review a message, as they would when rereading printed text. Ideas and information must therefore be delivered for easy comprehension and retention, so listeners will not only remember what was said, but know or believe a particular thing or be motivated to act on that information once the presentation is over. Oral presentations should (1) be simply structured, (2) be arranged around a specific purpose, and (3) clearly identify the dominant idea listeners are meant to retain. A presentation will have greater impact if supporting details are simplified and visuals are designed for readability at a glance. The advantage of the spoken word is that it provokes an immediate reaction and allows for instant feedback. Listeners' **non-verbal cues**—their moment-by-moment reactions—can help you gauge and modify your performance; their comments and questions will, in the end, tell you if you succeeded in getting your message across.

> **oral presentation** an informative or persuasive speech delivered using only notes and visual aids to guide the speaker's performance.

> **non-verbal communication** a form of communication that does not use words, only media such as gestures, eye contact, and tone of voice.

TYPES OF ORAL PRESENTATIONS

The term *oral presentation* covers a variety of speaking activities—ranging in length, formality, and style of delivery—which include the following:

- conducting workshops, seminars, and training sessions;
- addressing staff meetings;
- giving talks to clubs, societies, and organizations;
- making sales presentations;
- making a speech to a conference or gathering; and
- giving an oral report or briefing.

ANALYZING THE SITUATION AND AUDIENCE

An effective presentation starts with knowing what to expect of your surroundings and what the audience expects of you. Understanding the context for your presentation is essential if you hope to connect with the audience and achieve your purpose, whether that purpose is to inform, persuade, or simply convey goodwill. It is essential to keep your audience's needs, expectations, and perspective in mind in order to make appropriate adaptations.

How much assessment you need to do depends on whether you are speaking to colleagues, visitors, or outsiders. Preparing to speak to an internal business audience involves less analysis because your credibility is already established with listeners who know you. It is reasonable to assume they will be interested in your topic because it is relevant to shared business interests. However, speaking to outsiders presents greater challenges because it is harder to predict if your audience will be receptive and to determine what the audience's needs and expectations might be.

Who is your audience?

- Why will they be there and what will they expect from you?
- What is their attitude toward you and your subject? Will there be resistance? How can you counter any resistance?
- What is your organizational role and relationship to your audience? Is your rank in the organization above or below your listeners?
- Will there be decision-makers in the audience? What are their concerns?
- Are there tensions or conflicts within the audience?
- How knowledgeable will audience members be in the subject area? How much should you explain?
- How will this topic appeal to this audience?
- How can you relate this information to audience members' needs? What questions will they want you to answer?

What is the speaking situation?

- What is the purpose of your presentation? What underlying concern has necessitated it?
- What level of formality does your organization usually expect from people giving oral presentations?
- In what surroundings will you make your presentation? Is the setting formal or informal?
- How large is the room? Will it be equipped with a microphone or PA system? What are the acoustics and seating arrangements like? What are the visual-aid facilities and how are they placed relative to the audience?
- How much time has been allotted for your presentation? How long will listeners expect you to speak?
- Is your presentation the prime attraction (the only presentation to be given) or will there be presentations from other speakers? How does your presentation tie in with the actions or topics of other participants?
- What will happen before and after your presentation?

An effective presentation is designed around a specific purpose. That means you should have something clear and definite to say and a reason for saying it.

STRUCTURING PRESENTATIONS

The structure of your presentation is important. Without the integration and coherence that good organization provides, listeners can easily lose the thread of your argument and miss important points. A simple, effective structure that accommodates three to five key ideas is the best way to keep your listeners with you. Three common types of structure are suitable for an oral presentation:

- logical,
- narrative, and
- formal.

Logical Structure: Any presentation worth listening to must be logical in its approach. Listeners should be able to easily understand how each point you make relates to your purpose. You can use signpost words (*my first point, my next point*) to guide listeners through your presentation to show how what you have said relates to what comes next.

Narrative Structure: The ability to tell an accurate, credible, and compelling story can influence the acceptance of policies, procedures, and ideas. At the management level especially, this skill is valued. Turning your information into a good story can grab attention and make what you have to say memorable. Because statistics alone are abstract and often hard to grasp, narratives provide an important way to ground the information. In order for a storyline structure to work, however, the story itself must be well told, interesting, and relevant to your objectives.

Formal Structure: Skilful handling of repetition can aid meaning and retention. This is the idea behind the most common structure for presentations, with its three familiar divisions:

- introduction—tell them what you are going to tell them,
- main sections—tell them, and
- conclusion—tell them what you have told them.

Any informative presentation should contain supporting details—facts, statistics, and other forms of evidence—to back up your main points. Visual aids help to show listeners what you mean, working on the old assumption that a picture is worth a thousand words.

DEVELOPING A THREE-PART PRESENTATION

1. **Introduction:** An effective introduction prepares your audience to understand your ideas and makes them want to listen to what follows. Use your opening remarks to (1) arouse interest, (2) identify yourself and establish your credibility, (3) make your purpose clear, and (4) preview your main points. Part of your introduction can also be reserved for background information or a statement of how you will proceed. Don't forget that your opening remarks provide you with an opportunity to build rapport and establish common ground with your audience, making it clear why they should listen.

    Aim to hook your listeners in the first ninety seconds. In a world of sound bites and instant messaging, audiences have come to expect fast starts and immediate rewards for their attention. You can capture your audience through strong content and energetic delivery, but first make it easy for your audience to want to listen by choosing a relevant and interesting speech title that sets up positive expectations about what you have to say. Dull, lifeless speech titles repel potential listeners before the first word has even been uttered. A title with an element of surprise or novelty can make a presentation sound enticing and worth listening to.

You may want to introduce your topic with an attention-getting device, depending on the situation:

- State an unexpected statistic or fact, or point out an intriguing aspect of your topic.
- Ask a question that raises an issue you will address.
- Display a key visual aid or perform a demonstration, perhaps one that involves the audience.
- Cite a relevant quotation.
- Tell a joke or anecdote, but only if it is fresh, appropriate, and relevant to the situation (and never make a joke at the expense of the audience).

2. **Body:** The body of your presentation should develop your main theme and focus your audience's thinking. Always base your content on the most recent data available—fresh information usually gets the most attention. Whether your presentation is persuasive or informative, you should balance information with context and analysis, so your talk is more than just a torrent of facts. Give specific examples and offer properly attributed quotations from respected authorities, paraphrased if necessary in language the audience will easily understand. Anticipate questions and incorporate the answers into your presentation. Depending on your material, you may present your ideas and bring together facts in any of a variety of ways:

- chronological order—develop a timeline,
- topical/logical order—relate parts to the whole or introduce points in order of importance or reverse order,
- spatial order—map ideas visually,
- journalistic questions—ask *Who? What? Where? When? Why?* and *How?*,
- problem–solution—demonstrate that a problem exists and offer a solution or range of solutions,
- exclusion of alternatives—argue for the remaining option,
- causal order—explain a series of causes and effects,
- comparison/contrast—base assessment on similarities and differences,
- pro–con—review the arguments for and against a certain thing, and
- process—identify a sequence of steps or stages.

No matter which method you choose, you should clearly announce each point as it comes so listeners will know when you have completed one point and begun another.

3. **Conclusion:** Don't simply stop talking and walk away. You should end by helping your audience understand the significance of your presentation and remember its main points. Your closing comments should be brief—a quick summary developed in one of the following ways:

- Restate the main issues you want the audience to remember.
- Restate the point you started with in order to frame your presentation.
- Issue a challenge or call to action (this is suitable for persuasive presentations).
- Ask a question for the audience to think about.

Your conclusion should bring the presentation full circle and leave the audience with a positive impression of you and your ideas, so never end it prematurely just because you are rattled or nervous. Your introduction and conclusion may be the last parts of your presentation you write, but they are also the most crucial in helping your audience understand the value of your ideas.

ORAL PRESENTATION OUTLINE

Planning a presentation can be challenging, especially if you have to keep track of a number of points. Use the following template to prepare an outline or expand it to suit your needs.

Title _____

Purpose _____

I. **INTRODUCTION**

    A. Device to gain attention _____

    B. Establish credibility _____

    C. Involve audience _____

    D. State purpose _____

    E. Preview main points _____

    Transition _____

II. **BODY**

    A. First main point _____

        Supporting details   1. _____

                          2. _____

                          3. _____

    Transition _____

    B. Second main point _____

        Supporting details   1. _____

                            2. _____

                          3. _____

    Transition _____

    C. Third main point _____

        Supporting details   1. _____

                            2. _____

                          3. _____

    Transition _____

III. **CONCLUSION**

    A. Summary of main points _____

    B. Closing device _____

    C. Question period _____

USING VISUAL AIDS

visual aids typically charts, graphs, and tables used to present data in clearly understandable and appealing ways.

Visual aids help you to show what you mean. Not only do they clarify and emphasize your material, they increase its impact, helping to aid retention and involve your audience. As well as supplementing the spoken word, they also serve as an aid to your own memory, eliminating the need for additional notes and, along with it, helping to improve your poise, delivery, and self-confidence.

Oral presentations enhanced by visual aids are more persuasive, credible, and professional. It is therefore important to use good visual aids whenever possible and to know how to use them effectively so they enhance your message rather than detract from it. After all, the audience is supposed to listen to you and not be too distracted by your props and technology, which are best used in a supporting role.

General Tips for Presentations

- Never allow visual aids to dominate so much that they prevent you from connecting with your audience or getting your message across.

- Use aids sparingly for maximum impact; don't confuse your audience by using more than 12 visuals per presentation.

- Make your visuals consistent in size, font, contrast, and spacing. Type should be boldfaced and no smaller than 30-point size.

- Limit the amount of information on each visual to avoid clutter and confusion: simple graphs and charts to show data trends; no more than two illustrations per visual; no more than five or six numbered or bulleted points; and no more than 35 words on seven lines.

- Prepare each visual carefully and proofread it for accuracy.

- Give each visual aid a title that makes a point.

- Test audiovisual equipment in advance and check the optics of the room to ensure all participants have unobstructed views of the materials you plan to use.

- Put up your visual aid only when you are ready to talk about it, and give your audience a few moments to digest the information it supplies.

- Comment on—but do not read from—what you show, and match your delivery to the content of the visual. Remove the visual as soon as you are finished with it.

TYPES OF PRESENTATION AIDS

The type of visual aids you use to support your presentation depends on their cost, the formality of the situation, and the flexibility you need to convey your ideas and connect with your audience.

Chalkboard, Whiteboard, and Blank Flip Charts

Chalkboards, whiteboards, and **flip charts** are flexible and useful aids, suitable for small audiences (under thirty) and informal presentations. Speaking and writing at the same time can be a challenge. If you speak first and then write down what you have said, there may be odd lapses in your delivery. Post only your most essential points and write legibly, in letters large and distinct enough to be clear to everyone in the audience. Then explain what you have written, standing to the side and turning to the audience. Avoid speaking into the board or flip chart—the audience likely won't be able to hear you. The main disadvantage of these aids is their messiness: whiteboards require dry-ink markers that can smear and smell unpleasant; cleaning whiteboard and chalkboard surfaces can be a nuisance and often will leave you ink-stained or in a cloud of dust.

flip chart a large stand-mounted writing pad with bound pages that can be turned over at the top.

Prepared Flip Charts and Posters

Prepared flip charts and posters are the most basic of aids. They must be large enough to be seen by the entire audience and clear enough to communicate your points. Visuals must always look professional. In general, prepared flip charts and posters are suitable for audiences of up to forty or fifty, and they can be used to display fairly complicated material. Their main drawbacks are their size, which makes them awkward to carry around, and their low-tech appearance, which makes them less appealing to technically savvy audiences.

Overhead Projector Transparencies

Although computer-based presentations have largely replaced the use of overhead transparencies, you may encounter a situation where transparencies are recommended or preferred. These versatile visuals can be prepared cheaply on a copier or computer and easily stored for future use. The **overhead projectors** used to display them are widely available and allow an image to be projected in varying sizes, so it is visible to even the largest audience. Overlaying transparencies—the technique of placing one item on top of another—is useful for adding or modifying data. Despite these obvious pluses, overheads are decidedly low-tech. Any presentation supported by them can seem outdated and less than cutting-edge. To use this aid to best advantage, keep the lights on as you show your transparencies (so the audience stays awake) and speak loudly enough for your voice to be heard over the hum of the projector fan. Focus the image and check the backup bulb before you begin to talk, then make sure you stand to one side so you don't block the audience's view of the screen. It is never a good idea to read from transparencies. Limit the number of transparencies you show to curb your reliance on them at the expense of other delivery techniques.

overhead projector a device that projects the enlarged image of a transparency onto a screen.

FIGURE 12.1   INEFFECTIVE Transparency

Overhead Transparencies

This is an example of an ineffective transparency.

Well-planned overhead transparencies add interest and help to clarify the message you deliver in your presentation. Effectively designed transparencies communicate quickly and clearly. There are several important guidelines to follow in creating overhead transparencies.

Use consistent type style, **Size**, and spacing.

Use a readable font.

Use a series of overlays to explain a complex system or to elaborate on the base.

Limit the amount of information, keeping the number of bulleted or numbered items to five or six per transparency. Avoid overloading bulleted or numbered items. Do not attempt to communicate too much information. Use a series of transparencies to explain a complex point or topic.

Use boldface type that is at least 30 points in size (letters of at least ¼ inch in height).

Cover **ONE** idea per transparency.

Keep the image clear, simple, and uncluttered, with as few lines as possible, and ensure that every element contributes to the communication objective.

Enlarge charts, graphs, and illustrations to fit the 8 by 10–inch transparency format.

Replace or enlarge lettering in charts, graphs, or illustrations not specifically designed as transparency originals.

FIGURE 12.2 EFFECTIVE Transparency

GUIDELINES FOR CREATING OVERHEAD TRANSPARENCIES

- Keep the image clear, simple, and uncluttered.

- Ensure every element contributes to the communication objective.

- Use a consistent and readable boldface font (30 points or larger) along with consistent spacing.

- Focus on one idea per transparency—no more than five or six bulleted or numbered items.

- Use overlays or a series of transparencies to explain complex topics or systems.

- Enlarge charts, graphs, and illustrations to fit the 8 by 10–inch format.

Videos, Films, Models, and Samples

Films and videos are most effective in the form of short clips, introduced strategically to reinforce key points or concepts. While a well-made clip may be memorable, such an aid should not be allowed to take over the presentation. If a product is being discussed, it can be displayed and manipulated to demonstrate its use and capabilities.

Handouts

Distributing handouts that summarize your presentation plan or provide a permanent record of graphs and other data can greatly enhance the audience's understanding and retention. Typical handouts include outlines, articles, brochures, summaries, speaker notes, and even printed copies of PowerPoint slides (featuring two, three, four, six, or nine slides per page). It is important to time the distribution of materials for minimal disruption. Unless participants need the handout to understand what you say, such materials should be given out in advance or at the end—not in the middle of your presentation, when the sound of rattling papers can drown you out.

Multimedia and Computer Visuals

PowerPoint presentation software offering standard templates and other features that aid in the design of integrated text and effective visuals.

Computer-based presentations are the medium of choice for business people today. Graphic programs such as **PowerPoint** now make it possible to deliver a dynamic, professional-looking presentation and tell your story visually in several ways:

- as an onscreen slide show (complete with transition effects)
  - viewed on your laptop monitor by just a few people or
  - viewed on a big screen by a large audience (multimedia projector required);
- on paper (audience handouts with one or several images per page);
- on overhead transparencies; or
- output to 35-millimetre slides.

The capabilities of PowerPoint make it easy for you to create slides with a variety of formats, such as bulleted lists, numeric charts, tables, or organizational charts (pie, bar, and line charts). You can design slides that not only incorporate text, graphics, and artwork, but also include audio clips, animation, and video features. PowerPoint's *build* capability enables you to add, highlight, or reposition text and incorporate visual effects right up until the time you present. Once you have designed and assembled your slide show, you can take the further step of publishing your presentation on the Internet or your company's intranet.

DESIGNING A POWERPOINT PRESENTATION

With its many features, a PowerPoint presentation is sure to impress, but its slickness can sometimes fail to engage an audience. Don't let the "wow factor" of an electronic presentation overshadow what you have to say. The following are a few tips for making the best of what PowerPoint has to offer:

template a stored pattern for a document from which new documents can be made.

- **Use templates.** PowerPoint comes stocked with **templates** for constructing slides quickly and easily. These combine borders, fonts, and colours for optimal visual effects and offer guidance on a variety of layouts. Once you gain confidence in using PowerPoint, you can customize templates to suit your needs.

- **Choose a colour scheme** that relates similar elements, highlights important points (warm colours are good for this), and permits good visibility with available room lighting. Use dark backgrounds (with light text) only in darkened rooms. Dark text on light backgrounds is best for well-lit rooms. Restrict yourself to four or five colours.

- **Keep slides simple**, with a maximum of seven lines of text and no more than seven words per line. Use boldface, sans serif type in consistent point sizes for easy readability. Cramming too much information on a slide makes it difficult for your audience to read and listen at the same time and is an annoying source of eye strain; interspersing or combining text with visual elements can allow viewers to absorb information more readily.

- **Put titles on slides** so you can find them easily during your presentation. If you plan to save your presentation, name your files so you will remember what they contain.

- **Don't use too many slides.** A slide marathon can induce boredom and put your audience to sleep. Consider the amount of information your audience can absorb in the allotted time. Count on spending two or three minutes discussing each slide.

- **Create an agenda slide** with a list of hyperlinked topics pertaining to specific areas of your presentation. This will help your audience grasp where you are in your presentation.

- **Use transitions and animation**—effects such as dissolve, fade, vortex, or wipe-out—to keep the eyes of your audience focused on the screen between slides and reveal bulleted items one at a time so audience members won't be tempted to read ahead. You can also dim previous items. It is usually best to use one transition effect consistently rather than over-dazzling viewers with excessive use of animation.

- **Proofread the slides** before your presentation. If you are printing the slides to use as handouts, print a copy in advance to make sure there are no errors. Handout pages feature smaller versions of your slides.

- **Use the Outline View and Slide Sorter** features to see the structure and big picture of your presentation and reorganize slides easily. Slide Sorter can help you gauge the flow of your presentation and its graphical elements; with Outline View you can see charts on the slides in miniature.

- **Produce speaker notes** to help remind you what to say about each slide. You can set up notes to appear on a second monitor or you can print them. When printed, each page will show the slide on the top half and the accompanying prompt notes on the bottom half. Consider using these notes as handouts.

- **Back up your work.** Don't let your time and effort in developing a presentation go to waste because of a system failure. Copy everything to a USB flash drive or a Zip disk, or write your files to a recordable CD-ROM. Take printouts of your slides with you to your presentation for ready reference if your equipment fails.

- **Rehearse the slide show.** To ensure your slide show fits the allotted time, you can do a dry run and have PowerPoint record the timing. You can then edit or eliminate slides, as needed.

- **Never read from a slide**—instead maintain eye contact with the audience as you explain and amplify each slide you display. Never assume that a slide is self-explanatory or will compensate for weak content.

FIGURE 12.3   Sample PowerPoint Slide

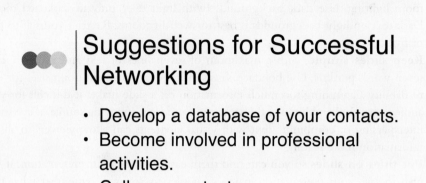

METHODS OF DELIVERY

Whichever method of delivery you choose for your presentation, it should bring out the best in your material and not call attention to itself at the expense of what you have to say. The following methods are the most common ways of delivering a speech to a group:

1. **Manuscript Method:** When you have to present extensive or complex data, with no margin for misinterpretation, you may need to prepare a script, which can be read from in full. Because it may be difficult to keep an audience with you as you focus on the printed page, make an extra effort to maintain as much visual contact with the audience as possible, looking up as you begin an important point or sentence. The script itself should be typed in large letters and tripled-spaced for easy readability at a glance. Remember that text read aloud can sound boring and expressionless due to flattened inflection, so try to inject some life into your voice by changing your tone appropriately and marking your script to indicate where special expression is required.

2. **Memorization:** While memorizing a speech can enliven the connection with the audience, this method can also backfire if you find yourself struggling to recall the exact words you have painstakingly committed to memory. Listeners can easily detect slip-ups and expressions made stale from constant repetition. For both you and your listeners, this has the effect of focusing attention not on what you have to say but on your ability to remember it. Unless you have years of acting experience, you may want to limit yourself to memorizing the general shape of your presentation, its key points, and your opening remarks instead of every word you plan to deliver.

3. **Impromptu Speaking:** Other situations—an informal gathering or celebration—might call for a short **impromptu speech**, made on the spur of the moment

impromptu speaking
a delivery method in which the speaker makes remarks without the aid of prepared notes.

without the aid of prepared notes or the benefit of advance notice. Listeners will not expect new information or specialized knowledge, only the ability to put a new spin on something you already know. A few pleasant, well-chosen remarks, delivered in less than two minutes, are usually all that is required.

4. **Extemporaneous Method:** Most oral presentations benefit from a combination of thoughtful preparation and a spontaneous, natural delivery style that engages the audience and holds its interest. Somewhere between ad libbing (which leaves too much to chance) and reading aloud word for word (which can lull listeners to sleep) is **extemporaneous speaking**—a form of delivery that sounds fresh and comfortable yet maintains a sense of order from the planning you have done.

Working with memory aids, such as small cues cards, can boost your confidence. They are often just enough to jog your memory, giving you the prompting you need so you can expand on the details. You should be able to fit an outline of your presentation on a single card, along with any quotations or statistics, lettered as large as possible in bold ink and highlighted for quick reference. An additional card can be used for each main section of your presentation, but don't make the mistake of writing out your speech in full. The purpose of this memory tool is simply to prompt you to your next main point. If you have had sufficient practice, you may be able do without the cards altogether. The immediacy your material gains from extemporaneous delivery helps to ensure your message gets across, whether your purpose is to inform or persuade your listeners.

> **extemporaneous speaking** a method of delivery in which the speaker relies on notes rather than manuscript memorization.

REHEARSING A PRESENTATION

Practice sessions can help your delivery go more smoothly—reducing nervousness, improving performance, and giving you the opportunity to judge your time and refine your content. Once you have drafted your presentation and prepared your visual aids, you are ready to practise the presentation itself.

- Practise aloud on-site or set up conditions that closely resemble those in which you will be speaking. Familiarize yourself with using your visual aids, integrating them and noting how long it will take to introduce each item and explain a particular point.
- Time yourself. Deliver your speech aloud, staying within the time permitted to you and noting where to pause. Make any adjustments, cutting out or adding material to ensure your presentation is the right length.
- Master your topic. Know your material well enough to be able to speak confidently without relying word for word on a script. Over-preparing by writing out your presentation in full and then memorizing it can kill spontaneity. Your delivery will be livelier if you speak from a note card that helps you familiarize yourself with the sequence of the material. Don't count on your ability to wing it or ad lib your way through an entire presentation.
- Record yourself or ask a friend to listen to your presentation and give you feedback. Rehearse in front of a mirror. Videotape yourself to detect mannerisms that might be distracting. Aim to develop a well-pitched speaking voice.
- Get a feel for the room. Inspect the seating arrangement and, if you plan to use them, make sure the sound system and audiovisual equipment are working properly. Set up or position a screen for optimal viewing.

- Learn stress-reduction techniques. Because shallow breathing can make you feel dizzy, breathe deeply several times before you begin. Visualize your success as a speaker. In the days or hours leading up to your presentation, you may find it helpful to try these techniques.
  - Practise breathing from your diaphragm (the muscular part of your respiratory system) with a simple exercise. Lie on your back and place your hand on your stomach. With your mouth closed, inhale through your nose and feel your stomach rise; exhale slowly, and feel your stomach fall. Try to spend the same length of time exhaling as inhaling, counting to yourself if you have to. Once you are comfortable with the technique, practise while sitting in a chair. You can do this exercise inconspicuously while you are waiting to be called to speak.
  - Attune yourself to your body's tension patterns by doing a muscular relaxation exercise. Lying on the floor, clench and unclench each muscle group several times, starting with your right and left fists, and progressing to your forearms, shoulders, neck, and so on. Focus on the difference between tension and relaxation.

DELIVERING A PRESENTATION

When the time comes to deliver your presentation, make every effort to be at your best and project a poised, professional image. If public speaking makes you nervous, put mind over matter and focus on your material and rapport with the audience. Stay in control of the situation, rather than allowing it to control you. Being confident and speaking in an animated way, with genuine enthusiasm for your topic, can give your words staying power. Here are a few tips for overcoming nervousness and reaching your audience:

1. **Dress appropriately.** It is important to look the part if you want to have credibility and be taken seriously. Wear comfortable, professional-looking clothing and adjust it in private beforehand (e.g., straightening a tie or skirt) so you don't appear dishevelled. Check your grooming for telltale signs of sloppiness (such as stains or stray hairs) and remove any large pieces of jewellery that might interfere with a microphone, should you require one.

2. **Arrive ahead of time** to familiarize yourself with your surroundings. Test the acoustics and decide where you can position yourself to be visible to the entire audience.

3. **Maintain good posture and move in a relaxed, controlled, natural way,** making an effort not to appear stiff and mechanical, like a robot. If you remain seated during a presentation, sit without slumping in order to improve your voice projection. If you're on your feet to speak, stand up straight and relax your shoulders. You can take a step or two to one side for emphasis at key transitional points, but otherwise stand without swaying from side to side. Avoid unnecessary hand gestures (such as waving, fidgeting, or jamming hands in pockets). The same goes for inappropriate facial expressions (exaggerated grinning or grimacing)—anything that might be distracting.

4. **Pause to collect yourself before beginning.** Adjust your notes, take a breath, maintain your poise, and take control of the situation. Look at the audience, not at your notes, as you make your opening remarks. Commit the first minute of your presentation to memory so you can speak unaided.

5. **Maintain eye contact** and use it to build rapport and gauge audience interest. The eyes of your audience members are a barometer of their interest, telling you if the audience is involved and "getting it." Listeners staring at the floor and looking around are visual cues that tell you your audience has tuned out. It may take time to get comfortable with your audience, so start by looking for a friendly face and making eye contact for a few seconds before you move on to someone else. Trying to scope out an audience all at once can make you appear nervous, so have direct eye contact with a number of people in your audience then glance from time to time at a the whole audience while speaking.

6. **Avoid long sentences and polysyllabic words.** Instead use concrete language and short, active-voice sentences that follow natural, conversational speech patterns.

7. **Speak in a clear, audible voice, but don't shout.** Maintain reasonable volume and aim for good, natural voice projection, gauged to the size of the audience and venue. Keep your head up and open your mouth slightly wider than in normal speech. This is a good way to prevent yourself from mumbling. If your voice won't be amplified, ask "Can you hear me at the back of the room?" as you begin.

8. **Pace yourself accordingly,** slowing down slightly for emphasis and speeding up slightly to convey enthusiasm—but always keeping the speed that comes with nervousness in check. Speak slowly enough to enunciate words clearly and prevent them from running together. If you are running out of time, don't speed up so much that listeners cannot follow what you are saying or mistake your haste for nervousness. You can make your content fit into the time you have left by editing your material as you go.

9. **Shape your phrasing and use inflection to give meaning and add interest.** Your pitch—or tone of voice—should sound natural and match your content. Use inflection—a downward emphasis at the end of sentences—to counteract the monotone that results from nervousness and also to emphasize key points. Never phrase a statement like a question, by raising your voice at the end. This habit can make you sound uncertain and nervous, sapping your listeners' confidence in what you have to say. Speak with conviction, as though you believe in what you are saying, to project your confidence and credibility.

10. **Never use slang or bad grammar.** Your credibility is on the line—speaking in an unprofessional way is the fastest way to lose it.

11. **Pause briefly to collect your thoughts** and create emphasis rather than resorting to fillers or verbal tics (such as *um*, *like*, and *ah*). Plan your transitions ahead of time so you can move easily from one topic to the next.

12. **Remember that you are a living, breathing human being**—not a statue. Don't stand as if transfixed by your audience. Remain calm and poised and remember to breathe (from the diaphragm rather than taking small gulps of air). Animate your delivery by integrating voice and gestures, leaving one hand free to point to visual aids. Gesture and move your body when you need to shift to major points. Be professional but let your personality shine through.

13. **Bring your presentation to a close.** Thank your audience and make materials available to them. Take questions and make yourself available for follow-up discussion, if necessary.

HANDLING QUESTIONS

Questions from the audience can help you gauge the effect and outcome of your presentation, and give you a second chance to get your message across. Audience members may want to obtain additional information, get clarification on a point you made, or express another point of view.

How you deal with questions depends on the formality of your presentation and the rapport you have with your audience. When speaking to a large audience, you can usually hold questions to the end. A question period afterwards can help to eliminate interruptions that can reduce momentum. During informal presentations, you may pause for questions at intervals, allowing you to check that the audience is still following you. Inviting spontaneous questions keeps audience members involved and prevents them from becoming too passive.

As you begin your presentation, make it clear how, if at all, you intend to handle questions. In taking questions, stay in control so the interaction is productive, not just a free-for-all:

1. **Listen carefully to the entire question.** If a question is confused or hard to hear, ask the questioner to repeat it or repeat or paraphrase it yourself for the audience. This has the added benefit of buying you time if you have to consider or formulate your answer—but don't automatically repeat every question that is asked of you.

2. **Separate strands of complex or two-part questions.** Disentangle parts of a question and deal with them one at a time.

3. **Ensure your answers are long enough, but not too long.** It might be tempting to launch into another speech during an end-of-presentation Q&A, but refrain from doing so—you might wear out your welcome. On the other hand, short answers can sound curt, even rude, so find a happy medium between the two. Relate your answer to the concerns of the questioner.

4. **Don't feel you have to answer every question.** There is usually no harm in admitting that you do not have an answer. In some cases, you can say the answer will come later in the presentation or you can throw the question to the audience for feedback and discussion.

5. **Never put down a questioner,** even if a question seems silly or has been fully answered during the presentation. It may be helpful to ask the questioner to explain further.

6. **Be firm with overzealous questioners.** Don't allow a persistent or long-winded questioner to monopolize the proceedings. Wait for a pause and politely interrupt, asking the questioner to briefly summarize the question being asked. The longer this person remains on a soapbox, the more frustrated other listeners will become.

7. **Stay on topic.** Don't allow yourself to be drawn off topic by an unrelated question or to have words put in your mouth. In the case of the former, say that the unrelated question is interesting and mention that you will be prepared to answer it later.

8. **Don't start by assuming a question is hostile.** Keep your cool and avoid sarcasm when challenged by an angry questioner, even if it means making an extra

effort not to reciprocate any unpleasantness in your response. If you overhear nasty asides from the audience, single out and ask the person responsible to share his comments with the group. If asides turn to heckling, you have several options: finesse your way out of the situation with a humorous reply, give a serious answer, carry on as if you have not heard the remark, appeal for a fair hearing, or ask that the heckler be ejected.

9. **End by thanking the audience for their questions and feedback.** Show that you value the question period as part of the communicative process.

TEAM-BASED PRESENTATIONS

Working together in a group of two or more can enhance the scope and complexity of a presentation, but it can also make the presentation more difficult to plan and execute. When there is a lack of coordination, speakers might end up contradicting or repeating each other, or not covering key topics. The presentation can lose its focus and clarity. Such problems can be avoided with proper planning and team effort.

Quick Tips for Team-Based Presentations

- Come to an agreement about who will cover which topic areas (conducting research, providing visual materials and handouts) and decide how the group will be governed (by majority rule, by consensus, or by shared leadership).

- Establish ground rules for the group, and give priority to presentation development meetings.

- Develop a work plan and set deadlines, working backward from the date of the presentation.

- Know what opinions each person will express to better prepare you to deal with questions and avoid controversy; agree how questions are to be handled.

- Allow time for rehearsals; plan the use of visual aids and how each person can help others use them; coordinate all presentation parts and visuals for consistency; and identify handover cues when one person takes over from another.

- Appoint a team leader to introduce speakers and help the group maintain its focus.

- Use previews, transitions, and summaries to help the audience understand how parts of the presentation interrelate. Provide a bridge to the next presenter with an introduction such as "Vanessa will now discuss time management."

- Adhere strictly to the allowed time for each speaker, but be flexible enough to accommodate last-minute changes and defer to the expertise of other group members.

SPECIAL-OCCASION PRESENTATIONS

From time to time, business people are involved in award-ceremony presentations, acceptances, and commemorations. Speaking for themselves or their companies, they may be asked to

- introduce or thank speakers/award recipients,
- propose toasts,
- give impromptu or after-dinner speeches, or
- deliver keynote addresses.

special-occasion presentation a speech made in appreciation, in acceptance of an award, in commemoration of an event, or by way of introduction.

An effective **special-occasion presentation** is tailored to the specific needs of an event. As a special-occasion speaker, you should anticipate what the moment requires you to say and be conscious of the impression you create. In making an introduction, for example, you should focus attention on what is to come—not on yourself. If public speaking scares you, you can follow a simple script:

> *I am pleased to introduce* (name of speaker) *from* (company/organization), *who is* (position, relevant achievements and experience).
> *Please join me in welcoming* (name of speaker).

Show that it is an actual pleasure and a privilege—not a chore—to perform the introduction. Your remarks should be congenial, gracious, brief, and most of all genuine, based on concrete facts rather than generalities.

Checklist for Oral Presentations

Strategy

- ☐ Does the opening device spark interest and engage the audience?
- ☐ Does the introduction establish credibility or provide background, as needed?
- ☐ Are ideas and approaches adapted to the audience's needs?
- ☐ Do presentation methods involve the audience?
- ☐ Does the degree of formality suit the situation?
- ☐ Does the conclusion provide a compelling sense of closure?

Content

- ☐ Do facts and information relate to the presentation's purpose?
- ☐ Is the supporting material specific and relevant?
- ☐ Does the presentation fulfill its purpose and provide information the audience finds interesting?
- ☐ Is care taken to clarify ideas that might be misconstrued or prove harmful to the speaker or the speaker's organization?

Organization

☐ Is an overview of the main points provided?

☐ Do verbal signposts announce transitions to major points? Are these transitions sufficient and logical?

Visuals

☐ Are visuals well designed, interesting, and appropriate for the size of the audience and room? Does each one supply the right amount of information without over-cramming data?

☐ Is each visual aid legible and error-free? Is it introduced at an appropriate point in the presentation?

☐ Do the visuals add to the presentation and enhance its meaning?

Delivery

☐ Is there direct and comfortable eye contact with the audience?

☐ Are voice, non-verbal cues, and gestures used effectively? Is the right tone and level of language used in addressing the audience?

☐ Are questions fielded effectively?

☐ Is the presentation paced according to the audience's level of understanding and interest?

☐ Does the speaker communicate interest in, and enthusiasm for, the topic?

☐ Does the speaker project confidence and professionalism? Have signs of stage fright been kept under control?

●● Organizing and Managing Meetings

Every year, a greater percentage of the average workday is spent in meetings. It is hardly surprising that the ability to work and communicate effectively in groups is a skill in increasingly high demand. How you perform in meetings—based on what you say, how you say it, and how you interact with others—provides clues to how competent you are and how ready you are to assume responsibility, solve problems, and work as part of a team. Meetings can be good for your profile, but they can also be good for groups as a whole, bringing leaders to the forefront, providing networking opportunities, and strengthening staff and client relations.

A meeting should be time well spent—a productive exercise that yields results and may even be enjoyable. For these goals to be met, a meeting has to be purposeful and properly managed, and it needs to draw on the strengths and input of its participants. Meetings can have one purpose or several of the following in combination:

- to give, share, or pool information;
- to brainstorm, develop, or evaluate ideas and policies;
- to find the root causes behind problems, solve problems, and solicit feedback;

- to make decisions (through consensus or voting) or help others make them (through consultation);
- to delegate work or authority;
- to develop projects or create documents collaboratively; and
- to motivate members and encourage teamwork.

TYPES OF MEETINGS

Meetings come in all shapes and sizes. They can be conducted face to face or through teleconferencing. They can also be hosted online with a program such as NetMeeting. They can be **internal,** involving only company personnel, or **external**, including outsiders. Meetings can differ substantially in the way they are run. **Formal meetings** operate by strict rules, under the guidance of a leader. Items up for discussion are pre-set by an agenda. Any motion must be introduced formally before it can be debated and voted on. Formal minutes then provide a record of each motion, vote, and action taken. **Informal meetings** are run more loosely, making them good forums for problem-solving, brainstorming, and team building. It may not even be necessary to hold votes if there is general agreement or consensus.

PREPARING FOR A MEETING

Poor planning and mismanagement can turn meetings into colossal time-wasters. It pays to make sure every meeting matters and has a clear reason for being convened. Behind-the-scenes planning can set the tone for what is to come and help you to make the best possible use of your time when participants finally sit down to meet. Consider the following elements before you call a meeting:

1. **Purpose:** There should be a good reason for calling a meeting. Define the task and make it clear to all participants. Do this at least two days in advance by distributing an agenda or supporting materials (see point 6). Keep in mind what you want to achieve, but don't weaken your effort by expecting to accomplish too much. Narrow the focus of the meeting by limiting the number of items on the agenda.

2. **Alternatives:** Consider if the meeting is truly necessary or if the same work can be accomplished without a meeting. Don't call a meeting if the same result can be achieved with a memo, group e-mail discussion, or a phone call, or if you can accomplish something on your own. Unnecessary meetings result in lost productivity.

3. **Participants:** Every person at a meeting should have a reason for being there. Limit participation to people who are most essential—those who will make the decision, implement it, or provide information crucial to decision-making. A meeting should be called off if not enough key people will be available to attend. If a meeting goes ahead without a few key participants, they should be e-mailed in advance for their views and contributions.

   Keep in mind that the purpose of a meeting often determines its size. Problem-solving is done most effectively in groups of five to fifteen, where opinions and ideas can be exchanged freely. Large groups of twenty-five or more are too big for anything more than the presentation of information or motivational purposes.

internal meeting
a formal meeting that involves only personnel from within an organization.

external meeting
a formal meeting that involves outsiders in addition to company personnel.

formal meeting a scheduled meeting that operates according to a pre-set agenda under guided leadership for the purposes of achieving specific goals.

informal meeting
a small, sometimes unscheduled meeting that may operate without strict rules.

4. **Location:** Deciding where to hold a meeting—in your office, in a board room, or off site—depends on several factors:

- the kind of environment you prefer,
- how well participants get along and interact,
- how much space you need for the group, and
- how much you need to be seen as being in control.

Meetings are not simply convened; they are staged and strategized. Choosing the right location is a matter of balancing practical concerns with the "politics" of meeting. For instance, holding a meeting in your office can give you greater perceived control over the proceedings, especially if you keep distractions (ringing telephones, interruptions) to a minimum. Conducting a meeting on neutral ground—away from the office—equalizes relationships, sparks creativity, and makes it easier to tackle controversial matters. Keep in mind, though, that the environment has to be quiet enough for you to carry on a normal conversation. Going to a client's office can show that you are committed to her professional needs.

Whatever location you settle on, the table and seating arrangement should enhance the flow of information and ideas—not create communication barriers. A seating arrangement can set the tone for a meeting and also unexpectedly shift perceptions of who holds more power.

Small Meetings

- Sitting behind a large desk plays up your status, power, and authority. Naturally, it also makes you less approachable and can intimidate anyone on the other side of the barrier.
- Barrier-free seating (i.e., chairs arranged across from each other or in a circle) creates a peer relationship and promotes discussion.

Medium-Sized Meetings

- Seating around a boardroom table has a hierarchy all its own, even though it can promote discussion by putting participants face to face. The person at the head of the table has the greatest perceived power. People at either side have lessening degrees of power the further away they are from the ends of the table.
- Seating around a circular table makes everyone more or less equal and promotes open discussion.
- Don't leave seating arrangements to chance if relations between meeting participants are known to be difficult. Put opponents at a distance from one another.
- When you plan to use a boardroom, be sure to reserve it before announcing your location. Inform participants immediately of any change of location.

Large Meetings

- The further away the speaker is from the audience, the more formal the meeting seems. Conversely, meetings where a speaker is close to, or part of, the audience have a more intimate feel.
- Speaking from behind a podium adds formality to the proceedings.
- Chairs set up in conventional rows create a formal setting; if seating is in an arched or semicircular pattern, it results in a more casual setting.

5. **Scheduling:** Establish when the meeting will begin and end. This is ideally a time convenient to key decision-makers or a time that fits in with personal working styles. Although meetings can be scheduled at any point during the day, some times will naturally be better than others, leaving participants primed to contribute—and not distracted by other matters or fatigued by the workday. Unless there is an urgent matter to be dealt with, informal meetings should be set for less busy or less stressful times, when managers or senior staff members aren't facing deadlines. Long meetings of more than two hours usually include a short break (five to ten minutes) to prevent fatigue and information overload.

agenda a document that establishes the purpose and goals of a meeting and outlines what the meeting will address, thereby helping to focus the group.

6. **Agenda:** An **agenda** is a tool for focusing the group—a written document that sets the order of business for a meeting, briefly describing items to be covered, identifying who is responsible for them, and allocating a time period for each agenda item (see Figure 12.4). An agenda also gives participants the particulars—when the meeting will take place (date, start time, end time), where it will be held, and what preparation they should do beforehand. A copy of the minutes of a previous meeting is sometimes also included when a group meets regularly or when a meeting is a continuation of an earlier one.

Distributing an agenda several days in advance gives participants a chance to prepare questions and formulate opinions. An agenda distributed in advance of a meeting should be accompanied by a cover memo that outlines the meeting's purpose; its date, time, and location; the names of people invited; and instructions on how to prepare. Before an agenda is finalized, it is usually a good idea get input from key presenters and participants—people who might have useful items to add and estimates of how much time they will need. Because everyone who attends a meeting has a stake in its success, keeping participants informed and involved in the process can help ensure a productive outcome.

CONDUCTING A MEETING

Under the right conditions, a meeting can spark great ideas—and lasting business relationships. When bright and well-informed people are given the chance to collaborate fully, there can be a huge payoff in the form of productive decisions and launched initiatives. However, collaboration can only happen in the right environment—when a meeting is well run and boosts the morale of its participants. Leading or facilitating a meeting successfully is therefore one of the most important tests a manager faces and requires meticulous preparation. While there is no blueprint for the perfect meeting or guarantee that a few eyes won't glaze over from time to time, following certain steps can help you to achieve better meetings that let you build consensus and accomplish what you set out to do—and more.

Leading a Meeting

- Distribute a detailed agenda in advance. This gives each participant time to make a list of questions; be prepared to support and respond to various points of view.
- Assign responsibilities: appoint a minute-taker to document the proceedings in a concise yet thorough way; ask someone else to write on a flip chart or computer to record information that needs to be viewed by everyone.

FIGURE 12.4 Sample Meeting Agenda

AGENDA

Jack Pine Resort and Conference Centre
Staff Meeting, January 12, 2010
9:00 a.m. to 10:30 a.m.
Conference Room 4A

I.   Call to order; attendance

II.   Approval of agenda

III.   Approval of minutes from previous meeting

		Presenter	Allotted Time
IV.	Committee reports		
	A. Corporate golf retreat package	Jorge Suarez	15 minutes
	B. Wireless upgrades	Brenda Holz	10 minutes
	C. Parking lot expansion	Mia Bergman	5 minutes
V.	Old Business		
	A. Facility maintenance	Rick Ellers	5 minutes
	B. Safety review	Lu Gan	5 minutes
	C. Overdue accounts	Jamal Smith	5 minutes
VI.	New Business		
	A. Marketing strategy	Ahmed Riyad	15 minutes
	B. New accounts	Jamal Smith	5 minutes

VII.   Announcements

VIII. Chair's summary; adjournment

- Establish ground rules (e.g., be on time, turn off your cellphone, don't use your Blackberry) and stick to them. Make sure to start and adjourn on time. If time runs out for a specific item, decide on it or leave it for a later discussion.
- Build momentum and focus the group by keeping to the agenda. Identify action items and avoid getting sidetracked by peripheral issues or ramblers—summarize what they have said, politely direct them back to the agenda, and move on. An idea doesn't need rehashing six or seven times for it to be considered thoroughly.
- Speak up, make eye contact with others around the table, and stay relaxed. Your behaviour sets the tone for the entire meeting and can put others at ease and help them remain focused and involved. Analyze non-verbal cues to determine if meeting participants have second thoughts or reservations about the decisions being made.

- Handle difficult people. Keep hostile participants in check by encouraging a healthy respect for the facts and establishing zero tolerance for name-calling, sulking, and personal attacks. Try to remain neutral in disputes, making sure the loudest members of the group don't dominate the discussion.
- Encourage full participation. Ask group members for their input rather than simply letting people volunteer their opinions and ideas. Respect the views of others by listening carefully and helping participants feel valued; allow room for opposing viewpoints and consider ways of doing things that are different from your own. Acknowledge and respond to what people say.
- Discourage anyone who interrupts. Instruct interrupters to let others finish before they chime in.
- Deal with conflict, but realize that because a group is composed of individuals with different attitudes and personalities a degree of conflict is inevitable, even valuable. It can stimulate creative thinking and challenge passive **groupthink**.
- End with a summary or recap in which you paraphrase all decisions and assignments and look ahead to future actions. Raise questions, ask for feedback, and clarify any misunderstandings. Tell participants when they can expect to receive copies of the minutes and set a time for the next meeting.
- Follow up on action items at the next meeting.

Participating in a Meeting

- Increase your profile by making eye contact with influential people and sitting toward the head of the table if you expect to have something important to say. Link your comment to the remarks of a leader or to something that has just been said.
- Be an **active listener** and demonstrate that you have heard and processed what has been said—and left unsaid. This involves tuning into underlying feelings, perspectives, and ideas.
  - Be actively interested—body language and facial expressions can signal attentiveness: learn forward, face the speaker, make eye contact. Nod your head when the speaker makes a point that seems particularly important. Don't let distractions get the better of you.
  - Pay attention to the speaker's gestures, facial expressions, and tone of voice—identify the feelings you think you hear.
  - Jot down the occasional note but avoid excessive note-taking and other distracting gestures, such as looking at your watch repeatedly.
  - If offering a reaction on something said, repeat in your own words the speaker's point of view and feed this back to the speaker in your response.
  - Make a mental list of questions you have—then ask for information or clarification.
- Interact and contribute when you have something to say—and be sure to speak up. Offer to help solve problems.
- Try not to dominate the discussion or get involved in arguments. Don't be defensive, disruptive, or overly territorial—let others have their say.
- Make it easy for others to take you seriously. Speak clearly and directly, in a well-organized way, so others will find it easy to listen to you. Do your homework and be prepared to support your point of view.

groupthink the practice of thinking or making decisions as a group, whereby conformity is rewarded and dissent punished; the result of groupthink is often poor decision-making.

active listening listening that demands close attention to the literal and emotional meaning of a message and a level of responsiveness that shows the speaker of the message was both heard and understood.

MEETING MINUTES

Meetings may be conducted formally or informally. Formal meetings adhere to a system of parliamentary procedure known as Robert's Rules of Parliamentary Procedure (from a book of the same name). For meetings conducted in this way, a proper procedure for transcribing **meeting minutes** has to be followed. Formal minutes record the following information:

- name of the group or committee holding the meeting;
- date, time, and place of the meeting;
- topic/title/kind of meeting (a regular meeting or a special meeting called to discuss a particular problem or subject);
- names/number of people present (for groups of ten or fewer, list names of attendees and absentees);
- statement that the chair was present (include time at which the meeting was called to order);
- statement that the minutes of the previous meeting were approved;
- description of old business;
- summary of new business and announcements;
- record of reports (read and approved), discussions, resolutions (adopted or rejected), motions (made, carried, or defeated), votes (taken or postponed), and key decisions;
- list of assignments and due dates;
- time the meeting was adjourned;
- date, time, and location of the next meeting; and
- name and signature of the secretary (the person recording the minutes).

Templates and software programs are available to assist you in compiling minutes. For instance, you can use PowerPoint Meeting Minder during a slideshow to record the minutes of your meeting and print them afterward.

Informal minutes are written for small groups and can be distributed by e-mail or as hard copy. They briefly summarize discussions, report decisions, and outline proposed actions.

GROUPWARE-SUPPORTED MEETINGS

In addition to conventional face-to-face meetings, there are now numerous technologies and computer tools, known as **groupware**, that can facilitate meetings when group members cannot get together in the same place—or even at the same time. Web-based meetings and online virtual conferences eliminate the inconvenience associated with holding long-distance meetings and can help groups collaborate, exchange information, and reach decisions. Many companies use the following technologies to conduct training programs or team-building seminars, or put colleagues in touch for planning or product and policy development.

- **Web-conferencing** is synchronous communication. It enables sound and images recorded by cameras at different locations to be sent in real time to other locations. Participants can view images on a large screen, a television screen, or desktop/laptop computers. Some web-conferencing technologies also enable participants to interact.

meeting minutes a written record of what occurred at a meeting, who attended it, and when and where it was convened.

groupware software designed to facilitate group work by a number of different users.

web-conferencing synchronous web-supported communication allowing for the real-time transmission of sound and images to other locations.

- **E-mail meetings** allow participants to respond at different times and make the meeting process more democratic by doing away with facilitators and the interruptions that controlling personalities can cause. However, e-mail meetings can suffer from the same problems that e-mail in general suffers from: there is no guarantee that messages will be read and have enough detail to be useful.

To get the most out of a meeting facilitated by some form of groupware, keep in mind the strategies listed in the following box.

Groupware Quick Tips

- Familiarize yourself with the technology you will be using to participate in the meeting or conference. Download and test any required software or plug-ins.
- Schedule time to participate. Even though you will not have to leave your office, you should set aside a block of time, just as you would for a face-to-face meeting. If you plan to take part in a long-distance synchronous (real-time) meeting, double-check the timing and see if the meeting originates in a different time zone.

⬤⬤ Communicating by Telephone

The telephone is an important business tool—and a link that is worth learning to use properly. It helps, first of all, to make the distinction between types of calls. Personal calls, often fuelled by the recreational use of cellphones, sometimes have no other purpose than to fill time. Business-driven calls, on the other hand, are much more time-sensitive and direct. Following the rules of telephone etiquette for business can help you send the right message to your associates and leave a good impression on those you call.

MAKING CALLS

Like any communication channel, the telephone can both help to increase productivity and reduce it. Make sure every call you make is necessary and offers the best way to get your message across when compared with other channels.

- Keep a list of frequently called numbers. Be accurate in dialling them or programming them into your speed dial.
- Identify yourself. When placing a call to someone who does not know you, give your name and identify the organization you represent.
- Give each call your full attention. Refrain from interrupting a call to carry on a conversation with someone in your office or laying the phone on the desk without putting the call on hold. Handle interruptions politely, asking permission to put someone on hold.
- Plan what you will say. Make mental or written notes of topics you intend to cover, information you need to obtain, and objections you may encounter. Forgetting a

point may result in having to call back. Anticipate what you might say if you reach someone's voice mail.

- Be positive, courteous, and accurate. To get ready for the call, visualize the person to whom you will be speaking. Your voice should sound animated, not flat or canned.
- Leave clear messages. When someone is unavailable to take your call, leave your name (including the correct spelling, if necessary), business title, company name, phone number, and a brief message (including the best time to reach you). Include an extension number to spare the caller the inconvenience of consulting your company's phone directory. Don't rush your message just because you are being recorded.
- Mind your telephone manners. Don't eat or chew gum while talking on the phone—it's rude, and will make it difficult for the person at the end of the line to hear you.
- Place calls when others are likely to receive them. It helps to have established a specific callback time when returning a call in order to avoid telephone tag. Otherwise, return calls promptly or redirect them elsewhere as needed.
- Learn to end a conversation. As the caller, it is your responsibility to close the conversation and keep yourself from rambling. You can end your call professionally by using a closing phrase (*I'm glad we resolved this concern*) and stating the action you will take. Show courtesy and refrain from using slang.

RECEIVING CALLS

- Make an effort to answer your phone within two or three rings—before the caller is tempted to hang up.
- When answering a call, identify yourself with your full name and department affiliation (*This is Accounts Receivable. Paul Kwon speaking.*). You may also begin your greeting with *good morning* or *good afternoon*—just be sure about what time of day it is.
- Avoid taking calls during meetings. Each activity deserves your full attention.
- Use proper telephone language. The tone of your voice tells callers a great deal. Without realizing it, you can signal something you did not intend and end up sounding abrupt, indifferent, or defensive. Be aware of the negative effects certain phrases can sometimes have on callers and opt for language that is positive and appropriate.

☒	☑
Hang on a second, okay?	May I put you on hold?
Who are you anyway?	May I say who is calling please?
What? WHAT? (when you cannot hear the person on the other end of the phone)	I am having difficulty hearing you. Can you please repeat that?

- Be professional in explaining why you have answered a call intended for a colleague. Don't give out privileged information that might embarrass a co-worker (e.g., *he's gone to the washroom* or *his mouth is full*). Instead simply say, *she's away from her desk at the moment* or *she is unavailable to take your call at the moment* and indicate when the person will be available to take the call.

- Excuse yourself when you have to step away from the phone for a moment to obtain information the caller has requested.
- Don't leave callers on hold indefinitely. Even a short time on hold can seem like an eternity. Remember to ask the caller, *may I put you on hold?* before doing so and thank the caller for waiting when you pick up again. Don't leave the caller on hold for more than 30 or 45 seconds, about the time it takes to record a second caller's name and number. If it is taking longer to find the information you need, give the caller the option of continuing to hold, transfer the person to another party, or offer to call back at a specific time.
- Apply active listening skills to evaluate the tone of the caller's voice and assess what is said.
- Learn to use the phone system. Lost or misdirected calls can result in frustration and lost business. Explain what you are doing and ask for permission when you transfer a call—and give the name, department, and extension number of the person the call is being transferred to in case the call is lost.
- Take accurate, confidential phone messages and deliver them promptly. A good phone message includes (1) the name of the person for whom the message was left, (2) the caller's name, department, and company, (3) the date and time, (4) a message, and (5) instructions (*please call*, *URGENT*, or *will call back*).

USING VOICE MAIL PRODUCTIVELY

Voice mail is both a convenience and an annoyance. Help callers use this tool effectively to reduce the incidence of telephone tag:

- Identify your voice-mail number clearly on your business cards.
- Prepare an appropriate greeting as your outgoing message—friendly, informative, and professional. *Hi, this is Jane Yang of True Blue Marketing. I'm in the office today but away from my desk. Please leave your name, number, and a brief message and I'll return your call shortly.*
- Re-record your greeting to reflect changing circumstances (e.g., you're on holidays or out of the office for an extended period). If appropriate, leave a contact name and number (of a colleague) for callers to use in emergencies.
- Test your message.

●● Dealing with the Media

Dealing with the media can be tricky at the best of times. When you speak with reporters or journalists, your image and that of your company is on the line. Many companies hire public-relations officers specifically for the purpose of maintaining a positive public image. While it is tempting to assume a reporter will tell the story you would like the public to hear, in all likelihood the reporter will write whatever story he wants. It is up to you to guide the reporter to your story and take responsibility for what comes across in an interview. Under your guidance, a media interview can be an opportunity to build goodwill and deliver specific messages to specific audiences through the filter

of a journalist. Here are ten rules for getting the best out of an interview—and not letting a reporter get the better of you.

1. **Prepare by anticipating the questions you might be asked,** especially the
   tough ones. Be aware of recent events that might affect what you have to say.
   Decide how candid you will be—which facts are for public consumption and
   which facts are not.

2. **Know your story, practise telling it, and stick to it.** A good story, crystallized
   into no more than three key points or a few hard-hitting sentences, does wonders
   for a message-driven interview. Try to relate the reporter's questions to one or
   more of your key points.

3. **Tone is very important**—it defines the impression you make. Stay calm and be
   positive and helpful, never overreacting to a reporter's attitude. Avoid negative or
   defensive language, keeping in mind that reporters find this kind of language very
   quotable.

4. **Assess what information will be valuable to the reporter,** but don't release
   facts or figures that should not be made public. Begin with a brief position statement that sets the tone for the interview. If you don't know the answer to a question, say so and offer to follow up later; if you cannot respond, explain why (*the
   matter is under consideration* or *it's in litigation*).

5. **Don't get too technical.** Avoid buzzwords and acronyms. Instead use language
   that both the reporter and the audience will understand.

6. **Speak in sound bites,** limiting your answers to between five and twenty words.
   Because what you say may be edited, don't flood your answers with too many
   details. Short answers are highly quotable and may help you get your message out
   more effectively.

   > **sound bite** a short, quotable extract from a recorded interview that is edited into a news broadcast.

7. **Tell the truth.** Remember that nothing is off the record. In cross-examining you,
   a reporter may be trying to find holes in your argument. Answer or refocus the
   reporter's question, but don't let the reporter put words in your mouth. Correct, as
   non-threateningly as possible, any misstatements made by the reporter.

8. **Be alert and on guard.** Avoid speculating, making off-hand comments, or saying anything you don't want attributed to you. You have to be able to stand behind
   what you say.

9. **Make transitions to your key points as you respond,** keeping the interview
   on track and moving back to what is most important, especially if you are interrupted. The following phrases can help you take the initiative:

   - *While _____ is important, don't forget _____. . . .*
   - *Another thing to remember is . . . .*
   - *Let me put that in perspective.*
   - *What I'm really here to talk to you about is . . . .*

10. **Look your best but be yourself.** Most reporters prefer to speak to a real person
    rather than a slick spokesperson rehearsing the official company line. Be engaged in

the interview and show your enthusiasm, using examples to enrich your story. Let the reporter ask questions; don't try to give all your information immediately.

Quick Tips for Television Interviews

- Only look at the camera when instructed to do so. At all other times, look at the interviewer and maintain eye contact to show your interest. Poor eye contact can denote guilt, boredom, or fear.

- Be camera-ready. Dress conservatively yet comfortably, avoiding all black, all white, and small prints (they can create a strobe effect). Remove glittery, oversized jewellery and take bulky pens out of your pockets. Gesture naturally and avoid fidgeting—and check your appearance for stray hairs and so on before you go on air.

- Speak clearly and distinctly, pausing strategically to avoid fillers such as *ah* and *um*. Remain seated (even after the interview is over) and lean slightly forward in your chair to project energy and interest.

WORKSHOPS AND DISCUSSION FORUMS

1. **Introduce Yourself to Your Class.** Give your name and some basic information. If you find this activity intimidating, you may want to follow a simple script: Hello, my name is _____. I have enrolled in (name of course) because _____ ____, with the ultimate goal of _____. Once you and your classmates have introduced yourselves, you can change the activity so that your role is now to introduce a classmate. Pair with a partner and conduct a quick interview to learn as much as you can about the other person. Complete the activity by performing a brief, professional introduction.

2. **Group Discussion—Face Your Public-Speaking Fears.** What scares you about public speaking? In groups of five or six, discuss your fears about speaking in public, then share strategies you have discovered to reduce situational stress.

3. **Apply Oral Communication Skills in Your Career.** How will you use oral communication skills in your future employment? Interview a professional in your field and share your findings with your classmates. Uphold ethical standards in conducting your interview by asking permission to quote the interviewee.

4. **Give an Impromptu Talk.** Give a brief talk (three to five minutes) on one of the following topics, selected at random or selected for you by your classmates:

   i) *The best part of my current/future job/field/industry is . . . .*

   ii) *The best way to find a job is . . . .*

   iii) *The person I most admire in the field or industry I hope to work in is . . . .* (or *The successful person I most admire is . . . .*)

5. **Meeting and Team-Building Exercise: Design a Banner or Logo.** In groups of five or six, hold meetings to work out the design of banners or T-shirts that represent the values and strengths of each individual team. Designate a scribe to keep minutes and a chair to lead the discussion as you consider

   - what the team stands for,
   - how it wishes to be seen, and
   - how the banner or logo can help others see the team in a different way.

The design can include a combination of symbols, colours, and shapes, as long as there is a clear reason for incorporating each element. Draw up a prototype. At the next class meeting, each team will briefly present and discuss the merits of its banner or logo (visual aids are recommended). After reviewing each design, debate how well each team achieved its purpose through its design. Submit prepared minutes of the meeting to your instructor.

Variations: Propose a slogan or radio advertisement that represents the values of the team.

6. **Meeting and Team-Building Exercise: Lay Down the Law.** In pairs or groups of three or more, work together to suggest a new law, well supported by reasons for needing such a law. Appoint a group leader whose job it will be to ensure that each member has input into the discussion, then write the law in clear, unequivocal language that will not be subject to misinterpretation. Introduce the law to your class in a short presentation aided by handouts or visuals.

7. **Meeting and Team-Building Exercise: Commitment to Change.** In pairs or groups of three or more, identify a problem in your community or at your school. By sharing ideas and experience, discuss how this situation could be improved and devise a plan for implementing constructive change.

8. **Meeting Exercise: Round–Table Discussion.** In groups of five or more, experiment with different types of seating arrangements for meetings. Start by setting up seats and rows, with the audience positioned to face a speaker standing at the front of the room. Use this arrangement for information sharing, problem-solving, and decision-making (a list of possible topics for each session is included below). Next try a U-shaped arrangement, with participants facing each other and the group leader seated at the head of the table. Repeat the process of information sharing, problem-solving, and decision-making. Afterward, reorganize the room set-up for a round-table discussion. What are the advantages and disadvantages of each arrangement?

   - Share information about effective listening skills or telephone etiquette.
   - Solve a problem that affects campus life or your community.
   - Agree on a new parking policy for your college or a revamping of the menu selection for your school cafeteria.

WRITING IMPROVEMENT EXERCISES

1. **Speak Like a Professional.** Record a one- or two-minute item from a radio or television news broadcast. Note the way the professional announcer or broadcaster has used inflection and enunciation to reinforce meaning and add emphasis. Write out what was said, underline keywords, and then read the script aloud into an audio recorder. Try to emulate the speaker's delivery while using your natural voice and giving appropriate downward emphasis at the end of sentences. Photocopy the broadcast transcript and read it aloud in front of your class.

2. **Polish Your Delivery.** Select a published article (one-page maximum) from a trade journal, business publication, or newspaper and practise reading it aloud, polishing your delivery so it is smooth, well pitched, and free of pauses and fillers. If you like, record your recitation and play it back.

3. **Change How You Think of Yourself as a Public Speaker.** On the left-hand side of a piece of paper, write down any negative thoughts you have about how you speak. On the right-hand side, write down positive thoughts that counter them.

   Negative: The audience will be able to tell that I don't have public-speaking experience.

   Positive: Good preparation will compensate for the fact that I don't have public-speaking experience.

   Make these positive thoughts your public-speaking mantra. If you have any negative thoughts as you prepare, say "stop" to yourself and substitute a positive alternative.

4. **Overcome Your Public-Speaking Fears.** Prepare a set of cards representing various stages in the

presentation sequence (e.g., practising your speech, being introduced, giving your speech). Look at each card and visualize the corresponding stage of your presentation to determine which activity causes the most stress, then try to combat that anxiety and calm yourself with breathing or muscle-relaxation exercises. Repeat the process until you no longer experience stress when you contemplate any aspect of giving a speech.

5. **Analyze Your Audience.** Imagine that you must deliver a briefing to the management and staff of a small company. Reread the criteria in "Analyzing the Situation and Audience" on pages 407–8, then decide how you can meet the needs of so diverse a group.

6. **Prepare a Short, Informative Presentation.** Design a five- or ten-minute informative presentation incorporating at least one visual aid in which you explain how to do one of the following:
   - Deal with conflict at your school or workplace
   - Prepare for an interview
   - Drive a bargain or budget for your school expenses
   - Overcome common types of telephone miscommunication
   - Use time more effectively in meetings
   - Balance the demands of work and school

7. **Prepare a Persuasive Presentation.** Prepare a five- or ten-minute presentation in which you persuade your audience to buy a consumer product you enjoy using or in which you advocate a particular action your audience can take. Focus on building credibility and capturing attention to help you make your case and incorporate visual aids that will help you show what you mean.

8. **Compose a PowerPoint Slide.** Write a short bullet point (of no more than seven words) suitable for use on a PowerPoint slide entitled, "What Not to Wear on TV." The point you write should summarize the following information:

   > Unless you want to create odd optical effects, you should make an effort to avoid plaid, stripes, herringbone, checkerboard, and white. These patterns and colours tend to photograph poorly.

9. **Design a Concise Visual Aid.** Write a series of bullet points (no more than seven words per line)

suitable for use on a PowerPoint slide or overhead transparency that summarizes the following information. Remember to add a suitable title:

   > We have four specific corporate goals in the year ahead. The first is to introduce new product lines, including cardio equipment and weight-lifting equipment. Our second goal is to see our company become a worldwide leader. However, if we are to achieve this goal, our company must expand geographically. Plans are now underway to establish operations in South America and Europe. Finally, we would like to continue 20 per cent and higher sales growth.

10. **Introduce a Speaker.** Imagine that you have been given the responsibility of introducing a celebrity or business/community leader who has accepted an invitation to speak at your school or organization. Prepare and deliver your remarks. Make sure to introduce yourself, the guest speaker, and the title of the speech. Include any necessary background information.

11. **Practise Your Special-Presentation Style.** Assume that you have been elected to give a short, impromptu speech at an event honouring a friend or classmate who has reached an important milestone or is receiving an award for service to the community. Explain why you admire the recipient and why the milestone or award is special.

12. **Prepare a Briefing.** Select a fairly substantial article (750 words or more) from the business or national news section of a daily newspaper. Prepare a brief oral presentation based on the article. If you require additional information, use the Internet to gather research by entering the article's keyword(s) into a search engine such as Google. Following your presentation, submit your outline (including an introduction, main body, and conclusion) to your instructor.

13. **Make a Group Oral Presentation.** Working with three or four classmates, plan and coordinate a group presentation on one of the topics listed below (or one of your choice with instructor approval). In advance of your presentation, submit a plan to your instructor that shows how you intend to allocate and share responsibilities.
   - Time-management techniques.
   - The advantages and drawbacks of teleconferencing.

- The advantages and drawbacks of wireless technology.
- A survey of job sites that offer the best employment opportunities in your field.
- PowerPoint: does it improve or undermine the quality of presentations?
- Is foreign ownership of Canadian companies a positive or a negative?

14. **Evaluate Oral Presentations.** Evaluate oral presentations given by classmates. Use the criteria in the "Checklist for Oral Presentations" on pages 424–5.

15. **Prepare a short PowerPoint presentation.** Select one of PowerPoint's features or functions and teach the rest of the class about it. Afterward, submit your PowerPoint notes.

16. **Evaluate the Handling of Questions.** Watch a news-related interview (as featured on shows such as *The Fifth Estate*, the magazine portion of *The National*, and *W5*) or press conference and assess the performance of an interviewee. How effectively does this individual handle tough questions?

17. **Evaluate a Meeting.** Attend the meeting of an organization on your campus or in your community (or a meeting at your workplace). Using the following checklist, assess how well the meeting was conducted.

☐ Is the meeting held in the right place, at the right time, with the right people?
☐ Does the meeting have and fulfill a specific purpose? Does the agenda reflect this?
☐ Are ground rules for the meeting properly enforced?
☐ Are participants encouraged to voice their opinions and ideas? Is the leader fair and does she help the group stay focused?
☐ Do participants know how to prepare for the meeting and how to follow up? Do they know what comes next?

☐ Is conflict dealt with in a fair and equitable way?

If the answer to any of these questions is no, write a brief review analyzing how the meeting could have been improved.

18. **Telephone Role-Playing.** With a partner, take turns placing and receiving telephone calls that correspond to one or more of the following scenarios:

i) *Answering for someone else.* Jenny Chow, owner of Fair Trade Coffees of the World, is calling her accountant, Joseph Li, about a reassessment of her most recent tax return. The call is answered by Amanda Sharp, the receptionist for Joseph Li. Mr. Li has gone to the spa for the afternoon. He has left instructions that his clients are not to be told of his whereabouts. Ms. Chow is an important client and her call must be handled as tactfully as possible.

ii) *Putting a caller on hold.* Brenda Rudnicki, manager and coordinator of Child's Garden Daycare, must place an emergency call to Spectrum Junior, a maker of non-toxic, washable paints, to find out how to safely remove large quantities of hardened paint from a child's hair. She has followed the instructions on the packaging exactly, but much of the paint still remains. The call is answered by customer-relations specialist Marie-Claire Lacasse. Because the colour in question, Dragon Purple, has gone on the market only recently, she must ask Ms. Rudnicki to hold while she confirms the removal procedure.

19. **Communicating by Phone: Outgoing Voice-Mail Message.** Using the appropriate audio device, record a friendly and professional voice-mail greeting that would be appropriate in the field or setting in which you plan to work. Play back the message and re-record it until you are satisfied with its tone and completeness.

ONLINE ACTIVITIES

http://www.

1. **Test Your Meeting IQ:** One of the diversions offered by EffectiveMeetings.com, this quiz consists of ten questions designed to help you successfully plan and lead your next meeting.
www.effectivemeetings.com/diversions/
meetingiq.asp

2. **Do You Suffer from Meeting Myopia?** Also from EffectiveMeetings.com, this quiz lets you find out how to overcome "meeting myopia" and learn to have more productive meetings.
www.effectivemeetings.com/diversions/
mm/index.asp

3. **Calculate the Cost of Your Meetings—Meetings as Corporate Investment:** Fill in the computer fields and click on the "calculate" button to determine the cost of the meetings you hold.
www.effectivemeetings.com/diversions/
meetingcost.asp

4. **Improving Your Active Listening Skills.** Watch the short video "Improving Your Listening Skills" by clicking several times on the "Next" button in the lower right-hand corner of the screen in order to prompt the video that will appear in the middle of the field. Identify the five approaches to listening, then find an example from your own life to match each approach.
www.idxlearning.com/marketing/idxready/
F127/

5. **Practise Your Listening Skills.** This site from the University of Leeds offers a range of resources to support active listening and interpersonal skills building, including a quiz for assessing listening skills and activities for gaining practice in watching and listening.
http://library.leeds.ac.uk/skills-interpersonal

Business Usage: A Style and Mechanics Guide

⬤⬤ Usage: Differentiating Commonly Confused Words

There are several categories of commonly confused words: homonyms (words that sound alike but have different meanings), non-standard words (that fall outside accepted usage), and words whose use depends on whether the nouns they are paired with are count nouns (naming persons, places, or things that can be counted, e.g., *computer*, *accountant*) or non-count (naming abstractions or entities that can't be counted, e.g., *advice*, *luggage*). The number sign (#) indicates entries below where the rules of count and non-count usage apply.

a/an Both *a* and *an* are singular indefinite articles. Use *a* before a consonant sound (*a report*) and *an* before a vowel sound (*an auditor*). **Special cases:** Use *an* before an acronym beginning with a vowel sound but not necessarily with a vowel (*an RSP, an MP, a URL*) or before a word beginning with a silent *h* (*an hour, an honest mistake*). If the *h* is pronounced, the word therefore begins with a consonant sound and requires *a* (not *an*): *a hospital, a hostile takeover*.

accept/except/expect *Accept* is a verb meaning "agree to" or "receive." *Except* is both a preposition and a verb. In its more common use as a preposition, it means "leaving out" or "excluding." As a verb, it means "to exclude." **TIP:** Let the *x* in *except* be a reminder of the *x* in *exclude*. Avoid the common word-processing error of typing *expect* ("regard as likely," "suppose") instead of *except*.

- I accept all terms of the contract except the last one.

accompanied by/accompanied with In these passive forms, *accompanied by* applies to both people and objects whereas *accompanied with* applies to objects.

- The president was accompanied by the general manager.

- The cheque was accompanied with [*or* by] a letter of apology.

advice/advise *Advice* is a noun meaning "words recommending a future action." *Advise* is a verb meaning "to give advice." **TIP:** Many verbs end in *-ise* (*advise, apprise, devise*) but only the nouns derived from them end in *-ice* (*advice, device*).

- She advised him to follow her advice.

affect/effect   *Affect* is a verb meaning "influence" and less commonly a noun with a specialized meaning used in the field of psychology. *Effect* is a noun meaning *result* and, less commonly, a formal and somewhat pretentious verb meaning "to bring about" or "create." **TIP:** *Affect* is used chiefly as a verb, *effect* as a noun. Think of the *-a* in *affect* as standing for its verbal action and the *-e* in *effect* as a convenient reminder of the *-e* in *result*.

- Restructuring did not affect morale; in the long term it will have a positive effect on productivity.
- The manager effected important changes in workplace safety.

aggravate/irritate   In colloquial usage only, *aggravate* and *irritate* are interchangeable. According to standard usage, *aggravate* means "make worse" and *irritate* means "annoy."

- The wildcat strike aggravated the already tenuous labour negotiations.
- Pointless messages on his voice mail irritated him.

agree to/agree with   *Agree to* means "give consent to." *Agree with* means "hold the same opinion" or "be in harmony with."

- The managers *agreed to* the changes.
- The managers *agree with* him about the timeliness of the plan.

ain't   *Ain't* is non-standard for grammatically correct equivalents such as *am not*, *is not*, and *are not*. It is unacceptable in all forms of communication for the workplace.

a lot/allot/lots   *A lot* (never *alot*) is an informal way of expressing the idea of "many" or "a great deal"—terms that are in fact preferable in most business documents. *Allot* is a verb meaning "to distribute" or "dole out in portions." *Lots* is unacceptable, non-standard usage.

alternative/alternate   *Alternative* is an adjective that means "available as another choice" or "unconventional" (as in *alternative medicine*). It is also a noun meaning "one of several possibilities" or the freedom to choose between them.

- They optioned several alternative energy sources.
- She had doubts about the plan but disliked the alternatives even more.
- He had no alternative but to terminate the contract.

Alternate is also an adjective, meaning "every other," and a stand-alone noun denoting a person or thing that substitutes for another. The verb *alternate* means "change between two things" or describes "two things succeeding each other by turns."

- Seminars were scheduled for alternate Tuesdays.
- Two alternates were named to the team.
- John alternated with Joanne as task-force chair.

a.m./A.M./p.m./P.M. The abbreviation *a.m.* stands for *ante meridiem* ("before noon"); *p.m.* stands for *post meridiem* ("after noon"). Neither should be used redundantly (as in *8:00 a.m. in the morning* or *3:00 p.m. in the afternoon*) nor with the adverb *o'clock*. Whether the *a.m.* and *p.m.* abbreviations are typed in capital (or small capital) or lower-case letters, the style you choose should be maintained consistently. To indicate the time of day, use figures, not words (*11:00 a.m.*). If the time is on the hour, the colon and zeros may be omitted; otherwise use a colon to separate the hour from the minutes (*11:30 a.m.*).

among/amongst These forms are interchangeable in all contexts. *Among* is by far more common, especially in North American usage, whereas *amongst* is more closely identified with British usage and has a somewhat old-fashioned or genteel quality. *Amongst* was once used with verbs conveying movement (*he distributed the memo amongst his co-workers*) but this usage is no longer common.

among/between (#) Use *among* with three or more people or items, *between* with two.

- There was a dispute among five staff members.

- The dispute between the company and its supplier has been resolved.

Use the objective case of personal pronouns (*me, you, him, her, us, them*) when they follow *between*.

- Between you and me, I think we should reconsider the merger.

amount/number (#) *Amount* indicates an uncountable quantity. Use it with nouns that name uncountable items (work, mail, equipment, money). *Number* indicates a countable quantity. Use it with countable nouns. **TIP:** *Amount* is never used with nouns ending in plural *-s*. Uncountable nouns always take singular form.

- He had a number of reports to write—a considerable amount of work for a single day.

ampersand (&) Use the ampersand sign (*&*) only in abbreviations (*R&D* for *Research and Development*, *M&A* for *mergers and acquisitions*) and in the registered names of organizations where it commonly appears (*Royal & SunAlliance Canada*, *Procter & Gamble Canada*, not *Procter and Gamble Canada*). The ampersand should not be substituted for *and* in text.

- Their company has long made use of federal government grants to fund R&D.

appraise/apprise To *appraise* is to "estimate the value of"; to *apprise* is to "inform people of a situation."

as/like *As* is a subordinating conjunction that introduces a subordinate clause.

- His performance in his new position has been outstanding, as [*not* like] everyone expected it would be.

Like is a preposition and is followed by a noun or noun phrase, not a subordinate clause. It is especially useful for suggesting points of similarity or comparison.

- Norcom, like Telstar, has expanded its foreign market.

If the comparison incorporates a prepositional phrase (beginning with *in*, *on*, or *at*), use *as* instead of *like*.

- In France, as in Germany, the unit of currency is the euro.

assure/ensure/insure   *Assure* means "convince," "promise," or "set someone's mind at rest." *Ensure* means "make certain." *Insure* means "guarantee against financial loss." **TIP:** Think of the noun forms of these verbs—*assurance* and *insurance*—to differentiate them more easily.

- She assured him that the team would meet the deadline.
- Her hard work ensured the success of the project.
- Their assets were insured for well over $1 million.

as to   This is an example of bureaucratic jargon. Use more direct substitutes, such as *on* or *about*.

- I reached a decision about [*not* as to] the new recruits.
- His remarks on [*not* as to] the team's performance were helpful.

averse/adverse   *Averse* (usually followed by *to*) means "opposed to." *Adverse* means "harmful" or "unfavourable." **TIP:** Think of the noun forms of these adjectives—*aversion* and *adversary*—to differentiate them more easily.

- She was averse to any plan that would have an adverse effect on efficiency.

backward/backwards   *Backward* and *backwards* are interchangeable adverbs meaning "toward the rear," "in reverse of the usual way," or "into the past."

- He counted backwards [*or* backward] from 10 to 1.

Only *backward* is used as an adjective meaning "reversed" or "slow to develop or progress."

- The CEO's backward policies are partly responsible for the decline in profits.

bad/badly   *Bad* is an adjective describing people, places, and things; also use it after linking verbs such as *feel*, *seem*, *appear*, *be*, *smell*, and *taste*.

- He felt bad [*not* badly] about the cutbacks.

Badly is an adverb used with all other verbs.

- The no-refund policy badly damaged customer relations.

beside/besides   *Beside* is a preposition meaning "next to," "near," or "at the side of."

- I sat beside him at the annual general meeting.

Besides is likewise a preposition but means "apart from" or "in addition to."

- No one besides the team leader liked the proposal.
- Besides balancing the departmental budget, the new manager improved employee relations.

Besides is also an adverb meaning "moreover," but this particular usage is more colloquial.

- The fund has performed well in the past. Besides, it promises even higher returns in the coming year.

between you and me/between you and I   *See* **among/between**

biennial/biannual/semi-annual   *Biennial* refers to something that occurs or recurs every two years. *Biannual* and *semi-annual* mean "twice a year."

biweekly/semi-weekly   *Biweekly* means "every two weeks"; *semi-weekly* means "twice a week."

both/each   *Both* means "the two"; it can be used in the following ways: *both consultants, both the consultants, both of the consultants. Each* means "every one of two or more persons or things." *Both* is plural; *each* is singular.

- She presented a $100 cheque to both of us to cover our expenses. [two people shared $100]

- She gave us each a $100 cheque to cover our expenses. [each person received $100]

bring/take   Use *bring* when an object is being transported from a distant place to a near place; use *take* when an object is transported from a near place to a distant place.

- Please bring the figures for the Anderson report with you to today's meeting.

- Please take these files with you when you go.

can/may   The once all-important distinction between *can* and *may* survives in formal writing. *Can* denotes ability, whereas *may* is reserved for requesting or granting permission.

- Can you finish the research today?

- May I help you with your research?

capital/capitol   *Capital* refers to the chief city of a country or province, to accumulated wealth or resources, and to an uppercase letter. In US usage, *capitol* refers to a building where lawmakers meet.

CEO/CFO/CIO/COO/CTO   These abbreviations require capitalization of all three letters and may be used on first reference depending on your audience or readership. Add lowercase *-s* to create the plural form (*CEOs*).

    CEO = chief executive officer
    CFO = chief financial officer
    CIO = chief information officer
    COO = chief operating officer
    CTO = chief technology officer

chair/chairperson/chairman   The gender-neutral *chair* and *chairperson* are preferable to the gender-specific and exclusionary *chairman*.

cite/sight/site   *See* **site/sight/cite**

company names   On first reference, write out the name of the company in full as it appears on company letterhead (where applicable, include *Ltd.*, *Inc.*). Afterward, use the company's shortened name (*Manulife* in place of *Manulife Financial Corporation*).

compare to/compare with   These forms are generally interchangeable. Use *compare to* to liken one thing to another by emphasizing the similarities of the items being compared. Use *compare with* to imply a greater element of formal analysis encompassing both similarities and differences:

- He compared the new security technology to a brick house.

- She compared e-business initiatives with more traditional approaches.

complement/compliment   *Complement* is a verb meaning "to go with or complete" and a noun meaning the "thing that completes" or "the full number needed." *Compliment* is a verb meaning "praise" and a noun meaning "a polite expression of praise." **TIP:** The first six letters of *complement* are identical to the first six letters of *complete*.

- His fluency in three languages complemented his skills as a communications officer.

- Impressed by his credentials, she complimented him on his fluency in three languages.

continually/continuously   *Continually* is an adverb meaning "occurring repeatedly." *Continuously* is an adverb meaning "going on without interruption." **TIP:** The letter *l* "occurs repeatedly" at the end of *continually*, so rely on the double consonant as a reminder of the word's meaning.

- He lost the goodwill of co-workers by continually interrupting meetings.

- The negotiators reached an agreement after bargaining continuously for five hours.

could of/could have   Helping verbs such as *could*, *would*, and *should* are paired with *have* to convey potential past action. *Could of* is non-standard, and therefore incorrect, usage.

council/counsel   A *council* (noun) is "an advisory or administrative body"; a *councillor* is a member of such a body. *Counsel* is both a noun meaning "advice" and "lawyer" and a verb meaning "to give advice." **Spell-Checker Advisory:** Only US English rejects the rule of doubling the final consonant before vowel suffixes. American-designed diagnostic software, which is often the default software, may flag *counselling* and *councillor* even though their spelling is correct.

- Town council considered amendments to zoning bylaws, but there was no consensus among councillors.

- The company lawyer counselled upper management on the ethics of the proposed changes.

courtesy titles   Courtesy titles (*Mr.*, *Mrs.*, *Ms.*) commonly appear before the addressee's name in the inside address and salutation of a standard business letter. When referring in text to an individual, on first reference use the full name without a courtesy title (*Mark Thompson*). Thereafter, refer to the individual by first name (*Mark*), surname (*Thompson*), or by courtesy title plus surname (*Mr. Thompson*).

criterion/criteria   A *criterion* is a standard or principle for judging something. *Criteria* is the plural form that is often mistakenly substituted for the singular, resulting in subject–verb agreement errors.

- There are several new criteria for performance reviews.

data   *Data*—"a series of facts or pieces of information"—is the plural of *datum*, a word that is uncommon and used only in technical writing. *Data* may be treated as a singular noun in all other cases.

- The new data is [*or* are] consistent with last year's findings.

defer/differ   *Defer* is a verb meaning "postpone" or "yield or make concessions to." *Differ* means "be unlike or at variance."

- According to the contract, they may defer payment for up to six months.

- On most challenging technology issues, the team leader deferred to his IT consultants.

- The CEO's position on first-quarter spending differed from the CFO's stance.

different from/different than   *Different from* is widely accepted and preferred in formal and professional writing. *Different than* is a colloquialism unsuitable for formal writing but otherwise acceptable when followed by a clause. The British usage *different to* is accepted but uncommon in North America.

- Their prices are dramatically different from those of their closest competitors.

- Please let me know if your staffing needs are different than they were a year ago.

differ from/differ with   *Differ from* means "be unlike"; *differ with* means "disagree" and usually suggests a disagreement between people.

- The manager's recommendations differed from hers.

- The task force members differed with each other over the wording of the agreement.

disinterested/uninterested   *Disinterested* means "impartial, unbiased, objective"; like *uninterested*, *disinterested* can also mean "not interested."

- The matter was referred to a disinterested third party for resolution.

- He was uninterested in the new program and decided not to volunteer.

dissent/descent   *Dissent* means "non-conformity" or "difference of opinion." *Descent* refers to family lineage, downward movement, or decline.

- There was dissent among committee members over the wording of the agreement.

- She packed away her laptop as the airplane made its final descent.

download/upload   *Download* means copy or transfer a document or software from a network to a computer or any other data-storage device. *Upload* means transfer data from a computer or data-storage device to the Net or a server. *Download* and *upload* are also nouns referring to the transferred files. In Canadian usage, *download* also means to shift costs or responsibilities from one level of government to another.

due to/because of   Use *due to* after forms of the verb *be*. In all other cases, use *because of*, which is generally preferred.

- The success of the project was due to the team's effort.

- The projected succeeded because of the team's effort.

e-/e-business/eBusiness/E-business   The prefix *e-* stands for *electronic* and is common to many recent hyphenated coinages: *e-learning*, *e-company*, *e-commerce*, *e-mail*. The *e-* is capitalized only when the word begins a sentence.

- Our e-business consulting team handles content management and monitors the day-to-day health of the system.

- E-business is the way of the future.

e.g./i.e./ex.   The abbreviation *e.g.* stands for the Latin expression *exempli gratia* ("for example"). It is often used in parentheses to introduce an example or to clarify a preceding statement. The abbreviation *i.e.* stands for the Latin expression *id est* ("that is to say"). Use it to expand a point or restate an idea more clearly. In formal writing, replace *e.g.* with the English equivalent, *for instance* or *for example*. The abbreviation *ex.* is non-standard.

emigrate from/immigrate to   *Emigrate* means "leave one's own country and settle in another." *Immigrate* means "come as a permanent resident to a country other than one's own native land."

eminent/imminent   *Eminent* means "notable, distinguished"; *imminent* means "impending, about to happen."

- The panel of speakers includes an eminent psychologist.

- A change in staffing procedures is imminent.

emoticons   These symbols, which combine punctuation marks to convey strong emotion or tone, are not recommended for most business correspondence. Among the best known are :-) (happy), ;-) (winking sarcasm), and :-o (shocked).

enquiry/inquiry   An *enquiry* is "an act of asking or seeking information"; an *inquiry* is "an investigation." Each is a variant spelling for the other.

etc./et al.   Commonly used at the end of lists, *etc.* is an abbreviation meaning "and the rest" or "and other things." Use it (as sparingly as possible) to refer to things, not people. If *etc.* comes at the end of a sentence, its single period is sufficient to create a full stop—there is no need to add another period. The abbreviation *et al.* stands for the Latin expression *et alii* ("and others" or "and other people") and is used in source citations for works with three or more authors.

explicit/implicit   *Explicit* means "expressed clearly, definitely, or in detail." **TIP:** To remember this meaning, think of the verb *explicate*, which shares *explicit's* word origin. *Implicit*, on the other hand, means "not plainly expressed but implied." Less commonly, it can also suggest a state of containment (often followed by *in*) or an unquestioning attitude.

- He gave explicit instructions that no one should interrupt the meeting.

- There was an implicit trust among co-workers.

farther/further   Use *farther* to suggest greater physical distance; use *further* to suggest greater time or a more abstract quality. Some writers prefer using *further* to suggest distance.

- How much farther is it to the airport?

- Her plan calls for further study.

few/little (#)   Use *few* ("not many") with countable items and *little* ("not much") with uncountable items.

- There were few complaints about the new procedures.

- The new proposal met with little resistance.

fewer/less (#)   These are the comparative forms of *few* and *little.* Use *fewer* ("not as many") with countable items (*fewer investments, fewer reports, fewer losses*). Use *less* ("not as much") with uncountable items and general amounts (*less money, less time, less input*).

- He has less work to do because he has fewer calls to answer.

fiscal/monetary   *Fiscal* pertains to financial or budgetary matters. *Monetary* pertains to money supply.

foreign words and phrases   Foreign words and phrases are used freely in certain disciplines, such as the law, where they are widely understood and integral to the vocabulary of the profession (e.g., pro bono, or "undertaken without charge"). Used out of context, however, foreign words and phrases may confuse readers, and in such cases they should be italicized (e.g., *sui juris,* or "having full legal rights or capacity").

former/latter   When referring to two items, use *former* to indicate the first and *latter* to indicate the second.

formerly/formally   *Formerly* means "in the past." *Formally* means "in a formal, structured manner."

- Jill was formerly an investment counsellor with Mathers-Acheson.

- He knew her to see her, but they had never been formally introduced.

forward/forwards/foreword   Both *forward* and *forwards* are adverbs meaning "to the front," "ahead," or "into prominence." *Forwards* is used to suggest continuous forward motion (*backwards and forwards*). *Forward* is preferred in most other cases.

- They decided to move forward[s] with the project.

Forward is also an adjective meaning "at or near the front," "advanced and with a view to the future," and "bold or presumptuous." In a specific business context, it refers to future produce or delivery (*forward contract*).

- Today's forward thinkers are tomorrow's CEOs.

A *foreword* is a preface to a book.

fund/funds   A *fund* is "a reserve of money or investments"; the term *funds* means "money resources."

gone/went   *Gone* is both the past participle of *go* and an adjective meaning "lost" or "used up." *Went* is the past tense of *go*. *Gone* is always preceded by an auxiliary verb; *went* does not require one.

- She went [*not* gone] to the meeting after Steve had gone [*not* had went] home.

good/well   *Good* is an adjective; *well* is both an adjective (meaning "healthy") and an adverb (meaning "effectively").

- Her interpersonal skills are good.

- He is a good judge of character.

- She is well today and will return to work.

- He performed well in the job interview.

got/have/have got   *Got* is a colloquial, non-standard substitute for *have* (*I got permission to proceed*). It should be avoided in formal business messages. *Must* or *have* are more acceptable substitutes for *have got*.

- He must [*not* has got to] submit a new application.

- We have [*not* have got] a week to gather the data for the report.

hanged/hung   *Hanged* means "executed by hanging." *Hung* means "supported or suspended from the top" and has many informal usages (*hung out together, hung out to dry*), most of them unsuitable for business correspondence.

- With the outlawing of capital punishment, no one has been hanged in Canada in more than forty years.

- They hung their coats in the reception area before the meeting began.

hardly   *Hardly* means "only just" or "only with difficulty." It should not be used with negative constructions.

Incorrect: I couldn't hardly believe the sudden upturn in the economy.

Correct: I could hardly believe the sudden upturn in the economy.

have/of   Use *have* (not *of*) after the verbs *could*, *should*, *would*, *might*, and *must*.

he/his   Decades ago, *he* was used whenever the sex of a person was unspecified.

- If anyone objects he will have to file a grievance.

- Each accountant has his own office where he is free to meet with clients.

Today, many regard this practice, known as common gender, as sexist; however, the effort to avoid discriminatory and exclusionary language often leads to awkward alternatives. To create gender-neutral sentences, consider using one of the following methods:

- **Replace the offending singular pronoun with the plural *they/their*.** This method, while it is expedient and gaining in acceptance, makes for incorrect grammar and fuzzy logic.

  - If anyone objects they will have to file a grievance.

  - Each accountant has their own office where they are free to meet with clients.

- **Replace the singular possessive pronoun with an indefinite article.** This method cannot remedy sentences in which the pronoun acts as a subject.

  - Each accountant has an office suitable for meetings with clients.

- **Recast the sentence using plural forms. Use indefinite pronouns (always singular) that don't require subsequent gender identification.**

  - Anyone who objects will have to file a grievance.

  - All accountants have their own offices where they are free to meet with clients.

- **Change *he* and *his* to *he/she* and *his/hers*.** Appropriate if used sparingly, this is the most awkward way to avoid sexist language. The construction *s/he* is not generally recommended.

heading   Headings used to organize long documents should be stylistically consistent by level throughout in terms of capitalization, italicization, typeface, spacing, and placement (centred or flush with left margin).

headquarters   *Headquarters* (abbreviated *HQ*)—the administrative centre of an organization—takes both singular and plural verbs.

homepage/home page   A homepage (also written as two words: home page) is the introductory page of a website.

http:// and **www**   The protocol *http://* may be omitted if *www* is part of the URL or web address.

I/we   *I* (singular) and *we* (plural) are first-person pronouns that help to establish the moderate informality of a personal business style. While personal pronouns are frowned upon in academic essays, *I*, *you*, and *we* can help business writers express themselves more directly and fluently in their daily tasking-centred messages. In each case, usage is determined by context and readers' needs.

- Use *I* for independent tasking or when you are the sole decision-maker.

■ Use *we* (i) for collaborative writing projects, (ii) when you write on behalf of a group or speak for a consensus, and (iii) when you have the authority to act as spokesperson for the policies and decisions of your organization. *We* should never imply the loftiness of the "royal We" or the condescension of *How are we feeling today?*

imply/infer   *Imply* means "to hint at, suggest, or insinuate without stating plainly." *Infer* means "to draw a conclusion from what is written or said." Generally, the writer or speaker *implies*; the reader or listener *infers*.

- While he didn't say so specifically, George implied that the negotiations were going well.

- The media inferred from George's comments that the strike would be settled by the end of the week.

incidents/incidence   *Incidents* is the plural form of *incident*, an event or occurrence that is either noteworthy or troublesome. *Incidence*, on the other hand, refers not to the event itself but to its rate of occurrence.

- Two recent incidents resulting in complaints against the department require further investigations.

- The increased incidence of absenteeism is cause for concern.

in regard to/in regards to/as regards/regards   The expressions *in regard to* and *with regard to* both mean "as concerns," making them interchangeable. *As concerns* is a somewhat stuffier expression meaning "about or concerning." *In regards to*, a misusage resulting from a confusion of these similar phrases, is considered incorrect. *As regards* is an acceptable phrase. *Regards* is an informal complimentary close.

Internet   Though web-related words are increasingly found in lowercase, this noun is capitalized, as is its abbreviation *Net*.

IPO   Use this abbreviation after a first reference that spells out in full *initial public offering*.

irregardless/regardless   Not to be confused with *irrespective* ("regardless of"), which is acceptable but somewhat stiff, *irregardless* is non-standard and incorrect; instead, use *regardless* (meaning "without consideration for").

it's/its   *It's* is a contraction of *it is*. *Its* is a possessive pronoun. Like other possessive pronouns (*his*, *hers*, *ours*, *yours*, *theirs*), *its* requires no apostrophe to denote possession.

- It's possible to reduce costs.

- The company hasn't released its year-end report.

kind/kinds   *Kind* is singular; the nouns and demonstrative pronouns (*this* and *that*) that agree with it are also singular. *Kinds* is plural; use it to indicate more than one kind. Use it with plural nouns and demonstrative pronouns (*these*, *those*): **this kind of file/those kinds of files**.

- This kind of retroactive agreement is rare.

- These kinds of retroactive agreements are rare.

kindly   *Kindly* means "please" in a polite demand or request (*Kindly refer to the enclosed documents*). While the courtesy *kindly* conveys is never out of place, some regard it as old-fashioned or overly genteel.

kind of/sort of   These informal expressions mean "somewhat" or "to some extent" and usually imply vagueness or looseness about the term to which they are applied.

later/latter   *Later* means "after a time." *Latter* means "the second-mentioned of two" or "nearer the end."

- Call me later about the arrangements.

- The project manager recently reviewed the Stewart and Young accounts and expressed serious concerns about the latter.

- His responsibilities require him to travel in the latter part of the year.

lay/lie   *Lay* is a verb meaning "to put or place something on a surface." It requires a direct object to express a complete idea. *Lie* means "to be situated in," "to recline," or "to be in a horizontal position." It does not require a direct object to express a complete idea.

The present tense of *lay* and the past tense form of *lie* are often confused.

	present	present -s	past	past participle	present participle
LAY	lay	lays	laid	laid	laying
LIE	lie	lies	lay	lain	lying

lay off/layoff   *Lay off* (written as two words) is a verb meaning "remove employees to cut costs or decrease the workforce"; *layoff* (written as a single word) is a noun.

lead/led   *Lead* is both a noun that names a type of metal and the present-tense singular form of a verb (pronounced *leed*) that means "to guide by going in front." *Led* is the past tense and past participle of *lead*.

- Teleway Inc. leads its sector in domestic sales.

- The department manager led a delegation at last year's equity conference.

lend/loan   *Lend* is a verb meaning "to allow the use of money at interest" or "to give someone the use of something on the understanding it will be returned." *Lent* is its past tense and past participle (*I lent, I have lent*). *Loan* is a noun meaning a sum of money lent as well as a verb meaning "to lend," especially "to lend money."

liable/libel/likely   *Liable* means "legally bound" or "subject to penalty or tax." *Liable* is also a synonym for *likely* ("probable") and *apt* ("have a tendency"), but this usage should be avoided in business messages, where it misleadingly implies legal liability or potentially unpleasant results. *Libel* is "a false and defamatory *written* statement." (*Slander*, on the other hand, refers to a "false, malicious and defamatory *spoken* statement.")

- His negligence left the company liable for damages.

- Given the defamatory nature of the newspaper report, the company sued for libel.

licence/license   As a noun, *licence* means "a permit from authority to use something, own something, or do something." Its variant U.S. spelling, *license*, is usually acceptable in Canadian usage. As a verb, *license* (and also *licence*) means "grant a licence (to a person)."

loose/lose   *Loose* is an adjective meaning "not tight" or "hanging partly free." *Lose* is a verb meaning "cease to have," "become unable to find," or "suffer a loss."

- A loose cable connection caused transmission problems.

- The telecommunications division has been losing money for years.

many/much (#)   Use *many* when referring to more than one item; use *much* with uncountable or single items.

- many: reports, accolades, responsibilities, suitcases, letters

- much: work, praise, responsibility, luggage, mail

may be/maybe   *May be* is a verb phrase expressing possibility. *Maybe* is an adverb meaning "perhaps" or "possibly."

- There may be plans for an additional support network.

- Maybe the company will be restructured next year.

media/medium   *Media* is a plural noun; *medium* is a singular noun. There is growing acceptance for the use of *media* as a mass noun with a singular verb.

- Marshall McLuhan claimed, "the medium is the message."

- The media are on our side.

- The media is on our side.

money/monies/moneys   *Money* refers to a form or medium of exchange—coins or banknotes. *Monies*, also spelled *moneys*, refers to sums of money.

myself/I/me   *I* is the subjective pronoun (meaning that it functions as a subject) and *me* is the objective pronoun (meaning that it functions as an object). To determine correct pronoun usage in sentences referring to two or more people, temporarily remove all pronouns and proper nouns except the pronoun in question:

- ☒ The draft proposal was revised by Jen and I.

- ☑ The draft proposal was revised by me.

- ☑ The draft proposal was revised by Jen and me.

Use the objective case if the pronoun follows a preposition:

- Everyone except Paul and me will attend the conference.

- Between you and me, the stock is undervalued.

Myself is the reflexive form of *me*. It refers to or intensifies *I* or *me*. In all other cases, avoid substituting *myself* for *I* and *me* in formal writing.

- I gave myself credit for finishing the report on time.

- The chair and I [*not* myself] offer our heartiest congratulations.

NASDAQ   This acronym stands for *National Association of Securities Dealers Automated Quotation System*, the second-largest stock market in the United States. It is also the abbreviation used after an initial reference to the *NASDAQ composite index*.

new economy/old economy   *New economy* refers to the Internet economy; *old economy* refers to the pre-Internet economy.

number   *See* **amount/number**

OK/O.K./okay   These informal forms of *all right* or *satisfactory* are acceptable in most types of e-mail but should be avoided in formal writing.

passed/past   *Passed* is the past tense of the verb *pass*. *Past* means "gone by in time" or "recently completed."

- She passed the test.

- He hasn't travelled in the past month.

per cent/percent/%/percentage/percentile   *Per cent* (also spelled *percent*) refers to "one part in every hundred"; it replaces the % sign (which is used only in statistical reports and on business forms) and usually follows a numeral (*30 per cent of the workforce*). *Percentage* likewise refers to a "rate" or "proportion" out of one hundred but usually follows a descriptive term (e.g., *a small percentage*). *Percentile* is a statistical term used for ranking a score in terms of the percentage of scores below. It usually refers to a variable resulting from the division of a population into one hundred equal groups.

- Shares climbed 15 per cent since the company reported a $200 million profit last week.

- There has been a drop in the percentage of investors who support the sell-off.

- He was in the top percentile for his age group.

practical/practicable   *Practical* means "useful," "sensible," or "designed for function." *Practicable* means "capable of being put into practice."

- His practical approach to debt reduction satisfied investors.

- Converting service vehicles to natural gas is not practicable in some regions.

practice/practise   *Practice* (less commonly spelled *practise*) is a noun meaning "a custom or way of doing something," "a repeated exercise that develops skills," or "the professional work of a doctor, lawyer, etc." *Practise* (less commonly spelled *practice*) is a verb meaning "perform habitually" or "be engaged in a profession, religion, etc."

- She will open a legal practice when she graduates with her LLB next year.

- He will need to practise his French before he transfers to our Montreal office.

precede/proceed   Both verbs, *precede* means "come before" and *proceed* means "go ahead with an activity" or "continue."

- A request for tenders precedes the selection process.

- Once you receive authorization, you may proceed with the project.

principal/principle   *Principal* is an adjective, meaning "first in rank or importance" and a noun meaning "capital sum" or "chief person" (especially the head of a school). *Principle* is a noun, meaning "rule" or "axiom." **TIPS:** The primary school saying, "the principal is my pal," is a helpful way of remembering the distinction between these homonyms. Both *princip**le*** and *ru**le*** have *le* endings and similar meanings.

- The principal was reinvested at a rate of 6.5 per cent.

- Her high principles helped her rise above the controversy.

Q1, Q2, Q3, Q4   These abbreviations for first, second, third, and fourth quarter of the year are appropriate in charts and internal documents, but in more formal documents they should be written out as *first quarter*, *second quarter*, *third quarter*, and *fourth quarter*.

quotation/quote   The noun *quotation* is "a reprinted statement made by another person or borrowed from a book or other source, usually enclosed in quotation marks." In business, it often refers to "an estimated cost" or "the current price of a stock or commodity." *Quote* is the informal abbreviated form of the noun as well as a verb. In business, the verb often means "to state the price of a job."

- She began her speech with a quotation from *The World Is Flat*.

- The quote [*or* quotation] for the project seemed unreasonably high.

- At the close of markets today, gold was quoted at $325.

rational/rationale   *Rational* is an adjective that means "sensible" or "based on reason." *Rationale* is a noun that means "the logical basis for something." It is often followed by *for* or *of*.

- A corporate sell-off was not the most rational course of action.

- By establishing a rationale for the new policy, he ensured the highest degree of compliance.

real/really   *Real* is an adjective; *really* is an adverb. Do not use *real* as an adverb if you want to avoid sounding folksy and colloquial.

- Our finest line of desktop organizers is crafted from real Cordovan leather.

- He said he was really [*not* real] sorry about the delay.

reason is because/reason is that   *The reason is because* is redundant. Use either *because* or *the reason . . . is that*

- The reason revenues grew was that [*not* is because] the company sold its poor-performing lending business.

- Revenues grew because the company sold its poor-performing lending business.

reason that/reason why   The expression *the reason why* is redundant. Use either *the reason that* or simply *why*.

- I don't know the reason that [*not* the reason why] he left.

- I don't know why he left.

regardless/irregardless/irrespective   *Regardless*, usually followed by *of*, means "without consideration of" or "despite what might happen." *Irregardless* is non-standard for *regardless*. *Irrespective*, also followed by *of*, means "regardless" or "not taking into account."

respectfully/respectively   *Respectfully*, a common but relatively formal complimentary close, means "with respect." *Respectively* means "in that order."

- I respectfully submit this report for your consideration.

- The first- and second-place rankings were awarded to Future Link Corp. and Emergent Technologies Inc., respectively.

since/because   *Since* usually relates to time. Avoid using *since* as a substitute for *because* if there is any hint of ambiguity, as in the following example: *Since* [meaning both *from that time* and *because*] *he got a promotion, he has spent more on luxuries.*

- He has received five job offers since his graduation last June.

site/sight/cite   *Site* is a noun referring to "a particular place," including a single source for files or services on the Internet. *Sight* is both a noun referring to the faculty of seeing or a thing seen and a verb meaning "observe or notice." *Cite*, also a verb, means "to quote or mention as an authority or example."

- The new site for our company offices will offer easy access to public transit.

- The sight of the month-old sandwich in the cafeteria made him ill.

- Analysts cited increased profit-taking as a reason for caution.

shall/will   *Shall* was once commonly used as a helping verb with *I* and *we* to express future action and with second and third persons to express intention or determination. *Will* was used, conversely, to express intention with the first person and the future tense in the second and third persons. Today, there is less confusion about when to use *shall* and *will*. Now less common, *shall* is still used to express a suggestion or pose a very polite question (*Shall we go?*). In legal documents, *shall* expresses obligation or duty (*The author shall revise the work.*), but the formality of the word makes it less suitable for most business messages. *Will* is now used with all persons to form the future tense and to express an assertion or a strong command.

should/would   *Should* expresses duty, obligation (*I should invest more of my disposable income.*), advisability (*He should seek legal counsel.*) or likelihood (*The markets should improve by the end of the week.*). It replaces *shall* in questions that ask what to do or request consent (*Should I revise the report?*). *Would* expresses habitual action (*He would call a meeting every Friday.*), a conditional mood (*The company would have met its targets if it had reduced overhead expenses.*), or probability (*Profits would exceed $1 million.* or *He would make a good CEO.*).

sometime/sometimes/some time   *Sometime* means "at some unspecified time in the future." *Sometimes* means "occasionally." *Some time* means "a span of time."

- The committee will meet sometime in May to make its final decision.

- He is sometimes late for meetings.

- Can you spare some time later this afternoon?

stationary/stationery   *Stationary* means "not moving." *Stationery* refers to writing materials and office supplies. **TIP:** the *e* in the ending of *stationery* should remind you of the *e*'s in *envelope* and *letter*).

suppose to/supposed to   *Suppose to* is non-standard for *supposed to*. The final *-d* and the preceding verb *be* are essential to convey the idea of a plan, obligation, or something that is generally accepted. *Suppose*, without *be* and the final *-d*, means "assume" or "be inclined to think." *I suppose so* is an expression of hesitant agreement.

- The meeting was supposed to take place last Thursday, but was postponed indefinitely.

- I suppose the profit warning will deter investors.

takeover/take over   *Takeover* is a noun that refers to "the assumption of control or ownership of a business," especially the sometimes hostile buying out of one business by another. *Take over* is a verb meaning "to control" or "to succeed to the management or ownership of" something.

than/then   *Than* is a conjunction that indicates comparison. *Then* is an adverb that shows relationships in time.

- The XJ copier is faster than the older AP model.

- We will do the costing, then submit a bid.

than I/than me   The choice of a pronoun can alter the meaning of a sentence. To check that the pronoun delivers its intended meaning, temporarily add the extra words that are implied.

- Hopkins likes golf more than I. [**in other words,** Hopkins likes golf more than I like golf]

- Hopkins likes golf more than me. [**in other words,** Hopkins likes golf more than he likes me]

that/which/who   These relative pronouns are key sentence builders because they introduce clauses that limit the meaning of the word or words they refer to. Relative pronouns add clarity by defining relationships and, because of this, should be retained in documents intended for translation. On the other hand, too many *that*, *which*, and *who* clauses create a cluttered and awkward syntax. For conciseness, especially in informal documents, revise wordy clauses by replacing them with equivalent modifiers.

Awkward: Place copies of claims that have been rejected in the tray that is red.

   Revised: Place copies of rejected claims in the red tray.

Awkward: The adjuster who handles small claims is the one that you should speak to.

   Revised: You should speak to the small claims adjuster.

It is important to distinguish between *that*, *which*, and *who*. **That** refers mainly to things or animals, but can also refer to a group of people (*The committee that revised the proposal received praise.*). *That* introduces restrictive clauses adding information essential to the meaning of the sentence. Restrictive clauses beginning with *that* are not set off with commas. **Which** also refers to things or animals, but introduces non-restrictive clauses containing information that is helpful but not necessarily essential to the meaning of a sentence. Non-restrictive clauses are set off with commas. Less commonly, *which* can also be used to introduce restrictive clauses. **Who** is a relative pronoun that refers to people.

- The report that you sent me yesterday is timely and well prepared. [*that you sent me yesterday* limits *the report* to a particular report].

- Your report, which I received yesterday, is timely and well prepared. [*which I received yesterday* just provides more information about the report].

- Analysts who recently predicted falling share prices are now optimistic about the stock's performance. [When not set off with commas, the restrictive clause *who recently predicted falling share prices* limits *analysts* to a particular group of analysts.]

- Analysts, who recently predicted falling share prices, are now optimistic about the stock's performance. [When followed by a non-restrictive clause set off with commas, the meaning of *analysts* remains general.]

themselves/themself/theirselves   *Themselves* is the only correct form of this plural reflexive pronoun.

there/their/they're   *There* refers to a position or place and is also used to indicate the existence of something at the beginning of an expletive sentence (*There is a new listing on the TSX.*). *Their* is a possessive pronoun. *They're* is the contraction of *they are*.

toward/towards   As prepositions meaning "in the direction of," *toward* and *towards* are equal and interchangeable. It is best to pick one spelling and use it consistently within a document.

unsolvable/insoluble/insolvent   Both *unsolvable* and *insoluble* mean "incapable of being solved." *Insolvent* means "unable to pay one's debts."

use to/used to   *Used to* is the only correct usage when referring to something that happened in the past—the *-d* ending in *used* is essential.

- He used to work for this company but now he heads up his own business.

wait for/wait on   *Wait for* means "await"; *wait on* can mean either "serve" or "await."

while   The subordinate conjunction *while* means "during that time" as well as "in spite of the fact that" and "on the contrary." If you are using it to concede a point, *while* must not deliver the unintended meaning of simultaneous action. Unless "during that time" is the intended meaning, replace *while* with *although*, *whereas*, or *despite the fact that*.

Ambiguous: While there are problems, I think we should proceed with caution. [This implies "proceed with caution only as long as the problems persist."]

Clear: Although there are problems, I think we should proceed with caution. [This means "proceed with caution in spite of the fact that there are problems."]

Ambiguous: I thought we should move ahead with the project while they had other ideas.

Clear: I thought we should move ahead with the project whereas they had other ideas.

who/that/which   *See* **that/which/who**

who/whom   The distinction between *who* (the subjective case of the pronoun) and *whom* (the objective case of the pronoun) is fast disappearing, especially in less formal contexts. *Who* is now the convenient multi-purpose choice for harried writers, but when more formality and absolute correctness are required, refer to the following case chart, then consider the type of sentence *who/whom* appears in:

Pronoun Case: who vs. whom:
  who = I, you, he, she, it, we, you, they **(all subjects)**
  whom = me, you, him, her, it, us, you, them **(all objects)**

---

who vs. whom in sentences that ask questions
1. Does the interrogative pronoun perform the action (*who*) or receive the action (*whom*) of the sentence?
2. If this is not clear, answer the question the sentence asks, then use the chart above to match up the correct form of *who/whom*.
    • Who was responsible for filing the Gustafson report? (**She**, not **her**, was responsible for filing the Gustafson report; therefore *who* is correct.)
    • Whom did *CanBiz Magazine* hire as its new editor? (*CanBiz Magazine* hired **him**, not **he**, as its new editor; therefore *whom* is correct.)
3. *Whom* commonly follows prepositions such as *to* and *for* (think of the salutation, *To Whom It May Concern*).
    • For whom was the memo intended? (The memo was intended for *them*, not *they*.)
    • To whom should the letter be addressed? (The letter should be addressed to *her*, not *she*.)

---

who vs. whom in sentences that make statements
The relative pronouns *who* and *whoever* (subjective case) and *whom* and *whomever* (objective case) are often the first words of subordinate clauses. To test for the correct pronoun, isolate the subordinate clause, then replace *who/whom* with the corresponding case of pronoun (see the accompanying case chart). Rearrange the clause to see whether a pronoun subject or pronoun object makes the most sense.
  • Original Sentence: Employees **who/whom** senior management encouraged reported greater job satisfaction.
  • Subordinate Clause: **who/whom** senior management encouraged
  • Trial Substitutions:

      ✗ senior management encouraged they = who

      ✔ senior management encouraged them = whom

- Correct Sentence: *Employees whom senior management encouraged reported greater job satisfaction.* You may drop *whom* from the sentence to lessen the formality: *Employees senior management encouraged reported greater job satisfaction.*
- Original Sentence: The award for business excellence goes to **whoever/whomever** contributes the most to the company in the next fiscal year.
- Subordinate Clause: **whoever/whomever** contributes the most
- Trial Substitutions:
  - ✔ she contributes the most = whoever
  - ✘ her contributes the most = whomever
- Correct Sentence: *The award for business excellence goes to whoever contributes the most to the company in the next fiscal year.* In this case, the objective-case-follows-a-preposition rule doesn't apply. The object of the preposition isn't a single word—*whomever*—but the entire clause beginning with the pronoun, so in this case the subject *whoever* is the only correct choice.

who's/whose   *Who's* is the contraction of *who is*. *Whose* is the possessive form of *who*.

- Who's eligible for the new training program?
- Our chief sales representative, whose name is Paul Sharma, will be glad to assist you.
- Whose phone is this?

your/you're   *Your* is a possessive adjective meaning "belonging to you"; *you're* is a contraction of *you are*.

USAGE EXERCISE

According to context, select the correct word in each set of parentheses:

1. He (*assured/ensured/insured*) me he would keep the (*amount/number*) of changes to a minimum.

2. The (*affects/effects*) of the (*take over/takeover*) were felt by many (*personal/personnel*). Those most (*affected/effected*) blamed (*backward/backwards*) policies.

3. After (*alot/allot/a lot*) of consultation with printers, the vice-president approved the new design for the company (*stationary/stationery*).

4. With (*fewer/less*) reports to file, there is (*fewer/less*) work to do.

5. She was (*suppose to/supposed to*) settle the dispute (*among/between*) the five committee members.

6. The delegates were accompanied (*by/with*) two members of the support staff.

7. In the (*past/passed*) year, the government has (*past/passed*) new labour legislation.

8. The hiring committee will meet (*sometime/some time/sometimes*) in the next week.

9. The dispute resolution committee agreed (*to*/*with*) the proposed changes.

10. Because the conference is held (*biennially*/*biannually*/*semi-annually*), Sean has two years to prepare his next study of investment trends.

11. (*As regards*/*In regard to*/*Regards*) your request to (*precede*/*proceed*) with the project, I fully support your initiative and ask that you move (*foreword*/*forwards*/*forward*) with the plan.

12. (*Between you and me*/*Between you and I*), I think the need for more (*capital*/*capitol*) is justified.

13. Lise (*could of*/*could have*) solved the problem if she had been (*apprised*/*appraised*) of the situation.

14. Every (*chairman*/*chairperson*/*chair*) of the advisory (*council*/*counsel*) has had (*his own*/*an*) office.

15. Our team's recommendations differed (*from*/*with*) (*theirs*/*there's*).

16. Mai Li plans to apply to (*a*/*an*) MBA program next year.

17. (*Compared to*/*Compared with*) his co-workers, Jorge performs (*well*/*good*) under pressure (*due to*/*because of*) his superior time-management skills.

18. The cancellation of the flight was (*due to*/*because of*) mechanical problems.

19. (*While*/*Although*) the financial officer (*who*/*whom*) he reports to is supportive, she plans to cut the budget for his department.

20. The committee is looking for applicants (*who*/*whom*) they feel are best prepared to promote our products in emerging markets.

◐ Abbreviations and Acronyms

ABBREVIATIONS

Abbreviations should be used sparingly—and only when their meanings are obvious to the reader.

- **abbreviated titles before and after names:** use abbreviations ending in periods for titles that precede names (Mr., Ms., Mrs., Prof., Dr., Hon.) or abbreviations for degrees and professional designations that follow names (CA, Ph.D., M.D., LL.B., Q.C.):

✔	✔	✘
Ms. Maria DaSilva	Maria DaSilva, CA	Ms. Maria DaSilva, CA
Dr. Paul Lui	Paul Lui, M.D.	Dr. Paul Lui, M.D.
Hon. Peter Kent		
	Thomas McKay, Jr.	
Rev. Ian Wilding		
Prof. Iqbal Khan	Iqbal Khan, Ph.D.	Prof. Iqbal Khan, Ph.D.

- **abbreviations of months:** abbreviate all months with the exception of *May*, *June*, and *July* when the month is written in text and is followed by a numeral (*Oct. 5, Jan. 28, June 17*). Use full spelling for the month if it appears on its own or if it is followed by a year (*December; March 1998*). Do not abbreviate months in letter datelines.

- **abbreviations of provinces and addresses:** use standard abbreviations of provinces (as opposed to the two-letter Canada Post abbreviations: AB, BC, MB, NB, NL, NS, NT, NU, ON, PE, QC, SK, YT) for provinces written in text accompanied by the name of a town or city (*the Markham, Ont., plant will be expanded*) but not for province names appearing alone (*the Ontario plant will be expanded*). Spell out words such as *street*, *boulevard*, and *avenue* in all inside addresses and in text when no number is part of the address (*please visit our Hastings Street office*).

In general, make abbreviations as clear as possible. If necessary, add periods to abbreviations that might be mistaken for words or typographical errors (e.g., *a.k.a.* or *a.m.*).

ACRONYMS

An acronym is a shortened form created from the first letters of a series of words. It is pronounced either as a single word (e.g., *WHO* stands for the World Health Organization; other examples are NATO and CANDU) or by letter (by-letter acronyms, such as the CBC or RCMP, are called initialisms) and in most cases does not require periods. If an acronym is well known, use it without explanation; otherwise spell it out parenthetically on first reference: *CPA* (*Certified Public Accounts*), *AFP* (*Association of Fundraising Professionals*). Acronyms are often used for the following:

- **names of corporations and banking institutions**

    IBM   CIBC   BMO   RBC

- **names of organizations and government agencies**

    CSIS   NATO   UNESCO   CPP   CBC   CSA   CRTC   CAW   CDIC

- **abbreviated phrases and compound nouns**

RSVP	(répondez s'il vous plaît)
FAQS	(frequently asked questions)
VIP	(very important person)
ASAP	(as soon as possible)
SUV	(sport utility vehicle)
RFI	(request for information)
RFP	(request for proposal)
radar	(radio detecting and ranging)
modem	(modulator/demodulator)
MS	(multiple sclerosis)
RAM	(random access memory)
CSB	(Canada Savings Bond)
GIC	(Guaranteed Investment Certificate)
RRSP	(Registered Retirement Savings Plan)

Numbers

Numbers may be expressed as words or as figures. In general, numbers up to and including ten are expressed as words; numbers above ten are expressed as figures. There are exceptions to this rule.

- **EMPHASIS:** Numbers under ten may be written as figures in special financial contexts and data references (*The TSX is down 8 points.*).
- **PLACEMENT:** Write the number as a word if it begins a sentence. (*Fifteen council members attended the meeting.*) Hyphenate words that form a single number (*Seventy-eight applications have been submitted.*). If the number consists of more than two words, consider revising the sentence so that the number is not at the beginning (*On average, 75 employees apply for this program each year.*).
- **MONEY:** Use figures to express sums of money greater than one dollar. (*The deluxe staplers cost $22.95 each.*) Omit the decimal and zeroes when expressing whole dollar amounts (*The starting salary is $50,000.*).
- **BIG FIGURES:** Write million or billion as a word instead of a figure with multiple zeroes. The number that precedes *million* or *billion* is expressed as a figure (*The company committed $2 million to the project.*). Figures in the millions are generally rounded off to one decimal place, but care should be taken to avoid possible misrepresentation (*Average compensation reached almost $5.5 million this year.*).
- **AGES:** Use words to express ages (*The preferred age for early retirement is fifty-five.*) unless the age follows a name (*Joan Brennerman, 62, is the top candidate for CFO.*).
- **RELATED NUMBERS:** Express related numbers (referring to items in the same category) in the form used for the larger number (*Four of the five candidates have graduate degrees.* and *We are prepared to retire 7 vehicles from our current fleet of 32.*). Express the first related number as a word if it falls at the beginning of a sentence (*Seven of history's 10 largest bankruptcies occurred in 2001 or 2002.*).
- **CONSECUTIVE NUMBERS:** Differentiate consecutive numbers that modify the same noun by expressing the first as a word and the second as a figure (*She purchased four 20-year bonds*). If the first number consists of more than two words, express the number as a figure (*200 12-page inserts*).
- **DECIMALS AND PERCENTAGES:** Use figures to express decimals (*9.75*). For amounts less than one, put a zero before the decimal (*0.5*) unless the decimal itself begins with a zero (*.08*). Avoid using more than two decimal points in text. Also use figures to express percentages along with the word *per cent* (*a 10 per cent drop*) or followed by the % symbol in statistical reports (*a 5% increase*). Use the % sign with each individual number (*The share-return price shrank to 45% from 57% the previous year.*). Spell out the percentage at the beginning of a sentence (*Thirty per cent of area residents opposed the development.*).
- **SIMPLE FRACTIONS** are expressed as words in text (*Three quarters of Canadians have Internet access.*) and are hyphenated when used as modifiers (*He sold his one-quarter share in the company.*).
- **TIME:** To express clock time (with *a.m.* or *p.m.*), use figures (*a meeting will be held on February 4 at 2:00 p.m.*). To express periods of time, use words (*The company has manufactured optical instruments for sixty-five years.*) or use figures for emphasis of important financial or contractual terms (*a 30-day money-back guarantee*).

- **DATES:** Use figures when the number follows the name of the month (*January 15*) and use ordinals (*1st, 2nd, 3rd*) when the number precedes the name of the month (*We will meet on the 15th of January.*). Do not use ordinals in European or military-style datelines (*15 January 2010*).
- **WEIGHTS AND MEASUREMENTS** are expressed with figures (*each unit weighs 2.2 kg; the office is 5 kilometres from Vancouver International Airport*).
- **TELEPHONE AND FAX NUMBERS:** For telephone and fax numbers in Canada and the United States, put the area code in parentheses and insert a hyphen after the exchange, for example *(416) 555-2167*; if extensions are essential, place a comma after the telephone number followed by the abbreviation *Ext.* or *ext.* For internal numbers, include only the extension, for example *Please call Terry Simpson, ext. 445*. Periods may also be used in place of more conventional punctuation *416.555.2167*.
- **ADDRESSES:** Write street numbers in figures, except for the number one.
- **CHAPTERS AND SECTIONS:** Use figures to designate chapter and section numbers. Capitalize the word before the number (*Chapter 7, Section 3*).

Quick-Reference Number Chart

Words	Figures
numbers ten and under	numbers above ten
numbers that begin sentences	numbers that begin sentences (3+ words)
small fractions	weights, measurements
ages	ages that appear after names
periods of time	clock time
	addresses
	sections, chapters, pages
	decimals, percentages
	money

NUMBER USAGE EXERCISE

Correct number usage errors in the following sentences:

1. 45 of the 75 applications for the advertised position were submitted electronically.

2. Project development was documented through a series of 5 10-page reports.

3. Our small electronics division had revenues of $32,900,000.00 in the latest fiscal year, an increase of fifteen per cent over the previous year.

4. When the price of gasoline rose to one dollar and twenty cents a litre, 3 media outlets in the greater Halifax area reported that price gouging was to blame.

5. The association's first conference on biomedical ethics, scheduled for January the tenth, is expected to draw more than three-hundred-and-fifty participants.

6. Our 5 Calgary-area sales centres were among the top 20 dealerships in the country for the 4th consecutive year.

7. Pure Citrus Products was charged with false advertising when it was found that its Premier™ Juice product line contained only .5 per cent real fruit juice.

Capitalization

- **PROPER NOUNS:** Proper nouns, which name specific people, places (geographic locations), and things, should be capitalized. References to language, culture, or ethnicity (*French*, *Indonesian*) should also be capitalized. Common nouns, naming general categories, are not capitalized unless they fall at the beginning of a sentence.

Proper Noun	Common Noun
First Canadian Place	office tower
Nova Scotia Community College	community college
Air Canada	airline or air carrier
Hinduism	religion
Lake Athabasca	lake

- **BUSINESS AND PROFESSIONAL TITLES:** Capitalize business titles only when they precede names or appear in inside addresses, salutations, signature blocks, official documents, and minutes of meetings—not when they follow names or appear alone in running text.

  - Ms Shauna Kovick
    Director of Human Resources
    Technion Enterprises, Inc.
    Ottawa, ON K4W 2E9

  - Sincerely,

    David McHenry
    Corporate Travel Administrator

  - Stephanie Di Castro, director of marketing, devised the new campaign.

  - Vice-President Leung has been assigned to head our Winnipeg operation.

  - Please consult the district manager before drafting the RFP.

  Note that the style guidelines of individual organizations may operate according to different standards.

- **DEPARTMENT AND DIVISION NAMES:** Capitalize the names of committees, departments, and divisions *within* your organization. It is customary in some organizations, however, to lowercase these names. If in doubt about which style your organization prefers, consult corporate style guidelines. Use lowercase for non-specific names of committees, departments, and divisions *outside* your organization.

    - The package was forwarded to our Project Management Division.
    - Antonio was recently transferred to our Accounting Department.
    - Their sales division was recently downsized.

- **ORGANIZATION NAMES:** Capitalize all words (excluding non-initial conjunctions and prepositions) in the names of public- and private-sector industries, educational institutions, government bodies, and social agencies, as well as charitable, non-profit, religious, and professional organizations.

Canadian Cancer Society	Environment Canada
HSBC Securities	Ministry of Transportation
Toronto District School Board	Hospital for Sick Children

- **PRODUCT NAMES:** Capitalize only trademarked items and manufacturers' names, not general products (*Canon copier*, *IBM computer*).
- **ACADEMIC DEGREES AND COURSES:** Capitalize specific degrees and courses as well as names of academic degrees that follow a person's name. Abbreviations for academic degrees are always capitalized. Degrees and courses referred to more generally are lower-cased.

    - Jason Jackson, M.B.A.
    - He earned a bachelor's degree in science.
    - He earned his Bachelor of Science degree.

- **BOOK TITLES:** Capitalize the initial word and all principal words (not articles, conjunctions, or prepositions) in the titles of books, articles, magazines, periodicals, newspapers, reports, government documents, films, songs, plays, and poems. The titles of major works or publications (such as books, magazines, and newspapers) should be underlined or italicized. The titles of all other works should be enclosed within quotation marks.
- **QUOTATIONS AND BULLET POINTS:** Capitalize the first word of quoted material that is a full sentence (*Debashis Chaudry said, "The company is remarkably different than it was a decade ago."*), but if the quotation is interrupted mid-sentence, do not capitalize the beginning of the second part. Do not capitalize the first letter of a quotation if the quotation itself is not a complete sentence (*The chair of the advisory board said that it was time to put an end to "fuzzy corporate accounting."*). Capitalize the initial word of a numbered or bulleted item appearing in list form.

- **E-MAIL AND COMPUTER FUNCTIONS:** Capitalize all e-mail and computer functions, as in *Click on* **Send**. Copy notations in e-mail (*cc, bcc*) are not capitalized.
- **NOUNS PRECEDING LETTERS OR NUMBERS:** Capitalize nouns that precede numbers or letters (*Flight 98, Gate 44, Room 3122, Table B*).

Quick-Reference Capitalization Chart

Do Capitalize	Do Not Capitalize
proper nouns	common nouns
courtesy or business titles preceding names	titles used as appositives titles used in place of names
internal department and division names	non-specific external departments, etc.
specific academic degrees and courses	general degrees and subjects
trademarked product names	common product names
compass points naming specific regions	compass points indicating direction
nouns followed by numbers or letters	
e-mail or computer functions	

CAPITALIZATION EXERCISES

Correct the following sentences by capitalizing words as required.

1. president siddiqui's favourite book is *the world is flat* by thomas l. friedman.

2. winnipeg-based enterprise press plans to launch its first french-language daily newspaper in the competitive montreal market.

3. As stated in article 5 of the senate report, our faculty of business will launch a new program called entrepreneurial studies in the 2011–2012 academic year.

4. the director of public relations will discuss the reintroduction of the gift-card program when she meets with the president next week.

5. tim hortons' famous double-double has helped the chain become the most profitable division of the us fast-food giant wendy's.

⬤⬤ Usage-Related Internet Resources

York University Style Guide (prepared by Marketing and Communications)—this useful Canadian style guide covers a range of topics and presents information modified from a number of sources, including the *CP Stylebook*.
www.yorku.ca/yorkweb/standards/language/

University of Calgary Style Guide (prepared by the Communications Office at the U of C)—this concise document offers guidance on spelling and capitalization from a Canadian perspective.
www.ucalgary.ca/news/styleguide

Also from the University of Calgary, the following site provides a list of the best online resources for citation guides and writing help:
http://libguides.ucalgary.ca/reference

Common Errors in English—homonyms, homophones, and usage queries briefly explained.
www.wsu.edu/~brians/errors/errors.html#errors

NetLingo: The Internet Dictionary—rules for the spelling and hyphenation of Internet terms, plus explanations of common acronyms.
www.netlingo.com

tiscali.reference—sponsored by a European Internet provider, this site features 1,600 detailed entries to help you make your wording precise.
www.tiscali.co.uk/reference/dictionaries/english

⬤⬤ Saluations and Complimentary Closes: A User's Guide

OPENING GREETINGS FOR E-MAIL

Salutations and complimentary closes are optional in e-mail messages but are fast becoming standard to a more personalized, reader-centred approach. Greetings and appropriate concluding remarks can soften otherwise abrupt messages, building goodwill and securing compliance. Vary the salutation and complimentary close to fit the tone, subject, and nature of the message and to reflect your relationship to the reader. For example, it is best to refrain from closing with *cheers* when your message contains bad news. Consider the degree of authority vis-à-vis friendliness you wish to project.

Formal	Less Formal	Informal
Dear	recipient's first name by itself	Hello (without using the recipient's name)
Good Morning Good Afternoon	Hi (without using the recipient's name)	(recipient's name incorporated within first line of message)
	Greetings	

CLOSERS FOR E-MAIL

Formal	Less Formal
Sincerely	Cheers
Best wishes	Regards
	Best
	Thanks (to show appreciation)

COMPLIMENTARY CLOSES FOR STANDARD LETTERS

Sincerely is universally accepted as the most appropriate complimentary close for standard business letters; however in certain circumstances, an alternative complimentary close may help you achieve a higher or lower degree of formality. Before making your choice, consider the following factors:

- workplace style guidelines and expected level of formality,
- your relationship to the reader and frequency of correspondence,
- tone and the nature of the message, and
- your position within the company hierarchy.

Here is a sampling of standard complimentary closes:

Very Formal	Somewhat Formal	Informal
Respectfully	Sincerely	Regards
Very sincerely yours	Sincerely yours	Best regards
Very truly yours	Cordially	Best wishes

Standard Phrases and Their Plain-Language Alternatives: A Quick-Reference Table

Standard Phrases (Wordy/Outdated)	Plain-Language Equivalents
are in receipt of	have received
are of the opinion that	think, believe
as per your request	as you requested, at your request
at your earliest convenience	soon, by (specific date)
enclosed herewith please find	enclosed
forthwith	without delay, at once
in the eventuality that	if
in view of the fact that	because
pursuant to your request	at your request
thanking you in advance	thank you

Grammar Handbook

Subject–Verb Agreement

Nothing detracts from the professionalism of business messages as severely as faulty subject–verb agreement. Verbs—"doing words" that show actions or states of being—must agree with their subjects both in number (singular/plural) and person (*I, you, he, she, it, we, you, they*). The primary rule is that singular subjects—those that name just one thing—require singular verbs, and plural subjects—those that name more than one thing—require plural verbs.

S RULE FOR THIRD-PERSON AGREEMENTS

There is a simple way to remember how to make correct subject–verb agreement that applies to singular and plural subjects in the third person (subject nouns that can be replaced by *he, she, it, one*, or *they*). Agreement with a singular subject in the third person is made by adding *s* to the verb:

- The author_ supports the subsidies.

The plural subject is formed by adding *-s* or *-es* to the noun, but no *s* is found at the end of the verb that agrees with it:

- The authors support_ the subsidies.

It stands to reason that only one element in the pair—either subject or verb—can end in *-s*. If both end in *-s* or neither ends in *-s*, then the error in agreement has been made.

FINDING THE SIMPLE SUBJECT

Part of the challenge in making subjects and verbs agree is finding the simple subject. To do this, ignore intervening phrases that begin with prepositions (words such as *in, at, of,* and *on*) and make the verb agree with the subject word that comes immediately before the preposition.

The **author** of the report **supports** subsidies. (singular subject/singular verb)

The **author** of the reports **supports** subsidies. (singular subject/singular verb)

The **authors** of the report **support** subsidies. (plural subject/plural verb)

COMPOUND SUBJECTS

Subjects joined by *and* take a plural verb.

- **The company and its subsidiary** manufacture appliances. (compound subject/plural verb)

Only subjects joined by *and* that name a single thing take a singular verb.

- **Red beans and rice** is his favourite dish. (singular subject/singular verb)

JOINING WORDS NOT EQUIVALENT TO *AND*

The following joining words are not equivalent to *and*—they do not alter the number of the subjects that come before them:

accompanied by	except	together with
along with	in addition to	with
as well as	including	

To determine verb agreement, simply ignore the nouns that follow these joining words.

- The **director**, as well as the managers, **is** pleased with the sales figures.

COLLECTIVE NOUNS AS SUBJECTS

Collective nouns—common in business correspondence—name groups of things or people: for example, *team, committee, group, family, class, number, audience, jury, couple.* Collective nouns present a challenge to verb agreement because they can be either singular or plural subjects depending on the dynamics of the group. Collective nouns are treated as singular to convey the idea of the group acting together and as plural to convey the idea of members of the group acting individually. Most often, they are treated as singular.

- The **committee is** meeting on Wednesday.
- The **committee are** unhappy with each other's proposals.

To clarify the idea of individual action within the group, add a plural noun such as *members.*

- The **members** of the committee **are** unhappy with each other's proposals.

An exception to the rule: *the number* . . . requires a singular verb; *a number* . . . requires a plural verb.

- **The number** of applicants **is** down this year.
- **A number** of applicants **are** taking MBA degrees.

SINGULAR SUBJECTS IN PLURAL FORM

Words such as *economics*, *ergonomics*, *human resources*, *measles*, *mumps*, and *news* are singular. Words such as *physics*, *mathematics*, *athletics*, and *statistics* are singular when they describe disciplines. When the word refers to multiple items, it is treated as a plural noun.

- **Statistics is** a required course for a degree in psychology.
- The new **statistics are** now available.

AMOUNTS AND UNITS OF MEASUREMENT AS SUBJECTS

When the subject names an amount (e.g., of time, money, distance, or weight) thought of as a single unit, the subject takes a singular verb.

- **Thirty dollars is** the closing price for a share of Computex.
- **Two weeks is** too long to wait for the estimates.
- **A five per cent increase** in sales **is** expected.

When the subject names an amount thought of in terms of individual things or persons, the subject takes a plural verb.

- **One-third** of the new employees **have** requested parking spaces.
- **Eighty per cent** of the programmers **are** satisfied with the current system.

TITLES, TERMS, AND ORGANIZATION NAMES AS SUBJECTS

Use a singular verb with the name of an organization, with a work cited by its title, and with words that make up a single term, even if the name, title, or term includes a plural noun:

- **Edgeworth, Flett, & Thompson LLP has** represented us for five years.
- ***The Eight Practices* is** a book that explores the subject of human capital.

SENTENCES BEGINNING WITH *HERE* AND *THERE*

Subjects follow verbs in sentences beginning with *here* and *there*.

- There **is a report** on that issue.
- There **are reports** on that issue.
- Here **are** the new sales **figures**.

SUBJECTS AND LINKING VERBS

Linking verbs—the verb *be* and verbs of perception and sense such as *appear, feel, seem, taste,* or *smell*—join subjects to words that supply more information about them. The verb always agrees with the subject that comes before it, not the descriptive words that follow it.

- His **concern is** low wages.

If this sentence is reversed, its subject is plural.

- Low **wages are** his concern.

EITHER . . . OR SENTENCES

When subjects follow pairs of conjunctions—*not only . . . but (also), neither . . . nor, either . . . or*—the verb agrees with the subject closest to it.

- Neither the employees nor the **president wants** to lose customers.
- Neither the president nor the **employees want** to lose customers.

PRONOUN SUBJECTS: *ANYONE, EVERYONE, SOMEONE, EACH, EITHER, ANY, NONE, SOME*

The following indefinite pronouns are singular and take singular verbs:

another	anything	every	everything	nothing	something
anybody	each	everybody	neither	somebody	
anyone	either	everyone	nobody	someone	

The following indefinite pronouns can be singular or plural, depending on the context:

all	more	none
any	most	some

- **Some** competition **is** unavoidable.
- **Some** of our competitors **are** downsizing.

ANTECEDENTS OF *THAT, WHICH,* AND *WHO* AS SUBJECTS

The verb agrees with the word to which *that, which,* or *who* refers.

VERB AGREEMENT AND THE PHRASES *ONE OF THE . . ., ONE OF THE . . . WHO,* AND *THE ONLY ONE OF THE . . . WHO*

Treat these constructions as follows:

- *one of the* + plural noun + singular verb

   One of the supervisors **is** touring the new facility.

- *one of the* + plural noun + *who (that, which)* + plural verb

   John is one of the **IT specialists who work** for our company.

- *the only one of the* + plural noun + *who (that, which)* + singular verb

   John is **the only one** of our IT specialists who **works** part-time.

EXERCISE: SUBJECT–VERB AGREEMENT

Underline the correct verb agreement in each of the following sentences.

1. Pressure from investors (*is, are*) partly responsible for the plan to reduce annual costs.

2. Changes in this policy (*is, are*) not expected for at least another year.

3. More than forty acquisitions in two years (*has, have*) made Briarcorp a market leader.

4. The president, as well as the CEO and CFO, (*anticipate, anticipates*) major changes in the year ahead.

5. Our current strategy of cutting staff in Western Canada and aggressively expanding in the East (*is, are*) controversial.

6. Copies of the manual (*is, are*) now available from accounting services.

7. Eighteen hundred dollars (*is, are*) a fair price for the latest Pentium 4 model.

8. Neither the biggest billboards nor the most eye-catching print campaign (*compensate, compensates*) for a flawed strategy that (*involve, involves*) withdrawing customer service.

9. Neither of the companies (*favour, favours*) a protracted series of layoffs.

10. We have canvassed several firms, but Thornton, Walters, & Estes (*is, are*) our first choice for legal services.

11. Anyone who (*requires, require*) clarification of the new health benefits package should contact human resources.

12. He is the only one of our sales representatives who (*has, have*) not completed the course.

13. Norstar is one of the companies that (*is, are*) cautious about overexpansion.

14. The number of customers satisfied with our services (*is, are*) up significantly this year.

15. Ninety per cent of our customers (*is, are*) satisfied with our services.

⬤⬤ Verb Tense Accuracy

Tense refers to the time of a verb's action. Each tense—past, present, and future—has simple, progressive, perfect, and perfect-progressive forms. These convey a range of time relations, from the simple to the complex.

Tense	For Actions	Examples
Present (simple)	happening now, occurring habitually, or true anytime	I walk; she walks
Past (simple)	completed in the past	I walked; she walked
Future (simple)	that will occur	I will walk; she will walk
Present Progressive	already in progress, happening now, or still happening	I am walking; she is walking
Past Progressive	in progress at a specific point in the past or that lasted for a period in the past	I was walking; she was walking
Future Progressive	of duration in the future, or occurring over a period at a specific point in the future	I will be walking; she will be walking
Present Perfect	begun in the past and continuing in the present, or occurring sometime in the past	I have walked; she has walked
Past Perfect	completed before others in the past	I had walked; she had walked
Future Perfect	completed before others in the future	I will have walked; she will have walked
Present Perfect Progressive	in progress recently, or of duration starting in the past and continuing in the present	I have been walking; she has been walking
Past Perfect Progressive	of duration completed before others in the past	I had been walking; she had been walking
Future Perfect Progressive	underway for a period of time before others in the future	I will have been walking; she will have been walking

SEQUENCING PAST TENSES

When one past action occurred at the same time as another, use the simple past tense in both instances.

- When our server **went** down, we **called** for support immediately.

Use the past perfect tense (*had* + past participle) to show that one past action preceded another.

- He **had left** the office by the time we **returned** from our meeting.

SHIFTS IN VERB TENSE

Shifts in tense are necessary to indicate changes in time frame; however, inconsistent or unnecessary shifts in tense create confusing and illogical sentences.

☒ When **he applied** for a loan, **we check** his credit history. (past/present)

☑ When he **applied** for a loan, we **checked** his credit history. (past/past)

⬤◯ Other Verb Problems

SPECULATING ABOUT THE FUTURE, MAKING RECOMMENDATIONS, OR EXPRESSING WISHES

The subjunctive is one of three "moods" in English. Formed by combining the base form of the verb with the sentence's subject (*work* instead of *works*; *be* instead of *am/ are*; *were* instead of *was*), it expresses conditions, requests, wishes, and speculation about future action that is improbable or unlikely. Once common but now mostly restricted in its use to formal English, it survives in certain well-known expressions: *so be it*, *as it were*, *far be it from me*. However ungrammatical the subjunctive sounds, use it in formal and mid-level writing in the following instances:

- when you use a clause beginning with *if*, *as if*, *as though*, or *unless* to express speculation rather than fact or describe hypothetical situations that are improbable or unlikely:

  - **Subjunctive**: If I **were** you, I would ask for assistance. (situation purely hypothetical—"I" cannot be "you")

  - **Subjunctive**: If he **were** to work tonight, he would finish the report on time. (speculation)

  - **Indicative**: If he works tonight, he will finish the report on time. (fact rather than speculation)

- when you use a clause ending in *that* to express recommendations, wishes, or demands:

  - It is important that a company representative **be** [not **is**] present to greet the dignitaries.

SPECULATING ABOUT THE PAST: APPROPRIATE USE OF *COULD, WOULD*

"Hindsight is 20/20," the saying goes, but speculation about action in the past is often difficult to express. In cause-and-effect sentences of this kind, the conditional verbs *could* and *would* belong in the independent clause describing conditions other than they are, not in the dependent *if/unless* clause describing the hypothetical situation that allows for that outcome.

> ☒ If she **would have** telephoned me, I **would have** faxed the information.

> ☑ If she **had** telephoned me, I **would have** faxed the information.

EMPHASIZING A MAIN VERB WITH *DO*

The helping verbs *do, does,* and *did* add positive emphasis to the main verbs they precede. To be effective, this construction should be used sparingly.

- Although there are no plans for expansion, the company **does** intend to modernize its current facilities.

Do, does, and *did* are used to ask questions and are paired with *never* or *not* to express negative meanings.

- **Do** you have experience in risk management?

- John **does not** advocate the expensing of stock options.

⬤⬤ Using Passive-Voice Constructions

The "voice" of a verb refers to whether the subject acts (active voice) or is acted upon (passive voice). The passive voice inverts standard **subject + verb + object** word order so that the original object (that receives the action) becomes the subject of the passive verb.

- active voice: The financial officer approved the budget.

- passive voice: The budget was approved by the financial officer.

- passive voice: The budget was approved. (The prepositional phrase containing the original active-voice subject is often omitted.)

The passive voice is formed in this way:

> a **form of the verb *to be*** (*am, is, are, was, were, be, being, been*)
>
> + **past participle** (for regular verbs, the base form of the verb + *-ed*)
>
> + (***by*** the agent of the action)

In business writing, the active voice is preferred and should be used whenever possible. There are circumstances, however, in which the passive voice is rhetorically useful.

CRITERIA FOR CHOOSING BETWEEN THE ACTIVE AND PASSIVE VOICE

- **Conciseness:** The active voice is more vigorous, concise, and direct than the passive voice. It is also less awkward and complicated. The higher word count of the passive construction can, with overuse, make writing sound weak and lacklustre. ACTIVE: *On Tuesday, Jinlu submitted his article to the managing editor.* PASSIVE: *On Tuesday, Jinlu's article was submitted to the managing editor.*

- **Emphasis and Disclosure:** The first element in a sentence has the most emphasis. The active voice emphasizes the actor; the passive voice minimizes or conceals the actor and emphasizes the recipient of the action or the fact of the action itself. ACTIVE: *Fiona did not complete the report on time.* PASSIVE: *The report was not completed on time.* Readers sometimes interpret this use of the passive voice as a sign of evasion or refusal to admit responsibility, so exercise caution in eliminating the final prepositional phrase. The passive voice is appropriate when the question of who performed an action is unimportant or irrelevant: *Bids will be accepted until the end of the week.*

- **Tact and Diplomacy:** The active voice is direct, often to the point of bluntness, playing up the personalities that figure in a refusal or denial. The passive voice minimizes the unpleasantness of negative messages by allowing for simple statements of fact, seemingly free of personal malice. ACTIVE: *We cannot activate your account at the present time.* PASSIVE: *Your account cannot be activated at the present time.*

- **Personal/Impersonal Style:** The passive voice minimizes or eliminates personal pronouns in instances where overuse conveys the impression of egotism or perceived personal conflict. ACTIVE: *I created this program to reduce cost overruns.* PASSIVE: *This program was created to reduce cost overruns.* Impersonal passive constructions—beginning with *it is*—may sound antiseptically official and bureaucratic: *It is felt that changes must be made.*

Use the active voice when you need to

- ☑ Write concisely

- ☑ Reveal the doer of an action

- ☑ Deliver positive or neutral news

Use the passive voice when you need to

- ☑ Emphasize an action, not who was responsible for it

- ☑ De-emphasize or soften bad news

- ☑ Take personalities (and their pronouns) out of the picture

⬤⬤ Avoiding Logically Mismatched Subjects and Verbs (Faulty Predication)

Subjects and their verbs (predicates) should agree in number and also make sense together.

☒ The purpose of the study assesses customer service preferences.

☑ The study assesses customer service preferences.

☑ The purpose of the study is to assess customer service preferences.

The first sentence is incorrect because a *purpose* cannot *assess*. Two other constructions make for similarly awkward sentences:

- *is when, is where*

   ☒ A recession is when the economy experiences a temporary downturn.

   ☑ A recession is a temporary economic downturn.

- *the reason . . . is because*

   ☒ The reason that we hired her is because she is creative.

   ☑ The reason we hired her is that she is creative.

   ☑ We hired her because she is creative.

Use either *the reason* or *because*, but not both, as this amounts to saying the same thing twice.

⬤⬤ Using Similar Phrasing for Items in a Series (Parallelism)

Use parallel grammatical forms to express two or more similar ideas or items in a series. Create balanced sentences by matching single words with single words (nouns with nouns, verbs with verbs), phrases with phrases, and clauses with clauses. Parallel phrasing—like other forms of consistency—improves readability and serves as an aid to memory.

☒ We held a meeting, discussed the matter, and a strategy was devised.

☑ We held a meeting, discussed the matter, and devised a strategy.

Add words necessary for logic and completeness. In the case of the first sentence below, *has . . . pursue* does not correctly form the past tense:

☒ The company has and will continue to pursue aggressive growth targets.

☑ The company has pursued and will continue to pursue aggressive growth targets.

   ☒ Alban has interned and worked for Apex Communications.

   ☑ Alban has interned **with** and worked for Apex Communications.

Balanced constructions can also be created using pairs of conjunctions: *either . . . or, neither . . . nor, both . . . and, not only . . . but (also)*. Equivalent grammatical elements must be used for each conjunction.

   ☒ She is not only developing a marketing program but the campaign will also be overseen by her.

   ☑ She is not only developing a marketing program but also overseeing the campaign.

PARALLELISM EXERCISE

Correct faulty parallel structure in the following sentences.

1. Respondents were asked to not only rank the importance of the recycling materials collected but also their preferences in the placement of recycling bins.

2. Neither the chair of the committee wants to seek bankruptcy protection nor its members.

3. Our intention is to develop a work plan, hire suitable people to staff the operation, and working out a schedule.

4. The team was asked to investigate where the raw materials might be available, what the price per unit tonne is, and what the cost to transport raw materials might be.

5. The task force on workforce diversity is committed to promoting an awareness and respect for cultural differences.

⬤⬤ Making Comparisons Clear and Logical (Sentences with *Than* or *As*)

Make sure sentences of comparison deliver the meaning you intend. Include all words required to clarify the relationship between the items being compared. Check the correctness of pronouns by mentally filling in implied words and phrases.

   ☒ Recent hires know more about instant messaging than their managers. (This implies a faulty comparison of *instant messaging* and *managers*.)

   ☑ Recent hires know about instant messaging more than their managers do. (This sentence compares recent hires' knowledge with managers' knowledge.)

   ☑ Recent hires know more than their managers about instant messaging.

Changing a pronoun can alter the meaning of a comparison sentence:

- Scott likes instant messaging as much as me. (Scott likes instant messaging as much as he likes the writer of the sentence.)

- Scott like instant messaging as much as I. (Scott likes instant messaging as much as the writer of the sentence does.)

Using Pronouns with Precision

Pronouns should be of the same case—functioning as subjects or objects—and agree in number and gender with the nouns they replace.

- Pronouns that replace subject words: *I, you, he, she, it, one, we, they, who*
- Pronouns that replace object words: *me, you, him, her, us, them, whom*
- Pronouns that indicate possession: *mine, yours, his, hers, ours, theirs, its*
- Pronouns that indicate reflexive action: *myself, yourself, himself, herself, itself, ourselves, yourselves, themselves*
- Demonstrative pronouns: *this, that, these, those*

AVOIDING VAGUE REFERENCES

Make sure pronouns refer clearly to preceding nouns. Unless a pronoun clearly renames a known antecedent, replace the pronoun with an appropriate noun. Indicate precisely who is responsible for the action of the sentence.

☒ On Bay Street, **they** make millions of dollars every week.

☑ On Bay Street, **stockbrokers/brokerage houses** make millions of dollars every week.

☑ **Bay Street brokers** make millions of dollars every week.

☒ **They** say the economy is recovering.

☑ **Financial analysts** say the economy is recovering.

This, that, and *it* must refer clearly to a readily apparent noun or phrase:

☒ Management disagreed with workers over benefits, but it was never settled.

☑ Management disagreed with workers over benefits, but the dispute was never resolved.

KNOWING WHEN TO USE *I* VERSUS *ME*

The old taboo against using *me* in combination at the beginning of a sentence—*Tom and me prepared the index*—leads many writers to avoid *me* and use *I* even when the pronoun is supposed to receive the action of the sentence. When two or more people are being referred to, determine what pronoun case to use by temporarily removing the other name with which the pronoun is paired:

> ☒ The new clients met with Peter and I.

> ☑ The new clients met with Peter and me.

Me is used after prepositions such as *between*, *after*, and *except*.

- Except for Lydia and me, everyone in the office has accountancy training.

- Just between you and me, the best time to invest is right now.

PRONOUN EXERCISES

Correct errors in pronoun usage in the following sentences:

1. Between you and I, I think the accounts manager has some explaining to do.

2. The change to two-factor authentication was suggested by Giorgio and I.

3. In China, they have a booming economy.

4. Milos and myself were responsible for organizing the team-building retreat.

5. The advantages of launching a clicks-and-mortar operation can outweigh its disadvantages, which requires further consideration.

◖◗ Correcting Modifier Mishaps

Modifiers—consisting of single words or entire phrases—refine the meaning of other words in a sentence: adjectives modify nouns; adverbs modify verbs, adjectives, and other adverbs. The key to using modifiers effectively is to make sure they relate clearly to the word or words they modify. Sentences with modifier problems are at best ambiguous and at worst unintentionally funny.

REINING IN MISPLACED MODIFIERS

The key to using modifiers without confusion is to keep the modifier as close as possible to the word or words it describes. If in doubt about where the modifier belongs, ask yourself, "What goes with what?"

> ☒ She sent a report to the department that was inaccurate. (The modifier seems to belong with *department*, not *report*.)

> ☑ She sent a report that was inaccurate to the department.

> ☑ She sent an inaccurate report to the department.

Placement of single-word modifiers such as *only*, *even*, and *hardly* can greatly alter the meaning of a sentence. Always position them next to the word(s) they modify.

- **Only** John asked for a 2 per cent salary increase. (no one else asked)

- John asked **only** for a 2 per cent salary increase. (he asked for nothing else)

- John asked for **only** a 2 per cent salary increase. (the salary increase was minimal)

When a modifier—especially a modifying phrase—seems to belong with the phrases that come both before and after it, reposition the modifier so it refers to only one phrase.

   ☒ He told her **on Friday** she would receive PowerPoint training.

   ☑ On Friday, he told her she would receive PowerPoint training.

   ☑ He told her she would receive PowerPoint training on Friday.

RESCUING DANGLING MODIFIERS

Modifiers are said to dangle when they fail to refer to or make sense with another word. Usually dangling modifiers are phrases that contain participles—present participles (ending in *-ing*), past participles (often ending in *-ed*), and infinitives (*to* + base form of verb)—but no subject. The easiest way to correct a dangling modifier is to follow the formula below and identify *who* or *what* performs the action of the initial participle phrase immediately after the phrase itself.

MODIFYING PHRASE: DOER/ACTOR + COMPLETE VERB

Stating the intended subject clearly saves the reader the trouble of guessing the missing word.

   ☒ Specializing in finance and international business, his credentials are impeccable.

   ☑ Specializing in finance and international business, he has impeccable credentials.

An equally workable means of correction is to change the modifying phrase into a dependent clause by (i) adding a subject, (ii) adding a subordinating conjunction, and (iii) making the verb complete.

   ☒ Reviewing the agenda, several errors came to her attention.

   ☑ Reviewing the agenda, she noted several errors.

   ☑ While she was reviewing the agenda, several errors came to her attention.

Dangling modifiers also sometimes result from unnecessary use of the passive voice. Use the active voice in the clause following the modifier.

- ☒ To qualify for a refund, a sales receipt must be presented.
- ☑ To qualify for a refund, you must present a sales receipt.
- ☑ To qualify for a refund, please present a sales receipt.

MODIFIER EXERCISES

Correct misplaced and dangling modifiers in the following sentences:

1. To ensure the safe operation of your vehicles, regular inspections by authorized mechanics are recommended.
2. After establishing specifications, the alternatives were weighed by the report committee.
3. To work in quiet and comfortable surroundings, the boardroom is the best place to go.
4. Committed to establishing a career, Anna almost applied for every job that was posted on monster.ca.
5. Our company was fortunate to find new headquarters in the city with two parking lots.
6. Our manager informed us in July no one will go on vacation.
7. We ordered a printer for our office that was unreliable.

●● Comma Usage

Quick-Reference Comma Chart

Use a comma	Don't use a comma
after a dependent clause that begins a sentence	between an initial independent clause and a subsequent dependent clause
Although his business failed, he learned a lot.	He learned a lot although his business failed.
before a dependent clause added to the end of a sentence as an afterthought	
We should meet next Thursday at 1:00 p.m., if you can spare the time.	
between coordinate modifiers that apply equally to the same noun	between modifiers that don't apply equally to the same noun
Ariel submitted a timely, thorough report.	A **delicious Italian** meal was enjoyed by the conference participants.

Use a comma	Don't use a comma
before and after parenthetical expressions, non-essential phrases, appositives, and interjections	before and after relative clauses beginning with *that*
The proposal, which took more than three months to develop, was enthusiastically received.	The report that addressed the failure of the initiative did not assign blame for deficiencies.
	singly between a subject and its verb
	The lecture will be held tomorrow.
between items in a series of three or more (the final comma before *and* is optional)	
St. John's, Halifax(,) and Moncton are key markets for our products.	
between two independent clauses joined by *and*, each with its own subject	between two independent clauses joined by *and* that share a subject
The **impact** of reduced health-care benefits on employee morale is considerable, and **we** will need to discuss the long-term consequences of this policy change at our next meeting.	Rinaldo took responsibility for the decline in sales and proposed a new marketing strategy.

Other Forms of Punctuation

SEMICOLONS AND COLONS

A **semicolon** consists of a period sitting atop a comma. Not surprisingly, it performs many of the same functions as the period and comma. Like a period, a semicolon can be used to join independent clauses, especially when the clauses are closely related or when a conjunctive adverb (a word such as *nevertheless*, *however*, *moreover*, or *furthermore*) links independent clauses.

- New ethics policies were adopted last year; they have been an unqualified success in helping our company promote values of honesty and transparency.

- The shipment of computers arrived today; however, it will be several days before the computer system is operational.

Like a comma, a semicolon can be used to separate items in a series. It is especially useful for separating items in cases where one or more of those items contain internal commas.

- Our company plans to establish operations in the following centres: Vancouver, the largest market for our sporting goods line; Calgary, the fastest growing market for our products; and Saskatoon, an emergent and underserved market.

A semicolon shouldn't be used to separate dependent and independent clauses or to introduce a list.

A **colon** is a punctuation mark that is primarily used to set off something to follow. Use it after an independent clause (complete thought) that introduces a list or a long quotation.

- Our director of human resources is responsible for overseeing the following areas:
    - recruitment and hiring,
    - employee benefits, and
    - payroll.

If an introductory statement ends in a verb (*are, is, were*) or a preposition (*in, by, at, to, for*), use no punctuation at all instead of a colon between the incomplete introductory statement and the text that follows.

- When proofreading a document
    - allow for a "cooling period" before you begin to read,
    - allow sufficient time to read slowly and carefully, and
    - make several passes over the document.

Colons are also used after salutations (*Dear Mr. Evans*:) and memo guide words (*To*:) and between titles and subtitles (*Technical Writing A−Z: A Common Sense Guide to Engineering Reports and Theses*).

APOSTROPHES

Apostrophes are used for two principal reasons: (1) to show possession or ownership and (2) to signal omissions (in contractions—*can't, it's, isn't, won't, they'll*). Adding an apostrophe in combination with -*s* to the end of most nouns (nouns that do not already end in -*s* or an *s* sound) communicates possession.

- Joanne attended the manager's meeting. (a meeting led or convened by one manager)

- I accepted the committee's decision. (*committee* is a singular noun)

- Marcia is a friend of John's. (in other words, *Marcia is a friend of his*)

Keep in mind, though, that there are many exceptions to this basic rule. When a noun ends in an -*s* or *s* sound, add only an apostrophe unless an extra syllable is needed for the sake of pronunciation.

- Joanne attended the managers' meeting. (the meeting of two or more managers)

- Two months' leave of absence seems generous. (*months* is a plural noun)

- The business's customer complaints line was deluged with calls. (extra -*s* added so the word *business* can be pronounced more easily)

Add -'s to each noun of two or more nouns when possession is individual.

- Paul's and Suleman's businesses have grown substantially. (Paul and Suleman each own a business; they do not own the businesses jointly.)

Add -'s to the last noun when possession is joint or collective.

- Irene and Madeline's business has been nominated for a prestigious award. (Irene and Madeline own a business together.)

PERIODS

Periods are used at the end of statements, mild commands, polite requests (that elicit actions rather than verbal answers) and indirect questions (that report asked questions).

- The restructuring of our central division led to a year of unprecedented gains. (statement)

- Return your completed application form to me by June 1. (mild command)

- Will you please send me a copy of your mission statement. (polite request)

- I asked if they wanted to upgrade their filing systems. (indirect question)

QUESTION MARKS

Question marks are used at the end of direct questions or after a question added to the end of a sentence.

- Have you considered telecommuting as a solution to your work-scheduling problems?

- The downturn in the real estate market should help our business, shouldn't it?

PARENTHESES

Parentheses interrupt the sentence structure, allowing you to add non-essential information or to gently introduce, almost in a whisper, an explanation, definition, reference, or question. Whatever is enclosed within parentheses tends to be de-emphasized, very much the opposite of dashes, which call attention to the set-off text. Some general rules apply: (1) never put a comma before an opening parenthesis, only after the closing parenthesis; (2) if a complete sentence in parentheses is part of another sentence, do not add a period to the sentence within parentheses, but do add a question mark or exclamation mark if it is required.

- The company blamed a high incidence of flaming (the exchange of hostile online messages) for the deterioration of employee morale.

- His impressive results on the CA exam (he had taken a leave of absence in order to devote himself to his studies) earned him accolades from his departmental manager.

DASHES

Dashes are high-impact punctuation—emphasizing the text they set off—but their impact is at its greatest only when they are used sparingly. Use dashes (1) to set off a list from an introductory statement, or (2) to emphasize information that interrupts a sentence. A general rule applies: don't use semicolons, commas, or periods next to dashes.

- His latest sales trip took him to the key markets in the Pacific Rim—Tokyo, Seoul, and Taipei.
- The practice of shouting—typing messages in all caps—offends many readers.

QUOTATION MARKS

Quotation marks are used primarily to enclose words copied exactly from a print source or transcribed from overheard speech or conversation. They are also used to enclose the titles of chapters or articles to give special treatment to words or letters, especially to unfamiliar technical terms or ironic words. Single quotation marks ('/') enclose quotations that fall within double quotation marks. When inserting a sentence's punctuation adjacent to quotation marks, place commas and periods inside the closing quotation marks, and place colons and semicolons outside the closing quotation marks.

- "The advantage of online retail," the president said, "is the reduction of storefront expenses."
- The term "authentication" has an ever-evolving definition given the development of new systems and technologies.
- The article entitled "Building a Team" was among the best offerings in the most recent issue of *Business Monthly*.

PUNCTUATION EXERCISES

Add correct and appropriate punctuation to the following sentences.

1. Will you please send me a travel expenses claim form
2. The introduction of a fast efficient system of online human resources management is a major advance for our company, isnt it
3. The following individuals have been selected for the conference panel to be held in a months time Preetasha Lai Hector Gonzalez and Vicki Nguyen
4. The departments leading sales reps are all friends of Johns
5. The secret to his success he shared it with us over dinner last night is his commitment to networking
6. Although the project ran over budget it was considered a creative breakthrough for the marketing team
7. Have you heard of the famous Italian design house Prada
8. The way forward the consultant said is to maximize resources without straining them

**Punctuating Sentences:
A Quick-Reference Chart**

1. *Independent clause.* *Independent clause.*
2. *Independent clause; closely related independent clause.*
3. *Independent clause dependent clause.*
4. *Independent clause, dependent clause that's an afterthought.*
5. *Dependent clause, independent clause.*
6. *Independent clause: independent clause explaining or advising.*
7. *Independent clause: list of items separated by commas or semicolons.*

Internet Resources: Grammar, Style, and ESL Guides

The Blue Book of Grammar and Punctuation—An online English reference guide including exercises and answer keys.
www.grammarbook.com

Guide to Grammar and Style—From the writing program at Rutgers University.
http://andromeda.rutgers.edu/~jlynch/Writing
www.world-english.org/grammar.htm

Guide to Grammar and Writing—An excellent interactive site: each grammar lesson includes exercises that can be submitted for online correction.
http://grammar.ccc.commnet.edu/grammar

OWL Online Writing Lab at Purdue University—Log on to the main page, then select "OWL Exercises." The site includes ESL-related grammar topics.
http://owl.english.purdue.edu

Grammar Girl: Quick and Dirty Tips for Better Writing—A useful resource on style, grammar, and punctuation.
http://grammar.quickanddirtytips.com/

APPENDIX C

Social Media and Networking

In this appendix you will learn to

1. Identify key social media tools, including blogs, social networks, micro-blogs, and video and photo sharing.

2. Identify benefits of social media for professional communication in business environments.

3. Communicate using social networking platforms and blogs and apply best practices and social media etiquette for business purposes.

4. Identify privacy issues related to social media use and management.

Social media has fast become an important dimension of everyday life, connecting us in a variety of ways like never before and changing the way we learn and do business. Social media has everything to do with engagement—with the world around us, with each other, and with our own thoughts and opinions. Navigating the social media landscape successfully brings a multitude of benefits, but it is also filled with many pitfalls and hazards that individuals and organizations alike must keep in mind.

Web 2.0 and the New Media Landscape

Far from putting an end to web technologies, the dot-com collapse in 2001 ushered in the Web 2.0 era—a second generation of Internet technology. From this point, the web grew to be more than just a platform where content and applications could be published by individuals, as it had been with Web 1.0. It became a platform for two-way communication, where content could be modified continuously by all users in collaboration.[1] Unlike Web 1.0, with its static websites, Web 2.0, with its blogs, wikis, and collaborative projects, was and continues to be about connection, engagement, and participation. The following table summarizes the evolution of web technologies.

TABLE 1   Overview of Web 1.0, 2.0, and 3.0 Technologies

Web 1.0	Web 2.0	Web 3.0
The "read-only" era	The "read-write" web	The "semantic" web
• No flow of communication from consumer to producer • No posting of comments • Static websites • Bookmarking • Hyperlinking	• Users publish their own content • Wikis, blogs, widgets • Video streaming • Easy exchange of music and video clips	• Information interpreted by machines (AI) • Users find, share, and combine information more easily • Natural language searches • Micro formats • Mobile devices • Cloud and grid computing • Personalized and contextual search

New functionalities in the Web 2.0 era, such as RSS (Really Simple Syndication) feeds for easy updating of content and Adobe Acrobat for adding animation and audio/ visual streams to web pages, allowed social media to evolve.[2] With these developments, Internet-based social technologies enabled the cost-free exchange of opinions, ideas, information, and user-generated content. People from around the world could connect online with others who shared similar goals and interests. In these new communities of interest, participants could interact not only with a site but also with each other and form broader social networks. With the opportunity to act as contributors and producers of published media rather than simply spectators or consumers of that content, people exploring the new social media landscape found rapidly evolving avenues and tools to communicate, collaborate, disseminate new ideas, and create Internet content.[3] In their roles as media makers and community participants, they became, and continue to be part of, what media scholar Henry Jenkins refers to as "participatory culture."[4]

What Is Participatory Culture?

Jenkins defines participatory culture as a culture with

- low barriers to creative expression and civic engagement,
- support and mentorship among members for each other's creations, and
- feelings of social connection between members and belief that their contributions matter.

Members can participate through *affiliation* (formal or informal membership in groups such as Facebook or Twitter), *expression* (producing new creative forms such as videos, zines, and mash-ups), *collaborative problem-solving* (working in formal or informal teams to develop new knowledge or complete tasks, such as through Wikipedia), and *circulations* (shaping the flow of media through blogging, micro-blogging, or podcasting).[5]

Being part of this new media landscape requires more than just the ability to read or use a computer. Other social skills, competencies, and "literacies" that are hallmarks of this culture include

- judgement—the ability to evaluate the reliability and credibility of information sources;
- networking—the ability to search for, disseminate, and synthesize information;
- collective intelligence—the ability to pool knowledge and compare information for common goals;
- transmedia navigation—the ability to follow the flow of stories across multiple media platforms;
- appropriation—the ability to remix and reconcile conflicting pieces of data to form a coherent picture; and
- negotiation—the ability to discern and respect multiple perspectives as shaped by the cultural differences of diverse communities.[6]

What Is Social Media?

There are many definitions of *social media*. Most commonly, the term applies to the interactive Internet-based and mobile-based tools for

- posting and sharing information (such as status updates, responses to blogs, and video and image comments),
- conducting conversations, and
- delivering and exchanging publicly available media content created by end-users, including content such as documents, presentations (SlideShare), photos (Pinterest), and videos (YouTube and Flickr).

These technologies—most significantly, a collection of social media websites that rank as the most visited sites in the world—facilitate connection, collaboration, and the creation of user-generated content (UGC), making content readers into content publishers. *Social media* can therefore also refer to the activity or activities that integrate technology and social interaction and to the content and contributions to the online spaces that are created in this way.

Immediacy and spontaneity underlie the social media experience. Social media allow individuals to see events and share in them as they happen. A breaking news story or headline can quickly spur responses on a social networking site such as Twitter, for example, far ahead of the response-rate that traditional news outlets allow for. The flow of information through social media can also be a strong predictor of trends and a means to listen to and measure public opinion.

Social media has changed the way businesses collaborate; network; learn; communicate with customers, employees, and stakeholders; and share ideas. The democratizing effect of social media, in giving everyone a voice, has helped to alter and soften traditional business hierarchies.

With social media applications numbering in the hundreds, it is best for businesses to be selective about the ones in which they choose to be active. Those decisions are often based on finding the best media for the message—the ones with the right degree of flexibility as well as the ability to reach the broadest user-base with the likeliest interest in the product or service.

The next few pages provide an overview of four kinds of social media and their relevance and use in business and professional activities: blogging, social networking, micro-blogging, and photo/video sharing.

BLOGS

Blogging is the earliest form of social media.[7] A blog is a special kind of website, usually managed by one person, with date-stamped entries in reverse chronological order. A blog typically represents one topical and timely content area or takes the form of a personal diary. It allows for more social interaction, engagement, and feedback than static Web 1.0 technologies through the posting of visitor comments in response to the blog entries.

Blogging for Business

From leading-edge blogging applications such as WordPress (2003) to more recent blogging websites such as Tumblr (2007), the blog concept has carried over to companies that use their own blogging applications for keeping employees, customers, and shareholders up to date on important developments while at the same time reinforcing and building the company's image and brand. Corporate blogs represent a shift in the way companies interact with customers and have been shown to build trust, liking, and involvement.[8] There are three different kinds of corporate blogs:

- intranet blogs,
- event blogs. and
- product blogs.[9]

Intranet blogs can be used by a company's employees on a daily basis to share opinions and expertise on products and to launch discussions of interest to other employees.[10] Blogging can connect workers with each other, even across continents; reduce communication costs; and boost morale and employee retention. It has the added benefits of attracting a younger demographic to the company workforce and making it easier for organizations to identify and draw on the special skill-sets of its workers. Blogging can also be a tool for spotlighting work accomplishments and gaining career advancement, with functions such as hashtags helping employees to draw management's attention with words that best describe their achievements. Blogging in Canadian organizations is on the rise. Five years ago, Toronto-Dominion Bank revamped its internal website into a social media platform supporting blogs, chat forums, and surveys. The site also includes the option for employees to leave comments both on blog pages and at the end of news items.[11]

For event and product-related blogs, best practices include

- writing about topics that matter to customers,
- educating customers by offering trend and industry news rather than just news of product launches,
- writing from a personal perspective rather than a seller's or brand-message perspective, and
- providing a view that complements but is different from press releases and other brand-based communications.[12]

While blogs tend to be mostly text-based, links can be added for image and video content. Additionally, CEOs often maintain blogs on their company websites, in part to improve transparency and reinforce positive perceptions of corporate social responsibility.

SOCIAL NETWORKS

Social networking describes a website application that facilitates communication and social interaction through one-to-one or one-to-many conversations between people. Social networking sites such as MySpace (2003) and Facebook (2004) enable users to connect by sending e-mails or text messages and by creating personal profiles featuring blogs, photos, and audio and video files that they then invite friends to access.

Social Networking for Business

Companies use social networking sites for a variety of purposes:

- to create brand communities;
- to keep stakeholders and shareholders up to date on products;
- to promote products and services, especially to targeted demographic groups;
- to publicize events, product launches, and contests; and
- to carry out marketing research.

Business has been quick to capitalize on and harness the power of social media. The social media campaign is an increasingly exploitable marketing tool because it provides access to current and potential customers in the millions without the cost of advertising. Nonprofits and charities likewise use social media sites to publicize their missions and to seek donations and volunteers as part of integrated fundraising campaigns.

Social networks have changed the way businesses interact online, transforming "customers" and the general public into "fans." Facebook, a giant among social networking sites, offers businesses the benefits of "word-of-mouth" marketing through four basic steps based on the same "liking," "commenting," and "friending" principles that apply to its personal profiles and online socializing: building a page, connecting with people, engaging the audience, and influencing friends of fans. Of similar relevance to business, LinkedIn is a popular social network for professionals; its Canadian user-base grew to more than 3 million in 2011.[13] This site's primary purpose is to link professionals to each other and to organizations.

Businesses that use Facebook effectively adopt a series of best practices. Consider the following when designing a Facebook page or group:

1. Update your page frequently.
2. Stay on topic—let the focus be your business and what makes it interesting to your customers.
3. Keep your message brief and relevant to fans and the target audience.
4. Use links and images, but keep the design clean and limited to essentials, letting the brand stand out.
5. Ensure the correctness and appropriateness of content and the way it is expressed—and do the same for customer content.
6. Keep the tone spontaneous and informal.
7. Signpost your company's expertise.
8. Make it interactive and engaging—encourage feedback and relationship-building through polls, user-generated content, promotions, surveys, and other forms of interaction.
9. Make some content exclusive to Facebook.

TABLE 2   Quick-Reference Descriptions of Selected Social Networking Sites

Site	Description
Blogstser	Blogging community featuring specific-interest blogs
Delicious	Social bookmarking service for storing, sharing, and discovering web bookmarks
Facebook	Social networking service for connecting and engaging with others via a profile page
Flickr	Online photo management and sharing application
Fotki	"Organic, fat-free" photo/video sharing site
Foursquare	Location-based mobile social network that helps users share and save places they visit
LinkedIn	Business and professional networking service
MySpace	General social networking site (gradually declining in popularity)
Pinterest	Online content-sharing service for organizing and sharing photos and videos that users love, with standard social networking features
Qapacity	Business-oriented social networking site and business directory
Reddit	User-generated news links
Talkbiznow	Web-based business community providing business services for small businesses and professionals
Twitter	Micro-blogging service
Yammer	Social networking service for office colleagues
Yelp	Site for reviewing and discussing local businesses

Different generations use social media in different ways. The digital divide between digital natives (those born after 1968 who grew up using online technologies) and digital immigrants (those born before 1968 who have had to adapt in learning these technologies) in part explains why some platforms are more popular than others among certain age groups.

MICRO-BLOGGING

Micro-blogs, such as Twitter, allow users to send out short text-like bursts of information to a community of followers in real time. Twitter combines this format with a news-feed function. In its maximum of 140 characters, a "tweet'" has a twofold function: it is both a message and a means of initiating a conversation with followers, who are expected to tweet in response.

Micro-blogging for Business

The short, snappy, instantaneous nature of Twitter communication makes it highly suited for sharing the latest, time-sensitive information. This two-way flow of communication helps in reputation- and trust-building. Business professionals and their organizations can use Twitter in a number of ways:

- to monitor the competition and their latest projects and initiatives,
- to monitor customer satisfaction and public perception of their organizations,
- to share and find professionally related knowledge and resources,
- to support employee and management communications,
- to monitor existing customers and prospect and engage new ones,
- to perform industry trend watches, and
- to prospect and recruit new hires.

To realize the full potential of the Twittersphere, consider the following guidelines:

1. Create a professional-looking profile and username and strive for a genuine, likeable tone.

2. Ask questions and respond in real time.

3. Be selective and professionally minded in what you tweet; focus on industry news and research, conferences and professional development opportunities and outcomes, or a professionally related article or question.

4. Retweet what you find interesting, reply publicly, and encourage retweets to acknowledge and show appreciation to followers.

5. Incorporate links, ideally shortened ones, and share photos to provide a fuller context for a business story or information burst.

6. Be strategic in the pace and timing of your tweets—do not send out so many at once that it overloads your followers' feeds.

PHOTO/VIDEO SHARING

Content communities such as YouTube, Pinterest, Instagram, and Flickr allow for the sharing of rich media content—multimedia, photography, and video—between users within broad, diverse audiences. Users are not required to create profile pages. Video- and photo-sharing sites carry the risk that copyrighted material will be shared, but most major sites take steps to ban illegal content. Another well-known content community is SlideShare (for electronic slide presentations).

Photo/Video Sharing for Business

Organizations use photo/video sharing sites in a number of ways:

- to share press announcements and keynote speeches with employees and investors;
- to upload company photos, public service announcements, and commercials;
- to post recruiting videos; and
- to capture client, customer, and public feedback on company enterprises, products, and services (comments must be monitored).

Encouraging users to post videos, often for contests, is another way organizations use highly popular sites such as YouTube, with users in the millions, to carry the brand name forward.

The Downside of Social Media

There is a good deal of euphoria and enthusiasm surrounding the use of social media, but that does not necessarily cancel out the problems associated with these platforms and applications. There are three key areas of social media that employers struggle with:

1. Time theft

2. Malicious or damaging employee comments made about employers

3. Leaks of confidential information[14]

Social networking is a powerful and popular tool, but it can also be a great time waster, with social media addictions sometimes cutting into work hours. The need to communicate and to stay connected can be overpowering. The fear of missing out by not remaining online can be detrimental to workflow and productivity. Employees used to sharing details of their personal lives through Facebook or Twitter posts may not understand the potential employment consequences of using social media to express beliefs and views about their work lives, especially when those views have the potential to expose their businesses to harm or risk. There may well be truth to the saying "The Facebook walls have ears." Even a casual remark or snippet from an online conversation can be used against a business by its competitors. Corporate takeovers have been fuelled and collective bargaining negotiations have been jeopardized by leaks of this kind.

In the new social media landscape, it is important for employees to know how to use—and how and when not to use—social media. Faced with the dilemma of social media abuse, employers such as the Government of Ontario have taken the radical step of banning Facebook.

Contrary to popular belief, Facebook and Twitter are not private. Employers may check viewable Facebook profiles or even ask for access to a job applicant's Facebook page before hiring. For this reason, job- and promotion-seekers and those who value their professional reputations should avoid posting potentially embarrassing words and images and be mindful of the online identities and profiles they create. Posts and comments made long ago can have surprising staying power and remain searchable, creating a need for professional "web scrubbers." In Canada, labour law protects job-seekers from employers asking for personal information, including social media passwords. Applicants approached for this kind of information have the right to refuse. It is equally within an employer's rights to search for employee information that has not been properly locked.[15]

Social media have the unexpected disadvantage of making it harder for organizations to control their message and conversations about their product or activities. Social media platforms not only function as channels for positive, business-enhancing communication, but also carry risks for impression management and reputation, especially when disgruntled customers or employees, through comments, have easy means to voice complaints in a way that can influence public opinion against an organization or its products and services. Likewise, a failed social media campaign or one that has caused a backlash is hard to eradicate, even when controversial, misleading, or offensive product ads have been taken down.

⬤⬤ Social Media Resources

Center for Social Media—This site is for an organization at the American University that showcases and analyzes public media for public knowledge and social action.
http://www.centerforsocialmedia.org

Chris Brogan on Media Starter Tips to Grow Your Business—In this short video, media marketing expert Chris Brogan, author of *Social Media 101*, discusses best practices for businesses in using new media.
http://www.entrepreneur.com/video/222749

Social Media Experts on Twitter—Sidneyeve Matrix (@sidneyeve), Chris Brogan (@ChrisBrogan)

Social Media Blog—Henry Jenkins's blog.
http://henryjenkins.org

⬤⬤ Activities and Applications

1. **Adapting to Twitter Style:** On your class's Twitter page, as set up by your instructor, tweet:

   a) a rule for using Twitter or social media effectively

   b) a principle, concept, or learning outcome from today's class

   c) a synopsis or description of your communications course

   d) a promotional message for your college or university

   e) a summary of last week's class

   f) a summary of a news story provided to you by your instructor or searched by you and your team members

2. **Analyzing a Facebook or Twitter Campaign:** In a small group, find an example of a Facebook or Twitter campaign for a consumer product or nonprofit fundraising organization. Analyze the elements of this campaign and prepare a brief, five-minute group presentation in which you review its major features and approach and identify a possible target audience. How is the main message, as delivered through social media, different from the message as communicated through the organization's website or other media?

3. **Creating a Personal Profile:** Create a mock-up of your Facebook or LinkedIn profile, then revise and upgrade it to make it more professional and business-ready.

4. **Creating a Corporate Blog Post:** Create a blog post for a corporate website about a recent work-related achievement or professional-development milestone related to your skills or education.

5. **Writing for Blogs:** Find a news story or press release and compose a blog post for a corporate website.

6. **E-Fundraising with Facebook:** Find a Facebook page for one of your favourite charities and compare its design and message to what is found on the correspond-

ing website for the organization. How does the message change across modalities? How would you describe the message and design of the information in each case?

7. **Exploring the Twittersphere—Deciding Who to Follow:** Log on to your Twitter account, perform a search, and find three hashtags (#) and/or users (@) connected to your program, discipline, or future career. Who/what would you consider following? Decide who can help you learn more and connect better. Here are a few steps and considerations that may help you choose:

a) Browse interests and review Twitter suggestions about who to follow.
b) Discover your friends on Twitter; if their professional interests are similar to your own, check who they are following.
c) Check the profile to ensure the bio corresponds to your interests.
d) See how many tweets and followers they have.
e) Review some of their recent updates.
f) Check who they are following—this can lead you to others with interests similar to your own.

Photo Credits

Notes

Chapter 1

1. Friedman, T.J. (2006). *The world is flat: A brief history of the twenty-first century*. New York: Farrar, Straus, and Giroux, p. 85.
2. Ibid.
3. Baron, N.S. (2008). *Always on: Language in an online and mobile world*. New York: Oxford University Press.
4. Friedman. (2006). *The world is flat*, p. 236.
5. About Facebook. Retrieved from www.facebook.com/press/info.php
6. Tweets from the top. (2009, May 22). *Globe and Mail*.
7. Rothwell, J.D. (1998). *In mixed company: Small group communication, instructor's manual/test bank*. Fort Worth, TX: Harcourt Brace.
8. Bugental, D.E., Kaswan, J.W., Love, L.R., & Fox, M.N. (1970). Child versus adult perception of evaluative messages in verbal, vocal, and visual channels. *Developments in Psychology, 2*, 376.
9. National Communication Association. (n.d.) Communication defined. Retrieved from http://www.natcom.org/index.asp?bid=1339
10. International Communication Association. (2006). History. Retrieved from www.icahdq.org/aboutica/history.asp.
11. Weaver, W. (1949). Introductory note on the general setting of the analytical communication studies. In C. Shannon & W. Weaver (Eds.), *The mathematical theory of communication* (p. 3). Urbana, IL: University of Illinois Press.
12. DeVito, J.A. (2008). *Interpersonal messages: Communication and relationship skills*. Boston: Pearson, p. 13.
13. Ibid.
14. Mehrabian, A. (1981). *Silent message* (2nd edn). Belmont, CA: Wadsworth Publishing, p. 78.
15. Argyle, M., Salter, V., Nicholson, H., Williams, M., & Burgess, P. (1970). The communication of inferior and superior attitudes by verbal and non-verbal signals. *British Journal of Social and Clinical Psychology 9*, 222–31.
16. Mast, M.S. (2002). Dominance as expressed and inferred through speaking time: A meta-analysis. *Human Communication Research 28*, 420–50.
17. Riggio, R.E. (2005). Business applications of nonverbal communication. In R.E. Riggio & R.S. Feldman (Eds.), *Applications of nonverbal communication research* (pp. 119–38). Mahwah, NJ: Lawrence Erlbaum Associates.
18. Hall, E.T. (1959). *The silent language*. New York: Doubleday.
19. Ekman, P., & Friesen, W. (1975). *Unmasking the face: A guide to recognizing emotions in facial expressions*. Englewood Cliffs, NJ: Prentice-Hall.
20. Partly based on Johnson, M. (2003, Winter). The psychology of ethical lapses. *Management Ethics*. Canadian Centre for Ethics & Corporate Policy. Retrieved from www.ethicscentre.ca/html/management%20ethics%20-%20Jan%202003.pdf
21. Hall, E.T. (1976). *Beyond culture*. New York: Doubleday.
22. Office of the Privacy Commissioner of Canada. (2009). A guide for individuals: Your guide to PIPEDA. Retrieved from http://www.priv.gc.ca/information/02_05_d_08_e.cfm
23. Baron. (2008). *Always on*.

Chapter 3

1. Stinson, S. (2003, June 17). Software takes the "bull" out of jargon, *National Post*, A 12.
2. *Canadian Defamation Law*, copyright © Lloyd Duhaime, 1996, 20 May 2003, www.duhaime.org/ca-defam.htm.

3. Ober, S., et al. (1999). Telling it like it is: The use of certainty in public business discourse. *The Journal of Business Communication*, *36*(3), 280.

Chapter 4

1. Guffey, M.E. (2001). Business communication: Process & product (3rd Canadian edn). Scarborough, ON: Nelson Thompson Learning, p. 151.

Chapter 10

1. Tufte, E.R. 1983. *The visual display of quantitative information*. Cheshire, CT: Graphics Press, p. 51.
2. Insurance Board of Canada. (2009). Incident and accident reporting. Retrieved from http://www.ibc.ca/en/business_insurance/risk_management/incident_and_accident_reporting.asp

Appendix C

1. Kaplan, A., & Haelein, M. (2010). Users of the world, unite! The challenges and opportunities of social media. *Business Horizons 53*, 61.
2. Kaplan & Haelein, 60.
3. Miller, V. (2011). *Understanding digital culture*. Thousand Oaks, CA: Sage Publications Ltd., p. 87.
4. Jenkins, H., et al. (2006). Confronting the challenges of participatory culture: Media education for the 21st century. Chicago: The MacArthur Foundation, p. 8. Retrieved from http://digitallearning.macfound.org/ atf/cf/%7BE45C7E0-A3E0-4B89-AC9C-E807E1B0AE4E%7D/JENKINS_WHITE_PAPER.PDF.
5. Jenkins et al., p. 3.
6. Jenkins et al., p. 4.
7. Kaplan & Haelein, p. 63.
8. Dwyer, P. (2007). Building trust with corporate blogs. ICWSM 2007 Conference. Retrieved from http://icwsm.org/papers/2--Dwyer.pdf.
9. Dugan, K. (2004). Emerging corporate blog models. Retrieved from http://prblog.type pad.com/stratetic_public_relation/2004/11/emergingcorpor.html.
10. Kolari, P., et al. (2007). On the structure, properties and utility of internal corporate blogs. ICWSM 2007 Conference. Retrieved from http://ebiquity.umbc.edu/_file_directory_/papers/341.pdf.
11. Johne, M. (2011, October 21). Firing on all cylinders with social media. *Globe and Mail*, p. B15.
12. Lionel Menchaca, quoted by Lee Oden. (2011). Big business blogging, the right way, Intel #ISMP. Retrieved from http://www.toprank blog.com/2011/07/big-business-blogging-dell.
13. Hartley, M. (2011, June 16). LinkedIn helping companies recruit "the rock stars." *National Post*, p. FP14.
14. Neilsen, C. (2012, March 31). The double-edged sword of social media. Panel discussion, Faculty of Business, Ryerson University.
15. McQuigge, M. (2012, March 28). Company wants your Facebook password? Just say no. *Globe and Mail*, p. B19.

Index